809.8973
St94
1982

STUDIES IN THE AMERICAN RENAISSANCE

1982

FRONTISPIECE
Thoreau's letter of 21 June 1856 to Calvin Greene.
Courtesy NjP

STUDIES IN THE AMERICAN RENAISSANCE

1982

Edited by JOEL MYERSON

BOSTON:
TWAYNE PUBLISHERS

STUDIES IN THE AMERICAN RENAISSANCE

EDITOR

Joel Myerson

EDITORIAL ASSISTANTS

Robert Morace (1974–1975)
Robert E. Burkholder (1975–1979)
Stephen Garrsion (1979–1981)
Caroline Bokinsky (1981–1982)

The editor would like to thank the College of Humanities and Social Sciences and the Department of English of the University of South Carolina, and especially George L. Geckle, for their support.

STUDIES IN THE AMERICAN RENAISSANCE examines the lives and works of mid-nineteenth-century American authors and the circumstances in which they wrote, published, and were received. The Editor welcomes biographical, historical, and bibliographical articles on the literature, history, philosophy, art, religion, and general culture of America during the period 1830–1860. Editorial correspondence should be addressed to Joel Myerson, Department of English, University of South Carolina, Columbia, South Carolina 29208.

STUDIES IN THE AMERICAN RENAISSANCE is indexed by *America: History and Life, American Humanities Index, American Literary Scholarship/An Annual, American Literature, Historical Abstracts*, and the MLA *International Bibliography*.

Copyright © 1982 by G. K. Hall & Co.
All rights reserved

ISSN 0149–015X
ISBN 0–8057–9015–2

STUDIES IN THE AMERICAN RENAISSANCE is published annually by Twayne Publishers, A Division of G. K. Hall & Co., 70 Lincoln Street, Boston, Massachusetts 02111, and is available on a standing order basis. The price of this volume is $30.00. Orders from individuals must be accompanied by payment.

First Printing, September 1982

CONTENTS

ILLUSTRATIONS	vii
LIBRARY SYMBOLS	ix
Victor Cousin: Still Another Source of Poe's Aesthetic Theory? Glen A. Omans	1
The Hidden Journey of *Arthur Gordon Pym* Richard Kopley	29
Bronson Alcott's "Journal for 1837" (Part Two) Larry A. Carlson	53
Jones Very's "Epistles to the Unborn" Phyllis Cole	169
George Ripley's Unpublished Lecture on Charles Fourier David A. Zonderman	185
James Freeman Clarke: Notes Toward a Comprehensive Bibliography Leonard Neufeldt	209
The Journals of Convers Francis (Part Two) Guy R. Woodall	227
The Preparation of a Poet: Puritan Directions in Emily Dickinson's Education Rowena Revis Jones	285
A Calendar of the Correspondence of Henry D. Thoreau Carolyn Kappes, Walter Harding, Randy F. Nelson, and Elizabeth Witherell	325
Withdrawal and Resumption: Whitman and Society in the Last Two Parts of *Specimen Days* William Aarnes	401

Biographical Technique in Horace Traubel's *With Walt
Whitman in Camden* 433
    Tibbie E. Lynch

BOOKS RECEIVED 445
    Caroline Bokinsky

CONTRIBUTORS 467

ILLUSTRATIONS

Frontispiece: Thoreau's letter of 21 June 1856 to Calvin Greene.

Plate One: Alcott's entry during Week XVIII (30 April–6 May) on philosophy.   60

Plate Two: Alcott's entry during Week XVIII (30 April–6 May) about Hiram Fuller.   67

Plate Three: Alcott's entry during Week XIX (7–13 May) on the reception of *Conversations*.   73

Plate Four: Alcott's entry during Week XXI (21–27 May) about the "Symposeum."   79

Plate Five: Alcott's entry during Week XXII (28 May–3 June) on F. H. Hedge.   88

Plate Six: Alcott's entry during Weeks XXVII–XXXVIII (2 July–30 September) about re-opening his school.   98

Plate Seven: Alcott's entry during Week XLI (15–21 October) on W. L. Garrison.   104

Plate Eight: Alcott's entry during Week XLVII (26 November–2 December) reviewing the past year.   131

Plate Nine: William Sweetser's letter of 21 July 1852 to Thoreau.   352

Plate Ten: Thoreau's letter of 26 July 1852 to William Sweetser.   353

Plate Eleven: Thoreau's letter of 22 September 1856 to B. B. Wiley.   371

LIBRARY SYMBOLS

CCS	Scripps College
CCamarSJ	St. John's Seminary
CSmH	Henry E. Huntington Library
CU-B	Bancroft Library, University of California, Berkeley
CtGreB	Bruce Museum, Greenwich, Connecticut
CtW	Wesleyan University
CtWaG	Gunn Memorial Library, Washington, Connecticut
CtY	Yale University
DFo	Folger Shakespeare Library
DLC	Library of Congress
ICarbS	Southern Illinois University
IaU	University of Iowa
InNd	University of Notre Dame
InU	Indiana University
MAJ	Jones Library
MB	Boston Public Library
MBN	Boston Museum of Science
MBU	Boston University
MCR-S	Schlesinger Library, Radcliffe College
MCo	Concord Free Public Library
MCoA	Concord Antiquarian Society

MCoMx	Middlesex School, Concord, Massachusetts
MH	Harvard University
MHarF	Fruitlands Museums, Harvard, Massachusetts
MHi	Massachusetts Historical Society
MPlPS	Pilgrim Society, Plymouth, Massachusetts
MSaE	Essex Institute
MWat	Watertown Free Public Library
MWatP	Perkins School for the Blind
MWiW-C	Chapin Library, Williams College
MeHi	Maine Historical Society
MiKC	Kalamazoo College
MnM	Minneapolis Public Library
NjP	Princeton University
NBu	Buffalo and Erie County Public Library
NHi	New-York Historical Society
NN	New York Public Library
NNC	Columbia University
NNPM	Pierpont Morgan Library
NNPa	Paulist Fathers Archives, New York, New York
NRU	University of Rochester
OKentU	Kent State University
OMC	Marietta College
PHC	Haverford College
PHi	Pennsylvania Historical Society
PSt	Pennsylvania State University
RPB	Brown University
TxU	University of Texas
ViBlbV	Virginia Polytechnic Institute and State University

ViU	University of Virginia
VtMiM	Middlebury College
VtU	University of Vermont

VICTOR COUSIN: STILL ANOTHER SOURCE OF POE'S AESTHETIC THEORY?

Glen A. Omans

SCHOLARS OF AMERICAN LITERATURE have apparently never taken as significant, Poe's two references to the French philosopher, Victor Cousin.[1] The first of these appeared in Poe's review of R. H. Horne's "Orion" in *Graham's Magazine* for March 1844. In the review, Poe describes as the aim of poetry to exalt the reader's "soul" into "a conception of pure beauty" by appealing to his "sentiment of the beautiful—that divine sixth sense which is yet so faintly understood—that sense which phrenology has attempted to embody in its organ of *ideality* —that sense which is the basis of all Cousin's dreams—that sense which speaks of God through his purest, if not his *sole* attribute—which proves, and which alone proves his existence."[2]

Poe's second reference to Cousin appeared only five months later in "Mesmeric Revelation," in the August 1844 *Columbian Magazine*. This time the reference to Cousin is negative. Vankirk, speaking about his attempts to believe in immortality, says: "I had been advised to study Cousin. I studied him in his own works as well as in those of his European and American echoes. The 'Charles Elwood' of Mr. Brownson, for example, was placed in my hands." But Vankirk has not been helped by his reading: "I was not long in perceiving that if man is to be intellectually convinced of his own immortality, he will never be so convinced by time the reference to Cousin is negative. Vankirk, speaking about his the mere abstractions which have been so long the fashion of the moralists of England, of France, and of Germany" (*Works*, 5:243).[3]

The first of Poe's two references to Cousin strikes us as the more important. It suggests that Poe has read Cousin and that this reading may have reinforced, if not actually originated, some of Poe's key aesthetic ideas. Poe's use of the expression "the sentiment of the beautiful" indicates Cousin's major work on aesthetics, his *Cours de philosophie ... sur le fondement des idées absolues du vrai, du beau, et du bien*, a series of lectures given at the University of Paris in 1818 and published in

1

1836,[4] in which Cousin's term for the aesthetic faculty, "*le sentiment du beau*," is the exact equivalent in French to Poe's expression. Poe had already used the phrase "the sense of the beautiful" in his April 1842 review of Longfellow's *Ballads and Other Poems* and would use it again in "The Poetic Principle," both times, as in his review of Horne's "Orion," in connection with a belief in an ideal beauty which is a guarantee of the immortality of the soul and the existence of God: "An important condition of man's immortal nature is thus, plainly, the sense of the Beautiful." The "burning thirst" which man feels for "the beauty beyond the grave," "belongs to the *immortal* essence of man's nature. It is equally a consequence and an indication of his perennial life.... It is a forethought of the loveliness to come." The artist's urge to create is "inspired with a prescient ecstasy of the beauty beyond the grave" as he struggles to "anticipate" in his own work "some portion of that loveliness whose very elements, perhaps, appertain solely to Eternity" (*Works*, 11:71–72; 14:273–74).

Poe has in mind here the usual Platonic dualism: on one hand the descendent world of phenomenal reality defined by matter, space, and time, and perceived by the bodily senses; on the other hand, the transcendent realm of immortal and immutable ideas, conceived only by the human reason in its highest reaching. It is a concept that Poe could know directly from Plato's dialogues, if not from any number of Neoplatonists. It is interesting to note, however, in connection with Poe's use of the phrase "sentiment of the beautiful," that Cousin, too, freely mingles Platonic concepts with traditional Christian beliefs and applies them to the subjects of art and artistic creation in a way that resembles Poe's own ideas and even phrases in several striking ways.

Cousin's lectures were divided into three sections on "the True," "the Beautiful," and "the Good." His discussion of aesthetics begins with the "*Dix-neuvième Leçon*," in which he posits the ideas of Beauty, Truth, and Good as "absolute ideas" which are manifestations "of the unchanging and infinite Being" (*du beau*, p. 190; Daniel, p. 26).[5] Cousin insists throughout his discussion on the same relationships between God, or heaven, and these absolute ideas that Poe assumes in his reviews of Longfellow and Horne, in "The Poetic Principle," and in "To Helen," "Israfel," and "Al Aaraaf:" "God is the metaphysical substance of... the Good, the Beautiful, and the True, conceived of in the unity of their essence.... But God is impenetrable: reason cannot approach his nature; it is needful that He make himself known by a medium accessible and intelligible. That medium is the idea of the good, the true, and the beautiful, the *logos* of Plato" (*du beau*, p. 261; Daniel, pp. 130–31). Cousin describes existence, then, as a hierarchy, with God at the top, the absolute ideas as mediating links, and the natural forms which reflect these ideas on the lowest level: "Beneath the Supreme Being, one finds supreme Beauty, which is least distanced from the Infinite but which is already very far from it; from there, from degradation to degradation, one descends to real beauty" (*du beau*, p. 207; my translation). The hierarchy can also be viewed in reverse. The lowest natural forms are symbols of the ideas of which they are manifestations, and beyond these ideas, of the Infinite or God, the origin of the ideas. "The Idea of the Beautiful," notes Cousin, "is one of the most glorious manifestations of Absolute Being, a grand medium between God, nature and man" (*du beau*, p. 190; Daniel, p. 38).[6] Beauty, then, has the power "to raise us to the ideal, ... to raise us to the Infinite, or to God" (*du beau*, p. 223; Daniel, p. 81). "Nature will probably appear to us the starting point of the ideal, and God the Being to whom it tends. God and nature will thus be, as it were, the two worlds between which the ideal will remain suspended" (*du beau*, pp. 193–94; Daniel, p. 42).

Since the artist's raw materials are the beautiful sights, sounds, and scents of the natural world, which are themselves symbols of ideal beauty, the artist's challenge is to use these earthly forms to evoke ideal beauty by means of his finished work of art. By so doing, he will lead his audience back through the ideal to a conception of the Infinite. "To elevate the real to the ideal is the mission of art," Cousin affirms (*du beau*, p. 267; Daniel, p. 140).[7] Since "God is the source of all Beauty ... the loftiest aim of art is to arouse the sentiment of the infinite" (*du beau*, p. 226; Daniel, p. 85). Art is "the representation of the absolute, the general, ... the ideal" (*du beau*, p. 300; Daniel, p. 183).

But the artist must refine the forms of natural beauty, must order and arrange them so that they evoke the idea of beauty more clearly, more inevitably, than they do in their natural state. The absolute idea of Beauty, Cousin argues, "can make itself visible in the bosom of nature, but it is always veiled and imperfect. It shines more brightly in the works of man, because the arm guided by intelligence approaches nearer to the model the mind has conceived" (*du beau*, p. 190; Daniel, p. 38). "Genius rends and reconstructs nature, in order to make it more like the idea" (*du beau*, p. 226; Daniel p. 137). "Art is nature destroyed and reconstructed: genius is taste no longer the appreciator of natural beauty, but the creator of beauty ideal and superior to the former" (*du beau*, p. 264; Daniel, p. 133).[8] Because "Beauty is an absolute idea, and not a copy of finite, accidental, and imperfect nature" (*du beau*, p. 190; Daniel, p. 38), Cousin urges the artist to seek, by means of his imagination, "beneath nature for the absolute idea of Beauty which is found hid there" (*du beau*, p. 239; Daniel, p. 103): "Endeavor to appreciate by your taste the beauty presented you in nature; but do not be contented with this merely meditative opinion which belongs chiefly to the philosopher; display your genius; set the ideal free from the enthrallment of the real, and bring back the absolute afresh clothed in purer forms" (*du beau*, p. 301; Daniel, p. 185).

Poe's ideas, if not always his phrases, are interestingly similar to those of Cousin. In the moment of creation, says Poe, the artist is motivated by no "mere appreciation of the beauty before us," "by no sublunary sights, or sounds, or sentiments," but by a "wild effort to reach the beauty above," by the "thirst for supernatural BEAUTY—a beauty which is not afforded the soul by any existing collocation of earth's forms—a beauty which, perhaps, *no possible* combination of these forms would fully produce." The soul "struggles by multiform novelty of combination among the things and thoughts of Time, to anticipate some portion of that loveliness whose very elements, perhaps, appertain solely to Eternity" (*Works*, 11:72–73; 14:274).

Poe emphasized several times that the artist's basic work is to combine material forms so as to suggest the ideal. As early as October 1836, in the *Southern Literary Messenger*, Poe bluntly asserted: "There is no greater mistake than the supposition that a true originality is a mere matter of impulse or inspiration. To originate, is carefully, patiently, and understandingly to combine" (*Works*, 14:73). He first linked the technique of patient craftsmanship with the search for the ideal in his April 1842 review of Longfellow, when he described "the attempt to satisfy" the thirst for supernal beauty "by *novel combinations, of those combinations which our predecessors, toiling in chase of the same phantom, have already set in order*" (*Works*, 11:73). In his review of Horne's "Orion," in juxtaposition with his reference to Cousin, Poe repeated the phrase describing the artist's attempt to "quench" his thirst for beauty through "novel combinations of beautiful forms (collocations of forms) physical or spiritual" (*Works*, 11:256). In his discussion of the function of the imagination in his article on N. P. Willis, Poe noted: "The pure Imagination chooses . . . only the most combinable things hitherto uncombined;— the compound as a general rule, partaking (in character) of sublimity or beauty, in the ratio of the respective sublimity or beauty of the things combined" (*Works*, 12:38). The idea of patient artistic combination is, of course, the basic thesis of "The Philosophy of Composition."

Poe's concept of the act of creation as a "struggle" to "combine" elements on a descendent or "real" level parallels Cousin's own emphasis on the craft or labor of the artist. Says Cousin: "Question the artist as to what passes in his mind when he produces a great work: he will reply that he abstracts, that he combines" (*du beau*, p. 238; Daniel, pp. 101–102). "The artist must know how to work with matter ... in such a way as to make it express the immaterial.... One should say to artists: If you do not know how to work with matter so as to elevate yourselves to the ideal, you will not be superior to nature" (*du beau*, pp. 269–70; my translation).

Both Cousin and Poe are in further agreement that the artist who fails to at least partially apprehend the supernal loveliness, or, worse, does not even attempt to do so, can claim to be no more than a poetaster. Cousin asserted: "Although art may be free, it must not aim ultimately at anything besides moral Beauty.... Thus, the artist who, seriously regarding nature, should be satisfied to copy it faithfully, would fall from the rank of an artist to that of a mechanic" (*du beau*, p. 268; Daniel, pp. 140–41).[9] Poe's statement of the same idea seems to directly echo Cousin's. The poet's "sense of the Beautiful" is delighted by "the manifold forms and colours and sounds and sentiments amid which he exists." But a "mere oral or written repetition" or "*record* of these forms and colours," though "a duplicate source of delight," is "not Poesy." "He who shall merely sing with whatever rapture, in however harmonious strains, or with however vivid a truth of imitation, of the sights and sounds which greet him in common with all mankind—he, we say, has yet failed to prove his divine title" (*Works*, 11:71; 14:273).[10]

Perhaps an indication of Cousin's actual influence on Poe is that before Poe could have read Cousin's *Cours de philosophie* of 1836, Poe spoke of "the sentiment of Poesy," in his review of Drake and Halleck in the *Southern Literary Messenger* (April 1836), as being aroused by natural physical objects: "Thence spring immediately admiration of the fair flowers, the fairer forests, the bright valleys and rivers and mountains of the Earth—and love of the gleaming stars and other burning glories of Heaven." Poe's concept of the less tangible ingredients of the poetic sentiment is intellectual rather than transcendental: "Poesy is the sentiment of Intellectual Happiness here, and the Hope of a higher Intellectual Happiness hereafter." Poe's footnote attributing this idea to the "Hymn to Intellectual Beauty" indicates Shelley as his inspiration at this time (*Works*, 8:282–83). Conspicuous by its absence is Cousin's idealistic dimension which Poe began to assert in his April 1842 Longfellow review, after he would have had an opportunity to read Cousin. He repeated it again in "The Poetic Principle" (*Works*, 14:273–74) and restated it in his "Marginalia" in 1849, each time directly contradicting the association of poetry with nature that he had established in his Drake-Halleck review: "Were I called upon to define, *very* briefly, the term 'Art,' I should call it 'the reproduction of what the Senses perceive in Nature through the veil of the soul.' The mere imitation, however accurate, of what *is* in Nature, entitles no man to the sacred name of 'Artist' " (*Works*, 16:164).

Cousin and Poe again agree, however, that it is practically impossible for even the true artist to attain the pure ideal in his work of art. The best that can be hoped for is a partial approximation, for human consciousness is trammeled by the world of matter. Cousin emphasizes that though the idea of beauty may shine "more brightly in the works of man" than in nature, "still the idea can never be entirely unfolded" by the work of art (*du beau*, p. 190; Daniel, p. 38). Thus he prepares his students to accept defeat: "Each work of art is but an approximation: the final expression of the ideal is in the Infinite, is in God. There is an unbridgeable chasm between God and the limit at which human efforts fail.... You will never attain the true ideal in itself; ... you struggle in vain to purify the real, to raise it to its greatest height. The absolute is always too high and too pure, and you will never reach it" (*du beau*, p. 207; my translation). Poe first suggested that the artist's attempt to embody the ideal in his work of art could never be fully realized in conjunction with his reference to Cousin in Poe's review of "Orion." Poetry, he said, "is the imperfect effort to quench this immortal thirst" for beauty (*Works*, 11:256). He made a more emphatic promise of defeat in "The Poetic Principle": "When by Poetry—or when by Music, the most entrancing of the Poetic moods—we find ourselves melted into tears—we weep them ... through a certain, petulant, impatient sorrow at our inability to grasp *now*, wholly here on earth, at once and for ever, those divine and rapturous joys, of which, *through* the poem, or *through* the music, we attain to but brief and indeterminate glimpses" (*Works*, 14:274). And, of course, this idea is the central theme of "Al Aaraaf" and "Israfel."

Cousin and Poe are also in close agreement as to the effect a work of art that even imperfectly suggests the ideal will have upon the reader, viewer, or listener. Cousin notes that the artist, in the act of creation, "experiences a *special* sentiment, awakened by the idea of the Beautiful; a sentiment disengaged from all desire, elevating and giving warmth to his soul.... The result of his work is to excite in the spectator the same sentiment of Beauty by which he himself has been possessed" (*du beau*, p. 239; my translation).[11] Poe's statements about the effect of pure poetry use the same idea of elevation and also refer to the receptive faculty as the "soul." In the same paragraph in which he cites Cousin in his review of Horne's "Orion," Poe notes that Tennyson's "Oenone" "exalts the soul ... into a conception of pure *beauty*, which in its elevation—its calm and intense rapture—has in it a foreshadowing of the future and spirtual life" (*Works*, 11:255). Two years late, in defining, in "The Philosophy of Composition," the effect a poem ought to convey, Poe insisted on that "pleasure" "at once the most intense, the most elevating, and the most pure" which is experienced "in the contemplation of the beautiful. When, indeed, men speak of Beauty, they mean, precisely, not a quality, as is supposed, but an effect— ... that intense and pure elevation of *soul* ... which is experienced in consequence of contemplating 'the beautiful'" (*Works*, 14:197–98). Poe used similar phrases to restate the same idea in "The Poetic Principle" (*Works*, 14:266, 275).

Both Poe and Cousin feel that the potential confusion between this pleasing elevation and excitement of the soul and the distinctly nonethereal excitement one experiences in the arousal of one's physical passions threatens the concept of the pure effect of ideal beauty which a work of art should induce. Thus both men emphasize the difference between the reaction of the grosser human emotions to sensual stimuli on the descendental level, and the pure excitation of the "soul" when it is elevated to a transcendent perception of ideal beauty. Cousin insists that "the property of Beauty is not to excite desire but to repress it. ... Nothing that is an object of desire is Beautiful; and nothing that is Beautiful excites desire" (*du beau*, pp. 218–19; Daniel, pp. 73–74).

> He who allows himself to be unsettled, moved, or troubled by a material object will never be an artist; if the physcial emotions enter as elements into [the artist's] work, upon seeing it we must feel the same sensations. But, should the productions of art move us with desire for the physical objects which are portrayed in the composition? Does not the imagination of the artist seek, within nature, the absolute idea of Beauty which is hidden there? ... The artist sees only the Beautiful where the sensual man finds only the alluring (*du beau*, pp. 239–40; my translation).

Poe argued this point in the context of his reference to Cousin in the "Orion" review. It was to prove the point "that poetry and *passion* are discordant" that Poe cited Tennyson's "Oenone" as an example of a poem which "exalts the soul not into passion, but into a conception of pure *beauty*, which in its elevation ... far transcends earthly passion," and then went on to present Cousin's "sentiment of the beautiful" as the "divine sixth sense" which experiences ideality in a high and pure aesthetic reaction which has nothing in common with the passionate response (*Works*, 11:255–56). Eight months later, in a review of the poetry of Amelia Welby, Poe asserted that "a passionate poem is a contradiction in terms" (*Works*, 11:277). Once again it may serve as an indication of Cousin's actual influence on Poe to note that, before Poe could have read Cousin, he expressed the idea in his Drake-Halleck review in April 1836 that though poetry "has no inevitable, and indeed no necessary co-existence" "with the *passions* of mankind," still poetry could "modify," "exalt," "purify," and even "inflame" those passions (*Works*, 8:283).[12] Later, in "The Philosophy of Composition," with the possible support of Cousin's position, Poe stressed that the arousal of passion was "absolutely antagonistic" to the experience of ideal beauty, introducing a separate faculty, the "heart," which is stimulated by passion, to distinguish carefully the passionate reaction from the higher excitation and elevation of the "soul" (*Works*, 14:198). In "The Poetic Principle," Poe added a further illustration of the difference between a grossly passionate response to art and a purer, higher excitation, by contrasting sexual passion to an idealized Platonic love: "The manifestation of the [Poetic] Principle is always found in *an elevating excitement of the Soul*—quite independent of that passion which is the intoxication of the heart.... For, in regard to Passion, alas! its tendency is to degrade, rather than to elevate the Soul. Love, on the contrary—Love—the true, the divine Eros—the Uranian, as distinguished from the Dionaean Venus—is unquestionably the purest and truest of all poetic themes" (*Works*, 14:290). In making this distinction, Poe aligned himself more closely than ever with Cousin, for Cousin had used the same contrast between love, "that pure and disinterested love which we call the Sentiment of the Beautiful" (*du beau*, p. 233; Daniel, p. 94), as symbolic of the true nature of the pure aesthetic experience, and passion, a lower, grossly sensual response to natural stimuli: "Physical sensibility chokes the sentiment of the Beautiful. Love pure, love disinterested, is the chief element, the true foundation of the imagination. We agree, undoubtedly, that physical sensibility is necessary, as the *occasion* for the development of imagination; but... pure love at last must... give warmth and vitality to the composition" (*du beau*, p. 240; Daniel, pp. 103–104).

Cousin also anticipates Poe in insisting that poetry should eschew attempts to be "useful" or "true," or to promote a moral effect or sentiment:

> Finally, I will examine a theory which confounds the Beautiful with religion and morality, and, consequently, the sentiment of the Beautiful with the moral and religious sentiment. According to this theory, the end of art is to make us better men, and to lift up our hearts to heaven.... [But] the Beautiful excites an internal, distinct, and special sentiment which has reference only to itself; Art is no more the servant of religion and of morals than of the useful; art is not an instrument but rather an end in itself (*du beau*, pp. 223–24; my translation).[13]

Cousin thus provided strong support for Poe's solitary attack against "the heresy of *The Didactic.*" (*Works*, 14:271), "which turns to prose (and that of the very flattest kind) the so called poetry of the so called transcendentalists" (*Works*, 14:207–208), the lesser kind of poetry Poe felt Longfellow and others were writing: "It has been assumed... that the ultimate object of all Poetry is Truth. Every poem, it is said, should inculcate a moral; and by this moral is the poetical merit of the work to be adjudged. We Americans especially have patronised this happy idea; and we Bostonians, very especially, have developed it in full" (*Works*, 14:271).[14] Poe's counter argument in "The Poetic Principle" is that "The demands of Truth are severe. She has no sympathy with the myrtles. All *that* which is so indispensable in Song, is precisely all *that* with which *she* has nothing whatever to do.... He must be theory-mad beyond redemption who, in spite of these differences, shall persist in attempting to reconcile the obstinate oils and waters of Poetry and Truth" (*Works*, 14:272; see also *Works*, 11:70, 254).

Both Poe and Cousin hasten to add a qualifying clause to their prohibition against moralizing. In "The Poetic Principle," after the aggressive statement quoted above, Poe softens his position: "It by no means follows, however, that the incitements of Passion, or the precepts of Duty, or even the lesson of Truth may not be introduced into a poem, and with advantage; for they may subserve... the general purposes of the work:—but the true artist will always contrive to tone them down in proper subjection to that *Beauty* which is the atmosphere and the real essence of the poem" (*Works*, 14:275–76; see also *Works*, 11:67–68, 71; 14:198). Cousin, too, adds his qualification in the midst of his insistence that beauty and morality should not be combined. And, like Poe, he ends his exception by returning once again to his basic position. Cousin refuses to reject the possibility that art can make us better persons and raise our hearts toward heaven,

> because the Beautiful is one form of the Infinite just as is the Good. So that by elevating us toward the ideal, Beauty also raises us toward the Infinite, toward God. But, I maintain that the form of the Beautiful is distinct from the form of the Good; and if art promotes moral perfection, it does not seek to do so, it does not pose this as its true end.... I do not mean that the pure and disinterested sentiment of Beauty cannot be the noble ally of morality and religion; ... but these sentiments must not be confused (*du beau*, pp. 223–24; my translation).[15]

It would give a false impression, however, and do a disservice to Poe's originality to suggest that he simply took over all of Cousin's ideas. Poe's aesthetic position contrasts with Cousin's in important ways. Armin Staats, the only other critic to suggest that Poe might have been influenced by Cousin, argues that Poe derived his schema of the three divisions or faculties of "the world of mind"—"the pure intellect, taste, and the moral sense" on which his distinction between the effects of beauty, truth, and morality is based, from Cousin.[16] Poe introduced his schema and the argument based upon it in his April 1842 review of Longfellow, repeated it with modifications in "The Philosophy of Composition," and returned to his original 1842 version in "The Poetic Principle": "We place *taste* between the intellect and the moral sense, because it is just this intermediate space which, in the mind, it occupies. It is the connecting link in the triple chain.... Just as conscience, or the moral sense, recognises duty; just as the intellect deals with *truth*; so is it the part of taste alone to inform us of BEAUTY. And Poesy is the handmaiden of Taste" (*Works*, 11:70; 14:198, 272–73). I have argued elsewhere that Poe's schema very closely resembles that proposed by Immanuel Kant in the "Introduction" to his *Critique of Judgment*, in which Kant places the aesthetic judgment (*Urteilskraft*) as the mediating and linking faculty between the intellect (*Verstand*) and the pure Reason (*Vernunft*).[17] Kant is a much more likely source of Poe's schema than Cousin, for Poe consistently describes and applies his schema in the same way that Kant consistently discusses his. Cousin had obviously read some Kant. One of Cousin's works is an interpretation of Kant's *Critique of Pure Reason*,[18] and in his *Cours de philosophie* of 1836 he cites Kant at least twice, both times to contradict him (*du beau*, pp. 217, 274; Daniel, pp. 71, 149). But Cousin is inconsistent in his interpretation of just what the mental faculties involved in the creation and perception of art are and rearranges (one might say "garbles") any schema of faculties he may have taken from Kant; so Cousin never reproduces a schema that at all closely resembles the one consistently used by Kant and Poe. Early in his discussion of "the Beautiful," Cousin argues that the physical senses (*la sensibilité*) perceive that which is "agreeable" or physically desirable while the "judgment" (*le jugement*) perceives that which is beautiful (*du beau*, pp. 208, 228; Daniel, pp. 60, 90). Here the faculties are those used by Locke and Hume rather than by Kant in the *Critique of Judgment*. Poe does not include the senses in his schema at all. A few pages later, Cousin uses Kant's concept of a linking faculty in making "the sentiment of the Beautiful" "intermediate" (*intermédiare*) between "the sensation of the agreeable" and "the judgment of the Beautiful" (*le jugement du beau*) (*du beau*, pp. 216–17; Daniel, pp. 69–70). But here the mediating faculty is not Kant's aesthetic judgment nor Poe's "taste," nor are the two faculties mediated between at all Kant's *Verstand* and *Vernunft* nor Poe's "intellect" and "moral sense." Moreover, Cousin does not make clear what the difference is between "the sentiment of the Beautiful" and "the judgment of the Beautiful."

In the one passage from Cousin's *Cours de philosophie* of 1836 that Staats cites in support of his contention that Poe derived his concept of the three faculties of the mind from Cousin, Cousin does seem at first glance to resemble both Poe's and Kant's schema in placing "the sentiment of the Beautiful between the rational judgment [*le jugement rationnel*] which determines it, and the fact of physical sensibility which occasionally serves as its escort, but with which it is never confounded" (Staats, p. 39; *du beau*, p. 231; Daniel, p. 91). But it is difficult to discern just what Cousin means by his faculty of "rational judgment." Does he mean the concept of the "rational" to be taken in the sense of Kant's *Verstand*, or of Kant's *Vernunft*? Both could be translated into French and English by the term "*rationnel*" or "rational." In either case, the combination of intellect-judgment, or the combination Reason-judgment, links faculties which Poe and Kant keep carefully separate. Even if one assumes that Cousin's *jugement rationnel* is somehow equivalent to Kant's *Vernunft* and Poe's "moral sense" and that Cousin's "sentiment of the Beautiful" is equivalent to Poe's "taste" and Kant's *Urteilskraft*, the third of Cousin's faculties is the physical sensibility which is again closer to the triad of faculties used by the English empiricists than to the third faculty of *Verstand* or "intellect" used by Kant and Poe.

Cousin's inconsistency becomes even more apparent in his discussions of the faculty of "taste." At the outset, Cousin's concept of "taste" is different from Poe's. What Poe means by "taste" is not easy to grasp, but it seems roughly equivalent to what Kant indicates as "aesthetic judgment."[19] It does not seem to be synonymous with "imagination," a term Poe largely discarded as he came to rely more and more on the concept of "taste." For Cousin, however, "taste" and "genius" are two aspects of the imagination: "taste" is the faculty which appreciates beauty; "genius" is the faculty which creates art (*du beau*, pp. 263–64, 267; Daniel, pp. 133, 136–37). Cousin describes "taste" as made up of "three essential elements": "sensible intuition" (*l'intuition sensible*), "reason" (*la raison*), and "the judgment and the sentiment of the Beautiful" (*le jugement et le sentiment du beau*) (*du beau*, p. 264; Daniel, pp. 133–34). By now, one has become impatient. Cousin combines here "the sentiment of the Beautiful" and "the judgment of the Beautiful" into one "element" when originally, in a different triad of faculties, he had the former as "intermediate" between the latter and the physical senses. Cousin also now includes the physical senses in his new triad along with "reason." The impression that Cousin is carelessly throwing terms and concepts around is confirmed when only a few pages later, Cousin observes that "the three conditions of taste are, the sentiment of the Beautiful, reason, and the representative faculty" (*du beau*, p. 272; Daniel, pp. 144–45). One is forced to conclude that whatever Cousin may think or mean, he cannot be the source of Poe's consistently applied schema of "intellect, taste, and the moral sense."

However, the major conclusion of Poe's and Cousin's aesthetic position is exactly the same—that the only valid intention of the artist is to produce through the work of art the experience, or "effect," of pure, ideal beauty, rather than compete with philosophy, morality, or religion. Poe concludes: "the *creation* of BEAUTY...[is] the essence of all Poesy" (*Works*, 11:73); "Beauty is the sole legitimate province of the poem" (*Works*, 14:197); "The struggle to apprehend the supernal Loveliness—...on the part of souls fittingly constituted—has given to the world all *that* which it...has ever been enabled at once to understand and *to feel* as Poetic" (*Works*, 14:274). Cousin insists that "art is its own end, as religion and morals are their own end" (*du beau*, p. 215; Daniel, p. 6); "Art should have only one aim, to excite the sentiment of the Beautiful" (*du beau*, p. 226; my translation);[20] "We must have religion for the sake of religion, morality for the sake of morality, art for the sake of art" (*du beau*, p. 224; my translation). Poe's slogan is arrestingly similar to Cousin's: "Under the sun there neither exists nor *can* exist any work more thoroughly dignified—more supremely noble than...this poem which is a poem and nothing more—this poem written solely for the poem's sake" (*Works*, 14:272).

Allowing for the happy accident that Poe originated for himself an expression that was to become a cliché in the later nineteenth century, it is interesting to conjecture where else but in Cousin Poe might have found this phrase in the 1840s. At least five scholars credit Cousin with having originated the expression *"l'art pour l'art"*: Albert Cassagne, L. M. Findlay, Paul Janet, Alfred Michiels, and Louise Rosenblatt.[21] Joel E. Spingarn notes, however, that the phrase appears in the *Journal Intime* of Benjamin Constant as early as 1804.[22] Since Poe never refers to Constant in either his works or his letters,[23] Constant seems an unlikely source of Poe's phrase "this poem written solely for the poem's sake." Findlay notes that Coleridge used the English phrase "beauty for its own sake" in his essay "On the Principles of Genial Criticism Concerning the Fine Arts" in 1814,[24] and that Leigh Hunt commented on Keats' "revelling in real poetry for its own sake" in the *Examiner* for July 1817.[25] Poe could have read Coleridge's essay when it was republished in Cottle's *Early Recollections* of 1837.[26] Findlay also notes that the French critic Desiré Nisard commented on "the theories of 'art for art's sake'" in an essay on Lamartine in the *Westminster Review* for January 1837.[27] Thus, a strong case cannot be made for Victor Cousin as the only possible source of Poe's statement. However, we can note that when Poe used the phrase in "The Poetic Principle" in 1848, Cousin's works had been very popular in Europe and the United States for about fifteen years.

Cousin's lectures were immediately successful because of his eloquence and enthusiasm as a lecturer, and because the mixture of ideas from Plato, Christian Neoplatonists, Kant, Schelling, Shaftesbury, Thomas Reid, and Dugald Stewart which Cousin called "Eclecticism" constituted an optimistic philosophy which made God and the Platonic ideals seem accessible to any person of normal intelligence. A writer in the *Christian Review* for December 1838 noted that Cousin's lectures, "delivered before an audience of several thousands, were received with an *éclat* and applause hitherto unexampled in Paris; they were taken down at the time of delivery by a stenographer, corrected by the author, and were circulated in the daily journals, from one end of the kingdom to the other." The writer concluded that "few men in France have attracted more attention in the literary world, and few have done more in that country to ... arouse the general attention to liberal and philosophical studies."[28] Cousin soon became known internationally, particularly in the United States where he attracted considerable attention and caused some controversy during the 1830s and 1840s. Vankirk's statement, in "Mesmeric Revelation," that he had studied Cousin "in his own works as well as in those of his European and American echoes" (*Works*, 5:243), indicates that Poe was aware of the influence and coverage that Cousin was experiencing during Poe's own career as editor and reviewer.[29]

The earliest critical notices of Cousin in America seem to have been by A. H. Everett in the July 1829 *North American Review*, Charles J. Ingersoll in the January 1830 *Christian Examiner*, and an anonymous writer in the December 1831 *American Quarterly Review*.[30] In 1832, Henning G. Linberg published Cousin's *Introduction to the History of Philosophy* (a translation of the first thirteen lectures of Cousin's *Cours de philosophie* of 1828, not to be confused with the *Cours de philosophie ... sur le fondement des idées absolues du vrai, du beau, et du bien* given as lectures in 1818 and published in 1836). In 1834, Caleb Sprague Henry translated Cousin's *Elements of Psychology* (a translation of lectures sixteen through twenty-five of volume 2 of Cousin's *Histoire de la philosophie au dix-huitième siècle*, 1829), and Sarah Austin published a translation and abridgment of Cousin's *Report on the State of Public Instruction in Prussia*.[31] These translations were immediately popular[32] and stimulated a favorable discussion of Cousin's ideas in the *American Monthly Review*, the *North American Review*, the *American Quarterly Observer*, the *Literary and Theological Review*, the *Quarterly Christian*

Spectator, the *Methodist Quarterly Review,* and the *Ladies' Repository* between 1832 and 1842.³³

Many of the thinkers associated with the Transcendentalists were particularly interested in Cousin's more philosophical and less traditionally Christian views on religion and ethics. Between 1836 and 1840, Orestes Brownson, whom Poe cites as a popularizer of Cousin in "Mesmeric Revelation" (*Works*, 5:243), became Cousin's advocate in long articles in the *Christian Examiner* and the *Boston Quarterly Review*.³⁴ In 1838, George Ripley edited and translated *Philosophical Miscellanies from the French of Cousin, Jouffroy, and Benjamin Constant,* the first two volumes in his series of *Specimens of Foreign Standard Literature*.³⁵ Ripley also taught a class which studied Cousin at Brook Farm.³⁶ William Ellery Channing read Linberg's translation of Cousin's *Introduction to the History of Philosophy*.³⁷ Cousin was cited twice in the *Dial*, once by Theodore Parker in April 1842 and once by Emerson in April 1843.³⁸ In 1842, James Murdock, surveying the influence of Cousin's philosophy in the United States in chapters 13 and 15 of his *Sketches of Modern Philosophy, Especially Among the Germans*,³⁹ portrayed the philosophy of the Transcendentalists as little more than an importation of Cousin's Eclecticism. Murdock claimed the Linberg's translation of Cousin's *Introduction to the History of Philosophy* was "the great store house from which" Brownson, Emerson, and Parker "have derived their peculiar philosophical opinions, their modes of reasoning, and their forms of thought and expression." Murdock concluded that anyone who "would understand the Transcendental writers, must first understand, if he can, the French philosopher Cousin and the German pantheists."⁴⁰

Spokesmen for more traditional Christian opinion, who associated Cousin with "Germanism" and atheism and so, like Murdock, with the Transcendentalists, began to attack Cousin as part of their campaign against the group. James W. Alexander, Albert B. Dod, and Charles Hodge, in what became a famous article, used the occasion of a review of Linberg's and Henry's translations of Cousin to also attack Emerson's Divinity School Address in the January 1839 *Princeton Review*.⁴¹ Cousin was also brought into the Ripley-Norton controversy. In a review of Andrews Norton's *A Discourse on the Latest Form of Infidelity* (1839) and of Ripley's reply, *A Letter to Mr. Andrews Norton, Occasioned by his Discourse before the Alumni of the Cambridge Theological School* (1839), Hodge, once again writing in the *Princeton Review* and obviously supportive of Norton's position, attacked Cousin as atheistic and dangerous to traditional Christian belief.⁴² These two articles were republished as a pamphlet, edited by Norton, entitled: *Two Articles from the Princeton Review, Concerning the Transcendental Philosophy of the Germans, and of Cousin, and its Influence on Opinion in this Country* (1840). In a review of this pamphlet, Brownson defended Cousin and Ripley's position in the July 1840 *Boston Quarterly Review,* while a reviewer who referred to himself as a Transcendentalist in the July 1840 *Christian Examiner* attacked both Cousin and the authors of the pamphlet.[43] Ripley himself replied in Cousin's defense in the October 1840 *Dial*.[44]

But the Transcendentalists themselves were soon disenchanted. Cousin was often regarded as an "explainer" and clarifier of the ideas of Kant,[45] whom American and British readers initially found obscure. But as Transcendentalists like Parker and Frederic Henry Hedge began to master Kant for themselves, they realized that Cousin's interpretation of Kant's ideas was freely mixed with his own, often to the point that Kant was made to adopt a position much the opposite to that he really held. Moreover, careful scholars in general began to object to Cousin's tendency to use terms loosely and to indulge in empty but pompous verbiage. Already in 1838, Emerson, in his address on "Literary Ethics" at Dartmouth College, noted "an optical illusion" in the "great pretensions" of Cousin's Eclecticism.[46] Murdock complained of Cousin's "great inconsistency of terminology," "lax use of language," and "confusion of thought and obscurity of statement."[47] Francis Bowen, in a sharp review of Linberg's, Henry's, and Ripley's translations of Cousin, in the July 1841 *North American Review,* criticized Cousin's "liking for bold and splendid generalizations, rapidly formed and confidently stated."[48] Other articles critical of Cousin appeared in the *Christian Review* in December 1838 and March 1839, and in the *Hesperian* in April 1839.[49] Cousin was ridiculed in another article in the April 1842 *North American Review,* which took apart Thomas Chalmers' treatise "On the Wisdom, Power, and Goodness of God."[50] Even Brownson, as he moved away from the Transcendentalist point of view and toward Roman Catholicism, became critical of Cousin in articles in the *United States Magazine, and Democratic Review* in May and June 1843 and *Brownson's Quarterly Review* in January 1844.[51] Eventually, he rejected Cousin completely in an article in the June 1867 *Catholic World*.[52]

Even at the point of Cousin's highest esteem in the United States, however, the many articles on him and the works by Cousin chosen for translation dealt entirely with his psychological, moral, and religious ideas. No doubt this particular focus was a result of the specific interests of the Transcendentalists and their opponents. Yet it does seem strange that Cousin's work on aesthetics, the *Cours de philosophie... sur le fondement des idées absolues du vrai, du beau, et du bien,* though considered by some scholars as his "most famous work,"[53] was not translated into English until 1848, four years after Poe referred to Cousin and "the sentiment of the beautiful" in *Graham's Magazine*. Before 1848, the only reference to Cousin's aesthetic ideas in American journals was three summarizing sentences in the "Eclecticism" article in the December 1838 *Christian Review*.[54] In all the controversy surrounding Cousin in the United States, there was little of direct interest or of use to Poe. It would seem, then, that to the extent that Poe knew Cousin's *Cours de philosophie* of 1836, he had read it in the original French text.

Poe would have had little trouble in doing this. Several scholars have assumed that Poe could read French easily. They cite as evidence that Poe studied French, as well as Latin, Greek, Spanish, and Italian, at the University of Virginia and that at the end of the university session at Christmas 1826, Poe had "a record for excellence in Latin and French."[55] Edith Philips, Burton R. Pollin, Jacques Barzun, and Célestin Cambiaire argue that Poe's knowledge of French was poor, but they succeed only in showing that when Poe quoted from French sources or originated French expressions of his own, he sometimes made mistakes.[56] The ability to compose original statements in French and the ability to read a French text are two different skills of different degrees of difficulty. Régis Messac, the French scholar who has most thoroughly studied the influence of French literature on Poe, examines Poe's knowledge of French with careful skepticism and concludes that while Poe's ability to write and speak in French must remain in question, his ability to read French is demonstrated by the many untranslated French texts that he seems to have known well: "Notre auteur, en somme, devait être capable de lire n'importe quel texte de français courant, c'est-à-dire qu'il dispose d'un vocabulaire passif assez étendu. Il est même capable—ce dont il se montre très fier—de distinguer certaines nuances assez délicates dans le vocabulaire courant."[57] Poe's frequent use of French expressions in his works, such as the quotations from Crébillon the "The Purloined Letter" and from Voltaire in "Al Aaraaf," or the statement in French at the end of "The Duc de L'Omelette,"[58] reveal his ability to *read* complex statements in French well enough to use them intelligently, meaningfully, and appropriately in contexts of his own. Arguments as to whether Poe found the quotations by actually reading Crébillon and Voltaire, or some more popular source, and as to whether Poe may have borrowed the expressions in "The Duc de L'Omelette" from a French text are beside the point. Poe's two letters to Frederick W. Thomas, in which Poe assumes his own ability to read French, were written in 1841 and 1842,[59] five years after the publication of Cousin's *Cours de philosophie* of 1836 and three years before Poe's references to Cousin in his review of "Orion" and in "Mesmeric Revelation." Surely Poe, aware of Cousin through the controversy surrounding him in the United States, and hearing of the publication of a new text by Cousin dealing, for the first time, with aesthetic theory, would have been able to secure this text in the United States several years after its publication in France and read his way through it.

Thus, the evidence suggests that Poe could and did read Cousin's *Cours de philosophie...sur le fondement des idées absolues du vrai, du beau, et du bien* in the original French. But I am reluctant to reach the simple conclusion that Poe lifted a number of his critical ideas directly from Cousin, almost without acknowledgment or modification. We have seen how Poe rejected Cousin's argument where it was garbled or contradictory. It is certain, however, that Poe and Cousin stand cheek by jowl on nine major issues, four of which Poe first discussed in connection with Cousin's name in Poe's review of Horne's "Orion." Thus, a reading of Cousin's explicit discussion of the separation of beauty from truth and morality makes Poe seem less original in this position than he appears from an exclusively American point of view. When Jesse Cato Daniel's translation of Cousin's work appeared in the United States in 1849, it must have had the effect of reinforcing Poe's critical position, ironically at the time of his death. Here, suddenly, was a Frenchman who supported the solitary American in his stand against the massed forces of the Transcendentalists. So much has been written on Poe's influence on the French *Symbolistes* that it is interesting to conjecture about Poe's own debt to a French philosopher, especially since the French themselves seem to have overlooked this reverse "French connection." However, in 1853, Cousin "severely corrected" his earlier lectures on the True, the Beautiful, and the Good and republished them in French. O. W. Wight's translation of Cousin's revised lectures, published in New York in 1854, sounds at times so much like Poe that one is forced to consider the possibility that Cousin was, in turn, influenced in his revisions by Poe's critical essays which perhaps were originally shaped by Cousin.[60]

One conclusion I would like to make concerns not how much Poe was influenced, or borrowed, or adapted, but how many of the major, seminal works of his time Poe read, absorbed, and used. I have argued, here and elsewhere, that some of Poe's important aesthetic ideas may have come from Kant's *Critique of Judgment*.[61] Other of Poe's ideas may have been derived from Locke, Coleridge, A. W. Schlegel, Madame de Staël, and Charles Villers.[62] If we also accept the possibility that Poe incorporated Cousin's ideas into his critical theories, we must think of Poe as a scholar rather than a hurried journalist. In a few brief essays, he condensed ideas that were current in the best works of the British, German, and French intellectual traditions. If this fact tends to diminish Poe's originality, it must also enhance his reputation as a critic working in the context of the most recent, contemporary, international trends of thought, as a "comparativist" worthy of the modern application of the term.

NOTES

1. Books and articles on sources of Poe's aesthetic theories, and on French influences on Poe in particular and American literature in general, which do not discuss Cousin as an influence on Poe include: Margaret Alterton, *Origins of Poe's Critical Theory* (Iowa City: University of Iowa, 1925); Célestin Pierre Cambiaire, *The Influence of Edgar Allen Poe in France* (New York: G. E. Stechert, 1927); Robert D. Jacobs, *Poe: Journalist and Critic* (Baton Rouge: Louisiana State University Press, 1969); Georges J. Joyaux, "Victor Cousin and American Transcendentalism," *French Review,* 29 (December 1955): 117–30; Émile Lauvrière, *Le Génie morbide d'Edgar Poe: Poésies et Contes* (Paris: Desclée de Brouwer, 1935); Walter L. Leighton, *French Philosophers and New-England Transcendentalism* (Charlottesville: University of Virginia, 1908); Régis Messac, *Influences françaises dans l'oeuvre d'Edgar Poe* (Paris: Picart, 1929); Patrick F. Quinn, *The French Face of Edgar Poe* (Carbondale: Southern Illinois University Press, 1957); Isaac Woodbridge Riley, "La Philosophie Française en Amérique: De Voltaire à Cousin," *Revue Philosophique,* 84 (November 1917): 393–428; Louis Seylaz, *Edgar Poe et les premiers symbolistes français* (Lausanne: Imprimerie La Concorde, 1923); and G. R. Thompson, *Poe's Fiction: Romantic Irony in the Gothic Tales* (Madison: University of Wisconsin Press, 1973).

2. *The Complete Works of Edgar Allan Poe,* ed. James A. Harrison (New York: Thomas Y. Crowell, 1902), 11:256–57. All further references to this work will appear in the text.

3. Poe made one other reference to Cousin in a review of "The Poetry of Rufus Dawes" in *Graham's Magazine* for October 1842, but here the reference is to the contents of Dawes' poem "Geraldine" rather than a substantive citation of Cousins works or ideas (*Works,* 11:136).

4. Victor Cousin, *Cours de philosophie professé à la Faculté des Lettres pendant l'année 1818, sur le fondement des idées absolues du vrai, du beau, et du bien* (Paris: L. Hachette, 1836). All further references to this work will appear in the text.

5. Cousin's lectures on "the Beautiful," lectures 19–29, were translated in 1848 by Jesse Cato Daniel, *The Philosophy of the Beautiful from the French of Victor Cousin* (London: William Pickering, 1848; New York: Daniel Bixby, 1849). I have used Daniel's translation throughout the following discussion except in a few instances where I have emended it to come closer to the exact wording of Cousin's original French. All references to Daniel's translation will appear in the text and will be to the New York edition, which has a different pagination from the London edition.

6. See also Cousin's final statement in his discussion of "the Beautiful": "the absolute, the ideal, the pure idea of the Beautiful; this is one of the manifestations of Infinite Being—of God" (*du beau,* p. 301; Daniel, p. 185).

7. See also, "Art is the power of realizing the ideal" (*du beau,* p. 194; Daniel, p. 42).

8. See also: "Art is a perfected nature that conceives of unity beneath variety, of the general with the particular, . . . the absolute within the relative, the ideal within the real, and that strives to reproduce the object of this conception but by means of forms more faithful" (*du beau*, p. 300; Daniel, p. 183). Because "the Beautiful is concealed *beneath* the real" (*du beau*, p. 189; Daniel, p. 36), ideal beauty must be "evolved from real Beauty by an immediate abstraction which perceives the one in the other" (*du beau*, p. 206; Daniel, p. 57).

9. See also Cousin's warning to the artist: "If you shut yourself up within the narrow boundary of the individual and the variable, your works will vanish and be forgotten like all that is changeful. That you may live for ever in the hearts of other men, lay hold on that which never passes away, the absolute, the ideal, the pure idea of the Beautiful" (*du beau*, p. 301; Daniel, p. 185).

10. Margaret Alterton claims that Poe derived this idea from Plato's dialogue between Socrates and Glaucon at the beginning of Book 10 of *The Republic* in which Socrates "ridicules the apparent creations of him who creates by repeating exactly what is before him" (*Origins*, pp. 129–30). Alterton bases her claim on the superficial resemblance between the mirror image used by Plato in Socrates' statement: "There are many ways in which the feat [of imitating nature directly] might be quickly and easily accomplished, none quicker than that of turning a mirror round and round" (*The Dialogues of Plato translated into English with Analyses and Introduction by B. Jowett*, 3d ed. [London: Oxford University Press, 1892], 3:308), and Poe's image of "the eyes of Amaryllis . . . repeated in the mirror" which immediately precedes Poe's statement, "He who shall merely sing . . ." in his April 1842 Longfellow review and in "The Poetic Principle." But the basic conclusion of Plato's discussion is the very antithesis of Poe's. Socrates argues that no poet is capable of elevating the reader to an experience of ideal beauty because poets are only imitators of surface reality: "Must we not infer that all these poetic individuals, beginning with Homer, are only imitators; they copy images of virtue and the like, but the truth they never reach? . . . The imitator or maker of the image knows nothing of true existence; he knows appearances only" (*Dialogues of Plato*, 3:314). Thus, concludes Socrates, "we are well aware that poetry being such as we have described is not to be regarded seriously as attaining to the truth" (*Dialogues of Plato*, 3:323).

Alterton then notes that "Coleridge expresses very much the same idea [as Poe] and doubtless drew on Plato for the point" (Alterton, *Origins*, p. 130n124). She then quotes from *Biographia Literaria*: "Images, however beautiful, though faithfully copied from nature, and as accurately represented in words, do not of themselves characterize the poet. They become proofs of original genius only as far as they are modified by a predominant passion; or by associated thoughts or images awakened by that passion; or when they have the effect of reducing multitude to unity, or succession to an instant" (*Biographia Literaria*, ed. J. Shawcross [Oxford: Oxford University Press, 1907], 2:16). Coleridge clearly did *not* draw on the cited passage from Plato for this idea; nor does Coleridge's idea particularly resemble Poe's. Coleridge is not discussing the influence of ideal vision on the creativity of the poet but rather the importance of passion and the artist's unifying capacity in shaping a work of art. However, in his brief essay "On Poesy or Art," Coleridge does state an idea that resembles Poe's: "If the artist copies the mere nature, the *natura naturata*, what idle rivalry! If he proceeds only from a given form, which is supposed to answer to the notion of beauty, what an emptiness, what an unreality there is in his productions. . . . Believe me, you must master the essence, the *natura naturans,* which presupposes a bond between nature in the higher sense and the soul of man" (Coleridge, *Biographia,* 2:257). I would argue that the rhythm and phrasing of Poe's statement are closer to those of Cousin than Coleridge. (Cousin: "The artist who . . . should be satisfied to copy [nature] faithfully would fall from the rank of an artist to that of a mechanic"; Poe: "He who shall merely sing . . . with however vivid a truth of imitation, of the sights and sounds which greet him in common with all mankind—he, we say, has yet failed to prove his divine title.") However, "On Poesy or Art" was first published in volume one of Coleridge's *Literary Remains* in 1836 (Coleridge, *Biographia,* 2:317), so that Poe would have had the opportunity to read it and use the cited passage as the source of his own statement made in 1842.

11. See also Cousin's similar statement: "If art has for its great purpose the picturing forth of moral beauty, the result is that it excites in other minds the sentiment of the Beautiful which the artist possesses" (*du beau,* p. 268; Daniel, p. 141).

12. In his comments on the incongruity of poetry and passion in his review of Horne's "Orion," Poe twice cited Coleridge as an authority who supported his position: "Although we agree, for example, with Coleridge, that poetry and *passion* are discordant, yet we are willing to permit Tennyson to bring, to the intense passion which prompted his 'Locksley Hall,' the aid of that terseness and pungency which are derivable from rhythm and from rhyme"; "If, with Coleridge, who, however erring at times, was precisely the mind fitted to decide a question such as this—if, with him, we reject *passion* from the true—from the pure poetry . . . with how much greater reason shall we dismiss all else?" (*Works,* 11:255, 256). This repeated attribution suggests that Coleridge rather than Cousin is the source of Poe's concept. However, Margaret Alterton notes that "the idea does not appear to come from Coleridge" and cites F. C. Prescott to support her (*Origins,* p. 127n113; Frederick Clarke Prescott, *Selections from the Critical Writings of Edgar Allan Poe* [New York: Henry Holt, 1909], p. 345). Derek Mossop, in "Poe's Theory of Pure Poetry," *Durham University Journal,* n.s. 17 (March 1956): 60–61, is also hard put to find the idea in Coleridge but suggests Coleridge's comments on Shakespeare's "Venus and Adonis" in which Coleridge describes the poet as "unparticipating in the passions, and actuated only by that pleasurable excitement which had resulted from the energetic fervour of his own spirit" (Coleridge, *Biographia,* 2:15). In his essay "On the Principles of Genial Criticism Concerning the Fine Arts," Coleridge defined the experience of beauty as a "simultaneous intuition of the relation of parts, each to each, and of all to a whole: exciting an immediate and absolute complacency, without intervenence, therefore, of any interest, sensual or intellectual" (Coleridge, *Biographia,* 2:239). Neither of these quotations, however, seems strong enough to justify Poe's association of his unequivocal view that "poetry and *passion* are discordant" with Coleridge.

In the third paragraph of "On Poesy or Art," Coleridge discussed the relationship between poetry and passion somewhat more fully. Though he insisted that all the "materials" of poetry "are from the mind, and all its products are for the mind," he did feel that poetry was an "apotheosis" of natural passions that are indicated by and associated with poetic images. Thus while poetry "recalls the sights and sounds that had accompanied the occasions of the original passions, poetry impregnates [these sights and sounds] with an interest not their own by means of the passions, and yet tempers the passion by the calming power which all distinct images exert on the human soul" (Coleridge, *Biographia*, 2:254). This concept of poetry as having a tempering and calming effect on the original passions may, perhaps, be what Poe had in mind in his earlier view, expressed in his Drake-Halleck review in 1836, that poetry could "modify," "exalt," and "purify" the passions. But Coleridge's discussion does *not* support Poes claim in the same passage that poetry could "inflame" the passions. Moreover, Poe's and Coleridge's views on the relationship between poetry and passion soon diverged to opposing extremes. While Poe asserted in "The Philosophy of Composition" that the stimulation of passion and the experience of ideal beauty were "absolutely antagonistic," Coleridge, in chapter 17 of *Biographia Literaria*, discussed passion as an essential element in artistic creation. Though "the property of Passion is not to *create*," Coleridge felt, it can "set in increased activity." Under "the unusual stimulation" which is "the appropriate effect of strong excitement," the "heat of passion may produce" new "connections of thoughts or images" in the poet's mind (Coleridge, *Biographia*, 2:42). In chapter 18, Coleridge described "the *origin* of metre" as "the balance in the mind effected by that spontaneous effort which strives to hold in check the workings of passion." The result is a "salutary antagonism" between passion, and "the will and judgement . . . for the foreseen purpose of pleasure." Thus, in every poem, there "must be not only a partnership, but a union; an interpenetration of passion and of will, of spontaneous impulse and *voluntary* purpose" (Coleridge, *Biographia*, 2:49–50). This discussion by Coleridge may be the basis of Poe's willingness "to permit Tennyson to bring, to the intense passion which prompted his 'Locksley Hall,' the aid of that terseness and pungency which are derivable from rhythm and from rhyme." But why does Poe, in his "Orion" review, want to seem to disagree with Coleridge when he agrees with him that there is a pleasureable tension between meter and passion, and seem to agree with Coleridge "that poetry and passion are discordant," when, in chapter 18 of *Biographia Literaira*, Coleridge concludes that poetry "does always imply PASSION: which word must be here understood in its general sense as an excited state of the feelings and faculties" (Coleridge, *Biographia*, 2:55–56)? The only plausible explanation of Poe's otherwise meaningless confusion is that it is intended to camouflage the source and extent of Poe's borrowings from Cousin. This would not be the only situation in which Poe used this subterfuge. I have discussed elsewhere Poe's apparent attempts to conceal his debt to Immanuel Kant (" 'Intellect, Taste, and the Moral Sense': Poe's Debt to Immanuel Kant," STUDIES IN THE AMERICAN RENAISSANCE 1980, p. 131). Henry A. Pochmann comments on Poe's obvious silence about the many resemblances between his own stories and those of E. T. A. Hoffmann (*German Culture in America 1600–1900* [Madison: University of Wisconsin Press, 1957], p. 716n186); and Régis Messac discusses Poe's tendency to "camouflage" his borrowings from other French sources (*Influences*, p. 57).

13. Cousin returns to this point a few pages later: "A man ceases to be an artist when he devotes his pencil, his chisel, or his lyre to any other purpose than the production of the Beautiful. So that, although Beauty can avail men otherwise than by unfolding within them a pure sentiment, the true artist never proposes any other end beside this sentiment" (*du beau*, p. 230; Daniel, p. 90).

14. For other Poe statements against "the heresy of *The Didactic*," Longfellow, and the Transcendentalists, see *Works*, 11:67–69, 253–54; 12:5–6, 41–43, 89–106; 13:1–13, 129.

15. Cousin's Platonic argument here and elsewhere that ideal truth, beauty, and good are three co-equal manifestations of the Infinite, such that the effect of each separate ideal is mingled with the effects of the other two, is the basis of his frequent use of the expression "moral beauty." Actually, Cousin vacillated considerably between the position that the True, the Beautiful, and the Good are separate ideals, so that art should aim only at an experience of pure beauty, and the position that truth, beauty, and good merge into one universal ideal, and that art, therefore, should combine the experience of truth and goodness with that of beauty. Elsewhere in the *Cours de philosophie . . . sur le fondement des idées absolues du vrai, du beau, et du bien* he says: "If the True, the Beautiful, and the Good appear to us to be distinct, it is not the case that they truly are, but rather that they are presented to us in different material forms. The True exists in and of itself; when the True is realized in human action, it becomes the Good; when the True is presented to us in sensible form it becomes the Beautiful. The mysterious unity which links these three ideas is the absolute, is God himself" (*du beau*, p. 298; my translation). Albert Cassagne, *La Théorie de l'Art pour l'Art en France* (1906; rpt. Paris: Lucien Dorbon, 1959), p. 43, says that this vacillation was due to pressure put on Cousin by the French clergy to give more importance to the place of morality in art. The result is consistent ambiguity in Cousin's *Cours de philosophie* of 1836 about the relationship between art, the *beau idéal*, and didactic intent which may have had some influence on Poe's own qualification of his otherwise radical position that "the obstinate oils and waters of Poetry and Truth" could not be reconciled.

16. Armin Staats, *Edgar Allan Poes symbolistiche Erzählkunst* (Heidelberg: Carl Winter, 1967), pp. 38–40. My thanks to Michael Bachem, Department of German, Temple University, for helping me to translate this work.

17. "Poe's Debt to Kant," pp. 123–68.

18. Victor Cousin, *Leçons sur la philosophie de Kant* (Paris: Ladrange, 1842).

19. "Poe's Debt to Kant," pp. 134–36.

20. See also: "The true artist has but one aim, to awaken the pure sentiment of the Beautiful" (*du beau*, p. 222; Daniel, p. 79); "Art must have no master but itself, and aim only at the expression of Beauty" (*du beau*, p. 281; Daniel, p. 159).

21. Cassagne, *Théorie*, pp. 38–39; L. M. Findlay, "The Introduction of the Phrase 'Art for Art's Sake' into English," *Notes and Queries*, n.s. 20 (July 1973): 247; Paul Alexandre René Janet, *Victor Cousin et son oeuvre* (Paris: Calmann Levy, 1885), p. 93; Alfred Michiels, *Histoire des Idées littéraires en France au dix-neuvième siècle* (Paris: W. Coquebert, 1842), 2:102; Louise M. Rosenblatt, *L'idée de l'art pour l'art dans la littérature anglaise pendant la période victorienne* (Paris: H. Champion, 1931), p. 10.

22. Joel E. Spingarn, "L'Art pour L'Art," *Modern Language Notes*, 25 (March 1910): 95.

23. See Burton R. Pollin, *Dictionary of Names and Titles in Poe's Collected Works* (New York: Da Capo, 1968).

24. Coleridge, *Biographia*, 2:236, 305.

25. Findlay, " 'Art for Art's Sake,' " 247.

26. Coleridge, *Biographia*, 2:305.

27. Findlay, " 'Art for Art's Sake,' " 247.

28. "Eclecticism," *Christian Review*, 3 (December 1838): 591–92. These remarks match closely the opening paragraph of a well-known review of Cousin's *Cours de*

philosophie of 1828 by Sir William Hamilton in the *Edinburgh Review,* 50 (October 1829): 194–221.

29. Information and bibliography on the Cousin vogue in America can be found in: George J. Joyaux, "Victor Cousin and American Transcendentalism," *French Review,* 29 (December 1955): 117–30; James Murdock, *Sketches of Modern Philosophy, Especially Among the Germans* (Hartford, Conn.: J. C. Wells, 1842), pp. 149–55, 178–82; Isaac Woodbridge Riley, "La Philosophie Française en Amérique," *Revue Philosophique,* 84 (November 1917): 393–428; René Wellek, *Immanuel Kant in England, 1793–1838* (Princeton: Princeton University Press, 1931), p. 262; Pochman, *German Culture,* pp. 102–109, 553–57n322–89. However, none of these sources discusses Cousin's aesthetic ideas and none of them suggests a connection between Poe and Cousin.

30. A. H. Everett, "History of Intellectual Philosophy" (a review of Cousin's translation of *Oeuvres de Platon,* 1822–28, and Cousin's *Fragmens philosophiques,* 1826, *Cours de philosophie,* 1828, and *Nouveaux Fragmens philosophiques,* 1828), *North American Review,* 29 (July 1829): 67–123; Charles J. Ingersoll, "National Literature" (originally "A Discourse concerning the Influence of America on the Mind, being the Annual Oration delivered before the American Philosophical Society, at the University in Philadelphia, October 18, 1823"), *Christian Examiner,* 7 (January 1830): 269–95 (Ingersoll's single reference to Cousin occurs on p. 292); "Cousin's Philosophy," *American Quarterly Review,* 10 (December 1831): 291–311.

31. Cousin, *Introduction to the History of Philosophy,* trans. Henning Gotfried Linberg (Boston: Hilliard, Gray, Little, and Wilkins, 1832); Cousin, *Elements of Psychology: Included in a Critical Examination of Locke's Essay on the Human Understanding,* trans. Caleb Sprague Henry (Hartford, Conn.: Cooke, 1834); Cousin, *Report on the State of Public Instruction in Prussia,* trans. Sarah Austin (London: Effingham Wilson, 1834). Henry's twenty-six page "Introduction" gives a convenient summary of what Americans understand Cousin's "Eclecticism" to be (Pochmann, *German Culture,* p. 102).

32. The second edition of Henry's translation of Cousin's *Elements of Psychology,* published in 1838, was used as a textbook at Harvard and elsewhere; see a review of this edition in the *Biblical Repository and Quarterly Observer,* 2d ser., 1 (January 1839): 247–48, and Francis Bowen, "Philosophy of Cousin," *North American Review,* 53 (July 1841): 1.

33. "Griffin's Remains," *American Monthly Review,* 1 (January 1832): 22–23; "Cousin's Philosophy," *North American Review,* 35 (July 1832): 19–36; "Literary Intelligence," *American Quarterly Observer,* 1 (July 1833): 177; "Prussian Schools," *American Quarterly Observer,* 3 (December 1834): 354–56; "Cousin's Elements of Psychology," *Literary and Theological Review,* 1 (December 1834): 690–91; "Cousin's Psychology," *Quarterly Christian Spectator,* 7 (March 1835): 89–127; A. H. Everett, "*Cousin's Rapport sur l'état de l'Instruction Publique,*" *North American Review,* 40 (April 1835): 511–36; "Cousin's Psychology," *Methodist Quarterly Review,* 3d ser., 1 (July 1841): 336–54; "Notice," *Ladies' Repository,* 2 (April 1842): 127.

34. See Brownson's "Cousin's Philosophy," *Christian Examiner,* 21 (September 1836): 33–64; "Recent Contributions to Philosophy," *Christian Examiner,* 22 (May 1837): 181–217; "The Eclectic Philosophy," *Boston Quarterly Review,* 2 (January 1839): 27–53; "Eclecticism-Ontology," *Boston Quarterly Review,* 2 (April 1839): 169–87; "*Fragmens philosophiques,* par V. Cousin," *Boston Quarterly Review,*

2 (October 1839): 435–48; and "Pure Reason-Rights-Duty-Free-Will," *Boston Quarterly Review,* 3 (April 1840): 193–208.

35. *Philosophical Miscellanies from the French of Cousin, Jouffroy, and Benjamin Constant,* trans. George Ripley (Boston: Hilliard, Gray, 1838). Only volume 1 contains material on and by Cousin: a forty-two-page "Introductory Notice" by Ripley, in which Ripley elaborately praises Cousin as a more successful philosopher than Coleridge; several short translations of Cousin entitled "Destiny of Modern Philosophy," "Exposition of Eclecticism," "The Moral Law and Liberty," "The Idea of Cause and of the Infinite," "Religion, Mysticism, Stoicism," and "Classification of Philosophical Questions and Schools"; and ninety pages of notes on the translations. Ripley's elaborate treatment of Cousin in this volume was republished in 1839 as volume 9 of *The Students' Cabinet Library of Useful Tracts* (Edinburgh: T. Clark, 1839), and, together with Linberg's and Henry's translations, became the source of many of the journal articles on Cousin which followed its publication. Ripley's book, for example, was enthusiastically reviewed in *New-York Review,* 3 (October 1838): 487–88; *Boston Quarterly Review,* 1 (October 1838): 433–34; *Knickerbocker,* 13 (April 1839): 353–54; *Ladies' Repository,* 1 (May 1841): 159; and *Methodist Quarterly Review,* 3d ser., 2 (April 1842): 165–92.

36. Pochmann, *German Culture,* pp. 37, 556n358.

37. Pochmann, *German Culture,* p. 83.

38. Theodore Parker, "Thoughts on Theology," *Dial,* 2 (April 1842): 488; Ralph Waldo Emerson, "Europe and European Books," *Dial,* 3 (April 1843): 513.

39. Murdock, *Philosophy,* pp. 149–55, 178–82.

40. Murdock, *Philosophy,* pp. 177–79.

41. James W. Alexander, Albert B. Dod, and Charles Hodge, "Transcendentalism," *Princeton Review,* 11 (January 1839): 37–101. The article attacks Cousin as anti-Christian and works hard to make him seem ridiculous (62–95).

42. Charles Hodge, "The Latest Form of Infidelity," *Princeton Review,* 12 (January 1840): 31–71. The attack on Cousin occurs on pp. 65–66 and 70–71.

43. Orestes Brownson, *"Two Articles from the Princeton Review," Boston Quarterly Review,* 3 (July 1840): 265–323; *"Two Articles from the Princeton Review," Christian Examiner,* 28 (July 1840): 378–89.

44. George Ripley, "Professor Walker's Vindication of Philosophy," *Dial,* 1 (October 1840): 256–60.

45. In a review of volumes 5 and 6 of Ripley's *Specimens of Foreign Standard Literature,* Samuel Osgood noted, "We are indebted to Cousin for our clearest ideas of modern German philosophy," in the *Christian Examiner,* 28 (May 1840): 137; G. E. Ellis published a translation of an article on Kant by Cousin which was originally published in *La Revue des Deux Mondes*: "Kant and his Philosophy," *American Eclectic,* 1 (March 1841): 276–87; and a reviewer sympathetic to the Transcendentalists used extensive quotations from Cousin to clarify a presentation of Kant's philosophy in "Spirit and Tendencies of the New School of Philosophy," *United States Magazine, and Democratic Review,* 15 (July 1844): 17–28.

46. *The Collected Works of Ralph Waldo Emerson,* ed. Alfred R. Ferguson et al., 2 vols. to date (Cambridge: Harvard University Press, 1971–), vol. 1, *Nature, Addresses, and Lectures* (1971), ed. Ferguson, p. 107. See also Emerson's journal for 1838, in which he notes that he found "a few memorable thoughts" in Ripley's *Philosophical Miscellanies from the French of Cousin,* "but by no means so many memorable thoughts as I have got out of many another book" (*The Journals and*

Miscellaneous Notebooks of Ralph Waldo Emerson, ed. William H. Gilman et al., 14 vols. to date [Cambridge: Harvard University Press, 1960–], 5:458).

47. Murdock, *Philosophy,* pp. 178–79.

48. Bowen, "Philosophy of Cousin," 6.

49. *Christian Review,* 3 (December 1838): 590–613; "Eclecticism," *Christian Review,* 4 (March 1839): 21–36; Rufus Dawes, "Swedenborg and Cousin," *Hesperian; or, Western Monthly Magazine,* 2 (April 1839): 482–83.

50. "Chalmers' *Natural Theology,*" *North American Review,* 54 (April 1842): 356–97. Cousin is specifically attacked on pp. 366–67, 375, 378, 386, 391, 394.

51. See Brownson's "Remarks on Universal History," *United States Magazine, and Democratic Review,* 12 (May 1843): 457–74 (Cousin is specifically discussed on pp. 467–74); "Remarks on Universal History," *United States Magazine, and Democratic Review,* 12 (June 1843): 569–86 (Cousin is specifically discussed on pp. 569–75, 580, 586); and "Eclecticism," *Brownson's Quarterly Review,* 1 (January 1844): 6–9. It is interesting to note that Poe published two pieces in the *Democratic Review* during the year following Brownson's discussion of Cousin in the same magazine—"Marginalia" in November 1844 (*Works,* 16:1–66) and his review of Amelia Welby in December 1844 (*Works,* 11:275–81). His reference to Brownson and Cousin in "Mesmeric Revelation" was first published in August 1844. It seems likely that Poe would have noticed Brownson's articles on Cousin in the May and June 1843 issues of the *Democratic Review.*

52. Orestes Brownson, "Victor Cousin and his Philosophy," *Catholic World,* 5 (June 1867): 333–47. Isaac Woodbridge Riley says that Cousin remained popular with the general reading public long after he had lost favor with the critics ("La Philosophie," 428). For example, a writer in *DeBow's Review* used Linberg's translation of Cousin's *Introduction to the History of Philosophy* as the center for five rambling articles on "The Science of History": *DeBow's Review,* 5 (January 1848): 58–64; (February 1848): 127–34; (March 1848): 211–20; (April 1848): 346–57; (May–June 1848): 445–54. Several new translations of works by Cousin followed Daniel's *Philosophy of the Beautiful* into print in the 1850s and 1860s: Orlando Williams Wright translated Cousin's *Course of the History of Modern Philosophy* (New York: D. Appleton, 1851; 2d ed., 1852; 3d ed., 1853), *Lectures on the True, the Beautiful and the Good* (New York: D. Appleton, 1854; enl. ed., 1861), and Cousin's edition of *The Thoughts, Letters, and Opuscules of Blaise Pascal* (New York: H. W. Derby, 1861); F. W. Ricord translated Cousin's *The Youth of Madame de Longueville; or Revelations of Court and Convent in the Seventeenth Century* (New York: D. Appleton, 1854); A. G. Henderson translated Cousin's *Philosophy of Kant* (London: J. Chapman, 1854); and Mary L. Booth translated Cousin's *Secret History of the French Court Under Richlieu and Mazarin; or, Life and Times of Madame de Chevreuse* (New York: Delisser and Procter, 1859; 2d ed., New York: J. Miller, 1871).

53. Frederick Will, "Cousin and Coleridge: the Aesthetic Ideal," *Comparative Literature,* 8 (Winter 1956): 65.

54. *Christian Review,* 3 (December 1838): 602. The three sentences were: "Man also possesses the ideal of the beautiful; and compared with its revelations, the coarse and imperfect representations of beauty which are found in nature, fade into insignificance. Accordingly, man begins also to model nature, after his own idea of the beautiful. This creates sculpture, painting, and poetry; and the beauty of art is pronounced to be as much superior to the beauty of nature as man is to

nature." Brownson's two articles in the *Boston Quarterly Review*, 2 (January, April 1839): 27–53, 169–87, were ostensibly reviews of Cousin's *Cours de philosophie professé à la Faculté des Lettres pendant l'année 1818*, but Brownson concentrated on Cousin's first four lectures, comparing Cousin's basic method to that of Locke and Kant, and said nothing at all about Cousin's aesthetic concepts.

55. George E. Woodberry, *The Life of Edgar Allan Poe* (Boston: Houghton, Mifflin, 1909), 1:32, 36, 70–71. See also James A. Harrison, *The Life of Edgar Allan Poe, Works*, 1:55; Una Pope-Hennessy, *Edgar Allan Poe, 1809–1849: A Critical Biography* (London: Macmillan, 1934), p. 43; Thomas R. Rees, "Why Poe? Some Notes on the Artistic Qualities of the Prose Fiction of Edgar Allan Poe," *Forum*, 12 (Spring 1974): 12; Edward C. Wagenknecht, *Edgar Allan Poe: The Man Behind the Legend* (New York: Oxford University Press, 1963), p. 117.

56. Edith Phillips says that many of the French expressions that Poe used, like *recherché* and *outré*, were clichés in English and that Poe used them in their accepted English sense, even when that sense was a corruption of the original French meaning. But Philips does not concern herself with Poe's longer statements in French, and she does not show that Poe could not *read* French ("The French of Edgar Allan Poe," *American Speech*, 2 [March 1927]: 270–74). Burton R. Pollin cites Phillips and Woodberry in support of his position but overplays Woodberry's argument that Poe sometimes used "bad French" (Woodberry, *Poe*, 1:179–80; Burton R. Pollin, *Discoveries in Poe* [Notre Dame: University of Notre Dame Press, 1970], pp. 10–11). Pollin then argues that Poe's many references to Victor Hugo and Béranger, which Poe used to give an impression of his "insouciant familiarity' with French literature and culture" were made with the help of English translations (p. ix). But Pollin admits that Poe made "authoritative allusions to the French originals" in a review of the Béranger translations (p. 54). One would also assume that in borrowing expressions in French from Hugo's *Notre Dame de Paris* with the help of a translation, Poe would have had to be able to read French well enough to correlate the equivalent English and French passages. Jacques Barzun cites two letters in which Poe suggests to Frederick W. Thomas that Thomas learn to read French by comparing "side-by-side translations continually, of which there are many to be found," as evidence that Poe used the same method ("A Note on the Inadequacy of Poe as a Proofreader and of his Editors as French Scholars," *Romanic Review*, 61 [February 1970]: 23–24). But a careful reading of the letters themselves shows that Poe is speaking of a case in which the would-be reader of French is not proficient in Latin and Greek, a situation, says Poe, which makes it "difficult" for one to learn a modern foreign language. It is clear that Poe is writing as one who knows French to one who does not, that Poe expects Thomas to understand that Poe has the " 'classical' education" that makes "the study of all additional languages . . . mere play" (*The Letters of Edgar Allan Poe*, ed. John Ward Ostrom [Cambridge Harvard University Press, 1948], 1:190, 192). Barzun also joins Woodberry and Philips in giving a list of Poe's mistakes in French and concludes: "Poe's French was from Stratford atte Bowe; the scraps of it scattered throughout his works show that when not quoting from an open book Poe stumbles" (p. 26). However, Barzun suggests here that when Poe "stumbles," he is quoting in French from memory! Barzun seems to support this impression that Poe knew French literature well when Barzun notes that Poe quoted Crébillon accurately in "The Purloined Letter," yet Crébillon was little known in the nineteenth century (26). The same point is suggested by Cam-

biaire's complaint (*Influence of Poe*, p. 263n1) that Poe's quotation from Voltaire in a footnote to "Al Aaraaf" is inaccurate (*Works*, 7:30). The real point is that Poe knew Voltaire, *in French*, well enough to quote him *à-propos*. The inaccuracy suggests that Poe was careless but also, perhaps, that he was quoting from memory.

57. Messac, *Influenses*, p. 17.
58. *Works*, 6:52; 7:30; 2:202.
59. Poe, *Letters*, 1:190, 192.
60. Wight, *Lectures on the True, the Beautiful, and the Good*, pp. vii–viii. For passages that seem to echo Poe, see pp. 131, 136, 169.
61. "Poe's Debt to Kant," pp. 123–36, 140–42.
62. Floyd Stovall, "Poe's Debt to Coleridge," *University of Texas Studies in English*, no. 10 (1930): 70–127; Alterton, *Origins*, pp. 68–79, 95, 99–106, 111–12; Albert J. Lubell, "Poe and A. W. Schlegel," *Journal of English and Germanic Philology*, 52 (January 1953): 1–12; "Poe's Debt to Kant," pp. 137–40, 151–53.

THE HIDDEN JOURNEY OF
ARTHUR GORDON PYM

Richard Kopley

IN A PREVIOUS ARTICLE, "The Secret of *Arthur Gordon Pym*: The Text and the Source,"[1] I offer a solution to the mystery of *Pym's* "shrouded human figure."[2] I suggest there that the phrase "human figure" links the polar apparition of *Pym's* climax with the Tsalal carving—a "representation of a human figure standing erect"—and I argue further that both of these may be linked with the Kerguelen's Land penguin—whose "resemblance to a human figure is very striking." Additional details, including that the underside of the penguin is white, the penguin appears most deceptive in the evening, and the penguin is often in close proximity to albatrosses, further link the penguin with the enigmatic specter, which is "of the perfect whiteness of the snow," which is encountered after "the darkness had materially increased," and which is preceded by "many gigantic and pallidly white birds." I then contend, with Charles O'Donnell, that the perilous voyage of Pym and Peters in their canoe at the end of the last chapter echoes the nearly catastrophic voyage of Pym and Augustus in the *Ariel* in the first chapter. In view of the fact that the *Ariel* encounters a ship, O'Donnell speculates that the "shrouded human figure" might be "a figurehead, sail, or prow of a ship." I concur: the final "human figure" is "shrouded" and "very far larger in its proportions than any dweller among men" precisely because it is the huge, white, wooden penguin figurehead of the ship the *Penguin*, which, as in chapter 1, will collide with, and then rescue, Arthur Gordon Pym. This argument is supported by various details in the text and tends to be confirmed by the newly found source, J. N. Reynolds' "Leaves From An Unpublished Journal." Not only does Reynolds' piece contain language singularly similar to that of Poe's *Pym*, but Reynolds' work also concludes with the rescue of men in the Antarctic by a ship named the *Penguin*. Thus, the source reinforces the reading advanced, the material explanation of *Pym*'s "shrouded human figure." If this explanation is indeed correct, then it should eventually lead to a new understanding of the symbolic identity of that figure, as well. In the present paper, I propose to continue the investigation by using close textual analysis to discover the symbolic identity of *Pym*'s "shrouded human figure." By doing so, I intend also to illuminate the whole of Poe's extraordinary novel.

The material explanation of the "shrouded human figure" directs our attention to Poe's extensive description of penguins in chapter 14. Most of the penguin passage is derivative, but Poe's revealingly divergent assertion that the penguin resembles a "human figure" is original.[3] It is necessary here to observe another tellingly divergent statement in Poe's penguin passage: "In short, survey it as we will, nothing can be more astonishing than *the spirit of reflection* evinced by these feathered beings" (3:157; my italics).

"The spirit of reflection" is a phrase which cannot be found in the penguin passages Poe relied upon from *Symzonia* and *A Narrative of Four Voyages*.[4] This phrase, like the phrase "human figure," is apparently an original insertion of Poe's. This insertion does clarify the nature of the puzzling penguin figurehead of *Arthur Gordon Pym*. Like the penguin of Kerguelen's Land, the penguin figurehead also possesses "the spirit of reflection"; however, in this case, it is not a seeming thoughtfulness which is implied. Rather, not uncharacteristically, Poe is punning: the penguin figurehead of *Arthur Gordon Pym* serves as a mirror.

It is important to add that the penguin figurehead appears not only in the last chapter as the "shrouded human figure," but also, implicity, in the first chapter, when the *Penguin* runs into the *Ariel*. The figurehead is not described here because Pym did not see it—he states that he had been so terrified by the warning shouts of unknown origin that "without having once raised my eyes to learn the source of my alarm, I tumbled headlong and insensible upon the body of my fallen companion" (3:10).

The presence of the penguin figurehead in the first and last chapters of the book and its figurative identity with a mirror help reveal the underlying structure of *Arthur Gordon Pym*. Clearly, Poe believed in "the power of symmetry"; the book, like Pym's canoe, is "modelled with the bow and stern alike" (3:233-34). More specifically, the book begins and ends with the penguin figurehead, which also functions as a mirror. Thus, the essential structure of the book emerges: two huge mirrors face one another across the expanse of the text, reflecting all that is in between, as well as each other, infinitely.

The Hidden Journey of Arthur Gordon Pym 31

Here it is apparent that Poe tried in *Pym* to make a "possible attempt at an impossible conception" (16:200): he tried to approach the infinite with finite language. In *Eureka*, Poe wrote, "The human brain has obviously a leaning to the 'Infinite,' and fondles the phantom of the idea. It seems to long with a passionate fervor for this impossible conception, with the hope of intellectually believing it when conceived" (16:275). Accordingly, the "phantom" of Pym's final journal entry, the "shrouded human figure," which is the penguin figurehead, which is one of the endlessly reflecting mirrors, is also, in fact, the "phantom of the idea" of infinity. It is a hint of that which is longed for, but impossible to reach.

The "leaning to the 'Infinite'" does take a quite particular form in *Pym*—Poe indicates covertly that the double mirrors endlessly reflect the image of one specific event in the narrative. This becomes clear with a close reading of the episode which constitutes a microcosm of the entire novel, Too-wit's confrontation with double mirrors on board the *Jane Guy*:

> There were two large mirrors in the cabin, and here was the acme of their [the natives'] amazement. Too-wit was the first to approach them, and he had got in the middle of the cabin, with his face to one and his back to the other, before he fairly perceived them. Upon raising his eyes and seeing his reflected self in the glass, I thought the savage would go mad; but, upon turning short round to make a retreat, and beholding himself a second time in the opposite direction, I was afraid he would expire upon the spot. (3:183)

The source for this passage is a similar passage in Morrell's *A Narrative of Four Voyages*, in which the native king and three of his men are also surprised by a mirror on a ship.[5] However, Morrell wrote of only one mirror; Poe added the second mirror in *Pym*, thereby duplicating the double mirrors of the first and last chapters. In this crucial passage, Poe carefully encapsulated the essential structure of *Arthur Gordon Pym*.

The missing element of the hitherto undetected structure of *Pym* is the analogue of Too-wit. This may be determined by attending to Too-wit's position—"in the middle of the cabin, with his face to one and his back to the other." If *Pym* is conceived to be the cabin, with a mirror at either end, then only that which is "in the middle" remains to be discovered.

Pym is composed of twenty-five chapters. The middle chapter of the book, chapter 13, is made up of a number of journal entries which describe Pym, Peters, and Augustus trying to survive on board the wreck of the *Grampus*. These journal entries cover a two-week period, from

24 July to 7 August. In the middle of this period, on 1 August—and in the eleventh of the twenty-two paragraphs of this chapter—Pym's wounded friend Augustus dies: "We now saw clearly that Augustus could not be saved; that he was evidently dying. We could do nothing to relieve his sufferings, which appeared to be great. About twelve o'clock he expired in strong convulsions, and without having spoken for several hours" (3:140).

It is Augustus who, at midday, is "in the middle" of the two mirrors of *Arthur Gordon Pym*: he is the analogue of Too-wit. The use of the word "expire" with regard both to Augustus and Too-wit reinforces this connection. Augustus is the missing element in the long-unrecognized structure of *Arthur Gordon Pym*. It is the image of the dying Augustus which is endlessly reflected in *Pym*'s huge double mirrors.

Moreover, it seems reasonable to suggest that these infinite reflections of the dying Augustus represent Pym's own infinite memories of his best friend's death. Thus, like "The Raven," *The Narrative of Arthur Gordon Pym* is a work which concerns, most fundamentally, "*Mournful and Never-ending Remembrance*" (14:208).

Here the "leaning to the '*Infinite*'" is very focused. It is the infinitely distant original moment of the death of Pym's friend Augustus which is longed for, but impossible to reach. Pym wishes to return to that irretrievable moment on 1 August so that he may die along with his lost friend. In order for this point to be developed further, a fuller solution to the mystery of *Pym*'s penguin figurehead must be provided. The vital connection which remains to be made is that between Pym's friend Augustus and Poe's brother Henry.

Marie Bonaparte was the first scholar to observe the definite parallels between Augustus and Henry Poe. For example, she notes that Augustus was two years older than Pym, just as Henry was two years older than Poe. Augustus told Pym stories of adventure, and Henry told Poe such stories, too. Both Augustus and Henry were given to drinking. Both were ill. And just as Augustus died in Pym's presence, so did Henry die in Poe's presence. Finally, in this context, Bonaparte specifies the date of Henry's death, 1 August, thereby implying a further critical parallel between Augustus and Henry Poe.[6]

In a slender, valuable, 1926 volume, *Poe's Brother*, Hervey Allen is credited with the discovery of the date of Henry Poe's death.[7] However, he never connects Augustus with Henry; instead, he links Augustus with Ebenezer Burling, Poe's boyhood friend.[8] Certainly there are similarities between these two; no doubt Burling was one model for the character of Augustus. Marie Bonaparte acknowledges this; however, she views Burling as "a substitute for Poe's elder brother."[9] She argues that it is actually Henry Poe, Poe's real elder brother, who is the primary model for the character of Augustus. By bringing forth the similarities between Augustus and Henry already enumerated here, and by suggestively noting Allen's own discovery, Henry Poe's date of death, which is the same as that of Augustus, Bonaparte effectively demonstrates the clear correspondence between Pym's friend Augustus and Poe's brother Henry.

This correspondence has been mentioned by other critics as well: Harry Levin cites the drinking parallel; Roger Forclaz and Richard Wilbur each note the facts of the age difference and the inclination to tell stories; Norma Jean English Walker refers to the shared date of death.[10] Critics have come to realize what Marie Bonaparte first suggested—even as Arthur Gordon Pym represents Edgar Allan Poe, Augustus represents Henry Poe. This point may be further confirmed by acknowledging additional significant parallels which have not been recognized before.

One of these parallels is that just as Pym and Augustus were, in many ways, doubles, so were Edgar and Henry Poe. Many critics have commented on the doppelganger motif in *Pym*, the most explicit evidence of which is Pym's assertion that "our intimate communion had resulted in a partial interchange of character" (3:18).[11] However, this motif has not yet been related to a similar one in the lives of Edgar and Henry Poe.

William Henry Leonard Poe, whom Edgar reputedly described as having "far more of the Poe nature" than he had,[12] published under his own name poetry by Edgar, wrote fiction about Edgar, and even called one of his characters "Edgar-Leonard."[13] Edgar reciprocated not only by writing in *Pym* about Henry, but also, earlier, by attributing to himself the adventures of Henry, and at one point by calling himself "Henri Le Rennet."[14] These details suggest that between Edgar and Henry Poe, too, there may well have been a "partial interchange of character." The "intimate communion" between them which contributed to this "partial interchange" forms the substance of the second unnoticed parallel.

Marie Bonaparte quotes an important statement Pym made with regard to himself and Augustus—"We occupied the same bed" (3:5); she later mentions that Edgar and Henry Poe shared the same room.[15] However, she fails to go beyond this to make an even more important connection. In 1831, Poe was sharing an attic room with his brother Henry in his Aunt Maria Clemm's apartment on Mechanics Row, Wilks Street, in Baltimore.[16] Considering the crowded and impoverished circumstances of the household,[17] as well as the custom of the time, it is likely that, like Pym and Augustus, Edgar and Henry Poe did share the same bed.[18]

Both these new parallels further confirm the correspondence between Augustus and Henry Poe. The second of these parallels also affords a new insight into the cryptic fragment of Augustus' message which Pym was able to read: *"blood—your life depends upon lying close"* (3:41). Literally, Augustus is here informing Pym that he should keep still. But this is not all; David Ketterer adds, "In view of the extreme amount of deception in *Pym*, it is very likely that the phrase, 'lying close,' contains a pun."[19] Certainly Augustus may be advising Pym not to speak the truth, and Poe may be acknowledging the possible deceitfulness of fiction, yet another reading of this punsome phrase is plausible, one which shows just how closely Poe did "lie" in *Pym*. Arguably, it is Pym's lying physically close to Augustus, as he did when he and Augustus (like Poe and his brother) shared the same bed, upon which Pym's life depends.

The way in which Poe recurrently employs the phrase "lying close," or variations of this phrase, tends to validate this interpretation. For instance, Pym's dog Tiger is said to be "lying close" to Pym in the hold of the *Grampus* (3:43), recalling Augustus' having told Pym that he was "tired . . . of lying in bed on such a fine night like a dog" (3:6). Fittingly enough, when Pym does escape from the hold, he once again shares the same bed with Augustus (3:74). The "lying close" of these two friends seems to be suggested further on in the novel when Poe twice notes that the ship the *Grampus* was *"laid* to under a *close*-reefed foresail" (3:80, 83; my italics). It is clearly alluded to in chapter 9, as Pym, Augustus, Peters, and Parker manage to survive on board the wreck of the *Grampus*: "Although we *lay close* together, no one of us could see the other, or, indeed, any portion of the brig itself, upon which we were so tempestuously hurled about" (3:100; my italics). This reference is soon repeated, with Peters serving as a surrogate Pym: "Augustus spoke, asking Peters, who *lay closest* to him, if he thought there was any possibility of our being saved" (3:101; my italics). Later, it is Pym, once again, who lies close to Augustus (3:109).

In terms of the novel alone, this pattern may be read as a hidden expression of Pym's profound need for the deep personal relationship he shared with Augustus, most frequently experienced in their bed. While it is possible that a specifically homosexual relationship may be implied, this does seem unlikely; little evidence is available to support such a view. Rather, it seems probable that Pym needed a private, warm, and brotherly comradeship.

The Hidden Journey of Arthur Gordon Pym   35

In terms of Poe's life, this pattern may be construed as evidence of Poe's own need for such comradeship. In spite of Henry's sickness and drinking, Poe must have cherished the "intimate communion" he was able to share with his brother in their bed in Maria Clemm's attic room. The loss of what Poe refers to in "A Descent Into The Maelstrom" as "my loved brother" (2:246) must have been a painfully wrenching one.

Poe's response to that loss was the creation of *Pym,* a magnificent memorial to the brother he had adored. The mysterious apparition of the climax of the book, the "shrouded human figure"—which is a penguin figurehead, which is one of the endlessly reflecting mirrors, which is an emblem of infinity—is, more particularly, not only the infinite reflection of the death of Augustus, but the infinite reflection of the death of Henry Poe as well. The endlessly reflecting mirrors of *Arthur Gordon Pym* represent Poe's own infinite memories of the death of his brother Henry.

Pym's finite fall on the island of Tsalal into the arms of the brotherly Peters, which echoes his earlier fall on the *Ariel* upon the body of Augustus, is followed by his infinite fall, near the South Pole, into the "shrouded human figure," one of the two mirrors which, like Pym's memory, endlessly reflect the death of Augustus. Pym seeks the unreachable moment of Augustus' death in order that he may die along with him. So, too, does Poe fall through his own infinite memories of the death of Henry Poe, seeking, but never finding, the original moment of his brother's death so that he may die along with Henry. It is this impossible quest which is the hidden journey of *Arthur Gordon Pym.*

In 1832, very shortly after Henry's death, Poe came close to acknowledging his need to die along with his brother. In a suppressed section of "Metzengerstein," Poe wrote of one "Lady Mary," "The beautiful Lady Mary! How could she die?—and of consumption! But it is a path I have prayed to follow" (2:371). William Bittner clearly links this "Lady Mary" with Poe's brother Henry, who had himself recently died of consumption.[20]

It seems reasonable to suggest here that Poe wished to die along with his brother, as Pym wished to die along with Augustus, so that he might maintain their precious "intimate communion." Poe wished to "lie close," even if it could only be in the grave. Augustus' message is ironically reversed; for Poe, "lying close" depended upon his death.

Poe sought the day of his brother's death so that he might die along with him, but 1 August 1831 was forever gone. However, it was also infinitely remembered. By embodying his infinite memory of 1 August in *Pym,* Poe was attempting to preserve and commemorate that long-lost day. It may be reasonably argued that Poe further attempted to honor that day by carefully planning for the copyright of the novel. After all, that book, whose core is the tragic death of Poe's brother, was deposited for copyright exactly seven years after Henry's death, on 1 August 1838.[21] In memory of his intense personal loss, Poe erected this extraordinary monument. *The Narrative of Arthur Gordon Pym* is a remarkable example of profound mourning transmuted into a complex and moving work of art.

Still, it is true that Poe's love for Henry was not unqualified by other emotions. While it may be a bit presumptive to argue, as Marie Bonaparte does, that Poe was jealous of his brother,[22] it does seem fair to contend that Poe felt guilt towards his brother. A number of literary allusions in *Pym* suggest this.

I speculate in my earlier article that the call "Tekeli-li!" may actually be the sailors' cry of "Tack-a-lee!";[23] additionally, it should be noted that critics have often considered the cry to be an echo of the biblical warning (Daniel 5:24-28), "Mene, Mene, Tekel, Upharsin."[24] That Pym was "found wanting" is borne out by the similarities between his story and that of the "Ancient Mariner," often observed by critics.[25] The novel's connections with Coleridge's "The Wanderings of Cain" further corroborate one's sense of Pym's guilt. In this poem, Coleridge's Cain encounters a "human shape" whose skin is "like the white sands"; it is none other than Cain's dead brother, Abel.[26] A common feature of both of these works by Coleridge, as well as *Pym*, provides additional confirmation. The "naked hulk" of "The Rime of the Ancient Mariner" and the "ships with naked masts" in "The Wanderings of Cain" are, at least in part, adumbrations of the cursed death ship, the specter ship, the "Flying Dutchman."[27] Accordingly, both ships may be linked with the "Dutch trader" (3:114), the "Flying Dutchman" of chapter 10 of *Arthur Gordon Pym*.[28]

Like "The Rime of the Ancient Mariner" and "The Wanderings of Cain," the tale of the "Flying Dutchman" is a tale of great guilt. Poe emphasizes this point in his version of the "Flying Dutchman" in *Pym* by writing that the terrifying ship is fronted by a "tawdry gilt figurehead" (3:110). By associating "gilt" with the word "figurehead," Poe is also linking guilt with the penguin figurehead, the mirror which infinitely reflects the death of Augustus, who is identifiable with Poe's brother Henry. The guilt so linked may reasonably be said to be that of the viewer of that mirror, Arthur Gordon Pym—that is, Poe himself.

The cause of this guilt may initially seem mysterious. Not only did Pym not harm Augustus or wish him harm, he actually saved Augustus' life in the *Ariel* episode and later cared for him when he was wounded.

Likewise, Poe tended his sick brother Henry. It may be argued, however, that Pym's guilt arose because he did not continue to "lie close" to Augustus; he did not die with him. This may be argued as well with regard to Poe and his brother Henry. Both Pym and Poe were profoundly guilt-ridden precisely because they survived.

Poe punishes Pym (and himself) by taking him to Tsalal. This island is Pym's Hell. Sidney Kaplan makes this point well in his introduction to *Pym*: "Tsalal is Hell; its water is Styx, a kind of dirty, imperfect blood flowing thickly 'in distinct veins, each of a distinct hue,' which do not commingle." Of the Tsalalians themselves, Kaplan writes, "They do not fear the 'formidable' serpents that cross their path; they pronounce the names of their land and king with a 'prolonged hissing sound.' "[29] Grace Farrell Lee concurs, stating, "Tsalal is easily recognized as an imaginative portrayal of Hell." She goes on to note the remarkable warmth of Tsalal, and the fire and explosion on board the *Jane Guy* which suggest the flames of Hell. She observes the Hellish blackness of Tsalal, and, before she quotes Kaplan himself, goes on to connect the Tsalalian water with the rivers of blood characteristic of the underworlds of English and Scottish folklore.[30]

This perceptive view of Tsalal may be developed even further. For example, hidden in the translation of the word formed by the Tsalalian chasms, " 'To be shady' " (3:244), is a near-anagram which attests to Tsalal's true nature: "To be Hades."[31] The character of Too-wit further supports this view.[32] Although Augustus and Too-wit are analogues inasmuch as they are both positioned midway between double mirrors, Augustus is Pym's brotherly friend, while Too-wit is the scheming and duplicitous leader of the Tsalalians, whom Pym considers "the most barbarous, subtle, and bloodthirsty wretches that ever contaminated the face of the globe" (3:200). Even as Augustus and Too-wit are analogues, they are also diametrical opposites. This becomes increasingly apparent upon consideration of the massacre on Tsalal.

Too-wit and his warriors, feigning friendship with the men from the *Jane Guy*, managed to kill all but Pym and Peters. Most of Pym's shipmates were destroyed in a ravine by an artificial landslide which was brought down upon them. The well-armed crew had been willing to follow the natives to this ravine, in part, because the Tsalalians were seemingly unarmed. The murderous Too-wit had even reassured the crew that "there was no need of arms where all were brothers" (3:201). These deceitful words help clarify the Augustus-Too-wit opposition.

Augustus, whose arm was wounded, was truly a brother to Pym; Too-wit, who was armed with a landslide, was a vicious killer only pretending brotherhood. Tsalal is most crucially Pym's Hell in that it is the land of false brothers. Pym is effectively punished there for having survived his brotherly friend Augustus. On that infernal island, he is subjected to the brutal and diabolical violation of the fraternal bond he so dearly valued.

If this were all, then perhaps the argument that Todd Lieber advances, that Pym eventually rejects brotherhood for "pure solipsistic selfhood," might be plausible.[33] Yet this is not all, and Lieber's argument is, finally, fallacious. Not only does Peters, the surrogate Augustus, remain Pym's brotherly friend; the ideal represented by Augustus, and believed in by Pym, also persists.

The Tsalalians feared white. Their alarmed response to whiteness— the cry "Tekeli-li!"—suggests the source of their fear: the white "shrouded human figure" itself, around which echoed the same cry. Apparently the natives had encountered and been much dismayed by the white "shrouded human figure," which is actually the white penguin figurehead of the ship the *Penguin,* which infinitely reflects the dying Augustus. Ultimately, these false brothers had been terrified by the true brother.

In the heart of the island of Tsalal were the chasms; within the third chasm was the carving of "a human figure standing erect, with outstretched arm" (3:225). By virtue of the identical phrasing used, this "human figure" is identifiable with the "human figure" of Pym's last journal entry, which is the penguin figurehead of the ship the *Penguin,* which again, infinitely reflects the dying Augustus. Thus, even on the Hellish island of Tsalal, the ideal of true brotherhood endured.

And Pym and Peters do leave Tsalal. Pym states that they were initially prevented from taking "the sole path by which we could hope to attain the shore in the proper point" (3:211). The near-spoonerism, "sole path," reveals their eventual destination—the South Pole. Upon finally taking possession of a canoe and escaping from the natives, Pym and Peters do voyage southward, realizing that, "Only one course seemed to be left open for hope" (3:236).

The repetition of the word "hope" in these passages is critical. In varying forms, the word appears thirty-eight times in *Pym,* which is nearly once every six pages in the 245-page Harrison edition. The word permeates the book. While Poe's particular usage of the word does not usually suggest its secret, on two occasions Poe provides contexts which do almost give it away. His first hint of the word's significance occurs in the "Preface" to *Pym*: "I could only hope for belief among my family" (3:1). This suggested family connection becomes quite specific in

The Hidden Journey of Arthur Gordon Pym 39

Poe's clearest clue, neatly planted in his description of the four men on board the wreck of the *Grampus*: "At intervals we called one to the other, thus endeavouring to keep alive hope, and render consolation and encouragement to such of us as stood most in need of it. The feeble condition of Augustus made him an object of solicitude with us all" (3:100). With this passage's striking juxtaposition, the secret of the word "hope" in *Pym* may emerge. It is really Pym's brotherly friend Augustus who, like hope, Pym and the others were trying to keep alive. Augustus may be identified with the word "hope," or, more revealingly, with its anagram, "H. Poe."

It is, indeed, H. Poe who permeates *Pym*.[34] And it is entirely fitting that Poe's last usage of the word "hope," already cited, is, "Only one course seemed to be left open for hope," for that one course does lead Pym and Peters to the mysterious "shrouded human figure," the infinite reflection of H. Poe.

Having expiated his guilt for not dying with Augustus by visiting Hell, Pym is now permitted to approach his dying brotherly friend. Reunion, "lying close," is impossible; approaching closely is not. Pym may voyage backwards through his infinite memories of Augustus' death, increasingly nearer to the actual time sought. For Poe, as well, "lying close" with his brother was impossible. Yet, one imagines that by writing *Pym*, Poe, too, was able to journey backwards through his own infinite memories of the death of his brother Henry, approaching closely that ever-elusive, irretrievable moment.

The discovery that Henry Poe is central to *Pym* leads to a corollary discovery: Henry Poe's own modest literary work seems to have influenced *Pym*. Also, Henry's writing sheds some light on his relationship with his brother.

Hervey Allen and T. O. Mabbott published some of Henry Poe's work in their fine book, *Poe's Brother*. In one story included there, "The Pirate," Henry Poe fancifully refashioned the unhappy romance of his brother and Elmira Royster. While the tale itself relates far more closely to Poe's "Tamerlane," its language does curiously resemble, on occasion, the language of *Pym*.

After the sick narrator is considerately sent ashore by the Poe-like pirate, he asserts that "here I was treated kindly."[35] Poe's Pym asserted that "Dirk Peters treated him [Augustus] with some degree of kindness" (3:54), and, later, that "Dirk Peters treated Augustus all this day with great kindness" (3:75). After telling his story, Henry Poe's pirate collapses: "He stopped short—and suddenly clasping his hands to his forehead, he reeled and sunk senseless on the floor."[36] Poe's Pym described his own collapsing in similar terms: "I sank, utterly exhausted, upon the mattress" (3:34), and, later, "Gasping for breath, I fell senseless to the deck" (3:129).

While these parallels are not conclusive proof of Poe's debt to his brother's writing, they may at least be supportive evidence. However, even this is questionable; actually, Poe may only have been borrowing from his own work. According to Allen and Mabbott, Henry Poe may well have composed "The Pirate" using letters about the Elmira Royster incident written by Poe himself.[37] Still, there are links between other works, attributable solely to Henry Poe, and Edgar Poe's *Arthur Gordon Pym*.

Henry Poe wrote a story called "Recollections," in which the narrator searches Spain for his long-lost brother. He observes a young man, a ship's captain, come ashore in a storm to elope with a woman from a convent. Henry Poe's narrator notes that among the men who await their captain is "a tall, herculean fellow."[38] Poe's Pym wrote that Dirk Peters' limbs were "of Herculean mould" (3:51-52). The captain and his lady return in his boat to his wind-blown ship, but the ship itself is wrecked on a reef "where the foam in the occasional light of the moon shone with a terrific whiteness."[39] At the conclusion of the story, the narrator finds the body of the lady washed ashore, as well as that of "the love-sick captain." Here, the narrator declares, "when I brushed the sand from his brow, what was my horror on discovering the countenance of my *long-sought Brother!*"[40]

"Recollections" may well have been another influence on Poe's writing of the conclusion of *Arthur Gordon Pym*. The "terrific whiteness" certainly corresponds with the "perfect whiteness of the snow," and the narrator's climactic discovery of his dead brother corresponds with Pym's climactic discovery of the "shrouded human figure," the penguin figurehead of the ship the *Penguin*, which infinitely reflects Pym's dying brotherly friend, Augustus.

Yet another one of Henry Poe's short works may have contributed to Poe's creation of *Pym*'s mysterious denouement—his version of Psalm 139. In "Psalm 139th," Henry renders the original eleventh and twelfth verses thus:

> If of the darkness I should say,
> 'Twill surely veil me—lo! the night,
> Pierced by the all-pervading ray—
> Around me shines with radiant light.[41]

Henry Poe's depiction of the psalmist glowing in the night with the penetrating light of God may well have conduced to Edgar Poe's vision of the white "shrouded human figure," the reflection of Augustus/ Henry, which emerged after "the darkness had materially increased." The biblical cadence and phrasing of this final journal entry of *Pym* definitely make this connection even more plausible.

Using a phrase of Henry James', John Livingstone Lowes has argued that a writer's reading remains with him in "'the deep well of unconscious cerebration.'" Lowes goes on to say that this "deep well" sustains and nourishes a writer's creative work.[42] The correspondences presented here suggest that the writing of Poe's brother was, if not part of Poe's conscious thinking, at least a significant feature of Poe's own "deep well." That Edgar Poe's unconscious knowledge of Henry Poe's work should have affected his own literary endeavor is very much to be expected, for, as has been demonstrated, Poe's loss of his much-cherished brother was at the heart of his writing of *Arthur Gordon Pym*.

The fond relationship that existed between Henry Poe and Edgar Poe which is implied in Poe's *Pym* is also intimated in Henry Poe's writing. The sympathetic portrayals of the tragic Edgar-like heroes suggest such a relationship; a related clichéd expression in a piece entitled "Monte Video" hints at this as well. Henry Poe writes here that as he and a companion became very friendly with two total strangers, "we were almost as well acquainted as if we had been brothers."[43]

Although no explicit references by the adult Henry Poe to his brother Edgar exist, a clear verbal message once sent by young Henry through his aunt to the then-distant four-year-old Edgar Poe is preserved in a letter written by that aunt, Eliza Poe. Henry's message does provide substantial evidence of his feeling for his younger brother: "Henry frequently speaks of his little brother and expressed a great desire to see him, tell him he sends his best love to him and is greatly pleased to hear that he is so good as [sic] also so pretty a boy as Mr. Douglas [a friend of the Allans] represented him to be."[44]

Allen and Mabbott are absolutely right when they assert, in *Poe's Brother*, that Henry Poe's writing "suggests, in fact proves, a much closer and more significant and affectionate contact between the two young brothers than has ever been suspected heretofore."[45] It was Edgar Poe's loss of that contact, that "intimate communion," which animated his creation of *The Narrative of Arthur Gordon Pym*.

Mourning for the loss of one's brother, often involving a wish to die along with that brother, is clearly a dominant theme in American literature. This theme is an essential feature of the works of Thoreau, Whitman, Wolfe, Bellow, Gardner, and many other American writers. Perhaps its most painful articulation occurs in Wolfe's novel, *Look Homeward, Angel,* after Eugene's brother Ben has died: "We can believe in the nothingness of life, we can believe in the nothingness of death and of life after death—but who can believe in the nothingness of Ben?"[46]

American writers attempt to overcome "the nothingness of Ben" not only by recreating their own lost brothers in their works, but also by creating new brothers in the world. After all, it is the reader to whom the writer reaches as a brother. And as many of us respond in kind to the author, we may also find new brothers in other readers. And we may find ourselves reaching out as brothers in our own writing. In this way, "intimate communion" is reborn, and the lost brother of American literature is continually recovered.

Yet it must also be observed that, in *Pym*, it is not the lost brother alone whose recovery is sought. Finally, Poe's hidden journey in *Arthur Gordon Pym* takes him beyond Henry. This becomes clear upon consideration of Poe's one explicit statement regarding his feelings for his brother. Responding, in October or November 1829, to John Neal's praise of his poem "Heaven" (later entitled "Fairyland"), Poe wrote, in part: "there can be no tie more strong than that of brother for brother—it is not so much that they love one another as that they both love the same parent—their affections are always running in the same direction—the same channel and cannot help mingling."[47] There can be little doubt that the parent referred to here is the mother of both Edgar and Henry Poe, Elizabeth Arnold Poe. Considerable evidence is available regarding the feelings of these sons for their common mother.

Edgar Poe once wrote that his mother was for him "a string to which my heart fully responds."[48] According to an acquaintance of his, he had once said "that he owed to his Mother 'every good gift of his intellect, & his heart.'"[49] He offered further praise in these words concerning his mother's profession: "no earl was ever prouder of his earldom than he of his descent from a woman who, although well born, hesitated not to consecrate to the drama her brief career of genius and beauty" (12:186).

Further evidence of Poe's affection for his mother is that he treasured always his miniature of her, as well as her mysterious correspondence, both of which he had received when she died.[50] Poe's 1827 visit to Boston may have been inspired, in part, by a third much-valued item in this small legacy from his mother, a painting of Boston Harbor, for on the back of this painting she had written, "For my little son Edgar, who should ever love Boston, the place of his birth, and where his mother found her best and most sympathetic friends."[51]

Henry Poe shared Edgar Poe's adoration of their mother. A friend of Henry Poe's, F. W. Thomas, asserted, "He often deplored the early death of his mother."[52] Henry wrote directly of his feelings for his mother in a small poem, itself prompted by his own legacy from his mother, a pocketbook containing locks of hair of his father, his sister, and his mother. The lines of this poem pertaining to his mother reveal not only Henry's love for her, but also his presence at her death-bed:

> My Mother's [hair], too!—then let me press
> This gift of her I loved so well,
> For I have had thy last caress,
> And heard thy long, thy last farewell.⁵³

As Poe acknowledged, the two brothers were closely bound by a mutual love for their lost mother. As Allen and Mabbott write, she was "much idolized" by them both.⁵⁴ Inasmuch as Edgar Poe loved his brother because he and Henry both loved the same parent, their mother, *The Narrative of Arthur Gordon Pym* is a memorial not only to Henry Poe, but to Elizabeth Arnold Poe, as well. This conclusion is well-corroborated by a number of details in the novel itself.⁵⁵

Pym and Augustus first met at the academy of Mr. E. Ronald (3:5). As Richard Wilbur has pointed out, "Ronald" is an anagram of "Arnold," Elizabeth Poe's maiden name.⁵⁶ Furthermore, the name of the boat Pym and Augustus sailed in together, the *Ariel*, came not only from Poe's familiaritry with Shakespeare, Milton, and Shelley, but also from a more personal source: in the Powell's Company's 1807 production of *The Tempest*, Mrs. Poe played the part of Ariel.⁵⁷

The cry "Tekeli-li!," already linked here with "Tack-a-lee!" and "Mene, Mene, Tekel, Upharsin," has its immediate source in another of Mrs. Poe's theatrical efforts. In an appendix to *Edgar Allan Poe,* Quinn discloses that on 23 March 1811, Mrs. Poe played the part of Christine in a play entitled *Tekeli*.⁵⁸ This connection has also been observed by David Jackson and Burton Pollin.⁵⁹ However, an interpretation of this discovery remains to be offered.

The *Charleston Courier* of 23 March 1811 reveals that Mrs. Poe did indeed play the part of Christine in *Tekeli* on 23 March; the *Courier* of 22 March shows that an earlier performance of this play, hitherto unnoticed, had been scheduled for 22 March.⁶⁰ Nevertheless, this earlier performance of *Tekeli* does not seem to have taken place. The play shared a bill with another play, *Jane Shore*; on Friday evening, 22 March, the *Charleston Times* announced: "THE Public are respectfully informed, that in consequence of the bad appearance of the weather, the Play of JANE SHORE, is unavoidably postponed until further Notice."⁶¹ Refunds for seats purchased to *Jane Shore* are made available. No listing for a performance of *Tekeli* that evening appears in this issue. Rather, the 23 March performance of *Othello* and *Tekeli* is announced, followed by the reassuring words, "No Postponement on account of the weather."⁶²

The *Charleston Courier* of Saturday morning, 23 March, provides similar information.⁶³

On 23 March 1811, Edgar Allan Poe was two years, two months old, and traveling with his mother.⁶⁴ Whether Poe would have remembered his mother's performance in *Tekeli* from his earliest childhood is impossible to determine. Robert Adger Law has argued, in another context, that Poe was probably familiar with back issues of the *Charleston Courier*.⁶⁵ It may therefore be conjectured that in order to discover the date of the performance of *Tekeli*, Poe read back issues of the *Charleston Courier* for 1811. By doing so, Poe would probably have found the original 22 March listing for *Tekeli*, and, not realizing that this particular performance had been cancelled, he might well have taken 22 March to be the true date of his mother's performance. Consequently it is on 22 March that Pym hears the albatross cries of "Tekeli-li!"

In *Tekeli*, Poe's mother played the part of a young bride.⁶⁶ Accordingly, it may fairly be argued that the mysterious white "shrouded human figure" of *Arthur Gordon Pym*, which appeared heralded by birds crying "Tekeli-li!," compellingly represents Poe's poignant image of his deeply beloved mother appearing on stage as Christine in *Tekeli*—an incomparable vision, resplendent in bridal white.

That the "shrouded human figure" is both brother and mother confirms what Poe's words regarding his brother have already suggested. By reaching out for his brother, Poe was also reaching out for the parent he and his brother had both loved, their mother, Elizabeth Arnold Poe. The first of August, the day of his brother's death, was, finally, a window for Poe on an earlier time—8 December 1811, the day of his mother's death.⁶⁷

Poe's mother's death is the covert concern of chapter 10 of *Pym*, the critical "Flying Dutchman" episode. Even as the death ship reinforces one's sense of Pym's guilt, it reveals the source of his possible salvation: his dead mother.

Marie Bonaparte has noted the connection between *Pym*'s "Flying Dutchman" and Poe's mother. She begins to unravel the "unfathomable mystery" (3:114) by linking the disease and death of the ship's crew with the disease and death of Mrs. Poe.⁶⁸ To substantiate this connection, Bonaparte observes that some of the putrefied corpses on board the ship were indeed female. However, she is mistaken when she claims that this detail was "dictated by the unconscious." This chapter is consistent with the rest of the novel; it, too, is quite consciously crafted.

Poe's selection of an uncommon version of the "Flying Dutchman," one involving a plague of yellow fever, is evidence of Poe's conscious crafting in this chapter.⁶⁹ The plague of yellow fever further ties the

The Hidden Journey of Arthur Gordon Pym   45

"Flying Dutchman's" crew to Poe's mother. While it is usually maintained that Mrs. Poe died of consumption, it is also asserted by both Susan Archer Weiss and Hervey Allen that malarial fever contributed to her decline.[70] Hervey Allen also claims that Mrs. Poe's own mother may have died of yellow fever itself.[71]

In view of this connection between the "Flying Dutchman's" dead crew and Poe's dead mother, it is wholly fitting that when Pym and Augustus see this crew, Poe writes, as Pym, "we could not help shouting to the dead for help!" (3:112). Their cries are, in fact, the cries of Edgar and Henry Poe for their passionately longed-for dead mother.

In *Arthur Gordon Pym*, Poe is reaching through his brother to his mother. His profound wish is to return to the moment of his mother's death, 8 December 1811, so that he might die along with her. He wishes, intensely, to "lie close" to his mother so that he might regain the remembered "intimate communion" of his early childhood.

This argument is supported by remarkable parallels within the text. Pym's conjecture regarding the death of the crew of the "Flying Dutchman," which, as has been suggested, represents the death of Poe's mother, bears a striking resemblance to the later conjecture regarding the death of Pym himself. These correspondences may be noted in the following passages:

Chapter 10

From the saffronlike hue of such of the corpses as were not entirely decayed, we concluded *that the* whole of her company had *perished* by the yellow fever, or some other virulent disease of the same *fearful* kind. *If* such were *the case* (and I *know* not what else to imagine), *death,* to judge from the positions of the bodies, must have come upon them in a manner awfully *sudden and* overwhelming, in a way totally distinct from that *which* generally characterizes even the most deadly pestilences with *which* mankind *are* acquainted. *It is* possible, indeed that poison, *accidentally* introduced into some of their sea stores, *may* have brought about the disaster; or that the eating some unknown species of fish, or other marine animal, or oceanic bird, might have induced it—but it is utterly useless to form

Note

The circumstances connected with the late *sudden and* distressing *death* of Mr. Pym *are* already well *known* to the public through the medium of the daily press. *It is feared that the* few *remaining* chapters *which* were to have completed his narrative, and *which* were retained by him, while the above were in type, for the purpose of revision, have been irrecoverably lost through the *accident* by which he *perished* himself. This, however, *may* prove not to be *the case,* and the papers, *if* ultimately found, *will* be given to the public. (3:245; my italics) conjectures where all is involved, and *will*, no doubt, *remain* forever involved, in the most appalling and unfathomable mystery. (3:114; my italics)

This mystery, too, may indeed be fathomed. Evidently, Pym met with the same death that had been met with by the crew of the "Flying Dutchman." And, since the death of that crew represents the death of Poe's mother, it may justifiably be affirmed that, through Pym, Poe was able to die in the same way as his mother had died.

These extraordinarily similar passages reveal that, if not in time, at least in manner, Poe did finally manage, through his fiction, to "lie close" to his mother. By means of this, his only novel, Poe did ultimately attain the cherished "intimate communion" of mother and son, of which the "intimate communion" of brother and brother had been an incarnation. Here, the hidden journey of *Arthur Gordon Pym* comes to an end; Edgar Allan Poe is home at last.

NOTES

1. Richard Kopley, "The Secret of *Arthur Gordon Pym*: The Text and the Source," *Studies in American Fiction*, 8 (Autumn 1980): 203–18.

2. *The Complete Works of Edgar Allan Poe*, ed. James A. Harrison (New York: Thomas Y. Crowell, 1902), 3:242. All further references to this work will appear in the text.

3. Kopley, "The Secret of *Arthur Gordon Pym*," 205.

4. Adam Seaborn (pseud.), *Symzonia* (Gainesville, Florida: Scholars' Facsimiles and Reprints, 1965 [1820]), pp. 30–35; Benjamin Morrell, *A Narrative of Four Voyages* (New York: J. & J. Harper, 1832), pp. 50–53.

5. Morrell, *A Narrative of Four Voyages*, p. 396.

6. Marie Bonaparte, *The Life and Works of Edgar Allan Poe* (London: Imago Publishing Company, 1949 [1933]), pp. 296–97, 326.

7. Hervey Allen and Thomas Ollive Mabbott, *Poe's Brother* (New York: George H. Doran, 1926), p. 93.

8. Hervey Allan, *Israfel* (New York: Farrar & Rinehart, 1934), pp. 79, 338.

9. Bonaparte, *Poe*, p. 296.

10. Harry Levin, *The Power of Blackness* (New York: Alfred A. Knopf, 1958), p. 112; Roger Forclaz, "A Voyage to the Frontiers of the Unknown: Edgar Poe's *Narrative of A. Gordon Pym*," *American Transcendental Quarterly*, no. 37 (Winter 1978): 53; Richard Wilbur, Introduction, *The Narrative of Arthur Gordon Pym* (Boston: Godine, 1973), p. xi; Norma Jean English Walker, "A Study of the Relation of Poe's 'The Narrative of Arthur Gordon Pym' to the Development of His Craft as a Writer" (Ph.D. diss., University of Illinois, 1974), p. 87.

11. Patrick F. Quinn, *The French Face of Edgar Poe* (Carbondale: Southern Illinois University Press, 1957), pp. 196–200; Levin, *The Power of Blackness*,

p. 111; Leslie Fiedler, *Love and Death in the American Novel*, rev. ed. (New York: Stein and Day, 1966), p. 395; Joseph J. Moldenhauer, "Imagination and Perversity in *The Narrative of Arthur Gordon Pym*," *Texas Studies in Literature and Language*, 13 (Summer 1971): 268-73; William Peden, "Prologue to a Dark Journey: The 'Opening' to Poe's *Pym*," in *Papers on Poe*, ed. Richard Veler (Springfield, Ohio: Chantry Music Press, 1972), p. 90; Daniel Hoffman, *Poe Poe Poe Poe Poe Poe Poe* (Garden City, New York: Doubleday, 1973 [1972]), pp. 261-70; Wilbur, Introduction, *Pym*, p. xii; Barton Levi St. Armand, "The Dragon and the Uroboros: Themes of Metamorphosis in *Arthur Gordon Pym*," *American Transcendental Quarterly*, no. 37 (Winter 1978): 62.

12. *John Henry Ingram's Poe Collection at the University of Virginia*, ed. John Carl Miller (Charlottesville: University of Virginia Press, 1960), p. 90.

13. For information on Henry's publishing under his own name poetry by Edgar, see Allen and Mabbott, *Poe's Brother*, pp. xiv, 30, 43, 50, 78-79. For further details on Henry's writing fiction about Edgar, see Allen and Mabbott, *Poe's Brother*, pp. 31-32, 53-59, 63-67, 78-80. For the particulars of Henry's usage of the name "Edgar-Leonard," consult Allen and Mabbott, *Poe's Brother*, pp. 32, 53-59.

14. For references to Edgar Poe's attributing to himself the adventures of Henry, see George Woodberry, *The Life of Edgar Allan Poe* (Boston: Houghton, Mifflin, 1909), 1:72-73; Allen and Mabbott, *Poe's Brother*, pp. 24-25; Allen, *Israfel*, p. 211; Bonaparte, *Poe*, p. 55. For references to Edgar Poe's alias, "Henri Le Rennet," see Allen and Mabbott, *Poe's Brother*, p. 30; Allen, *Israfel*, pp. 161, 163; Bonaparte, *Poe*, p. 36; Arthur Hobson Quinn, *Edgar Allan Poe* (New York: Appleton-Century-Crofts, 1941), p. 116.

While the source for the name "Henri" is plain, the source for the name "Le Rennet" is not. However, it may be legitimately speculated that this half of Poe's alias came from the name "Reynolds." After all, Robert Almy has affirmed that Henry Poe, a resident of Baltimore in 1826-27, was probably familiar with the ideas of J. N. Reynolds, also a resident of Baltimore at that time, and that Henry may well have communicated these ideas to Edgar (see "J. N. Reynolds: A Brief Biography With Particular Reference to Poe and Symmes," *The Colophon*, n.s. 2 [Winter 1937]: 235). Furthermore, T. O. Mabbott has suggested that Edgar Poe may have visited Henry in Baltimore in 1827 (see *Tamerlane and Other Poems* [New York: Columbia University Press, 1941], p. xii). Lewis Leary concurs with Mabbott's view (see "Miss Octavia's Autograph Album and Edgar Allan Poe," *Columbia Library Columns*, 17 [February 1968]: 9-15). It may be conjectured that the name "Le Rennet" derived from the name of this man about whom Poe had heard much, and with whom Poe may have had the opportunity to speak, J. N. Reynolds. If this is so, then Poe's coupling of his brother's name with that of Reynolds in his alias may suggest a degree of perceived similarity between the two men. Consequently, Poe's death-bed cries for Reynolds may also have been, in part, cries for Poe's dead brother Henry. While this cannot be proven, Poe's usage of Reynolds' work in *Pym*, a book which so centrally concerns Poe's brother Henry, may be taken as support for this hypothesis.

15. Bonaparte, *Poe*, pp. 297, 326.

16. Woodberry, *Poe*, 1:86-87; Allen, *Israfel*, pp. 256-57; Quinn, *Poe*, p. 186. There is disagreement as to whether Poe lived with his aunt earlier, in 1829. For the affirmative position, see Woodberry, *Poe*, 1:55, and Allen, *Israfel*, p. 203. For

the negative position, see Quinn, *Poe*, p. 151. It is interesting to note that Allen argues that Poe lived briefly with Maria Clemm in May 1830, receiving mail addressed to him in care of his brother Henry (see *Israfel*, p. 215). Woodberry and Quinn assert only that Poe stopped in Baltimore at this time (see Woodberry, *Poe*, 1:67; Quinn, *Poe*, p. 168). It should also be observed that Allen appears to be mistaken in identifying Maria Clemm's address as "Milk Street." Quinn's identification of the address as "Wilks Street" (pp. 186, 188) is supported by May Garrettson Evans, who refers to "the Wilk Street home of Mrs. Clemm" in "Poe in Amity Street," *Maryland Historical Magazine*, 36 (December 1941): 377.

17. Allen, *Israfel*, pp. 203–204, 257.

18. Hervey Allen holds this view; he imagines the situation well in *Israfel*: "Undressing under the eaves of the low-ceilinged room, Poe brushed them [his clothes] and folded them carefully, before he lay down by the side of the brother whose face was flushed, but whose hands and feet had already begun to take on an eternal cold" (p. 206).

19. David Ketterer, "Devious Voyage: The Singular *Narrative of A. Gordon Pym*," *American Transcendental Quarterly*, no. 37 (Winter 1978): 27.

20. William Bittner, *Poe: A Biography* (Boston: Little, Brown, 1962), p. 86.

21. J. V. Ridgely and Iola S. Haverstick, "Chartless Voyage: The Many Narratives of Arthur Gordon Pym," *Texas Studies in Literature and Language*, 8 (Spring 1966): 69. The entire copyright entry for *Pym*, which includes the 1 August 1838 deposit notation, is reproduced and reconsidered in Alexander Hammond's essay, "The Composition of *The Narrative of Arthur Gordon Pym*: Notes Toward a Re-examination," *American Transcendental Quarterly*, no. 37 (Winter 1978): 9–20.

22. Bonaparte, *Poe*, p. 326.

23. Kopley, "The Secret of *Arthur Gordon Pym*," 209.

24. Levin, *The Power of Blackness*, p. 118; Sidney Kaplan, Introduction, *The Narrative of Arthur Gordon Pym* (New York: Hill and Wang, 1960), pp. xviii–xix; Wilbur, Introduction, *Pym*, p. xiv.

25. Killis Campbell, "Poe's Reading," *University of Texas Studies in English*, 5 (October 1925): 169; Allen, *Israfel*, p. 337; Bonaparte, *Poe*, pp. 315–17; Edward H. Davidson, *Poe: A Critical Study* (Cambridge: Harvard University Press, 1957), p. 180; Levin, *The Power of Blackness*, p. 114.

26. *The Poetical Works of Samuel Taylor Coleridge*, ed. James Dykes Campbell (London: Macmillan, 1914 [1893]), pp. 112–16. "The Wanderings of Cain" has also been linked with Poe's "Silence—A Fable" by Floyd Stovall in "Poe's Debt to Coleridge," *University of Texas Studies in English*, 10 (July 1930): 79.

27. *The Poetical Works of Samuel Taylor Coleridge*, pp. 100, 114. John Livingstone Lowes discusses the connection between the spectre ship of "The Rime of the Ancient Mariner" and the "Flying Dutchman" in *The Road to Xanadu* (Boston: Houghton Mifflin, 1927), p. 512.

28. Grace Farrell Lee has made the connection between the death ship of "The Rime of the Ancient Mariner" and that of *Pym* in "The Quest of Arthur Gordon Pym," *Southern Literary Journal*, 4 (Spring 1972): 27. It is interesting to find in a book published several years after *Pym* a description of the "Flying Dutchman" "rolling along like the white shrouded ghost of a giant" (Nautical Superstition: The Flying Dutchman," in *Tales of Shipwrecks and Adventures at Sea*, ed. James Lindridge [London: William Mark Clark, 1846], p. 732). While the use of this language may be merely coincidental, it is also possible that this

language was suggested by the conclusion of *Pym*. Another story in this volume, "The Robinson Crusoe of the Polar Regions" (pp. 97–104), may also have been influenced by Poe's *Pym*.

29. Kaplan, Introduction, *Pym*, p. xix.

30. Lee, "The Quest of Arthur Gordon Pym," 29–30.

31. This wordplay, along with other aspects of *Pym*, seems to have been picked up by Vladimir Nabokov in *Pale Fire* (New York: Lancer Books, 1966 [1962]). In speaking on death, the poet John Shade writes that he "tore apart the fantasies of Poe" at the "Institute of Preparation for the Hereafter," an establishment about which his friend commented, "I really could not tell / The difference between this place and Hell" (pp. 36–39). Furthermore, Shade remarks that in trying to foresee death, "Maybe one finds *le grand neant*" (p. 39). This French phrase sounds rather close to "le geant blanc," the French expression for the "shrouded human figure." For a discussion of other parallels, including that of the "tall white fountain" of *Pale Fire* (p. 42) and the "limitless cataract" of *Pym* (3:241), see Thomas LeClair's article, "Poe's *Pym* and Nabokov's *Pale Fire*," *Notes on Contemporary Literature*, 3 (1973): 2–3.

32. The name "Too-wit" ultimately derives from Shakespeare's *Love's Labor's Lost* (V.ii.918). However, according to Killis Campbell in "Poe's Reading," while Poe often quoted from Shakespeare, he never quoted from this particular play (174–75). A likelier and more immediate source is Coleridge's "Christabel," a poem with which, Campbell rightly observes, Poe was quite familiar (169). "Tu-whit!—Tu-whoo!" the midnight cry of the owls in "Christabel," further links the "jet black" chief (3:181) with darkness. Also, the painful separation of brotherly friends in "Christabel," Roland and Sir Leoline, echoes the theme of the lost brother in Poe's *Pym* (see *The Poetical Works of Samuel Taylor Coleridge*, pp. 116–24). It should be added here that the phrase "to wit" may be found in the official copyright entry for Poe's novel (see Hammond, "The Composition of *The Narrative of Arthur Gordon Pym*," 11).

33. Todd M. Lieber, "The Apocalyptic Imagination of A. Gordon Pym," *Endless Experiments: Essays on the Heroic Experience in American Romanticism* (Columbus: Ohio State University Press, 1973), pp. 168–69.

34. This association of the word "hope" with Poe's dead brother seems to occur early on in Poe's work. The play "Politian," which Poe was writing in 1832 (Allen, *Israfel*, p. 278), contains a description of the Lady Lalage rather similar to Poe's later description of the dying Augustus:

"Politian"

Pym

It [the mirror] speaks of sunken eyes, and wasted cheeks, And Beauty long deceased—remembers me Of Joy departed—Hope, the Seraph Hope, Inurned and entombed!—now, in a tone Low, sad, and solemn, but most audible, Whispers of early grave untimely yawning For ruined maid. (7:65)

His eyes were sunk far in his head, being scarcely perceptible, and the skin of his cheeks hung so loosely as to prevent his masticating any food, or even swallowing any liquid, without great difficulty. (3:139)

In this context, "the Seraph Hope" may actually be a reference to Poe's recently deceased brother, H. Poe.

35. Allen and Mabbott, *Poe's Brother*, p. 55.
36. Allen and Mabbott, *Poe's Brother*, p. 59.
37. Allen and Mabbott, *Poe's Brother*, p. 31.
38. Allen and Mabbott, *Poe's Brother*, p. 66,
39. Allen and Mabbott, *Poe's Brother*, p. 67.
40. Allen and Mabbott, *Poe's Brother*, p. 67.
41. Allen and Mabbott, *Poe's Brother*, p. 74.
42. Lowes, *The Road to Xanadu*, pp. 52–59.
43. Allen and Mabbott, *Poe's Brother*, p. 46.
44. Allen and Mabbott, *Poe's Brother*, p. 20.
45. Allen and Mabbott, *Poe's Brother*, p. 33.
46. Wolfe, *Look Homeward, Angel* (New York: Charles Scribner's Sons, 1929), p. 557.
47. *The Letters of Edgar Allan Poe*, ed. John Ward Ostrom (Cambridge: Harvard University Press, 1948), 1:32.
48. *Letters*, 1:78.
49. John Carl Miller, *Building Poe Biography* (Baton Rouge: Louisiana State University Press, 1977), p. 140.
50. Allen, *Israfel*, pp. 11, 13, 20.
51. John H. Ingram, *Edgar Allan Poe: His Life, Letters, and Opinions* (New York: AMS Press, 1971 [1886]), p. 5.
52. J. H. Whitty, "Memoir," *The Complete Poems of Edgar Allan Poe* (Boston: Houghton Mifflin, 1911), p. xxi.
53. Allen and Mabbott, *Poe's Brother*, p. 41.
54. Allen and Mabbott, *Poe's Brother*, p. 81.
55. It should be noted that Pym's mother, who responds hysterically to her son's traveling (3:18), is based, in all likelihood, on Poe's stepmother, Mrs. Frances Allan, rather than on Poe's natural mother, Elizabeth Arnold Poe. Quinn does mention Mrs. Allen's "nervous temperament" (*Poe*, p. 117), and Hervey Allen writes that when Mrs. Allen learned that Edgar intended to leave Richmond after his heated quarrel with Mr. Allan, "she . . . must have created a scene, for she prevailed on Mr. Allan to stop Poe's departure" (*Israfel*, p. 160). Poe's stepmother, as represented by Pym's mother, is clearly an integral part of the novel. However, it is Poe's natural mother, Elizabeth Arnold Poe, the original lost mother, who is the greater concern of *Arthur Gordon Pym*.
56. Wilbur, Introduction, *Pym*, p. xi.
57. Quinn, *Poe*, p. 715.
58. Quinn, *Poe*, p. 723.
59. David K. Jackson and Burton R. Pollin, "Poe's 'Tekeli-li,'" *Poe Studies*, 12, no. 1 (June 1979): 19.
60. *Charleston Courier*, 23 March 1811, p. 3, col. 3; 22 March 1811, p. 2, col. 2.
61. *Charleston Times*, 22 March 1811, p. 3, col. 3.
62. *Charleston Times*, 22 March 1811, p. 3, col. 3.
63. *Charleston Courier*, 23 March 1811, p. 3, col. 3.
64. Allen, *Israfel*, pp. 11–12.
65. Robert Adger Law, "A Source For 'Annabel Lee,'" *Journal of English and German Philology*, 21 (April 1922): 344–46.

66. Theodore Edward Hook, *Tekeli; or The Siege of Montgatz* (London: C. and R. Baldwin, 1806). A description of the costumes in a later British production of the play states that Christine wore a "white muslin petticoat and apron" (see Theodore Edward Hook, *Tekeli; or The Seige of Montgatz*, in *Cumberland's British Theatre, London 1825–55*, 30 no. 2, p. 9).

67. Allen, *Israfel*, p. 19.

68. Bonaparte, *Poe*, pp. 320–21. Poe used this phrase "unfathomable mystery" mockingly; his actual attitude toward such an attempt at bogus mystification is evident in his rather sarcastic reference to the phrase " 'veiled in impenetrable mystery,' " used by Theodore S. Fay in his novel, *Norman Leslie* (8:57). In *Pym*, the mysteries are carefully worked out and, ultimately, fathomable. As Poe remarked through Legrand in "The Gold-Bug," "it may well be doubted whether human ingenuity can construct an enigma of the kind which human ingenuity may not, by proper application, resolve" (5:131–32).

69. For a possible source for Poe's rendering of this uncommon version of the "Flying Dutchman," see one of Sir Walter Scott's notes to "Rokeby," in *The Poetical Works of Sir Walter Scott* (Philadelphia: J. Crissy and Thomas Desilver, 1837), p. 234. Carroll D. Laverty mentions Coleridge's "The Rime of the Ancient Mariner" as a general influence and cites Charles Singer's *A Short History of Medicine* (New York: Oxford University Press, 1928), p. 275, as a text which discusses this particular version of the "Flying Dutchman," in "Science and Pseudo-Science in the Writings of Edgar Allan Poe" (Ph.D. diss., Duke University, 1951), p. 272.

70. Susan Archer Weiss, *The Home Life of Poe* (New York: Broadway Publishing Company, 1907), p. 5; Allen, *Israfel*, p. 17.

71. Allen, *Israfel*, p. 6.

BRONSON ALCOTT'S "JOURNAL FOR 1837"
(PART TWO)

Larry A. Carlson

THE SECOND AND CONCLUDING PART of this edition of Bronson Alcott's "Journal for 1837" covers the months of May through December.[1] As his journal entries for this period reveal, Alcott continued to suffer personally as well as professionally because of the hostile reactions to his teaching methods and his recently published *Conversations with Children on the Gospels*. His reputation assailed and enrollment in the Temple School steadily dwindling from quarter to quarter, he encountered further troubles and problems, all of which affected him profoundly. Having already sold his library to help meet expenses, Alcott was also forced to move his school to a smaller, less attractive room. During the summer, when his debts became unmanageable and when he fully realized that his experimental school would ultimately fail, he experienced a serious physical and emotional collapse. Upon recovering he became increasingly withdrawn; and as the year drew to a close, he tried to shut out the difficulties of the present by thinking more and more of the future, believing that in 1838 his controversial ideas would be more acceptable. Alcott was mistaken, however, for the injurious charges made against him in 1837 were not soon forgotten.

Following the pattern established during the early months of 1837, the reviews of the *Conversations* and his school that were published during the remainder of the year indicate clearly that Alcott's critics were numerous and vocal, his apologists few and ineffectual. For example, even his cousin and lifelong friend, Dr. William Andrus Alcott, would not fully endorse his experiment in "moral culture." Writing about the Temple School in the May number of the *Annals of Education* (7:233-34), Dr. Alcott commended his cousin's efforts to promote "the moral or spiritual nature of man" but refused to pass judgment on "the actual merits or demerits of the school." No such restraint was shown by Joseph T. Buckingham in the 9 May issue of the *Boston Courier* (p. 2), one of the city's most powerful dailies. Having once before used his position as editor to attack Alcott and the *Conversations* (29 March, p. 2), Buckingham again wanted to leave no doubt in the public's mind about what he felt was the malignant influence of Alcott. He averred that "the 'Conversations on the Gospels' is a more indecent and obscene book, (we say nothing of its absurdity) than any other one we ever saw exposed for sale on a bookseller's counter." Buckingham also included the recent remarks of a local clergyman who, when asked about the *Conversations*, is reported to have said, *"one third was absurd, one third was blasphemous, and one third obscene."*[2]

Alcott's most eloquent defender during this period of 1837 was James Freeman Clarke, editor of the liberal *Western Messenger*. In his review of the second volume of the *Conversations* in the May number of the *Messenger*, "Mr. Alcott's Book and the Objections Made to It" (3:678–83), Clarke stated that, notwithstanding any limitations in Alcott's theories and practices, "we maintain him to be a prophet." Like Emerson and others, however, Clarke was unable to convince the public of either the sincerity or the desirability of Alcott's cultural mission. Perhaps the most perceptive assessment of Alcott's shortcomings that was published in 1837 is an unsigned review of the *Conversations* that appeared in the November issue of the *Christian Examiner* (23:252–61). The writer acknowledged Alcott's "genius" and on the whole approved of the principles and goals of the Temple School but expressed genuine doubts about Alcott's practical ability to implement his highly speculative theories about education. Alcott's greatest weakness, the writer argued, was his constitutional tendency to dwell on the general to the exclusion of the concrete: "He prefers abstraction to the natural form of ideas." (Even Alcott's most loyal supporters were forced to concede this point.) By November, however, the debate had already been settled, on moral not technical issues. The public clearly would not countenance a "prophet" who so boldly challenged traditional beliefs about God, man, and nature.

Alcott felt the inevitable consequences of all this criticism more keenly each month. As parents continued to withdraw their children from his school, he could no longer afford to pay the yearly rent of $300 for the spacious quarters in Room 7 of the Masonic Temple, which he had enjoyed and taken great pride in since the opening of his school on 24 September 1834. When his 1837 summer term began on 22 May, Alcott reluctantly moved his school to Room 3 in the basement of the Temple, a small room that rented for $100 per year. Even more damaging to his pride, only eleven students (one nonpaying) enrolled during the summer, a third of his usual number.³ Depressed and painfully aware that the "tide of sentiment"⁴ was set against him, Alcott considered quitting his school after the summer session and moving his family to Scituate. In fact, he even asked his brother-in-law the Reverend Samuel J. May, a Unitarian minister in Scituate, to look for a place for them to live.⁵

One of the most anguished decisions that Alcott did carry through was declining to give the 10 June dedicatory address at Hiram Fuller's Greene Street School in Providence. Fuller, a successful young teacher and headmaster who had been a devoted admirer of Alcott for over a year, initially made the request during the fall of 1836, several weeks before the first volume of the *Conversations* was published. Immediately after accepting the invitation, Alcott began working on the speech with zeal and continued to do so throughout the winter.⁶ However, following the devastating attacks on the *Conversations* and the Temple School during the spring of 1837, he selflessly decided not to jeopardize the reputation of the Greene Street School by having it become publicly associated with him. Even though delivering the address probably would have given him much needed recognition and helped repair his badly damaged image, he refused—as an act of conscience—to risk the possible consequences to Fuller.

The cumulative effect of all these unsettling difficulties was more than he could withstand. Demoralized, emotionally and physically exhausted, and knowing that his credibility was destroyed, Alcott collapsed in July, unable even to write in his journal. After recuperating from his breakdown he wishfully thought that he might be able to rebuild patronage for his school. But at this point the damage to his reputation was irreparable: by the end of December, during the winter quarter, only seven students were attending the Temple School.⁷ Public and private opposition to his views remained firm.

Fortunately, Alcott had other outlets for his ideas and other sources of intellectual stimulation, which prevented his personal and professional crisis from being even more debilitating. For example, he looked forward to and enjoyed attending the meetings of the Transcendental Club, even if the quality of discussion did not always strike him as being the "highest or worthiest."⁸ In addition, he savored opportunities to correspond and converse with old friends, especially Margaret Fuller, Anna Quincy Thaxter, Convers Francis, William Henry Furness, William Russell, and of course Emerson. His friendship with Emerson, whom he saw and corresponded with on a frequent basis, continued to be his most significant source of gratification. Emerson, who regarded Alcott as "the most extraordinary man and the highest genius of the time,"⁹ faithfully provided moral and emotional support throughout this bleak period in his friend's life. Alcott also received encouragement from an enthusiastic admirer in England, James Pierrepont Greaves. A disciple of Pestalozzi, Greaves had read and was quite impressed with *Record of a School*; he wrote to Alcott in September to find out more about the Temple School and Alcott's teaching methods.[10] Alcott believed that "testimony" from fellow educators like Greaves would eventually "give confidence to [his] own faithless country men."[11]

Alcott also found solace in making plans for the future. Of special note are two projects that he felt sure would bring him success in 1838: publishing "Psyche" and offering a course of discussions on "Self-Culture." By the end of 1837 his manuscript of "Psyche," which he described as "a prose poem on the nature and wants of the Soul during its infancy and childhood,"[12] had grown to over four hundred pages. As his journal entries for the latter part of 1837 indicate, Alcott devoted more and more time to writing and revising "Psyche" as his school continued to languish. Encouraged by Emerson, who promised to finance its publication, he had high expectations for the salutary effects of the book. Always the optimist when contemplating the future, Alcott believed that "Psyche" would not only help restore his badly marred reputation but also "regenerate institutions; and transfigure man into the pure and unsullied image of his nature."[13] Likewise, he hoped that "acting on the age, by more direct means"[14] would also change public opinion. What he had in mind was complementing the ideas in "Psyche" by holding a series of conversations on "Self-Culture." Underpinning these hopes was his mistaken belief that the mere passage of time would make his controversial ideas more acceptable to society. As 1838 approached, Alcott felt sanguine about the future: he believed that "Psyche" and his conversations on "Self-Culture" would turn his fortunes around.

"Psyche" was never published, however, and his conversations on "Self-Culture," which he held at Lexington and Hingham during the fall and winter of 1838, did not alter the public's unfavorable image of him. The problem with "Psyche" was a practical one, as Emerson pointed out after seeing the final draft in June 1838: it was not well written, much of it was irremediably abstract, and it suffered from "a want of unity of design."[15] Alcott's conversations on "Self-Culture" did not improve his fortunes for the simple reason that neither his radicalism nor society's opinion of it had changed in the intervening year. Of all his future disappointments, however, the most bitter was having to close the Temple School in June 1838. Although he started a similar school in his own home during the fall of 1838, it too had to be closed, in 1839, because of public opposition to his ideas and practices. When this school closed, Alcott's career as an educator was finished. Alcott's own limitations and society's vociferous refusal to accept his controversial ideas, dramatically evident throughout 1837, continued for years to haunt him and to control the direction of his life.

[311] May.
Week XVIII. [30 April–6 May]

Notice of School.

Dr. Alcott inserted my Quarter Card of Study and Discipline, for the spring term of school, in the May number of the "Annals of Education", which appeared on the first of the month. He made some remarks in connexion, on the importance of Moral Culture; and the efforts of those, [312] who, in this country, have striven to promote it. His commendation is, however, quite measured as regards my endeavors, from the fact that he does not apprehend them.[16] He has confidence in my intentions; approves my methods generally; but distrusts the principles that guide me in practice. He is afraid of my theology; looks with some alarm upon the supposed philosophy which I espouse. In this, he is not alone. Most of the party, whose opinions he represents, regard me, so far as they know *me*, or apprehend my purpose and principles, in a similar light. *Trinitarians* know not what to make of me; *Unitarians* distrust me; *Unbelievers in Spirit*, cannot, of course, countenance me. Thus am I alone; both in the theological and philosophical world;—a few of the Free and Simple [313] minded, of no name or sect, speak in my favour; while the practical and sensible, of all parties, find much in my theory and practice to commend.—This is agreeable. It indicates that there is somewhat of the *Universal* in me. I would hope, that, when men shall shake themselves free from conventions and customs, there shall be found truth, unalloyed by error, in my principles, with less of imperfection in their administration, than in other systems.

As yet, my principles and purposes, have not found admission into the public Journals. I have wrought in secret. The "Annals of Education" has scarce named my enterprize. I think the time has now come when these shall be made [314] topics of popular interest. I have sent copies of my Book to all of the respectable Journals of the day; and suppose that most of these will notice it. The "Ch. Examiner" has already promised to do so. An article, I have understood, has been written, but, so severe in spirit, that it has been witheld. In the number for July next, some notice, if not review, will doubtless appear.[17]—By this means, the opinions of the press may be gathered. Party interests, will, no doubt, affect the views taken; yet, in spite of this, there will, I fancy, remain much to commend itself to the good sense of the community; and the book find its place among the publications of the time.

[315] *Visit Mr. Bro[w]nson & Mr. Walker.*

I passed an evening, during this week, with Mr. Br[o]wnson; and, with him, called and spent an hour with Mr. Walker [,] "Editor of Ch. Examiner".[18] Both these gentlemen are friends of human culture; yet with neither, do I find that hearty sympathy which I desire. They are men of fair talents; generous purpose; yet destitute of that deep and fervid enthusiasm, that kindling genius, which ennobles our nature and fits it for the happiest action on the age. My intimacy with them is not unmixed with the doubts and suspicions;—[19] associations—that pride of intellectual gifts, and indifference to the more gracious endowments of the soul, that prevail among the debased many. They[20] make themselves merry with the divine, in our nature, more than befits my taste. [316] They espouse the cause of the vulgar many, rather than that of the noble few. They make light of the visions of genius;—speak contemptuously of some of the most brilliant minds of the time: These they count shallow; blown with vain and silly conceits. Against the castles of these, they aim the heavy metal of their logic, and, what with this, charged with ridicule, they fain hope to demolish the baseless fabrics of their genius. Both chop logic: both are men of understanding; neither apprehends the being of poet or seer. The high works of poetic genius; the marvels of holiness; these are beyond their grasp. Both are good and useful men. They eschew belief in other than bare and barren Reason—which, as the life of the Eclectic school, they make the God of Philosophy, and refuse credence to all else. As [317] writers in the "Ch. Examiner," they strive to defend these doctrines. An article from the pen of the former has just appeared in the No. for May, in which the distinction between modern spiritualists, as these are represented among us, is attempted.[21] There are a few minds, whose views do not, in all respects, coincide with the doctrines of the Eclectic School. These have been named after the German School of *Transcendentalists*;—a name, among us, at this time, indicative of all that is fanciful, wild, and undevout. Those who adopt these views are assumed as wanting in good sense,—unworthy the name of philosophers, and without the graces of genuine piety. They are called Pantheists. Emerson, Hedge,[22] Furness, and myself are classed in this number.

[318] Thus there are the Eclectic,—the Transcendental—and the Rational doctrines—each having their representatives among us. In each of these, spiritualism reveals itself as the antagonist of the sensual philosophy which has so long had the ascendancy among us. These three forms of spiritualism appear among the adherents of every Christian sect among us. The tendency of the age is obviously toward spiritualism; and, though our language, our literature, science, arts, and institutions, are, at present, all tinged with the material elements, yet the spiritual is destined to have the ascendant—This, is finding its way into religion, literature, and education, and will soon spread itself over science, art, and civil institutions. Materialism is passing away before its light and life.

[319] Mr Walker informed me that a review of the "Conversations" had been promised from Mr. Hedge of Bangor, and that he had expected it for the May No. of the "Examiner,' but that Mr. H. had failed.[23] He spoke of having a review of it from another gentleman, inclining to spiritualism; and hoped to notice the work in the No[.] of the 'Examiner["] for July.—I have heard several ministers speak well of the book, and doubt not that, from some

PLATE ONE
Alcott's entry during Week XVIII' (30 April–6 May) on philosophy.
Courtesy MH

quarter, it will meet with justice. I should think ministers would find suggestions to aid them in their professional labours. The book, I fancy, will be found useful both to them, and to teachers of Sunday schools and parents. It is already adopted as a class book in some of the Sunday schools. Children, I know, will be interested in it. Teachers will find subject-matter for conversation with their pupils; and the *method*, I conceive, to be invaluable.

[320] *Dr. Henry More's "Philosophical Collections."*
DR. H. MORE   I borrowed of Mr. Walker the Philosophical writings of Dr. H. More. Some of his works I had read. A short time since, I read an interesting sketch of his life prefixed to a collection of his poems. His great poem on the Soul called "Psyche-Zoae," I have never read. His works, with the exception of Vol 1st of the 'Divine Dialogues", are not in the "Atheneum". There is, however, an able review of his poems, with large extracts, in the Retrospective Review, which I have read. The volume of "Philosophical Collections" contains the following treatises:[24]

>Antidote against Atheism.
>Discourse on Enthusiasm.
>Letters to Descartes.
>Immortality of the Soul.
>Cabbala.

[321] Dr. More was a great and good man. Of the writers of his time he stands among the first. He was an eminent divine; a poet of no mean pretensions; and a devout man. He espoused the doctrines of Plato, and defended the principles of Descartes' philosophy. He was cotemporary with Descartes and with Cudworth, the celebrated author of the "Intellectual System".[25] I read his works with some interest, although my opinions of him, as a philosopher, are by no means raised, on a view of his works. With many men of his age, he partook largely of the spirit of fanaticism; and, in his Discourse on Atheism, brings forward as proofs of the immater[i]ality of the soul, numerous relations of witches and ghosts. No man was more credulous surely than he. He seems to place almost equal confidence in these statements, with his logical arguments from psychology and physiology.

[322] Here is a specimen of his style of thought and diction, from his poem on the "*Preexistence of the Soul.*"

>Like to a light fast lock'd in lanthorn dark,
>Whereby by night our wary steps we guide
>In slabby streets, and dirty channels mark;
>Some weaker rays from the black top do glide,
>And flusher streams perhaps thro horny side:
>But when we've passed the peril of the way,

>   Arrived at home and laid the case aside,
>   The naked light how clearly doth it ray,
>   And spread its joyful beams as bright as summers' day.
>
>   Even so the soul, in this contracted state,
>   Confined to these streight instruments of sense,
>   More dull and narrowly doth operate;
>   At this hole hears, the sight must ray from thence,
>   Here tastes, there smells; But when she's gone from hence,
> [323]   Like naked lamp, she is one shining sphear,
>   And round about her perfect cognoscence,
>   Whate're in her horizon doth appear;
>   She is one orb of sense, all eye, and aiery ear.[26]

In his "General Preface" he says; "I should commend to them that would successfully philosophize, the belief and endeavour after a certain principle more noble and inward than Reason itself, and without which Reason would faulter, or at least, reach but to mean and frivolous things. I have a sense of something in me while I thus speak, which I must confess, is of so retruse a nature, that I want a name for it, unless I should adventure to term it *Divine Sagacity*, which is the First rise of successful reason, especially in matters of great comprehension and moment; and without which, a man is, as it were, in a thick wood, and may [324] make infinite promising attempts, but can find no open champain, where one may freely look about him every way, without the safe conduct of this good genius."[27]

"The beginning of Reason is not reason, but something better." Aristotle.

Here seems to be the same nature intended that I denote by *Instinct*, whose free action is *Faith*; or, as termed by Dr More *"Divine Sagacity;"* or by Socrates—his *"genius or demon."* The distinction made by modern philosophers does not satisfy me. The Eclectics have the *"Spontaneous and Reflective Reason"*: Schelling has *"Intellectual Intuition"*: Jacobi, *"Faith"*.[28] And this latter seems to me the better phrase. It agrees with the phraseology of the present version of the N[ew] Testament, and is an intelligible word. Dr More was a spiritualist of the highest order. [325] Had he lived a century later he would have been called a Transcendentalist. I shall peruse his works more fully.

My reading, since the year opened, has been scanty. I have scarce read a single work. In this respect, I am apt, of late, to err. While residing in Philadelphia, I read a good deal. Having access to the Public Library, and more leisure than since, I took the benefit of it. At present, I make much too light of the thoughts of the eminent of past time. I seek their society too seldom. Of works of modern date, I would not take much heed. I deem them shallow.

I would waste no time over them. But the great of Time demand my respect. *Plato* I have honoured. *Aristotle* I have [326] not wholly slighted.²⁹ *Bacon* has come under my eye at times.—Yet I do not derive the good from the speculations of other minds, that some are ready to do. I do not readily take the view of another. I am ever seeking to subordinate all facts and theories, to my own scheme of things. Writers benefit me in the way of suggestion;— afford me sympathy;—and give confidence in my own statements—It is consoling to find that the mind, at various ages, and under all possible aspects, and circumstances, has taken similar views of truth. It shows how trifling is the influence of time and of institutions, on the vision of great minds; how these rise above all circumstances to behold the self same truths, and, at their eras, to publish these to the world. *Truth is of no age nor nation; it is ever contemporaneous with genius and virtue.*

[327] *Rev. Mr. Francis.*
MR. FRANCIS   Rev. Mr. Francis of Watertown called on me this week, and expressed interest in my enterprize, and sympathy with me, in this present hour of proscription and misapprehension.³⁰ He had read my book with great pleasure, and seemed aware of its true purpose and character. He was sorry that any thing should interfere with the prosecution of my enterprize; and seemed pleased with my purpose of continuing my school, amidst the clamour. He hoped the time would come when I should have classes of young persons, whose characters I might form to grace and beauty, by conversations and lectures—Such an event will, I trust, favor my intention in autumn, when I mean to propose it.

[328] I became acquainted with Mr. F. at our 'Symposeum" in autumn last, since which time, I have seen him but little. He is one of our most worthy and sensible ministers. His learning is extensive. Few men among us are more erudite, or possess an understanding more robust, or more amply furnished. His judgement is just; he is free from all imaginative or fanatical bias; and yet possesses the power of apprehending the highest gifts and products of genius. I value his friendship and apprehension of my purpose, as of great importance. His influence with the sensible and moderate will further my ends. He will be a friend to justify my character and purposes, in relations where others have exerted counter influences.

[329] Mr. F. brought me a note from my friend Miss. Thaxter,³¹ who is spending a few days with him at Watertown. Miss T. is one of my earliest friends in this quarter. I insert, in this place, a portion of her note:—

"I wish particularly to let you know how much satisfaction and delight, I feel in hearing Mr. Emerson, (who preached here on the last Sabbath,)³² talk of you. He is the only³³ individual with whom I have conversed, who seems to me justly to appreciate and entirely to sympathize with you; and is not the appreciation and sympathy of such a being as Mr. E. worth infinitely more than the hosannas of the multitude? He seems to stand aloof from them, in the calm upper region of his own pure, holy, and blessed thoughts, and to look, with a vision undimmed by the mists [330] of prejudice and passion, on the stir of the great Babel, "without feeling its whirl". The approbation of such an one, when, as in your case, it is the *echo* of conscience, must be of priceless value. (—I write the following sentences of this note because I feel their truth, and not in the pride of arrogance or vain glory.)—While Mr. E. depicted in one of his sermons, with the glowing eloquence of simple truth,—*the only true life,—the life of life*, the consciousness of spiritual progress,—of approximation to the Infinite source of Light and Life—you were present to me, as (one of the) living quickening spirits, among those in the midst of whom I am placed, as most fully accomplishing your mission. What if the burden of the earth's sufferings, privations and toils, of reviling and persecution are heaped upon you? You will bear them, "as an angel does his wings [331] to elevate and glorify not to depress." And I must regard you not with sadness and regret, but with satisfaction and congratulation. Miss *Fuller* was with Mr Emerson.— Mr. *Hedge* passed last night with Mr. Francis, and talked a great deal and very delightfully. I am amused with the different effects produced upon me by the atmosphere of these two persons.—Mr. H and Mr E. They both excite and elevate my spirit; but Mr E's influence distils, like the early dew; your whole being is refreshed and fertilized without your being conscious of the process. I wished you had been here exceedingly with these gentlemen. I wish daily more and more that you knew Mr. *Francis*."

Miss Thaxter is most sincerely and intelligently interested in my purpose [332] and views; and, intimate as she is with some of the most promising and useful minds of the time, performs the part of a friend. Her clear and descerning mind, corrects many of the misapprehensions, that fly about on the wings of busy rumour, detrimental to my good name, and the advancement of truth and justice. Of the women of our time, I know of none, who take a more simple & candid view of my character and purpose. She is a person of devout and chaste spirit; free from all prejudice, bigotry, and intent on whatever shall shed light upon the welfare of humanity. She sympathizes with the purest, the highest, and the noblest, unaffectedly contemning the mean, the degraded, and conventional.

[333]   *Majesty of Holiness.*
GREATNESS Imposing is the spectacle of a character standing alone amidst misapprehension and obloquy, in a senseless and unbelieving age—in an age when simple faith and youthful enthusiasm, expose the posses[s]or to suspicion and contempt. There is a majesty in such a mind; a grandeur in its solitary greatness, that seems the more inspiring, the more awful, from the contrasts that beset it. It pleads its own divinity. It assures the beholder of the reality of nobleness. It invests the scenes of its trial with enduring glory.

Yet such is ever the condition of all true greatness: Such is the marvel of all holiness that overtops the apprehension of [334] the time. It is solitary and friendless. But always doth the Divinity, in its kindliness, look down complacently on such, to console them amidst the barrenness and isolation of their state. While men pass by heedlessly or contemptuously, *He* puts within the souls of such, a wealth of forbearance, a faith of perserverance, a serene and self-confiding reliance, which, not obloquy nor injustice, persecution nor neglect, can exhaust nor overcome. Let the world make up its worst face, and pronounce its severest words, at such a man, and he shall but walk the more erect; his countenance the more lovingly smile; his bearing become fuller of grace and gentleness. The gods oft walk on the earth, but ever in times of commotion, so that the vulgar behold them not till after their ascension; and then by the works they leave behind them on their way.[34]

[335] But, such is the community of mind, such the identity of all free and reverent thought, that no man can, at any time, be wholly without sympathy. The soul is ever a familiar nature to a thoughtful spirit, and all its products, however varied or fantastic, possess a common likeness. All great natures know them; they see in them some alliance with themselves. They separate the form from the substance; they strip this of the garb of individuality, and deck it in the universal costume. There is ever a relation between opposites; & the finest genius ever detects this, making what before seemed separated by wide, if not impossible extremes, to unite and flow into one nature. Genius destroys all difference, all antagonism, contrarieties, in nature, making these all to flee before its revealing light. It weds the universe to its God. All [336] natures are allied. In the products of all minds it perceives some affinity, for it apprehends the law and the order of Spirit. Great men know each other though they look across oceans, and backward through centuries. They need not the trifling circumstance of time and space, to bring them in connexion with each other—Genius is cosmopolitan, and as old as God: it is co-eval with Spirit, and presided at the conception of things. Space and time are but the sequel; the universe but the product, of its action. Genius imitates God: it obeys and completes the will & work of its Father. It is God exercising his art in the human soul on the elements of nature. It announces to all beholders the eternal Law by which God shall manifest his Will among things. It is the art of Spirit.

[337]   *Walk with Rev Mr Ripley.*
RIPLEY I took a short walk with Mr. Ripley during this week. I am pleased to find him so cordial. He seems to enter the movements of the time with not a little of interest and intelligence. Of the ministers of this city, he is, perhaps, the most in favour of fair and free discussion. He tells me that his brethren have been considering the subject of *freedom of discussion*, at their weekly meetings, during their two last sittings; and that they have been led to it, by the manner in which my book has been spoken of, and my enterprize, in the public prints. From him I learn that these gentlemen, with a few exceptions,

regard me as an interloper into the theological fold; and deem this a fit occasion to make their [338] sentiments known. They do not countenance my speculations; nor look with friendly eyes on my enterprize. Beside this, the teachers of public schools of the city, owing to the freedom of remark in which I indulge on the present state of education among us, owe me no good will; and hence a favorable moment has come for a movement against me. There is already a strong sentiment unfriendly to me and my purpose. But amidst this, are most worthy and wide advocates of my principles and course. Neither the ministers, nor teachers, with their allies, can, I fancy, defeat my plans. They may delay my course; render it necessary for me to modify, in some particulars, my general intention, but cannot put it beyond the notice, nor sympathy, of my patrons and friends. I shall succeed.

[339] *The Week.*

At the close of another week, I cast up its sum as noted on these pages:—

    1—Notice of School in "An. of Edn."
    2—Visit Mr. Brownson & Walker.
    3—Dr. H. Mores Philosophical Collections.
    4—Call of Rev. Mr. Francis.
    5. Walk with Rev Mr. Ripley.

I wrote also in answer to Mr. Fuller of Providence, who, since my declining to give the opening discourse at the commencement of his school, (which I have done, from a fear of affecting his enterprize unfavorably at this juncture)[35] is desirious of securing Mr. Emerson for that occasion, and wishes me to encourage his presence. I shall do so.[36]

[340] At much sacrifice of feeling I have declined making use of this occasion for the declaration of my views and principles on *human culture*. This school is[37] formed on the model of mine. Gladly should I have spoken at its opening, but for the fear of endangering its ultimate prosperity. It matters little, however, in *what name* the good work comes before the world. The right, and fit, and improved, thing *Is*. It has passed from Idea into act: the thought is embodied, and so built to itself a house. I hope that it will prove a worthy and successful work. M[r.] Emerson could say fit things on the occasion. His introduction would do the work honour; and aid in its prosperity.—Go good child of mine, and try thy fortune amidst these Sharpers and Shavers of all that is visible and corporeal.

[341]   May.
                    Week XIX. [7–13 May]

Preach for Mr. Barnard.
WARREN ST. CHAPEL   On Sunday morning [7 May], I preached to the children

PLATE TWO
Alcott's entry during Week XVIII (30 April–6 May) about Hiram Fuller.
Courtesy MH

of the Warren Street Chapel.[38] I attempted to make them acquainted with the *"reality of the Soul"*, by drawing illustrations of its action from their own experience. They gave good attention. I believe that I succeeded in making them apprehend this divine nature, in some of its most affecting [342] operations—in the want of sympathy—the thirst for knowledge,—and the aspiration for goodness.—Children are seldom addressed on topics of deep and primary value, in terms fitted to their apprehension. Too often, are they treated with the formal and technical abstractions of theology, as viewed by adults, who have lost all genuine sympathy with their minds, and are, of course, unable to interest them. Religion is not made a living, breathing agency, adapted to the wants and temptations, the circumstances and ages, of childhood; but often, if not almost always, a formal, dead, and distant, influence. Little is done to show its connexion with the joys and sorrows of life, and make it a familiar in the young heart. The soul is left, in all its mysterious faculties, without explanation, or apprehension. We have little instruction of a genuine character.

[343] But there are indications of better things. Children are becoming subjects of deeper and more reverent study. Our infant, Sunday, and parish schools, are drawing the attention of the community. And although, there has not, as yet, been any very clear views taken of the nature and wants of the young mind, by those engaged in their instruction and superintendance, a sympathy has been enkindled in their welfare; and the want begins to be felt of something more philosophic and trustworthy to guide our efforts for their culture. The *churches for children*, like that of Warren Street, have already done not a little to quicken an interest in this respect.—This is now in a very flourishing state. Some of the best of our citizens are interested in it; the teachers are intelligent; and the children [344] numerous, and, generally, well-behaved and attentive. A fine and well-constructed building is erected for the purpose; and I see no reason why this institution should not prepare the way for others, even better adapted to the minds of the young. I fancy that all these movements are preparatory to that state of the public mind for which all my own efforts have been directed—when children will have their rightful place in the regards of the community, and fit means taken to ensure their innocence from violation, by arming them with the knowledge and virtue, that shall fit them for the ends of their being.—This time is near. Our chief concern is to know by what means best to meet its wants, & further its ends.—But the minds are not. All have lost the simple vision, and cannot see.

[345] Truly there are few minds remaining to us unperverted. False education has despoiled the soul of its rich gifts of innocence of simplicity and faith. The maxims and ways of the world, have been, too early, enstamped upon its ductile nature, and the sense of its original holiness has thus died almost from its consciousness. Of course, there are few among us, clothed with these native powers, which fit the soul for happy and efficient action on the young. We have lost the ability to apprehend its action. We do not sympa-

thize with its inmost life. It is a nature all unknown to us. Its holiness, its innocence, its simplicity, its faith in the divine, are unseen realities to our closed senses. Our eyes are hidden that we cannot behold these. It is too holy for us to approach. It shrinks from [346] our unhallowed grasp. We cannot touch it. We cannot apprehend its pure and simple instincts. We cannot answer its deepest and highest wants. We leave it all defenceless; exposed to the evils and ills of life; and what wonder if it fall from its first estate, while thus tempted and forsaken; thus left without protection, or cherished by an apprehending sympathy.—Educate it, with such views, and in such ignorance and perverseness, we cannot. Or, if we seek to assist it, we can render but small service, and this, but to its humblest and lowest faculties. We pervert its higher and nobler, while calling forth its lower, faculties. We weaken all its forces. We drain it of its essential virtue; we dim its lustre; and perpetuate but ourselves—Man, glorious in his original nature, endowed and expanded in genius, we do not disclose—Philosophy presides not at his culture.

[347] I feel assured of having ascertained the want of the age, in this respect, and that the community will, at some future day, accept the views of the young mind, and adopt the means of unfolding it, which I have sketched, and, as far as the time would permit, carried into actual operation, in my own enterprize. My books will slowly do their work. My professional labours, in this metropolis, will aid in the same purpose. Bye and bye, it will be seen that I have done the thing needful for the young mind, and my day of actual usefulness will have dawned. How soon this will come, I cannot say. Powerful prejudices, it seems, are to be overcome. Much false philosophy, and more erroneous practices, springing from it, are to be undermined. Professional pride will oppose it. Bigotted sectarianism [348] will seek to bring it in disrepute: traditionary superstition, and formal custom, will treat it with contempt; but all these leagued against it, shall only call forth its truth and power. The soul will be heard amidst all the clamour which these may call forth. Human nature is more mighty than human opinion; and will, in fit time, subvert all that is false in theory, or foul in practice. Let it but act freely; let its action be submitted to the observation of reverent and sagacious minds; let genius interpret its acts, and the true and immutable law of its developement shall be discovered as the guide to all practice on a nature so deep, so divine, so mighty. The philosophy of Human Culture, shall be set forth in its principles and order.

[349] *Correspondence.*
ITEMS. I had some correspondence with friends, by letter, this week. I wrote to Mr. Emerson apprizing him of my purpose of spending Monday and Tuesday of next week [15 and 16 May] with him.[39] Also, to my brother residing in New York. From my mother living in Connecticut, I recd. a letter.[40] Rev. Mr. Furness[41] of Philadelphia wrote to me; Miss E. P. Peabody[42] of Salem, and Mr Emerson.[43] Mr. G. Bradford, a friend of mine, called on me. Mr. Smalley, a teacher from the vicinity of Boston, passed a morning in my

school, witnessing my methods and processes of teaching.[44] I had an hour, also, with Miss Thaxter who passed the day in town, being now on a visit to her friend Mr Frances of Watertown. I also closed my spring term, intending to open the summer term of my [350] school on Monday May 22, having a vacation of a week, in the interim. I shall occupy a smaller room in the Temple, for the coming term.

Mr. Furness writes as follows in relation to my book and the manner of its reception:—

"I saw the violent attacks in the newspapers, but they did not furnish me with any additional inducements to write to you, as I could not conceive of their having any effect upon you but to make you smile; and the influence upon the book must have been to increase its sale. The idea that there is anything in those pure pages of yours calculated to injure any mind young or old, is utterly preposterous. And that newspaper remarks were not worth reading. When I say I had not pa- [351] tience to read the newspaper criticisms, I do not mean to imply that they excited any feeling, but merely that they did not interest me. The longer I live the more fixed is my persuasion that the world of men is divided into those with eyes, and those without; with various grades between the two. And when men are so blind as so utterly to misapprehend your work, there is no help in *words*. *Eyes* are wanted, and these must come from the Father of Spirits.

I am afraid I expected too much from your Book. I expected it would furnish me with eyes. I was impatient constantly for a more full exhibition of your personal views. The children say striking things. But the difficulty is, that Truth being to their minds & to yours like an atmosphere "brooding over you like light", you are consequently unable to understand the darkness in which we grope, and which so many of [352] us mistake for broad noon-day. I cannot but think infinite service has been done to these children if you have only succeeded in giving spirit, in their minds, precedence of sense. The world may not understand them now or ever, but you have helped to keep them at the true point of view, and though they should not be able to adjust this life to their mode of thought, still what is this life but the merest fraction."[45]

Mr. F. regrets that I did not begin with the public life of Jesus, reserving his birth and childhood, till these could be seen in the light of the former. This might have been better as the order of publication, and the impression on this age more favorable; but the result will prove the same in the end.—The worldly-wise, consulting temporary con- [353] siderations, do often secure present ends, at the expense of general integrity, and future influence. But a wise man, while he braves no opinion or usage of the world without thoughtful heed, omits no occasion for uttering saving truths at whatever peril. He sees beyond the present. He foresees the consequences of his word or of his act, as it affects a coming age, not as it shall affect himself. Truth has a reputation to sustain though often at the loss of that of the individual, who espouses her cause. This is the sacrifice she calls upon the brave to make. Truth is entire and she asks of her followers that they be entire, that they obey the order of her divine law, not the caprice of custom or of opinion.

[354] Truth is prudent. But her prudence is above all low and temporary cunning. She sees[?] deeper than the surface, and takes in more than the present. She pierces the mists that envelope the mind's [word], as a tenant of the present age, and takes in the results of the future—There is a prudence (so called) that puts out the worlds' eyes—a wisdom, that eats the fruits of its own folly. These are counterfeits. Truth is for all times. The usages of no era can chain it. It is free, and will break through all restraints save those which it imposes on its own free will. Who is he that would check the course of the peerless luminary of day, by daring to thrust his hand into the wheeling spokes of his chariot, as he rides forth to give the light to the nations? Even such is he that attempts to stay the course of truth, in its circuit through the world of thought.[46]

[355] Among other things, in his letter of this week, *Emerson* has the following:—

"In the few moments broken conversation I had with you a fortnight a[go][47] it seems to me you did not acquiesce at all in what is always my golden view for you, as for all men to whom God has given the ["]vision and the faculty divine";[48] namely, that one day you would leave the impracticable world to wag its own way, and sit apart and write your oracles for its behoof. Write; let them hear or let them forbear; the written word abides, until slowly & unexpectedly and in widely sundered places, it has created its own church; and my love and confidence in that silent muse is such, that in circumstances in which I can easily conceive myself placed, I should prefer some manual or quite me-[356]chanical labour as a means of living that should leave me a few sacred hours in the twenty four, to any attempts to realize my idea in any existing forms called intell[ec]tual or spiritual, where, by defying every settled usage in society, I should be sure to sour my own temper".[49]

My friend sympathizes more intently in my speculative than in my practical genius. I would fain give my powers fit exercise in each of these modes of action. I would realize and embody my Idea as fully as my time shall suffer. Still it may be, that the speculative more than the practical element, predominates in me; and that it were wiser to obey my friend. Time shall decide for me.

[357] Yet to act on my age is an irrepressible instinct of my nature. I am restless without finding scope for the exercise of this instinct. I desire to see my

Idea not only a *written*, but a *spoken* and an *acted* Word—a *Word Incarnate*. And though I may dream of future action, long after my Idea shall have passed from me on its mission, yet would I behold, what is given me to see with these eyes of flesh. I would act on my kind. I would test the might of my Ideas by putting them in conflict with present abuses and usages; and thus *seeing* them work. If I mistake not, something of this vision shall be vouchsafed me. I shall set my thoughts in acts; not content with the use of the pen alone.

[358]   *Further Notice of the 'Conversations"*
In the "Boston Courier", of this week, appeared another notice of the "Conversations," from the Editor, who has not failed to make known his opinions of the character and tendency of this work, on former occasions. The article of this work, on former occasions. The article of this week, will serve to make known more fully than before, the respectability of those persons who speak in favor of the Book.[50] It is much more moderate and respectful in tone and manner; and shows that the work is gaining in public estimation, by the discussions to which it has given rise, both in private circles, and in the public prints. It indicates that the work has been read, and something known of its real character. I insert it in this place:

[359][51]

[360]   *Reading.*
DR. MORE   During this week I looked over the work of Dr. More. His 'Cabbala" is an ingenious interpretation of the Mosaic Cosmogony.[52] But he overlays his fine thoughts with so much learning, and is withal so fanciful, that the impression on the mind, from a perusal of his writings, is somewhat broken. He seems to me to have substituted the analogies of fancy, for the verities of the imagination.[53] This is indeed the common fault of every fine genius. It is apparent in Plato, and, in more modern times, in Swedenbourg.[54] Dr. More, as the Swëdish Cabbalist, encumbers his thoughts with so many analogies, that the reader is often puzzled to discriminate the apparent from the real. Full faith he does not obtain.—Yet often does he assert the [361] supremacy of his mind over the imagery that encumbers it. His love of the marvellous is immense: his credulity amazing, even when we take him in connexion with the age in which he lived and wrote. This subtracts much from the pleasure of reading his works.—I have not yet read his Essay on the Immortality of the Soul—a work, wherin his genius, I imagine, displays itself to best advantage. He was a psychologist of a high order. The soul was a favorite study of his. His life was beautiful. He was deeply devout. He was much loved by his friends; and stood high in the lists of great and good men.—With the pure of all time, he adopted the sentiment, so simply announced by Jesus as the condition of all knowledge, "If any man will know of the doctrine[?] let him do the will of the Father."[55]

May

358   Week XIX   1837

"*Further* Notice of the Conversations."

In the 'Boston Courier,' of this week, appeared another notice of the "Conversations," from the Editor, who has not failed to make known his opinions of the character and tendency of this work, for some occasions. The article of this week, will serve to make known more fully than before, the respectability of those persons who speak in favor of the Book. It is much more moderate and respectful in tone and manner; and shows that the work is gaining in public estimation, by the discussions to which it has given rise both in private circles, and in the public prints. It indicates that the work has been read, and something known of its real character. I insert it in this place.

PLATE THREE
Alcott's entry during Week XIX (7–13 May) on the reception of *Conversations*.
Courtesy MH

[362] *Wyse on Education.*
I read also the first vol. of a work just published in London on Education. Mr Wyse is a member of the English Parliament.[56] He takes a civic rather than moral or philosophic view of his subject. In this volume, he discusses *principles* chiefly. He defines education as "the perfecting of human nature by the practice of duty." He seems familiar with the writings of the French and German educators; and gives copious notes in which he speaks of their views and methods. These notes constitute to me the chief value of his book. He is a believer in the perfectibility of man, and, with all of his school, utters noble truths. Vol. second is not yet published. In this, he purposes to discuss *Methods of Instruction.*

[363] As yet we have no work on the philosophy of human culture. Man has not been investigated to this end in all the departments of his being. The data are not collected. Nature nor the Soul are as yet made known to us. Pestalozzi did much for the sentiments, and gave us some light into the spirit of intellectual culture. Basedow and the Philanthropists, improved some of the methods of addressing the soul.[57] The institutions for training the deaf and dumb; the blind; and asylums for the insane, with infant schools, have been of some use in this respect.—But we are far from apprehending our subject, and cannot, of course, dispose of the order and means of unfolding him into the full perfection of his being.—This is the triumph of a future age.

[364] All systems, to be worthy and successful, must spring from a knowledge of man. The more this nature is studied, the purer our practice upon it. No man can develope the soul that does not apprehend the soul. No man can inspire so divine a nature without being himself inspired. To know the soul is the condition upon which its developement depends. And to inspire this knowledge by self-developement, is the end of education. No man can know whose intellect shall not be quickened by the inspiring agency of a pure life, conforming his act to his Idea, in all things. *Education,* in its broadest and fullest sense, is the realization of the highest conceptions of the soul, by the developement of all its faculties in unity, according to their order of growth.

[365] *View of the Week.*
The week has glided by, leaving for my eye, the following insertions of things and events on these pages.

    1. Preach for Mr. Barnard.
    2. Correspondence
        —Wrote to Rev. R.W. Emerson.
        — "   to my Brother.
        —Recd Letter from Rev. Mr. Furness.
        — "   from Mr. Emerson.
    3. Notice of "Conversations" in B. Courier.

4—Reading
   —Dr. Mores Philosophical Collections
   Wyse on Education.
5—Close of Spring Term of School.

Besides the sympathy arising from these sources, I have dwelt much, in thought, on my relation to this age, [366] to ascertain, if possible, the readiest means of acting upon it to best advantage. Next week I am to see *Emerson*. Among the topics that shall interest us will be this most absorbing one. In the light of his mind, I may more clearly descern my own; and thence my work, and the time for my faculties to discharge their duty to the race.— Such vision doth one spirit give to another when there is a loving and apprehending union. On the wide earth there doth exist *one* soul in which a man shall see his own. Let him find this, and thenceforth, as time needs, take counsel for his course. If he fail of this, as most shall, then let him hold frequent and loving communion with the highest and holiest in his own soul, so shall he never be without sympathy or solace, nor in doubt.

[367]

20
May.
Week XX. [14–20 May]

Visit Emerson at Concord.

VISITS.   I spent a few days with Mr. Emerson at his own house in Concord.[58] I left home on Monday morning [15 May], and returned on Friday afternoon [19 May]; having seen Mr. E. at Concord, and Mr. Frances at Watertown. With the latter I spent a night, taking his house on my way home. During my visits to [368] these gentlemen, various topics of interest were discussed. Little difference of *opinion* seemed to exist between us: the means and method of communicating with the age were the chief points of difference. *Emerson*, true to his genius, favors written works. He holds men and things at a distance; pleases himself with using them for his own benefit, and as means of gathering material for his works. He does not believe in the actual. His sympathies are all intellectual. He persuades me to leave the actual, devote myself to the speculative, and embody my thoughts in written works.—*Frances*, on the other hand, inclines more to the actual; sympathises in the wants and pursuits of men. Emerson idealizes all things. This idealized picture is the true and real one to him; all else is nought. Even [369] persons are thus idealized, and his interest in them, and their influence over him, exists no longer than this conformity appears in his imagination. Beauty, beauty, this it is that charms him. But beauty has pure and delicate tastes, and hence all that mars or displeases this sense, with however much of truth or of goodness it may be associated, is of no interest to the mind. Emerson seeks the beauty of truth: it is not so much a quest of truth in itself, as the beauty thereof: not so much the desire of being holy and true, as of setting forth in fit and graceful terms, the beauty of truth and holiness. With him all men and things have a beauty; but this is the result of his point of vision, and often falls wide of the actual truth. To give pleasure, more than to impart truth, [370] is his mission. What is beautiful in man, nature, or art, this he apprehends, and with the poets power sets forth.

His genius is high and commanding. He will do honour to his age. As a man, however, this visit has somewhat modified my former notions of him. He seems not to be fully in earnest. He writes and speaks for effect. Fame stands before him as a dazzling award, and he holds himself somewhat too proudly, nor seeks the humble and sincere regard of his race. His life has been one of opportunity, and he has sought to realize in it, more of the accomplished scholar, than the perfect man.—A great intellect, refined by elegant study, rather than a divine life, radiant with the beauty of truth and holiness. He is an *eye*;[59] more than a *heart*—an *intellect*, more than a *soul*.

[371]   *Western Messenger.*

In the "Western Messenger" for the present month, appeared a notice of my Book, with a refutation of the charges brought against it in the public prints. This was from the pen of the editor. Beside this article of some length, he has the following under the head of "monthly record."

"*A Suggestion*—We perceive the editor of the 'Boston Courier' recommends that Mr Alcott be presented to the Grand Jury on account of his Book. We respectfully suggest, in addition, that the indictment be in the words of that formerly found against Socrates the son of Sophroniscus. In Xenophon's memorabilia Chap. 1, it runs thus:—"Socrates is accused of not believing in the Gods in [372] which the city believes, but introducing other divinities; he is also accused of corrupting the young." The two cases would be exactly parallel. Or perhaps the form as given by Plato, (Apol. Soc. 3.) would be thought more suitable. "Socrates is accused of searching out things under the earth, and above the heavens; of making the worse appear the better reason, and of teaching others the same."[60]

Emerson told me that he now considered my purpose and character as standing right before the public. The articles in the 'Messenger" and "Ch Register', having done me good justice. This further article of the Editor of the Messenger adds still more to the impression in my favor.

[373]   *Arrangement of School Room.*

I put room no 3 in the Temple in order for opening my school therein on Monday next [22 May]. It is quite small, being adapted, by this arrangement, for 18 or 20 pupils. This number will not exceed the number of my present pupils. Indeed it may not be much more than 10 or 15 during this Summer Term.[61] Always this is a scanty quarter. Parents are leaving the city for their summer residence; some do not choose to enter their children for a shorter time than a full quarter. Add to this, the pres[s]ure of the times,[62] and increase of terms at present in my own case, with the state of popular feeling on account of my Book, and the causes are told.

[374] *The Week.*
Being vacation of school, I note the following items:—

> Visit Mr. E.merson at Concord.
> Visit Mr. Frances at Watertown.
> Notice of Conversations in "West Mess.'
> Prepare Room No 3 for school.

Thus I have passed another week, seeking sympathy of thought and purpose. Some I have found. Yet not as I would like. Indeed, I scarce hope to find it at present. Opinions novel like mine, purposes unprecedented, are not likely to find sympathy, or advocacy at once. I wait alone and in faith.

[375]
21
May.
Week XXI. [21–27 May]

Opening of School in Room No. 3.
On Monday [22 May], of this week, I opened school in Room No 3 in the Temple. But 10 of my pupils remain with me. These will, I fancy make up my number for the present quarter. And, after the August holidays, I know not of any addition. Thus am I left with a third of my usual number. And these may be withdrawn at the end of the [376] present quarter, leaving me to close my doors. The tide of sentiment sets strongly against me, I may be unable to withstand it, for a time, but seek retreat in contemplation, or in some form of action less affecting the popular interests, or caprice.

But, should it come to this, good will have been done. I shall but have failed in my actual enterprize from the misapprehension of the public. The theory remains unassailed, and I can renew my efforts for its demonstration, at some future day, when the public mind shall have been divested of its present misapprehensions. There are those who feel the benefits of my action; who do not enter into popular views; whose influence still makes in my favor.

[377] Beside this testimony, my books contain a record of my practice, so that this is not lost. Currency will be given to the principles and methods which have here been adopted, and general education receive the benefit. It matters less, whether the enterprize continue, since all, most valuable, has been thus far recorded and preserved. Truth will thus bespeak favor for herself; and make herself respected as is meet. Labours like hers, of which I have been the instrument, will not be suffered to perish. They will abide, and honour the divinity in whose service they have been performed. Bye and bye, when the

scales shall fall from the eyes of men, then will they apprehend the work which was wrought in their presence, but which they did not perceive in their blindness. In such way, shall all things be made equal.

[378] Blindness cannot be cured at once. Though the world be a dunce, and a brute, we do not enlighten and elevate, by treating it as such. Wisdom is charitable. It has faith. It bears, and believes, hopes and endures. It knows that no act, or word, no purpose, nor idea, shall fail of its end, if meant for good, and have its full acceptance. For nothing true, nothing good, nothing noble, can perish. It cannot remain hidden. It contains within itself the principle of its own perpetuity, and though evils, errors, usages, may hide its lustre for a time, it shall come to the light, and command regard at last. The soul will out. Nature cannot confine; man cannot emprison it. Opinions, like clouds, do but obscure the sun for a day; its rising beams chase away all mists and vapours, in the end.

[379] It is easy for a combination of men, acting on public opinion, to embarrass and finally defeat the special plans of an individual. Through that modern organ, the press, they can give the law to popular sentiment. Professions can assail members: a man may give himself a thousand tongues, and find his words flying on the wings of rumour wheresoever he choose.

But all things right themselves in the end. Error and misapprehension are ephemeral. Facts alone are abiding, and no cunning, nor subterfuge, can hide these from finding the light. God's truth will make its own fortune in the world. But give it time and it asserts its honour. The foolish are in haste to make every thing appear or beseemeth good in their short sightedness. Truth is patient, and [380] makes no hurried feints. It has eternity to work in, and this gives it time to complete its purpose—to make all visible; adjust all temporary injustice; correct transient misapprehension.

Opinion may check the specific action of an individual: the man may withdraw from the actual; but if he have a thought or a principle, this shall speed on its errand, and do its behest, without his accompaniment. And this shall live and perpetuate itself. Nothing can compete with it. It will run and be glorified. Men may oppose it, after the instrument be withdrawn from their sight, but it grows the stronger by their assault.—Thus doth God take all worthy and noble things into his own hands, and pledge his omnipotence for their success.

[381] *Proposed meeting of the "Symposeum".*
LETTER TO EMERSON   I wrote a letter to Emerson, apprizing him of the proposed meeting of like minds, on Monday next [29 May] at Rev. Mr. Ripleys.[63] These meetings, given to conversations on topics of high moment, were deemed quite profitable, as well as interesting, when last held, during the

PLATE FOUR
Alcott's entry during Week XXI (21–27 May) about the "Symposeum."
Courtesy MH

summer and autumn of 1836. We purpose to renew them. The following gentlemen are expected to attend.

1—	Rev	Mr. Ripley	8—	Rev	Mr Dwight
2—	"	" Hedge	9—	"	" Bartol
3—	"	" Emerson	10—	"	" Robbins
4—	"	" Brownson	11—	"	" Stetson
5—	"	" Frances	12—	"	" Parker
6—	"	" Furness	13—	"	" Putnam
7—	"	" Clarke	14—he never came[64]		

[382] These gentlemen are all intent on advancing the honor and interests of humanity. They comprise the few among us that take higher and diviner views of the soul, than men have been wont to take in past times. They incline to the spiritual doctrines, each taking his own view of subjects. We propose to meet and disclose to each other our views and purposes; to receive and impart light, if light we have among us to confer. I value this opportunity as one of benefit to myself. It puts me in possession of the current genius of the time; acquaints me with its cherished purposes and means of action, and thus brings my own mind in communion with its comates. The action of these minds on each other will be healthful, and give unity to the action of all. Soul will become known to soul as best befits itself[.]

[383] *Note from Miss Fuller.*

Miss Fuller, having had some of my MS. Journals for perusal during her stay at Groton, returned them this week. In a note she says;

"I thank you for the look you have esteemed me worthy to take into your views and feelings, and trust you will never have reason to repent your confidence, as I shall always rejoice in the intercourse which has been permitted me with so fair a soul.[65] You will find on the first blank leaf of your journal, a little poem, which expresses some part of what has been suggested to me by the record of your life. You will, I hope, pardon the liberty I have taken in writing it there, as the leaf can easily be taken out, if the thoughts there inscribed do not please you."—[66] I insert the poem—

[384] *Light and Warmth.*[67]
from the German of Schiller.

The noble man walks forth,
Untroubled by low fear or doubt,
Visions which in his soul have birth
He hopes to meet without;
And consecrates, with generous feeling warm,
To do his faith's behests, a faithful arm.

> But, if awhile he tries
> To act upon this narrow stage,
>   He finds his strength will not suffice
> To save his heavenly heritage;
>   Must guard his heart so carefully
> Love can scarce ever get the key.

[385]
>   Not always the clear rays
> Of truth suffice to keep us warm,
>   Well for those who the face
> Of Wisdom see without hearts' harm!
> Would the Gods have their darlings safe from ill,
> The World-man's Eye must aid the Enthusiasts' Will.

        Translated by S.M.F for Mr. Alcott,
               May 18, 1837.

Miss F. soon enters upon her labours with Mr Fuller of Providence. On the first of June, his House is to be dedicated, and the school to open immediately.[68] Mr. Emerson has been invited to give the opening descourse on that occasion. I hope he will do so. It will be a fit moment to speak a word for the soul, and few men can do better justice to the subject than Mr. E. Mr F. invites me to be present, which I shall like if nothing seem to be in the way. Founded as this Institution [386] is on wise and liberal principles, I take an interest in its success. As yet, it is too much in a state of infancy to be regarded in any other light than as a promise of better things in Education. Mr. F is earnest and prudent in his efforts, and will, I doubt not, advance its interests. I hope the community will sustain him in his purpose. I feel a kind of paternal interest in this enterprize, as my own genius is more simply and visibly at work in it, than in other institutions of our country. Mr. F. adopts the spiritual doctrines, and is one of the few young men among us, who have risen to the perception of the high and sacred vocation of teacher, and worthily devotes his fine genius to its duties. His associate, Miss Fuller, is one of the first in point of native and acquired talent among us.

[387]   *Letter to Mr. Fuller.*

    I wrote to Mr. Fuller with a view of ascertaining the state of his institution at this time, and to signify my interest in it. In this letter I said;

"This clamor and stir seems to have intimidated some, and will, I fear, break up my School. But the Book sells I believe, and what I cannot do in one way, I may perhaps in another. The tide of opinion sets strong against me, and I may be unable to withstand it; but this cannot hurt the principles which I advance or hinder their diffusion in the end. Your institution will I trust be another form of the same Eternal Verity. You open your school under the most favorable auspices; and will, I am sure, be found worthy of the high trust which you assume. [388] I may be called to retire from the field of actual labour; but the good work will go on and prosper, without my hands. The renovating agency shall speed on its glorious behest; and it gives me joy even in his hour of comparative discouragement, to see the fulfilment of hope. Whatever is true, is pure, is noble, shall never perish. It contains within itself the pledge of its perpetuity. Though hidden for a time it shall come to the sight, and demand and receive reverence & honor, at last.—I shall be glad to hear from you, and learn whatsoever betides yourself, or the noble enterprize in which you (more worthily than most of your years) are so ardently engaged".[69]

Mr. Fuller is the only young man upon whom the doctrines and discipline of human culture, as displayed in my Books, have made an [389] impression so abiding as to find their way into actual teaching. The "Record of a School" first quickened his mind, and, under the light of this influence, he has been pursuing his way; and now is about entering upon an enterprize every way worthy of his genius, and of the city that gives its aid. A large and most commodeous house, built at considerable expense, and furnished according to his idea of elegance and convenience, has been the result of his exertions. Into this he takes 150 pupils, of both sexes, from the age of 3 to 18 years, and is assisted by competent teachers, at high salaries. To Miss Fuller he awards $1000 per ann[um]; and to his associate in the department of languages $1500—sums equal to those given to the teachers of the Boston Schools. The primary department, in this institution is one of great interest. [390] Into this he receives 50 or more small children, who are placed under the care of a special teacher, subject to his general supervision.—He has been in the practice of using the "Conversations on the Gospels" as a morning exercise, and all his methods are in the spirit, and most, in the form, of those practiced upon in my own school.—I cannot but look upon this enterprize with considerable interest. I shall be glad to see how another will receive and apply the principles that have so long guided my own practice; how these will affect the minds of those upon whom they shall be brought to bear. A man who sympathises with the young so sincerely, whose simple soul is all in harmony with theirs, must do them good; and can scarce fail, so long as he is true to his own nature.

[391] *Revision of 'Psyche".*
PSYCHE. I began to prepare for revising my MS. of *Psyche* for the press. As time wastes, and nothing of interest presents itself in the actual, I find my mind turning inward, and asking for fresh and free exercise. My school can[not] interest me, at present, save as a means of living; my number of pupils being so much reduced, and all idea at present given up, of resuming the 'Conversations on the Gospels"; or of attempting any thing new in demonstration of theory. I meet my pupils daily for useful labour whereby bread shall come for my family; not as subjects of large and generous experi-

ment in the principles and methods of education. I need action of mind for my hours of absence from the school room. [392] This I shall find in revising my MS of the work on the Soul of Childhood, which I incline to call 'Psyche". I wish to rewrite much of it; make large additions, with some omissions; arrange the whole according to some obvious law of order; and fit it for the eye of others, when the time shall come to give it to the world. I am sure of having said somewhat for humanity in these sheets. I have, I fancy, touched the maternal sense, and, if successful, shall not have written in vain. Mothers are the arbiters of the souls' infancy and childhood; and can I but diffuse my genius into their souls, it will flow out upon those committed to their care, and adorn, as well as bless, the inmates of the nursery.[70] In that hope, I have written Psyche. Drawing inspiration from a living child, as it [393] unfolded its life under my observation, I have sought so to present the phenomena of its pure consciousness to the mother, as to make her feel the divinity of its being, and the sacred mission to which she is called. In this, I have, I fancy, not wholly failed. Several of my friends have borne testimony to the faithfulness with which my plan has been executed and approved of its idea.[71]

"Psyche" is intended as a prose poem on the nature and wants of the Soul during its infancy and childhood, and the duties which devolve on mothers from a view of its endowments and destiny. I have sought to keep the philosophy of the piece somewhat in the background, anxious rather to address the heart, through the imagination, than to make formal appeal to the understanding. [394] I have wished to sing a song of the soul in the ear of the mother, and charm her into a sense of infant purity and holiness, so that the little ones who move before her senses, and appeal to her for sympathy, shall claim her affectionate regard, and grow more and more pure and lovely, under the smile of her guidance.—As yet the spirits' song for the behoof of childhood has not been sung by any bard. In no language is it written. The soul has been without an interpreter during the earlier stages of its terrestrial career. No worthy notes have been raised in its behalf. It has been without friend. It has plead in vain for sympathy. Love, such as angels were wont to bestow ere it became a tenant of flesh, it hath sought for in vain. It hath found no parent on earth. Its corporeal mother hath not fed its [395] yearning spirit with heavenly fare, and it hath suffered thereby. Could words, fit for its celestial purity, be found, and find response in the maternal heart, a good work would be done for the world. Childhood would appear in its true loveliness. Human nature would assert its divinity in the advancing stages of life; and men would learn that not to infancy and childhood alone, were given the sacred boon of innocence.

The influence of such a work, executed in a manner befitting the conception, on education, not only in its earlier statges, but upon the whole form[?] of human culture, would, I conceive, be most happy. It would show the value of the soul: open out the sacred ministry of human life, with all its manifold occasions for growth and glory; and send [396] a quickening and renewing force into all interests affecting the welfare of the soul. It would give man a point of sight from which to view himself, his relations, and duties. It would unfold new resources for the growth of society. It would regenerate institutions; and transfigure man into the pure and unsullied image of his nature.

Such a work, I would write. Such a service would I do for my kind. Of course, but few of my contemporaries would apprehend the nature, or trace the scope of my work, in all its features. But something worthy would be done. The souls' mission and destiny might be sketched with some faithfulness to a mother's vision. Psyche might be seen in the glory of her being, while reposing on the maternal bosom, [397] or plying its early faculties on the things of the domestic scene. Maternity, with its holy duties and divine consolations, might be set forth; and the true and simple souls that custom and culture have spared us, joy in the bequest thus given them.

I set myself then to this work, during this hour of misapprehension and reviling, without. In it, I can find release from the clamour of those who know me not, and would make my good appear as the evil deed. I will address myself to maternity. Here is a pure and divine sense. Touch it tenderly, reverently, and in the sympathy which it can feel, and the world is regenerated. I go here for solace, for sympathy, for useful labour, and the divine approval.—The time shall [398] come when deeds, actual rather than contemplative, shall call me away. But now am I without hands in the wide earth. My genius yokes me to angelic natures, and I bid adieu to the beasts of earth, who know me not, since I no longer herd with them, nor affect their manners, nor speak well of their creed. These corporeal members shall find sustenance; but not at the cost of my virtue. I will peril nought divine. I will chaffer not in the world's marts. God sendeth the corn and the rain; and he that trusts, shall not want for these, nor for shelter, nor raiment, peace and hope.[72]—The faithful soul hath no fears.—The pure soul no evils—the wise spirit seeth through all disguises; penetrates the clouds of sense, and eyes the Divinity. It is above want, and misapprehension, & defeat.

[399]   *Burden of the Week.*

The week ends. I have been busy as usual, and much in my wonted way. Memory would note the following entrances on these pages, from the interests of the same:—

    1. Opening of School in Room No 3.
    2. Proposed meeting of 'Symposeum."
    3. Note from Miss Fuller.
    4. Letter to Mr. Fuller.
    5. Revision of Psyche.

I find our residence in "Cottage Place" quite agreeable. The children enjoy it highly. And the effect on health and spirits is very salutary. The walk of fifteen or twenty minutes gives me needful exercise. Living as we do most simply: breathing the [400] pure air, and in the presence of natural scenery, we feel the good influence. We have little of art or of elegance to deck our simple mansion. But who needs these, as he needs content and peace! I should enjoy them. I love beauty. I feel enriched and honoured by its presence, but I can yet dispense with it. It costs me some feeling nevertheless. My little room, with my 10 pupils, and some of the remnants of my former more magnificent mansion, with which it is in great contrast, gives me unquiet reflections. But these soon disappear with the presence of worthy and just estimates of my true position as a man and a teacher. I feel honored by the manner in which these have been yielded, and see in the sacrifice, the glory that belongs to simple intentions and pure deeds.

[401]
22
June.
Week XXII. [28 May–3 June]

Psyche.

Besides my mornings at school, I gave some time during this week, especially my afternoon and evening hours, to the preparation of Psyche. In this, I feel my interest reviving, and if I make it in form and spirit, what [402] a Psyche should be, I shall not have thought and written in vain. Yet much remains to be written. Important facts and principles are barely[?] touched. My mind has taken broader views and deeper insight, since this first draught. There remains much filling up. And I find nothing wanting save the time for uninterrupted thought. I see not when this is to come. Sunday gives me whole and full day; besides this, I have none, save now and then as chance favors. Still I do something by way of filling up the outline that I have sketched. And shall do as best I may, time and occasion favoring or otherwise. Now and then, can I steal an hour from the morning before my school opens; and long settings at night (such has long been my habit) accomplish the rest.

[403] ### Anniversaries.

This week, being the season for the convening of the annual meetings of various societies, is usually a period of interest; to religionists especially. I attended some of the various meetings. But with little satisfaction. Sectarianism—bigotry—shallow and narrow views; noise, display, flourish of purpose, and of rhetoric—with less of earnestness and wisdom, seemed to predominate in these assemblies. Still I learned something from all. These are the phenomena of the time; a sage observer shall see under these movements, purposed or planned, the predominating spirit of his age. They indicate the hour on the Human Clock: now is the striking time—what's o clock? What's

[404] o clock? good and worthy, sirs[?], secretaries, presidents, agents, ye who announce the hour for all the various audiances who come each to hear his own clock strike. Verily, the hour struck, varies widely from the true hour, yet the world carries home the time of day, and waits in all patience, nothing doubting, till the year come round again, to learn his time of day again; not knowing (how should he) that the machinery hath been set long before, by interest, bigotry, and all the time-tinkers, of which all ages are full, to strike as they willed it.—God holdeth no anniversaries—marshals no associations to set the hours, or note the progress of that true index that ever defines the hour on the dial of time. And every true man heeds not others. He distrusts their accuracy. Whats' o clock for the human race, all over the world; not for me, and mine, here under [405] tropic, or pole, age or year; whats' o clock for all the world, at all places, and times; whats' o clock for eternity. Therein is the true time; and God ever setteth the Horologe that marks the hour for the human race. Look! Yet look not outward over space, or backward or forward in time—to tropic nor pole, age nor year, look into thine own soul: cast the hours that thy hand hath passed over, and learn thy true time for thyself. Regulate this by the true, not the false time, survey the Eternal Dial, and thou shall not be stunned by the alarm-bells; or lose thy reckoning amidst the lying hours of thine age. God keepeth thee in order by his own hand, and keeps thy reckoning plain for thee, if thou wilt but open thine eyes and see; yield thy faith and be true to the inward![73]

[406] So I refused to be enlight[en]ed as to the true time by these various time pieces, whose striking rang loudly all the week. I attended, however, the meetings of these;

    1. American Unitarian Association.
    2. Social meeting of Sunday School Teachers.
    3. Boston Sunday School Society.
    4. Book and Pamph[l]et Society.
    6. Anti-Slavery Convention.[74]

On Monday afternoon [29 May], I attended, also, the *meeting of gentlemen friendly to new and worthier views of men and things*, at Mr. Ripleys. Most of the gentlemen, named at page 381 of these notes, were present, and we separated to meet again in August next, probably at Concord.[75] (Spirited Conversation, on various topics—Religion, chiefly.)

[407]   Dr. Howe.

I found in a Discourse delivered by Dr. Howe of the Institution for the Blind in this city, before the Boston Phrenological Society, the following paragraph, designed to cast ridicule on my enterprize and method. The Discourse is on the "Social Relations of Man", and was pronounced at the time of the most noisy excitement about my Book.[76] He says;—

"I am not disposed to point out or reason from extreme cases; if I were, I need not go out of this city; nay, in this very building, you may find, at ten o clock to-morrow, a grave and solemn assembly of philosophers, whose first suit of jacket and trousers is not yet worn out—of four year old matrons, who are brought in four-wheeled baskets; you shall hear them addressed as men and women, whose reasons are perfected, and questions [408] put to them that would severely tax the causality,[77] comparison, and ideality, of mature minds. Nay! You will hear these mewling-pewling philosophers questioned upon the most abstruse and mystical points of religious belief, and their answers carefully recorded, to be published for the benefit of our stupid old generation which is called on to receive instruction from these babes and sucklings! You will pardon my allusion to this subject, it is too absurd for serious notice; but I could hardly avoid it, for, as the old philosophers have it, the propinquity of time and place forced it upon me."

Words! Words! Dr. Howe never heard a conversation—never saw the philosophers, or conversed on the subject with their teacher.

[409] Mr Hedge

I had pleasant conversation with Mr Hedge, both at "Symposeum,"[78] and at one other interview, during this week. I found more agreement with him than I had supposed would prevail. On education, we had most conversation. He misapprehends me somewhat on this topic. He inclines more to scholastic instruction—favours more the ancient doctrines of Aristotle, than of Socrates or Plato. But his is a mind of a fine order of powers. Of the younger members of the clergy, he is one of the most gifted. Emerson and Hedge promise more than others amongst us. With Furness, Brownson, and Ripley, they constitute the best talent in the liberal church. I can communicate freely with all these.

[410] Sum.

1. Revising "Psyche."
2. Attending anniversaries.
4. Notice of Dr Howe.
5. Symposeum.

Besides this, Mr. Fuller came to town to spend a few days, preparatory to the dedication of his school, which takes place next week. Mr Emerson gives the Descourse on that occasion. I shall attend unless something transpires to prevent. The occasion may be made one of great importance, both in its bearings on the special interests of M[r.] Fuller, and the spreading of simpler and worthier views on the culture of human beings.

June

1837   Week XXII.   409

Mr Hedge.

I had pleasant conversation with Mr Hedge, both at "Symposeum," and at one other interview, during this week. I found more agreement with him than I had supposed would prevail. On education, we had most conversation. He misapprehends me somewhat on this topic. He inclines more to scholastic instruction — leaning more the ancient doctrines of Aristotle, than of Socrates or Plato. But his is a mind of a fine order of powers. Of the younger members of the clergy, he is one of the most gifted. Emerson and Hedge promise more than others amongst us. With Francis, Brownson, and Ripley, they constitute the best talent in the liberal church. I can communicate freely with all these.

PLATE FIVE
Alcott's entry during Week XXII (28 May–3 June) on F. H. Hedge.
Courtesy MH

[411]
23
June.
Week XXIII. [4–10 June]

Mrs. A.

I gave this week mainly to 'Psyche'. Blessed Creature she takes all my time, and hence my thoughts, turned from the fleeting and passing interests, of the outward and corporeal life, find little of thing or show, to notice on these sheets. To add still more to my self-isolation, Mrs A. passed the week with her brother at Scituate, returning with him after his visit during the anniversaries. Here she intended passing a few days; but, being suddenly [412][79] indisposed, she continued through the week. The fine air and influences of the country, being more favorable to her health and spirits than those of the city.—Since our return to Boston from Philadelphia in 1834, she has scarce slept a night, scarce passed a day, from the city. Her cares, meanwhile, have been many; her health by no means firm; and, added to these interests, her mind has been unequal to the toils and anxieties that she has been called to assume. With a large family of children, during a part of this time, and during the whole, restricted by pecuniary resources, and hence in bodily comforts, she has had little time left her for quiet contemplation, little scope has been given to the free and full action of her fine powers. She has been a great sufferer; and none have entered into her state. Alone, unassisted, scarce seeing her way clearly, seeking for light, for quiet, yet called by imperious needs, away from the [413] sources whence these are to come, her days have passed away without satisfaction or solace, save that which faithful discharge of present needs seemed to require. Her own soul, and those of her family, have suffered loss thereby. Her early education and sphere of action were by no means suited to call forth the practical qualities most needed to be exercised in the discharge of labours like those devolved upon her. And hence, she has been a learner late in the school of discipline.[80] She has battled with the actual, and, so intent is she to discharge her duties worthily, that she wastes much of her strength, from her very ardour of pursuit and endeavor. This visit, by removing her from the scene of her toils, and giving her a view of her relations from a different quarter, will serve to refresh and enlighten. It will do her good.—I wrote her, once or twice, this week. In one of my letters I dwelt, at some length, on the dispensa-[414]tions of discipline and trial through which she had been called to pass, and sought to point out the need of submission to its austere ministries, in order to reap its blessed fruits, of moral strength, and religious hope. God is fitting her, by his providence, for great Duties and results, and although, as yet she has not seen the order of his will, yet the time draws nigh, when her darkness shall be turned into light; her distrusts into faith, her anxieties into peace, and quietude of soul. Then will she apprehend those events and disciplines which brought her into my arms, and bound her lot with mine, in those austere labours, which yield neither outward profit, nor noisy applause, but the silent and unspeakable rewards of simple, sincere, and constant fidelity to principle. Blessed day, this! For her, for our children, and for me!

[415] *Letter to Mrs A.*

(Copy)

My Good Wife!

Again have you been called to the mothers' trial of suffering, yet without her reward![81] Well, so be it! The Allwise Desposer doth best ever; and though short sighted man scarce apprehend the purpose, yet the sequel ever makes the dispensation clear, and the discipline most blessed. The thought has just come to me, that God is working out for you, (despite all your seeming distrust of a wise and beneficent ministry) a great and divine charge! You know it not, my friend, you ask light! light! in the thickness of the darkness;[82] but this deep cry for light, though at present witheld, shall be answered, when the good work shall be [416] wrought out upon you,—a work so great that to know it in progress would foreclose its blessed results. Know! who knows truly? None but God. To man it is not given to know save in part:[83] he is to believe. Faith is his life.—The very pulse that quickens—the hearts' life of life! Mystery is written on all things: how deeply on the soul! and its corporeal comate also. To me, spending my brief & yet busy day; yea, my recurring years, on this same *driad nature*, there yet remains deep and unpierced mysteries. Not the less sincere, earnest, constant is my faith: Yea it waxes more and more strong. Without mystery there can be no faith.[84] And if no faith, where is love—where constancy, devotion—all that makes life sacred and enduring.—Your *Knowalls'*, are assassins. I am afraid of them. O, for a world of believers—simple, docile, meek, souls, who distrust not;[85] who do not, like modern [417] professors, who good people, tell the All Wise, and All True, 'Thou art silly, thou liest!["] Let me lie with God, than be wise and true with such. Nine tenths of the world are in this predicament; what wonder should you be free of the popular rage. But you are wise and faithful at heart. Head! head! that head is the sinner. What doth it lack? Quiet. And this you are soon to have. And God is bringing it about in his own good way. Blessed quiet will it be, after the perplexities and trials of a life spent as yours has heretofore been. A long, and an austere discipline, but worthy its cost.

Yours in hope,
and faith.

A.B.A.

Mrs A.B. Alcott
Scituate.

[418] Change of scene is sometimes quite equivalent to change of soul! We then survey our duties from a new point of sight. We look back upon them as a second person, as an observer. We see how we look engaged in them—what figure we cut,—wherein we fail,—wherein we might improve; and thus change our course. What we want is, to free our souls from those pursuits which, not seldom, wind their meshes about us, and ensnare[?] us, until we are unable to extricate ourselves, though conscious that we are entrapped. God intends nature and friends, and other souls, not as agencies to bind us to special spots, or duties, but to quicken within us new and nobler prospects, and sober[?] reputations—ideal views[?]. Too often, does the soul emprison itself in its wonted labours; and it needs all the quickening of Nature, green and fresh, of friends, and providences, to rouse us from our stuper, and free us of our fetters.

[419] Dedication of School.
Mrs A's absence prevented by attending the dedication at Providence on Saturday [10 June] of this week, as I had purposed. Quite as well doubtless for the principles; though I should have enjoyed the sight of those who bear witness to them, and the view of the rooms. At some future day, however, I shall, perchance, be thus honoured and pleased.

Mr. E[merson] passed through town on his way; but I did not see him, as I intended. I wrote him during the week, but received answer concerning his intentions, at too late an hour to see him.[86] The meeting took[?] place at 4. P.M. on Saturday, in one of the churches. Arrangement for a general attendance on the services were made, and, when I shall hear of results, doubtless, they will be most favorable in truth, and appearance.

[420] The day is not far distant, I trust, when occasions like the present will be frequent; when men of the finest genius will come forward to speak a quickening word for human culture. From this hour doth there exist on earth, a symbol of a true, living Church, wherin the young are cared for, provided for, and their rightful place assigned them, in the order of human regards. From this day, doth Spiritual Culture, assume a rank among the interests of practical life; a Church stands in sight; and words worthy of the dread nature it aims to uphold[87] are spoken before the nations.—Do I dream! Am I too hasty in imagination! vainglorious in spirit! Hope[,] when inspired by purity and devotion, shall be swallowed up in faith. I will hope, and my prophecy shall become history. Principles wrought into the life, which give life to the soul, shall commend themselves to the soul, and make friends of [421] its deepest instincts, which, conscious of their value, and feeling their suitableness to supply its needs, shall become known, respected, loved, wrought into institutions, and mould the manners of the young soul.—Thus shall my mission be made manifest, and my present deed, though vilified, approve itself to the sense of mankind. It may yet appear that, although my school

in this city was deemed unworthy of confidence and support, yet did it contain the seed of new and productive life, that, nor wrong, nor persecution, nor obloquy, could hinder from springing into greenness and fruitage.

No[.] 7. is *not*; but Green[e] Street School in Providence, *is*![88] Where the loss! None, if so be the principles unfolded in the former are taught and enforced in the latter, as I would fain hope.

[422] Burden of Week.

1. Revising 'Psyche"
2. Mrs. A's visit and illness.
4. Dedication of Mr. Fuller's School.

This has been a most busy and full week.[89] I have been most intent on "Psyche." My mind is more and more charmed with the labour. I feel it fit and worthy. I have made some progress in copying and arranging topics. I shall swell the work beyond my original plan—seeking to attain more by its composition than was taken into view, while writing the original MSS.—I have the *Idea* now I think. It is clear, and perfect in its great outlines, and I see the specific, and separate, members of it.

[423] 24
June
Week XXIV. [11–17 June]

I rode to Scituate and brought Mrs. A. home; taking my youngest child [Elizabeth] with me—the same whose gentle spirit inspired my "Psyche." She was deeply pleased, all the way, at beholding the serene visage of nature, with her varied phases of verdure and animated creatures. Her carol of joy and gladness rang all the time. So vital and simple is the bond that unites Nature and the soul!

[424] Emerson.
Mr. Emerson called on me, on his return from Providence. He tells me that the exercises of the day were conducted in good order and taste; that the enterprize of Mr F[uller] bids fair, that his teachers are persons of good acquirements and manners; the people interested in Mr F; and the house one of the best in the US. He promised me the perusal of his descourse, and that he shall not refuse to publish it, although it is not what he wishes it, having been prepared in haste; and not yet complete in all its parts.—This descourse, if at all worthy the author, or of the occasion, will do good to the great interest of human culture. I trust it will be given to the public.[90] And, in connexion with some account of the school.

[425]   *Notice of Con. in Babtist Quarterly.*

    I observed a notice of the Conversations on the Gospels in the Christian Review, a periodical conducted by D[r]. Knowles of the Babtist Church. and Pres. of the Newton Theo. Institution. He speaks with moderation concerning the Book: and closes with a "regret that so much fine paper, and good printing, beautiful type, have beeen wasted[.]" Among other things, he says, that "the interpretation of the Scriptures is surely not the province of the author of the book."[91]

    All the world has been commenting on these same Scriptures, and, especially, on those of the Christian Dispensation, ever since their first dictation; with what success let sectaries, and the popular creeds, and lives of professing Christians, answer. An individual, with the senses of a few simple minded children to aid him, joins with the whole race, and let his testamony with theirs, be of its own value. It does good to hear a new & fresh word spoken, now and then, in the stupid and settled state of thought among us.

[426]   *Visit of my mother.*

    My mother, now more than 60 years of age, came from Wolcott, this week, to spend a few months with me. During the last year, her health has been quite low; she is now restored, and, with fresh mind, and renovated body, comes to spend her time with me. It makes me young to see her. She seems thoughtful; her mind intent on subjects of deep interest, and, (what leaves a pleasant impression on my mind), she is quite free from all bigotry or fanaticism, on religious subjects. She is perfectly free in her sentiments; ready to hear from all quarters, seeks more light, and believes most ardently and firmly, in the reality of virtue. Her amiable disposition, and fresh affections, withal, make her an agreeable companion. And she is *mother*. This name be honoured. Whoso dishonoreth it; whoso belies the filial sentiment, is lost to hope. Distrust him. The essential prop, yea, the very root of vital piety[?], is wanting.[92]

[427]   *Burden of the week.*

    I note these items on the foregoing sheets for this week:—

        1. Return of Mrs A. from Scituate.
        2. Emerson's return from Providence.
        4. Notice of Conversations in "Ch. Review"; &
                                         I add, as chief,
        5. Writing 'Psyche".

    Busy, indeed,—the bee not more so—was I during this whole week upon "Psyche." I copied much from the original MS.[,] wrote several new chapters, and attained to a fuller notion of the order and disposition of its parts. As I dwell on it, the whole becomes more interesting to me. I feel it to be a worthy representation of some of my thoughts, and [428] an acceptable offering to not a few persons, and those most worthy and sensible, among us. At present, the *Idea of the work* stands thus:

Proem.

Introduction.
(Theory of Revelation)

Book i.	Book iii.
I. INNOCENCE.	III. GENIUS.
Spring.	Autumn.
Initiation.	Culture.
Book ii.	Book iv.
II. TEMPERANCE.	IV. HOLINESS.
Summer.	Winter.
Nurture.	Discipline.

[429] Under these subdivisions, I purpose to treat of the prime facts and principles of the soul; and illustrate the same, by a narrative of the experience of my little ones, as preserved in my Psychological Journals,[93] and also to give the spirit of the seasons, by weaving their imagery into the whole frame work of the Book. Thus, do I fancy, that I shall produce a *Psyche*. As an introduction to the whole, I shall give a Theory of Revelation, and let the Body of the work follow as a specimen of the same, as regards the spirit of Childhood—To complete fully my work will require some time. I know not how my idea may enlarge, or be modified in its forms, as I belabour it. The employment is delightful, and I shall pursue it, so long as it holds its charm over me.

[430] My mind has been so much taken up with Psyche, that I have written little, elsewhere, especially on these pages. Thought now throws itself into forms adapted to my work. What once went into the Journal, is now, either omitted, especially as I engage scarce in the Actual—(my school being now a matter of secondary interest with me—) or is preserved for "Psyche". During the week, I have written several new chapters. On the subject of *nurture*, I had little in the original MS: and the department of the work, now arranged a[s] *Genius*, was nearly wanting. On both of these, I fancy that I have something of vital interest to say.

[431]
                    25-26
                    July.
            Weeks XXV[–]XXVI.   [18 June–1 July]

                    Psyche.
   More busy, if possible, during this period, than heretofore, on Psyche. The book enlarges by addition of much copied matter, both from the original MS. and from Journals of Children. I transcribed nearly all of the original Psyche. Besides, I wove into the work, at fit places, as explanatory of principles, brief, yet bold [432][94] sketches of events in my own life, as relief to the delicate fineness of that of Agatha, or the babe.[95] By this means, I hope to ensure greater freedom both in style of diction, and in the utterance of thoughts of sturdier feature. And thus shall I produce a worthier Psyche than was at first projected—a work serving as a string upon which to suspend some opinions of mine that I would send abroad. The free style of composition will I fancy aid the reception of the truths which it embodies. As I proceed with the thread of my story, I find fit occasion to speak of principles, and purposes, not only in their general bearing, but also in relation to much that has been widely misapprehended in my practice, as a teacher, and educator.

[433]   *Items.*
   While engaged thus busily on Psyche, other things will scarce find entrance. I shall live quite to the *soul.*

   I continue to spend five hours daily at my school. My numbers remain about the same, and will I fancy.

   During these weeks, I recd. letters from Miss S. Peabody[96] of Salem; and, also, from Miss M. Fuller of Providence. To both of these correspondents, I must soon write in reply.—Miss F. expresses herself pleased with the prospects of things in Providence: thinks well of Mr. Fuller, and writes in faith, as regards my principles of education. Mr. Emerson, whom I also saw this week, tells me she writes a similar word to him.[97]

[434]   *Misses Grimké.*[98]
   I heard Miss A. Grimke speak on Abolition of Slavery in [word(s)]. A graceful and eloquent speaker—and a well considered descourse.—This woman (Angelina!) realised my conception of a woman. Intellectual powers of a high order; graceful speech; elegant manner; beautiful person: tasteful dress; and deep, divine, piety. She is surely a noble creature.—Her sister, somewhat older, and of plainer features, was distinguished chiefly by her fervent piety, & Christian spirit. Such forms of human character shed enduring glory around our nature! They give assurance of the power that woman is destined to wield, when she shall be free[?] and cherished as she deserves.—Angelina! fit name for the sex, as God designed it!

[435] Burden of these weeks;

Psyche—Psyche—Psyche.
I find more uninterrupted pleasure in composing and arranging this same Psyche, than I have heretofore been wont. Giving myself more freedom, and inclining to a bolder style of thought and expression, my genius gets scope and play. I feel a truer satisfaction as regards the execution—a thing, I have seldom pleased myself in, heretofore.—I need quiet, uninterrupted hours, in order to dispose of my inner stores, to my taste. Composition, as an art, is a great and divine study; only the pure and true can compass it; and give thought a tongue! I wish to seize the [436] law of my mind when it succeeds in practice. My case is not, I fancy a hopeless one. I sometimes utter, as I would, the thought that I have. And, I think I perceive an improvement, from week to week.—It has taken me long to compass this end.

---

[437] 27-38 [27–39: 2 July–30 September][99]

Interruption.
At this period, I was arrested by desease, which confined me to my room for several weeks.

On recovering my strength, I visited my brother in law Rev. S. J. May at Scituate. With him I passed a fortnight. Returning, and passing a few days with my family, I then visited Rev. Mr. Emerson at Concord where I spent a week, and saw Rev. Mr Hedge while [438] in the family of Mr E. Again returning, and remaining with my family, in Cottage Place, a few days, I passed a week in Worcester, attending the anniversary of the Am. Ins. of Instruction. I also visited Hingham, with my mother, to see some relatives residing in that place. With my friend, Mr Wm Russell, from Phila., I had pleasing times.—In these excursions and intimacies, my inner being found somewhat of interesting topic, and quickening insight. Yet feebleness of body shut out *some* light. Agreeable excitement, but scanty nurture, was the benefit to me. I talked and heard talking; but was not strengthened thereby as is my wont.[100]

The *"Symposeum"* also met during this period, at Mr Emersons; and at Mr Clark[e]s'[,] Newton. I did not say or hear what seemed highest or worthiest. More persons were present than usual.

[439] Present were—Emerson: Hedge: Ripley: Frances: Stetson: Clarke: Dwight: Robbins: Putnam: Parker, &c.

Subject, at both interviews: "Does the Species advance beyond the individual."[101]

—The race, I hold pre-exists in individuals. Genius is, at its epoch, everybody: it is the species. Time does but popularize it. Biography is the seed of History. All its materials spring from the Soul, and the deeds of genius, comprise the staple of all biography, all history. Napoleon was the French Revolution. Washington the American. Both are now species, now individual. The question is one. One man is now every man. And in time every man becomes one.

[440] Reopening of School.
On Monday Sep. 3. I reopened school at No 3 Temple.[102] Six pupils attended. With these I begin the fourth year of my enterprize, and await its future fortunes. It is too early to form opinions regarding its success. I flatter myself, meanwhile, that, by and by, a change will set in my favour: that I shall not be hindered, by the misapprehensions that now beset me. I shall teach, in some form. Some of my friends, advise preaching. Yet I fear to put on the chains of a profession; my mind inclines to a more simple form of action. The pulpit becomes me not. It is too formal. I await my hour, and with it, fit deeds, in the light of clear ideas—Let me now do the small work that offers without; and ply my mind worthily on truths within.

[442] 39[103]
October.
Week XXXIX. [40: 1–7 October]

Fortunes.

Quiddle, quiddle, on half dozen souls, at No 3. Temple—to this am I doomed.[104] And how soon the wise, in plenitude of wisdom, shall shine favour on outcast, time shall show, as ever. Perchance, these shall grow suddenly generous, forgiving as venal, the [443] errors of its ill fated child. Yet, meanwhile, here he is, in tub, with corn, rain, sun-shine, lamp shine; and fire shine. But how long these shall be vouchsafed, oracle saith not. But instead omens of ill do appear. *Tub* saith, "thou yieldest no rent, and standest in danger of ejectment with all thy tublings." *Cistern-cock* saith, "thou shall not quench thirst, unworthy, for thou dost not pay for thy tank:" *Corn* cleaves to hand of clutching seller, and crieth, " not for thee, nor thine; thou art a shirk, and showeth no hard hand": *Sun* threatens to withold his face, and saith, "I will honour thee[?] with peep at barred window sometime soon; *Fire*[105] smouldereth, "thou art lazy, and dost not ply thy saw, or return aught to the woodman": while *lamp* sayeth, flickeringly, "Shall I shine for thee, when thou fuelest me not? Destitute! thou hast nought available about thee." And so, only *moonshine* remains, and he taketh [444] this as fit emblem (so sayeth the age) of his wan and leaden shine, and feedeth on (so called) moonbeams.

PLATE SIX
Alcott's entry during Weeks XXVII–XXXVIII (2 July– 30 September) about re-opening his school.
Courtesy MH

Yet needs must, and shall, all Soul-lovers subsist. God in good providence, though oft austere, orders bread and shelter for such. Submit in hope[,] brave and faithful Soul; thou shall not hunger, nor thirst, nor need aught. Feed on thy deeds. Hope in thy purpose. Let principle house thee, and truth light thy dwelling. The wide spacious world may not be thine to possess; nor the things thereof; wouldst thou chaffar thy jewels for it, as these. Thou art more than a world-holder; thou art a world-upholder, then why fear for thy ground plot; is not all safe in thine hands: and soled under thy boot: art thou not rich in rents of honour, and true glory! Thy farm is sown: [445] and dost thou not sing ha[r]vest home when thou wilt. Hast thou not cunning in thy soul; yea, even in thy fingers; brave then thy fortune, whatsoever it be; and bear thyself nobly.

And thus, would this soul of mine, beset with such hindrance, and doomed to such quiddlings in the actual, retire within itself, and drink light and life from Gods, not *world-spoiled*, nor *world holding*. An *"Idea"* hath fed and cheered me amidst hours of destitution. I have decked it in mine own fashion, with manners of my choice circle; and now doth it make face to my age. Go forth my bantling; sing thy best song in the ear of thy time; perchance thou shalt win some[106] to those truths that uphold and cherish Soul: and if thou bringest aught of corn or wine, in thy left hand, God be praised. Take passport *"Psyche"* and run on thine errand.[107]

[446]   40
October.
Week XL. [41: 8–14 October]

Psyche.

My mind is quite busy in putting these papers in order for the eye of others, when fortune shall favour their publication. I have now arranged them in accordance with the law of human growth; and the successive topics treat of most of the great needs of life. Thus ordered they make a work of 444 [447] pages, MS, and in any fit form, will make a comely volume. As I read these pages from time to time, they seem to have wherewithal to quicken the mind of this age. Not a formal treatise on grave and profound topics, but a simple, unpremeditated work, speaking in easy, earnest,—sometimes quaint tones, is this, and, as such, fitted to the tastes of the time. I fancy that a mother;—an ardent girl;—an enthusiastic young man;—a loving wife;—a devoted husband,—a father;—moralist;—theosophist;—especially teacher;—as all, indeed, who yet reverence their nature, and the ends of life, would take up such a volume, and read with profit and delight. I have therein given some of my most considered opinions, and in a style that shall ensure them, I trust, from contempt.— Not that I have said much that now seems worthiest, [448] best, yet, not wholly unsuited to my age. And I feel willing to let it show its face in the world, hoping to send better after it at no distant day.

"The Cross! the Cross!" this is the theme that I would set forth, in all its beauty, and fitness, to the sense of my kind. I would disclose its deep and divine significance. I would show the depths of the human soul for living enjoyment; its discipline thereto of divine sacrifice, and, needs must be, of sorrow and want. I would point out the relations of Duty as the ministries for selfinsight and self-culture.—Such a work I have had on my mind for some time; and have, (I believe) adverted to it in some prior page of my Journals.[108] [449] And such a work, I think, is needed. Duty should be brought back, from its vagrant, or sordid[109] forms, to the simple, needful, relations of life. Family—home,—trade,—profession,—pursuit,—should be set forth, amidst all their appropriate and graceful disciplines. And then the soul won[?] from the service of sense, or usage.—To such a work will not the desultory *'Psyche'* be fit introduction?

Yet, I know not that publisher or public shall be found for my works. But I can prepare them.—I can let them ripen under my eye, and, perchance, they shall, one day, find access to their age, and yield living fruit for famishing souls. To me, at any rate, they furnish delightsome labour, amidst hours of seeming uselessness, and misapprehension. Think, O soul; write, O hand! [450] Ply all thy faculties worthily. Hast thou not a deed to do before the nations. Hast thou not an Idea to reveal to thy kind; and, if needs must be, prove its identity with thine own being, by living, enduring, suffering, yea, dying for it? Thou knowest that thou hast. Thy familiar genius; thy divinest instinct, deceiveth thee not. Hast thou not from a youth sought wisdom, and adored virtue, as the guerdons of thy ambition, the most precious, most beautiful, of goods. And hath not all thy life long been a chase after these graces. Even in thy wanderings, was it not the promise of these that tempted thee in thy simplicity. Did not the divine dream of excellence fill all thy youth;—and shed its glories around thy head. Amidst thy perils was not this,[110] the abiding presance to thee. [451] Holiness and wisdom, are these strangers to thee, now when thou hast wooed, and won some graces from their exalted nature. Bea[u]ty! Charm! All hail! ye inmates of my soul. I love ye with all my hearts' devotion. I seek ye amidst all thoughts. On ye, I meditate by day and by night. Ye are my life. Your presance is the ornament of my sight. O let me be your meek and worthy minister here in this dark and unseemly age. Let me be worthy of sending your celestial radiance, unfolding your peerless beauty to my kind. As in my youth, so now in the waxing genius of my soul, let me be your lovers; and rain blessedness on my time. Let me be God's revelation of these attributes, which are your nature, to all beholders. Let me love Soul wherein these would ever shine. Let me [452] be ornament of truth and holiness in most familiar duties, and disciplines. Shall I not put on the Divine Image! Even so would the Divinity.

Haste thee! come away, O Soul! from communion with beasts. Fly! Burrow not. Dig not in mines. Be not covetous of fine ore. Array thyself in virtue.

Enrich thyself with wisdom. Ornament thyself in holiness. What hast thou to do with beasts; with the passions, desires of beasts? Doth not the Godlike stir within thee. Stir thou with it. Be it. Is not thy Father a God. And would he have his beloved child less: Be like thy Father, *Incarnate the Perfect* as he doth unceasingly, and thus becometh the Perfect. Be ye perfect, said thy Divinest brother, even as thy Father.[111] And so saith thy Instinct. [453] Live this forth as he did, and thus apprehend the counsels of thy Father; and thy filial relation to him. Lie on his bosom. Sit at his right hand. Know wherin is thy life, & will. Soul! thou hast an end; and a work; be up and doing! Let none despoil thee of thy faith. All things are possible to thee: Dost thou not believe.—Believe! God rides in the plenitude of his might, and the glory of his graces, in this same chariot of *Belief*. Wilt thou ride also with him. Be a believer, and thou careenest over the low walls of sense: thou breakest the fetters of usage; thou soarest, like the eagle; thou guidest the chariot of the[112] Sun! And the nations delight in thy shining! Faith! Belief! God!—

[454]
41
October.
Week XLI. [42: 15–21 October]

Household.

We live simply at our cottage in Cottage Place. Our means are small. And, but for some friends, who kindly send us family stores, now and then, we should not find support. Our family are now [455] of our own number only. We restrict ourselves mainly to a vegetable diet. Mrs A. performs all of her household duties, having dispensed with the little girl who had passed the summer with us. This she finds herself able to do; although a labour to which she had not been accustomed. She prepares our food, and all needful cleansing of wardrobe and apartments. The children seem to enjoy this domestic ministry; and all our household to prosper more than at former periods. They accompany me to school, wherein they spend the same five hours with me: the afternoon they pass at home in their amusements, or in aiding their mother. They make themselves quite useful, especially in the case of the little one [Elizabeth.] Anna is now reading in *"Frank"* with exercises in spelling and writing. Louisa is reading [456] in *"Gallaudets' Primer"*.[113] Elizabeth, the youngest, amuses herself in looking at *Pictures*, of which she has a fine variety. All three, seem unfolding in beauty, genius, and grace.

I write more or less daily. My writing, since my recovery, has been chiefly correction, of Psyche, or in such additions, as were suggested in revision of the work. Morning, afternoon, and evening, of each day, find me usually occupied on this MS: and, with exception of household cares, and my school, this work takes all my choicest hours, and best thoughts. Yet I do not originate much: I am chiefly performing the work of criticising my past thoughts, and arranging these in order. But this labour I shall soon complete. And then I am away to worthier labours. [457] I need more scope of thought. My sphere of action being narrowed, and supplying small excitement, I need the more to enter the inner world of life and labour. Self-trust—all other, seem withdrawn, or not proffered. Bye and bye, I must enter upon some investigations that shall tax all my faculties, and yield me constant and interesting labour. Work! Work! this alone shall suffice. I shall, I trust, be able to find wherewithal to eat, drink, and for raiment the old wardrobe shall suffice; in some sort I will appease the clamour of dues; and live for *soul.* The winter is coming. This is a season of mental labour with me. Shall I not write some chapters of the *"Cross"* during its bright hours, while lamp and fire shed propitious influence around, especially during long evenings? I shall see.

[458] MSS.

I wish times, public, and publishers, were more promising. I have sundry MSS. now by me that I should like to see in book, and circulated to the benefit (as I think) of public, and my own hungry belly. Yet compilers, authors, have no such organ; and should family depend on them, none the more. Like fire, like household: air, moonbeams, feed old and young of this genus. Others eat, drink, dress, make merry[,] ride, &c. Poor devel! An author (alias, book maker, —authors,—these are extinct) doth none of these. He lacks wherewithal; and so must not plead these, nor the needs thereof, in the presance of sovreign public, publishers! There is no market for mind now-a-days. Bring your matter by waggon loads, it [459] shall find ready and liberal purchaser; while poor pedestrian MS. pedlar, shall stroll to and from the great city, and find no favour with public's stockjobbers. Public wants no wares of this order: and so, poor devel! starves, or begs, or some kind sympath[i]zing friend sends pennies to save him from graveyard.

What have I. Let me enumerate some of my wares; with date of making.[114]

1st. *"Pictures of Thought,"* comprising Fables[,] Emblems, Parables, & Allegories, intended principally to aid the young in Self Insight and Self Culture. pp 308. 1834.

2. *"Pilgrims Progress"* adapted to the minds of children, being the allegory [460] divested of collateral doctrines, in the words of the original. pp 179. 1834.

3. *"Aids to Mothers"* in teaching the elements of Reading, Manners and Duty. Founded on the Text of Miss Ed[g]eworths' Frank. 1834. (First Idea)

4. *"Aids to Mothers"*—founded on an original Tale comprising the life of a child. Matured Idea (imperfect)

5. *"Gospels of the Life of Christ,"* illustrating the career of Spirit. p. 226. 1835.

6. "*Psyche*" in Four Books. 1836. p 503. (First Idea)

[461]   7. '*Psyche*," in Four Books. p 444. 1837. This, corrected and amended, with large additions.

These constitute my principal MS. beside my "*Journals*," which usually run on to 4 or 500 pp. yearly. Into the "*Psyche*" I have however incorporated portions of these Journals, chiefly from the pages of the last and ensuing years.—There are several volumes of "*Journals of the first and second years of the life of my children.*"115 But these I value chiefly as practice in observation & writing, as preparatory to the fuller "*Psyche*" now nearly written. Their positive value is small. My own Journals (ie of my life,) are but dots and indices, intelligible alone to myself. (I have written nought yet.)

[462]   *W.L. Garrison.*116

This gentleman spent an evening at my house during this week. I find, on more intimate acquaintance, a soul, free, devout, intent on the melioration of human woes, and eradication of human evils. He is not, by any means, narrowed in his views, by any popular interest. He sees *slavery* in its true bearings. More than any other man among us, he has exposed its evils, and brought the subject before the mind of the nation. But he sees other great national evils. And would do somewhat for their removal. His soul needs wider scope than this, now popular topic yields. He is too great and free a spirit for his party. They cannot apprehend the sweep of his purpose, and would cast him off.—His [463] political and theological views have already exposed him to the obloquy of politicians and priests. And a new topic of discussion seems now opening before him. I hope he will enter upon it. His clear perception of evils, and unsparing condemnation of these in the light of divine principles, eminently fit him for the work of reform. I found great sympathy with him, on most topics of conversation.

The day is not for distant when minds of creative genius,—true lovers of humanity—shall associate for its regeneration. To this every sign of the times now points. Men, intent on separate evils117 shall, at last, be led to the parent principle which is to kill every abuse and usage; and establish truth in the common mind.

[464]   42
                    October.
              Week XLII.   [43: 22–28 October]

              Foreign Correspondence.

I received, during this week, the following letter, from an English gentleman residing in London, (a stranger to me) making inquiries concerning my school; [465] and the principles by which it is conducted.118 From the account

PLATE SEVEN
Alcott's entry during Week XLI (15–21 October) on W. L. Garrison.
Courtesy MH

which he gives of himself, as well as from internal evidence afforded by his communication, he is obviously well acquainted with education; and intent on its improvements. I shall write soon, in answer to his inquiries. And it is encouraging to learn that my effort here, already begins to attract the notice of educators abroad, and that they honor me with so much of confidence, as to send across the water for information regarding it. Quite lately Mons. Vic. Cousin made similar inquiries, in a letter to a friend residing in this country. I fancy that views like mine, would find ready support both in France and England, and especially in Germany. At convenient opportunity I shall forward my books. Already a friend Rev. Mr. Brooks of Hingham, has sent to [466] Mons[.] Cousin, copies of my works, "the Record of a School," and the "Conversations on the Gospels.["] And Dr. Julius while in this country on a tour of examination regarding the spirit and forms of our institutions, desired me to inform him, from time to time, of the progress of my enterprize, and state of my own theories. This I have never done.[119]

Thus communication is opened, with distinguished patrons of education, in the three countries—England, France, & Germany. Meanwhile, I must write to Mr. Greaves in England, and Dr. Julius, sending them also copies of my books. Bye and bye, testimony in my favour, will come from the other side of the water, to give confidence to my own faithless country men.

[467] I fancy that editions of my books in the languages of these countries, would find readers, and a more ready apprehension than amongst us. Especially in Germany, where mind is less a marvel, and human culture[120] is a subject of deep study, would these works find favour. In due time, such results will come about. I need but wait. Whatever of truth, applied in simple and practicable forms, my works shall contain; or theory truly stated,[121] shall gain faith in the end. Nothing shall be suffered to fall to the ground.

I insert a copy of the letter, on the following page:

[468] Copy of Letter from Mr. Greaves.

49 Burton Street, Burton Crescent,
London, 16. Sep. 1837.

Dear Sir,

Believing the Spirit has so far established its nature in you, as to make you willingly coöperate with itself, in its Love operations, I am induced, without apology, to address you, as a friend and companion in the hidden path of Love's most powerful revelations. "The Record of a School", having fallen into my hands, through Miss H. Martineau,[122] I have perused it with deep interest, and [469] the object of my present address to you, (occasioned by this work), is to obtain a more intimate acquaintance with one, in our Sister land, who is so divinely and universally developed. Permit me therefore, dear sir, in simple affection, to put a few questions to you, which, if answered, will give me possession of that information respecting you, and your work, that, I think, will be useful to the present and future generation of men. Also, a mutual service may be rendered to ourselves, by assisting to evolve our own being more completely; thereby making us more efficient instruments for Love's use, in carrying forward the work which it has begun in us. The Unity himself must have his divine purposes to accomplish in and by us, or he would not have prepared us, as far as he has. I am willing, therefore, to withold nothing, but to receive, [470] and transmit all he is pleased to make me *be*; and thus, at length, to become an harmonious being. This he can readily work, in the accomplishment of his primitive purposes. Should you think that a personal intercourse, of a few weeks, would facilitate the universal work, I would willingly undertake the voyage to America for that purpose.[123] There is so decided and general similarity in the sentiments and natures expressed in the account of your teaching, that a contact of two spirits so alike developed, would, no doubt, prove productive of still further developement. Your School appears to work deeper than any we have in England; and its inner essential character interests me. If an american bookseller will send over any of your books to his correspondents here, I shall be happy to receive and pay for them.

[471] In the year 1817, some strong interiour visitations came over me, which withdrew me from the world, in a considerable degree, and I was enabled to yield myself up to Love's own manner of acting, regardless of all consequences. Soon after this time, I met with an account of the Spirits' work in and by the late venerable Pestalozzi, which so interested me that I proceeded, at once, to visit him, in Switzerland, and remained with him, in holy fellowship, four years. After that, I was working, with considerable success, amongst the various students in that country, when the prejudices of the self-made wise and powerful men, became jealous of my influence, and I was advised to return to England which I did. And have been working, in various ways of usefulness ever since, from the deep centre to the [472] circumference, and am now engaged in writing my conscientious experiences, as well as I can represent these in words; and also, in teaching all such as come within my sphere of action. Receptive beings, however, have, as yet, been but limited, and those who permanently retain, have been still less; yet, at present, there appears a greater degree of awakening to the central Love Sensibility than before. I see many more symptoms of the harvest time approaching in this country. There is, at present, an evident appearance of the Love seed, beginning to germinate.

Such of the following questions, as you may think calculated to throw any light upon what you are doing, I shall be obliged to you to answer; with any other [473] information you may feel disposed to supply, for the universal good.

Questions.

No 1. Do your instructions entirely follow the Universal Ideas;—and are they connected with any peculiar sect of religion?

2. Are you, yourself, satisfied with the results that appear?

3. Have you had many difficulties to encounter?

4. How early do you begin to act upon children?

[474] 5. Is a day-school, or a boarding school, best to carry out your views?

6. Have you found any one able to assist you?

7. Can mutual instruction avail any thing?

8. Does the moral influence decidedly dominate over the intellectual in the children?

9. Are parents willing to let you have the children?

10. What religious sect works most favourably with you?

11. What sect works most against you?

[475] 12. Do the children that have come from other schools show any preferance for yours?

13. To what age would you keep the children?

14. Do you consider that your mode of instruction could be nationalized easily?

15. Is your mode of teaching, compared with other modes, or is it estimated with relation to the end sought?

16. Do the children soon begin to perceive the power of the end that you have led them to?

17. Are inner tranquility, and inner thoughtfulness, results of the primary purpose?

[476] 18. Do you find that the exercise of the inferiour faculties neutralizes what you have done?

19. Can you make all branches of instruction relate to the primary purpose.

20. Do the girls make a greater progress under you than the boys; and are they more grateful for the results.

21. How do you rank music, singing, and dancing, as means?

22. Has sound a more universal influence than sight?

23. Are the poor children more easily acted upon than the rich?

[477] 24. Do the children feel at a loss when they are removed to other schools?

25. Can you act with more effect upon strange children, than upon your own?

26. Is the spirit of inquiry considerably deepened; and does it take an eternal, instead of a temporal direction?

27. How many scholars would you undertake to instruct in the manner you are acting?

28. Do you consider the mode in which you have fitted up your school-room as very beneficial?

29. Is it used for ordinary purposes, or only for instruction.

[478]   Observations.

I. The child has two orders of faculties, which are essential, and semi-essential: or, in other words, roots and branches.

II. Radical faculties belong to the interiour world; and the branchial to the exteriour.

III. To produce a central effect on the child, the radical faculties must be first developed: to represent this effect, the branchial faculties must be developed.

IV The radical faculties belong entirely to Love: the branchial to Knowledge & Industry.

V It is imperative upon us to follow [479] the determination of the radical faculties, and to modify the branchial always in obedience to the radical.

VI. It is the Child, (or the Love spirit in the Child,) that we must obey, and not suffer the parents or any one to divert us from it.

VII. Good is not to be determined by man's wishes, but God must originate and determine the wish.

VIII. The Preceptor must watch attentively for every[?] new exhibition of the Child's radical faculties, and obey these, as Divine Laws.

IX. We must every moment consider it as the Infinite perfecting the finite. All [480] that is unnecessary in the external must be kept from the child.

X. The Preceptors duty is, as far as possible, to remove every hindrance from the childs' way.

XI The closer we keep the child to the Spirit, the less it will want of us, or of any one else.

XII The child has an inward, Sacred, and unchangeable Nature; (which Nature is the Temple of Love.) This nature only, demands what it will give, if properly attended to: viz: Unfettered Liberty.

XIII. The Love germs can alone germinate by Love. Light and Life are but conditions of Love. Divine Capacities are made by Love alone.

[481] XIV. Love [e]ducation is, primar[i]ly, a passive one; and, secondarily, an active one. To educate the radical faculties, is, altogether, a new idea with teachers, at present.

XV. The parental end must be made much more prominent than it has been.

XVI. The conceptive powers want much more purification than the perceptive; and it is only as we purify the conceptive that we shall get the perceptive clear.

XVII. It is the essential conceptive powers that tinge all the consequences of the exteriour conceptive powers.

XVIII. We have double conceptions, and double perceptions; we are throughout [482] double beings, and claim the universal morality, as well as the personal.

XIX We must now educate the univeral moral faculties, as before we have only educated the personal moral faculties.

XX. It is in the Universal Moral Faculties that the Laws reside: and until these Laws are developed, we remain lawless beings.

XXI The personal moral faculties cannot stand without the aid of the univeral moral faculties; any more than the branches can grow without the roots.

XXII. Education, to be decidedly religious, should reach man's universal faculties—those faculties which contain the Laws that connect him with his Maker.

[484] These reflections (made on the other side) seem as worthwhile to make an observation upon. I shall be happy to hear it. Suggestions are always valuable, as they offer to the mind the liberty of free activity. The work we are engaged in, is too extensive and important, to lose any opportunity of gaining information.—If it should be inconvenient for you to reply to this letter, perhaps you will have the kindness to transfer it to the lady who wrote the book.[124] The earlier I receive your reply the better.—With good will towards you, and your important labours;

> I am, dear Sir,
> Yours, sincerely.
>
> J.P. Greaves.[125]

[485] Review of Conversations on the Gospels.

A brief, yet fair, review of the 'Conversations on the Gospels" came out, in the Nov. No. of the "Christian Examiner."[126] The writer virtually yields some of the points about which so much complaint has been made, and sets mainly to the statement of the value of the book, as an illustration of a true method of Religious Culture. This method he approves. He states the principles upon which this method is based. Yet he thinks the author imperfectly furnished to carry it into full and successful practice.—He thus closes his critique:—

[486] "To his genius, as displayed in the conception of this method of education, we would pay due tribute. It is what no apparatus of education could give. But, in order to do justice to the method, it is necessary to acknowledge that he is not accomplished in all points suffic[i]ently to carry it out.["]

Again:—

"The courage and manliness, and the confidence in his Idea, which led him to publish this first Practice, with all its crudities, of which, it is plain from his Preface, he was in some degree aware, is a ground of our assurance that he is more anxious that justice should be done to the *Method*, than [487] for his own personal reputation."

And again:—

—"the peculiarity of his own mind. He is not able to keep practically to his idea of letting the instincts of his childrens' minds lead him. He invariably chooses, for his subject of further questioning, those answers which touch upon the most speculative and least practical views. He even goes further. He prefers abstraction to the natural form of ideas. He does not go into outward nature when the children would lead him thither. xxxxx This imperfection of Mr Alcott's practice arises from the onesidedness of his own culture, perhaps, more than from his idiosyncrasy."

[488] Thus the reviewer. He takes but part of the purpose of the "Conversations" into view. He obviously makes small allowance for the difference between a recorded statement, and a verity! Nor the difficulties and hindrances under which this experiment was conducted.—Time, alone, shall show how far the author shall prove adequate to unfold his own Idea in successful practice. No final judgement can be made, in this particular, from examination of these imperfect conversations. The actual conversations could not be set forth in any *written* word. A teacher, and author, are different: Teaching and book, are not, always, complement of each other.

[489]   School.
My numbers are now ½ a dozen. And this is my complement, I suppose, for the present quarter. A few more may be added when families return to the metropolis from their country residence.

All changes must now, I fancy, affect the school favorably. It has fallen to its minimum of patronage, and is on its improvement. It has withstood whatever of hindrance the last year has yielded, and yet lives. I hold upon the age by such slender tie, till occasion offer for binding my Idea, around its practical needs, and for quickening its instin[c]ts to a sense of my purpose in its behoof.

[490] The age ever comes slowly into the presence or accepts the faith of individuals. It stands rather[?] in the presance, and dreads the visage of the many. Its Kings and priests, its prophets and teachers, are all of a past time. Wisdom built her temples for it and prescribed her laws, long since. Hence it hath no reverance for those who have made of wisdom a modern, and com-

mune with her in meditative insight, day by day. These it doth not know. And cannot till it hath lived the life of such. What a life of thought hath yielded, lives of thought must alike yield. The age becomes wise by copying examples of wisdom. And long does it toil ere it finds this in its midst. Ever is it groping amidst the sepulchers of the past, for the life that shines upon it, did it but see, from its true and living souls.

[491] Deepest wisdom is nearest. Not in the midst of the ages alone, but in the midst of every soul. Wouldst be wise, O man. Look then into thy soul, and thou shalt find wisdom. Yea more than did Plato or Jesus. For thus they waxed wise. So thou. Bring the ages into thy day. Behold eternity in it. Summon thy soul into thy presence: is not a greater than Plato or Jesus before thee! Thou mayest know this: those thou canst but fancy. Let thy instincts face thee. And when these shall put on their true features, becoming Ideas, and shall have been in and out before thee, as familiars, soon shall they knock at the doors of the ages, and gather all those who woo wisdom, as thou dost. What a noble company! Yet of how small esteem in the eyes of all others! Look, thou art amidst [492] the contemned, the persecuted, the slain. Thou beggest thy bread, and none careth for the riches of thy soul. All shun thee, at sight of thy rags!

Verily, wisdom doth ever find herself a beggar. She hath no where to lay her head. None seek her face. The ages are unworthy of her. They revile her. They cast stones at her. And when she speaketh most lovingly, pleads most earnestly, they turn aside, or pelt her with obloquy. And should she, as she ever doth, declare her saving truths, in the ears of her pers[e]cutors, or, do her divinest deeds in their midst, then do they slay her, in their anger and rage!

Behold the divine sign! She rises from her ashes, and sounds in the [493] hearts of her persecutors, the astounding words,—"I, wisdom, am eternal; and though ye lay violent hands on my outward form, and slay me, yet do I live; and will slay all that mock my counsels, or mar my forms!"

Whoso withstands wisdom braves God! The age that knows not its sages, nor listens to its prophets, shall soon come to dishonour.—I call on ye, O mine age, to do honour to thy saviours. Hast thou but one? Away with this canting impiety to the soul. One! Thou art a hypocrite, or a silly one. The soul is the saviour of souls. And always are souls in thy midst that would save thy sinking fortunes; pilot thee across the waves of change! Be saved! Save thyself rather. [494] But this thou canst not do, if thou givest not heed to thy wise men; or holdest them in contempt; or dost slay them.—On these depends thy life. They *are* thy life. Their wisdom is thy salvation. In them doth God hold rule in thy midst. Their faculties are God's divinest attributes. Reverance these. Hold by their counsels. And so shall thy days be prolonged!

But, O mine age! thou lackest wisdom. thine eyes are hidden. Thou art mad to stone the prophets. The seers are moon-gazers. Thou art ready to heap obloquy on them. Thou art Godless, Christless, insane, gluttonous, and a changeling. Thy deeds shall be heaped upon thee in the days of thy vengeance. Thou shalt be killed by those whom thou dost despise!—Wisdom slays Folly! Holiness kills Evil!¹²⁷

[495]
43
November.
Week XLIII. [44: 29 October–4 November]
Mr. Greaves.

I am glad to find the following testimony to the character and influence of Mr. Greaves, confirming the impressions which his letter to me had made upon my mind. They are taken from 'Letters of Pestalozzi on the Education of Infancy",—an edition of which was [496] first published in this city in 1830. They were translated from the original German, by a gentleman of this place, and appeared also in a series of articles in the "Am. Journal of Education", about the same time.¹²⁸

The translator says in his advertisement to the work:—

"These letters were addressed by Pestalozzi, to a Mr Greaves, an Englishman, who spent considerable time at his establishment, for the purpose of becoming acquainted with his principles, in order to put them in operation, in his own country."—"Mr Greaves was at the institution, at the period of Prof. Griscom's visit, and it was from him that the latter, chiefly derived the information concerning Pestalozzis' System," of which he speaks in his "*Year in Europe*".¹²⁹

[497] I regard this expression of confidence in my purposes and theories, from an associate and confidant of Pestalozzi, as a fact of more importance than any which has transpired since the opening of my career, as educator. A visit from him, would, indeed, be most agreeable; and, in my reply, I shall assure him of my strong desire to know, more intimately, one so deeply interested in man and favourably known, as a friend of human culture. I shall endeavour to transmit to him a statement of my purposes, views, and practice; which I can most easily do, in reply to his questions: and send him, beside, copies of my works.—The publishers should also transmit to some respectable house in London, some copies of these, on sale.¹³⁰ No copies have, I believe, as yet been taken from the country, unless by some friend, now [498] and then, for his own private use. Both the 'Record of a School", and the "Conversations on the Gospels," would find a few readers, I imagine, in England. Minds there must be, across the water, disposed to favor improved theories on the nature of man, and the means of unfolding his nature. This

would appear, in some degree, from the statements of Mr. Greaves, who deems the public mind on the[131] morn of a new birth of Ideas.—Opportunity of diffusing worthier views, both by books, and personal communication with the friends of the soul, will I fancy, soon be given me, in some form. A visit from Mr. Greaves, would be most gratifying, and become the means, perhaps, of extending worthier notions amongst my countrymen.

[495a] Foreign Correspondence.

On the day after writing the preceding sheet, of this record, I received a letter from a respectable bookseller in London, from which I extract the following, as befitting these pages:

"I have just recd. 3 copies of your 'Conversations on the Gospels," through Messrs Hilliard, Gray and Co. of your city, and am only sorry there were so few. The price, when the duty &c. is added, makes them rather expensive, and I think a sale might be effected of some, if you make them 6/ or not exceeding 6/6.—As Messrs Otis, Broaders, & Co. will be sending me a case, or, perhaps, Messrs Hilliard[,] Gray and Co. I shall be glad to receive a dozen copies, or more.[132] I have no doubt that, if properly advertised, they would [496a] sell well. I have had, and a few still remain, the "Record of a School." xxxx. I am much surprized that authors on your side [of] the Atlantic, do not make some arrangement with their works here. If I were to receive early sheets, I have the means of obtaining a premium for the monopoly of publishing, but this does not give copy right. If you will add a few copies of any other of your own works, I shall be happy to make them known. Should you require any English works, either new or secondhand, you may depend on my collecting and forwarding them to you, with despatch, and on the lowest terms.

I am, Dear Sir,
Yours, respectfully,

Richard J. Kennett.[133]

No 14.   York St.   Covent Garden.
October 5. 1837.

[497a] This is encouraging. The sale of these works has been scanty. Only about 300 copies of the "Conversations" have been desposed of, and the sale, at present, is by no means brisk. Of the "Record of a School", ½ of a[n] edition of 1000[?] copies was sold—the second edition, revised, and with additions, remains without purchaser.[134] It has never been advertised, as it should have been. The publishers, having no interest in these, beside that of seeing their names in the title page, take small pains to make them known, by generous advertisement, or circulation.

There is much need of a house given to the circulation of works, which, from their high literary, or philosophic character, do not meet with extensive favour, or yield immediate returns of profit, yet which should be before the community. A company formed for [498a] such purpose, might do much to encourage native genius, by presenting its claims to the world, in the publication of its works, and thus improve the national literature. For the want of such aid, genius may lack means; and the country lose the advantage arising from the diffusion of its light, in enduring works. At present, authors are too much at the mercy of illiterate and grasping publishers; who, in turn, are but the organs of popular sentiment, and dare not risk what is noble, for fear of losing patronage, or gaining a bad name; or, what is worse, engage in this pursuit, from motives of cupidity, and narrow self-interest. Publishers, instead of being timid slaves to popular sentiment, should aim, by the works they circulate, to correct its vulgarity, and give law to it. Such a house would be an honour to the nation.

[499]   Emerson.

Emerson is now doing something, as a substitute for such general aid. He is editing works of high literary value, and, through most respectable houses, presenting these to the community. "Carlyle's Sartor Resartus" was thus brought before the public. And now he is editing Carlyle's "History of the French Revolution."[135] In this wise, he does good with his moderate means. How much a man of fortune, possessing fine taste, and the philosophic vision, might do for the literature and morals of his country, by such generosity. How better could he devote his talent and means.

Emerson offers to publish by "Psyche", on his own responsibility, after he shall have brought the work of "Carlyle's" before the public.[136] I shall be glad to put it to press [500] under such favorable auspices, free from all pecuniary risk, as in my former work. I cannot publish at my own expense; and publishers, in the present state of the public mind concerning me, in this city, would hesitate as to the reception of my works. But for some friendly aid, of this sort, my works must lie, at present, in MS.

But, I fancy, the day of a more generous appreciation will come; when my name shall stand for somewhat in the booksellers ledger, and he be ready to publish whatever I may chance to offer to the public which he serves. It must be so. The age hath eyes. At any rate, it hath one, and this it shall chance turn, now and then, upon me, and my word. I shall not always be dependant, and helpless. My influence shall spread.

[501]   44
    November.
    Week XLIV. [45: 5–11 November]

Literary Labours.

I add, as appropriate topics are suggested, from day to day, chapters and paragraphs to my work, which, as yet, seems defective. It is not a fair transcript of my thoughts. It lacks fullness. It does not cover the ground over which my vision [502] has spanned. It is sketchy, and somewhat fragmentary, bearing the marks of the workman; and hence not a whole—a perfect work of art. Still, I hope to remove this defect, by supplying deficienc[i]es, filling seams, and giving to the whole, something of completeness and finish. As the sheets will lie by me, and daily pass under my eye, for some months to come, opportunity will then be given me for fit revision, before they go into the hands of the printer. At some future day, I hope to treat the great natures therein touched upon, in a more connected and philosophical manner. In this, I have aimed chiefly to speak quickening words, suggest worthy inquiries into the deepest subjects, and do somewhat to awaken in the sleeping intellect of the age, ideas and sentiments, befitting the dignity and end of the soul. I would touch the great interests of life: hint at great popular evils [503] and abuses, setting forth the divinity of principles. While the work shall, I fancy, commend itself to living and believing souls, it shall, doubtless, provoke evil-doers, and be an unspeakable offence to all, wedded to existing opinions, usages, institutions. The tribes of timeservers, shall cry out loudly against it. But yet I must speak. And speaking, utter my thought without marring its features, though these frown bold condemnation on the age. Plain speech is the sole vehicle of highest, divinest, truths. Shall a man, whose soul is fired with living ideas, authenticated by his holiest instincts, speak unworthily of these. Doth not conviction reprove all servile, or canting, speech, as belieing principles. Such a soul utters itself simply, yet faithfully. Self-insight hath opened its eye, and the visions that [504] dawn upon it, clothe its ideas in bold, lofty, commanding images. It hath an eloquence borrowed from nature. It hath an authority from heaven. And it sees beyond conventions, apprehending principles. Hence its seeming contempt of existing things, its outcry against existing evils, its rebuke of living men, and defects of human institutions. It frowns death, destruction, on such. It is bold for truth. Yet amidst all this lofty bearing, it hath a careless disregard of its own temporary interests, its fortunes, and name. It forgets self. It makes cause with principles. It lives in and for ideas. It takes their fortunes at heart. It hath no interest beside these. When these demand support, it braves all damage or insult; and would make its own reputation, by becoming one with the violated principle, and be seen in the light of contemned ideas. It falls, if need be, in [505] their defence. It dies that truth may receive its unwavering testimony, and thus declare its divine nature.

In this wise, do prophet, seer, shine divinest radiance on the world — Wisdom [and] virtue, beam forth serenely through their transfigured face, and the world, during the glorious trial, catch glimpse of the Godhead, who lives in the deep centre of noble souls. And thus doth God honour his cause on earth, in the sacrifice of his saints.

Yet man doth not now believe in the mighty force of his divine instincts. Saints die[?]; believers have once been. But saints are not, nor shall again be. There is no such power of self-surrender as once. Man [506] has lost the consciousness of his divinest faculties. He hath so long let these slumber in his soul, that he hath bereaved himself of their light. He deems this, indeed, the shining of another nature. He belies himself. The Godlike dies out of his consciousness. The prophetic faculty of his own soul, is transferred to a superior being. Seer, and saint, become superhuman, instead of human natures to him. He doth not know that he is sage, seer, saint, by virtue of his nature, would he but unfold his faculties, in harmony, fullness, by a life of divinest disciplines, by chastity, temperance, holiness, which quicken the Genius, that shall divine deep secrets of God, and unfold these, in living deeds, and words. Obey thy nature, O man! and thou shalt see, foresee, and enact, the Godlike. They hath [507] wondrous faculties. For doth not the Godhead ever stir in the deep instincts of the soul; evermore announcing the end that it should aim at, of becoming not only as God; but declaring the exercise of faculties, which, in their full developement, shall become God; thus preaching to man the divine force that he is, if he will but practice those disciplines that become himself.

I ask the reverent, inseeing soul, if it doth not feel a force stirring within it, that, in its fullness of accomplishment shall not be God. I ask such a soul, if God be other than the consummation of its own faculties; the full unfolding of its own wondrous nature? I ask him if God be other than the complement of himself? Doth he startle at the implied identity of his soul, with the object of his [508] deepest reverence, his holiest worship? In that fact I see the highest proof, given by his nature, of its union with God. He is startled at this identification of his own soul with God! Why? Because his nature is a mystery, too deep for him to fathom, in the darkness of his self-ignorance. He is too great to see himself in the dim and marrd image, which sin, hath imposed on him. His souls' vision is closed upon the grandeur and glory of its own being. Having denied God in this faith,[137] he sees not God in his intellect. He cannot approach himself. He stands at a distance. He sunders his divinest faculties from his soul, in his thought, and deems these God, for he cannot admit these to be his for lack of their exercise. To impose aught of his own perverted nature on God; or appropriate aught of Gods' attributes, to himself, he deems blasphemy. He sees nothing common [509] to each. He startles at the familiarity, and seeming irreverence of the soul, that hath found its identity with God, by an unfolding of his image and attributes through a life of divine disciplines. He knows not the attributes of his own soul, for he hath not *lived* them into his consciousness. His intellect hath not taken in the idea that is ever unfolded from it, by the practice of virtue, by pure aspirations, noble deeds, the worship of the Divinest in his soul, by the harmoneous exercise of all its faculties.

I call that man no[138] wise Christian, who belies the divinity of his nature, by denying the identity of his soul with God. I deem his creed false to the spirit of his master's teachings. He ever declared the union of his own soul with God, and, as constantly, denied all superiority [510] of nature, above others, I pronounce the man that sees not this intimate and divine union, yet destitute of the spirit of his master; and a vilifier of his holy religion. For this declares the eternity of the soul, and the dignity of man's nature. I say, that the Christian world is antiChrist. It speculatively denies the divinity of the soul. It casts off its divinest faculties; makes itself an outcast from their presence; and then yields these an idolotrous and false worship, by proffers of formal and heartless acts, wherin these faculties have no part. It changes the attributes of God, which constitute the life and truth of the soul, into death and lies.

Awake! Appear in the midst of this Godless Age, O divine Self! and shine life and truth, to dissipate idolatry and lies.

[511]   (Nov. 8)

Dr. Alcott.

This friend, and youthful intimate of mine, with his companion, came to reside in my family. For some years, we have seen each other but little: our pursuits have led us into spher[e]s of thought and action widely different, and this, aside from original bias, has widely separated us. Opinions differ. We now come to the same table—reside under the same roof. What the result of this intimacy shall be time shall prove.[139]

He is now busied in various literary & philanthropic interests. He edits the "Library of Health, or Teacher of the Human Constitution"—a periodical originating with himself: and exerting a good influence upon the corpo-[512]real welfare of society.[140] Education is a topic of interest with him, and he edits the popular Journal of the day, 'The Annals of Education". He is the author of several useful and popular works—the "Young Man's Guide"—"Young Mother"—"Young Wife. &c." His views are all of quite popular character. Distinguished by great industry, by good sense, and irreproachable morals, he exerts a good influence on the common mind.—We need the service of a mind, given to wider insight, deeper faith in ideas, an intenser enthusiasm, bolder statement of great principles; and a nobler confidence in human nature. Till such a soul appear, the great reform which the age demands, in education, shall not[141] begin. Where is he? Surely not among those, who now buzz before the public, as reformers in this department.

[513]   45
                              November.
                         Week XLV.   [46: 12–18 November]

                            Order of Life.

My household consists, at present, of seven souls—Myself, companion, three daughters, with my friend D[r]. Alcott, and wife. We offer them two rooms of our dwelling, and occupy the others ourselves. The house, though small, accommodates us all, with much of comfort. [514] I pay for it a rent of $250: for my school room, I pay $100, a year.—To meet the expenses of rents, and living, I shall receive, from the present number of pupils, should these continue under my care, $1000.[142] Dr Alcott is to pay $8 a week for his rooms and board, making $416 a year. As our living is simple, and we do our own work, our expenses must, necessarily, be much lightened.

The following is our present order for the day:

We rise at 5 o Clock. While Mrs A. prepares our morning meal, I call the children, and get them ready for the employments of the day. Dressing, washing, domestic chores, occupy the time till breakfast.

At half past 6. we breakfast. This consists of rice, bread, potatoes, cakes, pies, [515] fruits, nuts, &c. We use but little of flesh or fish, at any of our meals. Our drink is milk, or water, the latter chiefly. Butter, cheese, honey, we partake of sparingly. Vegetables we have in great variety. We have neither coffee nor tea.

From 7, till half past 8, the children are engaged in their plays, either in the parlour or play-room, or in assisting their mother about the affairs of the household. The little one, 3 years of age,[143] sometimes, passes this time with me, in looking at her pictures, conversing, or running about the house to watch others in their employments. I usually write or read. Sometimes saw or split my fuel.

At half past 8, the children are fitted for school. They accompany me. The distance from this, gives us fifteen minutes walk, and [516] we reach the Temple at 9 oclock. Here we spend the time till 1. oclock, with a recess of fifteen minutes, between 11 and 12,—during which, the pupils usually recreate themselves on the common.[144] The Card of exercises for the successive days of the week, appears on page 184, of this Journal. Yet from this, published for the spring term, occasional departures are made.

We leave the schoolroom for Cottage Place at 1. oclock, and reach this to sit down to dinner, at half past 1. Our dinner and supper are variations of the dishes of the morning. No additions are made of other articles. On my way from school, I, sometimes, order, or bring, needful things from the grocer's, or fruiterers. We rise from dinner at half past 2. having had conversation on topics of interest. Mrs A. prepares all our meals, and other household [517] work. She prefers this to the care of servants, were we able or desposed to employ such. Her labours, though constant and fatiguing, are dignified by the consciousness of duty, and are conducive to health, and virtue.

I spend the afternoon either in writing or study, surrounded by my family in the parlour; or when these are called into the kitchen, or other apartments, alone. At present the composition and arrangement of "Psyche" gives me employment for these hours. Sometimes, I walk into the crowded mart, however, calling at the bookstores; or reading at the Athaeneum. This I do for observation, as well as health. When disinclined for study, or walking, I saw wood in the cellar. The children are busied in their plays, either in doors, or, during fair weather, in the yard or court, which are free from all associates to vitiate their manners or minds.

[518] We sup at half past 5. The children immediately retire to their beds. I conduct them thither, and read, or converse, with the elder [Anna], for half an hour. The little one [Elizabeth], I see safely and comfortably, laid on her pillow. Mrs Alcott, having put her household in order, rejoins me in the parlour at 7. When disposed for conversation, or reading, we thus pass the evening till 9. Mrs. A. fatigued by her domestic toils, retires at this hour. The parlour is then free, and I enjoy the solitude, in meditation, study, reading or writing, till 11 oclock; when I retire to my bed chamber.

Thus my day—thus the order of my household. On Sunday, I usually give the whole day to thought, composition, writing and reading. But my reading is scanty. Psyche, Journal, school, and household, take up my time and thought.

[519] Thus, day by day, amidst this hour of small profit in the actual, do I live. Circumstances, age, do not favour such work as I have to do. Only, or chiefly, do I live in Idea. I order my life before mine own eyes, and those of my household. But the age will not employ me. I am an Idea without hands. I find no body for my thought amidst the materials of this age. It denies me timber. What shall I do but content myself with my lot, and await in patience the hour when the age shall give work for my faculties, and honour my art, supplying materials therefore—when souls shall be proffered, instead of bodies, and I shall practice my art on these, moulding them into figures of beauty, by wise disciplines.

Complain not, then my genius, thou shalt honour thyself in fit time, and do thy [520] deed before the ages. Ply well thy faculties; thou mayst fit thyself, by wise self-insight; by study of the times for future toils, when the age shall have risen to see thy purpose. This shall one day approach thee. Now at a distance, wait thou, and watch its tardy steps. Study its signs. Question it. Chide it. Counsel it. Shame it. Preach to it. Prophecy against it. Call it by its true name. Set in judgement on it. Note its usages, abuses, evils. Cry out against its institutions. Cast its destiny. Foretel its downfall. And open upon it the future time.

And thus shalt thou give thyself, O my genius, worthy employment, amidst hours of small profit. And write thou, and print thy thought, as it takes feature, to the eye of thy contemporaries. Set thy soul in type, and let the age read thee.

[521] Language.
Shakespeare has interested me lately, as a study of our language, in its freest and fullest aspects. I have read his works to enrich my own vocabulary. I find great profit therein. His page is th[o]roughly English.[145] Milton is, also, a good specimen. And the Sacred Volume is unsurpassed. Almost every fact that can come under the cognizance of the human soul, finds, in these writers, a worthy exponent, in the terms of our language.—Besides the study of these authors, as a means of enriching my vocabulary, I have also run over, by sight, many pages of our English Johnson.[146] I have run through several letters of the alphabet, looking out all words, under these, suited to [522] my needs, both in speech, written and colloquial. Shakespeare wrote our language in its purity. Numerous words, now gone out of use, appear in his page, and for which we have no substitutes; yet the facts for which they stand are, as ever, permanent elements of human life, and should find fit utterance in words. Treating of human nature, in its concrete phases, I search amidst our language for the terms that shall suit my needs. In modern writers, there is little, or nothing, to answer these. On the inmost functions of the soul, a deep silence prevails. Men have become ashamed of their instincts, or are awed by these and either slur these over, speak of them in secret places or prostrate themselves in superstition before them. Hence speech has grown tame; writing meagre: language doth justice but to some faculties & needs of man.

[523] I hold this to be unworthy of us. We must revive words gone into desuetude, and give all functions and needs of our nature fair utterance, both in colloquial and written speech. We must send abroad, those terms which have so long been closetted, and shut out of sight. The citizen, depraved in his functions, and thence fastidious in speech, must be shamed into simplic[i]ty and purity, by entering into the more cleanly and natural life of the country man, whose vocabulary truer to nature, shall be a simpler expression of soul. Cities, while they enlarge the boundaries of thought, and incorporate much of foreign value into a language, at the same time, degrade and cor-

rupt the functions of the soul, and hence throw out of use, terms, which in simpler modes of life, and in a state of comparative innocence, are used as fittest and best. They make [524] the soul ashamed of itself; and hence impoverish and corrupt speech. But this effect is temporary. Man, in earnest, falls back upon his instincts, and the soul utters itself in its fit words. The plain country man, saved from these incursions of corrupting influence, preserves both purity of soul and speech: Language remains uncorrupt: The citizen cannot wholly spoil it.

And the charm, as well as value, of works of genius, arises from the fact, that, in its productions, the human instincts[147] are worthily honoured in thought and utterance. Even amidst his corruption, the citizen, reads these, and refers to them as standards. He perceives their fitness to the needs and nature of the soul. Countryman and citizen speak the same mother tongue, [525] by reason of the common nature which they inherit.

Let a th[o]rough scholar, a man whose nature has not been stolen away by precedent, of books, but who sees man ever above, and of more value than the speech he employs, let such a man, leave the conventional city, (wherin nature, having profaned herself, is ashamed to acknowledge her misdeeds, but winks these out of hearing in speech,) and visit a rural district of simple people. Let him mark their speech; observe their manners. Shall he not find himself again in the presance of his proper nature, of which the city had well nigh bereft him. These people put themselves into their speech. They do not hide their souls. Words are things with them. [526] Their souls slide over their tongues. They are not hutched within, and hidden from sight. And in this simple, free, state of being, their language is more true to nature. They speak it in greater purity than the artificial citizen, or closetted bookworm. It is nearer to the soul. And the vocabulary of such is wider, at the same time that it is more faithful to the soul. They keep diction pure. A custom is like a book. I never hear a country-man speak without being reminded of the dignity of our common nature, and the richness of our common tongue. He reminds me of Shakespeare. He has retained his epithets. Language appears in its simpler, worthier forms. He deals with its staples. Its great words slip from his tongue.[148] The needs of the soul shine in his speech. His vocabulary is not shorn of woods, winds[,] waters, sky, toil, humanity. It hath a soul in it. Its images are of Gods' shaping. He deals [527] in the products of nature, and shames art, save when she, like him, is faithful in the uses and ends of nature. I would rather study simple country man, amidst scenes of nature, as dictionary of my native tongue, than commune with citizen, amidst his conventions, or read with professor, in college or halls, the tomes of library. There is life and meaning within it. It is devoid of pretense. It is mother-tongue.

Yet not in college or hall, in study of works of genius, in lexicon, or grammar, or even amidst simple countryman, shall fit language for the soul alone be mastered. These are but means, not causes, nor ends. A deeper, nobler, discipline yields this fruit[?], bestows this gift. Nature, book, college, professor, school are all dumb, and of no avail save as I find myself by use, or mis-use [528] thereof. I know not these, I am not benefitted by these, save as I know, and am a benefit to myself,—by self-insight, self-discipline. Life is opportunity, living is improvement of this opportunity. I live, not only amidst my opportunities, but must live in them; these must live in me. I must ply my faculties on these, as means to self-culture. All things exteriour are but occasions to the soul. The soul is itself cause. If it works, is pure[,] then all is ready for its use. All is significant. All run toward it. If idle, corrupt, it hath no material; all is dubious; every thing flees away from it. Self-insight sheds light over all around. It makes nature, college, school, lexicon, grammar, human beings, intelligible. Hence every man is his own dictionary. He defines his words, by his own living. He marks his soul by nature. If ignorant of this not, these shall yield him light. He hath no tongue, no written speech; and must remain speechless.

[529] Observation, pursuit, travel, thought, adversity,[149] condition,—these unloose the tongue of man, and discipline it to fit utterances. Language springs living from the needs of the soul.[150] The instincts, ever clamorous within the soul, claim light, interpretation: and to this end, nature, business, human beings, all the disciplines of life. And so the soul is tempted forth. And worthy dis[c]ipline shall familiarize it with all its faculties; supply its needs; and among these a chief one, language. But keep the soul active, and all things instruct. It is in the exercise of it[s] faculties, that genius, unaided by art, by colleges, schools,[151] reads nature and men around it, and drinks in their meanings, and finds fit utterance of this, in eloquent speech; often, indeed, giving law to language, because it wrought true to the soul, and, therefore,[152] satisf[y]ing [530] the mind of man; who feels[?] himself in it and accepts it as an expression of his nature. And thus genius ever makes the language of men; and from, time to time, renews, and improves it. It cleanses it from impurities. It gives the soul a clean tongue. It keep[s] it true to its instincts. He who rises to loftier views of the soul, sheds light into all low and vulgar avenues, and reveals the impurity that there hides itself from sight.

Every man of genius, enlarges the boundary of knowledge, and opens the eye of his age, yea, of all future ages, into the domain of the soul, and gives new notes to the human tongue, wherwith to utter itself, in fit speech. Henceforth the world uses his eye wherewith to see, and his tongue wherwith to speak.

[531]   46
                           November.
                    Week XLVI. [47: 19–25 November]

                    Genealogy of my Family
  I find the following facts regarding my family, in works treating of the early
history of N. England.

            In *"Prince's New England Chronology:"*
1630.—"The mortality increasing[,] many died weekly, yea, almost daily,
among whom [532] were Mrs Pynchon, Mrs Coddington, Mrs Phillips, and
Mrs Alcock," (now Alcott) "a sister of Mr Hooker.["] Mr Hooker came over
in 1633.

1630.   Oct. 19. ⎫
        Boston   ⎬ Mr George Alcock made freeman, at the General Court
                  ⎭ of Massachusetts Colony, with 108 others.

1632.—["]The "Roxbury Church Records" tell us that the people of Roxbury
(had) joined to the Church in Dorchester, till God should give them an opportunity to be a church themselves; and that Mr George Alcock, who came
over in 1630 and lived in godly sort, was by Dorchester Church chosen a
deacon, especially to regard the brethren of Roxbury, and after he joins the
Roxbury Church, is ordained their deacon.["][153]

[533]   In *"Mathers Magnalia"*.
1646.—Mr John Alcock graduates at Harvard University. This was the fifth
year after its foundation.

1659.—Mr. Samuel Alcock graduated.

1673.—Mr. George Alcock graduated.[154]

                    From Various Sources.[155]
  —Mr Thomas Hooker, was born at Murfield in Leicestershire in 1586. He
was a fellow of Emmanual College[,] Cambrid[g]e. He came to this country,—
New England, Boston,—in 1633. He settled at Hartford, Conn, in 1636.—Mr
George Alcock, married his sister, who died in 1630. Mr Alcock probably
accompan[i]ed him to Hartford from Roxbury: and from him my family,
who [534] settled in Hartford and New Haven, and afterwards, removed
to Wolcott, my native place in New Haven county.[156]

  My maternal ancestors first settled in Stonington, and New Haven, afterwards in Waterbury adjoining Wolcott, (then called Farmingbury) where

the name is yet common.¹⁵⁷ The Bronsons, or Brownsons, as it was originally, are numerous, as are the Blakeleys, with whom my grandfather, Amos Bronson, was connected by intermarriage. He settled in Plymouth where my mother was born. Both Plymouth and Waterbury join Farmingbury, or Wolcott.—The name, *Alcock*, was changed to *Alcott*, for sake of euphony, in my youthful days. The name is retained in England.¹⁵⁸

[535]   Psyche
As the weeks glide by, I find large additions made to my book. It is, indeed, the work to which my faculties have set themselves; and all else gathers around it, as a primary purpose. My school goes on as usual. My numbers are a dozen. I spend my five hours with these from day to day, and see them making progress in knowledge and virtue, though the progress be simple and slow, amidst the innumerable hindrances, domestic and social, as well as individual, which beset their course. I do much less than I would: But little can be done, in the present state of public sentiment among us. I must seek worthy labour in other ways. This I find in writing. The *Psyche* gives me employment.—Morning, afternoon, and eve-[536]ning. As I rise earlier than usual, by the present arrangement, I sometimes find time to write a sheet before the hour for school, besides preparing the affairs of household for the day. And there are moments, during the mornings exercises at school, when thoughts that glide into my mind, find hasty record. To preserve these in their freshness, I usually take my MS. to the school room. Some of my most satisfactory utterances have been suggested by exercises of my school, as, in conversations with my pupils, we touch upon subjects suited to my work. I would that every paragraph were a faithful transcript of life; of thoughts confirmed by experience, and seen in the full shine of Ideas. Only such are worthy of type. Only such do I intend to send to press. I would make a bock of inspirations; utterances of life and light, that shall quicken all readers.

[537] As I proceed in my work, I find myself weaving into the texture, anecdotes and passages of my life, which, when successfully drawn, give reality to what, without such statements, would become too abstract, for general reading. The children take much less space, than was proposed, in the first draught of my Idea. The Psyche becomes more and more adapted to the facts of adult life; and I hope to make it a fit transcript of the great needs, occasions, and interests of the soul, corporeal, mental, spiritual.

And thus I live, and purpose, and work. It seems like small performance. And yet what shall I do more? Nothing in the actual offers. I am driven into the ideal. My hands hang by my side. There is no [538] work for me to do amidst the conventions of my age; save the utterance of those thoughts, which (noblest of work) shall one day, sweep these conventions all away. I live in hope. I write in faith. I utter my word in confidence; and when time shall come that shall give me chance of fit publication, then shall these words go forth, as evidence of my labour, amidst this hour of solitary and obscure living.

My dwelling is in Cottage Place. Therein do I ply my faculties, as best I may. Amidst many needs and discouragements do I seek to do what seemeth right and fit, to my simple and growing family; and, day by day, sally forth, at hour of nine, to meet those who are yet left to receive my instruction.

[539] And there is joy in this labour: There is content in this, my lot. Henceforth shall I not look into my own soul, and ply well my own resources, come what hindrance there may. Shall I not, at some future hour of my terrestrial day, look back into this era, and find satisfaction in the retrospect. I did not yield to inaction. I did not despond, though desire for action on my age was an abiding, and living instinct of my soul; and my favorite scheme, for the time, was rudely assailed, and cast out of my hand.

Believe thou, o my soul! that all these hindrances, misapprehensions, needs, are but blessed ministries to unfold thy noblest faculties, and discipline thee into divinest virtues. Thou art hindered, that thou mayest baffle all these and [540] at last, prove the might that in thee lies. Thy work is great. Thou canst not compass it at once. Thou must have thy patience and trust proved, by these disciplines. And thus thyself be tried.—Perchance thou mayest be called to the trial of persecution,—of fire. Are there no signs of approaching dread. What say the times! Are not men of the day lost to truth! Doth not wickedness reign in high places.[159] Shall virtue, truth, wisdom, hol[i]ness, meet favour at its hands? The day of martyrdom hath already come! Even as I write, the land is bloody with the guilt of the slain, and slain for defence of truth—for the rights of the soul! One martyr hath fallen![160] Others may be ripening for their reward at the hands of a godless age. What shall hinder a man, like myself, true to his instincts, and frank, yea, bold, [541] in utterance, in action, from penalty of his simplicity. But that the truths which I utter regard more the intellectual and spiritual needs of man, than his corporeal,—but that their influence on the interests of the flesh, is not at once seen, I should expose myself to such fate.

But priests,—these do I gainsay. And these are deadly enemies to combat. These are, or shall be against me. I preach holiness, temperance, both in doctrine and deed. I expose the evils of the day. I call the age to account. Shall it bear it. Shall it not be provoked: and deal[161] vengeance on my head? Gluttons, drunkards, lechers, hypocrites, time-servers, worldlings, these shall fear to be offended. I would have my word a sword. Truth is ever a sword [542] to the wicked. It is brandished to strike evil and error dead. Shall not such natures seek defence: and this with diabolical weapons. What else hath these wherwith to fight?

Take up thy cross, and follow after Duty; ofttimes shall thy reward shine upon thee through the portals of the grave; and death is the angel, that shall conduct thee, amidst blood, flame, or crucifixion, to the courts of the blessed! Art thou ready, my soul! for the divine deed; then say the divine word. Shine lights upon the sins, and evils, and errors, of thy day, and if the hour of suffering come, prove thine own integrity, and be in this dread hour, a living light to all that shall behold or follow thee![162]

[543]

47
November
Week XLVII. [48: 26 November–2 December]

Vocabulary.

Language was a study with me during this week. Besides adding new matter to my Book,[163] I ran through the pages of Johnson's Dictionary, noting words of deep import, pertaining to the great needs and occasions of the soul. [544] In terms of this nature, our language is rich. All essential interests of our common nature, are represented in it. Its stores are ample. Yet most surprisingly have we cast these aside, on many of the great occasions of life, in current speech. And hence done much to impoverish language. There is little of pure English now spoken or written amongst us. And a man who shall give worthy specimen, in conversation or writing, will be deemed pedantic. We are slovenly both in speech and writing. The style of each is vulgar. It is shamefully impure. We give no proof of the riches of our tongue. Hundreds of words, all living with meaning, and exactly expressive of our commonest wants, and suited to commonest occasions, have fallen into desuetude. And we have no terms beside our current speech. Only in our Dictionaries, or in the Works of the Fathers of our Language, whose dialect we affect to despise, (especially in practice) [545] bear the only testimony to the riches of our common tongue. Both conversation, and Books, of modern date, disgrace us. Professedly wise and learned, we give small proof of either in our use of speech.

And why should we? The English Language is not studied, as a distinct branch of human culture. Slender provision is made for it, in our semenaries of learning. We have no professorships to this end. The time of students is wasted, chiefly, in the study of foreign languages, living or dead, to the neglect of his vernacular tongue. He studies no Classic as means of perfecting his own tongue. Greek, Latin, French, German, &c are studied chiefly as ends. Not as means of giving him expertness and accuracy in the use [of] his own native language. Of this he gains small knowledge, except by chance. [546] He comes not from the University, armed with the strength and grace, of his mother tongue. He stammers in this, and hath too often small proficience in foreign dialects. One great end of culture, a clear and free tongue, he hath not attained, by all his drillings at school. He cannot speak to his kind. His dialect is not English. It doth not touch the needs & occasions of life. It doth small honour to the deep instincts and nobler faculties of the soul. And the perfect end of scholastic influence is lost on him. He doth not put his Shakespeare into his dialect. His English dictionary hath small significance to him. He is more foreign than domestic in his diction. He touches not home. He stirs not the domestic affections, the familiar needs of men. And hence small is his influence. He is not educated. He is only drilled. He is not fitted for exerting a wide and deep influence [547] on his country men, or his age. It sees nothing desirable, or useful, or inspiring in him. And turns away, as of right it should to the mighty dead, in whose words and acts, it finds its own needs supplied.[164]

A man is not educated till he hath full and free use of all his faculties. The study of a great work, is but the study of a great soul, and should ever be made conducive to the developement of like greatness in the student. Study Shakespeare;—become Shakespeare;—think, act, speak, him. Then, indeed, is he studied, and study hath wrought its ends. Unless study of an author, reproduce the author in the student little is done. The study hath fallen short of its end. The thoughts, acts, words, of the author must be one with his. The author is, during this study, instructor. He is inspiration. He breathes himself into the soul [548] of his disciple. He lives in his faculties. And the disciple doth but reutter his living words, act his worthiest deeds. He reanimates the Shakespeare, the Milton, the Plato, the Jesus, whose works he studies. His faculties become one with the soul of these. He is living their life, seeing their thought, uttering their word. And when, in the light of these gifts, he looks out upon his age and time, he doth become a shining soul, that reminds his kindred of the wise and great with whom he hath held converse. His thought, his deed, his word, calls these into remembrance of his race. The wise, the good, again walk the earth, and show their faces to living men. Their dialect is spoken once more. Their enthusiasm burns again in the soul to do noble deeds. Their doctrines circulate in the minds of men and receive their willing faith. For Eternal Truth, Beauty, Good, have appeared again in worthy philosophies, in [549] rich literatures, noble moralities. Culture would do its work on the soul.

And hence the use of books as teachers. But there needs living teacher to make living book. Else the office is all sham. Professor must practice as well as profess. He must make the author studied live in the mind of the student. He must be the author, take his place, assume his authority, in the pupils idea. And thus interpret the authors thoughts, deeds, words. If he do not this, he is not professor, not teacher. And shall hinder the souls that he should help.

And all this holds true of all subordinate departments of instruction. No man can teach that hath not lived the doctrines, deeds, and hence learned the language of genius. Mere talent, which is but semblance, cannot do the work of genius. [550] The cobler mends, he doth not make the shoe. Numerous are the coblers that now belabour the human mind to small profit, in our colleges and halls. And how these do[165] mar and deform the faculties of our youth!

And shall, so long as they suffer it to be led astray from itself, by study of foreign, or vulgar literatures to exclusion of domestic and nobler disciplines. The speech of our day is vulgar. It partakes of the vulgar interests of the day. We are vulgar. Thought being vulgar, deeds become vulgar, and speech echoes it. Alas! the age hath fallen into the slough. It is begrimed with dirt. It doth not see by reason of the mire. Its mouth is full, and its diction bespattered with the foulness. What shall lift it out, and cleanse its face, its speech? Vision of its nobler faculties, and revival of its mother tongue.

[551]   Birthday.

November 29. completed my 38 year. One half of my days, gone, at most.[166] And small time remains in which to complete my terrestrial work, whatsoever it shall be. For, of this, not as yet, have I clear vision. Only in Instincts, that shine oft dim features of my Deed,—twin-yoked with Idea that inspires my Genius,—do I gain assurance of inner might, and foresight of occasion, that shall provoke this into actual day-light. Twilight shadows rest over it. Not, as yet, do I possess my Idea: behold my Deed, utter my Word.—But yet, as years glide by, shall these come into my sight, and take shape in the actual. My Instinct shall become a Deed, shining forth [552] in Idea announced in Word. I seek not now to provoke the future. Enough that assurance of noble deed, inspired thought, worthy word, is vouchsafed to me, and faith in might of soul that shall withstand all hindrance.

Yet now am I visibly idle. My hand is without service. The age hath no work for me. I stand with folded arms, desirous of doing some service for soul; but the age hath nothing of that sort on hand. It hath hands full of this for body. And, unhired, I gaze on labourer[s] around me. All hands, how busy! What noise of instruments! What roar of elements! Fool! Saith all the age didst thou think the soul, of which thou talkest, and for which wouldst fain labour, even unto death, hath aught like this. Thou speakest, mystically, of instincts, [553] faculties, whose needs these arts shall never supply. Behold all nature labours and lends her stores to supply all needs.—And so I look. And, verily, the human soul doth herein belie itself. It hath spread out all its faculties into a brawny arm, and lets off its instincts on nature, through cunning finger. Behold there, the Artisan, sooty Drudges, with iron apron, and leathern cap, midst smoke and cinders of Smithy, din of wheels, and roar of waters, transforming nature into shapes for corporeal uses. Fire glows; water roars amidst wheels, steam spits and plies enginery. He hath thousand hands all astir to feed, clothe, shelter, ornament, his body. And poor apprenticed Soul, blows clapping bellows for him all the while, nor heeds he hint of other toils. [554] Master Drudge holds him in durance, and checks all flights of thought transcending flue of Smithy. Grimly he saith, "work thou there lustily at bellows, and dismiss all inkling of soft-handed gentry, who eschew Smithy, and would never work. Blow, lublard, or I will turn thee from shop to starve.["]

Need may yet drive me into service of Drudges. Yet shall I retain my freedom, nevertheless. If the age give me no work on the soul, and, for lack of this, refuse bread, I can strike bargain with some cunning smith, for half of my time, and reserve remainder,—thus writing thinking and writing with work. I will blow coals for Drudges half of my day, and for Genius the other. Aye! Let me play cunning trick on grim face, [555] blow his smithy into a blaze, by live coal of mine, laid on his forge hearth, when he turns sooty lid to watch labours of shop. Too long hath this Vulcan sent dingy smoke flakes into the common atmosphere, and thereby blurred our sight, while noise of hammer ringing against anvil, or roar of forge, hath dinned our ears. He hath made fetters for our faculties, and bound these to bellows handle! Yes, burn Smithy.[167] I say. Worthy resolve this for birthday. Please God assist me in its furtherance.

I wait, with due patience, hour of deliverance from service of Drudges. As this year hath deprived me of opportunity of worthy labour in the actual, perchance the next shall restore me to my rights. Meanwhile, I do that which lieth nearest my hand,[168] and shall not complain.

[556] This year has been one of trial. It has been rich in discipline, and has done me good. I have been thrown inward upon my own resources, and have found these. My faculties have been sharpened for work. I have had much of self-insight. I have learned the dignity of standing alone before my age. Experience thus precious, I have cause to regard with thankfulness.—Doubtless the year upon which I now enter shall be equally rich in means of self-discipline. And my faculties strengthened by the events through which it shall conduct me.— Save me O ye destinies!, from idleness—from tame and servile engagements;— from compliance with the vulgar aims and pursuits of my age. Lift me above its low maxims, and make me a light shining amidst darkness;[169] so shall my year be one of blessing & reward!

[557]
48
December.
Week XLVIII.   [49: 3–9 December]

Conversations on Self-Culture.

Besides writing chapters and paragraphs for my book, I gave some thought, during this week, to my chances of acting on the age, by more direct means. My school affords me small employment. Its numbers [558] are now reduced to half dozen, at the opening of this winter term, commencing this week. Thus leaving me little hope of much longer employment in teaching. Boston, it would seem, hath nothing for me to do in this way.

PLATE EIGHT
Alcott's entry during Week XLVII (26 November–2 December) reviewing the past year.
Courtesy MH

Yet I believe something may be done by means of Conversations. To this end, I have allowed myself to dwell on this idea. At present, I incline to attempt something of this nature. Whether to hold private interview with the dozen or more individuals, who have already invited me to meet them weekly, for evening conversation, on means of Self-Culture; or to engage a hall, and invite all persons interested in self-improvement, by means of tickets, at a small charge, to such conversations, I have not, as yet decided. I have thought Sunday evening, a fit hour for such interviews.

[559] I take it for granted that there are, in this metropolis, many persons, especially amongst the young, who would find both pleasure and profit in such interviews. The interest manifested, during my first attempt last season, amidst all the disadvantages under which it laboured, seems to be proof of this. A second attempt, under more favorable circumstances, might, I fancy, be quite successful. It would add to the means of instruction during the long evenings of the winter. It would afford an agreeable variety.

I have long deemed Conversation as one of the most direct and effectual organs of instruction. And if such can be conducted before numbers, without losing its essential charm of simplicity, upon [560] which all its force depends, it might be made most conducive to public benefit, supplying the deficiency, as means of self-culture, of popular lectures, descources, and books, whose influence is ever of a passive nature; often, indeed, serving to lull the soul into vague dreams of knowledge and virtue, and thus despoil it of the great ends which these profess to accomplish. Conversation, by enlisting the faculties of several, and provoking discussion, by affording chance of free interchange between mind and mind, banishes all such effect, and gives life, light, to truth. I feel assured, that, with adequate assistance, which should ever ensure conversation, on the topics proposed, an audiance, might reap great good by spending an evening, now and then, in attendance.

[561] And there is the more need of such interviews, from the unsocial habits of our community. Very little of high, well sustained conversations, is practiced among us. The gift of speech is not ours. We hesitate, stammer, are shy of free utterance. Seldom are topics of worthy import discussed in worthy style. Colloquial gifts are rare. Our young men and women have little skill in this way. The fitness of our tongue for this end, is seldom shown forth.

I fancy that exercises of the kind proposed, would do somewhat to cherish a more easy & graceful style of conversation among us; as well as conducive to the higher end which I would aim at in holding such Conversations. Perhaps, a readier mode of bringing my views before the public, and [562] of testing their reception, could not be chosen. I should be present to hear and answer objections, remove false impressions, arising from broad and general statements, & make such qualifications, as these seemed to need.

Then should I publish and try my ideas, before sending them to press, and the freedom of comment here indulged in, open out to me choice insight into the human soul, both, in its popular and occluse aspects. I could make use of these conversations, as means of experimenting on the common soul, learning, before I committed thoughts to paper, in the guise of conversation, what reception truth shall have in my age. Here in, free, spontaneous speech, should I give utterance to my Self, and compose worthy passages, amidst the life and light of human countenance, for my future works.

[563] It was in such wise, that Plato, doubtless, first composed those divine Dialogues, in which he has embodied the wisdom and wit of his age, with the love of antiquity. He reproduced in those immortal works, the sentiments and words of his wise interlocutors. He put on record a worthy sample of the ancient style of Conversation. He gave specimen of worthy dialect. And, beside such testimony to this exercise of the human faculties, by the most learned, and wisest of the ancients, we have sacred example, in the records of the Gospels, of the divine colloquies of him whose mind was furnished above all former precedent, for the grace and glory of conversation. Highest authority are these to the fitness of conversation, as a means of utterance to divinest truths. And time is it that the practice of [564] such precedent were revived among us. It would be [a] most feasable substitute for the lazy, ineffectual, style of instruction, by means of descourse, lecture, and reading. Soul would thus treat intimately with soul. There would be interchange of thought. Many would engage in unfolding and illustrating the subject of consideration, instead of confining it to one. Its varied aspects would be brought into sight. It would be presented in its unity, and wholeness. The souls' varied faculties would[?] each answer, yea or nay, and this, audibly, to the reality or falsity of the statements; & thus truth shine forth from the action of the whole Soul. One mind would stand less chance of imposing itself on another. Faculty would qualify faculty, and the majesty of Ideas shine forth and declare their authority amidst the free [565] and full action of all the powers of the soul. Genius would irradiate such circle of attributes worthily engaged in practice of highest and divinest art.—Assuredly the soul puts forth its noblest graces, and displays its most glorious prerogatives, when engaged in spontaneous utterance of itself, inspired by the faces of its listening kindred, hanging delightedly on its eloquent lip. Then is it that it doth sweep the cords of it[s] own orphye lyre, and descourse heavenly harmony. Inspiration unseals the lip: and words winged with eloquence, send truths armed with arrowy might, to the soul of enraptured listener. The seraph descends and speaks to man in accents of angels. The soul is a burning coal on the altar of God.[170]

[566] But one deficiency stares me in the face, as regards the practicability of these exercises. I shall find it difficult to find those ready and competent to sustain me in such enterprize. Several there are, who entertain views some-

what in common with mine, and who, in private intercourse, descourse with ready freedom; yet these may be unwilling to stand forth in public, in defence of such doctrines, or even to attend conversations where these shall be discussed, though under most favorable circumstances. And without such assistance the thing should not be attempted, as I could not rely upon the audiance, without exposure to defeat. And then again, carping or ill-desposed persons, might intrude to throw stumbling blocks in my way. Doubtless something may be done to prevent this, by tickets of admittance to the course, thus excluding those who were not earnest seekers of wisdom, or who had cherished creed to defend.

[567] Yet amidst all the hindrances which seem to stand in my way, I deem this the most direct and feasible means of addressing myself to my age. Fewer hindrances check the action of my faculties in this form than in any other. I have made a first experiment, and this without failure. I am sure of ability. Not so as regards lecturing; in which I have small confidence, as means of benefit, except in singular instances, where the lecturer, as in the case of Emerson, approaches near the style of conversation, and by the force of his thought, as well as grace of manner, quickens the faculties, and suggests thought for after consideration. In connexion with the course of lectures on "*Human Culture*" which he delivers, during the winter,[171] my Conversations will, I fancy, furnish food for thought, and quicken the faculties of the hearer, to worthy exercise. Our [568] views are similar, and we should draw hearers of similar faculties, and modes of thinking. We might add our testimony to the good and true, each in his own way.

I shall consider on this subject, and if, on wiser thought, there seems to be chance of success, amidst seeming hindrance, I shall obtain a convenient Hall, and issue tickets to this end. I hope to settle this matter, so as to open my course, by January 1838.[172]

These will supply fit external excitement, and scope to my faculties, beside writing my book, during the ensuing season. Such scope I need, or I shall not grow.—Should the more public course fail, I shall adopt the private, according to request or, perhaps, carry on both at the same time.

[569] Emerson's Introductory Lecture on H. Culture.
Emerson gave the Introductory to his Course of Lectures on *Human Culture*, on Wednesday Evening [6 December] of this week. This first, was well attended, and promises attention from the elite of this metropolis to the course. I listened to it with great pleasure. It was a noble survey of the grounds and reasons of Self Culture, with fit statement of the apparatus of Nature and Soul to this end. It spread out a full view of this great discipline. Subsequent Lectures are to conduct the mind over the means of perfecting the different faculties, and realizing the whole of the soul, in consciousness.

These descourses, will, I doubt not, shed bright light on the human being, inspire [570] reverence for its ends, and provoke to those disciplines that unfold it into fullness. We need such utterances. Whatever leads the soul to regard with deep and felt reverance the divine faculties that stir within it, must make for the furtherance of human culture. At present, men have small regard for the soul. They have certain mystical, abstract, notions of God—of immortality, of retributive reward and punishment; yet these have as yet found no ground in their being, as the action of its faculties; but are deemed arbitrary natures, and operations, sundered from the nature of the soul. Men see not the illimitable nature of their soul, and thus apprehend not the facts of God, immortality, retribution. They have not that self insight, which results from culture of all their [571] faculties in unity, thus unfolding the Perfection of that nature, whose idea is God; whose faculties transcend time, and surpass the limits of space; and whose Ideal is ever so much in advance of its actual, that the sense of imperfection is ever present, and confirmed by all the rewards and penalties of endeavours to attain it, whether worthy or unworthy, as announced in the instinct of its growth, revealed ever in the depths of conscience. Men deem God other than the perfection of their soul. Immortality they regard as a gift, not possession of their soul. Conscience, as an erring Instinct of it. Hence all is arbitrary. God and Man are two. Soul and God are deverse natures. They are not coëternal. The sense of the perfect, which is the conscience of the soul, and proof of its power of actualizing this self perfection [572] by brave disciplines, which tempt forth and lift its faculties out of present and attained states, and ever setting up in the soul the court of judgements, by which all its acts are measured, with accompanying reward or penalty, all these are deemed counter operations and disciplines, under the influence of a superiour and separate being. The identity of the soul with God—the coworking ever of the Ideal with the Actual, whereby the soul measures its advance or lapse in Perfection, these are not clear[?][173] apprehensions in the souls of men at this day. An eternal duality separates the attributes of the soul from those of God, and ever checks all union of human & divine natures, as complement and counterpart of one another.

[573] Fuller light is soon to burst on the darkened and benighted faculties of men. He is to look into his own nature and apprehend its wondrous faculties. By self insight he is to see God. He is to find God in the attributes of his own soul. He is to behold this as a faculty of God: and God a complemental soul. By knowledge of his nature he is to see into those divine faculties which are its glory, & wherein the Godhead ever resides, ever the idea of the Perfect, whereof conscience ever inches[?] the presance. Divorced from itself, by reason of long departure from the sense of the perfect, by wide distance of actual from Ideal, the soul hath lost the sense of its divinity. Its God is out of it. It is not part of its faculties. It is made servant to subordinate faculties[?]. It limits itself [574] by terrestrial objects, and emprisons

itself in the senses, dates its existence to the hour of its advent into space, and loses all vision of future life beyond the grave, thus belie[i]ng its immortality. Ideas, eternal in their nature, thus clad in the habilaments of the grave; thus transmuted into perishing idols of sense, lose all life, and proclaim no longer to the soul, their heavenly lineage. Images of sense subvert ideas of soul. The Idea is wrapt in the Idol. Instincts, once quick with the life of God, and shining light into these Ideas, as their fit exponent and sign, become perverted by loss of unity, and the darken[e]d soul, unable to apprehend their significance, by reason of lapse of faculties, reads lies in the sacred utterances of the soul, no longer a law to itself, because it hath lost the vision of [575] its perfectibility, seeing only amidst the twilight darkness of faculties setting in the shades of evil and sin, of error and superstition. And thus wanders amidst shadows, graves, and death.

To lift the soul from this lapsed and darken[e]d state giving it vision of its own divine prerogatives, its union with the Perfect, its identity with this consummation of its faculties, and point to the noble disciplines that shall conduct more and more into the light of this Perfect Day, will be the issue, I trust, of these Lectures of Mr Emerson. No man among us has equal chance of doing justice to such divine themes. None has deeper insight into the soul, finds God more readily in its faculties; apprehends these more clearly in their action amidst the aids & hindrances of nature, and man; or has [576] gifts of speech to set these forth in worthier manner. Success to such high design!

But unworthy age this, of such teaching. On the young and hoping[,] these words of his, shall, however, make lasting impress. And the day shall come when doctrines, now urged with much of distrust, as to their reception, shall find ready & ardent desciples. The next age shall not be wholly atheist. A few godly souls are ripening amidst the reigning doubts, and godless impieties of this time, to shine belief and hope over the ashes of the departing age, and be a light to the risen generation.

[577]   Sequel.
After the lecture, I accompanied Mr Emerson to the house of a friend, and spent the remainder of the evening with several friends, Mr Dwight, Miss Fuller, (on a visit to Boston, from Providence,) Miss Sturges[174] &c. Conversation turned on various topics, Miss F. gave many interesting anecdotes of animal magnetism, which is now a subject of attention in Providence:[175] but nothing of a nature worthy of record.

I had some words with Mr E on my book, in which he takes an interest, and desires to bring it before the public when completed.[176] I shall be likely to spend the winter and spring I imagine, on the composition, and arrangement of this work, and shall not have it off my hands, a finished production, till late

[578] in spring, or beginning of summer. I shall not suffer it to show its face, till it shines with the light of thought, and beauty of truth and holiness. During the hours of winter, I hope to find times of sacred insight, wherein my thought shall find worthy shaping, and free utterance. Should I not have these visitings of the inner nature, my book must yet longer repose in the silence and seclusion of my own soul, till fit occasion call it forth. But yet I shall have such communion with self, in its inmost courts. If I live worthily, I shall see and speak worthily. What shall divert me from the intellectual and spiritual life that I would fain live. Nothing save vulgar self-indulgence; unworthy, or servile, obedience to the age, in deed or word, shall shed disastrous influence on my word.

[579] Meeting at Fanual Hall.
I attended a meeting at Fanual Hall, convened for the purpose of declaring the rights of speech and of the press, so lately invaded by the people of Alton, Ill. in their outrage on Rev. Mr. Lovejoy, which ended in the destruction of his printing press, and loss of his life. Dr. Channing, Hon. John Phillips, and other citizens, with one exception, friendly to the convocation of the meeting, addressed the citizens of Boston in defense of these rights. Wendall Phillips speaks[,] surprising all by his eloquence.[177]

But it saddens me to see the apathy of this community on the highest interests of the soul. A portion were against this meeting; And the doings thereof, were all unworthy the great purpose [580] of those who called it together. The jeopardy of our liberties, seems small matter by the many. The press is venal; speech is proscribed, and few among us seem alarmed in consequence.

But the time must come when men shall be awakened from such torper. Great principles are now riding in majesty through our land in the faculties of choice souls; and mobs, opposition, martyrdom, shall but cause these to shine the more brightly, in the face of unbelieving, persecuting, sluggish, souls, to quicken, awe, and inspire them, to a sense of their danger, and the need of energetic action.

[581]
49
December.
Week XLIX. [50: 10–16 December]

Greene Street School.
I heard Mr. Emerson's Lecture on Wednesday evening [13 December], on the *Hand, or Labour*["]; and Mr. Russells' on Saturday Evening [16 December] on the *Genius of Alfred Tennison*, with *readings* from his poetical works.[178] Besides these, I took [582] tea with Miss M. Fuller at the Tremont House. Miss M. spent the week in town. The school in Providence being in vacation. Mr. Fuller also passed an hour with me at my school room; and was of the company at Tremont House.

I learn, both from Miss F. and from others, of the prosperity of the school. 150 pupils are now in attendance. The most favorable impressions prevail concerning it amongst the people of Providence. I suppose, however, that the time must come for this, as all other institutions of like nature, to meet with prejudice and opposition. I have only to regret, in this case, that a course somewhat bolder were not pursued by those who conduct this institution, and a stand more manly, in the outset.

[583] The building, and interiour arrangements for instruction, are I believe, inferiour to none in N England.[179] The school will, I doubt not, in due time reveal its true character and purpose, and withstand all evils to which it may be subjected. Mr. F. is young, ardent, enterprising.[180] He has a good share of the New England prudence, and this, united with a love of the purest and best, will, I trust, [584] carry him successfully to the ends which he would attain.— I hope the day draws near, when institutions, for the culture of man, shall spring into existence among us, and these shall be encouraged by wise and generous patrons, enabling their projectors to demonstrate, by large experiment, the dignity and utility of thorough culture. Surely it is time, that the human being, amidst obje[c]ts of less moment, received some share of our attention, and means were taken, to unfold it into the beauty and strength, which are its native endowments. The glory of a people is in its specimens of human nature; not, chiefly, in improvements of soil, or secular advantages.

[585]   Generosity.

There is generosity in the world. And this sometimes in forms of alms. Amidst extremest needs, for which no means of relief were apparent, some friend sent me, this week, One Hundred Dollars. I know not, nor can I imagine, who is the generous giver.[181] But the gift came opportunely. Many small bills had become due. Duns became familiar to me. Almost daily, some unwelcome intruder of this sort, found entrance to my dwelling or schoolroom. And I had not wherewithal to answer the demand. This small sum, though it go but little way, was of timely use. It gave some relief. I shall, I trust, be able to bear through the winter, and find bread wherewithal to supply my family. My [586] friends (one or two) have furnished the wardrobes of my companion and children. I have checked all steps on my account to shop of taylor, and wear threadbare vestments, and shall so long as these cover nakedness. So shall we live.

But, amidst this hour of need, or rather of dubious dependance on goodwill of friends, I have been richer than at any former period. I have been never more busy. Never have I written more pages; never felt the free and independent exercise of my faculties, in more delightful con[s]ciousness. While the outward seemed cold, cheerless; while sun hid his beams, under frowning cloud, and nothing ripened for harvest, I have had calm, serene, sunshine, and harvested somewhat for future support. I have meditated, written, lived, in some sort, to soul.

[587] Society.
I have little society. I am quite recluse, seldom spending an hour from home. Indeed, I seem to be shut out, in good measure, from society, by the studies which I affect, and modes of thinking to which I incline. In these, small sympathy can be hoped. My thoughts run not in the popular current; but aside, often, against it. My reading and pursuits, are wide of such ends.

There are, however, a few minds with whom I hold community of thought and of purpose. Occasionally, I have sight of these, and time to say a word. But these are few, and times of communication unfrequent and seldom. I scarce feel the pleasures of [588] intercommunication. I still live quite alone. I go and come. Daily do I wend my course through the crowded thoroughfare, to my small schoolroom; pass my morning hours, with dozen or half dozen children; return, bringing wherwithal for bread on my arm, in market basket, and spend afternoon and evening, with children, wife, at home. And oft, do I rise, at crow of cock, to prepare our morning meal, and children for the day; or midnight taper glimmers at my window, as I pursue my vigils with book or pen, as family repose in my humble dwelling.—There is an austere romance in this, that oft adds serene quiet, elevated joy, to my lot. I find peace, employment, content. I toil on, amidst my age, and yet hope; and yet dream of fuller days, shining on souls beside mine own!

[589] Yet, nor friend, nor book, supplies my needs. I pick scanty sustenance from teaching, and gifts of friends. I interchange hasty word with congenial mind, yet from these sources, cometh not my comfort nor strength. No living man hath entered into my soul. No contemp[or]ary hath penetrated my purpose; beheld my aims; dreamed of my aspirings. Only to my sole self—to my innermost heart—are these things known. The friend, the age, apprehendeth them not. Of all contemporaneous minds, *Emerson* enters most deeply into my ends. But he seeth not all. He knows me not. *Brownson* hath vision of some of my aspirings. Others there are: men of talent; men of high purpose, and rising influence, who have glimpse of my purpose; and young men and women, a few, who hope, and turn their eyes on me. I am not without name, or interest.

[590] Yet now is my light hidden, and I cannot ascend the hill that shall send its shine abroad, over the vales below. I am in the vale. I dwell in quiet. I move not amidst stir of city. I lift not up my voice in high places. I commune the rather with the still small voice of my own heart; and would fain hire[?] wisdom from the frag[r]ent bloom of the valley. Time shall come, when this retreat shall not be vouchsafed me. I may be called away to more active work. Speculation shall open mine eyes to the scenes on which my feet are to press, and my hands work, at some future hour. So thank thee, seclusion, for the good, with which thou dost bless me. Accept[182] penury, obscurity, as noblest disciplines of thy faculties; and use these, to wise ends.

[591]   51
                    December.
                    Week LI.   [17–23 December]

                      Vision.
    The soul hath fitful action. Its vision is not ever equally bright, searching, final. Now, it seeth but in part; anow, the sight of the whole visits it. It burns, now dimly; now brightly: now flickers, and [592] almost dies out. The embers become seemingly cold,—there is no warmth on the hearthstone,—winter howls amidst leafless trunks—the sun vouchsafes but churlish and sidelong glances; and all is winter. But yet, even amidst the desolation—darkness—the taper dieth not quite out;—the spark lives in the dead embers;—there is promise of joy, and some sign of sun light, amidst cold and cheerlessness. Midnight shineth the departing day into the approaching—the cock betokens the dawn—the soul changes her heralds; and life, light, warmth, vision, do visit the faculties, which erewhile were lost in darkness, and shivering amidst rigour & sterility!

    I have added little to "Psyche"; for neither life, light, shining were given me for this while. Soul lost its brightness. [593] And I laid my oft-handled sheets in quiet repose in my book case, and seemed idle, amidst biding of my faculties.

    Amidst such discipline, in such mood, I heard Emersons' Lecture on the 'Head" or "Intellectual Culture";[183]—attended a meeting of friends of Free Speech, convened to commemorate the recent outrage on this, at Alton (Ill.);—and read "Boston Quarterly Review,"—the first number of which appears on 1st of January 1838:—its editor, my friend, *Brownson*,[184] and contributors, friends of human progress, most of them, friends of mine.

    These are all hopeful signs of [a] renewed era. I joy in the appearance of such. They are heralds of a new, and [594] believing age. Already doth the dawn streak the horizon, from the shining orb of diviner day, uprising in the East of the soul. A new age already preexists in the ideal of the rising minds of this; and the future shall cradle the young age, which is now being born, and shall grow into the image of his sires. Already hath the Old Time fallen into dotage, and soon shall drop into his grave; and few mourners doth he leave behind of his once revering family to bewail his loss. The new son hath small regard for the dying: He springs from another line; he hath other ideas, breeding, speech. And, I doubt not, shall have glorious career. All hail thou Age of Belief! I see the spectres of Doubt shimmer in the dark twilight, and, shrieking, disappear at the [595] the glorious shining of Faith. I hail the era of[185] Souls. The grave shall close over the ghost of the[186] godless Present; and the charnal house receive the souless skeleton of Atheist. No longer shall the Temples, in which Faith doth worship, bear [the] inscription, "God dieth," seize ye the inheritance that the Old Churl hath left for us," but "God liveth, live ye in the household wherein he shineth." Popular idols shall be thrown down, and a simple worship tax the faculties of living, devout, souls. Man shall know his use, the narrow creeds shall swell into fullness, and fit the faculties of his soul. God and man, and nature and life, shall be seen as one divine nature, revealing itself, in fit variety, and needful contrasts to feature its unity in its fullness.

[596] To the ushering in,[187] of this age, my faculties are pledged. I have features of it in mine own ideal. I have the young child already in my arms. And when the age hath Faith to apprehend his star, and proffer gifts of meet reverence, then shall I, with my brothers, consign him to the cradled Future, to be the hope and joy of all believing souls. Messiah shall come. Let the age prepare him nurture. Let wise men watch his star, and conduct themselves thereby to his cradle.—The young age is a son of God.[188] He knoweth his Father, and shall enter lovingly upon his Fathers' business,[189] nor cease until he hath cunni[n]gly fulfilled his mission. Behold, all ye who believed, his star! his advent!

[597] December.
Week LII. [24–31 December]

Revd. Mr. Brownson.

I gave this week to my Book, chiefly, as I did not open my school. Besides copying many sheets of the Psyche, and adding some new matter, I visited Rev. Mr. Brownson at Chelsea, spending Wednesday & Thursday [27 and 28 December] with [598] him. We conversed on many topics. Being editor of the 'Boston Quarterly Review," we had somewhat to say as regards to its prospective bearing on the public mind.[190] I have some hope of this work. The articles of the first number bid fair. The minds interested in it, are of sterling cast, and among the most influential of the day. Of these, all of whom are my most intimate friends are the following:—

> Rev. Geo. Ripley, Boston.
> Rev. John S. Dwight do.
> Rev. Wm. Channing do
> Rev. R.W. Emerson, Concord, Mss.
> Rev. F.H. Hedge, Bangor, Me.
> Rev. Caleb Stetson, Medford, Mss.
> Rev. Wm. H. Furness, Philad.
> Rev. Jas. F. Clarke[,] Louisville, Ky.[191]

[599] Besides these principal friends of[192] the work, there are many others. I hope a work so promising, will be sustained. It is much needed. Our Journals are deficient in elevation and spirit; have tame servility to the time; and, on most important subjects, utter not a word. This periodical, is of a bolder cast, and of more general scope. I hope its friends will sustain it.

Mr. Brownson is a man of great powers, fearless spirit, deep love of Humanity, and of more philosophical genius, than most among us. A Journal under his care will, I am assured exert a happy influence on the literature, religion, politics, and philosophy of the country. It will be an organ through which the free mind of the nation, can utter itself[.]

[600] There has been no public Journal open to me before this. All others were either pledged to sustain given opinions, or were timid of risking whatever should partake of novelty or bear strongly against existing opinions, usages, or institutions. Of course, I have written nothing for these, during the last several years. Perhaps I shall now avail myself of this Journal, should it continue, to speak on those topics, upon which my mind has been engaged for many years, on the doctrines and disciplines of Human Culture, as these shall be addressed by opinions, & institutions. Education, in its broad sense, includes the consideration of all opinions and institutions; and the grounds of these in Human nature, of which they are fruits and results.

[601]   Conclusion.

Items of the Year.

This week closes the year. I take a retrospective view of items of my history, during its passage.[193]

January.

	Commence Sacred Readings on Sunday.	p. 4.
	Quarter Card of Discipline & Studies of School.	" 12.
I.	Resume Conversations on the Gospels.	" 13.
	Emerson's Lecture on Art.	" 15.
	Conversation on Spiritual Renewal	" 19.
[602]	Correspondence, epistolary.	" 25.
	Emersons' Lecture on Politics	" 31.
II.	Conversation on Immortality of Soul	" 32.
	Distribution of "Doctrine & Discipline of Human Culture"	" 34.
	Graham's Lectures & Genius	" 36.
	Emerson's Lecture on Religion	" 47.
III.	Conversation on Immortality	" 53.
	Visit to Miss. M. Fuller	" 54.
	Sale of "Con. on the Gospels"	" 56.
	Theosophy	" 60.
	Emerson's Lecture on Society	" 67.

IV.	Conversation on Resurrection	"	68.
	School	"	72.
	Visit Miss M. Fuller	"	74.

[603] February.

	Close Sunday Readings	p.	75.
V.	Letter from a Patron of my School	"	79.
	Emersons' Lecture on Trades & Professions	"	81.
	Conversations on Resurrection	"	82.
	Emerson's Lecture on Manners	"	88.
VI.	Conversation on Miracles	"	89.
	School	"	92.
	My Faith and Purpose	"	93.
	Emerson's Lecture on Ethics	"	103.
	Emerson's Genius	"	106.
VII.	Visit to R.H. Dana	"	108.
	Conversation on Self Sacrifice	"	110.
	Publication of Vol II. "Con. on Gospels'	"	112.
	Close of Winter Term of School	"	114.

[604]	Conditions of Health	p.	117.
	Advance of Terms of Tuition	"	121.
VIII.	Emersons' Lecture on the Present Age	"	124.
	Conversation on Self Sacrifice	"	125.
	Proposed Change of Residence	"	135.
	The Hour	"	137.
	Rev. O.A. Brownson	"	141.
	Graham's Lectures on the Soul	"	145.
	Dr. Channings' Lecture on Temperance	"	147.
IX.	Emerson's Closing Lecture	"	150.
	Visit of Emerson	"	154.
	Conversation on Childhood	"	155.
	Opposition to my Conversations	"	156.
	Opposition to Mr. Graham	"	158.
	Notice of Con on Gospels in Ch. Register	"	162.

[605] March.

	Visit to Dr Channing	p.	168.
X.	Visit Rev. Mr. Ripley	"	170.

	Conversation on Culture	" 172.
	Literary Hopes	" 176.
	Bancrofts Lecture on Education	" 179.
	Conversation on Books	" 180.
XI.	Notice of Con. on Gospels in the Western Messenger	" 181.
	Quarter Card of School Studies	" 182.
	Letter from Boston School Committee	" 184.
	Reply to Boston S. Committee	" 190.
	Copy of Reply	" 191.
XI[I]	Visit to Dr Channing	" 192.
	Norton's Genuineness of Gospels	" 196.
	Notice of Con on Gospels in B. Advertiser	" 198.
[606]	Conversation on Religious Edn.	p. 202.
XII.	Letter from Emerson	" 204.
	Graham's Lectures on Diet and Regimen	" 206.
	Visit of Emerson	" 209.
	Visit to Miss M. Fuller	" 212.
	Notice of Conversations on the Gospels in	
XIII.	Bos. Courier	" 214.
	Notice in N.E. Galaxy	" 217.
	Conversation on Spirit	" 220.
	Arrangements for Removal	" 222.

April.

	Removal from Front Street no 26 to Cottage Place	
	no 1.	p. 225.
XIV.	Defence of Con. on the Gospels in the Courier,	
	by Emerson	" 231.
[607]	Notice of Conversations on the Gospels in Other	
	Prints	p. 233.
	My School and purposes	" 234.
	Lithographic view of my School[,] Room No 7.	
XIV.	Masonic Temple	" 241.
	Sale of my Library, and Catalogue of Books	" 243.
	Close of Conversations on Friday Evenings at	
	my room	" 247.
	Sunday Employments	" 259.
XV.	Note from Emerson	" 265.
	Excitement	" 269.

XVI.	Plans and Prospects	"	273.
	Notice of my School in S. Rose	"	279.
	Speculations	"	281.
[608]	Isolation of Genius	p.	285.
	Emerson's Sympathy	"	291.
XVIII.[194]	Letter from H. Fuller	"	295.
	Articles in Ch. Register	"	301.

May.

	Notice of School in Annals of Edn.	"	311.
	Visit Rev. Mr. Brownson and Dr. Walker	"	315.
	Dr. Henry Mores Philosophical Works	"	320.
XVIII.	Rev. Mr. Frances of Watertown	"	327.
	Miss A.Q. Thaxter	"	329.
	Greatness	"	333.
	Rev. Mr. Ripley	"	337.
	Preach for Mr. Barnard	"	342.
	Correspondence	"	349.
XIX.	Letter from Mr. Furness	"	350.
	Letter from Mr. Emerson	"	355.
	Notice of Con on Gos in B. Courier	"	358.
[609]	Reading of Dr. H. Mores' works	p.	360.
XIX.	" of Wyse on Education	"	362.
	Close of Spring Term of School	"	365.
	Visit Mr. Emerson at Concord	"	367.
XX.	" Mr. Frances at Watertown	"	368.
	Western Messenger	"	371.
	Open School in Room No 3. in Masonic Temple	"	376.
	Proposed Meeting of Symposeum	"	381.
XXI.	Note from Miss Fuller	"	383.
	Letter to Mr. Fuller	"	387.
	Beginning of revision of "Psyche'	"	391.

June.

	Anniversaries	"	403.
	Meeting of Symposeum	"	406.
XXII.	Dr Howes' Descourse	"	407.
	Rev. Mr. Hedge	"	409.

[610]	Mrs Alcott	p.	411.
XXIII.	Dedication of School at Providence. R.I.	"	419.
	Revision of Psyche	"	422.
	Ride to Scituate, Mass.	"	423.
	Emerson's Visit on returning from Providence	"	424.
XXIV.	Notice of Con on Gospels in Babtist Review	"	425.
	Visit of my Mother	"	426.
	Form of 'Psyche"	"	427.

July.

	Revising Psyche	"	432.
XXV–VI.	Correspondence	"	433.
	Misses Grimké	"	434.

[611]	July, August, September.[195]		

XXVII.
to
XL.

An illness confined me to my room
for weeks. While convalescing, I
Visited Rev. Mr. May[,] Scituate.
    ["] Rev. Mr. Emerson, Concord.
Attended Ann. of Am. Ins. of Instruction
        at Worcester, Mss.
Met with the Symposeum on two occasions; and
Opened School on Monday Sep. 3.

October.

XL.	Fortunes	p.	442.
XLI.	Psyche	"	447.
	Household	"	454.
XLII.	Manuscripts	"	458.
	Visit of W.L. Garrison	"	462.
[612]	Foreign Correspondence	p.	464.
	Copy of Mr Greaves' Letter	"	468.
XLIII.	Review of Con on Gospels in		
	Ch. Examiner	"	487.
	My School	"	489.

November.

	Mr. Greaves & Pestalozzi	"	495.

XLIV.	Letter from Mr. Kennett of London	"	496.
	Emerson's Generosity	"	499.
XLV.	Literary Labours	"	501.
	Dr. Alcott['s] residence with me	"	511.
XLVI.	Order of Life	"	513.
	Language	"	521.
[613]	Genealogy	p.	531.
XLVII.	Psyche	"	535.
XLVIII.	Vocabulary	"	543.
	My Birthday anniversary	"	551.

December.

	Idea of Conversations on Self Culture	"	557.
XLIX.	Emersons' Int. Lecture on H. Culture	"	569.
	Conversation with Emerson	"	577.
	Meeting at Fanuel Hall	"	579.
	Emerson's Lecture on the Hand	"	581.
	Russells' do on Tennison	"	581.
L.	Mr. and Miss Fuller	"	582.
	Greene Street School[,] Providence	"	583.
	Generosity	"	585.
	Society	"	587.
[614]	Vision	p.	591.
	Psyche	"	592.
LI.	Emersons' Lecture on the Head	"	593.
	Meeting of Friends of Free Speech	"	593.
	Boston Quarterly Review	"	593.
LII.	Writing Psyche	"	597.
	Visit Rev. Mr. Brownson, Chelsea.	"	597.

NOTES

1. The first part of this edition of Bronson Alcott's "Journal for 1837" is published in STUDIES IN THE AMERICAN RENAISSANCE 1981, pp. 27–132. Short titles are used for primary and secondary sources introduced in PART ONE; likewise, bio-

graphical information about Alcott's contemporaries is not repeated. Alcott's misnumbered lists on the following manuscript pages are not corrected: pp. 406, 410, 422, 427. The following silent emendations for the second part of this edition have been made for clarity:

61.15	treatises]	treastises
63.13	*contemporaneous*]	*contemporaryous*
76.23	of]	of of
77.22	the [376]]	the [376] the
84.2	renewing]	renewening
87.2	may]	may may
89.38	fitting her,]	fitting, her
92.34	prepared]	preapared
95.16	occasion]	occassion
95.38	wield]	weild
97.26	the [443]]	the [443] the
112.20	no]	not
112.30	mock]	mocks
112.32	to]	to to
117.16	at]	it
117.30	imposed]	impossed
124.14	of]	of of
130.4	my]	my my
136.8	to]	to to
141.36	principal]	principlal

Again, page references in the notes are keyed to the pagination of the manuscript journal.

2. Alcott identified the clergyman as Andrews Norton, conservative Unitarian spokesman ("Autobiographical Collection," p. 134).
3. "Autobiographical Collection," pp. 218, 227.
4. "Journal for 1837," p. 376.
5. See May's letter of 7 June 1837 to Alcott (copy, "Autobiography 1834").
6. "Journal for 1836," pp. 187, 189, 208, 233.
7. "Autobiographical Collection," p. 227.
8. "Journal for 1837," p. 438.
9. *JMN*, 5:328.
10. Alcott copied Greaves' letter of 16 September into his "Journal for 1837," pp. 468–84.
11. "Journal for 1837," p. 466.
12. "Journal for 1837," p. 393.
13. "Journal for 1837," p. 396.
14. "Journal for 1837," p. 557.
15. Letter of 28 June 1838 to Alcott (*Letters*, 2:138–41).
16. "School for Moral Culture," *Annals of Education*, 7 (May 1837): 233–34. Alcott fails to mention, however, that in another article in the same issue, "Story Telling in Schools" (217–19), Dr Alcott commends his use of parables as a teaching device. Alcott preserved a copy of his cousin's "measured" review in his "Autobiographical Collection" (p. 128).

17. No notice of the *Conversations* appeared in the July *Christian Examiner*, but an unsigned review was published in the November issue (see pp. 485–88 below).

18. Previously unidentified is the Unitarian minister James Walker (1794–1874), A.M., Harvard, 1817. Pastor of Charlestown from 1818 to 1839, Walker edited the influential *Christian Examiner* from 1831 to 1839. Although Walker was invited to join the Transcendental Club, it is unlikely that he ever attended (Myerson, "A Calendar of Transcendental Club Meetings," 206–207). Walker was later appointed Alford Professor of Natural Religion, Moral Philosophy, and Civil Polity at Harvard, and from 1853 to 1860 served as its president.

19. After "suspicions;—", "vulgar" is crossed out.

20. After "They", "cling more to the bestial, and" is crossed out.

21. Brownson's "Jouffroy's Contributions to Philosophy," *Christian Examiner*, 22 (May 1837): 181–217, complemented his earlier *Examiner* article on Victor Cousin (see note 119 below) and the Eclectics, "Cousin's Philosophy," 21 (September 1836): 32–64. The Eclectics, a group of nineteenth-century French philosophers led by Cousin and his disciple Théodore Jouffroy, believed that the history of philosophy was a synthesis of sensualism, idealism, skepticism, and mysticism. Brownson defended Eclecticism and carefully pointed out its differences from German Transcendentalism, which he felt emphasized idealism to the exclusion of other philosophical views. Alcott disapproved of the "superficial philosophy of France" as he later noted: "French thinking is not American thinking. Eclecticism is not deep enough for us. We ask a philosophy of life. We demand something more than a philosophy of criticism. We need an eye to read the facts of the present moment and in the light of our own life, not in the dim haze of opinions of those who have gone before us" ("Journal for 1838," p. 359). For a discussion of Eclecticism and American Transcendentalism, see Walter L. Leighton, *French Philosophers and New-England Transcendentalism* (Charlottesville: University of Virginia, 1908).

22. Previously unidentified is the Unitarian minister Frederic Henry Hedge (1805–90), A.M., Harvard, 1828, pastor of the Independent Congregational Society in Bangor, Maine, from 1835 to 1850. With Ripley, Emerson, and George Putnam (see note 64), he helped organize the Transcendental Club, known among its members as "Hedge's Club." In later years he edited the *Christian Examiner*, served as president of the American Unitarian Association, translated and promoted the study of German literature, and taught German and theology at Harvard. For further details see Stanley M. Vogel, *German Literary Influences on the American Transcendentalists* (New Haven: Yale University Press, 1955), pp. 113–18.

23. Hedge may in fact have been the author of the review "so severe in spirit" (p. 314 above) that it was withheld. In her letter of 6 April 1837 to Hedge, Margaret Fuller informed him that she had heard that he was "writing a piece to 'cut up Mr. Alcott'" and discouraged him from doing so (MB, Ms. Am. 1450 [79]).

24. In addition to the following five treatises, the second edition of *A Collection of Several Philosophical Writings of Dr. Henry More* (London, 1662) also contains a lengthy preface, a small portion of which Alcott quotes on pp. 323–24 below. (The compilers of the *National Union Catalogue*, 394:226, indicate that the title page of one of the copies of the second edition used to prepare their bibliographical information bears the signature "A. Bronson Alcott." Alcott may have later purchased his own copy or may have been given this one by Walker.) One of the most important figures of a group known as the Cambridge Platonists, the theologian and mystic Henry More (1614–87) wrote numerous polemical works combatting

the atheism and intolerance that he felt were creeping into the Church of England. In 1647 he published *Philosophical Poems,* in which "Psychozoia," a Spenserian allegory of the life of the soul, serves as the first of four parts of *A Platonic Song of the Soul,* an earlier version of which appeared in 1642. In 1668 he published *Divine Dialogues, Containing Sundry Disquisitions & Instructions Concerning the Attributes of God and His Providence in the World.* According to Flora MacKinnon, in her bibliography of More's publications (*Philosophical Writings of Henry More* [New York: Oxford University Press, 1925], pp. 235–45), the Boston Athenæum owned several volumes of More's works, but she does not indicate when they were acquired. The "interesting sketch" is unidentified. "Dr. Henry More's Philosophical Poems," an unsigned review-essay in the *Retrospective Review,* 5 (1822): 223–38, contains "large extracts" of More's poetry. Alcott first read More in the early 1830s while teaching in Philadelphia (*JBA,* p. 136n23). For an important contemporary appraisal of More, see Theodore Par¹·er's review-essay of Richard Ward's *Life of the Learned and Pious Dr. Henry More* (London, 1710) in the *Christian Examiner,* 26 (March 1839): 1–17.

25. Also a Cambridge Platonist, Ralph Cudworth (1617–88) published in 1678 *The True Intellectual System of the Universe, Wherein All the Reason and Philosophy of Atheism Is Confuted.* Because Alcott's reading of More's philosophical works was restricted to the 1662 collection, he did not know that in later years More's attitude toward Descartes had totally changed: the *Enchiridion Metaphysicum* (1671), in fact, was devoted entirely to refuting the Cartesian concepts of natural phenomena and the relationship between matter and space.

26. Stanzas 101–102 of "The Praexistency of the Soul" (1647), which More designated as an "appendix" to "Antipsychopannychia," the third part of *A Platonic Song of the Soul.*

27. "General Preface," pp. vii–viii. The following quotation, also from the "General Preface," p. ix, is More's translation of Aristotle. "Arist. *Moral. Eudem. lib. 7. cap. 14,*" the marginal gloss for the paragraph containing this quotation, indicates that it is from *Ethica Eudemia,* book 7, section 14.

28. Alcott's knowledge of the German Romantic philosophers Friedrich Wilhelm Joseph von Schelling (1775–1854) and Friedrich Heinrich Jacobi (1743–1819) may have been drawn from Sarah Austin's three-volume work on Goethe and his contemporaries, *Characteristics of Goethe* (London, 1833), copies of which were owned by both the Boston Athenæum and Emerson (Cameron, *Emerson the Essayist,* 1:320). Volume 3 contains discussions of both Jacobi and Schelling.

29. In 1835, assessing his "earlier attempts to set forth the principles of human culture," Alcott wrote in his journal: "I was then a disciple of Experience, trying to bring my theories within the Baconian method of induction, and took the philosophy of Aristotle as the exponent of humanity while my heart was even then lingering around the theories of Plato without being conscious of it. A follower of Aristotle was I in theory, yet a true Platonist in practice" (*JBA,* pp. 66–67).

30. Convers Francis (1795–1863), A.M., Harvard, 1818, Unitarian minister of the First Church in Watertown from 1819 to 1842 and thereafter Parkman Professor of Pulpit Eloquence and Pastoral Care at Harvard Divinity School, was a noted scholar of theology and German literature, an active member of the Massachusetts Historical Society, and a contributor to the *Christian Disciple,* the *Christian Examiner,* the *American Monthly Review,* and the *Unitarian Advocate.* Alcott's friendship with Francis began on 19 September 1836, when they met at Ripley's home for

the first real meeting of the Transcendental Club. For further biographical information, see William Newell, "Memoir of the Rev. Convers Francis, D.D.," *Proceedings of the Massachusetts Historical Society,* 8 (March 1865): 233–53, which contains a list of his publications, and Joel Myerson, "Convers Francis and Emerson," *American Literature,* 50 (March 1978): 17–36, which includes extracts from his journal.

31. Anna Quincy Thaxter (1796–1878), a close family friend from Hingham, later arranged for Alcott to hold conversations in her home town. "Of the few persons known to me, there are none of simpler faith, clearer apprehension, or purer charity than this lady" ("Journal for 1836," pp. 107–108). In his letter of 12 September 1836 to Sophia Peabody, Alcott expressed hopes of hiring Miss Thaxter as an assistant in his school to replace Margaret Fuller, who would be "temporary" (*Letters,* pp. 29–30); no evidence exists, however, to indicate that she ever worked for Alcott. A copy of Thaxter's letter of 3 May 1837 to Alcott is preserved in his "Autobiography 1834."

32. On 30 April Emerson exchanged pulpits with Francis, who preached in East Lexington (Myerson, "Convers Francis and Emerson," 24).

33. After "only" Alcott had written but failed to cancel "person" after writing "individual" above it.

34. This paragraph appears in somewhat different form in "Psyche" (2), pp. 259–60.

35. After "juncture", "of my affairs," is crossed out.

36. Alcott's decision not to deliver the forthcoming dedicatory address at his disciple's school was, as he explains below, a difficult one, for he had been working on the speech since the fall of 1836 when Fuller first asked him to give it ("Journal for 1836," pp. 187, 189, 208, 233). Emerson did substitute for Alcott on 10 June but apparently with some reluctance (see note 39 below). Fuller received Alcott's decision several weeks earlier and was relieved that Alcott had declined the invitation: in his letter of 17 April 1837 to Emerson, Fuller wrote, "Mr. Alcott from the best motives declines to act with us on the occasion. It would not do at present to identify the school with him—nor with any religious sect—So long as I have any thing to do with it, it must be free" (MH, bMS Am 1280 [1158]).

37. After "is" Alcott had written "the product of my Idea. It is formed on its model.". He crossed out "the product of my Idea. It is" and "its" and then added "the" and "of mine".

38. From 1837 to 1866 the philanthropist and Unitarian minister Charles Francis Barnard (1808–84), A.M., Harvard, 1831, served as pastor of the Warren Street Chapel, an engraving of which has been pasted in at the top of the page. Known as "the children's church," it was established to provide religious and secular training for disadvantaged children. Barnard's role in the project is discussed by Cyrus A. Bartol, "Ministry for the Poor," *Christian Examiner,* 21 (January 1837): 335–54. The only full-length study of Barnard is Francis Tiffany's *Charles Francis Barnard: A Sketch of His Life and Work* (Boston: Houghton Mifflin, 1895).

39. In his letter of 9 May to Emerson, Alcott also suggested that the Transcendental Club meet soon (for details of the 29 May meeting, see pp. 381–82 below) and noted that in a recent letter Hiram Fuller expressed "deep disappointment" with Emerson's apparent lack of commitment to deliver the dedicatory address at Fuller's new school in Providence in June (*Letters,* pp. 32–33). Emerson did deliver the address but appears to have stipulated some conditions for doing so that Fuller seems to have overlooked. For some evidence of the misunderstanding between Hiram Fuller and Emerson, see Emerson's letter of 19 April 1837 to

Margaret Fuller (*Letters*, 2:70). Alcott's account of next week's meeting with Emerson is preserved on pp. 367–70 below.

40. In his 7 May letter to Chatfield (1801–?), who moved from Connecticut to the Utica, New York, area in the 1820s, Alcott discussed the hostile reaction to the *Conversations* (copy, Alcott, "Memoir 1878," MH *59M–306 [23]). The letter to Alcott from his mother, Anna (1773–1863), probably confirmed her forthcoming trip to Boston (see p. 426 below).

41. Alcott copied part of Furness' letter into his journal on pp. 350–52 below.

42. Before helping to organize the Temple School and assisting Alcott in its operation from 1834 to 1836, Elizabeth Palmer Peabody (1804–94) taught at several private schools, studied Greek under Emerson, and for nine years served as amanuensis for Dr. Channing. While at the Temple School, she taught Latin, arithmetic, and geometry; in addition, she transcribed Alcott's conversations with his pupils, the early experiments with which she published in *Record of a School* (1835). She also recorded most of the discussions of the life of Christ that made up both volumes of *Conversations with Children on the Gospels* (1836–37). For a short while she lived with the Alcotts, probably as a form of compensation for her services. Her resignation from the Temple School in the summer of 1836 probably resulted from Alcott's continual failure to pay her, her ambition to start her own school, and her unwillingness to be associated with what she correctly surmised would be the scandal that developed over the *Conversations* and Alcott's teaching methods. After leaving Alcott's school she promoted the kindergarten movement, ran the successful West Street Bookstore, published the *Dial* for a short time, occasionally attended the meetings of the Transcendental Club, and during the 1880s became a member of Alcott's Concord School of Philosophy. Alcott and Peabody remained close friends, although after her resignation he changed the middle name of his third daughter, Elizabeth Peabody Alcott, to Sewall.

43. Alcott copied part of Emerson's letter into his journal on pp. 355–56 below.

44. After graduating from Harvard Divinity School in 1828, George Partridge Bradford (1807–90), Emerson's close friend, spent most of his life teaching. He occasionally attended the meetings of the Transcendental Club and later taught literature at Brook Farm. Mr. Smalley is unidentified.

45. In his 5 May letter to Alcott, Furness also mentioned that his wife had read the *Conversations* with "great interest" and "with a loving mind, fearing no heresy in you" (original letter, "Autobiographical Collection," p. 154).

46. This and the preceding sentence appear in slightly different form in "Psyche" (2), p. 244.

47. Because of a hole in this leaf the letters "go" are missing from "ago" on p. 355 and "ec" from "intellectual" on p. 356.

48. Wordsworth, *The Excursion*, Bk. 1, 1. 89.

49. In his 10 May letter Emerson, who had not received Alcott's letter of 9 May, also reminded Alcott of his "promise" to spend a few days in Concord (*Letters*, 2:74–75).

50. Buckingham's "Alcott's Conversations on the Gospels," *Boston Courier*, 9 May, p. 2, was written in response to an advertisement for the *Conversations* printed in the *Christian Register*, 6 May, p. 3, which contained a portion of Emerson's letter in the 4 April *Courier* and which gave as the source of the quotation not "R." (or Emerson) but the *Courier* itself. Fearing that the public would infer from the advertisement that he now endorsed the book, Buckingham pointed out that he

had introduced the 4 April letter with "an absolute disclaimer of the sentiments of the writer" and further added, lest there be any doubt about his position, that "the 'Conversations on the Gospels' is a more indecent and obscene book, (we say nothing of its absurdity) than any other one we ever saw exposed for sale on a bookseller's counter." He concluded his remarks by reporting another person's opinion: "We are told that a clergyman,—living at no great distance from Boston—when asked his opinion of the 'Conversations on the Gospels,' said, *one third was absurd, one third was blasphemous, and one third obscene.* And such, we apprehend, will be the deliberate opinion of those who diligently read and soberly reflect." For Alcott's identification of this clergyman as Andrew Norton, see note 51 below.

51. Once pasted in on p. 359, the review has since been removed. At the top of the page Alcott wrote "Transferred to 'Aut[obiographical] Coll[ection],'" where it appears on p. 134. Beneath the paragraph containing the remarks of the clergyman, Alcott wrote "Andrews Norton, D.D."

52. Originally published in 1653 and later included in his *Collection of Several Philosophical Writings*, More's *Conjectura Cabbalistica* is an explanation and defense of the Cabbala (Kabbala), a system of mystical Jewish thought believed to have been derived from Moses.

53. The terms "fancy" and "imagination," designating the mechanical and creative powers of the mind respectively, come from Coleridge's *Biographia Literaria* (1817), which Alcott first read in 1833 while teaching in Philadelphia.

54. While residing in Philadelphia Alcott first became acquainted with the works of the influential Swedish scientist, theologian, and philosopher Emanuel Swedenborg (1688–1772). Among the most important discussions of Swedenborg by the Transcendentalists are Sampson Reed, *Observations on the Growth of the Mind* (1826); F. H. Hedge, "Emanuel Swedenborg," *Christian Examiner*, 15 (November 1833): 193–218; and Emerson, "Swedenborg; or The Mystic," in *Representative Men* (1850), which explains Swedenborg's doctrine of "correspondence" between the material and spiritual worlds.

55. Cf. John 7:17.

56. The liberal politician and diplomat Sir Thomas Wyse (1791–1862) helped establish a system of national education in Ireland and was instrumental in founding England's Central Society of Education. A second volume of *Education Reform: or, The Necessity of a National System of Education* (London, 1836) was never published.

57. Basedow's followers, known as "philanthropists," were trained at his *Philanthropinum*, a model school that he established at Desau in 1774.

58. After Alcott left, Emerson, who had been suffering from a bad cold, noted in his journal: "Yet could I see plainly that I conversed with the most extraordinary man and the highest genius of the time. He is a Man. He is erect: he sees: let who ever be overthrown or parasitic or blind. . . . Wonderful is his vision. The steadiness & scope of his eye at once rebukes all before it, and we little men creep about ashamed" (*JMN*, 5:328).

59. After *"eye;"* Alcott erased "but not" and then substituted "more than"; in the same sentence, after *"intellect,"*, Alcott erased "not" and then substituted "more than".

60. In his review of the second volume of the *Conversations*, "Mr. Alcott's Book and the Objections Made to It," *Western Messenger*, 3 (May 1837): 678–83, Clarke stated that despite any shortcomings in Alcott's writings and teaching prac-

tices, "we maintain him to be a prophet." (A copy of Clarke's review is preserved in Alcott's "Autobiographical Collection," pp. 137–39.) Clarke's ironic suggestion in the same issue of the *Messenger*, pp. 715–16, that Alcott be charged like Socrates was a response to Buckingham's editorial comment in the 29 March *Courier*; Alcott preserved a copy of this ironic suggestion in his "Autobiographical Collection," p. 132.

61. Alcott's phrasing in his original sentence, "Indeed it may much be more than 10 or 15.", is obviously in error and has been emended. During the summer quarter, which ran until 29 July, only eleven students (one nonpaying) enrolled in Alcott's school ("Autobiographical Collection," p. 227).

62. A reference to the Panic of 1837, a severe economic depression that began in early May with the closing of many of the nation's banks as a result of the failure of the land boom. For background see Samuel Reznek, "The Social History of an American Depression, 1837–1842," *American Historical Review*, 40 (July 1935): 662–87, and William Charvat, "American Romanticism and the Depression of 1837," *Science and Society*, 2 (Winter 1937): 67–82.

63. In his 24 May letter to Emerson, Alcott also mentioned his "agreeable evening" with Convers Francis during the previous week and his resolution to continue teaching even though enrollment in his school had dropped considerably (*Letters*, p. 33).

64. Previously unidentified are Caleb Stetson (1793–1870), Theodore Parker (1810–60), and George Putnam (1807–78). Stetson, Emerson's classmate at Harvard, was minister at Medford from 1827 to 1848. Parker, who would be ordained on 21 June at West Roxbury, later became a noted scholar and abolitionist, his most important works including *The Transient and Permanent in Christianity* (1841), *A Discourse of Matters Pertaining to Religion* (1842), and his translation of De Wette's *Einleitung* (1843). Putnam, later the editor of the *Christian Examiner*, was then minister of the First Church at Roxbury. Obviously added after the 29 May meeting, "he never came" is written in a blank space that shows no signs of erasure. As Odell Shepard speculates, Alcott is probably referring to Dr. Channing (*JBA*, p. 92). Because Emerson's and Francis' journal records of the people who were present match exactly, Myerson believes that Clarke, Furness, Parker, and Robbins did not attend this meeting; Samuel Osgood (1812–80), who graduated from Harvard Divinity School in 1835, was also present (Myerson, "A Calendar of Transcendental Club Meetings," 201).

65. This appears to be the first of several occasions that Fuller borrowed Alcott's journals. After giving her the first 170 pages of his 1838 journal, Alcott explained why he found the practice so valuable: "I hand her these sheets; which, more than any other means, shall best apprize of the intents of her friend. It is the best substitute for epistolary correspondence—a mode of communication to which I am not sufficiently given; but which I deem most happily suited as a means of self-culture" ("Journal for 1838," pp. 175–76). Fuller also read Alcott's journal entries for the first seven months of 1839 (*JBA*, p. 136).

66. In her 18 May letter Fuller also agreed to correspond with Alcott, who apparently had written since her removal to Groton, and noted that his letters would be "very valuable" (MH *59M–312 [121]; a copy exists at MB, Ms. Am. 1450 [180]).

67. Fuller's translation of Schiller's "Licht und Wärme" was one of many translations that she did of German writers, her most important being that of Eckermann's *Conversations with Goethe* (1839). For further details, see Pochmann,

German Culture in America, pp. 440–47, and Vogel, *German Literary Influences on the American Transcendentalists*, pp. 126–43.

68. Fuller worked at the Greene Street School from its opening on 10 June 1837 until December 1838, when she returned to Groton, apparently dissatisfied with teaching.

69. This letter is printed in Wagner, "Eighty-Six Letters (1814–1882) of A. Bronson Alcott (Part One)," pp. 300–301.

70. For Alcott's interest in the importance of maternal influence on the development of children, see his three articles on the subject: "Maternal Instruction," *Unitarian Advocate*, 1 (1828): 304–308; "Maternal Instruction, Being a Review of *Hints to Parents*," *American Journal of Education*, 4 (January 1829): 53–58; "Maternal Influence," *Annals of Education*, 3 (January 1833): 16–24.

71. Of Alcott's friends only Emerson seems to have examined "Psyche" carefully. Alcott first gave "Psyche," then called "The Breath of Childhood," to Emerson on 1 February 1836 ("Journal for 1836," pp. 21–22). Emerson copied several passages from it into his journal (*JMN*, 5:122–23) and in his letter of 27 February 1836 to Alcott called it "original and vital in all its parts," noted that its major problem was "want of compression," and provided detailed suggestions for improvement (*Letters*, 2:4–6). Alcott gave "Psyche" to Emerson for a second reading, presumably with corrections, on 2 August 1836 ("Journal for 1836," p. 141). On 11 September 1836 Alcott noted in his journal after reading Emerson's recently published *Nature* that "Mr. E. adverts, indirectly, to my 'Psyche' (now in his hands) in the work" ("Journal for 1836," p. 188). (For the possible identification of Alcott as Emerson's "orphic poet," see Cameron, *Emerson the Essayist*, 1:325–28, 361–62.) After Emerson returned the manuscript in December 1836, Alcott mentioned in his journal that it also contained the "criticism of a female," whom he later identified at the bottom of the page as "Elizabeth Hoar," who had been engaged to Emerson's brother Charles before his death in May 1836. Alcott further noted that both Emerson and his friend "urge its publication," and that if Orestes Brownson and his wife, who now had "Psyche," both approved of it, he would publish it after completing the second volume of the *Conversations* ("Journal for 1836," pp. 237–38). For Emerson's final comments on "Psyche" and his promise to oversee its publication, see note 136 below. Sophia Peabody may also have read "Psyche"; see Alcott's letter of 23 August 1836 to her (*Letters*, pp. 28–29).

72. Cf. Joel 2:12–27.

73. The passage "what's o clock . . . to the inward" appears in slightly different form in "Psyche" (2), pp. 222–24.

74. For a complete list of meetings held in Boston during the 1837 "Anniversary Week," an annual convention time for Unitarian-sponsored societies, see the *Christian Register*, 27 May, p. 3.

75. The Transcendental Club did hold its next meeting in Concord, at Emerson's house, but not until 1 September (see pp. 438–39 below).

76. Founder of the Perkins Institution for the Blind, the noted humanitarian and teacher Samuel Gridley Howe (1801–76), who married the abolitionist Julia Ward in 1843, dedicated his life to helping the blind, deaf, and mentally handicapped. The following quotation is taken from Howe's *Discourse on the Social Relations of Man* (Boston: Marsh, Capen & Lyon, 1837), p. 24. According to the title page, the lecture was "delivered before the Boston Phrenological Society, at the close of their lectures," presumably during late winter or spring of 1837.

77. Directly above "casuality" Alcott wrote the same word.

78. That is, the Transcendental Club meeting that took place on Monday, 29 May, which Alcott mentions on pp. 381 and 406. Myerson, however, apparently relying on only the misleading monthly date "June" at the top of pp. 406 and 409 and failing to consider that pp. 401–10 cover the events of Week XXII (28 May–3 June) incorrectly concludes that this meeting was later than, and thus different from, the one on 29 May ("A Calendar of Transcendental Club Meetings," 201).

79. Irregularities exist with the running dates at the top of pp. 412–14: on p. 412 "June" has been written through what appears to be a partially erased "Psyche"; on p. 414 "June" has been written through what seems to be "July"; the running weekly dates on pp. 413 and 414 are incorrectly designated "Week XXI."

80. Abigail May Alcott (1800–1877), whose ancestors included the Sewalls and the Quincys, had been raised in a comfortable Boston household and was unaccustomed, as Alcott indicates, to the rigors of managing a family with a small income. Abba's brother, the Reverend Samuel J. May of Scituate, whom she occasionally visited and often turned to for advice, not only provided spiritual support for her and Bronson but on at least one occasion, in 1850, during another financial crisis, gave them money to pay house rent (*JBA*, p. 230). For further details about Abba, see Sandford Salyer, *Marmee: The Mother of Little Women* (Norman: University of Oklahoma Press, 1949).

81. Mrs. Alcott had just suffered a miscarriage; cf. her being "indisposed" on p. 412 above. This letter is printed in Wagner, "Eighty-Six Letters (1814–1882) of A. Bronson Alcott (Part One)," pp. 301–302.

82. Cf. 1 Kings 8:12.

83. Cf. 1 Corinthians 13:9–12.

84. Cf. Matthew 13:11, Mark 4:11, Luke 8:10.

85. The passage "The Allwise Desposer . . . who distrust not" appears in somewhat different form in "Psyche" (2), pp. 323–25.

86. In his letter of 6 June to Emerson, Alcott, apparently assuming that Abba would return before Saturday, indicated that he planned to accompany Emerson to Providence. Alcott also mentioned that he "wasted last week foolishly, and scandalously, at these glorifying and glorified anniversaries" (*Letters*, pp. 33–34).

87. After "uphold", "and revere," is crossed out.

88. Apparently Alcott was not yet accustomed to his new quarters in Room 3 of the Masonic Temple.

89. Indeed it had been "a most busy and full week," more so than Alcott reveals in his journal: Alcott had apparently considered quitting his school and moving his family to Scituate. In his letter of 7 June 1837 to Alcott, Samuel J. May indicated that he was looking for places for them to live (copy, "Autobiography 1834").

90. For the text of Emerson's 10 June "Address at Providence," which he did not publish, see *Early Lectures*, 2:189–204.

91. James D. Knowles (1798–1838), president of the Newton Theological Institution, a Baptist seminary, founded the quarterly *Christian Review* in 1836 and edited it until his death. In his review of the *Conversations*, published in the *Christian Review*, 2 (June 1837): 305–307, Knowles attacked Alcott's responses to his pupils for being "too mystical" and pointed out that some topics, notably the discussions of birth, were "improper."

92. After "wanting" Alcott had written "& rotten.", crossed it out, and then inserted a period after "wanting".

93. Alcott's "Psychological Journals" and "Journals of Children," which he mentions on pp. 431 and 461, are probably references to his manuscript collection "Observations on Childhood" (MH *59M–306 [1], [2], [3]), which he began immediately after the birth of Anna in 1831 and which constitute an earlier version of "Psyche."

94. Each of the running monthly dates ("July") on pp. 432–36 appears to have been written through some other word: on p. 432, through what seems to be a partially erased "Psyche"; on pp. 433–36, through what may be "June."

95. "Agatha" was apparently Alcott's favorite name for his youngest daughter, Elizabeth (see "Psyche" [2], pp. 167, 171, 185).

96. "I could not have imagined that those conversations about *Birth* which I recorded," wrote Sophia Peabody in her 9 June letter, "would not be received with reverence and thanks, by all who might have the privilege of either hearing or reading them. . . . Elizabeth [Peabody], also, feels the absurdity of the kind of fault-finding there has been,—it is only that the community have not yet arrived at a state pure enough to comprehend the essence of things." Sophia concluded her letter by expressing regret that Alcott had been forced to sell his "choice and beautiful library" but happily noted that his copy of *Biographia Literaria*, which she had borrowed and was about to return, was saved from the "general wreck" (Sanborn and Harris, *Alcott*, 1:222–24).

97. In her 27 June letter, Margaret Fuller also expressed regret that Alcott did not attend the dedication of Hiram Fuller's Greene Street School on 10 June, and she reminded Alcott that he had not, as promised, written to her (MH *59M–312 [122]; copies exist at MB, Ms. Am. 1450 [16], [181]). Fuller's "similar word" to Emerson is her letter of 6 June (MH bMS Am 1280 [2338]; copies exist at MB, Ms. Am. 1450 [19], [66]).

98. Sponsored by the Boston Female Anti-Slavery Society, the abolitionists and women's rights advocates Angelina Emily Grimké (1805–79) and her sister Sarah Moore Grimké (1792–1873) gave numerous public lectures in New England during the summer of 1837 as part of the American Anti-Slavery Society's efforts to submit petitions to state legislatures. Among other places during the last two weeks of June, they spoke at Roxbury, Weymouth, the Methodist Church on Boston's Church Street, and Lynn (Gerda Lerner, *The Grimké Sisters from South Carolina* [Boston: Houghton Mifflin, 1967], pp. 168–69).

99. See notes 101 and 103 below for an explanation of Alcott's dating errors and my procedure for correcting them.

100. Probable dates for Alcott's illness and subsequent visits are as follows: a letter to Emerson dated 25 July from Cottage Place mentioning that he was "just up from a severe indisposition" (*Letters*, pp. 34–35) confirms the termination of Alcott's sickness. Between 26 July and 28 July, the date of a letter he wrote to Abba from Scituate (printed in Sanborn and Harris, *Alcott*, 1:230–31), he arrived at his brother-in-law Samuel J. May's house to recuperate. In the same letter he mentioned that he hoped to return to "the cottage by Friday or Saturday of next week [4 or 5 August] at farthest." (If, however, he did stay a full "fortnight" at May's he would not have returned home until sometime between 9 and 11 August.) On 12 or 13 August he went to Concord to visit Emerson, who noted

in a journal entry for 17 August: "This morng. Mr Alcott & Mr Hedge left me. Four or five days full of discourse & much was seen" (*JMN*, 5:362–63). Unless he visited Hingham with his mother after returning from Concord, he remained with his family until going to Worcester to attend the annual convention of the American Institute of Instruction, 24–29 August, where he probably met his old friend William Russell. Alcott's 28 July letter from Scituate indicates that he planned to visit friends in Hingham on his return trip to Boston, but it could not have been with his mother, who according to the letter was staying with Abba and the children at Cottage Place. His visit to Hingham with his mother more than likely occurred between 6 and 11 August or between 18 and 23 August, the only substantial stretches of time available between his recuperation in late July and his attending the Friday, 1 September, meeting of the Transcendental Club (see note 101 below) and the opening of his school on the following Monday, 4 September. Two important omissions remain: Alcott fails to indicate who substituted for him at the Temple School during his illness; and he does not mention that he attended Emerson's Phi Beta Kappa address ("The American Scholar") at Harvard on 31 August, which he later recalled as having created in the audience feelings of "mixed confusion, consternation, surprise and wonder" ("The Transcendental Club and the Dial," 1).

101. After "the" Alcott had written "individuals composing it."; he crossed out "composing it.", erased the "s" on "individuals", and then added a period. The Transcendental Club met at Emerson's on 1 September (*JMN*, 5:373) and at Clarke's on 6 September (*JMN*, 5:375). Because pp. 437–40 of the journal were written (more than likely at one sitting in late September) as a summary of events for July, August, and September, the two meetings that Alcott mentions are unquestionably the same that Emerson reports. Myerson, "A Calendar of Transcendental Club Meetings," pp. 201–202, however, apparently relying on only the running dates at the top of pp. 438–39, which Alcott mistakenly wrote as "July, August" and "Weeks XXVII–XXXIV [2 July–26 August]," and failing to consider that pp. 437–40 cover events through September (the running dates "September" and "Weeks XXXV–XXXVIII [27 August–23 September]" appear at the top of p. 440), incorrectly concludes that the two meetings Alcott records (listed in the "Calendar" as numbers 8 and 9) were earlier than, and thus different from, those reported by Emerson (numbers 10 and 11). For a list of others who attended these meetings ("&c"), including Margaret Fuller and Elizabeth Palmer Peabody, see Myerson's entries under numbers 10 and 11 but note, because of Myerson's error, Parker is not included as a participant in either meeting. Putnam and Robbins did attend the meeting at Emerson's but probably not the one at Clarke's.

102. Alcott's error: Monday was 4 September. Alcott again placed an advertisement for his school in the *Christian Register* (2 September, p. 3) and copied it into his "Autobiographical Collection," p. 168.

103. On p. 611 below, under "Items of the Year," Alcott dated the section on "Fortunes," pp. 442–45, as "Week XL [1–7 October]" and the preceding material, pp. 437–40, as "Weeks XXVII–XL [2 July–7 October]." More than likely, however, pp. 437–40 were intended to carry the journal through Week XXXIX (24–30 September) because combined internal evidence on pp. 442–590 indicates that the dates introducing Weeks XXXIX–XLIX are exactly one week behind the actual ones. This discrepancy also explains the absence of a "Week L": Alcott's numbers

jump from "Week XLIX," p. 581, to "Week LI," p. 591. Although p. 442 is dated "Week XXXIX," Alcott did note a different month, "October," indicating that this section was probably composed during the first week of October. Under "Items of the Year" Alcott entered the correct dates for the material covered on pp. 442–590 but did not go back and revise the dates in the journal proper. On the basis of internal evidence, I have corrected Alcott's dates by bracketing the actual week numbers and days on pp. 437, 442, 446, 454, 464, 495, 501, 513, 531, 543, 557, and 581.

104. As a result of decreased enrollment in his school, Alcott was experiencing severe financial difficulties. In his letter of 6 October 1837 to Emerson, Alcott asked Emerson to pay in advance the tuition bill for Hillman Sampson, the son of a late friend of Emerson. Alcott hoped that Emerson would understand that his "needs, (which now stare me in the face somewhat more grimly than in times past) will be my excuse for troubling you with such intrusion, in advance" (*Letters*, p. 36).

105. After "*Fire*" Alcott crossed out "blazeth" and wrote "smouldereth" above it.

106. After "some", "from world-holder," is crossed out; in the same sentence, after "hand", "to thy fire" is crossed out.

107. This and the two preceding paragraphs appear in slightly different form in Alcott's letter of 9 October 1837 to Emerson. Alcott began his letter by thanking Emerson for his recent "favour," presumably the advance payment of Hillman's tuition: "Amidst my present fortunes it was quite a favour and bestowed in needful season" (*Letters*, pp. 36–37). Odell Shepard rightly observes that the passage on pp. 442–445 is "one of several in the Journal of 1837 that show the effects of a reading of *Sartor Resartus*" (*JBA*, p. 92n9).

108. Alcott first thought of writing "The Cross; or the Doctrine and Duty of Sacrifice," using as his text Matthew 10:38, in August 1836 ("Journal for 1836," p. 174).

109. After "sordid", "fancies or" is crossed out.

110. After "this,", "with her attendants of wisdom" is crossed out.

111. An echo of Matthew 5:48.

112. After "the", "Eternal–thou" is crossed out.

113. The first of many editions of *Frank*, a children's story, was published by the popular English novelist Maria Edgeworth (1767–1849) in 1801. Dr. Thomas Hopkins Gallaudet (1787–1851), pioneer educator of the deaf, published a number of primers, including *The Child's Picture Defining and Reading Book* (1830), *The Child's Book on the Soul* (1831), and *The Class-Book of Natural Theology* (1835).

114. None of the following manuscripts was ever published. Alcott's lifelong interest in allegory began in his youth when he first read Bunyan's *Divine Emblems* and *The Pilgrim's Progress*. Of the latter he once noted: "The book was, indeed, my dictionary. By it I learned the English tongue" (*JBA*, p. 111). During the previous year he wrote a preface and "Key to the Emblems" for Sarah Austin's translation of Friedrich Carové's *Story Without an End* (Boston: Joseph H. Francis, 1836); and he often read selections to his pupils from such allegorical works as Spenser's *Faerie Queen* and Krummacher's *Parabelin* (1805). For the final disposition of "Psyche" see note 136 below.

115. Probably "Observations on Childhood" (see note 93 above).

116. Alcott's long friendship with the abolitionist and reformer William Lloyd

Garrison (1805–79) began in 1830 when he, Garrison, and others met in Boston to establish the Preliminary Anti-Slavery Society, afterwards known as the New England Anti-Slavery Society.

117. After "evils", "and interests" is crossed out; in the same sentence, after "every", Alcott crossed out "such hindrance," and substituted "abuse and usage;".

118. The English Transcendentalist and reformer James Pierrepont Greaves (1777–1842), a copy of whose letter appears below, was a friend and noted disciple of Pestalozzi. During the 1820s Greaves served as secretary of the London Infant School Society; and in 1840, very much influenced by Alcott, he established near London the Alcott House, a school based on Alcott's theories and practices. This passage seems to indicate that Alcott forgot that he had read Greaves' Pestalozzian pamphlet *Exposition of the Principles of Conducting Infant Education* in 1828 (Shepard, *Pedlar's Progress*, pp. 84–85). Important contemporary discussions of Greaves include Ralph Waldo Emerson, "English Reformers," *Dial*, 3 (October 1842): 227–47, and Charles Lane, "James Pierrepont Greaves," *Dial*, 3 (October 1842, January 1843): 247–55, 281–96.

119. Previously unidentified are Victor Cousin (1792–1867) and Nicolaus Heinrich Julius (1783–1862). Though best known as the leader of the French Eclectic school of philosophy, Cousin was also an important educational reformer, serving in 1840 as the Minister of Education. His "Report on the Condition of Public Instruction in Germany, and Particularly in Prussia" (1831) eventually resulted in the complete reorganization of French schools from the elementary through the university levels. The innovative Prussian educator and reformer Dr. Julius had earlier visited the Temple School while touring America. After receiving a letter from Julius expressing an interest to be kept apprised of the Temple School, Alcott noted in a journal entry for 12 February 1836 that "Dr. J. is from a country where Education is made a popular branch of government, and is, of all men visiting us, best acquainted, perhaps, with the theory and practice of education. I take his interest as so much testimony in favor of my views and practice" ("Journal for 1836," p. 41). As late as February 1838, Alcott still had not written to Julius ("Journal for 1838," p. 121), probably because of the embarrassment caused by the hostile reactions to the *Conversations* and the Temple School.

120. After "culture" Alcott had written "in a higher state of improvement"; he crossed out "higher state of improvement" and substituted "subject of deep study" but failed to emend "in" to "is". This emendation has been made.

121. After "stated", "and based on the grounds of the soul" is crossed out.

122. The popular English author and reformer Harriet Martineau (1802–76), who visited Alcott's school in December 1835, gave a copy of *Record of a School* to her friend Greaves when she returned to London after a tour of America. Unlike Greaves, Martineau disapproved of Alcott's educational philosophy: "His system can be beneficial to none, and must be ruinous to many" (*Society in America* [London: Saunders and Otley, 1837], 2:278).

123. Because of declining health Greaves never did make a trip to see Alcott, although he did book passage to America in 1838 (Shepard, *Pedlar's Progress*, p. 329). Greaves died several months before Alcott's visit to England in 1842.

124. That is, Elizabeth Palmer Peabody, author of *Record of a School*. Alcott did give Greaves' letter to Peabody, who returned it with her letter of 22 December 1837. Peabody informed Alcott that her New York cousin Mr. Putnam could arrange to have fifty copies of *Record of a School* sent to any London publisher

(copy, "Autobiography 1834"). For details concerning Alcott's response to Greaves, see note 130 below.

125. In his article "A. Bronson Alcott's Works," *Dial*, 3 (April 1843): 417–54, Charles Lane, co-founder of the Fruitlands community, published Greaves' letter, which Alcott had apparently lent him. A copy of this printed version, excluding the twenty-two "Observations," is preserved in Alcott's "Autobiographical Collection," pp. 169–70.

126. "Alcott's *Conversations on the Gospels*," *Christian Examiner*, 23 (November 1837): 252–61, is unsigned. Alcott may have received an advance copy from his friend James Walker, editor of the *Examiner*, who had earlier promised to publish a review of the *Conversations* by a "gentleman, inclining to spiritualism" (see p. 319 above).

127. The material on pp. 490–94 appears in somewhat different form in "Psyche" (2), pp. 313–18.

128. Selections from the *Letters of Pestalozzi on the Education of Infancy* (Boston: Carter and Hendee, 1830) appeared earlier in the *American Journal of Education*, 4 (1829): 418–32, 548–55; the translator is unidentified.

129. In 1823 John Griscom (1774–1852), teacher and humanitarian, published *A Year in Europe*, an account of his tour of Great Britain and the Continent in 1818–19. Alcott read *Monitorial Instruction* (1825), one of Griscom's most influential Pestalozzian textbooks, shortly after its publication (McCuskey, *Alcott*, p. 185).

130. Because of his despair over the failure of the Temple School, Alcott did not write to Greaves until 26 April 1839 (Wagner, "Eighty-Six Letters [1814–1882] of A. Bronson Alcott [Part One]," pp. 304–306). Between September 1837 and April 1839, Alcott received further letters from Greaves; and in October 1838, William Oldham, acting on behalf of Greaves, sent several books to Alcott, including Greaves' *Three Hundred Maxims for the Consideration of Parents* (1827). Alcott did arrange with his publisher, James Munroe, to have a dozen copies of the *Conversations* sent to Greaves in the fall of 1837 but, as time passed, felt guilty that he had not written to Greaves ("Journal for 1838," pp. 119–21, 337–40).

131. After "the" Alcott crossed out "eve" and substitued "morn".

132. To prevent a possible misreading I have substituted a period for the comma that was placed between "more" and "I".

133. Although Alcott did have his publisher, James Munroe, send a dozen copies of the *Conversations* in the fall of 1837, Alcott himself did not write to Kennett, a London bookseller, until 26 April 1839. In his letter Alcott inquired about the possibility of having the *Conversations* or *Record of a School* republished in England, and asked Kennett to forward some books to Greaves and John Heraud (1799–1887), editor of the *Monthly Magazine*. The books included works by Alcott, Emerson, and Orestes Brownson (Wagner, "Eighty-Six Letters [1814–1882] of A. Bronson Alcott [Part One]," pp. 303–304).

134. Alcott had originally written what appears to be "one edition of 500" or "one edition of 700"; he crossed out "one", added "½ of a", and then wrote "10" through the first digit of the original number. According to Alcott's journal entry for 22 September 1836, one thousand copies of the *Conversations* were to have been printed ("Journal for 1836," p. 205); probably the same number of copies was printed for the first edition of *Record of a School* (Boston: James Munroe, 1835). The second edition of *Record of a School* (Boston: Russell, Shattuck, 1836) added, among other things, extracts from his students' journals. The five hundred

copies of the *Conversations* that remained unsold by 1841 were sold to trunk-makers at five cents a pound (Shepard, *Pedlar's Progress,* p. 295).

135. In 1836, at the suggestion of Le Baron Russell, a recent Harvard graduate, Emerson wrote a preface, albeit unsigned, to the first American edition of *Sartor Resartus,* which was reprinted from *Fraser's Magazine* (1833–34) and published in Boston by James Munroe. With Emerson overseeing production, the Boston firm of Charles C. Little and James Brown published Carlyle's *French Revolution* in late December 1837. Emerson's role in the publication of *Sartor Resartus* and *The French Revolution* is discussed by Joseph Slater in his edition of *The Correspondence of Emerson and Carlyle* (New York: Columbia University Press, 1964), pp. 16–21. The history of Carlyle's reputation in America is traced by Frank Luther Mott, "Carlyle's American Public," *Philological Quarterly,* 4 (July 1925): 245–64.

136. In late February 1838, with Carlyle's *The French Revolution* selling well, Emerson again offered to publish "Psyche" at "his own risk" ("Journal for 1838," p. 149). After spending the next few months revising the manuscript, Alcott gave it to Emerson for a final reading in June ("Journal for 1838," p. 257). But in his letter of 28 June 1838 to Alcott, Emerson advised, tactfully and painfully, against publication. He pointed out that, notwithstanding the book's "affirmation of the spiritual nature to an unbelieving age," it suffers "from a want of unity of design." Emerson did indicate, however, that if Alcott still wanted it published he would, as promised, make the arrangements (*Letters,* 2:138–41). Alcott preserved Emerson's letter and attached editorial comments in his "Autobiographical Collection," pp. 181–85, and noted in his journal: "I judge the counsel wise. And feel inclined, at present, to lay it aside, giving myself, the rather, to action, whereby I shall chance to ripen my faculties, and enrich my genius, for worthier composition, at some future day" ("Journal for 1838," p. 266). "Psyche" was never published. For further evidence of the difficulty of Emerson's decision see his letter of 28 June 1838 to Margaret Fuller (*Letters,* 2:142–43).

137. After "faith" Alcott crossed out "of his soul"; in the same sentence, after "his", Alcott crossed out "soul." and substituted "intellect.".

138. After "no" Alcott had originally written "Christian, whatsoever his profession, how specious soever his[?] creed[?], who denies . . ."; he added "wise" above "no Christian,", crossed out "whatsoever his profession, how specious soever his[?] creed[?]," and "denies", and then sustituted "belies" for "denies".

139. When Dr. Alcott and his wife finally left in March 1838, Bronson again remarked how far apart he and his cousin had grown but added that "this sundering of early associations is purely intellectual" ("Journal for 1838," p. 181).

140. Dr. Alcott's successful monthly *Library of Health, and Teacher on the Human Constitution* (1837–42) advocated vegetarianism.

141. After "not" Alcott crossed out "come to pass." and substituted "begin.".

142. Alcott's school accounts indicate that by the end of fall quarter, 25 November, only ten students were attending the Temple School: the initial six at $25 per term and four apparent latecomers, two at $10 and two at $12. Alcott fell far short of his projected $1,000 because of continuing problems with enrollment. His receipts for the 1837–38 academic year total only $549 ("Autobiographical Collection," pp. 227–28).

143. Elizabeth was actually two: her third birthday did not occur until 24 June 1838.

144. Located on Tremont Street, the Masonic Temple faced Boston Common.

145. After "English." Alcott had originally written "It is better than Johnson's Dictionary, as a study of our language."; he substituted "discipline in" for "study of" and then crossed out the entire sentence.

146. Alcott is apparently distinguishing Dr. Samuel Johnson (1708–89), poet, critic, and author of *A Dictionary of the English Language* (1755), from the New Haven, Connecticut, lexicographer Samuel Johnson (1757–1836), whose popular classroom text *A School Dictionary* (1798) simplified British spellings and employed stress marks to facilitate pronunciation.

147. After "instincts" Alcott crossed out "of the soul" and then added "human" above "the instincts".

148. After "tongue." Alcott crossed out "He has nature" and substituted "The needs of his soul".

149. After "adversity,", "indigence" is crossed out; in the same sentence, after "discipline", Alcott crossed out "the soul" and substituted "it".

150. After "soul." Alcott crossed out "Life," and then substituted "The instincts,".

151. After "schools,", "society of men," is crossed out.

152. After "therefore," Alcott had originally written "satisfied the taste of [530] and mind..."; he revised "satisfied" to read "satisfying" (but left out the "y"), crossed out "the taste of" and "and", and then added "the" before "mind".

153. The first part of Thomas Prince's *A Chronological History of New England* was published in 1736; in 1755 the remaining material was used in three sixpenny pamphlets. More than likely Alcott used the 1826 Boston edition, the only complete one, in which these three biographical items appear on pp. 313, 320–21, and 399, respectively. For the change of the family name, which was also spelled "Alcocke," "Alcocks," "Alcox," and "Olcott," see p. 534 below. According to James Savage, *A Genealogical Dictionary of the First Settlers of New England* (Boston: Little, Brown, 1860–62), 1:21, George Alcock (d. 1640), physician and member of the General Court, came to New England in 1630 with the Winthrop fleet accompanied by his wife and his brother Thomas. Because there were no carefully prepared genealogies at the time, Bronson did not know that he actually descended from Thomas, the details of which are discussed by Samuel Orcutt, *History of the Town of Wolcott (Connecticut) from 1731 to 1874* (Waterbury, Conn.: American Printing Co., 1874), pp. 231–38, 425–34. For information on Hooker see note 156 below.

154. Alcott took these names and graduation dates from Cotton Mather's *Magnalia Christi Americana* (1702), Book 4, which traces the early history of Harvard College. (Alcott probably used the 1820 Hartford edition.) Although land for Harvard had been set aside in 1636 and although the college was granted a charter by the General Court in 1640, the first class did not graduate until 1642, thus making 1646, by Alcott's calculations, the "fifth year." The only son of George Alcock and Thomas Hooker's sister, John Alcock (1627–67) was born in England, trained as a physician, and after graduating from Harvard moved to Hartford, where he taught school. Samuel (1637–77), George's son by his second wife, Elizabeth, was also a physician. John's son George (1655–77), a scholar and probably also a physician, later moved to London, where he died (Savage, *A Genealogical Dictionary*, 1:21–22).

155. Although the "Various Sources" are impossible to identify, Alcott undoubtedly had access to, and probably used, such standard works as James Savage's 1825

edition of Winthrop's *History of New England* and the 1815 edition of William Hubbard's *A General History of New-England* (*Collections of the Massachusetts Historical Society*, 2d ser., vols. 5–6). Alcott may have also consulted the manuscript records of the General Court and various Boston parishes.

156. Born in Marfield, the eminent Puritan divine Thomas Hooker (1586–1647) took his B.A. at Emmanuel College in 1608. In 1630, as a result of persecution by Archbishop Laud, he fled to Holland, where he remained until migrating to New England. George Alcock, who died in Roxbury, did not accompany Hooker to Connecticut, although his son John later moved to Hartford. George's nephew Phillip (1648–1716), Bronson's first Connecticut ancestor, moved to New Haven about 1660. In the right-hand margin following this paragraph Alcott later wrote: "(July 1853: See Genealogical Collection of Alcock)". He may have been referring to family papers now lost or to his manuscript collection of genealogical materials (MH *59M–306 [19], [20], [20a], [29], [30]). Following the death of his brother Junius in April 1852, Alcott became intensely interested in his ancestry; he joined the Massachusetts Genealogical Society in 1853 and spent a good deal of time talking with relatives and searching through church and civil records for genealogical information (*JBA*, pp. 261–64; Shepard, *Pedlar's Progress*, pp. 444–52).

157. At a later date, probably in 1853 also, Alcott crossed out "Stonington" and then inserted a question mark next to it; in the left-hand margin he added "Hartford", apparently to replace the cancelled "Stonington". A line stretching through the top parts of the letters "W", "t", and "b" of "Waterbury" indicate that Alcott may have intended to cancel this word too, though some Bro(w)nsons did in fact settle in Waterbury. In 1796 the parish of Farmingbury was incorporated as a town and named Wolcott.

158. Amos Bronson (d. 1819) married Anna Blakeslee (d. 1800), a variant spelling of Blakeley; and John Alcock (1705–77), Bronson Alcott's great grandfather, married Deborah Blakeslee (1711–89), who was probably related to Anna. For further, though incomplete, genealogical information about Alcott's maternal ancestors, see Savage, *A Genealogical Dictionary*, 1:189–90, 195, 279–80, and Orcutt, *History of the Town of Wolcott*, pp. 458–63.

159. Cf. Ephesians 6:12.

160. Probably a reference to the recent killing of the abolitionist Elijah Lovejoy (see p. 579 below).

161. After "deal" Alcott crossed out "retribution" and substituted "vengeance".

162. This paragraph appears in somewhat different form in "Psyche" (2), pp. 187–90.

163. That is, "Psyche."

164. This and the preceding paragraph appear in condensed form in "Psyche" (2), pp. 186–87.

165. For proper emphasis I have changed Alcott's phrasing from "do these" to "these do".

166. The context of this section would indicate that Alcott meant "at least" instead of "at most". Alcott's fear of a short life was ultimately unfounded: he died in March 1888, four months after his eighty-eighth birthday. 29 November was also his daughter Louisa May's birthday, her fifth in 1837.

167. The passage "Behold there, the Artisan . . . burn Smithy" appears in somewhat different form in "Psyche" (2), pp. 215–18.

168. Cf. Goethe, *Wilhelm Meister*: "Do the duty which lies nearest thee."

169. An echo of Luke 1:79, John 1:5, Acts 26:18, Romans 2:19, 1 Corinthians 4:5, 2 Corinthians 4:6, 2 Peter 1:19.

170. Cf. Isaiah 6:6–7.

171. Emerson's ten lectures on "Human Culture" were given on Wednesday evenings at the Masonic Temple from 6 December 1837 to 7 February 1838. For the texts of these lectures, see *Early Lectures*, 2:205–364.

172. Alcott did give a series of public conversations on "Self-Culture" in 1838 but not until October. For Alcott's list of the twelve topics covered at Lexington and Hingham, see his "Journal for 1838," pp. 471–74, and his "Autobiographical Collection," p. 189.

173. After "clear[?]", "and real" is crossed out.

174. Previously unidentified is "Miss Sturges," probably Caroline Sturgis (1819–88), a close friend of both Emerson and Margaret Fuller.

175. Interest in "animal magnetism" (hypnotism), popularized by the Viennese physician Franz Anton Mesmer (1734–1815), spread rapidly throughout Europe and America in the early nineteenth century. In New England the phenomenon was introduced by Charles Poyen, of the University of Paris, who lectured on the subject in Rhode Island during the fall and winter of 1836. For a history of the practice of animal magnetism in the United States, see *Abnormal Hypnotic Phenomena: A Survey of Nineteenth-Century Cases*, ed. Eric J. Dingwall (New York: Barnes & Noble, 1968), 4:2–78.

176. That is "Psyche," which would not be published (see note 136 above).

177. On 7 November the abolitionist Elijah Parish Lovejoy (1802–37), editor of the anti-slavery *Alton Observer*, was killed by a mob that set out to destroy his printing press. In response to the murder and the overt threat to first amendment rights, prominent Boston citizens held a protest meeting at Faneuil Hall on 8 December. The meeting was organized by Dr. Channing, who gave the opening address, and moderated by former Massachusetts Lieutenant-Governor Jonathan Phillips (1778–1860). The "one exception" Alcott refers to was Massachusetts Attorney-General James T. Austin (1784–1870), a member of Dr. Channing's congregation, who denounced Lovejoy's activities as seditious. Immediately following Austin's remarks a young lawyer named Wendell Phillips (1811–84), later a noted orator and delegate to the World Anti-Slavery Convention (1840), gave a stirring rebuttal. A transcript of his speech, regarded as his first significant one on abolition, is printed in *Old South Leaflets*, 4, no. 79, pp. 11–16. Summaries of the resolutions passed that evening were published in the *Boston Daily Advertiser*, 9 December, p. 2, and in the *Christian Register*, 16 December, p. 3. William Lloyd Garrison devoted several pages of the 15 December issue of the *Liberator* to the meeting and included extracts from the speeches of Channing, Austin, Wendell Phillips, and others. Alcott's admiration of Phillips grew over the years and is reflected in his article "Wendell Phillips," *Radical*, 3 (October 1867): 105–10. An unidentified newspaper clipping about the 8 December meeting is inserted in the front of Alcott's 1837 journal.

178. "Doctrine of the Hands," the second lecture in Emerson's series on "Human Culture," may have been read earlier in Lowell on 7 December (*Early Lectures*, 2:230). William Russell's lecture on Tennyson was apparently the fifth in his six-part series on English literature given on Saturday evenings at Chauncy Hall from 18 November to 23 December (*Christian Register*, 18 November 1837, p. 3).

179. An engraving of Hiram Fuller's Greene Street School is pasted in on the top half of the page.

180. Fuller was indeed "enterprising," more so than Alcott is here apparently willing to reveal. During November Emerson noted in his journal: "Fuller at Providence explained to me his plans, 'that he was to keep the school 5 years—income so much; outlay so much; then he should be able to go to Europe; &c, &c.' When I repeated all this to Alcott, he expressed chagrin & contempt. For Alcott holds the school in so high regard that he would scorn to exchange it for the Presidency of the United States" (*JMN*, 5:419). Fuller left the school in the early 1840s, married the daughter of a New York millionaire, and published the successful *New York Mirror* for a short time. His advocacy of the Southern cause during the Civil War, however, eventually led to his professional and financial ruin; he died in obscurity in Paris.

181. Although Alcott never identified the "generous giver," it may have been Emerson.

182. After "Accept" Alcott crossed out what appears to be "poverty," and then substituted "penury,".

183. Emerson's lecture on "The Head," the third in his series on "Human Culture," was delivered on Wednesday, 20 December, at the Masonic Temple. Emerson later revised the lecture and incorporated passages from it into his essay on "Intellect" (*Essays* [*First Series*], 1841).

184. Orestes Brownson's *Boston Quarterly Review*, which ran from 1838 to 1842, was an important Transcendental journal devoted to, as its "prospectus" indicated, "Religion, Philosophy, Politics, and General Literature" (*Christian Register*, 3 December 1837, p. 3). Besides Brownson, who did most of the writing, other contributors in the Transcendental circle included John Sullivan Dwight, Theodore Parker, George Ripley, Margaret Fuller, and Elizabeth Palmer Peabody. In the October 1841 issue (4:492–94), Brownson published Alcott's only contribution, "Orphic Sayings." For further information about Brownson's journal, see Gohdes, *The Periodicals of American Transcendentalism*, pp. 38–82, and Mott, *A History of American Magazines 1741–1850*, 1:685–91.

185. After "of", "Ideas; the time of" is crossed out; after "Souls", "; the body of life" is crossed out.

186. After "the", "doubting" is crossed out.

187. After "in,", "and shining" is crossed out.

188. The passage "All hail thou . . . son of God" appears in somewhat different form in "Psyche" (2), pp 299–301.

189. Cf. Luke 2:50.

190. The dangling construction is potentially misleading here: Brownson alone edited the *Boston Quarterly Review*. Brownson did indeed attempt to change public opinion on many issues, including Alcott's controversial theories about education. Brownson's review-essay on the *Conversations*, "Alcott on Human Culture," *Boston Quarterly Review*, 1 (October 1838): 417–32, is one of the most convincing defenses and explanations of Alcott's educational philosophy ever to have been published.

191. Between the names of Furness and Clarke, Alcott had written "Rev. Geo. Bancroft". Bancroft's name has been crossed out emphatically, probably at a later date following Alcott's apparent estrangement from him. After his refusal to dine with Emerson and Margaret Fuller at Bancroft's in December 1839, Alcott noted

in his journal: "Is it a meet place for me at the tables of the fashionable, the voluptuous, the opulent? Am I not rather at present living in rebuke to all such? Above the temptations, what have I to do amongst the Sadducees? . . . I seek the dwellings of the publicans, the workshops of the artisan, rather, and make my appeal to them with more of hope" (*JBA*, p. 137).

192. After "of" Alcott had written "mine, and of the work"; "mine, and" is crossed out but the second "of" is not. The emendation has been made.

193. Alcott's list of "Items" covered during the year is incomplete and occasionally inaccurate. No attempt has been made to note missing subject matter; however, dating problems are discussed. Because full spellings of abbreviated words appear in the journal proper or in the accompanying notes, shortened forms in the following section are not expanded.

194. The date should read "XVII."

195. See note 103 above for an explanation of dating problems with this section.

JONES VERY'S "EPISTLES TO THE UNBORN"

Phyllis Cole

AMONG EMERSON'S PAPERS at the time of his death were not only nine personal letters from Jones Very but also three formal prose "Epistles" entitled "To the Unborn."[1] Neither the manuscripts themselves nor any comment by Very or Emerson explicitly reveals the intent or date of their composition. But the oracular and systematic quality of this three-part text makes it appear much more than a private communication to Emerson, rather a chief public pronouncement of Very's 1838–39 season of creative and visionary madness. Edwin Gittleman conjectures reasonably that Very sent the "Epistles" to Emerson in the spring of 1839 to introduce and explain his poems, an edition of which Emerson was preparing that year.[2] But Emerson chose not to publish the "Epistles." They must have epitomized the quality in Very that he as editor wanted to play down, the apocalyptic Hebraism that led him to muse ironically in his journal about "John of Patmos in the shape of Jones Very."[3] For these short addresses are Very's Apocalypse as well as Epistles, his full revelation of divine ways as well as letters to the churches of Cambridge and Concord.

Modern students of the New England Renaissance will be more interested than Emerson was to hear Very speak as St. Paul and St. John; in fact the "Epistles" provide a crucial text for understanding Very's highly personal pietism and obsessive interest in the language of the Bible. Much of the last forty years' scholarship on Very has debated the particular quality of Calvinist conviction that informs his writing, even though this writing was produced within a Unitarian and Transcendentalist setting. And evangelical Calvinism, it has concurrently been seen, is one of the enduring patterns of American culture at least into the nineteenth century, constituting both a major pole of the "Protestant Temperament" broadly construed and an important way into Romantic sensibility more particularly.[4] Very's "Epistles" reveal him as a Calvinist both by temperament and by literary vocation. By temperament he pursues a radical perfection, explaining how the soul must be born again not once but twice out of the original "still-birth" of the body through a life of constant self-denial. And this spiritual ascent finds expression in literary work too, in a particular kind of reading and speaking, of Scriptural exegesis and prophecy. "Birth" takes place through a mystically informed reading of the "words of *God*," and this birth in turn enables one to speak as the word, with the truth-telling power of Paul and John and even of Christ.

Truth is what is at stake here, the truth both of God's text and of Very's. And in this concern Very appears to be speaking his own part in the miracles controversy that shook Cambridge and its environs from 1838 to 1840. Indeed it is possible to see the entire episode of Very's holy "insanity" as a special response to pressures within the intellectual culture of New England in the 1830s. Scriptural and personal authority were both in doubt. It was during 1837, Very's first year as Greek tutor and divinity student at Harvard, that Andrews Norton brought forth his long-awaited *Evidence of the Genuineness of the Gospels*, arguing for the truth of Christian Scripture but only as verifiable history. Emerson responded memorably in the summer of 1838 by arguing to the seniors of the Divinity School that Christian "Miracles" belonged not to the historic Jesus but to the Jesus in all living souls, to all "new-born bards of the Holy Ghost." In the next several months Norton and the Unitarians called Emerson's talk "the latest form of infidelity" while Brownson and Ripley prepared critiques of Norton and defenses of Emerson.[5] And in September Jones Very suddenly began giving a "spiritual interpretation" of Matthew 24—one proclaiming himself as Christ bringing judgment on the desecrated temple of Jerusalem—to whatever Harvard faculty and students he could corner. As the theological argument continued in more or less decorous printed forms, Very was sent off to the McLean Asylum and thence home to Salem for good. Charles Stearns Wheeler, who replaced Very as Greek Tutor at Harvard, observed the situation acutely: "Very does not believe even as Emerson does. Very bases all his insane notion of Christ's second coming in him upon the authority of the Bible. Emerson's faith allows for no authority ... to any man or book. Emerson can rise above and explain the enthusiasm of the Quakers and the raptures of the Swedenborgian, and the new-birth of the Calvinist. Very's insanity seems closely allied to these."[6] Very could find "authority" only in "enthusiasm," enthusiasm that Harvard perhaps rightly judged insane. And both the surrounding controversy and the enthusiasm were still alive by the spring of 1839, when Very sat down to vindicate the Bible and himself in the "Epistles."

In this statement Very takes the part neither of Norton nor of Emerson, but argues for an absolutism that neither could have countenanced, a latest form of fidelity in response to their two ambiguities. Norton, following Locke, had seen words as arbitrary signs produced by ever-changing circumstances; and therefore he had ruled out figurative expressions and momentary intuitions as sources of certainty, thus severely limiting the realm of the knowable. Emerson celebrated intuitive and symbolic modes of finding truth, but did not insist that such truth was absolute or unchangeable. Very's response to each is implied in the first paragraph of "An Epistle on Birth": he asks the reader to hear the word "for himself," but goes on to project the meaning of that word beyond dispute or reversal. Once the word is received it brings the hearer into a wholly new "world" from which he looks back at the former, now "finished" for him, "and predicates of its confusion order." Like the saints on the Last Day in Revelations, he is "dead in the Lord" with respect to his former life. Every birth is an apocalypse, apocalypse both as disclosure and as finality; and every saint is a prophet bringing order back to the confusion of others. His saving speech is the "Prayer" of the second Epistle; its effect is both a "quickening" of others not yet born and a self-perfecting by the saint to the second apocalyptic "birth of eternal life." And when the saint, now risen to complete identification with Christ, continues to address others, the "Miracles" of the third Epistle occur: miracles of apocalyptic, "face to face" encounter.

In his insistence on the new birth and the absolute truth of Scripture, Very was, as Wheeler saw, a "Calvinist." But in both respects Very's statement is idiosyncratic and personal, a romantic vision and not a doctrinal stance. The "Epistles" are in part a narrative of conversion, one which would have found a readier audience on the circuits of Second Great Awakening evangelism than in Cambridge or Concord. In December 1838 Very had in fact written such an autobiographical narrative to his Harvard classmate Henry W. Bellows.[7] But whereas the Bellows letter was psychological in its language, direct personal witness to a "change of heart" and "new will," the "Epistles" recast the experience of conversion into a more formal, personally distant imaginative structure. Here Very asserts the existence of three absolute "spheres" or "states" in an essentially Neoplatonic cosmology. He speaks in the first person with a claim to knowledge of all three, but presents the result rather than the experience of that knowledge. Each state, he emphasizes, includes a language and level of understanding of its own; and failures of communication are seen as separations of state. What the unborn consider "natural"—the realm of bodily enjoyment—is really "unnatural"; the truly "natural" must be a "body of denial," a gift of birth. Similarly, "world" is to the born a special place and meaning, one which unborn readers "know not." Very articulates the relationship among these states largely through a series of Scriptural figures and conceptual paradoxes. And as speaker he claims at least in the present the sole right to interpret such paradoxes: "Remember therefore," he warns, "that with the real meaning of Scripture, as with the commonest thing around you, *you* can as yet have nothing to do."

The "real meaning" of Very's Bible is then absolute but elusive. Again there is a partial parallel to this exegetical position within the Calvinist, not liberal, culture of New England: at Andover, Moses Stuart was presently engaged in a sophisticated effort to read Scripture as symbol pointing to the firm truth of orthodoxy.[8] But Very's actual reading of Scripture is much more private and rhapsodic—indeed delusional—than anything proceeding from Andover. Typological and covenantal history, the bedrock of New England orthodox readings of Scripture, falls away before an intensely Christ-centered vision of apocalypse realizable in the present moment. And Very's own voice hovers near the presence of Christ, moving finally, as he had in addressing Harvard the previous September, to complete assumption of Christ's words and power. Now, however, Very is not an angry Christ calling judgment down on the temple, but Christ exhorting and supplicating the people to experience birth.[9] The great New Testament texts on resurrection are his center; he echoes both Christ's parables of the kingdom and Paul's hymn to the coming time when "the dead shall be raised incorruptible, and we shall all be changed." Most fundamentally of all, though, he follows the drama of resurrection through the gospel of John: like Christ to Nicodemus in John 3, he tells how a man must be "born from above" to see the kingdom of God; and he ends by proclaiming, like Christ to Lazarus in John 11, "I am the Resurrection and the Life."

In claiming to be Christ Very is inviting the reader to be Christ too, for such identity is the essential attribute of all reborn or eternal life. At the same time, however, he does not imagine easy ways to the divine state any more than easy readings of Scripture; the burden of his argument is warning as well as encouragement. "You are permitted to see" the born, but "you are no more, ignorantly, to exult yourselves to their spheres, than you physically would do to those of the bright *shining* globes, which to your night-vision roll over your heads." Emotionally Very is, unlike Emerson, a separatist and preparationist. His system demands a reprobate, a large unborn multitude who will never transcend "night-vision"; the judgmental anger of his earlier outburst is not after all so far under the surface of this writing. And even in forwarding the work of resurrection Very insists on the traditional Puritan paradox of preparation for grace: though you must not "exult yourselves" upward, still spiritual growth is "dependent upon yourself"; the soul must "be willing," "quickening" through desire, sowing "bare grain" with no certainty that a harvest will follow. This is the work of self-denial, of clearing a place in the soul for grace to enter rather than moving toward grace.[10] Nowhere is Very more a traditional American Puritan than in these emphases on election and preparatory self-denial; for in his immediate culture Unitarians and Transcendentalists, Awakening evangelists and Swedenborgians, alike affirmed a more Arminian doctrine of the soul's capacity to will its own salvation.

In fact Very, in this drama of birth through denial, is recreating a Puritan imitation of Christ; and this imitation becomes the key to his quite un-Puritan proclamation of self as Christ. In the first Epistle the repudiation of body and sexual origin appears to be a rather traditional way of ascetic discipleship, of *following* Christ; in fact Very echoes Christ's injunction that whoever will follow must "*deny himself.*" But by the second Epistle self-denial has become self-crucifixion, full mystical participation in the "true body of Jesus Christ." And this body is "lifted up" (another Johannine term) in resurrected glory as in crucifixion. Humility, rather than Emerson's seizure of possibility, becomes a way to Emerson's end of godlike knowledge and power. Sacvan Bercovitch has described the historic emergence of the Romantic "American Self" as a movement that began in the Puritans' self-effacing obedience to Christ and culminated in Emerson's "deific creation *ex imaginatio*" of a Christlike self.[11] The compelling interest of Very's Puritan Romanticism is that it recapitulates such an emergence within its own rhetoric.

The personal center of this Romanticism, at once neurotic and brilliantly original, is the account of Very's own power as Christ, his own work saving the unborn. No soul can "exult" itself upward through his spheres, but once "lifted up" to Birth and Rebirth the soul can exert immense power downward to "draw all who are dead...to life." Such "action of the soul" is called "Prayer," the title of the second Epistle. Prayer is a continuation of self-denial and self-crucifixion, but now it is an act of love, of giving oneself for the life of others: "For this cause, says Jesus, I sanctify *myself; that* they also may be one even as we are one." In thus quoting Christ's priestly prayer from John, Very lays claim to atoning as well as self-redeeming power in his own habitual asceticism. "Love" as an "action of the soul" is not manifest in good works or communal relationships; it is a private contemplative condition "for the health of others." It acts as a magnetic emanation from the higher sphere to the lower, a sort of energy of divine love exerted directly by born and reborn God-Man. Very's figure for this life of Prayer—for his own life—is a tree rooted in decay and therefore green and fresh as it grows toward the upper air, "so that the influence of life shall ever be thrown around you, and be for the healing of the nations." This healing influence then extends outward and downward, back toward its own source in decay but now with the power of God on the Last Day to call upon the dead to "come forth."

Very's reborn soul is not self-reliant in Emerson's sense, because its absolute need and vindication is this saving work on behalf of others. On the other hand Very does not easily imagine a communion of saints, a joyfully reborn society. There is no room in his thought for truly collective experience. The crux, one which emerges explicitly in the final "Epistle on Miracles," is Very's yearning from his uppermost sphere for encounter with the other single souls that he will resurrect. Biblical metaphors multiply as he reaches out toward these unborn: he is their begetter and they his children; he stands as a stranger at their door and knocks; he is a fisher of men, a net thrown into the sea to catch "abundantly of every kind." Very projects a mask of unassailable authority in his ascetic quietism. He stands in an "unseen relation" to his intended converts and speaks to them "from within" as an "external influence," that is an influence from a higher sphere of being. Communication is mystical, not open to disproof. But when the "Miracle" of conversion takes place its test will be acknowledgment of Very's own mission and authority, "face to face" meeting between Very and the soul he has converted.

Emerson, Thoreau, and Whitman all worked changes on St. Paul by seeing their divinely charged worlds "face to face," making the apocalyptic revelation an immediate experience.[12] Very's imagining of a "face to face" meeting is significantly different from theirs: "Now you see me, if sight it may be called, externally with an unchanged spirit; then face to face. Now you *make* me what I am to you; then you shall see me as I *am*; for you yourself will be much like unto me. Then shall you know that it was *I* who called you forth from the grave; it was *I* who raised you from the bed of sickness; and *you will* arise and minister unto *me*." Alone among American Romantics, Very dares to imagine the face-to-face meeting from God's perspective; it is recognition of the divinity *in him* that will constitute the apocalyptic event. Very insists (as Christ did not) that he is the father of all who follow him, and as he looks for face-to-face recognition he assumes both a parental and a godlike position of strength for himself. Very is never the petitioner. But when this as-yet-unfulfilled moment of resurrection takes place, the risen Lazarus will "minister unto" Very the father-Christ.

The emotional need behind the mask of authority emerges most painfully in this demand for recognition and ministering love.

Indeed in an important sense Very's "Epistles" read as documentation of a personal pathology; his imagination has worked to create unambiguous, unassailable conditions of power for himself. "The lie is in the detachment," Emerson concluded about this John of Patmos; "and when he is in the room with other persons, speech stops as if there were a corpse in the apartment." Very's effort to ordain the conditions of human speech and meaning was, of course, a failure both personally and culturally: ambiguity rather than closure would become the more viable mode for discerning truth in literary and religious America. But Emerson saw too that this "exaggerated and detached pietism" was "true in itself... speaking things in every word"; only a bridge was needed "between Very and the Americans."[13] And with our longer retrospect, these "Epistles"—quintessential expression of Very's truth—appear even more integral to Very's America. Both their grandeur and their pathological quality belong to the history of the American "deific creation *ex imaginatio.*"

To the Unborn[14]

An Epistle on Birth

The meaning of the words of *God* can only be had by each one who hears for himself. They are the forms and light of the worlds given to each to dwell in as he advances and consequently are intelligible only to one move-in the same as with himself [*sic*].[15] What the word *world* means is therefore not to be understood by one who has never entered it, nor *fully* so even by one who has; but only uttered and comprehended by him who has passed into and through and out of it. He alone can *speak* to you of any thing who has ceased to do with that thing. Thus God, when He had made the world, is said to have *rested* from his labors and *called* it good. Whoever speaks then of that condition which is before the world, or of the world itself or of another, can only show it as good when *speaking*, or sent from the next following. His relations to the first have ceased, that is are finished in the regular order of nature; and he stands to *that* as perfect, he rests from his labors in it, and predicates of its confusion order. He is dead in the Lord and his works follow him.[16]

I write now of *the birth* into the world; I shall at some future period write of the *new* birth, or that which is when one has left the world and enters on that which is beyond. When I speak of *the birth into the world*, those to whom I write will say, "Are we not already born then, and in the world?" You are so as you understand these terms, but of *the birth* of Scripture,[17] and of *the world* in which I live, you know not; and it is, therefore, that you may know of *these* that I write to you.

To me, you were *dead* or *still born* into *what you call* the world; that is *your* bodies were begotten in enjoyment; and what you call your spirits naturally, as you would say, seek enjoyment. Your father and mother, or that which reminds you of them, this nature which they gave you, you know; and when *your* bodies and spirits are warred with by Him who is begetting you of another nature, you call *them* parents. By your still birth you are by inheritance opposed to the universal relations into which you are thrown, and this opposition continues until it ends in giving you a *new* body and spirit by which you recognize *God* as a parent. *This* is *the Birth*; the other was the *dead*-birth. *This* is your *natural* body; the other, the body of desire or enjoyment, your *unnatural* one. That *you* of which you *now* speak as living is then raised to life; its body is *the body of denial* or flesh of Christ which is now forming but which as yet has not supplanted that of enjoyment in which you now dwell. *This* is your *natural* body because you were[18] a conscious witness of its coming and became so by the denial of the other. *That* was the *unnatural* one, because you knew not whence it came; but you *found* yourself clothed and miserably so with it. As you know where this your *natural* body came, so will you also know where it shall go. As it is the body of Christ and your own natural body, so is it to be broken or crucified by a continuance in the denial by which it came. So shall it be raised and you a witness of it incorruptible, and in the *true* and *ever*-living likeness of Jesus Christ. But of the unnatural body of your desires, as it came you know not whence, so it goes you know not where. It was the seed which God first buried, that by its decay *you* might be *born*, a man fitted to listen to his word. These desires which form your unnatural flesh are the grain which you are now sowing; I say *you*, though the *you* which sows may not as yet be said to be. You know not that which shall be, but sow *as it were* bare grain; it is that you may labor in hope that I, who am what you shall be, write.[19]

Remember that you are now *the sown*, and not properly sowers, the seed of tares sown by the evil men of former generations, daily decaying by the sun and rain of Him who quickens you, that a new *you*, even a grain of *wheat*, may come out of evil and death.[20] Remember therefore that with the real meaning of Scripture, as with the commonest thing about you, *you* can as yet have nothing to do; save that the influence of the sight of those who there work may quicken in you the desire to become workmen, and the appearance of gifts around may fashion you more and more to become worthy to possess them. Those of whom you there read, or *think you read*, as well as the commonest things of your daily life, move and are, as I have thus shown you, in other worlds than your own, and only exhibited to your sight that you may be led to aspire to communion with them. Because *in this way* you are permitted to see them, you are no more ignorantly to exult yourselves to their spheres than you physically would do to those of the bright *shining* globes, which to your night-vision roll over your heads. *They* are the true orbs and, in this night of your spirits, are ever shining down upon you making clear and bright the heavens above. *You* must then *be born into the world,* before you can have to do with those who are there, or learn to use the gifts of it.

Jones Very

To the Unborn

An Epistle on Prayer

What has been before said of words will it is to be remembered apply equally well to *all* the words of sacred writ; for they are *sacred* for this reason.

Prayer is that action of the soul which begins at its *birth* and which consequently with the *unborn* has never begun. As the denial or death of what you now are will give you *birth,* so will prayer or the continuance in that denial give you the death again of that which is so born, by which death you attain unto immortality. The dead soul became a living and the living one has again changed its nature and become a quickening spirit, which remains or does not change. You may *increase* and *multiply* but you are still a quickening spirit. He who is *born* is alone said by God, or in scripture language, to *deny himself*. This is prayer and by it you show that you love the brethren, because you cannot love more than *this,* that you accomplish the entire denial of the life you have attained unto by being born. It is made for the *health* of others, because as you die, that is are attaining unto an eternal state of health or dying, they die; it is made for their increase in *riches,* because as you are poor by sacrifice they also will see their *false* riches and come and buy of you the enduring ones. That you shall continue, or as it is otherwise called stand in this state when you have by death or a perfect denial attained unto it, is the first and second commandment with promise. This is prayer, in sincerity *ever* to love your neighbor as *yourself*.[21] It has not really begun until then.

When *you* who are unborn are using words to which you give that name, there is no agency at work benefiting those for whom you thus speak. So far as in this or in anything else you are doing, if *you* may be said to *do* at all, you are dying or decaying, or in other words reviving and being raised to life, so far does this spirit act unseen on and for others. This is *your* prayer if you may be said to pray. If you rise or are lifted up, you shall raise and draw all who are dead to you and to life.[22] It is your words which are proceeding from your inward growth or backwardness that convey this influence to others unknowingly to yourself. Use what language you will you can never *say* anything but what you are. Whoever lives better than you knows what you are *really* saying whatever the sounds of your lips. The spirit will always work whether it be good or whether it be evil.

In the state of Love of which I have spoken, every *not-working* or not-quickening word calls you, says Jesus, into judgement, or to account. It is *idle* in this sense you are then considered; and, amid the sons of God, your cessation from work is instantly noted, even in *one* word. Pray always, writes the Apostle, to those in this state; that is bear always about with you, or be you always in that condition of dying, by which your words will make evident, that yours is the *true* body of Jesus Christ. The decay in which you are then rooted shall keep your leaves green and fresh, so that the influence of life shall ever be thrown around you and be for the healing of the nations. For this cause, says Jesus, I sanctify *myself, that* they also may be one even as we are one.[23]

Prayer then is the action by which the *living* live and quicken life and happiness in each other. Its beginning is also that *prelude* to action, too faint and low as yet to be heard and called by the name of prayer, by which you, the dead, are becoming, *unknowingly to yourselves*, the living, and drawing along with you those who are around you in your several spheres. Go on, until it has become the full and audible sound of one who actually lives and speaks; then shall the dead whom you have left hear your voice and come forth, and you yourselves rejoice that the Father hears you.[24]

Jones Very

To the Unborn

An Epistle on Miracles

The born are the begetters of the unborn, and those born *again* in their turn the fathers of the born. Who are the *Born* they only know who are so; who are those born *again* they only know who have witnessed the second birth. It is this *second* birth of eternal life of which Jesus said, "*I* am the Resurrection *and* the life, he that believeth on *Me*, though he were dead yet shall he live; and he that liveth and believeth shall never die." So say *I* to you to whom as the unborn I stand in a similar relation. *I* am your Resurrection and life; believe in the *Me* that speaks and you though unborn shall be born yet *again* and shall know the *only Begotten* of the Father. "He that receives *you*," said he to his disciples, "receives Me, and he that receives *Me* receives Him that sent *Me*."²⁵ These *Me's* and *I's* are the *I's* and *Me's* of persons in the different worlds or states of which I have spoken and which because they are used are confounded by you and you are led to think that the person who speaks is like yourself but gifted in some unaccountable manner with power over you. Instead of understanding that the person who speaks to you is external to the *you* he addresses from *within*; you transfer this power to an external influence over your *visible bodies* as you call them and believe that *these* are to be raised by him after their decay, not knowing that to him who speaks the *you* to which he is sent to speak is always the *body* to be raised. The power is indeed external to you, but it is from a want of knowledge *in what manner* it is so that you are thus led to wrest it to your own destruction. He who speaks is external to you; he speaks to you from without; but it is *outward from within* and *so* exerts an *external* influence over you. Behold *I* stand without and knock. The relation in which I once stood to you is changed, else I could not call upon you as a *stranger* to be received into your dwelling. I was *once* as you *now* are, but I am changed and *as such* exert this power of raising you from the dead; I, this *new I*, stand without *you*, that is the old *you* which I was, and knock. No man has power over that house in which *you* are except he has first bound or slain the strong man in it.²⁶ This strong man the former *I* was, which is now dead to my present self and gives *me* power over all such as I then was. But you will say, "Let me see *you* stand forth and exert this power." I answer I do thus work and in *these* words declare it. To myself *I* am raising you, but *you* do not see *me*; because if so I could not stand in *this unseen* relation. He who is *sent* unto you or *calls you* must always come from where *you* are not and remain unknown until you have realized what *he* is in your own nature, until your nature is raised in the image of his. There are heavenly places in Christ, that is, to be realized by denial, as well as those; you call such external to you.²⁷ He continually goes before you and prepares a way, and whither *he* goes you cannot come now, that is immediately—the *you* that you now are must first have been changed—then shall the *new* you follow where he goes. The body which I *now* have, and which is forming in you or upon that *you*, declares of itself that it is your begetter. It is my natural speech to call you my children; for the *me* which was to me, I gave up that you might have life; this I did then, and now I come in person with authority to claim you as mine.²⁸ *I* am the Resurrection; but who this I is which speaks, you the dead or unraised cannot know; but when that change in you which gives me power to declare this of myself has taken place, then shall you also declare it of yourselves and know that I speak in truth, for you will know me.

I hide nothing from you; as much as you *will* see that you shall see. But remember it is *hard* to be *willing*; be so long enough and you *see* of *yourselves*. I am loathe to enter *your* dwellings, but entreat me *much* and I will come in. One may forward you who is living the same life or passing toward the same life as yourself; he alone can raise you or act upon you with a power different from your own who lives that other life and has *already passed* before you into it.

Your growth is thus made dependent upon yourself. "What have *I* to do with *you*," said Jesus to his mother, "*my* time has not yet come to have to do with *you*." *You* therefore shall know *me* not by *this external* semblance of myself which I give you naturally in words by my own growth, but to know me in truth you yourself by a like increase in yourself must see me as I *am* from the eternal image there. As in a glass face answers to face, so will my heart then answer to yours. Now *you* see *me*, if sight it may be called, *ex*ternally with an unchanged spirit; then face to face. Now you *make* me what I am to you; then you shall see me as *I am*, for you yourself will be much like unto me. Then shall you know it was *I* who called you forth from the grave; it was *I* who raised you from the bed of sickness; and *you will* arise and minister unto *me*.[29]

Because you read of fishermen and tent makers, do not think that the words of *God* are to be interpreted by your own employments, similar only in name. Why when His children thus speak do the people, that is the *born*, *rage*, because they tell *them* that *they* must be born *again*; and the heathen, that is the *unborn*, imagine *vain* things, because they cannot understand at all the things of which they speak. James and John were *poor* fishermen, that is they were Jews or *born*, and yet refrained from teaching others as the scribes; and were rather mending their nets as though they *yet* were unprepared for the toilsome voyage they saw before them. It was to these poor fishermen in *spirit* that Christ came, that is that were *born again* and that so were made fishers of men such as they themselves had been before. So did Jesus send one unto the sea that he might take the *first* fish—since all were his—who would give him the money wanted for tribute. So again is the kingdom of heaven likened unto a *net* which a man, that is a man-child, threw into the sea and caught abundantly of *every* kind.[30]

True life is alone the product of decay; but while by enjoyment you are checking this process within you, you see an external life for which you provide earthly homes, lament over its disease, and bury with tears. The outward body is made by you immortal and you wonder where it departs. But he who *is really* dying never laments the perishing of the outward man, as from its decay is every putting forth that better body, even the incorruptible one of Jesus. It is that you stop this dying and thus are ceasing more and more to realize the coming of the *new* flesh in its stead that you lament and falsely believe in a future rising of the corruption you possess, instead of losing it in the incorruption which is your birthright. "A wicked and perverse generation," said Jesus of the Jews or *born*, "are clamorous for a *sign*, but no sign shall be given them except the *sign* of the prophet Jonas; as he was three days and three nights in the belly of the whale, so must the son of man remain in the heart of the earth." This he spoke of that decay or death of the natural flesh of desires which alone can give the wished for increase, and *this* is itself the true *sign*. *Thus*, falsely as I have said, will *you* believe and thus will you lament; for thus will your house be left desolate unto you until you shall welcome and say blessed is *he* that comes in the name of the Lord.[31]

Jones Very

NOTES

1. All of Very's letters to Emerson were sent, probably by Emerson's executor James Elliot Cabot, to William P. Andrews; Andrews (1848–1916), a Salem Clerk of Court and amateur poet, was preparing the "Memoir" and edition of Very's poems that appeared in 1883 (Boston: Houghton, Mifflin). Andrews later gave all his Very materials to Harvard philosopher and literary scholar George Herbert Palmer (1842–1933); in 1915 Palmer willed these, along with his rare books, to Wellesley College in honor of his late wife and former Wellesley President Alice Freeman Palmer. The "Epistles" have been quoted and commented upon several times, both by Andrews and by recent scholars: Edwin Gittleman in *Jones Very: The Effective Years, 1833–1840* (New York: Columbia University Press, 1964), pp. 325–30; Lawrence Buell in *Literary Transcendentalism: Style and Vision in the American Renaissance* (Ithaca: Cornell University Press, 1973), pp. 316–17; David Robinson in "The Exemplary Self and the Transcendent Self in the Poetry of Jones Very," *ESQ: A Journal of the American Renaissance*, 24 (4th Quarter 1978): 206–14. And they were transcribed as an appendix in Harry L. Jones' dissertation "Symbolism in the Mystical Poetry of Jones Very" (Catholic University of America, 1967). But they have not until now been fully edited or studied as a separate and complete text.

I want especially to thank Eleanor Nicholes, Wellesley College Special Collections Librarian, for her permission to publish the text and her warm encouragement of this project from its start.

2. Gittleman, *Jones Very*, p. 324.
3. *The Journals and Miscellaneous Notebooks of Ralph Waldo Emerson*, ed. William H. Gilman et al., 14 vols. to date (Cambridge: Harvard University Press, 1960–), 7:213.
4. For Very's Calvinism, see especially Ivor Winters' *In Defense of Reason* (Chicago: Swallow Press, 1943); Warner Berthoff, "Jones Very: New England Mystic," *Boston Public Library Quarterly*, 2 (January 1950): 63–76; James A. Levernier, "Calvinism and Transcendentalism in the Poetry of Jones Very," *ESQ: A Journal of the American Renaissance*, 24 (1st Quarter 1978): 30–41; and for a dissenting view, David Robinson, "Jones Very, the Transcendentalists, and the Unitarian Tradition," *Harvard Theological Review*, 68 (April 1975): 103–24. A suggestive psychological context for Very's pietism might be drawn from Philip Greven, *The Protestant Temperament: Patterns of Child-Rearing, Religious Experience, and the Self in Early America* (New York: Alfred A. Knopf, 1977), part 2, "The Evangelicals." In "Calvinism Romanticized: Harriet Beecher Stowe, Samuel Hopkins, and *The Minister's Wooing*," *ESQ: A Journal of the American Renaissance*, 24 (3d Quarter 1978): 129, Lawrence Buell suggests three characteristic traits of

nineteenth-century Calvinism as it affects literary sensibility: an acceptance of supernatural religion as given, a playing off of doctrinally rigorous religion against the "religion of love," and "on some level an equation between self-fulfillment and self-denial." The first and third of these describe Very admirably, and the second perhaps suggests the sentimentality against which his own masculine asceticism rebounds.

5. For the major documents of the miracles controversy, see *The Transcendentalists*, ed. Perry Miller (Cambridge: Harvard University Press, 1950), section 5. My interpretation of the events of 1838–40, emphasizing issues of linguistic and epistemological authority, is strongly influenced by the work of Philip Gura; to him I owe special thanks for letting me read the proofs of his recent book *The Wisdom of Words: Language, Theology, and Literature in the New England Renaissance* (Middletown, Conn.: Wesleyan University Press, 1981). See especially the introduction and chapters 1–2.

6. Quoted by Gittleman, *Jones Very*, p. 228; see also chapter 10.

7. In Harry L. Jones, "The Very Madness: A New Manuscript," *College Language Association Journal*, 10 (March 1967): 198–200.

8. See Gura, *The Wisdom of Words*, chapter 1; also "The Transcendentalists and Language: The Unitarian Exegetical Background," STUDIES IN THE AMERICAN RENAISSANCE 1979, pp. 5–7.

9. For a critical view of this self-perception in both the "Epistles" and the poems, see Robinson, "The Exemplary Self and the Transcendental Self," 207, 211–14.

10. See Norman Pettit, *The Heart Prepared* (New Haven: Yale University Press, 1966), chapter 1.

11. *The Puritan Origins of the American Self* (New Haven: Yale University Press, 1975), esp. pp. 164–65.

12. *The Collected Works of Ralph Waldo Emerson*, ed. Alfred R. Ferguson et al., 2 vols. to date (Cambridge: Harvard University Press, 1971–   ), vol. 1, *Nature, Addresses, and Lectures* (1971), p. 7; *The Writings of Henry D. Thoreau*, ed. Walter Harding et al., 5 vols. to date (Princeton: Princeton University Press, 1971–   ), *Walden* (1971), ed J. Lyndon Shanley, p. 98; Whitman, "Crossing Brooklyn Ferry."

13. Emerson, *Journals*, 7:213. See Gura's sense of "ambiguity," especially in his introduction and chapter 5.

14. In preparing a clear text of the "Epistles" I have sparingly corrected accidentals in the manuscript as I believe they would have been corrected for publication: Very's occasional misspellings and frequent misuse and overuse of commas and semicolons. I have preserved all of his emphatic underlinings, however, as an important element of style.

15. In the manuscript a line-end comes between "move-" and "in". Possibly Very made a transcriptional error here, leaving important words out of the sentence.

16. Cf. John 1:1–14, Genesis 1–2:2, Revelations 14:13.

17. John 3:3.

18. The manuscript reads "was."

19. Cf. Matthew 16:24, 1 Corinthians 11:24, 1 Corinthians 15:35–44.

20. Cf. Matthew 13:24–30, John 12:24.

21. Cf. I Corinthians 15:45, Genesis 1:22, Matthew 16:24, John 15:12–13, Matthew 22:37–40.

22. Cf. John 12:32.
23. Cf. Matthew 12:36, Ephesians 6:18, John 17:19-21.
24. Cf. John 5:28-29.
25. Cf. John 11:25-26, Matthew 10:40.
26. Cf. Revelations 3:20, 1 Corinthians 15:51, Matthew 12:29.
27. The manuscript reads "There are heavenly places in Christ that is to be realized by denial as well as those you call such external to you."
28. Cf. Ephesians 2:6, Mark 1:2-3, John 10:10.
29. Cf. Matthew 12:48-49 and John 7:6, 1 Corinthians 13:12, John 11:43-44.
30. Cf. Acts 4:25, Matthew 4:18-22, Matthew 17:27, Matthew 13:47.
31. Cf. 1 Corinthians 15:54, Matthew 12:38-40, Matthew 23:38-39.

GEORGE RIPLEY'S UNPUBLISHED LECTURE ON CHARLES FOURIER

David A. Zonderman

GEORGE RIPLEY had never read the works of Charles Fourier when he and a small band of followers formed their community at Brook Farm in the spring of 1841. He was familiar with Albert Brisbane's recently published book *The Social Destiny of Man* (1840); and he was impressed with this exposition of Fourierist social theory by the leading American authority on the subject. But he remained unconverted to the entire doctrine; Ripley was determined to carry out his own design for the Farm's communal organization.[1] His plan was a uniquely personal blend of Transcendentalism, Christian Socialism, and a pinch of hard-scrabble Yankee ingenuity.

Once settled at Brook Farm, Ripley turned to Fourier's original writings and was even more captivated with these writings of the master himself.[2] He saw many parallels between Fourier's theories and his own efforts at the Farm. Both men believed in cooperative labor, universal education, and the abolition of class distinctions. Yet Ripley was still hesitant to embrace the entire Fourierist system or to change his experiment into a phalanx. By the end of 1843, however, a combination of chronic financial instability and increasing internal bickering convinced Ripley that the Farm had to be restructured if it was to remain harmonious and economically viable.

At the same time that Ripley was concerned with problems at home, he was also being courted by leading Associationists such as Brisbane and Horace Greeley (Associationism was the American version of Fourierism). They needed his support, his talents as a writer and lecturer, and his influence among other communitarians, to bolster their movement. Throughout the summer and fall of 1843 Ripley helped these men to organize Associationist conventions where he publicly supported Fourierist social theory.[3] He also became convinced that

Fourierism would give his own project at Brook Farm the spiritual and practical direction it needed. His community would stand on the cutting edge of true social reform, attract new members and money from all over the country, and reorganize its own operations under the Fourierist doctrine of Attractive Industry.

Ripley's conversion did, however, have its slow and painful moments. He was well aware that some Farmers feared the coming of Fourierism. While he believed that the new movement would bring the Farm together as a true working community, he also knew that others saw Associationism as a threat to individual freedom. He was anxious not to trample on the sensibilities of those Farmers who opposed Fourierism—the transformation of the community had to be an exercise in unity, not division. Hence, he used all his efforts to persuade others to accept Associationism, just as he himself had been convinced, and he met with considerable success.[4]

Once Brook Farm was officially reorganized according to Fourierist doctrine in January 1844, Ripley turned his powers of persuasion toward the general public. He became a zealous missionary for the cause of Association. Throughout the following four years he headed various conventions on Fourier and Associative reform.[5] He edited and published the *Harbinger* from Brook Farm, and he contributed numerous articles to this principal organ of the Associationist movement. He also organized a lecturers' bureau and actively participated in it, along with other Brook Farmers such as John Allen, John Dwight, and John Orvis.[6] Orvis and Allen spoke throughout New England and the midwest; their speeches both raised money for the Farm and stimulated the formation of Associationist groups in the various towns they visited.

Although the lecture published below is not dated, it seems to fall into this period (1844–47) of Ripley's work in behalf of Fourierism. Octavius Brooks Frothingham made the only known reference to the manuscript (which is to be found today in papers relating to his biography of Ripley) and he placed the date of its composition sometime in 1845.[7] The lecture, by Ripley's own description, was intended as an introduction to the life and thought of Fourier. It was probably used as a means of acquainting the general audiences which Ripley addressed with the history and principles of Associationism, and may have served the added purpose of drumming up sympathy and support for Brook Farm. But it was not an elaborate exposition of Fourierist philosophy for the advanced student, nor was it a carefully orchestrated appeal for building new phalanxes. Ripley probably left most of the actual recruiting work to his travelling missionaries such as Orvis and

Allen. His own "forte was in the lecture series rather than the organizing lecture."[8] This manuscript, in fact, contains some evidence of its being part of one such group of talks.

The content of the lecture is heavily weighted toward biographical details of Fourier's life. Ripley wrote at great length about his belief that the exceptional power of intellect and intensity of emotion which Fourier showed as a child blossomed in his adult life and became the very tools which he used to create his social theories. It is difficult to know for certain where Ripley discovered all the details of Fourier's life which he revealed in his manuscript. He may have read the biography of Fourier which Charles Pellarin published, in French, in 1843.[9] More likely, he gleaned a number of stories about Fourier's youth from Albert Brisbane, who had become a frequent visitor to Brook Farm. Both Brisbane and Ripley were also engaged in translating a number of Fourier's notebooks and unpublished works, particularly for publication in the *Harbinger*, and it seems probable that still more biographical information emerged from this editing process.[10]

Ripley joined this lengthy discussion of Fourier's life with a summary of his theories and writings. This overview is perhaps the strongest part of the lecture; it is a remarkably clear presentation of the essential principles underlying Fourierism. It demonstrates Ripley's earnest effort to make this doctrine approachable, understandable, and acceptable. All the bizarre speculations concerning the future, which Fourier's critics often raised to question his sanity, were distilled out by Ripley. He, and Brisbane, had always been uncomfortable with some of the master's more outlandish schemes. So Ripley made no mention of oceans turning to lemonade or anti-animals populating a new world; instead, he focused on the enormous potential for social reform inherent in the Fourierist system.

This vast potential for positive change was found, according to Ripley, in both Fourier's discovery of the divine order of society and his desire to use such grand schemes as a means of elevating man above his present misery. Fourier was scathing in his criticism of human dishonesty and cruelty, and the institutions which perpetuate it, because he saw a better way to organize those social structures. He not only demonstrated, to Ripley's satisfaction, the ultimate bankruptcy of "civilization," but he also proposed new Associative values to replace the old ones he discredited. It was this constructive spirit in Fourier—his desire not to lose himself in theory and speculation, but to confront the reality of human existence and to consider how to rearrange society so that every person could reach his complete human potential—that made him such a unique and powerful force for social change. Fourier, Ripley proclaimed, brought the great social issues of the day back to where they belonged, back to the individual and his struggle for a meaningful life with others.

Some present-day readers may be uneasy with the effusive praise of Fourier at the close of Ripley's lecture. The rhetoric seems inflated and naive—and Fourier's theories now appear to be improbable and unrealistic. But this speech is essentially one visionary's tribute to another; as such, Ripley may be allowed his unbridled admiration for Fourier. For behind all those theories and postulates lay a man who sincerely believed that he held the key to unlocking an age of human justice; and behind all that laudatory prose lay another man who thought he could find that same key on a farm outside of Boston. These two men shared a sense of hope and faith in God's ultimate wisdom and man's infinite potential for improvement. Their unbounded optimism in an age of uncertainty was, in the end, all a dream. A dream which made their lives, and the lives of those who lived and worked with them, a little more humane.[11]

"Beware when the great God lets loose a thinker on this planet. Then all things are at risk. The very hopes of man, the thoughts of his heart, the religion of nations, the manners and morals of mankind, are all at the mercy of a new generalization."[12]

There is no man in the history of the 19th century to whom this language of one of our most original writers can be applied with so much propriety as to the great discoverer of the laws of social Harmony, Charles Fourier. In boldness, acuteness, and depth of thought,—in the vast compasses of his researches,—in the almost fearful power of intellect, with which he penetrated into the mysteries of nature, he stands unrivalled and unapproached on the records of scientific investigation. The results of his thought are not contained in any abstract, barren, metaphysical formulas. They apply directly to the most important institutions of mankind, to the practical organization of the social state, and to the fulfillment of human destiny on earth. They have already produced an earnestness of conviction, an enthusiastic devotion in a large number of minds both in Europe and in this country, such as no other cause inspires, and their ultimate effect, as we believe, will be the establishment of a social order adapted to develop the nature of man in a richness and majesty hitherto unknown, and to "cause the will of God to be done of earth, as it is in Heaven."

I propose in this Lecture to give a sketch of the life and system of the founder of the Associative School, premising that I shall hardly be able to present any details with which the student of writings on Association is not already familiar.[13]

Charles Fourier was born in Besancon, an ancient French city, on the 7th April, 1772, thus coming into the world the same year in which it was left by another profound observer of the laws of Universal Harmony, the illustrious Emmanuel Swedenborg. It is a pleasing imagination, at least, to suppose that the advent of the great thinker who first announced to the world the reality of a divine social code, no less determinate, no less immutable than that which governs the revolutions of the planets, was consecrated by the parting benediction of the sublime spirit whose earthly life was irradiated with the glorious visions of celestial beatitude and harmony.

The father of Fourier was a merchant in easy circumstances, enjoying a high consideration in his native city, and entrusted with the discharge of various functions of official dignity. He died in 1781, leaving his son the heir to a handsome competence.

From the earliest age, Fourier displayed the same firmness of will, the same integrity and freedom of thought, the same independence of traditional errors and social prejudice, which were such conspicuous traits of his character in subsequent life. "We have often heard him relate," says his devoted and intelligent disciple, M. Victor Considerant,[14] "that his mind was first impressed with the falseness of the existing relations of commerce at the age of five years, when he was punished by his father for telling the truth in regard to an irregular business operation, in which he had attempted to become a purchaser. This led him, even then, to take the vow of Hannibal against commerce; and herein, we may find the germ of his vast discoveries; for it was by seeking the method of introducing truth and honesty into the operations of trade that he arrived, at a later period, at the knowledge of Agricultural Association, the grand law of the Series as the condition of Harmony, and the immortal theorem of Attractions proportional to Destinies."

Another characteristic feature that was early developed was his hatred of all injustice and oppression. In his intercourse with his school mates, he proudly took the part of the weak againt the strong, and though by no means of a quarrelsome disposition, he never refused to grapple with those juvenile heroes who loved to signature[?] their courage by attacking boys of inferior physical force to themselves.

His aptitude for harmony was far above the ordinary rank. At College, he received the prizes for French themes and Latin Verses, although, it must be confessed, his talent and interest in this kind of literature were probably exhausted with the completion of his juvenile studies. His favorite pursuit was geography: he devoted his pocket money to the purchase of maps and charts; and often spent whole nights in poring over them. He was enthusiastically attached to the cultivation of flowers from his earliest boyhood. He loved to collect every variety of each species that he cultivated, and to attempt with them every method of culture of which they were susceptible. His room was crowded with flower pots of every size and quality, from common earthen to the finest porcelain; a free space only was left from the door to the window; every other spot was filled with his plants which formed a graduated series; and woe to the unlucky wretch who should be so awkward as to derange their symmetry or let fall one of these brittle objects of his fond idolatry.

Congenial with this passionate taste, was his ardent love of music. He not only played on several instruments, but was profoundly versed in the theory of music, and in various instances successfully tried his skill as an original composer. His admirable knowledge of musical harmony must have afforded him a singular facility in his investigations of social harmony; many of his most striking illustrations of the divine laws of society are drawn from this source; and experience has shown, that it is among those whose souls are most exquisitely susceptible to the sublime harmonies of sound, his vast system of the Harmonies of the Universe has found its most enlightened and earnest adherents. "Amongst other indications of reform in arbitrary methods," we are told by Mr. Doherty,[15] "he has given a plan of universal notation, by which all the different voices and instruments may give the same name to the same note, instead of employing seven or eight different keys on particular scales."

Another trait in the character of Fourier, during his childhood, in which we may detect a germ of the discoveries that have made his name immortal, was his sympathy with misfortune and distress. In after life this was not wasted in unfruitful sentimentality; it assumed the systematic form in which his genius delighted; and developed itself in a positive and rigid science, which affords the means as far as human power can do so, of removing suffering, anguish, and despair, from the earth. An incident is related, from this portion of his life, which illustrates the sincere, unostentatious kindness of his disposition. He was in the habit of filling his pocket with bread when he set off for school in the morning, and although he was a very moderate eater, he daily took away what seemed quite a large quantity, for a boy's luncheon. He would add a bit of cold meat to this, when he could get the chance, or some other article of food that might be conveniently carried. No notice of this was taken by his parents, or it was regarded only as a childish eccentricity, when one day after he had left Besancon for the first time, a poor and infirm old man, who had fixed himself a short distance from the house of his father, came and inquired after the young gentleman and wanted to know if he were ill or gone away. On being informed that he had left Besancon, the poor cripple burst into tears and said he had lost his guardian angel who used every morning to feed and comfort him. The first time Fourier wrote to his friends, he begged them to protect the old man, whom he had forgotten in the hurry of departure, and his request was complied with; but the helpless creature lost his all when he lost his comforter, and though still protected by his absent benefactor, he pined away and died, as much from grief, it is supposed, as from infirmity.

Upon completing his academical course, he was placed in a counting room at Lyons, although the mercantile profession was repugnant to his natural taste; his own inclinations giving him a decided preference for the employment of civil engineer. He gained the confidence of his employers, however, by his fidelity and accuracy, and at length was entrusted with the responsible function of travelling clerk or agent for several important mercantile houses. This pursuit was far more in accordance with his feelings than the monotonous, stationary life of a city, and it gave him the opportunity for indulging his passionate drive for travel and observation. The liberal patrimony which he had inherited made him independent of his commercial patrons, and enabled him to gratify his curiosity by visiting the most interesting places, and remaining as long as he wished in the most important European Capitals. In this way, he became familiar not only with the principal cities of France but also of Germany, Belgium, Holland, Switzerland.

Nothing that was remarkable escaped his observation in the course of his travels, nor was his memory less retentive than his other intellectual facilities were powerful and methodical. The climate, the soil, the rivers, hills, forests etc., the peculiarities of every province in every kingdom which he had visited, were regularly classed in his memory, and critically compared one with another. The number of inhabitants of each city and their respective pursuits of industry, the principal buildings, both public and private, their respective dimensions, beauties, and defects, the width and direction of streets, the height of houses, the nature of building materials, promenades, fountains, vistas, every thing notable in fact was seen by his observing eye, wherever he passed; and when once he had properly observed, he never forgot even the most trifling details. It often happened that those who visited him were astonished to hear him explain the defects of public buildings, the insalubrious distribution of streets, and the particular improvements which might be made in their native cities, through which he had passed only once or twice in his life, and then remained perhaps not more than a few hours. They had passed a great part of their whole lives in their native cities without ever noticing those details which he had pointed to them. "We remember," says Mr. Doherty, "an instance of this nature concerning Metz. One of his friends, a military engineer, who had long been stationed in that city, and who from his profession was well acquainted with it, on hearing him comment learnedly and familiarly on its beauties and defects, the deformities of certain buildings, and the improvements which might be easily made, was led to believe that Fourier had not only resided there many years, but that he had been employed as an Edile[16] of the city; on inquiring how long it was since Fourier had resided there, the answer was that he had never resided there at all; that he had only been there once in his life, about thirty years before that time; and that he then remained only one day in that city, he was either going to, or returning from Germany; arriving in Metz early in the morning, he was obliged to wait for an evening coach, and there, not knowing what to do with his time, he passed it in his usual recreation, that of observing the buildings and the neighboring country."

It would seem that his remarkable taste for geographical and architectural knowledge was connected with the mission which Providence had assigned to him of discovering the divine social order adapted to the nature of man, and destined to be established on the whole surface of the globe. He never saw a public or private edifice without noticing its proportions and arrangements, its peculiar beauties or defects, and the improvements of which it was susceptible. Every monument in Paris, and even in all the principal cities of France, was familiar to him; he could describe it from memory, even to minute details. His walking stick was regularly marked off in feet and inches, and every thing remarkable which met his eye was instantly reduced to measurement and calculation.

The native tendencies of his mind led him to the study of every branch of science. He was born with a peculiar affinity with Nature; he delighted in all her manifestations of grandeur and beauty; and his intellectual faculties found their appropriate nutriment in the analysis of her rich and magnificent phenomena. He made himself acquainted, as far as his pursuits would allow, with anatomy, chemistry, natural history, and physics, and availed himself of their results in illustration and proof of his discoveries in social science. He believed in the harmony of all truth, and from the contradictions which abounded in the pretended moral, philosophical, and political sciences, he was led to perceive the weakness of their foundations, and enabled to explain the absurdity of their claims. The study of the languages was the only one for which he appeared to have little attraction. He regarded the variety of languages as one of the signs of the social incoherence of the globe,—as one evidence among many others of the antagonism of man with nature, and the distance of the human race from the attainment of their destiny. "One of his earliest discoveries revealed to him the most simple sounds were forty eight in number, he saw the confusion which must necessarily arise from the fragmentary attempts to represent a compound multiplicity of these distinct sounds by means of twenty or thirty simple letters." His intuitive genius thus anticipated a brilliant discovery of more recent times which reduces the art of writing by sounds to an accurate science, and introduces harmony between the spoken and written symbols of feeling and thought.

His habits of study were those of an earnest and enthusiastic lover of truth. He became at once entirely absorbed in ever subject that commanded his attention. He could not leave it until he had sounded its depths. The idea of it haunted him, night and day; and took absolute possession of his soul. He might have replied, with Newton, to any one who asked him how he had arrived at his great discoveries, "By the force of thinking."

He early displayed his talent for invention. At the age of 19, he had conceived the plan of locomotion by railroads, which has since been carried out with such splendid results. He communicated his idea to certain engineers among his acquaintance; they at once pronounced the thing impossible; and treated his project with raillery and contempt. "At the age of 19" said Fourier, on relating the circumstance a few years before his death, "a man may be put down in his discoveries by the sect of Impossibilists; but later in life, it is another affair."

The idea of the Serial order as the law of Harmony was also suggested to his mind long before he undertook to apply it to the organization of Society. As we have seen in his cultivation of flowers, he wished to collect not only a Series of species but every variety of his favorite species. About the time of his leaving school, he procured a box of colors and, for several months, devoted himself to the study of how great a variety of shades he could produce by their different combinations. He carried this to so great an extent that he could designate every regiment in the army by the color of the facings of its uniform.

After several years of absence, Fourier returned to Besancon in the year 1793, having attained the age of 21. The storms of the French Revolution were now raging; but he was not impelled by the fiery blood of youth to take part in its scenes of horror and misery. Throughout his whole life, he cherished the most profound aversion to every disorganizing, destructive movement; he had no patience with the schemes of violent demagogues; and nothing could provoke him more than to confound his theory of social Harmony with the doctrines and plans of those radical politicians who, content with assaulting the venerable ruins of past ages, propose no better social fabric in their place. He kept himself completely aloof from all the parties of the Revolution, and never exhibited the least confidence in its results as an effectual remedy for the sufferings of the masses.

He remained at Besancon but one or two months, and having converted his patrimony of about $16,000 into cash, he invested the whole of it in colonial products, with a view to engaging in that branch of business in the city of Lyons. His purchases had scarcely been forwarded from Marseilles when the celebrated revolt of Lyons against the National Convention broke out. The consequences of this enterprise were disastrous to Fourier. The city was besieged, taken after a long resistance, and partially destroyed. The property of Fourier suffered a total wreck. His bales of cotton were used for temporary ramparts; his rice, sugar, coffee, and so forth, were appropriated to the service of the hospitals, and the nourishment of those who were engaged in the defense of the city. He was himself forced into the ranks, and throughout the whole duration of the siege, obliged to do duty as a common soldier. His life was exposed to great danger and on one occasion, the column to which he belonged being ordered to make a sally against the besiegers, nearly every man in it was cut to pieces, and it was almost by a miracle that he escaped unharmed.

After the city surrendered to the troops of the Convention, which it did at the close of a siege of more than 60 days, Fourier not only failed to obtain an indemnity for his losses, but was subject to imminent danger, on account of his involuntary participation in the revolt. He was thrown into prison and narrowly escape the scaffold. His perils, however, were not brought to a close with his release from confinement. He was still in the power of the unscrupulous Revolutionary agents, who were no less distinguished for their rapacity than for their cruelty. He was often arrested, on some frivolous pretence, and then discharged; and he thus remained for several weeks in apprehension of death. His petty tyrants would sometimes inflict on him four or five domiciliary visits in a day, and they never departed without depriving him of some of the few valuable articles which he still retained. He was thus robbed of his money, his clothes, his watch, and at last, of a beautiful collection of maps and charts which he had procured for his own use, and to which, with his passionate taste for geographical studies, he had attached a peculiar value. At length, he succeeded in eluding the vigilance of his tyrants, and escaped into the country; for some time he remained there in concealment; but finding no safety in the vicinity of Lyons, he returned to his natural home at Besancon.

He had passed through severe sufferings during the siege of the city, and the months subsequent to its capture. His health was impaired, although he experienced no depression of spirits on account of his pecuniary sacrifices. On returning to his native city, he abandoned the precautions he had used at Lyons, and impatient of concealment or restraint, appeared freely in all public places, until he attracted the notice of the government, and was again incarcerated as a suspicious person. He remained in durance for eight days, when by the intervention of a relative, who was one of the Revolutionary Committee of Besancon, he again obtained his liberty. He was, however, immediately compelled to enter the national service, by virtue of a decree of the Convention which presented the most stringent claims on the patriotism of the citizens. He was now enrolled in a regiment of light dragoons, and if like Coleridge in a similar condition, he displayed more talent than was becoming in a private soldier, his miltiary experience was no obstacle to his future scientific success. We may perhaps trace back to his recollections of the French Cavalry, some of the arrangements which he applies to the Juvenile Hordes,—the organized band of children; mounted on their fiery ponies, and waging a destructive warfare on the only perpetual enemy of Harmony that will remain in a true form of society. He joined the army of the Rhine and Morelle, and after remaining in it about two years, obtained his discharge, on account of ill health, in January, 1795.

About this time, he laid before the Minister of War some plans for facilitating the passage of the French troops between the Alps and the Rhine which were favorably received by Carnot. He also made proposals to the Directory concerning the organization of the army and its mode of subsistence, by which a stop would be put to the greediness of speculators, who were then amassing large fortunes at the public expense. His plans appear to have embraced the idea of a general social reform, although he was not acquainted with the scientific method which he discovered only two years afterward. Having visited Paris, for the purpose of recommending his project, but without success, he quitted that city in a few months, and resumed the employment of commercial agent.

At the commencement of 1799, we find him at Marseilles, charged with a commission by a mercantile house which had an important influence on the development of his ideas, and the discovery of his social theory. He was employed to oversee the destruction of a cargo of rice, by throwing it into the sea, which, in hope of realizing a large profit, had been kept in the warehouse of its owners, until it was completely spoiled. France had been suffering from exceeding scarcity during the past year, and notwithstanding the risk of famine among the people, those secret monopolizers of food had allowed their stores to rot, rather than sell them at a reasonable profit. This circumstance seems to have brought the speculations of Fourier to a crisis, to have crystalized the conceptions that had long been floating in his mind, and to have prepared a systematic form and embodiment to the great humanitary truths which had dawned upon his vision. Before the close of this year, he discovered the principles of Universal Movement, and attained a knowledge of the laws which regulate the earthly destiny of man.

He stood on the point which separated the past from the coming century. The age of protest, of denial, of skeptical criticism, of a barren and bloody sensualism was about to close. It had been marked by great intellectual acuteness, a bold assertion and exercise of freedom of mind, and a reckless denial of beliefs and principles that had been deemed sacred since the memory of man. But no substantial, vital, kindling truth had been revealed to supply the dreary want, which was every where felt. No thrilling hopes of the future inspired the soul with energy to overcome the prevailing heartlessness and frivolity of society. A vague dream of liberty had caused blood to flow in torrents, but no new paths had been opened for the career of Humanity. Was the century, now on the eve of being born, to bring with it a fresh hope for the destiny of our race, or, like those which had gone before, was it doomed to welter in the abyss of social chaos, until in their deep wretchedness, men should lose all faith in their own souls and in God? At this moment of transition between the Past and the Future, at this culminating point of the protesting and critical, though aspiring spirit of the 18th century, is it not a coincidence worthy of observation, that the mind of Fourier attained a perception of truth in the neglected but all essential sphere of social science, a perception pregnant with the fate of unborn generations which has already made a deep and broad mark upon our own age, and which before its close will commence upon the earth a reign of justice, harmony, love, and celestial joy, worthy again to call the angels from their starry abodes to chant "Gloria in Excelsis" over a regenerated world.

The attention of Fourier had been directed, from an early period of his life, to the complicated evils arising from the false arrangements of commerce. His own experience of mercantile life had shown him the temptations to fraud and duplicity which are inseparable from business as at present conducted. His natural love of truth and justice was constantly wounded by the common practices of his profession. Although he devoted himself with assiduity to the pursuits of trade, it was his most earnest wish to discover the means of substituting integrity, plain dealing, and mutual advantage in the transactions of business, in place of the artifice, concealment, and intense selfishness by which they were every where characterized. Besides the grosser immortalities which shocked his sense of justice, there were certain features of commerce that made a deep impression on his imagination and memory. His first visit to Paris was made in the year 1790. He was charmed, as we may well suppose, with the splendor of the public buildings, the magnificence of the monuments, and the imposing display of wealth and grandeur; but these did not blind him to the wretchedness of the masses, and to the enormous prices that were extorted from them for the necessaries of life. A circumstance of an apparently trifling character produced a great effect upon his mind as a specimen of the revolting anomalies of trade. He was extravagantly fond of fruit, and perceiving a favorite apple in the market, was led to inquire its price; he found that he would have to pay seven pence a piece for a kind of apple which he had often purchased in the country at the rate of three farthings a dozen.[17] This fact gave a new impulse to his mind, and stimulated his desire, already intense, to discover the true laws of commerce, and hence to ascertain the true relations of human society.

It is a singular fancy that as an apple, according to the beautiful Hebrew legend, tempted the mother of mankind to the first sin, it was also an apple that suggested to the mind of Newton, the Laws of Material Harmony, and to Fourier, the more sublime laws of Social Harmony, by which our globe is to rise from the ruins of the Fall,—to be transformed from a wilderness of tigers and monkeys, foxes and snakes, to a high imperial abode,—an abode worthy of Man, in the dignity of his primeval nature,—of Man, no longer doomed to creep and toil and cheat, in subjection to another's will, but the owner of himself and the owner of the soil,—of Man, no longer the drudge of bloated monopoly, but the free and joyous cultivator of his mother earth,—of Man, nursed in the lap of luxury and delights, from which not one is excluded, where the sleep of pampered wealth is not disturbed by the wail of famished babes and starving old men,—of Man, standing by the side of his equal glorious sister Woman, and seeing in the integral development of her nature, her willingness, her purity, her freedom, her social and pecuniary independence, the surest guarantee of his own.

From that time to 1799, the epoch of his grand discovery, a period of 9 years, he was constantly devoted to the accomplishment of his task; but all his efforts were without success; he found no issue to the gloomy labyrinth; the more he advanced in science and a true knowledge of the world, the more his hopes were chilled by the deep shadow of impossibility. He did not, however, yield to despair; like a holy prophet of truth, he labored to fulfill his mission unconscious of its comprehensive and vast extent; and as we have seen, was aroused to more earnest investigation by the spectacle of monopoly forcing the people to starve, while an abundance of food was suffered to rot in the secret hordes of relentless speculation.

His first inquiries concerning commerce led him to perceive the evils of separation and antagonism of individual interests. Hence, he inferred the necessity of agricultural Association and of wholesale trade to the introduction of truth, equity, and economy, in productive industry. But this discovery only increased the difficulty of realizing his favorite project of commercial honesty. It involved the necessity of associating human beings with their natural instincts and tastes, their varieties of character and disposition, their crude conceptions and conflicting opinions; no means of doing this was known; but Fourier was persuaded that such a science was possible; and needed only to be discovered in order to be susceptible of immediate application. When he reflected on the immense advantages of economy, rapidity, equity, education, science, and universal prosperity, which would be realized by Association, he could not doubt that Providence had preordained this order of society as the natural destiny of man, and he believed that these preordained laws of Association were permanently revealed in the general laws of nature. He found that Attraction and Repulsion were the two great principles by which the Creator governs the world, and in order to obtain a complete knowledge of these laws, he resolved the study simultaneously the highest and lowest order of creation in the Universe. He considered the stars as the highest order of creation, mankind as the middle term, and the inferior animals and insects as the lowest step in the scale. He supposed that there must be certain general laws of unity common to these three orders of existence or it would be impossible for them to compose our harmonious whole; and he hoped that by studying all that was known in the positive sciences concerning them, he might discover the natural laws of relation which combine them in an integral unity. His principle instrument in the work of discovery was a sort of algebraic calculation by which he supposed every law that was common to any two of these general terms must be common to the third; and he never abandoned any branch of study until he had discovered those principles of nature which were common to the medium and the two extremes.

His first discovery was the universality of distribution, according to a law of ascending and descending progression, in every order of creation, from the highest to the lowest degree of animate and inanimate beings. This Law of Progressive Distribution he termed Series; accordingly, the first grand axiom which he established was this, "All the Harmonies of the Universe are distributed in Progressive Series."

Having observed perfect analogy in the different orders of creation in the Universe, he was led to infer that as the Creator was one and the same Being, Infinite and Eternal in his attributes, there must necessarily be a principle of unity and analogy in his creations; that the Creation must necessarily be a reflection of the attributes of the Creator; that the Creator being all in all, it was impossible for him to paint or represent any thing but himself in the Creation. From these considerations, Fourier derived the second grand axiom which is at the foundation of his system, "The Creator being one Infinite Harmonious Being, every thing in nature must be an imitation of his own attributes."

Moreover, we are to remember that attraction and repulsion are the universal laws of nature; that God is the original author and distributor of all sorts of attraction; and hence, we may justly infer, that the respective faculties or impulses of attraction and repulsion in all orders of beings,—the primary, essential, necessary tendencies of their nature, are distributed exactly in proportion to their respective functions in the general harmony of the Universe; the affinity which binds the atom, the attractive power which governs the planets, the affections which bind human beings to each other in society, are only so many different modes of the one universal law of attraction and repulsion; and from this induction Fourier derived his third general axiom, namely "The permanent attractions and repulsions of every order of beings in the creation, are exactly in proportion to their respective functions and real destinies in the Universe."

The principles are summed up in the comprehensive formula with which every student of the Associative School is familiar.

1. The Series governs Harmonies
2. Universal Analogy

3. Attractions proportional to Destinies

Here is the whole secret of Fourier's philosophy. His vast system of sublime theories concerning the nature of man, the Providence of God, the Harmonies of the Universe, the action of Human Passions, the organization of society, and the destiny of our race, is only a development of these vital, pregnant principles in their largest application. If we would understand the magnificent conceptions of Fourier, we must meditate on the central truths which formed the guiding light of his investigations, until we have succeeded in penetrating their spirit, and they become visible to our minds in all the depth and fulness of their significance. When we first hear these principles announced, they may not impress us with their originality. We may fancy that nothing new has been made known to us. We may wonder that so vast a system has been evolved from such simple data. We certainly shall not at once perceive the profoundness of their meaning, or the extent of their application. To do this would require the gigantic intellect of their author. But if we have learned how fruitless have been the attempts of philosophers to solve the mysteries of the Universe; how much their researches for truth have resembled the "sports of children playing on the sea shore, and content with picking up a smoother pebble or a more beautiful shell than their companions, while the great ocean of truth lay all undiscovered before them;" if we have clung to the faith, in every hour of darkness and skepticism, that the Universe is under the control of the wisest laws, and that the soul of man is the noblest manifestation of the Creator, we have a mental preparation for the reception of these sublime discoveries; we may cherish a forefeeling of their importance which will lead us to give them a reverent welcome; and approach the study of them with the genuine modesty of science, enjoined by Lord Bacon, when he said "it was as necessary to become a little child to enter the Kingdom of philosophy as it was to enter the Kingdom of Heaven."

It was in this spirit that Fourier pursued his inquiries concerning the designs of Providence in the Creation of the Universe. He cherished the most unwavering faith in the wisdom, justice, and goodness of the Creator. He believed in the universal operation of his laws, and inferred from his benevolence and power, as displayed in the Harmonies of Material Nature, that there must be a divine social code, adapted to the constitution of Man, and in obedience to which he would find the true perfection of his being and the fulfillment of his destiny. The life of Fourier was consecrated to the discovery and illustration of this divine social code. He saw clearly that there was no remedy for human suffering, degradation, and wretchedness, but in an order of society that should be in accordance with the divine will. Accordingly, he never aims to construct an ideal form of society; he deals in no hypothesis; he never indulges a philosophical fancy, like Plato, in framing imaginary republics, or invokes the genius of poetry, like Sir Thomas More, to people utopias with visionary beings; but concentrates the whole force of his intellect on the single question, What is the social order designed for man by the Creator of the Universe? Nothing diverted his attention from this inquiry. He pursued it with the devotion of a prophet who felt that the interests of humanity were staked on the issue. He took no counsel of man. His mind seems to have been absolutely free from prejudices. He brought a virgin soul to commune with the eternal source of truth. He entered the career of discovery like one new born. No splendor of reputation, no force of authority, no magic of sympathy, no charm of traditional opinion could seduce him from his allegiance to God. He rejected, with a stern indignation, every pretended science that bore the impress of human weakness and folly, and trusted to no evidence but the manifestation of the Creator in the Laws of the Universe. With his eagle eye, he looked with unblenching gaze on the Majesty of the Sun, and was not blinded by the surpassing brightness of the Original Source of Light.

From the epoch of his great discovery until the year 1808, Fourier made no publication of his ideas. With the patience of one conscious that he was in possession of a system of truth which could not be impaired by time, he waited for a favorable occasion to present his discoveries to the world. The first work in which his system is set forth, entitled "The Theory of the Four Movements and of General Destinies," was published in 1808.[18] This work is not to be regarded as an elaborate exposition of his discoveries. It was intended only as a general introduction to a voluminous treatise in which his theories were to be fully exhibited in a scientific form. Nor were his views at this same time so completely elaborated as to enable him to present them in their full connections, proportions, and limitations. At a later period of his investigations, he was not in the habit of referring to this work as an authoritative expression of his doctrines; and, indeed, he was so conscious of its defects and omissions, that he wished to withdraw it from circulation, at least until he should have the opportunity to give it a complete revision, and arrange it in a more accurate and systematic form. The student of Fourier will however always recur to this book with peculiar delight. It was written in the first glow of enthusiasm, when the mind of the author was all on fire with the magnitude of his conceptions, and before the ardor of his genius was chilled by the neglect of the world. The introduction, in which he describes the gradual progress of his discoveries, the principles which he adhered to in conducting his inquiries, the manner in which one truth after another dawned upon his sight, and the stupendous results to which he had arrived by simple fidelity to nature, is a masterpiece of composition. As a specimen of literary autobiography, I know not where we should look for its parallel. It is written in a style of singular ingenuousness, though of massive power; unfolding the most sublime powers of the Universe with a simplicity that is itself sublime; and displaying a proud consciousness of the magnitude of its truths while it disclaims all merit on account of their discovery. The key which this volume presents to the philosophy of history possesses an almost magical power; it shows the law which has presided over the progress of our race, of which you have had an eloquent illustration in a former Lecture;[19] and gives order and consistency to the general course of Humanity throughout the ages. Its criticisms on the falseness of the present arrangements of commerce, on the duplicity and disorder which prevail in the holiest relations of life, on the impotence of political regulations to secure the happiness of the mass, are of the most pungent and biting character. No one can read them without suspecting, at least, that the most cherished institutions of Civilized society are at war with the designs of Nature, that the foundation on which they rest is hollow and worm eaten, and that any powerful agitation of opinion would lay the whole fabric in ruins. Its delineations of a better order of society are adapted to awaken the most inspiring hopes, and although they suggest a condition of manners in future ages of Harmony inconsistent with existing usages, no sound and pure mind can fail to recognize the truthfulness, refinement, and reverence for Humanity, which pervaded the mind and purposes of the writer.

This work, however, like most of the eminent productions of original genius, was too far removed from popular conceptions of the age in which it appeared to meet with general recognition or appreciation. It was not until the lapse of eight years, that Fourier found a congenial mind to understand his principles and share in his convictions. In 1816, he formed an acquaintance with Just-Muiron,[20] a man whose name will be remembered with gratitude and respect as the first who welcomed the doctrines of Universal Unity, and who, from his earliest initiation into their profound significance, devoted himself to their promotion, with a calm and judicious energy worthy of their cause. Just-Muiron was endowed by nature with a critical, investigating spirit; the necessities of his mind impelled him to the boldest inquiry; he had devoted himself, with a rare fidelity, to the earnest pursuit of truth; he was familiar with the writings of the most celebrated sages, philosophers, and moralists, of all, in short, who had pretended to explain the destiny of Man and the secret of the Universe; but the result was so far from inspiring him with a vital faith, that he fell into a state of utter skepticism, of intellectual despair. In this condition, he for the first time read the Theory of the Four Movements in 1814. It caused the scales to fall from his eyes. It gave him that light which he had sought so earnestly without success. It breathed a fresh life into his soul, and gave an unwonted hope and charm to his existence. After endeavoring in vain to find the obscure author of this immortal work, he at length succeeded in 1816 in ascertaining his residence, and at once addressed him in a letter, expressing the effect that had been produced upon his mind by the perusal of his work, and inquiring as to the further progress and development of his ideas. Fourier replied to him in a simple and friendly manner, informed him of the obstacles which had prevented any publication since 1808, and added that he was then employed on a complete Treatise concerning his theory of Attraction, which could not appear under two years at soonest. Fourier continued his labors on this work until, by the liberal aid of Just-Murion, he was enabled to bring it before the public in the year 1822.[21]

The theory of Universal Unity, originally appearing under the modest title of a Treatise on Domestic and Agricultural Association, contains the record of Fourier's vast discoveries concerning the laws of universal movement, and their application to the true organization of Human Society. Its leading principle that[?] the Universe is constructed on the model of the human soul coincides with the axiom which the celebrated German philosopher Schiller unsuccessfully attempted to expand into a system, and seems to have been dimly foreshadowed in the doctrine of spiritual and material correspondences which holds a conspicuous rank in the teachings of Swedenborg. Assuming this principle as a clue to the labyrinth of science, Fourier unfolds the order of distribution throughout the Universe, and presents the law which governs the destiny of all created beings. In his bold and magnificent theories, however, he never loses sight of the great practical object of his work,—the elevation of Humanity by the establishment of a social organization in accordance with the immutable laws of God. The first step in the demonstration of this process was an exact analysis of the passional nature of man. This was a subject that had been strangely overlooked in the speculations of philosophers. They had devoted their inquiries to the origin of ideas, had sought to explain the functions of [the] human soul by abstract metaphysical subtleties, but had wholly ne[glected] to investigate the essential springs of action which make ma[n what] he is, and determine his earthly destiny. Fourier has analyzed th[e] desires, tendencies, or attractions of human nature, with the t[?][22] scientific observation, and laid the foundation of a rational psychology which leads to the most important practical results. The soul, in its original unity, may be regarded as a living force tending to Universal Harmony. The moment we observe its manifestations, we find them divided into three great branches, Sensation, Affection, and Intellect, which exhaust the sphere of its spontaneous action. The Sensitive Passions, corresponding to the Five external senses, connect us with the material world, impel us to the pursuit of material order and harmony, and find their legitimate centre in the true action and gratification of the external senses. The normal development of these five sensitive passions, although not forming the highest aim of the soul, is an essential condition of the true well being of man. It lies at the foundation of all human prosperity. Their claims cannot be overlooked or slighted without defrauding[?] nature. It is a false and perverted spiritualism which seek to develop the higher nature of man by sacrificing the ties which bind him to the material world. We might as well hope to quicken and invigorate his intellectual faculties by cutting off his limbs or putting out his eyes. Next in order, be the four Affective Passions, which comprise the sphere of the moral feelings, or the sentiments which connect the individuals of our race with each other. These are the ties which unite men in the relations of equals, of inferiors and superiors, the relation of the sexes, and of parent and child, or the passions of friendship, of ambition or reverence, of love and familism. These two orders of attractions, or original passion, compose the primary springs of action in man. His fundamental wants grow out of them. They furnish the motives for industry and suggest the method of its true organization. As the light and regulator of these Cardinal Passions, we find three others, belonging to the intellectual sphere, which Fourier terms the Cabalist, the Composite, and the Alternating Passions, but which, considered in reference to their mode of operation, may be called the tendency to Analysis, to Synthesis, and to Observation. The united, proportional, harmonious action of these twelve radical attractions or passions brings the nature of Man into Unity with itself, with external Nature, and with God, raises him to the loftiest degree of perfection which he is capable of reaching, crowns him with the happiness for which his whole being perpetually yearns, and fulfills the designs of a beneficent Providence in placing him on the globe. The desire, common to all passions, of universal harmony, the grand pivotal passion of the soul which aspires to the Absolute, to the Infinite, to God, is called by Fourier, Unityism, and is regarded by him as the source of the religious sentiment, and the spring of the holiest and noblest developments of the soul. "This passion is the full development of all faculties in voluntary equilibrium, in which they lose their individual characters in one celestial or angelic union of dignity, simplicity, serenity, and sympathy, as the colors of the solar spectrum lose their individual peculiarities in one celestial unitary color,—white. Unityism is so perfect in all its bearings, that you cannot see the individual passions of which it is composed, and yet no one is wanting. It is sublime simplicity and we can only hope to see it perfect when society is harmonized. Those who have it imperfectly developed are as the grey dawn of morning compared with the noon day sun."

From this analysis of the essential attractions of the soul, Fourier deduces the conditions of attractive industry, the arrangement of labor by groups and series, and the general system of social organization. His views of society thus composes a comprehensive and perfect whole. The Phalanx, with all its elaborate details, its scientific provisions, its vast economies, its harmonic arrangements for the satisfaction of human wants, and the development of human nature, is a practical embodiment, in organic institutions, of the fundamental attractions of the human soul. It is evident that Fourier had a clear perception of the great problem to be solved in the organization of society. No one can, with any shadow of justice, deny him this merit, whatever opinion he may form of the soundness of its solution. This perception in itself is an important step in social progress; and strange as it may seem, has been altogether wanting in previous speculations on the subject. The problem may be stated in the briefest form, Given human nature,—what is the form of society best adapted to its harmonious development? No one will pretend that this problem has found its solution in either of the four great periods into which society has been divided: Savagism, Patriarchalism, Barbarism, Civilization. The disciples of Fourier maintain that he has given the true law of its solution, in Integral Association, based upon attractive industry in groups and series. This question begins to attract the attention which it deserves; compared with it, all other topics of political or social economy are of trivial importance; and it will undoubtedly form the prominent subject of discussion and interest for the present century.

After the publication of the Theory of Universal Unity, Fourier devoted himself to the further illustration of its principles, and to procuring means for their practical illustration. His whole life was consecrated to this purpose. Nothing could divert him from the attempt to accomplish his mission. He succeeded, however, only in planting the seed of truth in the hearts of a devoted band of disciples. Like most discoverers of new truth in the history of the world, he was not permitted to enter the promised land which he had conquered for Humanity by years of toil and sacrifice in the wilderness.

His health which had been gradually failing since the year 1831, suffered severely during the winter of 1836. The spring brought with it only a temporary relief, and in the ensuing autumn he was so far reduced as to be unable to leave his chambers. He was unwilling to accept of medical advice, although he had several distinguished physicians among his friends. He carried his spirit of independence and his unwillingness to give trouble to such an extent, that he declined all offers of assistance from his friends, and insisted on being left alone. It was only with difficulty that they obtained his consent to allow an aged female servant to visit his room from time to time, in order to ascertain his wants. The 8th and 9th of October, he presented a slight appearance of amendment. On the evening of the 9th, the domestic remained with him till midnight, he showed no symptoms of change; but on returning at 5 o'clock in the morning she found him in a kneeling posture by the side of the bed; and on speaking to him, she ascertained that life was entirely extinct.

Thus closed the earthly career of one of the few original men, whom the Creator raises up to form an epoch in the history of Humanity. His life was sincere, earnest, disinterested, inspired with a religious love of truth, an ardent faith in the goodness and wisdom of God, and a holy devotion to the elevation of man.

The personal history of Fourier is interesting only on account of the system of truths which he was permitted to discover and make known to the world. No man was ever more free from all taint of individual ambition; he lived not for himself, but for science; he did not consult his fame, his interest, or his ease, but was absorbed in the contemplation of the eternal laws of the Universe; and having made the discovery which unfolded the destiny of man on earth, he was unwilling to use it as an instrument of personal celebrity, and even protested against its being designated by his name.

His system, we believe to be of the utmost importance to the welfare of man, because it is founded on the essential principles of human nature. It lays a broad basis for social harmony, spiritual elevation, and universal happiness, in a just and natural arrangement of labor,—the only legitimate source of the material satisfaction which the highest welfare of man demands.

Ripley's Unpublished Lecture on Charles Fourier   205

In the words of an eloquent expounder of [undeciphered], "it announces to the trodden and worn millions of the laboring classes, who in all ages and nations have cried to man in vain for relief in the agonies of their distress, the great word of Attractive Industry. After centuries of hopeless degradation, of remediless wrongs and sufferings, they have at length received the assurance that their destiny is not forever to a debasing, monotonous, repugnant, ill paid, painful, and disease-producing toil; in filthy and pestilent shops; under cruel taskmasters; from night to morning, without relief or change; at cutthroat competition, each man with his fellow; and all for a niggardly stipend, never enough to secure a man, much less his family, against sickness and old age, but always keeping him in anxiety on the brink of starvation and death. The tidings have gone forth that Industry must be organized and already the Purveyor to this glorious Host of brave and disciplined Workers and Doers has gone before to provide its food and habitations. Let a seven fold chorus of rejoicing go up from the myriads whose emancipation is at hand."

Nor in the relations of industry alone, does the system of Fourier contemplate a change which shall elevate man to a more lofty eminence than he has ever attained. By the introduction of truth and integrity into the arrangements of commerce, by the establishment of elegance, refinement, and abundance in the supply of our material wants, by placing woman in a more dignified, responsible, and independent position than she can now enjoy, by applying a system of universal education to all orders of society, by creating an entire unity of interest between the classes that are now torn so wildly assunder by the diversity of occupation, culture, and taste, by cherishing the moral sentiments of our nature, and expanding them to a degree of strength and purity which is impossible in the poisonous atmosphere of our present selfish and antagonistic civilization, and by the influence of a sublime religious spirit, manifested in all the attractive charms of a unitary ritual, combining the austere devotion to truth claimed as characteristic of the Protestant with more than the imposing magnificence and thrilling appeals to the senses and the heart in the Catholic service,— this vast and comprehensive system of social unity aims at the realization of integral harmony among men, at the fulfillment of those glorious hopes for humanity which in every age have stirred the noblest souls with inappeasable yearnings, inspired the loftiest visions of holy prophets, and caused the whole creation to travail in pain until now waiting for the manifestation of the Son of God. Well may we apply to this far reaching system of justice and humanity, the words of the great Roman Orator, in a deeper and broader significance than they were used by him to describe the sentiment of patriotism, "Caritas omnes caritalis complictens," The charity including all others in its wide embrace.

This system, we believe, finally, to be the practical embodiment of the Christian spirit in the relations of society. This view was earnestly and strongly insisted on by Fourier, almost, as it was, with his dying breath.

Born in the midst of the infidelity and materialism of the last century, he never yielded to its influence. His religious convictions stand forth in bold relief on every page of his writings. He bowed in reverence before that name, which the Christian adores as above every name. In one of the last chapters written by him, describing the triumphs of Universal Association, he exclaims, "These are the days of mercy promised in the Word of the Redeemer. Blessed are they which do hunger and thirst after righteousness for they shall be filled. It is verily in Harmony, in Associative Unity, that God will manifest to us the bounteous immensity of his Providence, and that the Savior will come according to his word in all the glory of his Father; it is the Kingdom of Heaven that comes to us in this terrestrial world; it is the reign of Christ; he triumphs; he has conquered evil. Christus regnat, veriet imperat. Then will the cross have accomplished its two fold destiny, that of consolation during the reign of evil, and that of Universal Banner when human Reason shall have accomplished the task imposed upon it by the Creator. Seek ye first the Kingdom of God and his righteousness;—the Harmony of the Passions in Associative Unity. Then will the Banner of the Cross display with glory its device, the augury of victory. In hoc Signo vinces; for then it will have conquered evil, conquered the gates of Hell, conquered false philosophy, and national indigence, and spurious civilization, et portae inferei non prevalebient."

("To Charles Fourier, then, we give our warmest gratitude for having under God taught us the true method of Associative progress on the Christian principles, including both social and individual advancement. He has introduced a new truth to the human race; he has given a new direction to human thought; he has turned the current of human opinion; he has evoked the spirit of a new era; in short, he is what his French name indicates, Fourier—the Harbinger.")[23]

Such was the man, whom future ages will crown with ever blooming honors as the immortal discoverer of the Laws of Social Harmony, of the conditions of fulfilling the destiny of man on earth. While he lived, he endured the usual fate of men of genius who have obtained glimpses of truth and beauty beyond the prevailing opinions of their day. His faith was a stern and solitary one; with a nature capacious as the firmament, he trod the wilderness alone; no troops of friends gathered round the old age of the austere thinker to cheer him with their gratitude; no blandishments of the senses diverted him from the aim of his glorious calling; but there alone, companionless, in poverty, in neglect, deeply conscious of the degradation of the world, and of the sublime designs of the Deity, with a high faith that the present social chaos would give place to scenes of surpassing harmony and joy, he wrestled through the darkest watches of the night with the angel of truth, until like the patriarch of old he saw the blessing descending from above as the day was about to break and the shadows fled[?] away.

At the present moment, the name of Charles Fourier, though uttered by many with terror, and by many with reproach, can no longer be regarded with indifference or neglect. His advent has formed a new era in the history of Humanity. His presence has left a broad and deep impression on the course of the ages. Already his significance begins to be felt by the noblest minds. Already is he hailed as the great social deliverer, by an increasing multitude, who have received from his doctrines of Universal Unity, a generous impulse to self-devotion, which stirs the deepest heart of their being. Already is he welcomed, with a lofty enthusiasm, by high-souled men, with genius kindred to his own,—by the oppressed and insulted laborer, who longs to stand on his own free soil, and share the abundant fruits of Attractive Industry,—by woman, who demands that the Mother of our race shall be placed in a position of social honor and pecuniary independence, for which civilization offers her only the pretended homage of spectral smiles and hollow flatteries,—by the fiery heart of youth whose generous instincts proclaim that the present state of social slavery, degradation, poverty, meagreness, and morality, and spiritual death can never be appointed destiny of man.

Honors will continue to gather round this illustrious name. The philosopher will extol him as the penetrating intellect which broke through the shackles of custom and prejudice, and opened the primal fountains of truth. The poet will build the lofty rhyme to bless his memory. The holiest works of Art will be consecrated to the illustration of his fame. But the most sublime tribute that will be offered to Charles Fourier will proceed from the graceful, swelling hearts of men in ages of Social Harmony, when, in the full enjoyment of the promised blessings of the combined order, on each annual return of his Birth-day, the Rising Sun will be saluted as the gilds [undeciphered] the [undecipered] of each gorgeous Phalanstery with its rising[?] beams, [wi]th hymn and song and choral dance, in honor of Fourier,—[the P]rophet of Universal Harmony—of Fourier, the annointed Apostle [of hu]manity—of Fourier, the Harbinger, as his very name signifies, of a bright and blessed day.[24]

NOTES

1. Charles Crowe, *George Ripley: Transcendentalist and Utopian Socialist* (Athens: University of Georgia Press, 1967), p. 70.

2. George Ripley and George Bradford, "Philosophic Thought in Boston," *The Memorial History of Boston*, ed. Justin Winsor (Boston: James R. Osgood, 1881), 4:313.

3. Crowe, *Ripley*, pp. 170, 202.

4. For a more complete examination of this entire discussion concerning Fourierism at Brook Farm, including the conditions prompting the change and Ripley's own conversion, see my undergraduate honors thesis, "Brook Farm at the Crossroads: The Debate Over Fourierism" (Amherst College, 1980).

5. Crowe, *Ripley*, pp. 203–204.

6. Crowe, *Ripley*, p. 206.

7. Octavius Brooks Frothingham, *George Ripley* (Boston: Houghton, Mifflin, 1882), p. 181.

8. Crowe, *Ripley,* p. 206.

9. C. Pellarin, *Charles Fourier, sa vie et sa théorie* (Paris, 1843). This is actually a second edition, and the first edition may have been published in an earlier year. An English translation of the first part, *The Life of Charles Fourier,* was published in 1848.

10. Frothingham, *Ripley,* pp. 184–85.

11. The manuscript of Ripley's lecture is copyright 1982 by the Massachusetts Historical Society and is edited with permission. I am grateful to Louis L. Tucker for assistance. In the following diplomatic transcription, Ripley's cancellations and interlineations have not been so indicated, his punctuation has been regularized for clarity, and his abbreviations (such as '&' for 'and', 'Chn' for 'Christian', and 'Cht' for 'Christ') have been silently expanded. I am extremely indebted to Joel Myerson for his patience and generosity in guiding the preparation of this manuscript.

12. "Circles," *The Collected Works of Ralph Waldo Emerson,* ed. Alfred R. Ferguson et al., 2 vols. to date (Cambridge: Harvard University Press, 1971–), vol. 2, *Essays: First Series* (1979), p. 183.

13. The preceding three paragraphs form an unnumbered introductory page.

14. Victor Considerant (1809–93) was one of the leading Fourierists in Europe, and published a number of works on Associative theory.

15. Hugh Doherty (d. 1891) was an editor of the London *Phalanx* and edited the 1851 English translation of Fourier's *The Passions of the Human Soul,* as well as a critical introduction to the theory of attractive Industry.

16. An Aedile was an inspector of public buildings in the Roman Empire.

17. The last sentence of this paragraph and the following entire paragraph were added by Ripley on an unnumbered page.

18. *Théorie des quatre movemens et des destinées générales. Prospectus et annonce de la déscouverte* . . . (Leipzig [Lyon], 1808).

19. This reference is an indication that this lecture was probably delivered as part of a series of lectures.

20. Jean Claude Just-Muiron (1787–1881) is generally regarded as the first disciple of Fourier.

21. *Traité de l'association domestique-agricola* (Paris: Bossange, 1822) was also published under the title *Théorie de l'unité universelle.*

22. Portions of this sentence were lost when the manuscript was torn.

23. The parentheses and quotation marks are Ripley's. The following paragraphs, the last of the manuscript, are found on unnumbered pages. They may well be an alternate ending which Ripley considered using.

24. The corner of the end of this manuscript leaf is torn.

JAMES FREEMAN CLARKE: NOTES TOWARD A COMPREHENSIVE BIBLIOGRAPHY

Leonard Neufeldt

EMERSON'S VIEW THAT THERE IS NO END in any vital system applies to the work of bibliographers as much as to nature, and to their bibliographies, especially inventories of secondary sources. In the case of James Freeman Clarke (1810–88) all primary and secondary bibliographies are secure in the trait of incompleteness, which, I am quick to point out, characterizes this bibliography as well. Previously unknown Clarke autograph manuscripts continue to show up in likely and unlikely places, descendants of Clarke and literary estates of families unrelated to the Clarkes still hold an indeterminate number of Clarke manuscripts, and Clarke materials have recently been identified in several uncatalogued and partially catalogued collections of his contemporaries in libraries. Moreover, the nature and sheer volume of Clarke's publications, whether these were issued under his supervision or not, and whether in his lifetime or posthumously, makes an exhaustive list of first printings virtually impossible. The problem is compounded by desultory and unreliable book trade records and by equally inadequate records by Clarke's publishers and our scholarly libraries. In response to the growing stature of Clarke there have been scattered efforts at identifying scholarly commentary on him. Less than pullulative if combined, these efforts have extended our information of such scholarship while extending the list of scholarship itself. With an eye to the growing significance of Clarke in American Unitarian and Transcendentalist studies, I have attempted to compile a comprehensive survey of Clarke manuscripts and inventory of primary and secondary works.

I. MANUSCRIPTS

There is no comprehensive and accurate list of Clarke's manuscripts.

The most extensive inventory appears in Arthur S. Bolster, Jr.'s mammoth dissertation, "The Life of James Freeman Clarke" (Harvard University, 1953), which, because of the policy of the Harvard Library not to circulate Harvard dissertations, is accessible only if one visits the Pusey Library or orders a microfilm copy. The two other important surveys are the bibliography in Charles E. Blackburn's dissertation, "James Freeman Clarke: An Interpretation of the Western Years" (Yale University, 1952), and *American Literary Manuscripts*, 2d ed., ed. J. Albert Robbins (Athens: University of Georgia Press, 1977). Over the last three decades Bolster's and Blackburn's manuscript information has become largely obsolete, on the one hand because numerous manuscripts unknown to them have appeared since then, and on the other hand because several major collections then in private hands have since been divided and deposited at or donated to libraries in New England. Sad to say, Bolster and Blackburn are considerably more reliable and useful than *American Literary Manuscripts* (*ALM*), which is noninformative on the holdings in the Houghton Library, one of two enormous collections of Clarke's manuscripts, and is distressingly inaccurate on the holdings at the Massachusetts Historical Society, the other large collection. Furthermore, *ALM* failed to consult the Andover-Harvard Theological Library, the third largest trove of Clarke's manuscripts. Also overlooked were the archives of the Unitarian Universalist Association headquarters on Beacon Street in Boston, which contain at least a few manuscripts of every well-known nineteenth-century American Unitarian minister.

Needless to say, one of the urgent needs is a reliable inventory of Clarke manuscript holdings. In a start toward that end I shall briefly survey the major collections.

A. THE HOUGHTON LIBRARY OF HARVARD UNIVERSITY (MH)

The holdings at the Houghton consist of a number of collections, and are, with minor exceptions, accurately described in three lengthy typed inventory lists compiled by the Houghton staff, one list prepared recently, the other two compiled in 1946 and 1959, respectively. Together the collections include close to 700 autograph letters by Clarke; more than 1,300 autograph letters to him; numerous postcards and autograph notes by and to him; better than 350 manuscript sermons, lectures, and essays (and numerous outlines, fragmentary drafts, and notes for the same); well over 500 pages of autograph poetry manuscripts; a number of translations, by Clarke and in his hand, of German poets; nine journal and diary notebooks or remnants of them;[1] some intermediate draft pages and parts of the final version of his novel, *The Legend of Thomas Didymus*; a preliminary draft of what appears to be the first chapter of another novel, which he never completed; a preliminary or intermediate draft of a short story; twelve leaves that were deleted from his autobiography (it is unclear who removed these pages); forty-seven college essays; account books, miscellaneous logs and records, scrapbooks, business statements, receipts, and deeds; and a folio scrapbook of the published versions of the correspondence between Clarke and his sister Sarah during his years in Louisville (these letters were published serially by Lilian F. Clarke in *The Cheerful Letter* from November 1903 to January 1910).

The manuscript sermons, lectures, and essays reveal some duplication, and a number of them exist in more than one version. On the cover page of many of these manuscripts is Clarke's chronological log of the number of times he delivered a particular address and where it was presented. For instance, the columnar tally on the cover of his lyceum lecture "Public Speaking" reports that he delivered the address eleven times at various lyceums, thus enacting the argument of the address. This lecture is an important document on the Transcendentalist art of conversation. It should also be noted that because the criteria of Clarke and his publishers for publishing his work may not agree, in many cases, with our judgment on the relative significance of individual compositions, a number of works important to scholars today were never published. There are, for example, major unpublished manuscripts on topics such as political theory and practice, women's suffrage, women's equality, abolitionism, temperance, cultural pluralism, penal justice, equitable taxation, honest elections, curbing of monopolistic practices, and many other controversial reform issues, as well as treatises on vocation, agriculture, science, and literature.

Other special features of the MH collections include abundant manuscript evidence of Clarke's activity in the writing of poetry and fiction, evidence of his interest in and knowledge of German, the diaries and journals, records of his editorial work with magazines and his contributions to scores of magazines and newspapers, his juvenilia, a separate box with fifty-five Louisville sermons chronologically arranged and another seven Louisville sermons included in other folders, evidence of his prolific and wide-ranging correspondence, indications of his business acumen and economic well-being, and much material related to his many energetic reform activities and liberal thought in theology, philosophy, politics, and economics. Of special interest to the biographer and critic is a leaf on which Clarke listed "My Teachers" in a column from one to thirteen: Channing, Carlyle, Coleridge, Wordsworth, Goethe, Margaret Fuller, Milton, Bacon, Scott, Rousseau, Socrates, St. Paul, and Cousin. In a revised list on the same leaf he added Christ as number fourteen, ranked Paul thirteen, and elevated Cousin to eighth, Margaret Fuller to fourth, and Wordsworth to second.

B. THE MASSACHUSETTS HISTORICAL SOCIETY (MHi)

Since the deposit more than a decade ago of the Perry-Clarke papers at the Massachusetts Historical Society and the acquisition of most of these materials by the Society in November 1979, this library has become virtually as important as MH in its holdings of Clarke's manuscripts. The Perry-Clarke collection represents a large portion of the papers of Clarke in the hands of grandson James Freeman Clarke during the period when Bolster completed his dissertation and, one year later, published it in book form (see III.A below). The Perry-Clarke papers, largely uncatalogued, include more than sixty-five autograph letters by Clarke; about 3,100 autograph letters and approxmiately twenty typescript letters to Clarke; some 570 manuscript sermons, lectures, and essays, and sermon and lecture outlines and notes[2] (some of the outlines and notes are in his wife's hand); and close to 1,600 bills, receipts, deeds, and other records of business transactions. Of the manuscript sermons and lectures, sixteen texts proper are missing but the cover leaves have survived. Of the sermons, 165 were published by Henry Parker, editor and publisher of the Boston *Saturday Evening Gazette*, which from 1873 to 1888 published about 475 of Clarke's sermons.

Until all nineteenth-century manuscript collections at MHi connected even remotely with Clarke are exhaustively catalogued and cross-referenced, no one will know how much Clarke correspondence and perhaps additional manuscript items currently lie buried in other collections. The most important of these collections are the Bellows papers, which are only selectively catalogued and include a substantial amount of uncatalogued Clarke correspondence (my random check indicates more than twenty autograph letters by Clarke and more than fifty to him) and the Archives of King's Chapel, a substantial portion of which has been deposited very recently at MHi. Several other collections also contain correspondence both by and to Clarke. Some of these, including the Ezra Stiles Gannett papers and the T. J. Coolidge Deposit, are currently being catalogued.

Noteworthy features of the MHi holdings include: a vast collection of sermons Clarke preached at the Church of the Disciples from its inception in 1841 (under his guidance); prolific evidence of his activties as editor of and contributor to magazines and newspapers; deeds and records of his purchase of Brook Farm in 1855 and the subsequent leasing out and other uses of it; extensive records of his investments in railroads, banks, and real estate and of his large loans (usually at ten percent) to a number of clients in the east and midwest; evidence of his scrupulously honest business practices; and some indications of his intolerance for economic exploitation, concentration of wealth, and unfair taxation (more than once he expressed in letters and notes that he favored income taxation). Like the collections at MH, the Perry-Clarke papers show an enormous, wide-ranging, and sustained correspondence and clear evidence of his eventual popularity in Boston, impressive stature and influence in America, and his full sense of his popularity and influence. The papers also provide insight into the extent of his advocacy of reforms, in which he persisted until his death.

C. ANDOVER-HARVARD THEOLOGICAL LIBRARY (MH-AH)

Smaller in quantity than the MH and MHi holdings, the Clarke materials at Andover-Harvard are, nonetheless, impressive. They include 168 autograph letters by Clarke; six autograph letters to him (undoubtedly additional letters to Clarke are buried in collections not as yet completely catalogued); some forty manuscript lectures, sermons, and essays, plus notes, fragmentary drafts, and remnants; a bibliography, in Clarke's hand, of Herder's works; a file on the controversy in the Church of the Disciples over the Clarke-Theodore Parker pulpit exchange in the winter of 1844–45; other information on the Church of the Disciples, including a brief typed history compiled in the 1940s with the help of selective recall and church records; and eighteen letterpress copies of Clarke's letters in the AUA secretary's letterbook written while Clarke served as secretary of the association. The autograph letter count includes twenty-five letters to secretaries of the AUA (bound in the AUA Letterbooks), for which Harvard's index is helpful but incomplete.

D. THE HUNTINGTON LIBRARY (CSmH)

Manuscripts include: one poem by Clarke, one journal that records a journey to California, thirty-six letters by Clarke, two letters addressed to him, and one quotation copied by him. The Clarke document noted in *ALM* is actually an essay on Clarke (John Fiske, *A Candid Theologian*).

E. UNITARIAN UNIVERSALIST ASSOCIATION (MBUUA)

At least as important as the CSmH collection of Clarke manuscripts are the Clarke materials at the Unitarian Universalist offices and archives on Beacon Street in Boston. The archives contain ten autograph letters by Clarke, a number of letters addressed to him (e.g., there are four Parker letters to Clarke in the Theodore Parker folders), valuable information on the Church of the Disciples, and a letter by Clarke's wife to the Reverend E. B. Willson shortly after Clarke's death, the request in which helps to explain why his correspondence has in large part been preserved and collected by the Clarke family. The text of her letter to "My dear Mr. Willson" reads:

> Among the papers of my husband I have found these letters which I send you, thinking that you may like to have them again.
> If you have any letters of Mr. Clarke's to give me I shall be very grateful for them.[3]

Indications are that Anna Clarke received more letters than she returned to correspondents whose letters Clarke had filed.

F. OTHER SIGNIFICANT HOLDINGS

Boston Public Library: forty-three autograph letters by Clarke, eight letters to him, and several autograph manuscript poems; American Antiquarian Society (not reported in *ALM*): eight autograph letters by Clarke, two record books from Clarke's ministerial days in Louisville (in the church papers of the First Unitarian Church, Louisville), and probably some correspondence to Clarke in several other collections; Schlesinger Library of Radcliffe College: nine autograph letters by Clarke, three letters to him; Washington University Library: eight or more autograph letters from William G. Eliot to Clarke. For the other Clarke holdings in the United States, all of which are very small, see *ALM*.

For Clarke's Transcendentalist views and his literary theories and criticism, scholars should consult the materials at MH, MH-AH, and MHi. Especially illuminating for the Transcendentalist scholar are manuscript addresses such as "A Friendly Letter et cetera to Theodore Parker" (MH), "The Influence of Great Souls in History" (MH), ["The Law of Nature and the Spiritual Life"] (MH), "The Law of Equilibrium" (MH), "Origin of the World by Evolution, Emanation and Creation" (MH), numerous lectures on women's suffrage (MH), "Miracles" (several versions at MH and MHi), "Conformity and Transformation" (MHi), "Immortality" (MHi), "Positivism, Comte and Spencer" (MHi), "The Religion of Science" (MHi), "Lecture on Poetry" (MH-AH), and "Realism & Idealism in Art" (MH-AH).

II. PRIMARY TEXTS

The first substantial and truly useful primary bibliography appeared in Bolster's dissertation, "The Life of James Freeman Clarke." Thanks to Joel Myerson's entry in *First Printings of American Authors*, ed. Matthew J. Bruccoli et al. (Detroit: Gale, 1979), an extensive inventory of Clarke's books and pamphlets is now available (4:93–107). Myerson's ninety-seven titles represent the bulk of Clarke's publications and include the titles of special interest to the literary scholar. A definitive primary bibliography, however, is still an unrealized prospect. Some pamphlet publications are not available in library collections in the United States, including the Library of Congress. Compounding the problem is the incomplete, inconsistent, and at times erroneous information in the OCLC data bank and the *National Union Catalog of Pre-1956 Imprints*, particularly in the latter. Many of Clarke's writings appeared solely in serial form or in collections co-edited with colleagues or collected and edited by a colleague. A monumental and undoubtedly onerous task facing the bibliographer is to identify and compile the vast array of Clarke's essays, sermons, editorials, letters, regularly featured columns, special reports, poems, and other items in the scores of serials to which he contributed material (a number of which he edited for a time). In this section I will deal with separately published works by Clarke, serialized texts, and collections to which Clarke contributed or which he compiled or edited.

A. BOOKS, PAMPHLETS, AND EDITIONS

Myerson's checklist in *First Printings* makes the task here a relatively easy one. What follows is merely an addendum to the titles listed by Myerson. To the extent possible, these additional titles are arranged according to date of publication. Undated publications for which I could not determine the date of printing are listed at the end. Because numerous Clarke texts were published in more than one form or edition, I have listed in each case what to the best of my knowledge is the first printing. For example, several of the sermons published separately in the

1890s or the first six years of the decade that followed were included in the collection *Transfiguration of Life* in 1909, then subsequently published as tracts by the American Unitarian Association.

A Protest Against American Slavery. Medford, Mass.: n.p., 1845. Composed by Clarke, signed by 123 ministers.
Charge at the Ordination of T. W. Higginson. N.p.: n.p., 1847.
An Important Question. Boston: Office of the Christian World, 1847.
James Freeman. Discourse at Dedication of Freeman Place Chapel. [Boston?]: n.p., 1850.
Is Evil Eternal? A Reply to Dr. Mansel. N.p.: n.p., 1864.
The Hour Which Cometh and Now Is. Boston: William V. Spencer, 1868. Includes eight new sermons not in *The Hour Which Cometh and Now Is* (Boston: Walker, Wise, 1864).
One God, The Father. N.p.: n.p., 1878.
A Collection of Twelve Sermons Preached at the Church of the Disciples. Boston: n.p., 1884.
Messages of Faith, Hope and Love. Boston: George H. Ellis, 1885.
Memoir of Ralph Waldo Emerson. Boston: n.p., 1886.
Anarchy and Law. Boston: George H. Ellis, 1887.
From Faith to Faith. Boston: George H. Ellis, 1887.
A Happy New Year. Boston: George H. Ellis, 1887.
Ministry of the Letter and the Ministry of the Spirit. Boston: George H. Ellis, 1887.
The Mutual Obligations of Science and Religion. Boston: George H. Ellis, 1887.
The Pew System and the Free-Seat System. Boston: George H. Ellis, 1887.
Rejoice Evermore. Boston: George H. Ellis, 1887.
A Sermon on Scolding. Boston: George H. Ellis, 1887.
Temperance Efforts and Temperance Methods. Boston: George H. Ellis, 1887.
The Wrath of the Lamb. Boston: George H. Ellis, 1887.
Be Not Weary in Well-Doing. Boston: George H. Ellis, 1888.
The Broad Church. Boston: George H. Ellis, 1888.
Christ and Other Masters. Boston: George H. Ellis, 1888.
The Hereafter—23 Answers by as many Teachers. Boston: George H. Ellis, 1888.
Homes in Heaven and on Earth. Boston: George H. Ellis, 1888.
The Joys of Christmas. Boston: George H. Ellis, 1888.
The Mind of Christ. Boston: George H. Ellis, 1888.
The Old and New View of the Hereafter. Boston: George H. Ellis, 1888.

The Transformation of Years into Life. Boston: George H. Ellis, 1888.
What God Gives He Gives Forever. Boston: George H. Ellis, 1888.
Woman Suffrage: Reasons For and Against. Boston: George H. Ellis, 1888.
Church-Going: Past, Present, and Future. Boston: American Unitarian Association, [188?].
Selections from Sermons Preached to the Church of the Disciples. Boston: Lowell & Co., [188?].
What Do Unitarians Believe About God? Boston: George H. Ellis, 1890.
What Do Unitarians Believe About Jesus Christ? Boston: George H. Ellis, 1890.
What Do Unitarians Believe About Sin and Salvation? Boston: George H. Ellis, 1890.
What Do Unitarians Believe About the Holy Ghost? Boston: George H. Ellis, 1892.
The Resurrection of Jesus. Boston: George H. Ellis, 1900.
The Genuine Prayer. Boston: George H. Ellis, 1901.
Salvation by Character. Boston: George H. Ellis, 1905.
God Loves all Souls. Boston: American Unitarian Association, 1906.
Keep the Bible. Boston: American Unitarian Association, 1906.
The True Self is the Best Self. Boston: American Unitarian Association, 1906.
What is Heaven? Boston: American Unitarian Association, 1906.
Conference Sermon, Preached at the First Meeting of the National Conference of Unitarian and Other Christian Churches, April 4, 1863. Boston: George H. Ellis, 1909.
The Blessings of Our Knowledge and of Our Ignorance in Regard to a Future State. Boston: George H. Ellis, 1910.
Not Unclothed, but Clothed Upon. Boston: George H. Ellis, 1910.
William Hull and the Surrender of Detroit. Boston: George H. Ellis, 1912.
Why Women Ought to Desire the Ballot. Boston: Lilian Freeman Clarke, 1913.
The Lessons of the American Civil War. Boston: George H. Ellis, 1916.
Many Mansions in God's House. Boston: American Unitarian Association, 1925.
What Good Has the Birth of Jesus Brought to the World. Boston: American Unitarian Association, 1926.
A Christmas Parable. Boston: General Alliance of Unitarian and Other Liberal Christian Women, 1926.
The True Doctrine of Liberal Christianity. Boston: American Unitarian Association, 1937.

The Fatherhood of God. Boston: George H. Ellis, n.d.
From the Old Faith to the New. Boston: American Unitarian Association, n.d.
How to Get Eternal Life. Boston: American Unitarian Association, n.d.
The Leadership of Jesus. Boston: George H. Ellis, n.d.
Unitarian Belief in Regard to the Supernatural Element in Christianity. Boston: George H. Ellis, n.d.
H. Ellis, n.d.
Unitarian Belief in Regard to Vicarious Sacrifice. Boston: George H. Ellis, n.d.
We Need to Know God. Boston: American Unitarian Association, n.d.
What do Unitarians Believe about Heaven and Hell? Boston: George H. Ellis, n.d.

In the case of six undated pamphlet publications, the texts of which also appeared in book-length collections, it has been impossible to determine which printing was the first one, the pamphlet or book form.

Charles Sumner. His Character and Career. Boston: n.p., n.d. Republished by George H. Ellis in 1911.
Do not be Discouraged. Boston: American Unitarian Association, n.d.
How to Get the Most out of the Coming Year. Boston: George H. Ellis, n.d.
Man Doth not Live by Bread Alone. Boston: George H. Ellis, n.d.
Old and New Views Concerning the Bible. Boston: George H. Ellis, n.d.
Some Reasons for Believing in a Future Life. Boston: n.p., n.d.

According to the Clarke family records at MHi the following six items were also published as pamphlets.

The Character of George Keats. N.p.: n.p., 1843.
Address Before the Agricultural Society. N.p.: n.p., 1865.
Address at the Dedication of the West Roxbury Soldiers' Monument. N.p.: n.p., 1871.
Materialism and Atheism. N.p.: n.p., 1882.
Unitarian Belief and Fellowship. N.p.: n.p., 1886.
Abraham Lincoln. N.p.: n.p., n.d.

B. SERIAL PUBLICATIONS

Many of Clarke's writings appeared in serial form (in some instances more than once) prior to being published in books or as pamphlets. Still more of his writings appeared solely in serials, which were for him as important a forum as the pulpit in the Church of the Disciples, the published pamphlet or book, or the American Unitarian Association. Indeed, the bulk of his writing appeared only in serials. Bolster's dissertation lists the majority of Clarke's writings printed in perodicals other than daily or weekly newspapers (pp. 664–720). These periodicals are the *Atlantic Monthly*, the *Christian Examiner*, the *Christian Inquirer* (later the *Liberal Christian*), the *Christian Register*, the *Christian World*, the *Dial*, *Harper's New Monthly Magazine*, the *Independent*, the *Index*, the *Monthly Religious Magazine* (later the *Unitarian Review and Religious Magazine*), the *North American Review*, *Old and New*, the *Quarterly Journal of the American Unitarian Association* (later the *Monthly Journal of the American Unitarian Association*), the *Radical*, and the *Western Messenger*. Clarke's contributions to the *Congregationalist* and *Galaxy* were overlooked by Bolster.

As editor of or regular editorial contributor to a number of these periodicals, Clarke was the author of more than 150 items in both the *Quarterly Journal of the American Unitarian Association* and the *Western Messenger*, more than 200 in both the *Christian Inquirer* and the *Christian Register*, and approximately 300 in the *Christian World*. Precise figures are impossible to ascertain because of the many anonymous contributions, a substantial number of which are probably Clarke's, and because of the fragmentary nature of Clarke's own records and the checklists prepared by family members after his death. Bolster's gargantuan list of Clarke's serial publications notwithstanding, a comprehensive—in the sense of complete—inventory still needs to be done.

The same holds true for Clarke's contributions to newspapers, for which no checklist or bibliographic survey has ever been attempted. In the secondary bibliography of his dissertation, Bolster lists several non-religious daily and weekly newspapers that offer insights into Clarke's era and region: the *Boston Daily Advertiser*, the *Boston Daily Evening Transcript*, the *Boston Daily Journal*, the *Boston Herald*, the *Boston Saturday Evening Gazette*, and the *National Anti-Slavery Standard*. All of these newspapers, however, also carried contributions by Clarke. The almost 500 sermons printed in the *Saturday Evening Gazette* is far and away the highest figure for items published by Clarke in any newspaper. Additional town and city newspapers to print work by Clarke include the *Boston Daily Bee*, the *Boston Post*, the *Boston Recorder and Telegraph*, the *Essex Register*, the *Louisville Literary Newsletter*, and the *Springfield Republican*. Undoubtedly there are others.

C. OTHER WRITINGS

Clarke's prominence in the Unitarian movement and his popularity as a writer made him a valuable addition to collections of essays by multiple contributors. Undoubtedly one of the reasons why his own writings have not been collected is his prolific production as a writer. He was also active as promoter and defender of literature and literary artists, and an ardent traveler to Europe whose travels occasioned both original work and compilations. For almost half a century the pastor of the Church of the Disciples, Clarke also compiled and translated works for use in the church (at the outset of his Boston pastorate he deliberately chose to be a liberal reformer without resigning from the pulpit as Emerson had done).

1. BOOKS AND PAMPHLETS TO WHICH CLARKE CONTRIBUTED:

"The Right Hand of Fellowship," in *The Kingdom of Heaven*, ed. William Henry Furness, pp. 31–36. Somerville, Mass.: Edmund Tufts, 1846.

Revolutionary Services and Civil Life of Gen. William Hull Prepared . . . by his daughter, Mrs. Maria Campbell, Together with the History of the Campaign of 1812 and Surrender of the Port of Detroit by his Grandson, J. F. Clarke. New York: D. Appleton, 1848, pp. 291–482; and Philadelphia: G. S. Appleton, 1848, pp. 295–482.

"Address," in *New England Historic Genealogical Society. Tercentenary Celebration of the Birth of Shakespeare*, pp. 11–52. Boston: n.p., 1864.

"Address of Rev. James F. Clarke, D. D.," in *Services in Memory of Rev. William E. Channing, D. D.*, pp. 39–44. Boston: John Wilson and Son, 1867.

"A True Theology the Basis of Human Progress," in *Christianity and Modern Thought*, pp. 35–60. Boston: American Unitarian Association, 1872.

"Religion Made for Man, not Man for Religion," in *Order of Services at the Dedication of the Fourth Unitarian Church of Chicago Together With Sermons Preached on that Occasion*, pp. 16–24. Chicago: Fergus Printing Co., 1873.

The Battle of Syracuse. Two Essays by James Freeman Clarke and Francis Ellington Abbott, pp. 1–11. Boston: The Index Association, 1875.

"The Bible," in *Unitarian Affirmations: Seven Discourses Given in Washington, D.C., by Unitarian Ministers*, pp. 27–80. Boston: American Unitarian Association, 1879.

"The Antislavery Movement in Boston," in *The Memorial History of Boston*, ed. Justin Winsor, 3:379–400. Boston: James R. Osgood, 1881.

Benjamin Peirce: A Memorial Collection, ed. Moses King. Cambridge, Mass.: n.p., 1881. I have been unable to ascertain the title and page numbers of Clarke's essay.

"Address," in *The Centenary of the King's Chapel Liturgy: Discourse by Rev. Henry Wilder Foote and Address by Rev. James Freeman Clarke, D.D.* pp. 23–34. Boston: George H. Ellis, 1885.

"Introduction," to Theodore Parker, *Views of Religion*, pp. v–x. Boston: American Unitarian Association, 1885.

"Dedication Sermon," in *Modern Unitarianism, Essays and Sermons* by J. F. Clarke, J. H. Allen et al., pp. 7–25. Philadelphia: J. B. Lippincott, 1886.

"Unitarian Belief and Fellowship," in *Unitarian Christianity*, pp. 2–5. Chicago: n.p., [1886?].

Constitution of the Defensive League of Freedom. Boston: n.p., n.d. Multiple collaborators.

"Selected Sermons," in *Treasures New and Old*, comp. Clara B. Beasley, pp. 114ff. Boston: American Unitarian Association, 1910.

2. EDITIONS:

Light on the Hidden Way, with an "Introduction" by Clarke. Boston: William D. Ticknor, 1886.

Memoirs of Margaret Fuller Ossoli, 2 vols., ed. with Ralph Waldo Emerson and William Henry Channing. Boston: Phillips, Sampson, 1852. Clarke edited "II. Cambridge." in vol. 1.

Jones Very, *Poems and Essays*. Boston: Houghton, Mifflin, 1886. Includes "Biographical Notice of Jones Very," pp. xxiii–xxvi.

3. TRANSLATIONS:

See Myerson, "James Freeman Clarke," *First Printings*, 4:106–107.

4. COMPILATION:

See Myerson, "James Freeman Clarke," *First Printings*, 4:106–107.

III. SECONDARY WORKS

A. PAMPHLETS AND BOOKS

Some of the books listed here deal only in part with Clarke. Studies with significant discussions of Clarke have been included; those with passing and fragmentary mention of Clarke are excluded. Titles are arranged alphabetically by author.

Albanese, Catherine. *Corresponding Motion: Transcendental Religion and the New America.* Philadelphia: Temple University Press, 1977.

Allen, Joseph H. *Sequel to "Our Liberal Movement."* Boston: Roberts Brothers, 1897.

Ahlstrom, Sydney E. *The American Protestant Encounter With World Religions.* Beloit: Beloit College, 1962.

Boller, Paul F., Jr. *American Transcendentalism, 1830–1860: An Intellectual Inquiry.* New York: Putnams, 1974.

Bolster, Arthur S., Jr. *James Freeman Clarke: Disciple to Advancing Truth.* Boston: Beacon, 1954.

Brooks, Phillips. *A Facsimile of a few Words Spoken by Phillips Brooks at the Time of the Death of James Freeman Clarke.* Boston: n.p., 1903.

Cameron, Kenneth Walter. *Transcendental Reading Patterns.* Hartford, Conn.: Transcendental Books, 1970.

Church of the Disciples: Seventieth Birthday of James Freeman Clarke. Boston: The Committee, 1880.

Cooke, George Willis. *An Historical and Biographical Introduction to Accompany* The Dial. Cleveland: Rowfant Club, 1902.

Cooke, George Willis. *Unitarianism in America: A History of its Origin and Development.* Boston: American Unitarian Association, 1902.

Dall, Caroline Healey. *Margaret and Her Friends.* Boston: Roberts Brothers, 1895.

Doten, Lizzie. *A Review of a Lecture by Jas. Freeman Clarke on the Philosophy of Ralph Waldo Emerson.* Boston: William White, 1865.

Frothingham, Octavius Brooks. *Transcendentalism in New England: A History.* New York: Putnams, 1876.

Fuller, Margaret. *Summer on the Lakes, in 1843.* Boston: Charles C. Little & James Brown, 1844.

Goddard, Harold Clarke. *Studies in New England Transcendentalism.* New York: Columbia University Press, 1908.

Gohdes, Clarence L. F. *The Periodicals of American Transcendentalism.* Durham: Duke University Press, 1931.

Goodnight, S. H. *German Literature in American Magazines Prior to 1846.* Madison: University of Wisconsin, 1907.
Heralds of a Liberal Faith, vol. 3, ed. Samuel A. Eliot. Boston: American Unitarian Association, 1910.
Hutchison, William R. *The Transcendentalist Ministers.* New Haven: Yale University Press, 1959.
Koster, Donald N. *Transcendentalism in America.* Boston: Twayne, 1975.
The Later Years of the Saturday Club, ed. M. A. DeWolfe Howe. Boston: Houghton Mifflin, 1927.
McKinsey, Elizabeth. *The Western Experiment: New England Transcendentalism in the Ohio Valley.* Cambridge: Harvard University Press, 1973.
Memorial of the Commemoration by the Church of the Disciples of the Fiftieth Birthday of their Pastor, April 4, 1860. Boston: n.p., 1860.
Myerson, Joel. *The New England Transcendentalists and the* Dial. Rutherford, N.J.: Fairleigh Dickinson University Press, 1980.
Peabody, Francis G. *Reminiscences of Present-Day Saints.* Boston: Houghton Mifflin, 1927.
Rusk, Ralph L. *The Literature of the Middle Western Frontier*, vol. 1. New York: Columbia University Press, 1925.
Stange, Douglas. *Patterns of Anti-Slavery Among American Unitarians, 1831–1860.* Rutherford, N.J.: Fairleigh Dickinson University Press, 1977.
Thomas, John Wesley. *Amerikanische Dichter und die deutsche Literatur.* Berlin: Goslar, 1950.
Thomas, John Wesley. *James Freeman Clarke: Apostle of German Culture.* Boston: John W. Luce, 1949.
Treasures New and Old, comp. Clara Bancroft Beasley. Boston: American Unitarian Association, 1910.
Venable, W. H. *Beginnings of a Literary Culture in the Ohio Valley.* Cincinnati: Robert Clarke, 1887.
Vogel, Stanley M. *German Literary Influences on the American Transcendentalists, 1810–1840.* Yale University Press, 1955.

B. ARTICLES

A number of the articles listed below feature and comment on unpublished Clarke manuscripts. The Clarke letters in Colville's two articles and in Thomas' article in the *Filson Club History Quarterly* are collected in Thomas' *Letters of James Freeman Clarke to Margaret Fuller.* The numerous notices in newspapers, magazines, and journals of Clarke's death, and the many obituary tributes and memorials have not been included here.

Albrecht, Robert C. "The Theological Response of the Transcendentalists to the Civil War," *New England Quarterly*, 38 (March 1965): 21–34.
Batchelor, George. "Unitarian Sin: The Transcendental Period," *Christian Register*, 73 (1 February 1894): 72–73.
Blackburn, Charles E. "Some New Light on the *Western Messenger*," *American Literature*, 26 (November 1954): 320–36.
Christian Register, 67 (14 June 1888). Entire issue on Clarke.
Colville, Derek. "The Transcendental Friends: Clarke and Margaret Fuller," *New England Quarterly*, 30 (September 1957): 378–82.
Colville, Derek. "A Transcendentalist in Old Kentucky," *Register of the Kentucky Historical Society*, 55 (October 1957): 325–29.
Gohdes, Clarence. "The *Western Messenger* and the *Dial*," *Studies in Philology*, 26 (January 1929): 67–84. Reprinted in his *The Periodicals of American Transcendentalism*.
Habich, Robert D. "James Freeman Clarke's 1833 Letter-Journal for Margaret Fuller," *ESQ: A Journal of the American Renaissance*, 27 (1st Quarter 1981): 47–56.
Howe, Julia Ward. "The Church of the Disciples: The Ministry of James Freeman Clarke," *Christian Register*, 70 (14 May 1891): 308ff. Also in *Services and Addresses at the Semi-centennial Celebration of the Church of the Disciples, April 27, 1891.* Boston: George H. Ellis, 1891.
Myerson, Joel. " 'A True & High Minded Person': Transcendentalist Sarah Clarke," *Southwest Review*, 59 (Spring 1974): 163–72.
Our Best Words, 15 July 1888. Entire issue of this Unitarian newspaper in Shelbyville, Illinois, on Clarke.
Peabody, Andrew P. "Memoir of James Freeman Clarke," *Proceedings of the Massachusetts Historical Society*, 2d ser. 4 (March 1889): 320–35.
Perkins, James H. "The Western Messenger: Devoted to Religion and Literature," *Christian Examiner*, 25 (September 1838): 37–42.
Shivers, Frank R., Jr. "A Western Chapter in the History of American Transcendentalism," *Bulletin of the Historical and Philosophical Society of Ohio*, 15 (April 1957): 117–30.
Stern, Madeleine B. "Four Letters from George Keats," *PMLA*, 56 (March 1941): 207–18.
Thomas, John Wesley. "The Fifth Gospel," *Modern Language Notes*, 62 (November 1947): 445–49.
Thomas, John Wesley. "A Hitherto Unpublished Critique of Goethe,

Written on the Occasion of His Death," *Journal of English and Germanic Philology,* 48 (October 1949): 588–94.

Thomas, John Wesley. "A Hitherto Unpublished Textual Criticism by James Freeman Clarke of Margaret Fuller's Translation of *Tasso,*" *Monatshefte,* 41 (February 1949): 89–92.

Thomas, John Wesley. "James Freeman Clarke as a Translator," *American-Germanic Review,* 10 (December 1943): 31–33.

Thomas, John Wesley. "James Freeman Clarke, Margaret Fuller and Emma Keats: Some Previously Unpublished Manuscripts," *Filson Club History Quarterly,* 28 (January 1954): 21–27.

Thomas, John Wesley. "New Light on Margaret Fuller's Projected 'Life of Goethe,'" *Germanic Review,* 24 (October 1949): 216–23.

Tucker, Louis L. "The Semi-Colon Club of Cincinnati," *Ohio History,* 73 (Winter 1964): 13–26, 57–58.

Williams, George H. "The Attitude of Liberals in New England Toward Non-Christian Religions, 1784–1885," *Crane Review,* 9 (Winter 1967): 59–89.

Wilson, John B. "Elizabeth Peabody and Other Transcendentalists on History and Historians," *Historian,* 30 (November 1967): 72–86.

C. DISSERTATIONS AND THESES

I have been able to identify eleven doctoral dissertations solely on Clarke or dealing with him to a significant extent. Five of these, revised to varying degrees, have been published as books: Albanese, Bolster, Myerson, Thomas, and Vogel. Bolster's book is a much abbreviated version of his dissertation and lacks virtually all of the bibliographic information of the dissertation, including the footnotes.

Albanese, Catherine L. "Charon and the River: The Changing Religious Symbols of Six American Transcendentalists." University of Chicago Divinity School, 1972.

Albrecht, Robert Charles. "The New England Transcendentalists' Response to the Civil War." University of Minnesota, 1962.

Blackburn, Charles E. "James Freeman Clarke: An Interpretation of the Western Years (1833–1840)." Yale University, 1952.

Bolster, Arthur S., Jr. "The Life of James Freeman Clarke." Harvard University, 1953.

Brickett, Elsie Furbush. "Poets and Poetry of New England Transcendentalism." Yale University, 1937.

Colville, Derek K. "James Freeman Clarke: A Practical Transcendentalist and His Writings." Washington University, 1953.

Green, Judith A. "Religion, Life, and Literature in the *Western Messenger.*" University of Wisconsin, 1981.

Habich, Robert D. "The History and Achievement of *The Western Messenger,* 1835–1841." Pennsylvania State University, 1982.

Myerson, Joel. "A History of the *Dial* (1840–1844)." Northwestern University, 1971.

Thomas, John Wesley. "James Freeman Clarke, Apostle of German Culture to America." Pennsylvania State University, 1942.

Vogel, Stanley M. "German Literary Influences on the American Transcendentalists, 1800–1840." Yale University, 1947.

In addition there is one master's thesis that includes material on Clarke: Theresa Layton Hall, "A Bibliography of the New England Transcendentalist Movement" (Columbia University, 1929).

NOTES

1. These are frankly disappointing: Clarke kept journals infrequently and haphazardly, and fire damage to some of the notebooks raises the possibility that journals and other personal records were destroyed by fire.

2. Peter Drummey, Assistant Curator of Manuscripts at MHi, has prepared preliminary lists of the manuscript addresses and essays.

3. Quoted with the permission of the Unitarian Universalist Association and Carl Seaburg, Director of the Information Office.

THE JOURNALS OF CONVERS FRANCIS
(PART TWO)

Guy R. Woodall

THIS INSTALLMENT of Convers Francis' journals covers the period from 1825 through 1863, the year of his death. For a discussion of Francis' life and the editorial method used in this edition of his journals, see "The Journals of Convers Francis (Part One)," STUDIES IN THE AMERICAN RENAISSANCE 1981, pp. 265–343.

Jan. 2d, 1825.— Preached at home: but as there was a very violent snow-storm, I deferred the communion & the new year's sermon to another Sabbath,[498] & delivered to 20 or 30 hearers two old sermons, from 11 Kings VIII, 13, & Matth. VIII, 1, 2, & 3.[499]—Read to the church after meeting the letter inviting us to attend Mr. Furness' ordination,[500]—& married three couples.—

Jan. 9th. 1825.— At home.—preached in the forenoon from 1 Thessalonians V, 19,[501] & administered the communion, wh had been deferred,—preached in the afternoon a new year's sermon from Psalm XC, 12.[502]—Felt animated & free all day.—

Jan. 16th, 1825.— Exchanged with Mr. [T. B.] Gannett of Cam. Port: preached there from Mark IX, 24, & Ecclesiastes III, 1.[503]—Was much struck with seeing among Dr. Chaplin's[504] insane patients a young man, named Erwin, who had formerly been one of my pupils.—

Jan. 23d, 1825.— At home: it being an excessively cold & blustering day, & the audience very thin, I preached two old sermons, instead of those wh I had prepared;—texts John XIII, 17, & Psalm CXIX, 136.[505]—

Jan. 30th, 1825.— At home,—preached from Matth. V, 2–13, & Matth. V, 13–17,[506]—the two first of a series, wh I have begun, of discourses on the sermon on the mount, expository & practical. I think they were heard with interest,—I hope with edification.

Feb. 6th, 1825.— At home; preached in the forenoon an old sermon with a new text (on account of a death) from Job V, 6,—& in the afternoon one of my series on the sermon on the mount, from Matth. V, 17–21.[507]—

Feb. 13th. 1825.— Preached at home from Prov. XXVII, 1, & Matth. V, 21–27.[508] This last I thought to be a good sermon, but the audience were sleepy.—

Feb. 20th. 1825— At home; preached from Matth. V, 33–38, & 11 Peter III, 3;[509]—the latter an old sermon, though I had another new one written, wh circumstances induced me to defer to another Sabbath.—

Feb. 27th, 1825.— At home; preached from 1 Corinthians XV, 20, & Matth. V, 38–43.[510]—I thought both these sermons good. After services, attended at the meeting-house the funeral of Susanna Bright, who died in Waltham, whither her parents had lately removed, but who belonged to this town. She was a remarkable instance of protracted suffering & of uncomplaining patience, having been confined to her bed for more than 7 years, & for a considerable part of that time enduring excruciating pain.—

March 6th, 1825.— Communion day: at home in the forenoon; preached from 11 Corinthians I, 5;[511]—in the afternoon exchanged with Mr. [S.] Ripley, & preached from Gen. I, 27.[512]—After meeting administered the communion to Mrs. Cochrane at her house.—

March 13th. 1825.— Exchanged with Mr. Barrett, who has recently been settled over the 12th Congre. church in Boston, a new society;—preached from 1 Timothy VI, 7, & Esther V, 13.[513]—,with pleasure & was heard with great attention.—This seems a very promising society.

March 20th. 1825.— At home,—continued my discourses from the Sermon on the Mount,—Matth. V, 43–48, & VI, 1–5.[514]—;—they appeared to excite very considerable interest.—

March 27th. 1825.— Exchanged with Dr. Lowell of Boston: sermons from Mark IX, 24, & Amos VI, 1.;[515] spent a pleasant day at Mr. Loring's.[516]

April 3d. 1825.— At home;—preached from Matth. VI, 5–16; & Jeremiah IX, 3.[517]—In the afternoon very stormy, & house very thin.—

Thursday, April 7th. 1825— Fast Day: in the forenoon at home,—preached one of my series on the Sermon on the Mount, Matth. VI, 15–19;[518]—in the afternoon exchanged with Mr. [S.] Ripley,—sermon from Zephaniah III, 5.[519]—

April 10th. 1825:— At Duxbury; preached for Dr. [J.] Allyn from John XIV,

15, & Esther V, 13.—[520]—Left my dear [wife] Abba then, & had pleasant visit. Mr. [William] Farmer of Cambridge preached for me.—

Friday, April 15th. 1825—   Preached a lecture for Mr. [T. B.] Gannett of C. Port, from John XIV, 15.[521]—

April 17th, 1825—   At home,—preached with much animation & interest from Matth. VI, 18–22,—& 22–24.—I was told the forenoon sermon was the best I ever preached.[522]—

April 24th, 1825.—   Exchanged with Mr. Brooks of Hingham,—preached from Genesis I, 27, & Philippians III, 13, 14.[523]—Had a pleasant day, & brought home my dear Abba after a visit at Duxbury.[524]—

April 29th, 1825—Preached my own Friday lecture from Luke XIX, 42.[525]—

May 1st, 1825—   At home; communion day; preached from 11 Timothy I, 10,[526]—on occasion of three deaths, a sermon, wh excited much interest. In afternoon exhanged with Mr. [S.] Ripley, sermon from Prov. I, 20.[527]—

May 8th, 1825.—   Exchanged with Mr. [T.] Gray of Roxbury,—sermons from 1 Timothy VI, 7, & Proverbs I, 20.[528]—Dined with Mr. Bussy,—& preached with freedom & animation.—

Friday, May 13th. 1825—   Preached a lecture for Dr. Foster from Philippians III, 20.[529]—

May 15th. 1825—   At home: continued my discourses on Sermon on the Mount, from Matth. VI, 24–34, & VII, 1–6.[530]—Not much interest either in myself or the audience.—Met the children after meeting.—

May 22d, 1825—   Exchanged with Dr. Harris of Dorchester; sermons from Romans II, 12 & Jeremiah XII, 1;[531]—spoke with ease & animation.—

May 29th. 1825.—   Exchanged with Mr. B. Whitman,[532] who is supplying for a new society in Chelmsford at the head of the canal; administered the communion there, & preached from John XIV, 15, & 1 Timothy VI, 7.[533]—Visited the wonderful establishment of the new factories in C., wh has arisen suddenly as if by the touch of an enchanter;—spent the time very pleasantly at Mr. C. Baldwin's.—

June 5th. 1825.—   At home, discourses from the Sermon on the Mount, Matth. VII, 6, & VII, 7–12.[534]—Day very rainy & audience small.

June 12th. 1825.—   Exchanged with Mr. Lamson of Dedham,—& by another exchange Mr. Walker of Charlestown preached in my pulpit: I preached at D. from Romans II, 12, & 1 Timothy VI, 7.[535]—

June 19th, 1825— Exchanged with Mr. Bigelow of Medford,—preached from Amos VI, 1, & Jeremiah XII, 1;[536]—had a very pleasant day among old friends.—

June 26th. 1825.— Preached for Mr. Brazer of Salem two sermons from Matth. VI, 9.[537]—Dr. Thayer of Lancaster[538] preached in my pulpit,—& Mr. B. in his.—

Friday July 1st. 1825.— Preached my own lecture from Hebrews IV, 4[539]—

July 3d, 1825.— At home, preached from Romans X, 10,[540] & administered the communion in the forenoon; & in the afternoon, instead of making my usual exchange with Mr. [S.] Ripley, preached at home from Matth. VII, 12.[541]—A very warm & fatiguing day.—

July 10th, 1825.— At home;—discourses from Sermon on the mount, Matth. VII, 13 & 14,—& VII, 15–24;[542]—an exceedingly hot day, & I was unable to preach with any energy.

July 17th. 1825.— At home; discourses from Romans XV, 13, & Matth. VII, 24–28.[543] There was a similarity between these sermons, wh made it irksome to preach them both the same day.—

July 24th. 1825.— Exchanged with Mr. Furness of Philadelphia, & preached at Brattle St. in Boston, where Mr. F. now on a visit at home is supplying, Mr. Palfrey being absent on his voyage to England.—My sermons were from Romans II, 12, & Matth. VI, 18, 19.[544]—Preached with freedom & energy.—

July 31st. 1825.— At home: forenoon sermon from Matth. VII, 28, 29, the last of my series on the sermon on the mount: afternoon from 11 Corinthians III, 17,[545]—composed principally from one of my old ones.

Aug. 7th. 1825.— Preached at Duxbury for Dr. [J.] Allyn from 1 Corinth. IV, 20 & 1 Corinth. XIII, 9,[546]—with a good deal of satisfaction to myself at least.— Mr. Farmer from Cambridge[547] preached, in my pulpit.—

Wednesday, Aug. 10th, 1825.— Preached before the Bay Association at Mr. Kendall's meeting house in Plymouth, from Matth. VII, 28, 29;[548]—& had a very pleasant visit.—

Aug. 14th 1825.— Exchanged with Mr. Young,[549] lately settled at the New South Church in Boston, & preached there from Matth. VII, 28, 29, & Matth. VI, 18–22.[550]—Felt interested in my subjects, & was animated.—

Aug. 21st. 1825— At home; day very rainy, & audience very thin;—& therefore I preached in the forenoon an old sermon from Luke XXII, 61, 62,[551] though I had 4 new ones on hand;—in the afternoon preached a new sermon from Ecclesiastes IX, 10.[552]—Rufus Allyn[553] called to see us after meeting.—

Aug. 28th. 1825. At home; sermons from Acts XV, 1, & Job. XXII, 21.[554] Though in the forenoon I thought I had a good sermon, I was heavy & obtuse in my feelings. Had 4 baptisms.—

Sept. 4th, 1825— At home in the forenoon, communion,—preached from John XV, 4; in afternoon exchanged with Mr. [S.] Ripley,—sermon from Philippians, I, 21.[555]

Sept. 11th. 1825.— Exchanged with Dr. Pierce of Brookline;—preached from Mark IX, 24, & Matth. VI, 18–22.—Spent an exceedingly pleasant day.[556]—

Sept. 18th. 1825.— At home,—preached two old sermons, though I had 3 new ones on hand,—to one I put a new text, Ezechiel XXXIII, 5,—the other was from Job. XXIX, 18.[557]—These I selected on account of their fitness to my purpose.— Attended 3 funerals today, one of wh was that of Mr. Spring.—

Sept. 25th. 1825.— Exchanged with Mr. [P.] Whitney of Quincy, preached from Philippians I, 21, & 1 Corinthians XIII, 9.[558]—Saw the venerable Mr. [J.] Adams, who in his old age has the singular felicity to see his son raised to the post of honour at the head of the nation, wh he himself once filled.—

Oct. 2d, 1825.— At home; preached in the forenoon an excellent sermon from Proverbs XX, 9,[559] written by John Allyn[560] & found among his papers;—in the afternoon a sermon from 1 Corinthians XII, 4.[561]—Female Society had their contribution.—

Oct. 9th, 1825.— Preached at Norridgewock in Maine (being on a visit to my sister)[562] at the Court House,—in the forenoon from John III, 3,[563] two sermons in one,—in the afternoon from 1 Cor. XIII, 9.[564]—These sermons gave rise to some discussion,—& were well received.—

Thursday, Oct. 13th, 1825.— Preached in the evening at Norridg[e]wock Court House from Amos VI, 1,[565] a practical, earnest sermon, much admired.—

Oct. 16th, 1825.— Preached at Hallowell for Mr. Everett[566] from Acts XV, 1, & Philippians III, 13, 14.[567]—The forenoon's sermon particularly much liked, & I hope useful.

In the evening of the same day, I preached the same sermon (by particular request) at Augusta in the Court House.—In a day or two afterwards, received a formal request from the most respectable people in Hallowell & Augusta to have it printed, wh I declined.—

Oct. 18th. 1825. Tuesday evening. Preached in Mr. [S.] E[verett]'s meeting house, Hallowell, a sermon from Gen. I, 27,[568]—wh I think one of my best, & I believe it was well received.—

Oct. 23d. 1825.— Preached in Portland for Dr. Nichols,[569] from Matth. VII, 28, 29, & Gen. I, 27.[570]—& had reason to think people were extremely pleased, though Dr. N. said not a word, not even to thank me for preaching.—

Mr. Noyes of Cambridge preached in my pulpit—the 3 last Sundays, or supplied for me.—

Oct. 30th, 1825.— Preached at home from Acts XIX, 9, & Romans VI, 21.[571] —The first of these sermons was in a great measure stolen from Sydney Smith,[572] & I had the comfort of being told by my sister[573] that it was the best I ever preached.—

Nov. 4th. 1825— A lecture at home from Matth. XI, 6.[574]—

Nov. 6th. 1825— Communion day; at home all the day; preached in the forenoon on our Sav's agony in the garden from Matth. XXVI, 38, a sermon wh I think very good: in afternoon from 1 Samuel XXV, 32, 33.[575]—

Nov. 13th, 1825.— In the forenoon at home;—sermon from Philippians IV, 13,[576] good & animated: in the afternoon exchanged with Mr. [B.] Whitman, who is now supplying for the 2d Society in Waltham, from wh Mr. Harding has been lately dismissed,—preached from John XX, 31.[577]—

Nov. 18th. 1825— Friday: preached a lecture for Dr. Foster, Brighton, from Romans II, 28, 29.[578]—

Nov. 20th. 1825.— Preached at home, in forenoon from Matth. XIV, 1, 2, & in afternoon from Psalm CXII, 8,[579]—the last a stolen sermon,—rather a bad practice,—though Paley[580] gives great latitude—"write one sermon & steal five."—

Thursday Nov. 24th. 1825— Thanksgiving day;—preached at home from Psalm LXV, 11[581]—what I thought a good sermon;—but it was a dull & heavy day to me.—

Nov. 27th. 1825.— Preached in Waltham for the Second Society, who are now destitute,[582] from Matth. XXV, 21, & 1 Corinth. XIII, 9.[583]—This society are just emerging into Unitarianism.—Mr. Kimball of Hingham[584] preached in my pulpit.—

Dec. 4th. 1825.— Exchanged with Dr. Foster of Brighton;—sermons from 1 Kings XII, 8, & Philippians I, 21.[585]—preached with great dissatisfaction to myself,—& was heavy & cold.—Baptized a child.—

Dec. 11th. 1825.— Preached at home from 1 Corinthians XIII, 11, & Psalm XXIV, 5.[586]—The first I thought one of my best sermons,—but I doubt whether others thought so. Miss Townsend from Boston was here on a visit.—

Dec. 18th. 1825— Had an exchange with Dr. Fiske of West Cambridge: sermons from Philippians I, 21, & Ecclesiastes III, 1.[587]—A very rainy day; & very thin audience.—

Dec. 25th, 1825.— At home: preached two Christmas sermons from Matth. II, 1, 2, & Galatians IV, 4,[588]—wh I though very good, but wh excited, I think, very little attention.—

Jan. 1st, 1826.— At home all day—communion in the forenoon, sermon from Roman XIII, 11,[589]—new year's discourse in the afternoon from Psalm XC, 9.[590] I thought both these sermons animated & impressive,—& scarcely ever spoke with more power.—I attended 3 weddings before meeting in the morning.—

Jan. 8, 1826.— Exchanged with Mr. [N. L.] Frothingham of Boston; sermons from Acts XV, 1, & Mark IX, 24.[591]—I was exceedingly heavy & foggy in the forenoon,—my brain feeling as if it were bound with iron.—

Jan. 15th, 1826.— Went to Duxbury, & preached for Dr. [J.] Allyn from Philippians I, 21, & Acts XV, 1;[592]—found them there in all the excitement, wh attends the project of settling a colleague; staid 3 days.—Mr. Wiswall of Cambridge[593] preached for me.—

Jan. 22. 1826.— Exchanged with Mr. Briggs of Lexington;—preached from Romans II, 11, & Ecclesiastes III, 1.[594]—Nothing particular.—

Jan. 29th. 1826.— At home: sermons from 1 Corinth. IX, 24, 25,—& Isaiah LXIV, 6.[595]—The forenoon sermon was one of my favorite sermons,—though I very much doubt whether it was so to the audience.

Feb. 5th. 1826.— At home: in the forenoon preached from Luke II, 29, 30,[596] wh I thought a very good sermon: & in the afternoon a sermon found among J. Allyn's[597] papers, from Acts I, 8, wh I thought much better.—

Feb. 12th, 1826.— Exchanged with Mr. [A.] Young of Boston; preached from 1 Cor. XIII, 11, & Philippians I, 21.[598]—It has seldom happened to me to have more animation & engagedness.—

Feb. 19th. 1826.— At home; sermons from Matth. X, 34, & Romans VII, 22, 23.[599]—I thought them good, but they excited no attention.—

Feb. 26th, 1826.— At home, with such a cold that I could hardly speak:—preached from Psalm XCVI, 9, & James II, 10.[600] In the forenoon sermon I recommended a change of our hymn book for the one lately published by Mr. Dabney.—

Friday, March 3d. 1826— Preached my own lecture from Acts IV, 13.[601]—

March 5th. 1826. Preached at home in the forenoon—communion day—from Acts II, 22,[602]—& in the afternoon at Mr. [S.] Ripley's from Matth. VII, 28, 29.[603]—

March 12th. 1826.— Exchanged with Dr. Lowell, & preached in the forenoon at Brattle St. Church, on another exchange with Mr. Jenks, from 1 Cor. XIII, 11,[604]—in the afternoon at Dr. Lowell's from 1 Cor. IX, 24, 25.[605]—Heard many compliments on my preaching to day, wh are dangerous things.—

Friday. March 17th. 1826— Preached a lecture for Mr. Bigelow of Medford from John XIII, 23.[606]—

March 19th, 1826.— At home in the forenoon,—sermon from James IV, 4.[607]— In the afternoon, exchanged with Pres. Kirkland, & preached at the College Chapel in Cam.,[608]—a thing, wh I had long dreaded, but wh, like other dreaded things, I found to be less in reality than in apprehension; my sermon was from Luke XVIII, 9 &c.[609]—

March 26th, 1826.— At home all day: sermons from 11 Corinthians VII, 1, & Job XIV, 14, 15.[610]—The last was a stolen sermon; & though Paley[611] recommends "to write one sermon & steal five", yet I doubt whether the practice, in any degree, be good.—

April 2d. 1826.— Exchanged with Dr. Holmes of Cambridge;—preached from Numbers XXXII, 23, & 1 Corinthians IX, 24, 25.[612]—Dr. H., being an orthodox man, is just able to settle the affair with his conscience, so as to be able to exchange with me,—& that is all;—how long even this will continue to be the case is quite uncertain.—

Thursday, April 6th. 1826.— Fast Day.—Preached at home in the morning from Isaiah XXXIII, 6,[613]—a sermon wh I thought very good.—In the afternoon preached at Mr. [S.] Ripley's from Matth. VI, 16–19.[614]—Mr. [B.] Whitman preached in my pulpit.—

April 9th. 1826.— At home: in the forenoon sermon from John XVI, 33,—& in the afternoon one of my old sermons abridged from Romans XIV, 17.[615]—

April 16th. 1826— At home,—sermons from Job XXVII, 8, & Psalm CXXI, 5;[616]—the last stolen, nearly all, from Butcher;—& both of them impressive & good.—

April 23d. 1826— Preached at Northampton to Mr. Hall's society[617]—from Luke XVIII, 9 &c. & Philippians I, 21.[618]—Mr. Crafts[619] preached for me. I excited but little interest at N. this day.—

April 30th. 1826.— Continued at Northampton, preached from Gen. I, 27, & 1 Cor. XIII, 11,[620] two of my best sermons, & they excited considerable attention. Mr. Crafts again preached for me.—Had a charming visit at N.—

May 5th. 1826—Friday. Mr. Bigelow of Medford preached my lecture, from Luke XXII, 15.—

May 7th, 1826— Communion day,—at home in forenoon—sermon from Ephesians II, 18,[621] animated & good: in the afternoon exchanged with Mr. [B.] Whitman of Waltham, & preached from Romans II, 11.[622].

May 14th, 1826.— At home all day; in the forenoon, sermon from Luke XII, 27,—& in the afternoon, an old sermon from Prov. I, 10;[623] I had a new one ready, but thought this would serve my purpose better.—Met the children after meeting, for the first time this season.—

May 21st. 1826.— Exchanged with Mr. [T. B.] Gannett of C. Port, but by another arrangement preached for Mr. Barrett of Boston, from Gen. I, 27, & 1 Cor. XIII, 9.[624]—Felt animated, & preached well. Mr. G. was in my pulpit.—

May 28th, 1826.— At home all day; sermons from 1 John V, 3,—& 11 Corinthians IX, 10.[625]—The forenoon sermon I thought a good one.—Attended to the children after meeting.—

June 4th. 1826.— Preached at Duxbury for Dr. [J.] Allyn, from Philippians I, 27, & Acts X, 33.[626]—I had the satisfaction of thinking that I did some good. Mr. Kent[627] preached for me.—

Wednesday. June 7th. 1826.— Preached the sermon at the ordination of Mr. Kent[628] as colleague with Dr. [J.] Allyn. The audience was very large, & the occasion highly interesting. My text was from 2d Corinthians I, 24.[629]—This is the first ordination sermon I have ever preached.—

June 11th, 1826.— Exchanged with Mr. Field of Weston, & preached from Numbers XXXII, 23, & James IV, 4.[630]—Audience indifferent & dull.—

Friday, June 16th, 1826. Preached a lecture for Mr. [T. B.] Gannett of C. Port from 1 John V, 4.[631]

June 18th. 1826.— At home: sermons from Prov. IV, 9, & Prov. XXVIII, 14,[632]—both of wh were more impressive & excited more interest than common.— Attended the children after meeting.—

June 25th. 1826.— Preached at Nashua Village in Dunstable N. H., to a new society connected with the Factories. It is a flourishing village, & bids fair to make a good society. Sermons from Philippians III, 13, 14, & Philippians I, 21.[633]—Mr. David Reed[634] supplied my pulpit.—

Friday, June 30th. 1826.— Mr. [T. B.] Gannett of C. Port preached my lecture from Mark XIV, 25.—

July 2d. 1826.— At home in the forenoon; sermon from 1 Corinthians III, 11,[635] & administered the communion. In the afternoon preached two sermons in Waltham, one for Mr. [S.] Ripley from Luke II, 29, 30,[636]—the other for Mr. Whitman from 1 Corinthians IV, 20.[637]—Mr. Ripley preached for me.—

July 9th. 1826.— At home all day: sermons from Hebrews II, 15, & Psalm LXIII, 6.[638]—The first of these, in wh I spoke of the death of the venerable John Adams I thought one of my best sermons.—

July 14th, 1826—Friday.— Preached a lecture for Dr. Foster of Brighton, from Ephesians II, 18.[639]—

July 16th, 1826— Exchanged with Dr. [E.] Porter of Roxbury; my sermons from Luke II, 29, 30, & Genesis I, 27.[640]—Preached with animation, & spent a pleasant day.—

July 23d. 1826.— At home all day; sermon in the forenoon from Romans XIV, 7,[641] in wh I spoke of Mr. Jefferson's death; in the afternoon from Psalm XCIV, 11,[642]—a stolen sermon,—& not a very good one.—

July 30th. 1826.— At home all day; preached from Job II, 10, & 1 Kings XVIII, 21,[643]—; the first I thought a good sermon,—though perhaps the other was the more useful.—

Aug. 6th. 1826.— Preached at Brattle St., Boston,—Mr. Palfrey not having yet returned from Europe;—in the forenoon from John XIII, 23, & then administered the communion; in the afternoon from Romans XIV, 7.[644]—Mr. Webster[645] was there, & his presence seems to give dignity even to religious services. Mr. Bigelow of Medford preached in my pulpit, & Mr. E. B. Hall in his.—

Aug. 13th. 1826.— At home all day;—sermons from 11 Timothy IV, 7, & Galatians V, 7 & 8.[646]—The last I thought peculiarly useful & direct;—I thought of certain persons in my parish, when I was writing it; & I spoke it with great interest.—

Aug. 20th, 1826.— At home all day—forenoon sermon from Deuteronomy VIII, 2,—an old sermon;—in the afternoon from Psalm XXXV, 13.[647]—Day very hot, & I felt no animation.—

Aug. 27th, 1826.— Preached at Duxbury on an exchange with Mr. Kent;—sermons from Philippians III, 20, & Ecclesiastes III, 1.[648]—It fills me with melancholy to see Dr. [J.] Allyn,—the wreck of what he was, & of what he ought to be.—

Sept. 1st, 1826— Friday:—preached my own lecture from John XII, 44, 45.[649]—

Sept. 3d, 1826— Communion: at home in forenoon, sermon from Luke XXIV, 32,[650]—baptism in the morning: afternoon exchanged with Mr. [S.] Ripley—sermon from Romans XIV, 7.[651]—Felt finely to day.—

Sept. 10th. 1826.— Preached in the Unitarian Church in Baltimore, whither I had gone to supply that pulpit for 6 weeks: sermons—in the morning from parable of the Pharisee & publican,—in the evening (for they have no afternoon service) from Romans II, 12.[652]—Nothing scarcely can be more grand or beautiful, than this church.—Mr. Hill from Cambridge[653] preached in my pulpit.—

Sept. 17th, 1826.— Preached in Baltimore; in the morning from Philippians III, 13, 14,—& in the evening from Genesis I, 27.[654]—Mr. Goldsborough from Cambridge[655] supplied for me.—

Sept. 24th, 1826.— In Baltimore; sermons from a passage in Job—"I shall die in my nest" &c, & from Acts XV, 1.[656]—Mr. [A.] Hill preached for me.—

Oct. 1st, 1826.— Preached still in Baltimore from Galatians V, 1. & from 1 Corinthians XIII, 11.[657]—two sermons, I believe, very acceptable,—the first having some reference to the peculiar circumstances of the society.—Mr. Stetson of Cambridge[658] was in my pulpit.—

Oct. 8th, 1826.— Preached in the Unitarian Church in Washington,[659] on an exchange with Mr. Little, who went to Baltimore; sermons from 1 Corinthians XIII, 11,[660] at wh Mr. Clay[661] & Mr. Barbour[662] were auditors, & from

Gen. I, 27.⁶⁶³—I felt a pleasure & animation in this day's preaching.—Mr. Jenks supplied my pulpit.—

Oct. 15th, 1826.— The last Sunday of my engagement in Baltimore, where I preached from Mark IX, 24,—& from 1 Corinthians X, 21.⁶⁶⁴—Mr. [A.] Hill was in my pulpit.—Thus closed my services in B., & I am afraid that the good wh I did bore no proportion to the time, wh I spent; though I hope my visit was not altogether useless.—

Oct. 22d, 1826. On my way home, I stopt to preach this day for my friend, Mr. Furness in Philadelphia; in the morning from 1 Cor. XIII, 11:—in the evening from Gen. I, 27.⁶⁶⁵—I am almost ashamed of preaching these sermons so often, but I think them good.—Mr. F.—made some judicious, & just remarks on the bad management of my voice, by wh I hope to profit.—Mr. Kimball of Needham preached in my pulpit.—

Oct. 29th, 1826.— At home again after my long absence, wh has made my own pulpit seem like an old friend. Preached in the forenoon from Ecclesiastes I, 8,⁶⁶⁶—a sermon wh I wrote in one day,—what I never did before;—but it was thought one of my best:—in the afternoon from 1 Peter III, 8, and old sermon,⁶⁶⁷ though I had a new one written; I took that on account of a collection for the Female Society.—

Nov. 3d. 1826.—Friday— Preached a lecture for Mr. [S.] Ripley in Waltham, from Ephesians II, 18.⁶⁶⁸—Mr. [B.] Whitman the same day preached my lecture.—

Nov. 5th. 1826.— At home; communion day; sermon in the forenoon from Philippians III, 7, 8, 9;—in the afternoon from Romans VIII, 28.⁶⁶⁹—Nobody took the least interest in either of these sermons,—wh in fact is now the case with almost every thing connected with me. I am already cast by as an old & tiresome thing.—

Nov. 12th, 1826.— Preached at home, in the forenoon from Psalm XLII, 4, a sermon wh possibly excited some interest, because I spoke of singing & going to meeting;—& in the afternoon from Matth. XX, 22,⁶⁷⁰ one wh I know did not excite a particle of interest.—So I go from Sabbath to Sabbath, nobody caring what I preach; & to most of my people probably, [a] post, if it could be made to utter any sounds, would do as much good as I do.—

Nov. 19th. 1826— At home all day; in the forenoon, sermon from 11 Samuel XII, 23,—in the afternoon what I thought a good sermon from Isaiah XL, 8;⁶⁷¹— but I was appalled at seeing Mr. Dabney in my pew. Very thin audience, & apparently no interest in those who were present.—

Nov. 26th, 1826.— Exchanged with Mr. [A.] Young of Boston,—& preached not at all to my own satisfaction from Job II, 10 in the forenoon, & in the afternoon from Galatians IV, 16.[672]—I dined with Mr. Rollins & baptized his child, Francis Torrey.—I am sure that I preached miserably to day.—

Nov. 30th, 1826.— Thanksgiving day;—preached at home what I thought a pretty good sermon from Psalm CXXII, 6;[673] but it apparently excited but little attention.—

Dec. 3d, 1826.— Preached at home in the morning, from Luke XXI, 1–5,[674]— an exceedingly plain, familiar sermon,—& on that account, I believe, it excited considerable attention: for the first time since I have been settled, there was no choir in the singing seats, the singers having in a most disgraceful faction combined to desert them.—In the afternoon I exchanged with Mr. Kent of Duxbury, & preached in Waltham, where Mr. K. was supplying on an exchange with Mr. [S.] Ripley:—sermon from Galatians VI, 7 & 8.[675]—

Dec. 10th. 1826.— Exchanged with Dr. Pierce of Brookline; preached in the forenoon from Romans XV, 13, & in afternoon from Luke XIV, 26[676]—Felt as if I had preached to some edification, & with some success.—Dined with the charming family of Rich. Sullivan.[677]—

Dec. 17th. 1826. Preached at home forenoon & afternoon from the same text, Job XI, 7.[678]—two sermons, wh I thought better than common, but I am afraid not much adapted to interest the hearers.—

Dec. 24th. 1826.— Preached at Lincoln, a parish lately vacant by the death of Dr. Stearns;[679] sermons from 1 Cor. III, 19, & Galat. VI, 7 & 8.[680]—Very cold. Mr. Jenks preached for me.—

Dec. 31st. 1826.— At home: sermons from Gen. I, 14, & John IX, 4[681]—the last an old sermon taken on account of stormy weather & thin audience.— Services adapted to the close of the year. Dr. [J.] Allyn made one of the prayers.—

Jan. 5th. 1827. Friday. Dr. [J.] Allyn preached my lecture,—an excellent sermon from Titus II, 11, 12, 13, 14.—

Jan. 7th. 1827.— At home: sermon in the forenoon from Hebrews X, 3,[682]— administered the communion: in the afternoon, Dr. [J.] Allyn preached a very good sermon for me from John VII, 16.—My sermon in the morning was plain, direct, & useful.—

Jan. 14th. 1827. At home all day: sermons from 1 Kings XX, 11, & Ephesians

IV, 22, 23, 24.[683]—The first of these, I have reason to think, is one of the best of my sermons, & made a pretty deep impression. But like every thing else I preach, it was, I suppose, forgotten as soon as uttered.—

Jan. 21st. 1827.— Exchanged with Mr. Stetson, & preached at Medford, from Mark IX, 24,—& 1 Kings XX, 11.[684]—I read Mr. S's answer, in the affirmative, to the invitation to settle in Medford, Mr. Bigelow[685] having some time since asked a dismission.—

Jan. 28th, 1827.— Exchanged with Mr. Brooks of Hingham;—sermons from Hebrews II, 15, & 1 Corinth. XIII,[686] 9. The first of these more especially, I believe, excited a deep attention.—Had a very pleasant visit at H.—

Feby. 4th. 1827. At home all day: forenoon sermon from 1 Peter I, 17, with wh I was pleased as one of my good sermons; afternoon from Luke XI, 37–41,[687]—rather ordinary & dull.—

Feb. 11th. 1827.— Exchanged with Mr. Palfrey of Boston; preached from Hebrews II, 15, & Ecclesiastes I, 8.[688]—These sermons I think very good, & they appeared to excite considerable interest.—

Feb. 18th, 1827.— At home; sermons from John IV, 9, & Proverbs XVII, 16.[689]—These were poor sermons, & the day a dull & unprofitable one. I am ashamed to say, I have not let learned the art of preaching.—

Feby. 25th, 1827 Exchanged with Mr. Ripley of Boston;[690] sermons from 1 Timothy VI, 7, & Luke XIV, 26.[691]—The audience very attentive. Learned that Mr. [T. B.] Gannett had received an invitation to settle in N. York.—

Wednesday, Feb. 28th, 1827.— Preached the Sermon at Mr. Stetson's[692] ordination in Medford, from Romans XIV, 17.[693]—

Friday, March 2d. [1827]— Preached my own lecture from 1 John I, 3.[694]—

March 4th, 1827.— At home in the forenoon,—communion service,—sermon from John I, 12, 13.[695]—Exchanged in the afternoon with Mr. [B.] Whitman of Waltham, & preached from 1 Kings XX, 11.[696]—

March 11th, 1827.— At home: in the forenoon, Mr. Kent of Duxbury, who was here on a *labor of love,* preached for me a very fine sermon from the passage—"men ought always to pray, & not to faint"; in the afternoon (Mr. K. being gone to Waltham), I preached myself from 1 Cor. VI, 12.[697]—

March 18th. 1827.— At home, & preached all day,—in the forenoon from Romans VI, 17, & in the afternoon partly an old sermon from Luke X, 36,

37,[698] with some additions on occasion of a collection taken in aid of the Greeks.[699]—I felt a more than common animation in the services.—Mr. Alexander was with us.—

March 25th. 1827.— Exchanged with Dr. Lowell of Boston; sermons from Job II, 10, & Ecclesiastes I, 8.[700]—I preached with a good deal of animation, but did not preserve the natural key of my voice. Spent the day with Mr. John Clark,[701] an old acquaintance.—

April 1st. 1827— At home; sermons,—one new from Acts XVIII, 17,—the other old, from James I, 13, 14.[702]—But little interest in my preaching today.—

April 5th—1827.— Fast Day.—Exchanged in the morning with Mr. [S.] Ripley of Waltham;—sermon from Jeremiah VI, 15:[703] preached at home in the afternoon the same sermon.—

April 8th, 1827.— Exchanged with Mr. Kent of Duxbury, who preached in W. Cambridge, & Dr. Fisk preached in my pulpit. My sermons were, at D., from 1 Cor. XII, 4, & 1 Kings XII, 8.[704]—A very pleasant visit at D.; but melancholy to see Dr. [J.] Allyn.—

April 15th, 1827.— At home all day: forenoon sermon, an old one, with a new text Ephesians VI, 4,[705] on religious education;—in the afternoon from James III, 17[706] rather a poor sermon.—

April 22d. 1827. Had agreed upon an exchange with Dr. Foster of Brighton for to day; but Mr. [T. B.] Gannett of C. Port interposed, took my place at Brighton, & I preached in his pulpit, from Philippians III, 13, 14, & Luke XIV, 26.[707]—Dr. F. preached in my pulpit.—

Thursday, April 26. 1827.— Preached the Thursday lecture in Boston for Mr. Palfrey, from 1 Peter I, 17.—

April 29th, 1827.— At home; my sermons were on true & false zeal, one from Romans X, 2,—the other from Galatians IV, 18.[708]—In the forenoon sermon I went on heavily, & felt,—as I have often done under such circumstances,—a reluctance to look any of the audience in the face; this might be explained, I suppose, on Smith's principle of a want of sympathy, real or imaginary.—Yet I thought them both good sermons, & appropriate to the present state of the religious community.—

Friday, May 4th. 1827.— Preached my own lecture from John XIV, 6.[709]—

May 6th. 1827.— At home in the forenoon,—communion; preached from

Mark X, 45[710]—wh I thought a good sermon. Afternoon exchanged with Mr. [B.] Whitman of Waltham,—sermon from 1 Peter, I, 17.[711]—

May 13th. 1827. Exchanged with Mr. Green of Lynn; sermons from Gen. I, 27, & Luke XIII, 23, 24;[712]—the first, though a good sermon, I have preached so often that I am tired of it.—The other was rambling & incoherent.—

May 20th, 1827.— Preached at home all day, from Mark IV, 26, 27, 28,[713]— wh I thought one of the best sermons I have ever written,—& from Luke IX, 55.[714]. I was much interested in the sermons all day.—In the evening I went to Boston, & preached the Sunday evening lecture, at Dr. [William Ellery] Channing's church, from Romans III, 20.[715] I experienced to a degree, of wh before I had no conception, the exhilirating effect of an immense audience by candle-light.—It was a new scene to me; & I can easily understand why some ministers love night-meetings.—

May 27th. 1827. Exchanged with Mr. Pierpont of Boston; a very hot, dull, stupid day: sermons from Hebrews II, 15, & Ecclesiastes I, 8:[716]—believe I did no good, & nobody liked me.—

May 29th, 1827.— Preached in Boston at Chauncey place[717] before the Society for promoting Xtian knowledge, piety, & charity,[718] in consequence of the failure of the appointed preacher, Mr. Allen of Northborough.[719] My sermon was an old one with a closing application, from Luke X, 21.,[720]—& the audience was so small, that the service seemed little better than a farce.—

June 3d. 1827.— Preached at Mr. Frothingham's in Boston[721] today, on an exchange with Mr. Wells,[722], who is supplying there, Mr. F. being absent on the tour of Europe. Sermon in the forenoon from 1 Corinthians III, 11,[723]— then administered the communion:—& sermon in afternoon from Mark IV, 26, 27, 28.[724] Spent the day at Deac. Foster's very pleasantly.—

June 10th. 1827.— At home; a dull & unprofitable day; I was not "in the spirit."—My sermons were from 1. Cor. XIII, 13, & Psalm LI. 3.[725]—The first I thought a good sermon, but believe it was not.—Baptized Mr. Leathe's family in the morning, & this was an interesting scene.—

June 17th, 1827. Exchanged with Mr. Green of Malden,—& preached from Philippians I, 21, & 1 Corinthians XIII, 9.[726] Mr. G's society is in a sad state of confusion & division, & he intends to be dismissed.—

June 24th. 1827. Preached at home; sermons from Joshua XXIV, 15, & Acts XVII, 11.[727]—These I thought useful, practical, & earnest sermons, & the exercises of the day were more interesting than usual to me.—

Friday, June 29th, 1827.— Preached the communion lecture at home, from Ephesians II, 4, 5, 6.[728]—

July 1st. 1827.— At home all day; communion in the forenoon, & sermon from John XIV, 21; in the afternoon an old sermon from 1 Cor. III, 19.[729]—The day was interesting, & I was more engaged than common.—

July 8th, 1827. Preached at Brighton from Romans X, 2, & Galatians IV, 18.[730]—two sermons, in which I felt interested.—Dr. Foster preached in C. Port, & Mr. [T. B.] Gannett in my pulpit.—

July 15th. 1827. Exchanged with Mr. Robinson of Groton,[731]—sermons from 1 Cor. XIII, 11, & Mark IV, 26, 27, 28,[732] & preached with animation & spirit.— Had a fine ride to Groton with Mr. Bigelow.[733]—

July 22d. 1827.— At home: two sermons in connexion from John XIV, 27.[734]— Heavy & dull in the forenoon, but animated in the afternoon.—

July 29th. 1827.— Preached at Dr. Channing's in Boston, & Mr. [T. B. Gannett, with whom I made an exchange, went to Concord N. H.—Dr. [W.] Ware of Cambridge preached for me.—My sermons, were from 1 Corinth. X, 31. & 1 Peter, I, 17.[735]—

Aug. 5th. 1827.— At home all day; preached in the forenoon what I thought a very good sermon from Ephesians II, 8:[736] in the afternoon, Dr. [J.] Allyn, who was here on a visit, preached for me from Luke XIII, 24, a sermon exhibiting no "imbecility".[737]—

Aug. 12th, 1827.— Preached at home all day,—forenoon from Prov. XXX, 5 & 6,; the afternoon's sermon was an old one from Isaiah V, 20,[738]—though I had another prepared.—This has been a dull, profitless day with me.—

Aug. 19th. 1827.— Exchanged with Mr. [H.] Ware [Jr.] of Boston: my sermons were from 1 Kings XX, 11, & 1 Peter I, 17.[739]—Spent a quiet, pleasant day, & preached with spirit.—

Aug. 26th, 1827.— At home; sermons, in the forenoon from Psalm LV, 19, one of the best I have ever preached,—in the afternoon from Matth. XV, 1–10[740] principally expository.—I have been satisfied & interested unusually with the services of this day.—

Friday, Aug. 31st. 1827.— My lecture was preached by Mr. Motte, a gentleman from Charleston S. C.,[741] lately a convert from Episcopacy to Unitarianism. He gave us a most excellent sermon from 11 Peter III, 18.—

Sept. 2d. 1827.— Communion day: preached at home in the forenoon from 11 Corinthians V, 18,[742] & administered the ordinance: in the afternoon exchanged with Mr. [S.] Ripley of Waltham, & preached from Mark IV, 26, 27, 28.[743]—

Sept. 9th. 1827.— Exchanged with Dr. [E.] Ripley of Concord, where I had three services & preached three sermons, from 1 Corinthians XIII, 11,—1 Kings XX, 11,—& Mark IV, 26, 27, 28.[744]—I labored all day under the pressure of a heavy, stupifying cold.—

Sept. 16th, 1827. At home; two sermons on the same text, Romans VIII, 9.[745] I thought them good,—but the morning sermon, to my feelings, went off heavily: my wife said it was because I was aware that it was above the mental standard of a great part of the audience. I believe this was the true reason.—

Sept. 23d. 1827. At home: preached from Acts X, 4, & from 11 Thessalonians III. 18.[746]—The first of these I thought a good sermon, because it was useful & intelligible, & I felt great freedom in the delivery of it.—

Sept. 30th, 1827.— At home; preached in the forenoon from John XVII, 3, & in afternoon from Hebrews XI, 24, 25.[747]—I am afraid it has been an unprofitable day, though I thought the sermons adapted to do good, when I wrote them.—

Oct. 7th, 1827.— Exchanged with Mr. Kent of Duxbury,[748] & preached from 1 Corinthians III, 11. & 1 Kings XX, 11.[749]—Mr. K. was at W. on a return from his wedding tour. I administered communion at D. & had a pleasant visit on some accounts, but painful on others.[750]—

Oct. 14th, 1827.— Exchanged with Dr. Pierce of Brookline, & spent a pleasant day, as usual, at B.—My sermons were from 1 Corinthians XIII, 11, & 1 Kings XX, 11.[751]—I was not satisfied with my preaching to day.—

Oct. 21. 1827.— At home: two sermons on the same subject,—Faith,—from Hebrews XI, 1, & Romans V, 1.[752] These were very plain & familiar sermons: the congregation very thin.—

Oct. 28th, 1827.— Preached at Lechmere Point for a new Unitarian society, who are building a church, & who meet meanwhile in the Court House: my sermons were from 1 Peter I, 17, & 1 Kings XX, 11.[753]—Mr. Noyes from Cambridge preached for me.—I did not succeed at all to day.—

Friday, Nov. 2d. 1827. Preached a lecture at home from Luke X, 21.[754]—

Nov. 4th. 1827. Communion day: at home in the forenoon,—sermon from 1 Corinthians V, 7,[755] administered communion; preached in the afternoon at Mr. [S.] Ripley['s] Waltham, from Psalm XXIV, 5.[756]—Mr. [B.] Whitman of W. preached for me.—

Nov. 11th, 1827— Preached at the new church in Saxonville parish, Framingham from Mark IV, 26, 27, 28, & 1 Corinthians XIII, 9.[757] A cold day; & few hearers.—Mr. Thayer, from the Cambridge School, preached for me.—

Nov. 18th. 1827.— At home: my sermons were from Psalm XIV, 1, & Psalm LI, 13.[758]—These I thought pretty good sermons, especially the first; the last was perhaps more useful, as being more practical & direct.—

Nov. 25th. 1827— At home; preached from Hebrews XII, 5, a merely tolerable sermon,—& from Proverbs XII, 26,[759] a very poor one, partly borrowed. I have not imparted much edification to-day,—I am afraid.—

Thursday, Nov. 29th, 1827.— Thanksgiving day: preached at home from 1 Samuel XV, 22,[760]—a pretty good, & I believe, a popular sermon.—This is the 9th. Thanksgiving since my settlement.[761]—

Dec. 2d. 1827.— Exchanged with Mr. [T. B.] Gannett of C. Port;—sermons from Ephesians II, 8,—& 1 Peter I, 17.[762]—The first of these was, I believe, very acceptable;—Mr. T[imothy] Fuller spoke very highly of it, & requested the loan of it: it was a plain & direct exposition of *grace*.—

Dec. 9th, 1827.— This day Mr. [Ralph Waldo] Emerson from Cambridge preached for me, though I performed the other services. His sermons were from 1 Timothy V, 4—"let them learn", & from 11 Chronicles XX, 20, "believe in the L. your G. &c"[763]—These sermons were distinguished by great felicity of thought & style, by rich moral eloquence, & by a fresh & fervent earnestness. It is delightful to see & hear such a young man as Mr. E.—

Dec. 16th. 1827.— At home in the forenoon; sermon from 11 Timothy III, 12,[764] a pretty good sermon. In the afternoon exchanged with Dr. [H.] Ware, & preached at the College Chapel from 1 Corinthians XIII, 11;[765] succeeded much better than I expected.—

Dec. 23d. 1827.— Exchanged with Dr. Lowell, & preached in his church from 1 Peter I, 17, & 1 Kings XX.[766] I was exceedingly dissatisfied with my preaching & all my services this day; I could feel no interest & impart none.—Spent the evening with Dr. Lowell at his house; he talked much & very well of the present state of religious parties in the community.

Dec. 30th,—1827. Last Sunday of the year, & of this book.—I preached at home all day from Deuteronomy IV, 32, & Colossians III, 23;[767]—the first rather too flourishing & fine,—the last plain & better.—

VOLUME TWO

August 11, [1835] Went with Mr. Hedge[768] to Concord to attend association meeting[769] at Dr. [E.] Ripleys: much good talk there: R. W. Emerson there; I found Mr. H. and Mr. E. were not, as I was, disappointed in Coleridge's Table Talk;[770] they saw little or nothing to be blamed in it; talked much of Coleridge.

[1835] With what graphic power does Tacitus sketch events and characters! the stern brevity and dark majesty of his style, his impatience of words, which leads him to make each one bear as much meaning as possible, so that a whole picture is crowded into a line or sentence, the keen insight of his mind into the springs of action, which seems to rive, as it were, the very hearts of those who were the managers of great concerns, qualify him admirably for the period he has taken. The *lactea ubertas* of Livy (as Quinctilian calls it) is poor, compared with the severe, almost fearful power of Tacitus.

September 19, 1836 Attended a meeting of several gentlemen at Mr. Geo. Ripleys house. The object of the meeting was to form a sort of society for the discussion of great subjects in theology, philosophy, and literature.[771]—We want more freedom of thought and expression, they say, than can be found in any of the present meetings of the day; we want congenial spirits to talk without fear or reserve on all topics.

October 3, 1836 Went to Boston & attended the meeting mentioned a fortnight ago.[772] It was at Mr. Alcott's;[773] present, Mr. A. Mr. Emerson, Bro[w]nson,[774] Ripley, Hedge, Clark[e],[775] Bartol[776] and myself. It was an interesting meeting & the discussion edifying: the question,—why has our country hitherto failed to produce the highest order of genius, especially in the fine arts? The remarks of Alcott, Emerson, Ripley and Hedge were admirable.

1836 I find that Geo. Ripley is publishing Discourses on the Philosophy of Religion;[777] besides, Brownson is out with his New Views,[778] and Alcott with Questions on the Gospels,[779] for children. Then there is Furness's book, Remarks on the Gospels;[780] so that it seems the spiritualists[781] are taking the field in force. I have long seen that the Unitarians must break into two schools,—the Old one, or English school, belonging to the sensual and empiric philosophy,—and the New one, or the German school (perhaps it may be called), belonging to the spiritual philosophy. The last have the most of truth; but it will take them some time to ripen, and meanwhile they will be laughed at, perhaps, for things that will appear visionary and crude.[782] But the great cause of spiritual truth will gain far more by them than by the others.

[1836–37] The life derived from a higher life, the incoming of power and help from above,—this has been man's feeling, persuasion, at all times, the world over. The volumes of heathen wisdom and religion are as full of it as the Christian. It is the spontaneous creed of divine affinities, the testimony, always speaking itself out, to the God in the man, which after all shames down materialism with its cunning arguments. It met me the other day in Pindar,— those lines so rich with divinity near the close of the Eighth Pythian Ode:

> Σκιᾶς ὄναρ, ἄνθρωποι · ἀλλ, ὅταν αἴγαλ
> Διόςδοτος ἔλθῃ,
> Λαμπρὸν φέγγος ἔπεστιν ἀνδρῶν
> Καὶ μείλιχος αἰών.

"Man is indeed the dream of a shadow; but when a god-given beam visits him, then his own being glows with a bright radiance, and around him is a lovely world."[783]

[ca. 1837] What time-shadows we live in and are surrounded by! In a still, beautiful day, such as we have had this autumn, I hear the leaves break away from their stems, and see them fall with a gentle whirl to the bosom of earth. So have the outward forms of men been dropping away around me, and the ever busy but silent work of decay has gone on. I hope that meanwhile my true being has not suffered loss. I hope even that its work has been a-doing, and its vitality been quickened. I hope—but how much more do I fear.

January 16, 1837 Dined at Mr. T's,[784] whose daughter told me of the meetings for conversation at Mr. Alcott's school-room,[785] and how gloriously he talked. Mr. T. said his daughter was one of a knot of *transcendental* young ladies, to which she replied, she did not know the meaning of that, but she loved to hear Mr. Emerson lecture, & Mr. Alcott talk—I commend her taste.

February 8, [1837] Read Mr. Waldo Emerson's exquisite article on Michael Angelo in the North American Review.[786] Was ever a mind cast in a finer mould, than E's? He seems to have already anticipated the purity of the spiritual state.

February 16, 1837 Went to Boston, in the evening to hear one of Mr. Emerson's course of lectures. The subject was "Ethics".[787] It was distinguished by all his usual peculiarities of beautiful thought and expression. There is a charm about this man's mind & his compositions, wh I know not how to explain, except by saying that it is the charm of hearty truthfulness & the simplicity of a pure, far seeing soul. His style is too fragmentary & sententious. It wants the requisite words or phrases of connection and transition from one thought to another; but has unequalled precision and beauty in single sentences. This defect, & his habit of expressing a common truth in some uncommon (is it not sometimes slightly fantastic?) way of his own, are the reasons perhaps that it is so difficult to retain and carry away what he says. I find that his beautiful things are *slippery*, and will not stay in my mind. Sometimes there is a homely familiarity in his illustrations, wh is not a little amusing. Among others things he said this evening, that young persons were apt to have a diseased love of speculating on questions, wh the mind in a pure and healthy state of action does not care enough about to recognize at all.—such as original sin, the origin of evil, etc. These things, he said, were "the mumps, measles & hooping-cough of the soul."[788]

March 28, 1837 In passing the site of our old meeting-house, I observed that yesterday and to-day the last remains of it had been levelled with the ground.[789] The old spire came down, and the cock bowed his head to the dust, after having for so many years stood manfully up amidst the winds of heaven, and turned himself round with silent significance to the various points of the compass. So my old church has vanished from the list of existing things, and is henceforth to be only a remembrance. It was a work of art, the manifestation of the idea of certain artificers, who lived more than eighty years ago. There is an interest attached to the humblest forms in which the genius of man makes itself apparent in outward shapes, however rude or coarse. Every church, every dwelling-house, every utensil we use in domestic life, every garment we wear, is the expression of an idea, a fragment in the great world of art, which has been building up ever since Adam. The individual forms and manifestations vanish; but art is ever reappearing, and clothing itself with other expressions. I believe, after all, I can never love my new church as I did the old one: it had some good historical associations; it had been consecrated by years of prayer and instruction; generations had come and gone, and had sought God and truth within its walls; old men were there, with their gray hairs, whose infant fronts had been touched with the water of baptism at that altar, and when we left it, it seemed to some as if the Sabbath were no Sabbath without it.

April 30, 1837 Exchanged with R. W. Emerson, preached at E. Lexington, where Mr. E. has the care of the pulpit.[790]

May 1, [1837] Among other things, I helped to plant several trees on the hill around our new church.[791]

May 29, [1837] Went to Geo. Ripley's, where I found a pleasant company, assembled by notice,[792] consisting of Mr. Hedge, Stetson, Bro[w]nson, R. W. Emerson, Alcott, G. Ripley Bartol, Dwight,[793] Putnam[794] & Osgood.[795] We had much social & philosophical talk; discussed several topics,—as what is the essence of *religion* as distinct from morality,—what are the features of the present time as to religion, etc. R. W. Emerson defined religion to be "the emotion of shuddering delight and awe from the perception of the infinite." Others said it was a "sentiment," others "a faith of reason." Yet, I think, when we came to explain, we all pretty nearly agreed.

June 21, 1837   Attended Mr. Parker's ordination at Spring Street,[796] where I preached the sermon, under the irksome influence of a hoarse cold, but succeeded in the attempt to speak better than I anticipated. Mr. Stetson of Medford gave a capital Charge, and George Ripley of Boston an exquisitely written Right Hand. It was altogether a pleasing and well-ordered affair, quiet modest and in good taste. I liked it better than any ordination I have attended for a long time.

July 31, [1837]   At noon Mr. T. Parker, now settled at Spring Street, called. We talked of literary and theological projects. He mentioned a plan which he had in this respect, and said that when a lad he had determined to become acquainted with the literature of every known language.[797] A gigantic project; but he is young and ardent. God speed him; a fine scholar!

November 30, 1837   Thanksgiving Day. Preached at home a rather ordinary sermon, to the last part of which, however, I gave some interest by expressing my indignation at the outrage recently committed at Alton, in Illinois, in the murder of Mr. Lovejoy for his abolition principles.[798] I could not in conscience omit the notice of such an atrocity, which is in fact but one of a long series.

December 6, 1837   To Boston, to hear Mr. Emerson's lecture. It was the first of his course this winter, on Human Culture & was occupied in a general explanation of the nature, means, extent, etc. of Culture.[799] Like all the lectures, sermons and writings of Mr. E., it was as a rich strain of music from the upper air. His fault is that of too quick and easy *generalization,*—the natural fault of a mind that dwells habitually on ideas and principles. But every sentence in it was a gem of thought. His description of the *ideal,* the universal aspiration towards the *better,*—was admirable, and what some of his statements are not, it was clear. He was perpetually opening such rich, lofty, far reaching veins of thought, that we sat breathless, as it were & the mind ached with pleasure in following him. The commonness & quaintness of some of his illustrations threw a peculiar coloring of homely wisdom over parts of the lecture, wh yet blended finely with the elevated spirituality of the whole. Nothing surprises me more than the inexhaustible beauties of Mr. E's style; you listen, expecting that, as in other men's writing, so in his an ordinary sentence will occur at least now and then; but it never comes; *every* sentence is a perfect one; showing the unconscious *artist,* as the most trifling turns in a fine status show the master hand of the true sculptor. To hear Mr. E. & to see the varying expressions of his heavenly countenance, while truth radiates from him, rather than is uttered by him, seems like breathing a better atmosphere than that of this world.

"L argior hic campos aether et lumine vestit.
"Purpureo; solemque suum, sua, sidera norunt."[800]

December 13, 1837 Went to Boston, went to hear Mr. Emerson's lecture, the second in the course. It was on that part of Culture, wh relates to the *hand*, "the doctrine of the hands,"[801] as he called it, including the forms of mechanical ingenuity & industry as manifestations, or promoters of the general human culture & It was less philosophical, less *transcendental*, (as the talkers of the day would say) than the first lecture; it was full of all pithy, quaint, humorous, & serio-comical remarks & illustrations, abounding in truth and wisdom; I suppose *practical men* (as they are called) must have liked it better than most of Mr. E's lectures.

January 3, 1838 In the evening went to Boston & heard another of Mr. Emerson's admirable lectures; it was on the Culture of the Social Nature,[802] full of his genius and beauty of manner, wh appears frequently like originality, when the thought itself is not new.

January 10, [1838] Went to Boston—left the party to attend Mr. Emerson's lecture, wh was on the *heart* as signifying *intellectual integrity*,[803]—i.e. that we must do things *from the heart*, we must *be*, & not *seem*. It was full of his rich moral eloquence, striking down deep into the truth which underlies all outside things. But after the lecture, I had some debate with him for saying that Walter Scott sometimes was not *real*, but acted the fine gentleman.[804] The *spiritual* men,[805] I find, are not disposed to do justice to Scott, because he lived so in the phenomenal, the outward; they will not allow him to be a *true man*, because he was not what they require. But why was not his development as true, hearty and real, as if he had been a spiritualist? It had as much reality, though it was different. I hold Scott to have been as true a *man* as Coleridge.

February 6, 1838 Went to Boston to attend Mr. Emerson's lecture. It was the last in the course, and was a most delightful survey or recapitulation of some of the principles of Human Culture.[806] I suppose every one present was sad to think it was the last; it was like a beautiful strain of music wh one would fain have continued indefinitely. I could not but think of Milton's exquisite description, for I felt as his Adam felt:

"The angel ended, & in Adam's ear"
(quoted from this line down to)
"With glory attributed to the high Creator"
(Par. Lost—Bk. VIII, 1–13.).

Mr. Emerson in this course of lectures has spoken of high things, & spoken of them as one filled with the pure inspiration of truth.

February 14, [1837] Went to Cambridge to hear Mr. E., who is to repeat his lectures there. Heard the lecture on the "doctrine of the hands,"[807] man's double-speeders,[808] as he called them,—the culture arising from labor. We had heard it before in Boston;[809] but it was as fresh and beautiful as ever.

February 22, 1838 To Cambridge to hear Mr. Emerson's lecture. It was on the culture of the *intellect*,[810]—what the intellect is, how it *grows* & what *we can do* for it. The lecture, on the whole, I think superior to any I have heard from Mr. E., more methodical & coherent,—at the same time full of lofty and far reaching views. The two practical directions to the student, have a room to yourself, and keep a journal.[811]

March 8, [1838] To Cambridge to hear Mr. Emerson's lecture;—it was on *the heart*, or the affections, the social nature,[812]—full to overflowing of beauty and truth; he closed with a description of a family of young, intelligent boys, struggling for education, and acquiring culture, amidst the rough training of poverty and hardship; nothing could exceed it for power of truth, & for felicitous sketching.[813]

March 15, [1838] To Cambridge to hear Mr. Emerson's lecture; it was the second part on the Affections, a noble and beautiful thing. I had heard it before in Boston.[814]

March 22, 1838 Went to Cambridge and heard Mr. Emerson's lecture on the heroic;[815] it was grand in accordance with the subject,—alluded to Lovejoy and the Alton murder.[816]

March 28, [1838] Went to hear Mr. Emerson's lecture on the culture of the moral sentiment, *the holy* in man. This is the lecture, wh, when delivered in Boston, alarmed some people not a little, as certain parts of it were supposed to deny the personality of the Deity & to border close upon atheism.[817] Strange what interpretations are sometimes put upon the words of a man, who is unique and original in thought and expression! So far from this lecture containing anything like atheism, it seemed to me a noble strain of fervent, lofty, philosophical piety. It was, like its topic, *holy*. The only idea of personality in the Deity, which he impugned, was, I think the vulgar idea, wh considers God as occupying space:—the personality wh consists in a *will* and *consciousness* (& what other personality can there be?) he seemed to me to express or take for granted, though, it is true, some of his incidental expressions might look differently. I thought that in one passage of the lecture he seemed to take away the distinct, individual existence of man, as a conscious being, after death, and resolve him into the All, the Divine Soul: but my impression is probably erroneous.[818] I wish exceedingly to see Mr. E. in private & hear him expound these matters more with all the sweet charm of his delightful conversation. After return from Cambridge, read and wrote, but not much; my head and heart were too full of Mr. E's lecture for that.

March 29, [1838] Went to C[ambridge]. with Miss M.[819] to hear Mr. Emerson. It was the last lecture of the course,[820] & that was the only sad thing about it: it gave a view of the obstacles to culture, the excitements to it, a noble conclusion to a noble course of wisdom & philosophical eloquence.

April 22, 1838 After services, Parker[821] came in from Waltham, and stayed till nine o'clock. Glorious man! and a glorious time my wife and I had. He talks most delightfully: such richness of thought, such warmth of heart, such inexhaustible information. His intellectual affluence exceeds that of any man I know, not only among his coevals, but among all others. The rapid expansion and powerful development of his mind, since he first came to me as a schoolmaster,[822] have been matter of amazement to me. God bless him, and spare his life to us.

September 10, 1838 Took tea at _____[823] a family belonging to the straitest sect of Boston conservatism. I found they had been taught by _____[824] to abhor & abominate R. W. Emerson as a sort of mad dog: & when I defended that pure and angelic spirit & told them he was full of piety and truthfulness, (as he is, no man more so) they laughed at me with amazement,—for no such sounds had penetrated their *clique* before.

September 22, [1838][825] Returned to Mr. Emersons, & spent the night.[826] There was abundance of good talk, wh I hardly know how to report. What a pure, noble, loving, far-reaching spirit is Mr. E.! When we were alone, he talked of his Discourse at the Divinity School, & of the obloquy it had brought upon him:[827] he is perfectly quiet amidst the storm; to my objections and remarks he gave the most candid replies, though we could not agree upon some points: the more I see of this beautiful spirit, the more I revere and love him; such a calm, steady, simple soul always looking for truth & living in wisdom, & in love for man, and goodness, I have never met. Mr. E. is not a philosopher, so called, not a logic-man, not one whose vocation it is to state processes of argument; he is a *seer* who reports in sweet and significant words what he sees; he looks into the infinite of truth, & records what there passes before his vision: if you see it as he does, you will recognise him for a gifted teacher; if not, there is little or nothing to be said about it & you will go elsewhere for truth: but do not brand him with the names of *visionary*, or *fanatic*, or *pretender*: he is no such thing,—he is a true, godful man, though in his love of the ideal he disregards too much the actual.

September 23, [1838] In the morning at Mr. E's, we talked chiefly on matters of natural science, where Mr. Russell[828] was continually giving us information & excellent remarks. I laughed heartily at a quotation made by Mr. E. in his arch, quiet way; Mr. R. had told us of a naturalist, who spent much time and pains in investigating the habits and nature of the *louse* on *the cod-fish*; "O star eyed science" said Mr. E. "hast thou wandered there?"

September, 1838[829] Spent the night at Mr. Emerson's. When we were alone, he talked of his Discourse at the Divinity School, and of the obloquy it had drawn upon him. He is perfectly quiet amidst the storm; to my objections and remarks he gave the most candid replies, though we could not agree on some points. The more I see of this beautiful spirit, the more I revere and love him; such a calm, steady, simple soul, always looking for truth and living in wisdom and in love for man and goodness I have never met.

Mr. Emerson is not one whose vocation it is to state processes of argument; he is a seer who reports in sweet and significant words what he sees. He looks into the infinite of truth, and records what there passes before his vision; if you see it as he does, you will recognize him for a gifted teacher; if not, there is little or nothing to be said about it, and you will go elsewhere for truth. But do not brand him with the name of *visionary*, or *fanatic*, or *pretender*: he is no such thing,—he is a true, Godful man, though in his love of the ideal he disregards the actual.

The next morning[830] we talked chiefly on matters of natural science where young Mr. R[ussell]. was continually giving us information. I laughed heartily at a quotation made by Mr. Emerson in his quiet way. Mr. R. had told us of a naturalist who spent much time and pains in investigating the nature of the louse on the codfish. "O star-eyed science," said Mr. Emerson, "hast thou wandered there?"

October, 1838 Is not that the very sublime of religious philosophy, which Plato says in his Theætetus: "We cannot be free from evil while in this world, and therefore we ought to fly out of it as soon as possible. The way to fly out of it is to become as *like God* as we can. By becoming just, wise, and holy, we shall resemble him most. God is infinitely just, and there is nothing on earth so like him as a just man."[831]

Shall I deem such truth as this the less divine, or the less inspired, because I find it in an ancient heathen? Had it been written within the covers of the Bible, it would have been quoted with exultation as coming from God, and worthy to come from him; is it less so because it is written in Plato? Is there any measure of inspiration but the presence of divine truth in the spoken or written word, approving itself to the common consciousness of man?

January 9, 1839 Then wife and I rode to Boston, to hear Mr. Emerson's lecture. It was on *Genius*.[832] Never before have I been so much delighted & excited even by this most delightful and exciting of all lecturers. It was a strain of inspiration, at once lofty and sweet, throughout. It was a burst of that power, of wh it treated. I was reminded of the often quoted line about Longinus,—"and is himself the great sublime he draws." Mr. E. gives one such a succession of the best things in condensed sentences, that we can scarcely *remember* any of them. He has not, like common writers, any of those dry, sandy spots, indifferent passages,—where one can rest for a few moments, & think of and remember the good things. Hence it is so difficult to give an account to others of what he says.

January 23, [1839]   We (i.e. my wife & I, W. White and Miss Meriam)[833] set off for Boston to hear Mr. Emerson.[834] The lecture was on the Tragedy of Life,[835]—full of good thoughts, finely said, and of wisdom happily expressed.— perhaps not so striking, however, either for originality or beauty, as some of Mr. E.'s lectures. The idea of Fate was well described and dwelt upon,—how it is the idea of childish or savage life and is outgrown in the progress of refinement, being dispelled by reflection: its difference from philosophical necessity, which is optimism, etc. of the sadness occasioned by death he said, we have nothing to do with our own death,—we have only to do with living:— the death of others saddens us, yet why should it? Sorrow, he said, after all belongs to the lower part of our nature, and is an element of weakness. Composure is the wise man's element, etc.[836]

January 30, 1839   To hear Mr. Emerson's lecture. It was on the *Comic* of Human Life.[837] It gave me on the whole but little satisfaction; the philosophy seemed not quite sound, & the illustrations & anecdotes were not so piquant and striking as his usually are. One, whose thoughts are usually so rich and beautiful, can afford to fail once in a while: it is rare indeed with him.

March 16, [1839]   We heard Mr. Emerson lecture at the Rumford Institute;[838] it was one of the winter's course delivered in Boston. "The Protest,"[839]— a most admirable exhibition of the disposition in young & ardent minds, in asserting their freedom, to protest against existing things. I have scarcely heard anything from E. wh I liked so well. The instances of Michael Angelo and Columbus finely set forth.[840]

February 2, 1840   W. came in this evening: told me among other things, that his aunt, Mrs ———[841] wished that Waldo Emerson had been among the lost in the steam-boat Lexington;[842] he is such a pestilent man!!

February 12, [1840]   With Sarah Clarke, Mary Channing, wife & Mrs Bartol[843] went to hear Mr. Emerson's lecture. It was the last of his course,—on "Tendencies"[844] with reference to the present Age; full of his good things, especially some keen remarks on the common foolish notions about *consistency*, said this consistency was "the hobgoblin of little minds."[845] There was more humor in this lecture than usual.

November 7, [1840] Spent the night at Mr. Emerson's.[846] We talked till a late hour; he read me extracts of letters from Mr. Carlyle about Heraud, Landor and others,[847]—very amusing and striking from C's peculiar style of writing. In conversation somehow I cannot get very nigh to Mr. Emerson: but after all, is not every person, by the nature of the case, *insular, alone*, as to the intellect? do people ever come together, except through the affections? I suspect not.

March 31, 1841 Among other reading, finished today Emerson's Essays,[848] a most remarkable book. It contains more closely packed thought, than anything I have read this long time. The style is altogether *sua more*, the most felicitous choice of words, so that every sentence is loaded with meaning & you cannot spare a word any more than you can spare a stone from the masonry of a compact, solid wall. Emerson's illustrations are arguments; they are not patched, or laid on the composition, but grow up from within it, as parts of its essential structure. There is in his mode of writing a constant use of figurative or allusive words, so that his sentences oftener suggest than tell his meaning; & this, I think, is the main cause of the alleged obscurity of his writings. The quaint familiarity, & the frequent allusion to the personal peculiarities or feelings of the author, without egotism, sometimes remind me of the manner of Montaigne, who, I know, is a favorite author with Mr. E. There will doubtless be a great outcry from some quarters about the sentiments expressed in these Essays, & with some of them certainly I can by no means agree. But nothing can be more disgusting than this ill natured clamor of passion and ignorance. It is of little consequence whether you agree with Mr. E. or not: he is the most *suggestive* writer we have & stirs the reader's mind more than any other,—& that is a great merit, worth all the smooth proprieties, & approved commonplaces in the world.

June 13, 1841 I find there is a great hue and cry about Parker's sermon at the ordination of Mr. Shackford:[849] he is accused of infidelity, &c.,—the old song over again; and one writer in the Puritan recommends that he be prosecuted under the law of the Commonwealth against blasphemy! Bravo! So mote it be! Would to God they would try their hand at this. Here is a man of sound Christian piety, of unequalled theological attainments, of the most Christ-like spirit, who is menaced with a civil prosecution and imprisonment. Why? Because he has said we may be Christians without believing all that is written in the Old and New Testaments! This in a community boasting of its entire religious freedom! And the Unitarians, too, open full-mouthed in the cry, as well as the Orthodox!

November 26, 1841 Went to Waltham, took tea,[850] & heard Mr. Emerson lecture on Poetry.[851] It had all his usual beauties, especially his magic felicity of style,—& some of his usual defects. How difficult it is to grasp and retain the nameless charm of that man's writing.

December 11, 1841   T. Parker came in to spend the night. We had much good talk about matters of learning, &c. In religious things he seems, notwithstanding his reputation of infidelity, more and more pious every time I see him. A mind so affluent in learning and high thought I have never known.

December 28, [1841]   Am reading the new volume of Emerson's Essays:[852] how nobly and beautifully he speaks out from a world, which seems to be all his own! such an exquisite master of English expression is nowhere else to be found. I have tried in vain to analyse his mind: does it not defy analysis?

February 12, 1842   My studies this week have been in Plato, whose Republic I have finished, and in Aristophanes, whose Birds I have begun. What an admirable thing is that close of the tenth book of Plato's Republic! The defenders of Christianity are wont to say that the heathen had no faith in a future life. I would ask where in the Bible they will find the doctrine of immortality and of retribution more fully and beautifully drawn out than in that part of the Republic just referred to? As if the development of the soul—especially such development as it received under Grecian culture—did not necessarily involve the faith in immortality. If we are told that the doctrine wanted the sanction of a divine authority in the teacher, and so was but a mere conjecture, then comes up the whole question concerning this thing called authority in the manifestation of truth to the soul,—a question not so easily despatched as some suppose.

April 9, [1842]   Have read Dr. Channing's remarks on the Creole case, just published,[853]—an excellent piece of argument, and breathing a pure moral spirit: it puts to shame the letter of our Secretary of State, Daniel Webster, and shows Channing in this case the better statesman of the two. Can it be that we shall have a war with England to sustain our slavery interest of the South? Μὴ γένοιτο.[854]

June 25, 1842   Received a letter from T. Parker which made me very sad.[855] His book (Discourse of Religion)[856] has drawn upon him, of course, great obloquy, and he complains bitterly of being cut off from fellowship and kindness. That he should be treated unkindly by Unitarians, whose doctrine is individual freedom, is abominable. But I find a great deal to regret in Parker's book, the more so because I love and admire the man so much. The spirit of it *seems* to be bad, derisive, sarcastic, arrogant,—contemptuous of what the wise and good hold sacred: nothing of all this did he mean, I am persuaded,—but it has that appearance. I wish very much that he had reserved the publication of it till years had brought more consideration.

Yet perhaps it is his destiny to become a reformer, and all this sharpness may be necessary to it. But I cannot sympathize with *it*, though nobody can think more highly of *him* as a pious man, and a rich, ripe scholar, than I do.

July 23, 1842   On Thursday I preached the lecture in Boston,[857] and the sermon, I believe, gave some satisfaction to those who have been disposed to accuse me of the horrible crime of transcendentalism! O the folly, as well as wickedness, of the *odium theologicum*! it is just as bad in the nineteenth as in the fifteenth or sixteenth century,—just as bad among Unitarians as among the straitest of the Orthodox.

August 21, 1842   It was a deeply trying day for me; but I made my way through it with less distress than I had expected.[858] It seemed like tearing up old roots and planting them again in a new place. Every family, every hill or valley, every walk in my parish, has a history; and all these little histories of the heart come thronging upon me, and make a child of me. May the Head of the Church be gracious to my dear people, and send them a good minister of Jesus Christ to take the place hitherto so imperfectly filled by me. I have enjoyed much at Watertown; and though frequently saddened at the ill success of my ministry, have likewise had bright gleams of encouragement.

September 24, [1842]   Cambridge has become my home; and if I can but succeed in serving the cause of the Lord by helping to train true servants for his Church, it will be a happy home. But oh! that *if* distresses me.

[December, 1842]   I have been to a wedding in Watertown, and these visits and occasions among my quondam parishoners awaken my love of the former times and places. Shall I confess it, the artless people of a country parish interest me more than what are called intellectual people. Perhaps it is because these simple people loved me, and looked up to me as a guide. The longer I live, the more weary of conventionalisms are mere intellect. I find little that deserves to be called wisdom, except the wisdom of an earnest, loving heart.

March 11, 1843   Last Sunday I preached at Watertown, and administered the Communion to my former church.[859] It was a day of great interest to me. My roots were struck so deep there, that when I am on the spot it seems as if I must continue to grow there. They have not yet settled a minister in my place.[860] I feel anxious about their welfare as a religious society. May God bless them and give them the spirit of love and of fidelity to the Gospel of Christ. I am sometimes distressed with thinking how little I did for them while I ministered there.

[1843?]   One or two unpleasant indications at the School have troubled me this week. The thoughtlessness of young men, even those preparing for the ministry, surprises me. I wish they know how much they have my happiness in their power: I am sure they would be more considerate.

March, 1844   Last evening the Divinity Students began a very interesting discussion of the Letter from the Unitarian Ministers of England to those of America on the subject of slavery.[861]

I was glad to find that almost all the School thought and felt strongly as antislavery men. Fenner[862] said that Garrison,[863] Wendell Phillips,[864] Edmund Quincy,[865] &c. were to these times what the prophets of old were to theirs. I said all I could to encourage them in their resistance to this sin of our land, and told them I hoped every member of the School would go forth into the ministry prepared to set his face as a flint against this terrible iniquity.[866]

May 22, 1847   From Athenaeus we learn that the Rhodians were accustomed to welcome the arrival of the swallow in the Spring with a solemn song, beginning as follows:

ἦλθ', ἦλθε χελιδὼν καλὰς ὥρας
ἄγουσα, καὶ καλοὺς ἐνιαυτούς,
ἐπὶ γαστέρα λευκά, κἠπὶ νῶτα μέλαινα, &c.

"The swallow is come! is come! with her plumage white on the belly & black on the back, the herald of fair seasons & happy years" &c. (*Deipnosoph.* lib. VIII. cap. 15).[867]—O blessed nature, what are all the agonies of our studies by the side of thee! mere foolishness.—I love the sacred words, even better, when I remember that, as our poet (the [ποιητής] by way of eminance among us) has said,—

"Out of the heart of nature rolled
"The burdens of the Bible old."[868]

January 15, 1848   I am glad to see an article in Blackwood about Mr. Emerson,[869] wh does that great and good mind so much justice, though still the writer by no means understands Mr. E. or knows how to estimate him fully. The comparison of some of E's sentences to the quaint and rich ones of Sir Thomas Browne seems to me just and happy.

August 5, [1848]   Today went to Concord to see R. W. Emerson, who has lately returned from England.[870] A charming conversation of two hours with him. The presence and the words of such a man are a quickening refreshment amidst the platitudes and the lies of the οἱ πολλοί[871] one meets with. He told me much in his charming way, of the men and things of London, of Milnes, Macaulay, etc. but especially of Carlyle, of whom he gave graphic descriptions.[872] He said that the authorship and literature of Carlyle were only accidental appendagés to his strong, burly, earnest, intense soul, which was made for action rather than for writing; he was, E. said, "a great iron triphammer with an Eolian harp for an accompaniment."—"he works great iron machinery to play his piano" &c.[873] E. went to Oxford, & was highly pleased with the scholars he found there; he thought well of the institution of fellowships as means of promoting a general and spreading intellectual culture.

1848 I find there is nothing I love so well as to preach to a plain country audience, a people without conventionalisms, and whose minds are not flyblown with the silly love of criticism. I believe I was made for the country, and I could be well content, with my family and library, to live and die in the obscurest village. This would be an unintelligible confession to make to one of our Bostonians, whether clerical or lay, who seem to me to think as Mascarille does in Moliere's *Precieuses Ridicules,*—"Pour moi je tiens que, hors de Paris, il n'y a point de salut pour les honnêtes gens."[874]

February 3, [1849] Mr. Emerson is lecturing in Boston & my wife goes to hear him;[875] it is, I understand the same sweet and lofty strain of intellectual & spiritual music, as ever; but how hard it is for any one, who hears & is charmed while he hears, to give an account of it! This comes inevitably from the character of Mr. E's genius: but I do not wonder that some think his lectures to be moonshine, because they cannot analyse them, or remember their parts: this is their mistake, but a natural one, for even his admirers are sometimes inclined to say of his fascinating words, in the language of Cowper—

> "Like quicksilver, the rhetoric they display
> "Shines as it runs, but grasped at slips away."[876]

September 1, 1849 I am reading again parts of Plato's Phaedrus. In Plato's remarkable description of the man, whose soul is conversant with the divine reality of things (τὸ ὄν), is there not something applicable, without any arrogant assumption, to such a man as R. W. Emerson (I mention Mr. E. rather as representative of a class, than as individual)?

> ἐξιστάμενος δὲ τῶν ἀνθρωπίνων σπουδασμάτων
> καὶ πρὸς τῳ θείῳ γιγνόμενος, νουθετεῖται μὲν ὑπὸ
> τῶν πολλῶν ὡς παρακινῶν, ἐνθουσιάζων δὲ
> λέληθεν τοὺς πολλούς.

1850 Sophocles, in a choral ode of the Coloneus, in a touching allusion to the miseries of his own old age, speaks of

> ἀπροσύμιλον
>
> γῆρας ἄφιλον,–2

a lonely old age without friends.

I have not yet reached what is called old age; but I have lived long enough to find that the friends of earlier years are missing, and their place is not filled by others, and that a sober *afternoon* light gathers around one, very different from the flush and gayety of the forenoon light. But I think I have sometimes enjoyed a moonlight evening as much as the brightest and fairest daylight.

Sometimes I wish that I had less of a yearning after sympathy and love, and that I could lock myself up in my own castle and care not for the world without. But I cannot, and, what is more, ought not. If the Christian hope blesses me, I shall never be ἄφιλος ;[879] for there is a Friend that never faileth.

November 22, 1851 In the "Elder Brother," one of the plays of Beaumont and Fletcher,[880] Charles the student thus describes the pleasures of his library:—

> "Give me leave
> T'enjoy myself; that place that does contain
> My books, the best companions, is to me
> A glorious court, where hourly I converse
> With the old sages and philosophers;
> And sometimes, for variety, I confer
> With kings and emperors, and weigh their counsels;
> Calling their victories, if unjustly got,
> Unto a strict account, and, in my fancy,
> Deface their ill-placed statues. Can I, then,
> Part with such constant pleasures, to embrace
> Uncertain vanities? No; be it in your care
> T'augment your heap of wealth: it shall be mine
> T'increase in knowledge."—Act I. Sc. 2.

In this spirited and loving plea for the pleasures of the library I may be allowed to feel some sympathy; for books have ever been my dear, dear friends. But so far from its being any credit to me, I have been blamed for loving them too much. And there are some amongst the ministers who flout me for it, as an unpractical taste. Well, so be it. I know that my books have been my solace, my nutriment, and my discipline. Along with them I have cultivated an acquaintance with all common things of every-day life, and have always loved the society of farmers and mechanics better (in general) than that of so-called intellectual men, and I think I have learned more from them. My books, I know, have never made me unpractical, nor interfered in the least with my vital interest and persevering labor in the ministry.

Thus much I feel bound to say for those treasures of the mind, embalmed in print, which, next to religion, have been the richest source of happiness to me, and for an acquaintance with which I thank God from my heart.

1851 I was impressed the other day with the following sentences in Cicero[881] about the injurious effect of *authority* in the relation between teacher and learner: "Non enim tam auctoritatis in disputando, quam rationis momenta quaerenda sunt. Quin etiam obest plerumque iis, qui discere volunt, auctoritas eorum, qui se docere profitentur. Desinunt enim suum judicim adhibere; id habent ratum, quod ab eo, quem probant, judicatum vident."[882] I have endeavored to act on this principle as much as possible in my duties at Divinity Hall. I have always told the young men that I wished to be with them as an elder brother, to go along with them in their studies and inquiries, giving such help and guidance as I could, not as a dictator, or authoritative teacher, displacing the action of their own minds to make room for that of mine, or giving them results to be accepted, instead of means and aids for arriving at their own results. This I have thought the true way; but I believe the way of *auctoritas* would have made me more popular, both among the students and in the Unitarian denomination, strange as it may seem. Most people like better to be told what to accept, than to be put upon finding it out for themselves.

[1851] On Wednesday I began to lecture again. There is something in this using the mind wholly *for others*, and with reference to others, which I do not like. It seems to nudge one's faculties on the elbow, and tell them that they are not to move at their own sweet will, but to produce a certain tale of brick for an employer. What would be the effect if the mind of every one were set free from tasks, and could flower out in musing, in speech, in writing, like shrubs and trees? We should have more true men and women, and fewer repeating-machines.

1852 On Thursday of this week was the annual Thanksgiving. I had no engagements to preach, so I walked to Medford. After the service, I went to the scenes of my childhood, the places about my father's house,[883] and lingered there a good while. The boys were playing at football, as I did with others on the same spot forty-five or forty-six years ago. A crowd of youthful recollections came over me and chained me to the spot. The world of that day, which seemed to have sunk under the tide of time, came up again, and lived as fresh as it were yesterday. There is to me an inexpressible charm in such remembrances: they have a deep tinge of melancholy. I think the sadness is more than the joy: but it is a sweet sadness.

Then I went to my mother's grave, in a retired part of the old burying-ground. "Mrs. Susannah, wife of Mr. Convers Francis, died May 7, 1814. Aged 48."[884] How much those words said to me! I stood there and wept like a child. I may well say like a child; for it was a little child that I stood by the grave of a dear, dear good mother. That early world of love and kind care all came back: my mother was with me again, and all that she did for me had the freshness of boyhood's feelings upon it again: acts of affection and of self-sacrificing toil for me returned one after another, like heavenly visitants. They *were* heavenly visitants. Blessed and dear mother, hadst thou lived to be with me now, how much better would I requite thy love than I did then!

Cowper's exquisite lines on "The Receipt of his Mother's Picture" came to mind with new beauty and force. The tears were in my eyes, and my heart was full all the way on my walk back to Cambridge.

January 27, 1855   Thursday evening, heard R. W. Emersons lecture in the course on Slavery;[885] it was characteristic of him, of course,—for all he writes is so; admirable in parts, wise and true in all,—yet not well adapted on the whole for popular impression, though there was some hearty applause:—what a deep power sometimes wells out from his face!

July 28, 1855   Went with Mrs R.[886] to R. W. Emerson's & had an altogether charming time of it; His brother, W. Emerson from N. York[887] was there. R. W. E. talked a good deal of Thomas Carlyle with whom he corresponds, & of Miss Bacon of New Haven.[888] He read a letter from the former, most characteristic and amusing, in wh C. complains, in his own quaint way, of his disappointment about Frederick the Great, of whom he is making a book & and [sic] who turns out, he says, to be no hero to him.[889]

[After 1856]   My father was for a great many years the most intensely industrious man, I think, that I ever knew. He devoted himself to his work with an eagerness and an unsparing exertion of strength which used to seem to me prodigious. He was a sturdy, sometimes rough, but kind and faithful. He had good common-sense, and a well-balanced judgment: his education had been very scanty, but he was always fond of reading, and picked up considerable information. His opinions sometimes became prejudices, and were strong. He was a great lover of right and freedom. The sound of the old Revolution, in which his father was a soldier, was still in his ears, and he detested slavery, with all its apologists and in all its forms. It was pleasant to hear him say, two or three weeks before his death, "I rejoice that my first Presidential vote was given for General Washington, and now my last for Colonel Fremont."[890]

August, 1857   I rose at half past three; took a long walk, and surrendered myself to the impressions of the hour. I seemed to be alone with God in this lovely universe; and the first faint tinge of the dawn, just undulating over the hills, was a reflection from the "light of His countenance."

Perhaps no hour affords so much true pleasure even to the senses as this. The eye is refreshed by the soft and gentle light, gradually deepening its blush, and unveiling while it enriches the near and distant landscape. There is no light to be compared with it. The ear is charmed with the blending of diverse sounds, all "discoursing excellent music,"—the song of the awakened birds, the "shrill clarion'" of the cock which comes piercing the silence from afar, the gurgle of near water and the hum of the fall at a distance, the occasional ringing and jolting of some wagon, early on its way to the city market, the perpetual whispering of the leaves to each other as the wind kisses them gently,— truly there are no voices like the mingled voices of a summer's morning. They remind me of the talk which hope and fancy used to hold with me in the hour of unconscious childhood. The smell is regaled with a fragrance which belongs to no other time, springing thousand-fold from flowers, grasses, trees, and which, as the hot day comes on, flies before it. The touch has its most refined enjoyment in the refreshing coolness with which that "chartered libertine," the air, embraces you all around, so that mere feeling becomes a delight.

April 10, 1858 (Saturday) Wednesday went with my wife to hear R. W. Emerson's lecture in Boston.[891] Many years ago that strain of the poet-philosopher fell upon my ear often, & it always brought a charm with it. Now, after a long interval, heard again, it seemed just the same thing. The subject was "Self-possession"; & think there was no idea wh I had not found in his lectures from 15 to 20 years ago, & and [sic] the very words were about the same. The old topics, subjectiveness and individuality,—we create all that we see,—we are lords of all that is. I had hoped to find by this time something else; but, I doubt, Mr E. never gets or has got beyond the old thought, however good that may be. The fault of his manner of discussing a subject seems to be that he never makes any progress in the subject itself: he empties before you a box or bag of jewels as he goes on, wh you may take and make the most you can of; but you find no progress in the subject, no opening out, expanding, motion onwards,—but instead thereof standing still & giving the utterance that comes at the moment. He might as well begin anywhere else & end anywhere else, as where he does begin and end. The mind of the hearer has not the satisfaction of moving steadily on till the consummation is effected,—sweeping forward till the march of thought is brought to its natural close.

October 2, 1858 Cattle-fairs & Agricultural shows are now the order of the day all over our Commonwealth. There was one at Concord, at which Mr. Emerson delivered the address,[892] marked with his usual felicity of thought and expression;—it is quite noticeable what a *practical* man he is,—just what people generally think he is *not*. I wish I had the privilege of seeing him more than I am ever likely to do in a world where every man has his own peculiar work, wh drives him to the wall.

August, 1859 On Wednesday I went to Concord, spent the night at Mrs [Sarah] Ripley's: called in the evening at Mr. Emerson's, who talked charmingly, among other things, "what great things this time has done for us in giving us two such works as Carlyle's Frederick, Tennyson's new poem, the "Idyls of the King", said he.[893]

May, 1861 Again to the hallowed spot in the Watertown village graveyard.[894] The place where her remains lie is now neatly sodded, with flowers growing over her bosom,—that bosom which it was a large part of my happiness to repose upon. The trees and bushes are well trimmed, and everything there looks neat, simple, and appropriate, *simplex munditiis,*—words, by the way, which I remember to have applied years ago as descriptive of her character and tastes, greatly to her delight.

I was alone, save with her silent presence. A little poem of Barry Cornwall's came home to my feelings with a wonderful sweetness, while the family thoughts were nestling about my heart:—

> "Touch us gently, Time!
>   Let us glide adown thy stream,
> Gently as we sometimes glide
>   Through a quiet dream.
> Humble voyagers are we
> Husband, wife, and children three,
> One is lost,—an angel, fled
> To the azure overhead.
>
> Touch us gently, Time!
>   We've not proud nor soaring wings;
> *Our* ambition, our content,
>   Lies in simple things.
> Humble voyagers are we
> O'er life's dim, unsounded sea,
> Seeking only some calm clime:
> Touch us gently, gentle Time!"[895]

August, 1862 At Mr. Emerson's, Mrs [Sarah] Ripley and I met a room full of most pleasant and high company: Mr. E. himself,—his brother William with his lovely wife,—Channing,[896] Elisabeth Peabody[897] etc—Emerson talked with me, (charmingly, as he always does) about the late Homeric controversy, or discussion about the principles of translation as applied to the Iliad, between Matthew Arnold & F. W. Newman.[898] This was altogether a very bright evening.

January 3, 1863 Read in the Eclectic Review a long, elaborate, would be philosophical article on R. W. Emerson,[899] which interested me as coming from an English critic, & representing English thought about one whom *we* have known from his boyhood all the way from his growth up to fame.

NOTES

498. See the entry of 9 January 1825.
499. "On the Self Ignorance of Hazael" and "On the Miraculous Cure of the Leper."
500. William Henry Furness. Neither Francis nor a delegation from Watertown was able to attend Furness' ordination, but a letter of fellowship was sent; see

"Records of the Church of Christ in Watertown," 2 January 1825, p. 24 (MWat).
501. "On Quenching the Spirit."
502. See the entry of 2 January 1825 and sermon "On Numbering Our Days. New Year's Sermon."
503. "The Mixture of Belief and Unbelief" and "Every Thing to Be Done in Its Proper Season."
504. Dr. James P. Chaplin (1782–1828) of Cambridgeport became famous as the head of a private establishment for the treatment of nervous disorders and insanity.
505. "The Union of Knowledge and Practice" and "On Compassion for the Wicked."
506. "On the Beatitudes. Sermon on the Mount. 1." and "The Disciples Compared to the Salt of the Earth, the Light of the World, Etc. Sermon on the Mount. 2."
507. "The Nature and Uses of Affliction" and "Jesus Came Not to Destroy the Law & the Prophets, Etc. Sermon on the Mount. 3."
508. "Boast Not of Tomorrow" and "Ye Have Heard That It Was Said—Thou Shalt Not Kill, Etc. Sermon on the Mount. 4."
509. "On Oaths & Profane Swearing. Sermon on the Mount. 5" and "On the Habit of Scoffing at Religion."
510. "Uses of the Resurrection of Christ" and "On Non-resistance to Evil, Etc. Sermon on the Mount. 6."
511. "Consolation Abounding by Christ."
512. "The Efficacy of Prayer;—'Ask, & Ye Shall Receive, Etc.'"
513. "What We Have on Coming into This World & What We Have on Leaving It" and "Haman & Mordecai."
514. "On the Love of Enemies. Sermon on the Mount. 7." and "On Secrecy in Doing Good, Etc. Sermon on the Mount. 8."
515. "The Mixture of Belief and Unbelief" and "On Moral Unconcern."
516. This is probably Ellis Gray Loring (1803–58), Boston lawyer and antislavery advocate, who left Harvard College in 1823 without taking a degree. He then studied law and became a member of the bar in 1827. On 1 January 1831 he and several others in Boston organized the New England Anti-Slavery Society, one of the pioneer abolitionist organizations in America. His decisive financial support kept the *Liberator,* William Lloyd Garrison's publication, alive.
517. "Ostentation, Vain Repetitions, Etc. in Prayer. Sermon on the Mount. 9." and "The Gradual Process of Evil."
518. "On Fasting with a Sad Countenance, Etc. Sermon on the Mount. 10. Fast Day."
519. "On Shame."
520. I have not been able to identify the forenoon sermon; the afternoon sermon was "Haman & Mordecai."
521. I have not been able to identify this sermon.
522. "On Laying Up Treasures on Earth & in Heaven, Etc. Sermon on the Mount. 11." and "The Light of the Body & the Light of the Mind, Etc. Sermon on the Mount. 12."
523. "Man Created in the Image of God" and "The Progressive Character of Religion."
524. Francis had left his wife, Abby, at Duxbury two weeks earlier when he was there to fill the pulpit of her father, John Allyn; see the entry of 10 April 1825.

525. "The Danger of Neglecting Religion."
526. "Life and Immortality Brought to Life by Jesus Christ."
527. "The Invitation of Wisdom."
528. "What We Have on Coming into This World & What We Have on Leaving It" and "The Invitation of Wisdom."
529. "On a Heavenly Conversation."
530. "Serving God & Mammon, & Care for the Future. Sermon on the Mount. 13." and " 'Judge Not,' Etc. Sermon on the Mount. 14."
531. "Men to Be Judged According to Their Means and Opportunities" and "The Prosperity of a Wicked Conscience."
532. Bernard Whitman (1796–1834), who was licensed to preach in 1824, was pastor of the Second Church in Waltham from 1826 to 1834.
533. I have not been able to identify the forenoon sermon; the afternoon sermon was "What We Have on Coming into This World & What We Have on Leaving It."
534. " 'Giving That Which Is Holy unto Dogs,' Etc. Sermon on the Mount. 15." and "The Efficacy of Prayer;—'Ask, & Ye Shall Receive, Etc.' Sermon on the Mount. 16."
535. "Men to Be Judged According to Their Means and Opportunities" and "What We Have on Coming into This World & What We Have on Leaving It."
536. "On Moral Unconcern" and "The Prosperity of a Wicked Conscience."
537. "On the Parental Character of God. No. 1." and "On the Parental Character of God. No. 2."
538. Nathaniel Thayer (1769–1840) was pastor of the Congregational church in Lancaster, Pennsylvania, from 1793 to 1840.
539. "Motives to Perseverance from the Services & Character of Christ."
540. "Believing Is Confessing Religion."
541. "Doing unto Others as We Would Be Done By, Etc. Sermon on the Mount. 17."
542. "The Strait Gate and the Narrow Way, Etc. Sermon on the Mount. 18." and "Beware of False Prophets, Etc. & Saying Lord, Lord, Etc. Sermon on the Mount. 19."
543. "Religious Hope" and "Building on a Rock & on Sand, Etc. Sermon on the Mount. 20."
544. "Men to Be Judged According to Their Means and Opportunities" and "On Laying Up Treasures on Earth & in Heaven, Etc. Sermon on the Mount. 11."
545. "How the Spirit of the Lord Is a Spirit of Liberty."
546. "On Experimental Religion" and "The Imperfection of Our Religious Knowledge."
547. William Farmer (1793–1862) was graduated at the Harvard Divinity School in 1822. Afterwards he preached in several states in New England.
548. "General View of the Sermon on the Mount."
549. Alexander Young (1800–1854) was graduated from the Harvard Divinity School in 1824. He was pastor of the Sixth Congregational Church (the New South Church) in Boston from 1825 to 1854.
550. "General View of the Sermon on the Mount" and "On Laying Up Treasures on Earth & in Heaven, Etc. Sermon on the Mount. 11."
551. "On Peter's Denying His Lord."
552. "On Diligence in Business."
553. Rufus Allyn, Francis' brother-in-law.

554. "The Exclusive Spirit of Bigotry" and "On Acquaintance with God."
555. "The Christian View of Life & Death."
556. "The Mixture of Belief and Unbelief" and "On Laying Up Treasures on Earth & in Heaven, Etc. Sermon on the Mount. 11."
557. I have not been able to identify the forenoon sermon; the afternoon sermon was "Thoughts Suggested by Death & Disappointment."
558. "The Christian View of Life & Death" and "The Imperfection of Our Religious Knowledge."
559. I have not been able to identify this sermon.
560. John Allyn, Jr., Francis' brother-in-law, lately deceased.
561. "On the Varieties of Rank Etc. in Life."
562. Lydia Maria Francis, Later Lydia Maria Child.
563. "On Having Fellowship with God. 1."
564. "Our Having Fellowship with God. 2."
565. "On Moral Unconcern."
566. Stevens Everett (1796–1853) was pastor of the Unitarian church in Hallowell, Maine, from 1824 to 1832.
567. "The Exclusive Spirit of Bigotry" and "The Progressive Character of Religion."
568. "Man Created in the Image of God."
569. Ichabod Nichols (1784–1859) was pastor of the First Church in Portland, Maine, from 1809 to 1855.
570. "General View of the Sermon on the Mount" and "Man Created in the Image of God."
571. "On Scepticism" and "The Duty of Learning Wisdom from Errors and Mistakes."
572. Sydney Smith (1771–1845), famed as one of the founders of the *Edinburgh Review* in 1802, was a frequent writer and lecturer on moral philosophy and, after 1831, a canon of St. Paul's.
573. Lydia Maria Francis, later Lydia Maria Child.
574. "On Being Offended in Christ."
575. "Our Saviour's Agony in Gethsemane" and "The Conduct of David toward Nabal."
576. "On the Strengthening Power of Christianity."
577. "The Design."
578. "External & Internal Religion."
579. "Of Herod in Connection with John the Baptist and Christ" and "On Establishing the Heart."
580. William Paley (1743–1805), English theologian and Philosopher, was the author of *The Principles of Moral and Political Philosophy* (1785), a book of lectures which became the ethical textbook at Cambridge; *View of the Evidences of Christianity* (1794), a collection of evidences to refute deism; and *Natural Theology* (1802), an argument for the existence of God.
581. "Gratitude for the Fruits of the Earth. Thanksgiving Sermon. 7."
582. See the entry of 13 November 1825.
583. "The Character & Reward of Faithful Servants."
584. Daniel Kimball (1778–1862) was ordained as a Congregational minister at Hingham in 1817 but never settled over any one church.
585. "On the Respect Due to Age" and "The Christian View of Life & Death."

586. "The Difference between the Present and Future State Illustrated by the Difference between Childhood and Manhood" and "On the Blessing of God."
587. "The Christian View of Life & Death" and "Every Thing to Be Done in Its Proper Season."
588. "The Visit of the Wise Men to the Infant Jesus. Christmas." and "The Fitness of the Time of Our Saviour's Appearance. Christmas."
589. "Admonition 'to Awake out of Sleep.' New Year."
590. "Our Years Spent as a Tale Etc. New Year."
591. "The Exclusive Spirit of Bigotry" and "The Mixture of Belief and Unbelief."
592. "The Christian View of Life & Death" and "The Exclusive Spirit of Bigotry."
593. William Daniels (Lot) Wiswall (1787–1853) was graduated from the Harvard Divinity School in 1821 and preached among several Congregational churches in New England, but was never settled over one congregation very long.
594. "God No Respecter of Persons" and "On Winter."
595. "Comparison Between the Grecian Games and the Christian Course" and "'Our Righteousness as Filthy Rags' Etc."
596. "On the Desire to Live until Certain Purposes Have Been Accomplished."
597. John Allyn, Jr., Francis' brother-in-law, lately deceased.
598. "The Difference between the Present and Future State Illustrated by the Difference between Childhood and Manhood" and "The Christian View of Life & Death."
599. "On Christ's Saying—I Came Not to Send Peace Etc." and "The Law in the Members and the Law of the Mind."
600. "Worshipping in the Beauty of Holiness" and "Offending in One Point Making Us Guilty of All."
601. "On Showing That We Have Been with Jesus."
602. "The Moral Characteristics of Our Saviour's Miracles."
603. "General View of the Sermon on the Mount."
604. "The Difference between the Present and Future State Illustrated by the Difference between Childhood and Manhood."
605. "Comparison Between the Grecian Games and the Christian Course."
606. "John, the Disciple Whom Jesus Loved."
607. "The Friendship of the World Enmity with God."
608. For another instance of Francis' apprehension about preaching in college chapel at Harvard, see the entry of 19 March 1826. After his appointment as a professor of divinity at Harvard in August 1842, Francis preached half of the daily sermons in chapel during his twenty years' tenure (Octavius Brooks Frothingham, *Recollections and Impressions: 1822–1890* [Boston: Putnams, 1891], p. 27).
609. "The Parable of the Pharisee & Publican."
610. "The Promises of Christianity Motives to Purity" and "The Patient Waiting of Job."
611. William Paley: see the entry of 20 November 1825.
612. "No Secrecy or Impurity in Sin" and "Comparison Between the Grecian Games and the Christian Course."
613. "Knowledge Essential to the Stability of Good Institutions."
614. "On Fasting with a Sad Countenance, Etc. Sermon on the Mount. 10. Fast Day."
615. "The Tribulations of the World Overcome, Etc." and "Xtianity Consists in 'Righteousness, Peace, and Joy in the Holy Ghost.'"

616. "On Hypocrisy" and "The Divine Protection."
617. Edmund Butcher: see the entry of 25 January 1824.
618. "The Parable of the Pharisee & Publican" and "The Christian View of Life & Death."
619. Eliphalet Porter Crafts (1800–1880) was graduated at Brown in 1821 and at Harvard with an honorary M.A. in 1825. Thereafter he held pulpits in East Bridgewater, Sandwich, and East Lexington, Massachusetts.
620. "Man Created in the Image of God" and "The Difference between the Present and Future State Illustrated by the Difference between Childhood and Manhood."
621. "Access to God in One Spirit."
622. "God No Respecter of Persons."
623. "Reflections on the Vegetation of Spring" and "The Enticement of Sinners."
624. "Man Created in the Image of God" and "The Imperfection of Our Religious Knowledge."
625. "The Love of God Expressed by Keeping His Commandments" and "Continual Increase the Christianity."
626. "The Duty of Professing Christians to Stand Fast in One Spirit, Etc." and "On the Manner of Attending Religious Worship and Instruction."
627. Benjamin Kent (1794–1859) settled in Duxbury as a colleague minister to John Allyn in 1826. After a short time he resigned because of bad health and became a school teacher in Roxbury.
628. For the invitation to the ordination, see "Records of the Church of Christ in Watertown," 28 May 1826, pp. 23–24 (MWat).
629. I have not been able to identify this sermon.
630. "No Secrecy or Impurity in Sin" and "The Friendship of the World Enmity with God."
631. "The Victory of Faith over the World."
632. "On Early Piety" and "Hardness of Heart.—Its Causes, Etc."
633. "The Progressive Character of Religion" and "The Christian View of Life & Death."
634. David Reed (1790–1870), Unitarian minister and editor, established the *Christian Register* in 1821 and conducted it for more than forty-five years.
635. "Jesus the True Foundation."
636. "On the Desire to Live until Certain Purposes Have Been Accomplished."
637. "On Experimental Religion."
638. "On the Fear of Death."
639. "Access to God in One Spirit."
640. "On the Desire to Live until Certain Purposes Have Been Accomplished" and "Man Created in the Image of God."
641. " 'Delivered before the Female Society' / 'For None of Us Liveth Unto Himself.' "
642. "The Vanity of Human Thoughts."
643. "Evil Bears Witness to the Wisdom and Goodness of God" and "On Partial and Undecided Obedience."
644. "John, the Disciple Whom Jesus Loved" and " 'Delivered before the Female Society' / 'For None of Us Liveth Unto Himself.' "
645. Daniel Webster (1782–1852) was living in Boston at this time; see the entry of 9 September 1821.

646. "The Christian Life Represented as Warfare" and "Sowing to the Flesh, and Sowing to the Spirit."

647. " 'Delivered before the Female Society' / 'For None of Us Liveth Unto Himself' " and "On Prayers as a Means of Self-Knowledge."

648. "On a Heavenly Conversation" and "Every Thing to Be Done in Its Proper Season."

649. "God Manifesting Himself through Jesus Christ."

650. "Reflections on the Account of the Walk to Emmaus."

651. " 'Delivered before the Female Society' / 'For None of Us Liveth Unto Himself.' "

652. "Men to Be Judged According to Their Means and Opportunities."

653. Alonzo Hill (1800–1871) was graduated from the Divinity School in 1826 and thereafter was pastor of the Second Parish in Worcester until 1871.

654. "The Progressive Character of Religion" and "The Exclusive Spirit of Bigotry."

655. I have not been able to identify Mr. Goldsborough.

656. "Thoughts Suggested by Death & Disappointment" and "Man Created in the Image of God."

657. "The Right and Duty of Free Inquiry" and "The Difference between the Present and Future State Illustrated by the Difference between Childhood and Manhood."

658. Caleb Stetson (1793–1870) was graduated from the Harvard Divinity School in 1827 and thereafter served Unitarian churches in Medford, Norwell, and East Lexington, Massachusetts, until 1865.

659. The Unitarian Church in Washington, D.C., was organized on 11 November 1821 with Robert Little as its pastor. Little served until 1827. The history of Unitarianism in Washington has been traced in Jennie W. Scudder, *A Century of Unitarianism in the Nation's Capital: 1821–1921* (Boston: Beacon Press, 1922).

660. "The Difference between the Present and Future State Illustrated by the Difference between Childhood and Manhood."

661. Henry Clay (1777–1852), lawyer and statesman, was at this time United States Secretary of State.

662. James Barbour (1775–1842), statesman, was at this time United States Secretary of War.

663. "Man Created in the Image of God."

664. "The Mixture of Belief and Unbelief" and "On Doing All to the Glory of God."

665. "The Difference between the Present and Future State Illustrated by the Difference between Childhood and Manhood" and "Man Created in the Image of God."

666. "The Eye Not Satisfied with Seeing, Etc."

667. "The Excellence of the Kind & Gentle Virtues."

668. "Access to God in One Spirit."

669. "St. Paul Counting All Things but Loss for Jesus Christ" and "All Things Working Together for Good to the Christian."

670. "The Voice of Joy and Praise in the House of God" and " 'Ye Know Not What Ye Ask.' "

671. "The Conduct of David on the Death of His Child" and "Thoughts Suggested by Autumn."

672. "Evil Bears Witness to the Wisdom and Goodness of God" and "On the Dislike to the Truth."

673. "On the Love of Country. Thanksgiving Sermon. 8."

674. "The Poor Widow and Her Two Mites."

675. "Sowing to the Flesh, and Sowing to the Spirit."

676. "Religious Hope" and "On Jesus' Requiring His Disciples to Hate Father and Mother, Etc."

677. Richard Sullivan was a leading layman in the Unitarian Church in Boston: see the entry of 8 February 1824.

678. "On the Incomprehensibility of God. 1." and "On the Incomprehensibility of God. 2."

679. Charles Stearns (1753–1826) was pastor of the Congregational church in Lincoln, Massachusetts, from 1781 until his death in July 1826.

680. "The Wisdom of This World" and "Sowing to the Flesh, and Sowing to the Spirit."

681. "The Heavenly Bodies Considered as Measures of Time. Last Day of the Year" and "New Year's Sermon."

682. "Remembrance of Sins Every Year."

683. "The Danger of Premature Confidence and Exhaltation Illustrated" and "'Putting off the Old Man and Putting on the New.'"

684. "The Mixture of Belief and Unbelief" and "The Danger of Premature Confidence and Exhaltation Illustrated."

685. Andrew Bigelow had moved to Washington, D.C., to become pastor of the First Unitarian Church.

686. "On the Fear of Death" and "The Imperfection of Our Religious Knowledge."

687. "On Religious Fear" and "The Reproof of Christ to the Pharisee for Making Clean the Outside, Etc."

688. "On the Fear of Death" and "The Eye Not Satisfied with Seeing, Etc."

689. "Reflection on the Enmity between the Jews & Samaritans" and "The Price to Get Wisdom in the Hands of the Fool."

690. George Ripley (1802–80) was pastor of the Purchase Street Chruch (Thirteenth Congregation) from 1826 to 1841.

691. "What We Have on Coming into This World & What We Have on Leaving It" and "On Jesus' Requiring His Disciples to Hate Father and Mother, Etc."

692. For the invitation by the church at Medford to Stetson's ordination, see "Records of the Church of Christ in Watertown," 18 February 1827, p. 25 (MWat).

693. "Xtianity Consists in 'Righteousness, Peace, and Joy in the Holy Ghost.'"

694. "On Having Fellowship with God. 2."

695. "To Receive Christ the Way to Become Sons of God, Etc."

696. "The Danger of Premature Confidence and Exaltation Illustrated."

697. "The Wisdom of Not Being Subjected to Any Desire."

698. "The Pleasure We Ought to Feel in the Moral Reformation of Our Fellow-Men" and "On the Parable of the Good Samaritan. No. 1."

699. Throughout the 1820s the Greeks were violently repressed when trying to escape Turkish rule. Western Europe and America gave the Greek patriots sympathy and material support, and such collections as the one Francis describes were commonplace in America.

700. "Evil Bears Witness to the Wisdom of Goodness of God" and "The Eye Not Satisfied with Seeing, Etc."

701. This is probably John Clark, Jr. (1796–1851), son of John Clark of Waltham, Massachusetts. Clark received his A.B. degree at Harvard in 1816 and his A.M. degree in 1819.

702. "Gallio's Indifference Considered" and "On the Source of Temptations & the Means of Resisting It."

703. "The Importance of a Lively Moral Sense in the Community. Fast Day."

704. "On the Varieties of Rank Etc in Life" and "On the Respect Due to Age."

705. "On the Religious Education of Children."

706. "The Wisdom That Is from Above."

707. "The Progressive Character of Religion" and "On Jesus' Requiring His Disciples to Hate Father and Mother, Etc."

708. "On False Zeal" and "On True Zeal."

709. "The Way, the Truth, & the Life."

710. "Jesus Christ a Benefactor and a Sacrifice. Communion."

711. "On Religious Fear."

712. "Man Created in the Image of God" and "On the Question 'Are There Few That Be Saved?'"

713. "Religion Like Seed Cast into the Ground, Etc."

714. "'We Know not What Manner of Spirit We Are Of.'"

715. "On Being Justified by the Deeds of the Law, Etc."

716. "On the Fear of Death" and "The Eye Not Satisfied with Seeing, Etc."

717. The First Church in Boston occupied the building in Chauncey Place from 1808 to 1868. For a brief history of the edifices of this church, see Frothingham, *Boston Unitarianism: 1820–1850*, pp. 26–28.

718. This Society, founded in about 1806 and existing until 1888, was established by residents of the Boston area for the purpose of publishing religious books and tracts. William Emerson, pastor of the First Church in Boston, was the first secretary of the organization. It was he who initiated the *Christian Monitor*, a quarterly publication of the Society.

719. Joseph Allen (1793–1853) was ordained in 1816 as pastor of the Congregational church in Northboro, where he remained until his death.

720. "Christianity Hid from the Wise & Prudent & Revealed unto Babes."

721. Nathaniel L. Frothingham preached at the First Church, meeting at Chauncey Place, in Boston.

722. George W. Wells (1804–43) completed a course of studies at the Harvard Divinity School in 1826 and did supply preaching before settling in Kennebunk, Maine, in late 1827.

723. "Jesus the True Foundation."

724. "Religion Like Seed Cast into the Ground, Etc."

725. "Superiority of Charity over Faith & Hope" and "The Duty of Remembering & Confessing Our Sins."

726. "The Christian View of Life & Death" and "The Imperfection of Our Religious Knowledge."

727. I have not been able to identify the first sermon; the second was "The Example of the Bereans Recommended."

728. "Sermon for a Communion Sabbath."

729. "The Connexion between Affection for Christ and Obeying His Commandments. Communion Service." and "The Wisdom of This World."

730. "On False Zeal" and "On True Zeal."

731. Charles Robinson (1793–1862) was pastor of the First Parish in Groton from 1825 to 1828.

732. "The Difference between the Present and Future State Illustrated by the Difference between Childhood and Manhood" and "Religion Like Seed Cast into the Ground, Etc."

733. Possibly Andrew Bigelow.

734. "The Peace Bequeathed by Jesus to His Disciples" and "Jesus Christ Not as the World Giveth."

735. "On Doing All to the Glory of God" and "On Religious Fear."

736. "Grace as Connected with Salvation."

737. John Allyn, Francis' father-in-law, was debilitating in mind.

738. "The Propensity to Add to Divine Truth" and "On the Mistakes of Mankind."

739. "The Danger of Premature Confidence and Exaltation Illustrated" and "On Religious Fear."

740. "Good Influences of Vicissitude & Change" and "The Disciples Accused of Eating with Unwashed Hands, Etc."

741. Mellish I. Motte (1801–81) was graduated at Harvard College in 1821. From 1828 to 1842 he preached for the South Congregational Church in Boston.

742. "The Doctrine of Reconciliation to God."

743. "Religion Like Seed Cast into the Ground, Etc."

744. "The Difference between the Present and Future State Illustrated by the Difference between Childhood and Manhood," "The Danger of Premature Confidence and Exaltation Illustrated," and "Religion Like Seed Cast into the Ground, Etc."

745. "On Spiritual Influences. 1." and "On Spiritual Influences. 2."

746. "The Union of Prayers & Alms" and "Paul's Valedictory Prayer Explained."

747. "Life Eternal in the Knowledge of God & Jesus Christ" and "The Choice of Moses a Good Example."

748. Benjamin Kent had become the colleague minister of the local minister, John Allyn, on 7 June 1826.

749. "Jesus the True Foundation" and "The Danger of Premature Confidence and Exaltation Illustrated."

750. Francis' address could have been caused by the failing health of his father-in-law, John Allyn.

751. "The Difference between the Present and Future State Illustrated by the Difference between Childhood and Manhood" and "The Danger of Premature Confidence and Exhaltation Illustrated."

752. "On Faith. No. 1." and "On Faith. No. 2."

753. "On Religious Fear" and "The Danger of Premature Confidence and Exaltation Illustrated."

754. "Christianity Hid from the Wise & Prudent & Revealed unto Babes."

755. "The Lord's Supper in Connection with the Passover."

756. "On the Blessing of God."

757. "Religion Like Seed Cast into the Ground, Etc." and "The Imperfection of Our Religious Knowledge."

758. I have not been able to identify the forenoon sermon; the afternoon sermon was "On Conversion."

759. "The Extremes of Indifference & of Despair under Trials" and "The Righteous More Excellent than His Neighbor."
760. "Improvement & Duty the Best Forms of Gratitude. Thanksgiving Sermon."
761. Francis was called to be pastor of the First Parish Church on 31 March 1819 and accepted on 8 May 1819; see "Records of the Church of Christ in Watertown," p. 3 (MWat).
762. "Grace as Connected with Salvation" and "On Religious Fear."
763. These sermons were, respectively, Emerson's "On Showing Piety at Home" (sermon no. 10) and "Change and Permanence" (sermon no. 6). Emerson was to preach the first of these twenty-seven times and the second twelve times (see Kenneth Walter Cameron, *Index-Concordance to Emerson's Sermons; with Homiletical Papers* [Hartford: Transcendental Books, 1963], 2:695, 704).
764. "Persecution of the Godly."
765. "Persecution of the Godly."
766. "On Religious Fear" and "The Danger of Premature Confidence and Exaltation Illustrated."
767. "Uses of Consulting the Past" and "Doing Our Duty unto the Lord & Not unto Men."
768. Frederic Henry Hedge (1805–90) was pastor of the Unitarian church in West Cambridge from 1829 to 1835 and in Bangor, Maine, from 1835 to 1850.
769. This was the Cambridge Association of Congregational Ministers, constituted of pastors of churches in Cambridge, Concord, Billerica, Brighton, Lowell, Lexington, East Lexington, Waltham, Watertown, West Cambridge, and Woburn.
770. The immediate interest in Coleridge was prompted by the recent publication of *Table Talk*, ed. H. N. Coleridge (1835). The American edition of *Table Talk* is still in Emerson's library at the Antiquarian House in Concord (*The Letters of Ralph Waldo Emerson*, ed. Ralph L. Rusk [New York: Columbia University Press, 1939]), 1:448; hereafter cited as *L*; Walter Harding, *Emerson's Library* [Charlottesville: University of Virginia Press, 1967], p. 64).
771. This was the first full meeting of the Symposium or Transcendental Club, which met at Ripley's home in Boston. The Transcendental Club grew out of a proposal by Hedge to Ralph Emerson that they meet with other liberal Unitarian ministers to form a "symposium" to discuss the "mood" of the times. To bring this club into existence, a planning session was held at the Willard Hotel in Cambridge on 8 September 1836. Present at this meeting were Emerson, Hedge, George Ripley, and George Putnam. Francis was one of eleven people present at the first meeting of the Transcendental Club. He, as the eldest, presided, and in the course of the evening proposed that the subject at the next meeting be "American Genius—the causes which hinder its growth, and give us no first rate productions" (Myerson, "Calendar of Transcendental Club Meetings," pp. 198–200). It is a matter of record that Francis attended fifteen of the remaining twenty-nine known meetings of the Transcendental Club, though he possibly attended a few more before the Club had its final meeting in the autumn of 1840.
772. The second meeting of the Transcendental Club was held on 3 October 1836, at Bronson Alcott's home in Boston. Shortly before the meeting, Alcott, in his inimitable style, penned Francis an invitation: "The children of light must need have concern to dispel the darkness which ever blinds the eyes of ages. There are too few in our day; and wisdom shall ever suffer by the absence of a single member of her striving circle" ([1836], MB).

773. Amos Bronson Alcott (1799–1888)—philosopher, pedagogue, and poet—was one of the most conspicuous members of the Transcendental circle.

774. Orestes Augustus Brownson (1803–76)—editor, essayist on religion and philosophy, and novelist—became well known as the publisher of the *Boston Quarterly Review* and *Brownson's Quarterly Review* between 1838 and 1865.

775. James Freeman Clarke (1810–88) was minister of the Unitarian church in Louisville, Kentucky, from 1833 to 1840, and of the Church of the Disciples in Boston from 1841 to 1886.

776. Cyrus Augustus Bartol (1813–89) was graduated from the Harvard Divinity School in 1835 and thereafter was pastor of the West Church in Boston until 1889.

777. Ripley, *Discourses on the Philosophy of Religion* (1836).

778. Brownson, *New Views of Christianity, Society, and the Church* (1836).

779. Alcott, *Conversations with Children on the Gospels* (1836).

780. Furness, *Remarks on the Four Gospels* (1836).

781. That is, the Kantian Transcendentalists or Intuitionalists as opposed to the Lockean Sensualists or Empiricists.

782. Francis was, of course, correct. A singular example of derision was that directed at Alcott and his Temple School; see the entry of 16 January 1837 and notes.

783. John Sandys translates these lines as "Man is but a dream of a shadow; but when a gleam of sunshine cometh as a gift of heaven, a radiant light resteth on men, aye, and a gentle life" ("Pythian Ode VIII, ll. 95–97," *The Odes of Pindar, including the Principal Fragments* [Cambridge: Harvard University Press, 1937], p. 269). For similar expressions of the transcendental idea that divine illumination is not peculiar to Holy Writ alone and that spiritual men in all ages have intuited great truths, see the entries of October 1838 and 12 February 1842.

784. The persons here cannot be identified with certainty, but it is possible that this was Levi Thaxter, a friend of Francis whose daughter Anna was a disciple and defender of Alcott (see F. B. Sanborn and William T. Harris, *A. Bronson Alcott, His Life and Philosophy* [Boston: Roberts, 1893], 1:224, 230–31).

785. In the autumn of 1834 Alcott opened a school at the Masonic Temple in Boston. His method of teaching was the conversation, and the thirty-seven children in the school were taught by Conversations on the gospels. Alcott was assisted by Elizabeth Palmer Peabody, who recorded most of the Conversations. These Conversations, published by James Munroe in 1836 as *Conversations with Children on the Gospels*, were, along with a second volume published in 1837, ridiculed and derided in pulpit and press as being absurd, blasphemous, and obscene. Public antagonism forced Alcott to close his school, and he turned to directing public conversations in and about Boston. For a fuller account of the Temple School and the Conversations, see Sanborn and Harris, *Alcott*, 1:171–234 and Odell Shepard, *Pedlar's Progress: The Life of Bronson Alcott* (Boston: Little, Brown, 1937), pp. 180–210.

786. "Catalogue of One Hundred Drawings by Michael Angelo," *North American Review*, 44 (January 1837): 1–16.

787. This is the first record of Francis' attending one of Emerson's lectures. The lecture, "Ethics," was the ninth in the "Philosophy of History" series, and was delivered on 16 February 1837 at the Boston Masonic Temple. For more on this lecture and the series, see William Charvat, *Emerson's American Lecture Engagements: A Chronological List* (New York: New York Public Library, 1961), p. 16; see also *The Early Lectures of Ralph Waldo Emerson*, ed. Stephen E. Whicher,

Robert E. Spiller, and Wallace E. Williams (Cambridge: Harvard University Press, 1959–72), 2:143–56: hereafter cited as *EL*.

788. See *EL*, 2:145.

789. The Old Meeting House was vacated on Sunday, 4 September 1836, and two sermons were preached on the occasion; on the following Wednesday, 7 September, the sermon dedicating the new building was preached. These sermons were printed under the title of *Three Discourses preached before the Congregational Society in Watertown; Two upon leaving the Old Meeting House, and One at the Dedication of the New, 1836*.

790. In the afternoon Francis preached a sermon on "The Tendency of Occasional & Transient Faults to Pass into Permanent Habits." I have not been able to identify the forenoon sermon. Emerson supplied the pulpit in East Lexington from 1835 to 1838. He was frequently away, but he was solicitous of securing good ministers to supply for him. For much on Emerson's connection with the church at East Lexington, see *L*, 2:6–251, 310, 340, and Myerson, "Convers Francis and Emerson," 24n.

791. The dedication of the new meeting house of the First Congregational Unitarian society in Watertown, Massachusetts, had been on Wednesday, 7 September 1836. The dedication sermon was based upon 1 Kg. 9: 3—"I have hallowed this house which Thou hast built." For more on the leaving of the old house and occupying the new, see the entry of 28 March 1837. The forenoon and afternoon sermons preached on the first Sunday in the new meeting house, 21 September 1836, were "Holiness Becometh the House of the Lord" and "Seeing a Vision in the Temple." The new church building lasted until the summer of 1841, when it burned down (Weiss, *Discourse*, pp. 36–37).

792. This was the fifth meeting of the Transcendental Club. For more on this meeting, see Myerson, "A Calendar of Transcendental Club Meetings," p. 201.

793. John Sullivan Dwight (1813–93) often supplied Unitarian pulpits in the Boston area, but became famous as a music critic and editor of *Dwight's Journal of Music*.

794. George Putnam (1807–78) was pastor of the First Church in Roxbury from 1830 to 1878.

795. Samuel Osgood (1812–80) was graduated from the Harvard Divinity School in 1835 and later served Unitarian and Episcopal churches in Rhode Island and New York.

796. I have been unable to locate the manuscript of the ordination sermon that Francis preached, but in it Francis recommended that Parker not neglect his studies. Henry Ware prayed that "his fondness for peculiar studies" never divert him from doing the Lord's work. At the ordination other prayers were made by Chandler Robbins and Francis Cunningham; Caleb Stetson delivered the charge; George Ripley extended the right hand of fellowship; and hymns written especially for the occasion by John Sullivan Dwight and John Pierpont were sung. John Quincy Adams attended as the delegate from Quincy, Massachusetts (Weiss, *Theodore Parker*, 1:98–99, and Octavius Brooks Frothingham, *Theodore Parker: A Biography* [Boston: James R. Osgood, 1874], p. 87). For an account of the invitation by the Second Parish in Roxbury and the acceptance of the church in Watertown to participate in Parker's ordination, see "Records of the Church of Christ in Watertown," 18 June 1837, p. 40 (MWat). Peter Clark was chosen as the delegate from Watertown to attend the ordination.

797. For Parker's settlement at Spring Street in West Roxbury, see the entry of 21 June 1837. For evidence that Parker had by 1837 achieved a proficiency in the major languages, living and dead, see Weiss, *Theodore Parker,* 1:72–73. Parker commanded Hebrew, Syriac, Greek, Latin, German, Dutch, Italian, Portuguese, Icelandic, Chaldaic, Arabic, Persian, Swedish, Anglo-Saxon, Russian, and "a smattering of Aethiopic."

798. Francis' sermon, taken from Ps. 27: 13, was "We Faint, but for the Goodness of the Lord. Thanksgiving Day." Elijah Parish Lovejoy (1802–57), Abolitionist editor, was shot and killed by a mob in Alton, Illinois, on 1 November 1837, while defending his press. His murder raised great indignation in the North (see the entry of 22 March 1838).

799. This lecture, entitled "Introductory," was the first in the series on "Human Culture" delivered at the Boston Masonic Temple in the winter of 1837–38 (*EL,* 2:213–14).

800. "Here an ampler ether clothes the meads with roseate light, and they know their own sun, and stars of their own" (*Aeneid,* book 7, ll. 640–41, *Virgil,* trans. H. Rushton Fairclough, rev. ed. [Cambridge: Harvard University Press, 1965], 1:550–51).

801. "The Doctrine of the Hands," delivered on 13 December 1837, was the second lecture in the "Human Culture" series (*EL,* 2:230). See the entry of 14 February 1838 for a later presentation of this lecture at Cambridge.

802. The lecture was "The Heart," delivered on the evening of 3 January 1838. It was the fifth in the "Human Culture" series (*EL,* 2:278).

803. The lecture, "Being and Seeming," on the evening of 10 January 1838, was the sixth in the "Human Culture" series (*EL,* 2:295).

804. Emerson had said: "Scott seems not to have been a great poet but to have had a one talent, a sort of *clairvoyance,* so that no man died to him but whatever he knew of the history of a house or hamlet or a glen instantly reproduced the ghosts of the departed in form and habit as when they lived, the moment he looked on the spot. This reverence for great men I think betrays our deep sympathy with the real" (*EL,* 2:307).

805. That is, "transcendental" as opposed to "empirical."

806. This lecture, entitled "General Views," here dated 6 February, should be 7 February; see Charvat, *Emerson's Lectures,* p. 17; *EL,* 2:357; and Eleanor M. Tilton, "Emerson's Lecture Schedule—1837–1838—Revised." *Harvard Library Bulletin,* 21 (October 1973): 397.

807. Neither Charvat, *EL,* nor Tilton lists Emerson's lecturing in Cambridge on this date. Myerson suggests that if Emerson lectured in Cambridge on Thursday this time, as he did for the other lectures in the series, the date would be 15 February ("Convers Francis and Emerson," 27n). This lecture, "Doctrine of the Hands," was the same one that Emerson had delivered as the second in the "Human Culture Series" in Boston on 13 December 1837 (Charvat, *Emerson's Lectures,* p. 17).

808. See *EL,* 2:230.

809. See the entry of 13 December 1837.

810. Neither Charvat nor *EL* has Emerson lecturing in Cambridge on this date but Tilton ("Emerson's Lectures," 397) does. This lecture, "The Head," has been previously given at the Masonic Temple in Boston on 20 December 1837, as a part of the "Human Culture" series (Charvat, *Emerson's Lectures,* p. 17; *EL,* 2:246).

811. See "The Head," *EL,* 2:261.

812. This lecture, "The Heart," was previously delivered on 3 January 1838, as the fifth in the "Human Culture" series at the Masonic Temple in Boston. For more on this lecture, see the entry of 3 January 1838.

813. Possibly the reference here is to Emerson's illustration using the family of the Italian poet Monti; see *EL*, 2:292.

814. This lecture, "Being and Seeming," was previously delivered on 10 January 1838, as a part of the "Human Culture" series in Boston at the Masonic Temple; see the entry of 3 January 1838.

815. This lecture, "Heroism," was first delivered at the Boston Masonic Temple in the "Human Culture" series on 24 January 1838. This lecture is not listed in Charvat or *EL* as having been given in Cambridge on 22 March, but it is in Tilton. "Emerson's Lectures," 397.

816. For Francis' personal interest in the death of the Abolitionist editor Elijah Parish Lovejoy, see entry of 6 December 1837. For Emerson on "brave Lovejoy," see *EL*, 2:327, 328.

817. This lecture, "Holiness," a part of the "Human Culture" series, was read first on 31 January 1838 at the Masonic Temple in Boston. It is given a questionable date of 28 March 1838 in Charvat, but Tilton ("Emerson's Lectures," 397), with Francis, dates it positively 28 March. For more on this lecture, see *EL*, 2:340.

818. After the lecture Francis talked to Ellis Gray Loring about what he thought Emerson had said. Loring, in turn, questioned Emerson about the nature of the deity. Loring learned and reported that Emerson "does not believe, or rather he positively disbelieves in anything outside of himself. He carries idealism to the Extreme, Consequently if there is a God, he is God. God & he are one"; Loring, further, said that Emerson allowed the possibility that "all minds might beat with one pulsation, as to be one & lose all (identity) consciousness" (Tilton, "Emerson's Lectures," 390; Myerson, "Convers Francis and Emerson," 29n).

819. This probably is Miss Merriam, a teacher in Watertown; see the entry of 23 January 1839 and Abby Francis' letter to Edward Emerson, printed in the introduction, above.

820. This lecture, "General Views," was earlier delivered on 7 February 1837 at the Boston Masonic Temple as the final part of the "Human Culture" series (Tilton, "Emerson's Lectures," p. 398; Myerson, "Convers Francis and Emerson," p. 28n).

821. Theodore Parker had probably been preaching on exchange that day with his friend Samuel Ripley.

822. Parker moved to Watertown in April 1832, to keep school and place himself under the tutelage of Francis (Weiss, *Theodore Parker*, 1:57–60).

823. Either Francis discreetly deleted the name in the original journal or his daughter left it out as she copied this entry for Edward Emerson.

824. The name has been omitted in Abby Francis' Manuscript.

825. Compare the entry from Abby Francis' Manuscript and the one of 23 September 1838 with the excerpt from Weiss for September 1838, below. Weiss obviously combined the two entries dated by Abby Francis 22 and 23 September.

826. Francis spent the next night with Emerson in Concord awaiting the next day to preach in Ezra Ripley's pulpit. In Ripley's place he preached sermon "He That Believeth on the Son Hath Everlasting Life" in the morning and "The Language of Action" in the afternoon.

827. Emerson delivered his "Divinity School Address" at Harvard on 15 July 1838. It seems certain that Francis did not hear the address when it was given, but

while the storm surrounding the lecture was still raging, Emerson sent Francis a printed copy of it about 21 August 1838, when it was published (*The Journals and Miscellaneous Notebooks of Ralph Waldo Emerson*, ed. William H. Gilman et al. [Cambridge: Harvard University Press, 1960–M], 12:180: hereafter cited as *JMN*).

828. John Lewis Russell, the naturalist. On 25 September 1838 Emerson recorded in his journal: "A good woodland day or two with John Lewis Russell who came here and showed me mushrooms, lichens, and mosses. A man in whose mind things stand order of cause and effect, & not in order of a shop or even a cabinet" (*JMN*, 7:86).

829. Compare this entry with those of 22 and 23 September, above. In this entry Weiss combined the two preceding ones, making only minor transitional changes.

830. At this place Abby Francis begins a separate entry, dated 23 September 1838, which has a slightly different beginning; see the preceding entry.

831. Paraphrase of *Theaetetus* 176 B. Harold North Fowler renders the whole passage as follows: "But it is impossible that evils should be done away with, Theodorus, for there must always be something opposed to the good; and they cannot have their place among the gods, but must inevitably hover about mortal nature and this earth. Therefore we ought to try to escape from the earth to the dwelling of the gods as quickly as we can; and to escape is to become like God, so far as this is possible; and to become like God is to become righteous and holy and wise" (*Plato with an English Translation* [Cambridge: Harvard University Press, 1952], 2:127, 129).

832. This lecture, "Genius," was the fifth of ten in the "Human Life" series that Emerson delivered at the Masonic Temple in Boston in the winter of 1838–39 (*EL*, 3:68).

833. Those who accompanied Francis and his wife were William Abijah White, brother of Maria White (afterwards Mrs. James Russell Lowell) and son of Abijah, an affluent farmer and merchant of Watertown; and Miss Merriam, a teacher in Watertown. See Abby Francis' letter to Edward Emerson, printed in the introduction, above.

834. At this place Abby Francis put a footnote marker and then noted at the bottom of the page: "Tho' I have not always quoted the *party* that went to hear the lectures, there were always a number of young people who went with my father —as well as my mother generally. A. B. F."

835. The lecture, "Tragedy," was the seventh in the "Human Life" series (*EL*, 3:103).

836. See *EL*, 3:111.

837. This lecture, entitled "Comedy," was delivered on 30 January 1839 as the eighth in the "Human Life" series (*EL*, 3:121).

838. The Rumford Institute was in Waltham, Massachusetts.

839. Emerson's lecture, "The Protest," was first delivered at the Masonic Temple in Boston on 16 January 1839 as the sixth in the "Human Life" series. He later delivered it in Concord on 27 March 1839. Neither Charvat nor *EL* lists this lecture as being delivered at any place other than at Boston and Concord (*EL*, 3:85).

840. See *EL*, 3:100–101.

841. The name has been omitted in Abby Francis' Manuscript.

842. The *Lexington* was destroyed by fire in Long Island Sound on 13 January 1840 (*L*, 2:250).

843. In order, these are Sarah Clarke, sister of James Freeman Clarke; Mary

Channing, daughter of William Ellery Channing, and later married to Frederic Augustus Eustis; Abby Allyn Francis, Convers Francis' wife; and Mrs. Cyrus A. Bartol, wife of the colleague minister of the West Church in Boston.

844. This lecture, "Tendencies," was the final one read at the Boston Masonic Temple in the "Present Age" series presented in the winter of 1839–40 (*EL*, 3:302).

845. See *EL*, 3:310.

846. Francis preached in Concord the next day for Ezra Ripley. He probably preached a morning sermon, but I have been unable to identify it; in the afternoon he preached a sermon entitled "Elisha, Vision of the Horses & Chariots of Fire."

847. The letters in which Carlyle described John A. Heraud, the English editor, and Walter Savage Landor, the poet-essayist, were probably those written on 1 April and 26 September 1840 (*The Correspondence of Emerson and Carlyle*, ed. Joseph Slater. [New York: Columbia University Press, 1964], pp. 264–65, 281; hereafter cited as *CEC*).

848. Emerson sent his first volume of essays to the printer on new year's day 1841. After it was published about the middle of March, Emerson sent Convers Francis, among about fifty others, a copy of it on 19 March (*JMN*, 7:546). Francis' copy of Emerson's *Essays*, inscribed by the author, is in the Widener Collection, MH.

849. Charles C. Shackford was ordained in South Boston at the Hawes-Place Church on 19 May 1841. Parker's sermon, now celebrated because it added fuel to the fire of the Miracles Controversy which had been raging for some time in the Unitarian church, was entitled "The Transient and Permanent in Christianity" based upon the text "Heaven and earth shall pass away; but my words shall not pass away" (Luke 21:33). Parker was castigated for the sermon from every quarter in the pulpit and press. Octavius Brooks Frothingham summed up the reaction: "The writers seemed all to use steel pens. The words 'infidel,' 'scorner,' 'blasphemer,' were freely bandied about. Parker's name was rarely spoken except in connection with Voltaire, Paine, and high priests of unbelief.... Friendly writers were hardly more than apologetic: hostile writers alone forebore to practice the virtue of moderation" (*Theodore Parker*, p. 158). See the entry of 11 December 1841 for more on Parker's reputation as a subject of discussion between Francis and Parker.

850. Undoubtedly he took tea at the home of his old friends Samuel and Sarah Alden Bradford Ripley.

851. The title of this lecture is not given in Charvat or *EL*, but quite likely it was "Nature and the Powers of the Poet," which was presented on 3 November 1841 in Concord. If this were the lecture, more on it is to be found in *EL*, 3:347.

852. This entry could, it seems, be 28 December 1844 instead of 28 December 1841, although Abby Francis seems to place it in the 1841 position. The "new" volume of Emerson's *Essays: Second Series* did not appear until October 1844. Francis had read *Essays* back in March 1841.

853. On 7 November 1841, seventeen slaves being transported aboard the American brig *Creole* out of Norfolk successfully rebelled against the officers, capturing the ship. The slaves were given sanctuary by the British in Nassau. In an official letter Daniel Webster, the Secretary of State, demanded that the British surrender the slaves and make redress, but the British refused. Channing, an ardent anti-slavery advocate, differed with what he felt to be pro-slavery posture of Webster and the federal government, and wrote a reply that was published in two parts as a pamphlet entitled *The Duty of the United States; Or Remarks Suggested by the Case of the "Creole"* (1842).

854. "May it not happen."

855. See Parker to Francis, 24 June 1842, Weiss, *Theodore Parker*, 2:183–84.

856. The highly controversial book was Parker's *Discourse of Matters Pertaining to Religion*, published in May 1842. It was an enlargement of a series of lectures delivered in Boston in the autumn of 1841. The book went through four printings and became Parker's best known and probably most influential work. The Boston Association of Ministers denounced the book as "vehemently deistical" and "subversive of Christianity as a particular religion" (Frothingham, *Theodore Parker*, pp. 161–62). In a letter to Francis on 5 May 1842, Parker stated that the book, then in press, had demanded fifty to eighty hours a week of his time for six weeks (Weiss, *Theodore Parker*, 2:181).

857. This sermon was entitled "Afar Off–and made Nigh by the Blood of Christ." The Thursday Lecture dated back to John Cotton, the second pastor of the First Congregational Church in Boston. Over the years the minister of the First Church regularly preached the lecture. Between 1825 and 1845 the Boston Association of Congregational Ministers, by courtesy of the First Church, supplied ministers to preach the lecture. After 1845 the minister of the First Church once again became responsible for the Thursday Lecture.

858. On this day Francis preached his farewell sermon at Watertown before moving to Cambridge to become Parkman Professor of Pulpit Eloquence and the Pastoral Care at the Harvard Divinity School. He had been pastor of the First Parish Unitarian Congregational Church in Watertown since 23 June 1819. His farewell sermon was "Standing Fast in the Lord." Francis tendered his resignation at Watertown on 13 August 1842 and it was formally accepted by the church on 21 August; see "Records of the Church of Christ in Watertown," pp. 54–55 (MWat).

859. The sermon was entitled "The Coming of Jesus in the Power and Glory."

860. Francis' final sermon as settled minister at Watertown was on 21 August 1842. It was not until 25 October 1843 that John Weiss was settled as the pastor of the church in Watertown.

861. The letter from the Unitarian ministers in England was a result of Samuel May's suggestion to them, when he was visiting abroad in 1843, that they send a letter of advice on slavery to their fellow ministers in America. Eighty-five British ministers signed the letter, and 130 American ministers signed a reply that protested rather than indicated acceptance of the advice. The letter promoted a discussion of abolition activity (Cooke, *Unitarianism in America*, p. 360).

862. Cornelius George Fenner (1822–47) was a student at the Harvard Divinity School from 1842 to 1845.

863. William Lloyd Garrison (1804–79), the noted abolitionist, started the *Liberator*, a journal devoted to the abolition of slavery, in 1831 in Boston. It was discontinued in 1865. He founded an anti-slavery society in 1832 in Boston and later served as president of the American Anti-Slavery Society from 1865 to 1870. He was also prominent in women's suffrage and other reforms.

864. Wendell Phillips (1811–84), Boston orator and abolitionist, was the best known orator of the abolitionists from 1837, to 1865, and president of the American Anti-Slavery Society from 1865 to 1870. He was also prominent in women's suffrage and other reforms.

865. Edmund Quincy (1808–77) was after 1837 active in the anti-slavery movement as an orator and editor.

866. Francis was not ostentatious in his opposition to slavery, but he quietly made his influence against the evil felt. Parker wrote to Francis when Francis was an old man to thank him for his great influence, saying: "Then, too, you early took a deep, warm interest in the antislavery enterprise when its friends were few, feeble, and despised; and you helped the great cause of human Freedom not merely by word and work but by the silent and subtle force of example, which sometimes is worth more than all the words and works of man; for while they may fail, I think the other never does" (3 February 1859, Weiss, *Discourse*, pp. 75–76).

867. See Book VIII, c. 60, *The Deipnosophists or Banquet of the Learned of Athenaeus*, trans. C. D. Younge (London: Henry G. Bohn, 1854), 2:567.

868. Emerson, "The Problem," ll. 13–14, in *The Complete Works of Ralph Waldo Emerson*, ed. Edward Waldo Emerson (Boston: Houghton Mifflin, 1903–1904), vol. 9, *Poems* (1904), pp. 6–7.

869. "Emerson," *Blackwood's Edinburgh Magazine* 62 (December 1847): 643–57.

870. Emerson was on a lecture tour in England from 5 October 1847 to 27 July 1848.

871. "The masses."

872. Thomas Babington Macaulay (1800–1859), English writer and statesman; Richard Monckton Milnes (1809–85), English poet; and Thomas Carlyle (1795–1881), Scottish essayist and historian, were only few notable literary men whom Emerson saw often in London in late winter of 1848.

873. On the use of the "iron triphammer" metaphor, see *JMN*, 10:179, 541, and "Impressions of Thomas Carlyle in 1848," *Scribner's Magazine*, 22 (May 1881): 89.

874. "As for me I hold that outside of Paris there is no salvation at all for upright people" (Moliere, "Les Precieuses Ridicules," scene 95 in *Ouvres de Molière*, new ed. [Paris: LeGrairie Hachette, 1875], 2:78).

875. Emerson was lecturing in Boston at the Freeman Chapel in his series "Mind and Manners in the 19th Century." The third in the series had been delivered on 29 January, and the fourth was delivered on 5 February (Charvat, *Emerson's Lectures*, p. 23). For a list of the topics in this series, which had been given in the previous year in England, see *L*, 4:80, 129.

876. "The Progress of Error," ll. 21–22, in *The Poetical Works of William Cowper*, ed. William Benham (London: Macmillan, 1908), p. 64.

877. "But, as he forgets earthly interests and is rapt in the divine, the vulgar deem him mad, and rebuke him; they do not see that he is inspired" (*The Dialogues of Plato*, trans. B. Jowett, 4th ed. [Oxford: Oxford University Press 1953], 3:156).

878. "Old age, unsociable, and friendless" (*Oedipus at Colonus*, l. 1236).

879. "Without a friend."

880. Between 21 July 1851 and 23 July 1852 Francis checked fifty-six titles out of the Harvard University library, among which was the *Works* of Beaumont and Fletcher ("Library Charging List for 1851–1852," p. 8, Harvard University Archives, MH).

881. Cicero's *Orations* was among sixty-five titles that Francis checked out at the Harvard University library between 23 July 1849 and 26 April 1850 ("Library Charging List for 1849–1850," p. 9, Harvard University Archives, MH).

882. "*De Nat. Deorum*, Lib. I, 5. For in discussing anything, the weight of reasoning, and not of authority, should be sought, since the authority of those

who profess to teach is on the whole a hindrance to those who wish to learn. For the latter cease to depend upon their own judgment, and take for granted the conclusions of those in whom they confide," [Weiss' note].

883. Convers Francis, Sr., a baker, moved to Medford from West Cambridge shortly after Convers was born in 1795. In 1800 his father built a new house and bakery.

884. Convers Francis' mother was formerly Susannah Rand, daughter of Barrett and Susannah Rand of Charlestown, Massachusetts. Convers Francis, Sr., and Susannah Rand married in 1788, when each was twenty-one years old.

885. Emerson delivered his "Lecture on Slavery" on 25 January 1855, at the Tremont Temple in Boston before the Massachusetts Anti-Slavery Society (Charvat, *Emerson's Lectures*, p. 30).

886. Almost positively Mrs. Samuel (Sarah Alden Bradford) Ripley, the widow of the half-uncle of Ralph Waldo Emerson. She had lived in Concord, Massachusetts, since 1846 when she and her husband moved into the Old Manse, his birthplace, from Waltham, where Samuel Ripley had been pastor of the First Congregational Church for thirty-eight years.

887. William Emerson (1801–68), Ralph Waldo Emerson's oldest brother.

888. Delia Bacon's *The Philosophy of Shakespeare Unfolded*, published in 1857 with an introduction by Nathaniel Hawthorne, attempted to show Francis Bacon's authorship of Shakespeare's plays. Emerson had given her a letter of introduction to Carlyle when she left for England to do research and helped her to find a publisher. Carlyle thought "truly there can [be] no madder enterprise than her present one." She died in a mental institution in 1859. A copy of her book is still in Emerson's library (12 May 1853, 8 April 1854, *CEC*, pp. 487–88, 502; Harding, *Emerson's Library*, p. 19).

889. From Chelsea, Carlyle wrote Emerson on 13 May 1855: "Frederick himself is a pretty little man to me, veracious, courageous, invincible in his small sphere; but he does not rise into the empyrean regions, or kindle my heart... and his history... is the most dislocated, unmanageably incoherent, altogether dusty, barren and beggarly production of the modern Muses, as given hitherto" (*CEC*, pp. 505–506).

890. Francis' father died on 27 November 1856, in his ninetieth year, in Wayland, Massachusetts, at the home of his daughter, Lydia Maria Child. Colonel John C. Fremont was the first candidate of the new Republican party in 1856. His anti-slavery position caused him to lose the Southern electoral votes, and he was defeated for the presidency by James Buchanan, the Democratic nominee.

891. This lecture, "Self-possession," was delivered on 7 April 1858 in Boston at Freeman Place Chapel. It was one of four in the "Intellectual Science" or "Mental Philosophy" series (Charvat, *Emerson's Lectures*, p. 34).

892. This lecture was "Man with the Hoe," delivered in Concord at the Middlesex County Fair on 29 September 1858 (Charuat, *Emerson's Lectures*, p. 34). It's quite likely that this was the last public discourse that Francis heard Emerson deliver.

893. Emerson called Carlyle's *History of Frederick the Second* "infinitely the wittiest book that was ever written." Tennyson's *Idylls of the King* showed "a supreme social culture, a perfect insight and the possession of all the weapons all the functions of a man." Copies of both works are still in Emerson's library (May 1859, *The Journals of Ralph Waldo Emerson*, ed. Edward Waldo Emerson and

Waldo Emerson Forbes [Boston: Houghton Mifflin, 1909–14], 9:195, 207; Harding, *Emerson's Library*, p. 269).

894. Francis' wife, Abby Bradford Allyn Francis, had died in Cambridge on 17 December 1860. Her grave and that of her husband are marked today by a single gravestone erected by the Historical Society of Watertown in 1944.

895. Bryan Waller Procter (pseud. "Barry Cornwall"), "A Petition to Time."

896. William Ellery Channing (1818–1901), the poet and essayist, married Ellen Fuller and settled in Concord near Emerson in 1842.

897. Elizabeth Palmer Peabody (1804–94), a close friend of Emerson, Alcott, Horace Mann, and, indeed, most of the Transcendentalists, liberal clergymen, and savants in New England in her time.

898. In his *On Translating Homer: Three Lectures Given at Oxford* (London: Longman, Green, and Roberts, 1861), Matthew Arnold precipitated a controversy by citing the failure of F. W. Newman to deal adequately with the nobility of Homer in his translations. Newman remonstrated in a pamphlet entitled *Homeric Translation in Theory and Practice. A Reply to Matthew Arnold, Esq.* (London: Williams and Norgate, 1861). Arnold carried the controversy on in a fourth lecture, which he published as *On Translating Homer: Last Words* (London: Longman, Green, and Roberts, 1862). For surveys of the Homeric controversy, see Sidney Coulling, *Matthew Arnold and His Critics: A Study of Arnold's Controversies* (Athens: Ohio Universty Press, 1974), pp. 62–99; Matthew Arnold, *On the Classical Tradition*, ed. R. H. Super (Ann Arbor: University of Michigan Press, 1960), pp. 238–53 (notes). Arnold sent Emerson his *Last Words*, which Emerson read and pronounced an "amiable" book (Emerson to Edward Waldo Emerson, 12 June 1862, *L*, 5:279).

899. "Emerson—the Conduct of Life," *Eclectic Review*, n.s. 3 (November 1862): 363–409.

THE PREPARATION OF A POET: PURITAN DIRECTIONS IN EMILY DICKINSON'S EDUCATION

Rowena Revis Jones

AS A NEW ENGLAND TOWN, Amherst, Massachusetts, for many generations has shared a dedication to learning derived in large part from its Puritan past. The Puritan ideal of education, based upon the immediate relationship of the individual to God, emphasized one's dependence upon the written Word as an essential means of grace. Every man and woman was responsible to seek his or her own salvation, and in order to do so had to learn first to read and reason.

Emily Dickinson was a part of this tradition. Born into a family loyal to both the Congregational church and the advancement of learning, she was raised in an atmosphere that encouraged her to develop both mind and soul. Intellectual fibre, a certain toughness of mind and spirit, permeates the poems of this daughter of Amherst. Self-respect, stubborn doubts, and hard-fought positions marked her manner of life as well as the insights and patterns of her expression. Sharp recordings of objective phenomena balance a sometimes overwhelming preoccupation with inner spiritual experience.

Such characteristics are consistent with at least three main directions that emerge from a review of Dickinson's educational background. All three stem to a significant degree from her Puritan heritage. First, the extreme importance of cultivating the mind was inculcated in Dickinson through family, school, and church. Second, a growing recognition of woman's intellectual capacity increased her educational opportunities and sense of self-worth. Third, the Puritan ideal of a union between mental culture and religious faith helped shape her most profound assumptions, desires, and concerns.

Both Samuel Fowler Dickinson and Edward Dickinson, as well as Emily's brother, William Austin Dickinson, were among the Amherst town fathers prominent for their contributions to the educational life of the area. The eldest Dickinson was a key figure in the founding of Amherst Academy and Amherst College. Himself a Dartmouth graduate, he shared with other village leaders a strong desire to improve the educational opportunities of area youth. He and one other citizen, Hezekiah Wright Strong, headed the original subscription list for Amherst Academy. Three years after its establishment in 1814, Dickinson, a member of the Board of Trustees until 1824, served on a committee charged with soliciting support for a permanent fund to help young men preparing to be ministers, and to endow an ongoing professorship for this purpose. Unable to raise enough public support for meeting these goals at the academy, the committee endorsed a constitution and bylaws for raising and managing a charitable fund that would help launch a separate institution of higher learning with the distinct aim of educating "indigent young men of promising talents and hopeful piety, who shall manifest a desire to obtain a liberal education with the sole view to the Christian ministry."[1] When the full board approved this proposal, under the conviction that just such a "Classical" institution, in cooperation with the theological seminaries and educational societies, was the most effective way of "civilizing and evangelizing the world,"[2] it initiated the establishment of Amherst College.

Once plans for the proposed college were underway, Dickinson was instrumental in getting it located in Amherst. He not only continued to give time and effort to support the infant college, but repeatedly donated his own financial resources. Samuel Dickinson's efforts, along with those of Colonel Rufus Graves, original secretary of the Academy Board of Trustees and a member of the committee that first conceived of a separate institution for advanced learning, led Amherst president Edward Hitchcock to write that these two "had more to do informing and executing plans for the founding of Amherst College than any other men."[3] Professor William Seymour Tyler reaffirmed Dickinson's contributions, saying that to him and Hezekiah Wright Strong, "beyond any other citizens of Amherst, the College afterward owed its origin."[4]

Edward Dickinson, a graduate of Yale, served on the executive committee of the Academy Board of Trustees from 1838 to 1860, and was treasurer of Amherst College from 1835 until his resignation in 1872. His son, William Austin Dickinson, succeeded him as treasurer until 1894. Thus, from the year Samuel Fowler Dickinson headed the subscription list for the academy through Austin's tenure as treasurer, three generations of Dickinsons served the academy and college for some seventy years.

Edward Dickinson's concern for the cause of higher education in Massachusetts and particularly at Amherst, was expressed further through his efforts to increase financial support from the Massachusetts Legislature during his tenure as a member of the House from January 1837 to April 1839. His letters home from Boston at this time reflect his desire to see the interests of the college successfully represented. On the college campus itself, he was held in high respect, receiving an honorary Doctor of Laws degree in 1863, heading the list of honorary pallbearers at the funeral of President Hitchcock in 1864, and officiating as acting president at the laying of the cornerstone of Walker Hall in 1868.[5] Annually for forty years,[6] he and Mrs. Dickinson held a commencement tea at their home which, according to a report in the *Springfield Republican,* was "one of the most ancient and most agreeable of the social festivities of the week at Amherst."[7] When Dickinson resigned as treasurer, the college trustees expressed their "profound sense" of the value of his thirty-seven years of service, marked as they were by "a fidelity and assiduity that could not have been surpassed, had he been managing his own estate."[8]

Edward Dickinson's interest in education was not limited to his service to Amherst College. In 1864 he urged the local citizens to appropriate funds to secure the Massachusetts Agricultural College in their town, and later he helped persuade the college trustees to accept this location and erect the original nucleus of what is now the University of Massachusetts–Amherst. While his own children were not yet old enough to attend school, he served as the only lay member of the local school committee,[9] and when Emily was ten, he called to order a meeting of "the friends of Education" in Amherst.[10]

A father so attentive to the needs of his community would not be likely to neglect those of his own family, and the evidence is ample that Dickinson desired for his children the best possible upbringing. His strong sense of responsibility for their development is particularly evident in a letter he wrote their mother from Boston in January 1838:

> My family is the object of my thoughts, & my exertions—and without them, there would be little to prompt me to make exertion. The duty which devolves upon us, of bringing up our little children as they should be, is an important one—and we can not realize too deeply, our obligation to study the best course—and adopt the best methods of instruction & government—& set before them the best example for imitation. They are a trust committed to our care—& we must discharge that trust faithfully. . . . To take a rational view of life, & the object of it, is, at once, to place almost any thing we value here, in the light of little importance—and if, as you believe, and I can't doubt, this life

is a mere preparatory state for another period of existence, how important, to act with reference to such a state—& yet how little we really do seem to consider it. I need not tell you that no day passes without my having some reflections on this subject, in connection with you, & our dear little children.[11]

Other letters written from Boston at the same time to Mrs. Dickinson and the children—William Austin, Emily, and Lavinia—reveal his solicitude for their health and manners, as well as their progress at school. "Keep school, and learn," he admonished the children, "so as to tell me, when I come home, how many new things you have learned, since I came away."[12] They were to consider themselves fortunate, he added, that they owned books, and had a school to attend.[13] He sent them reading matter also: a subscription to the *Sabbath School Visitor* for Austin and Emily, which he thought "would please them"; and another to *Parley's Magazine*, which contained "some interesting stories."[14]

Edward Dickinson's allusions to his children's early education reflect no distinction on his part between the importance of proper schooling for his young son Austin, and the attention he expects little Emily and Vinnie to give their lessons. Such impartiality might be dismissed on the basis of the children's ages, were it not confirmed by his continued interest in the education of not only his son, who eventually was graduated from Amherst College and Harvard Law School, but of his daughters as well, both of whom were to attend recently established female seminaries. In this respect, Dickinson was only one of many church and civic leaders in New England who by the 1830s were pressing for greater educational opportunities for young women.

Women in the New England Puritan culture were not regarded as necessarily mentally inferior by reason of their sex. In a comparison between Anne Bradstreet and Emily Dickinson, Karl Keller agrees that the Puritan faith provided women with a sense of their own value, equal to that of men, in the sight of God. Both New England women poets, Keller writes, shared in "an undercurrent of the culture, an assumption for two hundred years that woman too had to do something about her salvation—and on her own and within the range of her inherent possibilities and according to her physical and mental inclinations."[15] It was this assumption, Keller concludes, that "liberated" New England women and led them to assert the strain of independence he notes in the poems of Bradstreet and Dickinson.

Within Amherst itself, both church and school demonstrated their faith in the female intellect by promoting education for women. In 1820, a sermon addressed specifically "To the Females of the First Parish in Amherst, Massachusetts," affirmed that the gospel indeed emancipated women. The minister, Daniel A. Clark, reminded his congregation that "the moment the gospel abandons a people, females lose in a great degree their influence, their respectability, and their comfort: while, under its benign influence, they are wise, respectable and happy."[16] Although Clark regarded the wife as subservient to her husband in family relationships, he speaks indignantly of those who would disparage her mind. "The base suggestion, that as the female is confined at home, she needs no intellectual improvement, has long since been repelled," he claims.[17] While it is still true that "even in gospel lands they have never risen as high as they may,"[18] Clark declared to what must have been a sympathetic female audience, "happily we live in an age, when no man presumes to say, that the female mind possesses any natural imbecility, which must necessarily cramp its growth."[19]

Reminding them that their minds were "capable of indefinite enlargement" until they reached a heaven where knowledge would be complete,[20] Clark enjoined his hearers to examine their own values and not to seek to be "*first* in the *fashion*, lest they end up *last* in the *library*," if indeed they arrived there at all.[21] Perception, thought, reason, and judgment were to be enlarged by receiving ideas and by learning to think. His advice to the women was strong and direct:

> Every wise woman, then, will enlarge her mind; will read, and think, and reason. She will be especially ambitious to grow in the knowledge of God; will become acquainted with her own being, and with being in general; that she may be the more happy, and the more useful. Sisters, mothers, there lies a world around you, and within your reach, which it is your duty to explore. It rests with you to determine whether you will carry with you to the grave a contracted mind, or a mind large as the regions of space. Men have been found base enough, to libel your characters, and have pronounced the female sex made for servitude. The reproach is unmerited, and has been promptly repelled. It belongs to you to settle this question forever, and show the slanderer that you are capable of an intellectual dignity, which can look him into deserved contempt. Endeavour in yourselves, and your daughters, to give noble examples of female magnanimity; to reach that growth of thought, that shall make you and them blessings to unborn generations.[22]

In 1820 Emily Norcross of Monson had not yet become the bride of Edward Dickinson and a member of this church, but her future mother-in-law, Lucretia Gunn Dickinson, may have been in the congregation, as the Dickinsons were charter members of First Church. Her future father-in-law, Samuel Dickinson, was to express his view of female education a decade later: "A good husband will also *educate well his daughters*.... Daughters should be *well instructed*, in the useful sciences; comprising a *good* English education: including a thorough knowledge of our own language, geography, history, mathematics and natural philosophy. The female mind, so sensitive, so susceptible to improvement, should not be neglected ... God hath designed nothing in vain."[23]

Whether Emily Dickinson's own mother felt strongly on the subject of her daughter's education cannot be judged, though her concern for her family's health and happiness is evident, and she contributed generously to the life of her church and community. She does not appear to have been a literary woman herself. But Emily's father seems to have been in full accord with the position of his church's former pastor. Among the several books he chose for his daughter in later years is a small volume containing much the same view of female education that Clark had presented to the Amherst church. Originally using the rather unlikely title *Letters on Practical Subjects, from a Clergyman of New England, to His Daughter*, its author, William Buell Sprague, dwells at length on the need for young women to cultivate their God-given mental faculties, and the need of society to provide them opportunity and encouragement. Too long have even Christian parents and teachers overlooked this obligation:

> Especially has this capital error been committed in substituting what is called an ornamental, for a solid education; in taking more care to form the person than to form the mind; and the consequence of this has been that many a girl of fine talents has come forth to the world and shown us the fruit of a long and expensive education, in the marvellous dexterity she has acquired in the use of her hands and feet. But are not females gifted with the exalted attribute of reason as well as the other sex? And where has providence intimated that in one sex this gift is to be cultivated with the utmost care, and in the other is to be left in all the wildness and barrenness of nature? What if the sexes have not, in all respects, the same destination? What if man is destined to stand forth in the bolder walks of society; and what if woman has her station allotted her more exclusively, amidst the retired scenes of domestic life? This may be a reason why their education should in some respects be differently conducted; but it can never be an argument for leaving the mind of the female to rust with ignorance, or moulding her into a pleasant, animated plaything. If it be desirable that the mind of man should expand and strengthen by exercise, it must also be desirable that the female mind should share in some degree the same cultivation: otherwise the dearest, tenderest connexion of life, which ought to be but another name for the most absolute community of interest and feeling, will be converted into a unequal, unnatural league between intellectual refinement, and intellectual barbarism.[24]

Sprague does caution against the disputatious female, however. He, like his fellow-minister Clark, upheld a "womanly" ideal, which he felt would be most readily shattered in the arena of religious controversy. "I beg you," he wrote his motherless daughter, never to display what theological knowledge you may have acquired: "When a woman takes up the weapons of theological warfare, the native loveliness of the female is instantly eclipsed. The modest and retiring virtues, which are the chief ornament of your sex, always retreat from the din and clashing of religious combatants."[25] His own unfortunate encounter with one "sturdy female polemick" had strengthened his hope "that the time will never come, when the cause of truth will require the polemick influence of females."[26] Dickinson, preferring as she did to tell the truth "slant" and to remain private, would not have needed this particular advice.

At the same time, Sprague regards as essential an independence of mind, or that quality "which leads us to form all our opinions deliberately, and from the best light which we can gain, and then to adhere to them with firmness, until there shall be sufficient evidence to reverse our convictions."[27] At this point, Dickinson would have taken note.

A second reservation that Sprague holds regards the choice of reading matter for his daughter. He recommends the Bible, theology, and sermons such as those by "the immortal Edwards." A few works of fiction can be read to advantage, such as the novels of Richardson and Scott. But most fiction he considers dangerous, and he cannot encourage the addiction of young females to novel reading. Likewise, a few poets such as Milton, Cowper, and Thompson may be read with profit, but others, including most modern poets, "cannot be safely recommended as guides to youthful virtue."[28] The criteria by which Sprague judges are related to moral and religious influence. Edwards' sermons, for example, "though wholly destitute of ornament, are in the highest degree instructive, and contain perhaps, the most powerful appeals to the heart and conscience, which are to be found out of the Bible."[29] His distrust of modern literati would strike a similar chord in Edward Dickinson, who according to Emily warned his children against all books that would "joggle the mind."[30] Clearly, Dickinson chose to exercise independence of mind at this point. Also, her father did bring home books he thought would please his children. Belles lettres were represented among his own collection, though he preferred nonfictional works of history, politics, law, religion, and travel.

The stature accorded women by Puritanism, contributing as it did by the 1830s to a heightened emphasis upon their education, benefited Dickinson during her formal schooling. The system of free public education was long established in Massachusetts, and by this time girls as well as boys attended the Amherst "Primary School." Dickinson began school either here or with other "faculty children" at a Misses Nelsons' school, although it is just possible that she attended very briefly the Amherst Female Seminary, which was supported by area clergymen—among them Matthew T. Adam of First Church—and other citizens concerned for the education of their daughters. This day school was operated from 1832 until 1835, when it was destroyed by fire. Its enrollment exceeded expectations, reaching 191 pupils.[31] But it is recorded definitely that during at least part of 1840–41, Dickinson was enrolled in the "English course" at Amherst Academy. Between 1841 and 1843, she is listed in the "Classical course." In the next extant catalogue, for 1846–47, her name reappears under the English course. References in her correspondence indicate she attended during certain terms between 1843 and 1846. She was at the academy, then, intermittently for seven years.

Amherst Academy was strongly supported not only by the students' families, but also by others in the area, including many religious and civic leaders. Among its earliest promoters was Dr. David Parsons, second pastor of the Dickinsons' church, who donated the land on which the academy was built and served as first president of its Board of Trustees. Dr. Parsons was succeeded as president by Noah Webster, a leading citizen during his residency in Amherst from 1812–22. Dr. Parsons and Samuel Dickinson were among the trustees who originally opened the academy to both sexes, and Noah Webster had joined the Board while this policy was first in effect. As one local history points out, this step was taken "long before the era of woman's [sic] colleges, and [provided] the only avenue open to young women in search of a higher education."[32] When Emily Dickinson attended the academy it was coeducational, the Female Department having been reinstituted in 1838 after a lapse of fourteen years.[33] The "Prudential" or executive committee of the Board of Trustees included her father and also Aaron Colton, then the minister of First Church. Family, church, and community continued to stand behind her.[34]

But the most obvious impact upon the poet of the heightened interest in women's education at this period, is the opportunity she had to attend Mount Holyoke Female Seminary, just nine miles away in South Hadley. "I am fitting to go to South Hadley Seminary," she joyously announced in June 1846 to her friend Abiah Root, "& expect if my health is good to enter that institution a year from next fall. Are you not astonished to hear such news? You cannot imagine how much I am anticipating in entering there. It has been in my thought by day,

The Preparation of a Poet

& my dreams by night, ever since I heard of South Hadley Seminary."[35]

Mount Holyoke Female Seminary had been chartered just a decade earlier—on 10 February 1836. Although even the original trustees, who had contributed generously to its realization, considered the seminary the result chiefly of the efforts of one woman, an important factor in its founding was Mary Lyon's propitious timing. An increasing awareness in New England during the first half of the nineteenth century of a need to upgrade female education not only encouraged greater local support for coeducational district schools, but also helped establish a number of female seminaries as well as academies like the one at Amherst, open to both sexes. As Elizabeth Alden Green has observed in *Mary Lyon and Mount Holyoke: Opening the Gates*, the Puritans of the nineteenth century not only sought an inward state of consecration to God, but as "pragmatic idealists" they simultaneously devoted themselves to good works.[36] To New Englanders of piety, especially those who looked upon women as made in the divine image, the cause of female education could well have presented itself as a religious cause, a way of advancing the kingdom of God. This was most certainly true in the case of Mary Lyon, but she was not alone.

For two decades before Mount Holyoke opened, Mary Lyon had been actively involved in the movement for female education, as a district school teacher, as a student herself, and as a teacher and administrator in coeducational and female schools. She had attended Sanderson Academy in Ashfield in 1817, Amherst Academy in 1818, and a recently founded seminary for women in Byfield in 1821. Then after two years as preceptress back in Ashfield, she had gone in 1824 to Derry, New Hampshire, to serve at the newly opened Adams Academy for women, while also conducting her own district school in Buckland and Ashfield for part of each winter. From 1830 to 1834, she was assistant principal and acting head at Ipswich Female Seminary, which also had just been established.[37]

Mary Lyon's acquaintance with schools and educators across Massachusetts and beyond was wide, before she even conceived of the seminary at South Hadley. Her ten-year association with Zilpah Grant, the principal at Derry and Ipswich who shared the vision of a permanent seminary for women, was of particular importance. She had come into close contact also with at least three outspoken male supporters of education for women. In Ashfield she lived in the home of Thomas White, a trustee of Sanderson Academy who acted as her financial adviser, and helped her to go on to Byfield with his daughter Amanda and later return to Sanderson to teach. Squire White was a firm advocate of education for women; his daughter Hannah later assisted Mary Lyon and also taught at Ipswich and Amherst.[38] The contribution of Joseph Emerson, the Congregational minister who had founded the female seminary in Byfield in 1818, was even more pervasive. Not only Emerson's belief in a religious principle at the heart of all learning, and his insistence upon thorough and systematic preparation, but also his respect for the intellectual capacities of his women students impressed her deeply. Finally, among all who supported Mary Lyon in her efforts to advance education for women, her foremost advocate was Edward Hitchcock, in whose home she lived while teaching at Conway in the summer of 1823. Their association continued and strengthened so that after leaving Ipswich Seminary in 1834, Mary Lyon spent the winter with the Hitchcocks in Amherst. The arrangement allowed her not only the stimulation of conversation and study, but no doubt helped increase Hitchcock's support of her efforts during this period to launch a permanent female seminary. Hitchcock became Mary Lyon's chief spokesman in the Connecticut Valley, publicly defending her cause and principles before and after the opening of the seminary, which he served as a trustee from 1836 until his death in 1864.

In promoting female education, Mary Lyon was following a direction by now clearly marked within the New England culture. Not only were many educators, clergy, and civic leaders in agreement, but the general populace also gave encouragement. She sought her support from the broad middle class, whom she saw as united in its desire to provide schooling for its sons and daughters and to spread the gospel through an educated ministry. As she travelled the countryside soliciting contributions, she appealed to this desire by pressing the need to prepare well trained women teachers who would in turn strengthen the entire educational system. Gifts came in from those who could barely spare them, women as well as men.

But widespread as the sentiment for female education was in New England at this time, Mary Lyon also met indifference and hostility. As Daniel Clark had remarked to his congregation at the First Church of Amherst in 1820, women had not yet risen as high as they might. Mary Lyon herself acknowledged to Zilpah Grant that "many good men will fear the effect on society of so much female influence, and what they call female greatness."[39] A measure of her accomplishment lies in the degree to which such attitudes were overcome or set aside, and also to what Elizabeth Alden Green has described as her "unshakable belief in the capacity of young women to rise—physically, intellectually, spiritually—to the most arduous demands society would make."[40] It is this faith in female capabilities, as well as a sense of fair play and a belief in the importance of education, that is reflected most strongly in Mary Lyon's arguments for a permanent female seminary equal in endowment to institutions for young men. "The design of this enterprise," she explained to the public, "is to give our country an institution for females, founded on as benevolent and liberal a plan, and as permanent in its existence and character, as those for the other sex; an institution directly suited to aid in promoting the great work of renovating the world, as are our higher institutions for young men."[41] Throughout her year at the seminary, Emily Dickinson must have received every encouragement to "rise"; her own persistent striving after stature may well have been intensified under the influence of Mary Lyon and Mount Holyoke. The ideal to which she was called remained a "womanly" one, in that "domestic economy" and "female piety" were heavily stressed. But the academic requirements were made relatively stringent, evidently on the assumption that women were as capable as men of meeting them. Essential to the purpose of Mount Holyoke were selective admissions criteria, careful choice of textbooks and studies comparable to those at schools for men, and high standards for classroom performance, including thorough reviews and examinations. In view of the aims of Mary Lyon and her contemporaries, this final year of Dickinson's formal schooling must have helped educate her as to the dignity of her sex.

Emily Dickinson's year of study at Mount Holyoke brings forward the fact that the main direction of her education was overwhelmingly religious. The pursuit of education in the Connecticut Valley well into the nineteenth century took its tone of high seriousness from the aims of its promoters. Civic leaders such as Samuel Fowler and Edward Dickinson, clergymen such as those from the First Church of Amherst, and educators like Mary Lyon espoused learning not merely as a worthy end in itself, and extended it to women not simply to advance their status in society, but rather they established and supported and administered schools primarily so that by educating young men and women they might help direct their souls toward eternity. It was because he could not doubt "this life is a mere preparatory state for another period of existence," that Emily's father reflected so gravely upon the instruction of his little children. Small wonder that the poet reveals throughout her writing what Richard Chase has referred to as an "eschatological cast of mind."[42]

The religious character of Dickinson's education first emerges from her earliest textbooks: the Bible, *The New England Primer*, and her speller. From earliest childhood she was taught the Bible. Morning prayers, including Scripture reading, were an established part of the Dickinson household routine. The Bible's language, imagery, and concepts saturate her letters and poems from youth upward, indicating that she began hearing and reading it as a small child. Bible instruction in the Dickinson home was supplemented at the First (Congregational) Church, which Emily as a girl attended regularly with her family. She must also have been a pupil in the Sabbath School of which her grandfather had been one of the first directors. Proposed by Noah Webster and begun during the pastorate of Daniel Clark (1820–24), this school continued to stress Scripture memorization very heavily until at least 1850.[43]

Dickinson was familiar also with *The New England Primer*.[44] As she committed to memory the letters of her alphabet, she doubtless learned from the *Primer* the rhymes familiar to generations of New England children: "In Adam's fall / We sinned all"; "Thy life to mend, / God's Book attend"; "As runs the Glass, / Man's life doth pass." Bible verses beginning with different letters of the alphabet also helped reinforce her memory. The uncertainty of life and one's own need of salvation through Christ were among the themes of the earliest poems she must have heard; John Rogers' burning at the stake, illustrating well how straight a path of suffering the early martyrs trod, helped introduce her to the narrative form.

But the most significant feature of *The New England Primer* was "The Shorter Catechism, agreed upon by the Reverend Assembly of Divines at Westminster." This catechism consisted of a series of questions and answers formulated by English presbyters in 1643, and represented the doctrinal beliefs of both English and American Puritanism. In New England, children for generations continued to commit it to memory. "Our Puritan ancestors brought the Shorter Catechism with them," wrote Amherst College president Heman Humphrey, "and laid it on the shelf with the family Bible." He expressed his "own admiration of it, as the most lucid, guarded and comprehensive epitome of Bible truth, which I have ever seen; and as, in my judgment, the best family manual that the wisdom and piety of any body of uninspired men has ever given to the church." Children should continue to learn by heart its "true and fundamental doctrines," so that in their maturity the Spirit of God might work upon them effectually. "How delightful it is," observed this leading educator of nineteenth century Amherst, "to hear, as we sometimes do, the aged disciple, repeating with thrilling interest, and feasting his soul upon the definitions of *justification, sanctification, glorification,* and the like, which, three quarters of a century before, were imprinted upon his memory in the nursery."[45] Although she directed them to their own ends, throughout her life Dickinson used just such terminology and underlying concepts as appear in the Shorter Catechism to help shape poem after poem. The expressed desire for "redemption," "communion," "sanctification," and future fulfillment; the sense of inadequacy and isolation, distance, and awe, as well as the critical moments of spiritual revelation and exaltation wrought by "grace" appear in her art as mature transmutations of a close early acquaintance with *The New England Primer.*

One other source vital to the poet's early education would have been her spelling book. Noah Webster's involvement in the educational affairs of Amherst increases the likelihood that the famous blue-backed speller that he first published in 1783 was used locally. At an Amherst town meeting held 1 April 1833, it was "voted to refer to the General School Committee the power of retaining or excluding the Webster Spelling Book, as they shall deem expedient."[46] Neither the outcome of the vote, however, nor subsequent action of the committee on this issue is reported by the compilers of the records. So popular was the Webster speller at the time that from 1812 to 1822, when Webster lived in Amherst, proceeds from it provided almost his entire income. By the time of his death in 1843, approximately 20,000 copies were in circulation.[47] Its success has been attributed partly to Webster's deliberate inclusion of moral and religious instruction. "This distinguished philologist," wrote Amherst College historian William Seymour Tyler, "sympathized with the most puritanical of the founders in their religious faith and the fervor of their Christian spirit."[48] The "Moral Catechism" included in *The American Spelling Book* illustrates Webster's purpose, pointing young readers to God's Word as the source of moral law and admonishing them to grow into the image of their Heavenly Father, whose favor the pure in heart would enjoy forever.[49] His *Elementary* speller, which was issued several times between 1829 and 1845, continues to catechize: "The Holy Bible is the book of God"; "We are apt to live forgetful of our continued dependence on the will of God"; "It is a solemn thing to die and appear before God"; "Christ is the mediator between an offended God and offending man"; "God will impart grace to the humble penitent"; "The irresistibility of divine grace is disputed."[50]

Another speller, *The National Spelling-Book* by Benjamin Dudley Emerson, may have been used by the Dickinson children. At least two copies of this textbook were in the Dickinson library. This speller does not have as strong a theological cast as Webster's, but the reading lessons contain selections from the Bible and stress the importance of loving and obeying an all knowing, all powerful Heavenly Father.[51] Although it is not recorded what speller Dickinson actually used, the character of instruction offered in her pre-academy years could not have differed markedly from that which these texts offered.

As Emily Dickinson progressed to the academy and later Mount Holyoke Female Seminary, the essentially religious character of her education continued to be stamped by that singleness of aim that bound together church, school, and community in this portion of the Valley during the middle decades of the nineteenth century. "The cardinal fact about Emily Dickinson," as George Frisbee Whicher remarked, "is that she was a product of her time and place.... Her mind was shaped by church, school, and college, which in her time expressed with dynamic vigor the intellectual and spiritual energies of the Puritan tradition."[52] "Amherst Academy, Amherst College, and Mount Holyoke Seminary," Whicher explains in his biography of the poet,

> were alike conceived in the faith that the spread of Christian doctrines as interpreted by Orthodox Congregationalism would free the world of its miseries and corruptions. The explosive force of this conviction, thundered from a thousand pulpits, was incalcuable. It led thrifty farmers and shrewd lawyers, as well as devoted teachers and clergymen, to give more than they could afford to promote educational institutions and missionary enterprises.[53]

Not only did an impressive number of individuals in the community pledge financial support to the fledgling college but, as Thomas LeDuc has observed, just as "eloquent" are the many unsolicited donations of labor and material for the construction of its original building.[54] For, as LeDuc adds, the religious purpose of the college was rooted in the convictions of the Valley community:

> Here was the last frontier of Connecticut Puritanism; here the teaching of Thomas Hooker and Jonathan Edwards still furnished the rule of life. Unitarianism, a tidewater heresy, had scarcely reached the valley before the "second awakening" burst into flame and revived men's faith in faith. It was this new repentance that prepared the way for the opening of the college. The Congregational churches had kept the revival well in hand and had largely preserved the region for the orthodox.[55]

The close connection of the Dickinsons' church to local education reflected its position that learning and religious faith are inseparable.

When Edward Sereno Dwight, its minister from 1853 to 1860 and a member of the College Board of Trustees, argued that public education could work either good or evil, depending upon whether it encouraged an intelligence rooted in the religion of the gospel, he struck a chord that would have been familiar to this congregation.[56] Introducing an address on the "Relation of the [First] Church to the Educational Institutions of Amherst," Professor William Tyler observed that the Christian church historically had established and fostered education because of a "natural affinity between sound learning and true religion."[57] Following this tradition, "the officers and members of this church," claimed Tyler, "were the *founders* of Amherst Academy and Amherst College."[58] The academy, the favorite "eldest daughter of the church," "received its dower partly indeed from the Commonwealth of Massachusetts but chiefly from the church and the good people of Amherst."[59] Although a Congregational enterprise "born of the revivals and the spirit of missions that distinguished the first half of the present century," the college in the strictest sense was founded "by a single local church. Other churches helped.... But the ministers and members of this church took the lead. They bore the burden, *they* did the work."[60]

Tyler cited specifically the contributions several former members had made to the establishment of the academy and the college, including Hezekiah Wright Strong, Rufus Graves, and Samuel Fowler Dickinson. All three had been leaders in First Church, Dickinson having served as a deacon for forty years. Tyler elsewhere attributed the role of these men in founding the academy and college to their religious zeal. "The conversion of the world often pressed heavily upon his [Dickinson's] mind," Tyler wrote in his *History of Amherst College*, and he "saw in the Institution contemplated at Amherst, one of the agencies that would surely hasten the promised event."[61] President Edward Hitchcock also linked Dickinson's religious faith to his determination to establish the academy and endow within it a professorship for preparing ministers and missionaries, and then, when this did not materialize, to enlarge the original plan and found a college for this purpose. Dickinson "was a man of very decided religious principles," Hitchcock remarked, "and once satisfied that he was in the path of duty, his face was as a flint, and he remained one of the early Puritans."[62]

The singleness of aim shared by First Church, the academy, college, and also the community of Amherst, was strikingly illustrated at the laying of the cornerstone for the first college building in 1820. The community had helped make possible the event through their gifts of money, material, and labor. Dr. David Parsons, second pastor of the church and president of the Academy Board of Trustees, now over seventy years old and just retired from the pulpit, laid the granite cornerstone. This early minister, writes Tyler, "was among the most zealous and earnest advocates of the union of a high standard of scholarship with the highest type of evangelical religion."[63] Noah Webster, a member of Dr. Parson's congregation who immediately after this ceremony succeeded him as president of the Board, delivered an address. Ours is a ministry aimed at "extending and establishing the Redeemer's empire—the empire of Truth,"[64] he reminded those assembled. "This institution will grow and flourish, and become auxiliary to a thousand associations which Christian philanthropy has formed, to reclaim and evangelize the miserable children of Adam."[65] Finally, Daniel Clark, Parson's successor in the First Church pulpit, gave the sermon. Clark likewise envisioned the college as an arm of the church, "a fountain pouring forth its streams to fertilize the boundless wastes of a miserable world."[66] While it was the declared purpose of the college to help prepare young men for the ministry, in a more general sense its religious aim was shared by the academy that Dickinson was to attend. Indeed, the Academy Board of Trustees governed both institutions at the time the cornerstone was laid for the college they had conceived. The academy, in addition to providing instruction in languages, arts, and sciences, was at the same time to promote "morality, piety & religion."[67]

The role of the clergy in Amherst's educational life, and the importance of the ministry in the eyes of the entire community, makes even more clear the directions which Dickinson's formal schooling naturally would take. The local school committee consisted predominantly of clergymen. While some laymen such as Samuel Dickinson and Noah Webster were prominent in the establishment of Amherst Academy and College, two thirds of the original Academy Board of Trustees were Congregational ministers.[68] The majority of the principals at the academy when Emily Dickinson was a student were either ordained or headed for the ministry or mission field.[69] From among her preceptresses, Caroline D. Hunt was the wife of the pastor at North Amherst, and Rebecca M. Woodbridge was the daughter of the minister at Hadley. At the college, with only one exception the entire faculty under President Heman Humphrey (1823–45) were ministers;[70] during the administration of William Augustus Stearns (1854–76), still over half were clergymen.[71] Helping to fulfill the vision of a college which would help educate "indigent young men of piety and talents for the ministry," most of the students who enrolled before 1850 did indeed intend to become ministers.[72] This trend continued through the administration of President Stearns, so that during this period Amherst is said to have been graduating more future ministers than any other American college.[73]

Professors from the college not only delivered weekly religious lectures and preached alternate Sundays at the College Church, but also frequently filled the pulpit of the Dickinsons' church during the years Emily attended there. Professors Nathan Welby Fiske, William Chauncey Fowler, Joseph Haven II, Edwards Amasa Park, Julius Hawley Seelye, William Seymour Tyler, and Aaron Warner, as well as presidents Humphrey, Hitchcock, and Stearns are all known to have preached at the First Church between 1838 and 1860, the period in which Dickinson would have been most likely to hear them. Professor Park, Professor of Moral Philosophy and Metaphysics in 1835–36, won the poet's unqualified approval when he returned to Amherst and spoke at First Church some years later. "I never heard anything like it," Emily wrote Austin, "and don't expect to again.... How I wish you had heard him."[74] Park at this time was a professor at Andover Theological Seminary and a prominent figure in the Congregational Church. Since he has been described as an impressive orator whose "mere presence in the pulpit was majestic and fascinating,"[75] it is possible Dickinson was attracted chiefly by Park's rhetoric or personality. The substance of his sermon, however, would have reinforced the ideal of learning that permeated education at all levels in Amherst. An orthodox Trinitarian himself, Park upheld the necessity of systematized doctrine. Dickinson, who once remarked she did not "respect doctrines,"[76] apparently was in no way offended by the sermon that she heard. In one of his published addresses, "The Theology of the Intellect and That of the Feelings," Park calls for a balance of mind and heart, of those faculties necessary to the reasoning process and those that affect the "sensibilities," kindling the imagination and stirring the affections. In this sermon, he deplores

> a tendency of pietism to undervalue the human intellect for the sake of exalting the affections; as if sin had less to do with the feelings than with the intelligence; as if a deceived heart had never turned men aside; as if reason had fallen deeper than the will. Rather has the will fallen *from* the intellectual powers, while they remain truer than any other to their office. It cannot be a *pious* act to underrate these powers, given as they were by Him who made the soul in his image. Our speculative tendencies are original, legitimate parts of the constitution which it is irreverent to censure. We *must* speculate. We must define, distinguish, infer, arrange our inferences in a system.[77]

A second Amherst College professor who especially impressed the young Dickinson was Henry Boynton Smith, professor of Mental and Moral Philosophy from 1847 to 1850. In 1849, Smith addressed students at Andover on the topic "The Relations of Faith and Philosophy." Smith espoused an experiential faith based firmly upon a systematic theology. The "clear and articulate" system undergirding the New England Puritan theology is essential, he argued, for "if we believe in a God and are consistent thinkers, we cannot avoid believing in a sure and divine system of things: thus alone can we keep alive the divine agency and government, without which all theology would be unsupported."[78] Although insistent that religious faith claims internal as well as historic evidence and calls for a "response of the heart" along with rational conviction, clearly these two representatives of the Amherst College faculty at mid-century had by no means embraced revelation by intuition. Rather, they urged the conscious application of the mind to the operations of the soul.

Three Amherst presidents preached occasionally in the Dickinsons' church while Emily still attended, as well as at special functions she may have joined with her family. Heman Humphrey, Edward Hitchcock, and William Augustus Stearns all strongly upheld the Puritan ideal of a union between faith and learning. While she was only fourteen when Hitchcock succeeded Humphrey in April 1845, and twenty-four when Stearns took office in November 1854, the spirit if not the full substance of their educational goals could not have been lost upon her. And again, their words can be taken to demonstrate the direction of her own education in Amherst at that time.

Under his administration, Humphrey declared in his "Valedictory Address," trustees and faculty had continued to recognize "the importance of providing a holy, and thoroughly educated ministry."[79] Nearly all the colleges of New England, and others which had derived from them, had been founded and staffed by evangelical ministers and pious laymen, Humphrey reminded his hearers: "Woe to our posterity, woe to the church, woe to the country, woe to the world, should that day ever come, when this same religious influence should be withdrawn from our public literary institutions."[80] Only the "salt of divine grace" in the form of teachers who upheld the evangelical doctrines of the Bible could preserve the heritage represented in Amherst College.

Hitchcock succeeded Humphrey with a focus no less firm upon the significance of religious principles at the heart of education. Because they are of such "infinite moment," the highest aim of education must be to exalt them:

Everything, therefore, in literature and science, that discovers, illustrates, or confirms, the external principles of religion, swells into an importance proportionably great. It remains, then, only to show that the wide fields of learning afford us such illustrations over their entire surface, and the position will be made out, that the religious applications of literature and science, are the most important of all their relations; and that consequently, when we consecrate our property, our influence, or our lives, to the cause of education, we consecrate them to one of the noblest of all human enterprises.[81]

Measuring the field of polite literature by his religious principles, Hitchcock shared some of the same reservations that Edward Dickinson and William Buell Sprague held regarding writings that did not meet their moral and religious criteria.

President Stearns, who brought to his presidency an exceptionally strong educational background as well as wide experience in the pulpit, upheld the religious aims of the college founders. Central as are the cultivation of intellect and also conscience, he emphasized in his inaugural address, still religious education "infinitely transcends" them in significance. "The highest style of man cannot be produced without religion," he insisted, and this implied experience as well as "facts." The college must send forth graduates who are "men mighty in God" and "anointed with the Holy Ghost," whose minds have "come into connection with the divine."[82] Stearns felt a great sense of personal responsibility for preserving the traditionally orthodox stance at Amherst, declaring that he "should esteem it a calamity more dreadful than death, if, though any fault of mine, this College should receive a poise, even to the breadth of a hair, towards the transcendental atheism of the age."[83] If Dickinson was to be exposed to influences that might oppose or weaken the Puritan heritage, it would not be through the agency of Amherst College presidents or professors. who believed their mission as educators in the community must be to mold the minds of youth in patterns predetermined by orthodox Congregationalism.

Dickinson's instructors at Amherst Academy, though lacking the years, training, and experience of many of the college professors, were hired as "persons of good moral character; of competent learning and abilities; firmly established in the faith of the Christian religion." The by-laws of the academy required also that they were to "inculcate as well by example as precept" the "doctrines and duties" of that religion. The preceptor was to "open and close the school each day with prayer," and every student was to "uniformly attend upon the public worship of God on the sabbath."[84] In addition, the student was to attend a Bible exercise each Saturday morning.[85] Religion and learning were to be combined. Emily Dickinson would be taught here also to value not only her mind, but her immortal soul as well.

The regular curriculum at the academy during the years Dickinson attended was a broad one, including English, history, philosophy, theology, languages, mathematics, and natural sciences. She herself refers to studying history, Latin, German, mental philosophy, ecclesiastical history, algebra, geometry, geology, and botany.[86] Compositions she wrote at the academy were later praised by one of her teachers, Daniel Taggart Fiske, principal in 1842–43. The New Testament and *Paradise Lost*, required reading, are echoed in her poems and letters, though of course she had been introduced to at least the Bible much earlier.

Varied as this curriculum was, education at the academy had one dominant aim. A number of the textbooks listed in the catalogues for these years reflect the strongly religious orientation of Dickinson's academy education. *The Improvement of the Mind* by Isaac Watts (1674–1748) illustrates this focus well.

"Watts on the Mind" is listed in the 1840–41 academy catalogue as a text prescribed for the second, or lower, division of the English Department. As an entering student in the English course that year, Dickinson may have been introduced to Watts immediately, although it is difficult to imagine a ten- or eleven-year-old concentrating upon it long. But she must have studied it by the time she entered Mount Holyoke, where "a good knowledge" of Watts was required for admission.

Watts' "grand object," according to Mary Lyon's mentor Joseph Emerson in his introduction to an 1831 edition, was to help young persons "to subject every thought, power and pursuit to the empire of reason; to subordinate all to the service of God—in short, to prepare the mortal and immortal part of our nature, for the greatest possible usefulness and enjoyment both here and forever."[87] Watts himself bases his case for mental improvement upon human obligation and self interest. Not only are we accountable to God to exercise the reason He gave us, but our own "most important concern in the life to come" makes it "a matter of the highest moment for every one to understand, to judge, and to reason right about the things of religion."[88] Watts warns, however, against total reliance upon human reason alone, and enjoins his readers to pray for and depend upon divine assistance to "bless all your attempts and labors in reading, study and conversation."[89]

Throughout the text, Watts continues to balance the development and exercise of the finite mind against a reliance upon supernatural authority and revelation. Instructors of youth, he writes, are "to give them notice, how far the light of nature or mere reason will instruct us in these [Christian] doctrines and duties, and how far we are obliged to divine revelation and scripture."⁹⁰ He advises students to be open to new insights as they read from other authors: "Never apply yourself to read any human author, with a determination beforehand, either for or against him, nor with a settled resolution to believe or disbelieve, to confirm or to oppose whatsoever he says; but always read with design to lay your mind open to truth."⁹¹ Indeed, he deplores the narrowness of mind that results when persons are "trained up from their infancy in one set of notions," and "confined to one single track both in the civil and religious life, without ever hearing or knowing, what other opinions are current among mankind." Such persons tend to "judge and condemn at once." "If we are scholars," he explains, "we should also read the objections against our own tenets, and view the principles of other parties, as they are represented in their own authors, and not merely in the citations of those who would confute them. We should take an honest and unbiassed [sic] survey of the force of reasoning on all sides, and bring all to the test of unprejudiced reason and divine revelation."⁹²

"Exert care, skill, and diligence about every subject and every question, in a just proportion to the importance of it," Watts urges,⁹³ and weigh all points according to the evidence: "Even the most mysterious and sublime doctrines of revelation, are not to be believed without just reason; nor should our pious affections be engaged in defense of them, till we have plain and convincing proof."⁹⁴ Where reason is silent, on doctrines such as the resurrection, the Bible alone furnishes authoritative evidence.⁹⁵ And to aid a doubting Thomas to accept miracles, on occasion God will provide "inward and divine influences," "divine illuminations."⁹⁶ *The Improvement of the Mind* is based upon a careful consideration of natural and revealed revelation. It encourages the full development of the human reason, but limits its capacity to arrive at knowledge without divine aid. Thoroughly orthodox, it refers young minds to the Bible as the final rule of faith and conduct.

Watts discourages a disputatious or dogmatic tone. When inclined to be critical of an author, he advises, one should consider "how many are the beauties of such an author whom he censures, in comparison with his blemishes, and remember, that it is a much more honorable and good natured thing to find out peculiar beauties than faults."⁹⁷ Also, he denies that judgment should rest upon subject matter alone. Justness of sentiment, beauty of manner, force of expression, strength of reason, and "the weight of just and proper argument" must be appreciated.⁹⁸ However, Watts' own literary judgments appear to be based primarily upon the degree of "truth" contained in a work. His views on "poesy" are consistent with those expressed elsewhere in Dickinson's educational circle. The salutary effect it can have, in some cases on the moral and religious life, is its highest value. Rhyme aids the memory and can also "gloriously exalt the matter, as to give a sublime imagination, its proper relish and delight."[99] But a poet might better spend his time reading rather than writing, though "there may be seasons, when it is hardly possible for a poetic soul to restrain the fancy, or quench the flame, when it is hard to suppress the exhuberant flow of lofty sentiments, and prevent the imagination from this sort of style or language." Only at this season should the desire to write be indulged.[100] Curiously, Watts indulged this inclination with impressive frequency through his hymns. Dickinson, of course, made no attempt to restrain herself.

The editions of *The Improvement of the Mind* now preserved in the Jones Library at Amherst and the Williston Library at Mount Holyoke include questions and, in most cases, answers prepared by Joseph Emerson to help guide pupils through their recitations. "Hints" which Emerson offers regarding the use of Watts in schools suggest that a very thorough knowledge of the book was to be expected. Have the students read, reread, and review it, and then make it the subject of compositions, he recommends. Examine them faithfully at the end of each quarter, and repeat the course every two of three years. Lest all this not sink in, ask them "how far they have practiced the directions of Watts, and with what advantage." "Make the utmost efforts to impress their minds with the truths and doctrines inculcated," but "Encourage them to state with freedom their inquiries and objections."[101] A sampling of questions will illustrate the level and nature of learning for which a ten- to seventeen-year-old daughter of Amherst could be made accountable in the 1840s:

> What frame of spirit should we maintain, in order to advance in knowledge and mental improvement? (Quoted from Watts' text: "a virtuous and pious frame of spirit")
>
> What is implied in having a good heart? That we obey the law of God from the heart.
>
> What is there reason to fear, we should be left to pursue, if we do not seek the divine aid in the investigation of truth? (Quoted from Watts' text: "wild excesses of foolery," "strange extravagances of opinion," "temporal and eternal ruin")

How can prayer conduce to furnish our minds with knowledge? It tends to make us love it more ardently, to seek it more vigorously. . . .

What if we should never pass over a passage of scripture, without perfectly understanding it? We should probably never get through Genesis.

Why should we yield our assent to the declarations of God? Because he certainly knows, and cannot lie.

Why cannot God lie? Because he is unchangeably good.

On what subjects, are we more especially bound to judge for ourselves? On the most important subjects of religion and conscience.

Why? Because we must all give account of ourselves at the day of judgement.

What may be the effect of knowledge and mental improvement, without virtue and holiness? To sink the mind in disgrace and misery forever.—with virtue and holiness? To raise the mind to eternal honor and felicity.

Meaning of virtue? Practice of moral duties.—of holiness? Conformity of heart and life to the law of God.

How has God manifested his regard for poetry? A considerable part of the Bible was originally written in poetry.

How has Watts manifested his regard for poetry? By writing so much.

Poetic character of Shakespeare, Dryden and Byron? They are justly ranked among the greatest poets, that ever lived.

Grand objection to their poems? That from their immoral tendency, they are likely to do more harm than good, at least to some.

Meaning of transubstantiation? (Definition not supplied by Watts or Emerson, but evidently expected from the student. Elsewhere Watts dismisses it as a "popish" doctrine, but here he is pressing a need to use "plain and intelligible language" in religious discourse. He applies this principle elsewhere to the preparation of children's catechisms.)

Why is the Bible the best source of information, respecting the human mind? It was inspired by Him, who knows perfectly what is in man, and relates very much to the human mind.[102]

In May 1845 Dickinson was studying "Mental Philosophy," a "big" undertaking, as she admitted to her friend Abiah Root.[103] *Elements of Mental Philosophy* by Thomas Cogswell Upham[104] introduced her to "the two departments of the intellect and the sensibilities." Upham's primary emphasis is upon an understanding of these faculties rather than their cultivation as in Watts, but theological assumptions are present. The "benevolent affections," for example, include love for the Supreme Being, whom man was created originally to love. "Memory" is connected to the doctrine of a final judgment and future life, and "Moral Education" is judged important, embracing the knowledge of the Supreme Being and of religious truth. Whether or not Dickinson's reading of this textbook should be discounted, as Whicher recommends,[105] can be known best by evidence in her poems and letters. These strongly invite several correlations with words and topics examined by Upham, suggesting that he indeed may have helped stimulate her to speculate on connections of the mind with the material world; the nature of sensation and perception as sources of external knowledge; the power of suggestion; the nature of space, time, and eternity; consciousness as a source of internal knowledge; the nature of the memory; the processes of reason and imagination; the nature of the emotions, especially that of beauty, whether intrinsic or aroused by forms (as a circle), color and sound (as in music); and the nature of desires and human instinct.

According to an academy catalogue, the poet's study of church history, to which she refers in March 1847, was based upon "Goodrich's Ecclesiastical History." If she prepared herself to answer even a fair portion of the thirty-one pages of questions included in the 1835 edition of *The Ecclesiastical Class Book or History of the Church from the Birth of Christ to the Present Time*,[106] she gained an introduction to church history and doctrine that would be extensive for any layperson of her age. With her knowledge of this and of the Bible, whatever decision she might come to make regarding religious belief or her relation to the institutional church, that decision would be an intellectually informed one. And what use she was to make of theological language and concepts in her poems deserves very close scrutiny, for her education would have prepared her to apply them with careful distinction.

Academic excellence and a religious orientation were central in the education which Emily Dickinson was to be offered when she arrived in South Hadley at the close of September 1847. The minimum entrance age had been set the previous year at sixteen, with preference given to those at least seventeen. Over 500 applications reportedly were received for the fall of 1847; about 250 were admitted and actually enrolled.¹⁰⁷ The new students were examined promptly on their previous studies and classified on the basis of their performance. By 6 November Emily informed her friend Abiah Root, a number of girls had left, "on account of finding the examinations more difficult than they anticipated.... Perhaps you know that Miss Lyon is raising her standard of scholarship a good deal, on account of the number of applicants this year & on account of that, she made the examinations more severe than usual."¹⁰⁸ This steady upgrading of requirements, and the practice of placement by examination, had become by now important features of Mary Lyon's educational goals and practices.

After passing her entrance examinations, Dickinson reviewed the studies of the "Junior," or beginning, course so that she could begin at the "Middle" level before the first term ended. In addition to English grammar, this review entailed the study of Latin, history, algebra, geometry, and some botany. Those students not proficient in Latin, a newly adopted requirement for graduation, could take "English" courses in the philosophy of natural history and ecclesiastical history. By mid-August 1848, when she had completed three terms at the seminary, or the full year to which every entering student was expected to commit herself, Dickinson had completed also the studies of the middle class: Latin, physiology, astronomy, advanced botany, and rhetoric. Again, there was an optional study for those weak in Latin: Archibald Alexander's *Evidences of the Christian Religion*. Composition, reading, and calesthenics were a regular part of every student's program.¹⁰⁹ Dickinson, in letters over the year to her brother Austin and her friend Abiah Root, refers to transposing Pope's "Essay on Man," and to studying history ("Goldsmith and Grimshaw"), Euclid, algebra, chemistry, physiology, astronomy, and rhetoric.¹¹⁰

The textbooks used at the seminary in 1847–48 were widely used at other schools; several had been used at Ipswich, and a dozen were the same as those used at this time by students at Amherst College.¹¹¹ Their popularity alone, however, did not dictate Miss Lyon's choice, for she is known to have selected them with great care.¹¹² One criterion they met in common was their religious orientation. *Paradise Lost* was required reading at least for seniors, and of course there was the Bible, which Mary Lyon explicated for all the students almost daily. History, travel, and poetry were recommended reading, but novels, particularly popular fiction, were not approved.

The study of history, expanded beyond the history of the United States required upon admission to include ancient and contemporary world history, was based upon a philosophy of design and order. On the basis of her admiration for Jonathan Edwards' *History of Redemption*, this view accorded with Mary Lyons' own philosophy of history.[113] Worcester's *Elements*, which Dickinson probably had studied already in the English course at the academy, presents among the "uses" of history its tendency "to strengthen the sentiments of virtue," and also to exhibit "the conduct of Divine Providence." According to Worcester, not only will history, if truly presented, demonstrate the value of "promoting the good of mankind," but it also will reveal that a supernatural agency, of its own volition and for its own purposes, often intervenes to shape the course of human events.[114]

It is unlikely that Dickinson herself studied Marsh's *Ecclesiastical History* or Alexander's *Evidences of the Christian Religion* since these were intended primarily for those with less preparation in Latin than she had received at the academy. These books, however, strongly indicate the tone and direction of instruction at the seminary. Marsh also sees this world as "the theatre of the most divine operations." The old dispensation under Abraham is made to typify the covenant of grace. His account of church history reflects an adherence to Congregational orthodoxy: he condemns "heresies" extending from "the darkness of Popery" to the present-day views of Unitarians in eastern New England, defending in particular Christ's divinity and unique role as mediator, and the doctrine of human depravity.[115] Alexander's *Evidences of the Christian Religion*, used also at the academy, is a forthright defense of supernatural revelation as a valid source of human knowledge. Divine interposition through miracles and the plenary inspiration of the Scriptures are presented as wholly credible to the rational mind.[116]

The prominence of science courses in the curriculum at Mount Holyoke, although not unusual for the time, reflects Mary Lyon's own training and interest, and in no way counteracts her religious purpose. As Green remarks, Mary Lyon shared the enthusiasm of her close teacher, friend, and adviser, Edward Hitchcock, for "both science and salvation."[117] She herself had enjoyed abundant opportunity to study the natural sciences while living with the Hitchcocks in Amherst, where she attended lectures by not only her host but also other men of science. In 1846 Mary Whitman, teacher of chemistry and geology at the seminary, also spent a summer at the Hitchcocks in Amherst advancing her studies. Under the teaching of these women, interest in the natural sciences increased among the students at Mount Holyoke, and it is reasonable to assume that Dickinson shared it, especially since her poems reveal an unusual control of scientific data.

Science classes at Mount Holyoke were supplemented by lectures by a number of professors from Amherst and also Williams College. Foremost among these men was Hitchcock, now president of the college at which he taught for forty years. During these years he launched what Whicher labelled a "scientific renaissance" that must have been felt by every young person in the area. At the academy his textbook on geology was presented by the trustees as a gift to the library, and at the seminary it was the prescribed book in geology for seniors. Hitchcock was a frequent and regular lecturer at the seminary; Dickinson must have heard him on many occasions throughout her youth. She may also have joined the other students and young people from Amherst and South Hadley whom he led on botanical and geological surveys in the Valley.

As the leading representative of the teaching of science at Amherst and Mount Holyoke in the 1840s, Edward Hitchcock typified those "deeply religious men [and women] whose avowed object," according to Whicher, "was to exhibit the glorious handiwork of the Creator as manifested in the world of nature and who were themselves untouched by the materialistic implications of science."[118] At a time when scientific theory challenged orthodox assumptions regarding the origin of the universe and humankind, Hitchcock attempted to reconcile his scientific conclusions with the doctrine of a special creation. "An informed geologist himself," LeDuc asserts, "he was able to satisfy his students with a ready acknowledgement of demonstrated truth and with an interpretation of Scripture that harmonized with it. His own faith never wavered."[119]

One of Hitchcock's lecture series to Amherst College students between 1845 and 1849, published in 1850 under the title *Religious Lectures on Peculiar Phenomena in the Four Seasons*, has been examined by Dickinson's biographer Richard Sewall for the appreciative tone its author conveys in describing natural phenomena and for the abundance and precision of its scientific observations.[120] It is very possible that Dickinson heard these lectures as an Amherst girl, possibly while at the academy or at the seminary. The first of the series to be presented, "The Coronation of Winter," was delivered at both Amherst and Mount Holyoke, and was "admired on both sides of the Notch."[121] All four illustrate well not only Hitchcock's use of natural imagery, as Sewall demonstrates, but also the union of scientific observation with religious faith that characterized the instruction Dickinson was receiving.

Hitchcock implies his purpose at the start, by saying that he "feels that Natural Religion has not yielded all the fruits that may be derived from it, to feed the heart of piety; especially when those fruits are ripened and gathered under the bright sun of revelation."[122] He wishes to show how nature figuratively can point us to the "truth" of eternal life already promised literally in the language of the Bible. The apostle Paul, Hitchcock explains in "The Resurrection of Spring," is our authority for knowing that the resurrection body arises from the "germ" of what was laid in the grave, thus answering "the infidel's objection" that Dickinson was to repeat verbatim as a question: "with what body do they come?"[123] The biblical writer has explained that each resurrection body will possess "*a specific individual identity*,"[124] or in Dickinson's words, a "separate consciousness." But the "sudden and astonishing transformation"[125] that Paul says this spiritual body will undergo can be illustrated by numerous striking examples from nature. "The Resurrection of Spring" provides several of these, such as the metamorphosis of the insect. Although the analogy is not complete and is not intended to *prove* a doctrine already revealed through divine inspiration, it can serve to strengthen the believer's hope: "O, what a change, and what a vision! And to know too, that his own body, on earth so frail, and it may be so full of pain and infirmity, shall then come forth purified, ethereal, incorruptible, and adapted to be the residence of the sinless and immortal spirit, how delightful the anticipation."[126] One can just imagine the rapt attention young Emily would have paid to this lecture on the "flood subject" of personal immortality, charged as it was with assurance and anticipation.

The summer season likewise can be read as a prefiguration of heavenly glory. "The Triumphal Arch of Summer" refers most directly to the rainbow, "an emblem of the covenant of redemption," "of union and harmony in the midst of diversity."[127] In contrast to the rainbow, summer lightning and thunder may be taken to represent divine justice and remind us that the world does exhibit, here and there, "evidences of God's displeasure against sin." Yet there is hope, for while nature tells us "with a thousand tongues" that this "is a world of probation and discipline," it also is "a mere preparatory state for a final and far more exalted condition."[128] Hutchcock vividly depicts the fury of a thunderstorm in language that indeed may have inspired Dickinson's own description. The breaking of the clouds and the sunset that follows he presents as the harbinger of a glorious dawn, when darkness on earth will give way at length to the Sun of Righteousness.[129]

While "The Euthanasia of Autumn" teaches "the certainty of the decay and dissolution of our bodily powers" and "the brevity of human beauty and glory," it also points to the benevolence of God, which has thus spread rich beauty over the face of unwelcome decay, and made nature's party-colored winding sheet so attractive, that we smile with her as she puts it on. It is a beautiful example of that Infinite Benevolence which, though it could not but make nature remind us that we live in a fallen world, has yet so mingled mercy in the cup, that we drink it almost with pain, and are softened by the kindness that yearns over us in our misery, and throws many a bow of promise over the dark clouds that spread over the heavens.[130]

The tone of this passage is far more reverent than melancholy, itself suggesting that life has withdrawn only to reappear, and autumn is "only a change of state, and not the extinction of life."[131] It would invite the poet to a "Last Communion in the Haze," if not with God, then with nature.

Hitchcock placed "The Coronation of Winter" at the end of the published series, for far from signalizing the finality of death, winter illustrates the active agency of God. Winter too is change, but speaks more of permanence than decay. In this season also, the Christian—not the philosopher—can see God's "hand turning round the wheels of nature."[132]

Botany and astronomy as represented in the textbooks used by the junior and middle classes at Mount Holyoke would have reinforced further the religious orientation given Dickinson's earlier study of science at the academy. At both schools, Wood's *Class-book of Botany* would have pointed her to "the beauty and simplicity of the plan on which Creative Power is exerted in the production of the countless forms of vegetable existence," just as at the academy, Lincoln's *Botany* would have directed her "to behold the providence of God as ever active, and ever watchful over all, even the least of his works." Olmstead's *Astronomy*, used at both schools, was intended to glorify the omniscience and benevolence of the Creator, as Burritt's *Class Book of Astronomy* at the academy invited "a serious contemplation of the stupendous works of the Most High, which astronomy unfolds."[133] In science as in history, Dickinson's textbooks assumed a universal order originating in God, sustained by Him, and pointing ultimately to His glory.

Had Dickinson returned for the senior year at Mount Holyoke, she would have studied at least two books intended to reinforce a religious interpretation of natural phenomena: William Paley's *Natural Theology, or, Evidences of the Existence and Attributes of the Deity, Collected from the Appearances of Nature*, and Joseph Butler's *The Analogy of Religion Natural and Revealed, to the Constitution and Course of Nature*.[134] As it was, her education by now had provided her with a sound introduction to natural science, and an approach that would much more than encourage her to inquire as to its possible religious significance.

The feature of Dickinson's year at Mount Holyoke that has received the most attention is the "pressure" it put upon her to declare herself a Christian. Without question, the welfare of her immortal soul was uppermost in the minds of those under whom she studied. Religious instruction "was considered the most important object for which the institution was founded," confirmed Edward Hitchcock; "and, therefore, everything else was held subordinate to this."[135] This focus is reflected in the topic of the 1848 commencement address, delivered by Edward Beecher at the close of Dickinson's stay in South Hadley: "Christian Experience Indispensable to the Normal Development and Culture of all the Powers, and to a Complete Education."[136] Mary Lyon herself, explaining the "Tendencies of the Principles Embraced, and the System Adopted in the Mount Holyoke Female Seminary" to those from whom she was soliciting funds in 1839, emphasized the centrality of "religious culture":

> This lies at the foundation of that female character which the founders of this seminary have contemplated. Without this, their efforts would entirely fail of their design. This institution has been built for the Lord, that it might be peculiarly his own. . . . Public worship, the Bible lesson, and other appropriate duties of the Sabbath, a regular observance of secret devotion, suitable attention to religious instruction and social prayer meetings, and the maintaining of a consistent Christian deportment, are considered the most important objects of regard, for both teachers and scholars. The friends of this seminary have sought that this might be a spot where souls shall be born of God, and where much shall be done for maturing and elevating Christian character.[137]

Each of the means Mary Lyon mentions was observed during 1847–48. "At 9 we all meet in Seminary Hall, for devotions," Emily wrote Abiah Root. "At 4 ½ we go into Seminary Hall, & receive advice from Miss Lyon in the form of a lecture."[138] She visited the village church on Sundays with her classmates, and is reported to have joined at least one small group meeting during a mid-winter season of revival.[139]

By 1847–48 Mary Lyon had come to lay increasing stress on the salvation of souls. Following the example of Zilpah Grant and Joseph Emerson at their seminaries, she had the students classify themselves according to their religious condition at the beginning of the year. She then made those "without hope" her special concern throughout the year. Her lectures, as reported that year by three of the seminary teachers in a journal prepared for former students and staff now on the mission field, reflect the urgency of her desire, and theirs as well, for the conversion of their charges.

In letters to Abiah Root, Emily expressed her concern regarding her own lack of spiritual assurance,[140] but neither here nor elsewhere in her correspondence over the year is there any indication of strong resentment toward her spiritual counselors at the seminary. On the contrary, beyond an occasional note of homesickness or disappointment over being denied a minor request, she appears happy with the seminary and its staff.

The concerted effort of Mary Lyon and others to bring the students to a "decision for Christ," need not be interpreted as unusual "pressure." In the context of contemporary revivalism—Amherst College experienced six periods of marked revival between 1830 and 1850[141]—and the close association of education with evangelism in many seminaries and colleges at the time, Mount Holyoke was part of a pattern. And as Mary Lyon had pointed out in her 1839 fund-raising appeal, the seminary from its outset had been "embalmed by prayer in many hearts, and consecrated around many a family altar."[142] To most of the students who enrolled, Dickinson included, the religious life of Mount Holyoke Female Seminary, though perhaps intensified, was no different from what they had been raised to expect of a school.

Within the context of her early education and formal schooling, Emily Dickinson emerges as one who was strongly encouraged at every step to develop her mind. Family, church, school, and community dedicated themselves to her education to an unusual degree, convinced that all persons of both sexes were intended by God to grow in wisdom until, as the poet was to express it, their "statures touch[ed] the skies." A review of her education increases our understanding of Dickinson in at least three respects. Particularly since she apparently did well in studies that seem to have been comprehensive and demanding, it would be misleading to dismiss the poet as uninformed or not given to deliberate judgments. Neither the outward isolation of her life nor her emotional intensity and intuitive insight need minimize the strength of mind encouraged in her early years. Second, it is noteworthy that far from being denied the opportunity to receive a classical education by the fact of her womanhood, Dickinson benefited directly from the support of religious and civic leaders in New England who had been successful in promoting a high level of education for her sex. She was not, in short, as socially oppressed as some would make her out to be. Nor was the independence that marks the person and the poems necessarily a sign of rebellion or rage; she was taught to value her individuality and, with a humility appropriate to both sexes, to assert her judgment on the basis of evidence and reason.

But the most impressive conclusion toward which her education points is that from her earliest years onward, Dickinson was taught to regard all of life and learning from a religious perspective. Such an orientation was crucial to the direction of her thinking, her view of herself, and her responses to the universe. Also, to the extent that her teachers and textbooks defined for her the content of New England Congregationalism, they helped supply her with concepts and language that informed many of her finest poems.

Emily Dickinson was, to begin with, a daughter of Amherst. She was very much a part of her world, represented in the Connecticut Valley not only by the spires of Congregational churches but also by the educational institutions that in the mid-nineteenth century promoted with these churches a common religious heritage. Her poems in part grow out of and reflect the mental rigor, sense of personal worth, and consciousness of divine dimensions impressed upon her through a "Puritan" education.

NOTES

1. Records of the Board of Trustees of Amherst Academy preserved among the *Manuscripts* of Noah Webster, in Frederick Tuckerman, *Amherst Academy: A New England School of the Past, 1814–1861* (Amherst, Mass.: Amherst College Trustees, 1929), p. 30.

2. "Preamble" to "A Constitution and System of By-Laws for raising and managing a Permanent Charitable Fund, as the basis of an Institution in Amherst, in the County of Hampshire, for the classical education of indigent young men of piety and talents for the Christian Ministry," in Edward Hitchcock, *Reminiscences of Amherst College* (Northampton, Mass.: Bridgman and Childs, 1863), p. 161.

3. Hitchcock, *Reminiscences*, p. 5.

4. William Seymour Tyler, *History of Amherst College During its First Half Century, 1821–1871* (Springfield, Mass.: Clark W. Bryan and Company, 1873), p. 34.

5. *Springfield Republican*, 10 July 1863, 5 March 1864, and 11 June 1868, in Jay Leyda, *The Years and Hours of Emily Dickinson* (New Haven: Yale University Press, 1960), 2:81, 86, 131.

6. Martha Dickinson Bianchi, *The Life and Letters of Emily Dickinson* (Boston: Houghton Mifflin, 1924), p. 42.

7. *Springfield Republican*, 9 July 1873, in Leyda, *Dickinson*, 2:203.

8. *Amherst Record*, 17 July 1872, in Leyda, *Dickinson*, 2:188.

9. Amherst town meeting records, in Leyda, *Dickinson*, 1:18.

10. *Northampton Courier*, 28 September 1841, in Leyda, *Dickinson*, 1:71.

11. 21 January 1838, in Leyda, *Dickinson*, 1:43.

12. 7 January 1838, in Leyda, *Dickinson*, 1:40.

13. 13 January 1838, in Leyda, *Dickinson*, 1:42.

14. 7 and 16 February 1838, in Leyda, *Dickinson*, 1:35, 45.

15. Karl Keller, *The Only Kangaroo Among the Beauty: Emily Dickinson and America* (Baltimore: Johns Hopkins Press, 1979), p. 21.

16. Daniel A. Clark, *The Wise Builder: A Sermon Delivered to the Females of the First Parish in Amherst, Massachusetts* (Boston: Ezra Lincoln, 1820), pp. 17–18.
17. Clark, *Wise Builder*, p. 13.
18. Clark, *Wise Builder*, p. 17.
19. Clark, *Wise Builder*, p. 8.
20. Clark, *Wise Builder*, p. 13.
21. Clark, *Wise Builder*, p. 14.
22. Clark, *Wise Builder*, p. 8.
23. Address before the Hampshire, Hampden, and Franklin Agricultural Society, Northampton, 7 October 1831, in Leyda, *Dickinson*, 1:17–18.
24. William Buell Sprague, *Letters on Practical Subjects, to a Daughter*, 9th American ed. rev. and enl. (Albany, N.Y.: E. H. Pease & Co., 1851), pp. 33–34. The "original" title appears on an 1822 edition published in Hartford, Conn., by Huntington and Hopkins. Quotations are taken from the 1851 text, which is the one Edward Dickinson gave his daughter.
25. Sprague, *Letters*, p. 200.
26. Sprague, *Letters*, pp. 200–201.
27. Sprague, *Letters*, p. 100.
28. Sprague, *Letters*, p. 79.
29. Sprague, *Letters*, p. 90.
30. Dickinson to Thomas Wentworth Higginson, 25 April 1862, in *The Letters of Emily Dickinson*, ed. Thomas Johnson and Theodora Ward (Cambridge: Harvard University Press, 1958), 2:404. Dickinson's letters to Higginson frequently are given to overstatement.
31. *Catalogue of Amherst Female Seminary, For the Year Ending August, 1835* (Amherst, Mass.: J. S. & C. Adams). An "Emily Dickinson" of Amherst appears in this catalogue, but this evidence is inconclusive since there were other Emily Dickinsons in Amherst at the time. References to the seminary occur in Tuckerman, *Amherst Academy*, p. 96, and Leyda, *Dickinson*. 1:xxix. The earliest reference to Dickinson's school attendance occurs in a letter written by Edward Dickinson to his wife, 7 September 1835. Elizabeth Alden Green, in *Mary Lyon and Mount Holyoke: Opening the Gates* (Hanover, N.H.: University Press of New England, 1979), p. 13, cites four years as the usual age for starting in the district school. Emily was born 10 December 1830.

The most thorough account of the poet's schooling appears in Richard Sewall, *The Life of Emily Dickinson* (New York: Farrar, Strauss & Giroux, 1975), 1:335–67. This still can be supplemented very profitably, however, by the account in George Frisbee Whicher, *This Was a Poet: A Critical Biography of Emily Dickinson* (New York: Scribners, 1939), pp. 39–57.

32. *The History of the Town of Amherst, Mass. 1831–1896*, comp. Charles Morehouse and Edward W. Carpenter (Amherst, Mass.: Carpenter and Morehouse, 1896), p. 148.
33. Tuckerman, *Amherst Academy*, pp. 96–97. In 1840–41, thirty-five young men were in the Classical Department, and fifty-one in the English Department. Seventy-six young women were in the Female Department, twenty-seven pursuing the Classical, and forty-nine the English course. The fact that only ten fewer women than men were enrolled in Amherst Academy during Dickinson's initial year there adds testimony to the support of the community for the education of its daughters as well as its sons (*Catalogue of the Trustees, Instructors, and Students*

of *Amherst Academy. For the Academical Year Ending July 1841* [Amherst, Mass.: J. S. & C. Adams]). Catalogues for the academic years ending in July 1842, August 1843, and August 1847 are available also.

34. Daniel A. Clark, minister of the First Congregational Church of Amherst from 1820 to 1824, in a sermon delivered at the laying of the cornerstone for the first building at the college, urged the women present to support the fledgling institution. Such patronage would be to their own advantage, he argued, since they would be helping to spread a gospel which, "in addition to the promise of eternal life, renders them free, respected and happy in the life that now is!" (*A Plea for a Miserable World: I. An Address, Delivered at the Laying of the Corner Stone of the Building Now Erecting for the Charity Institution in Amherst, Massachusetts, August 9, 1820, by Noah Webster, Esq. II. A Sermon, Delivered on the Same Occasion, by Rev. Daniel A. Clark* [Boston: Ezra Lincoln, 1820], pp. 33–34).

Perhaps because they agreed with Clark's thesis that the status of women improved in conjunction with the spread of the gospel, the women of Amherst had supported the establishment of a charitable fund to educate young men for the ministry. An unpublished manuscript in the Boltwood Collection of the Jones Library at Amherst, dated 6 September 1814 and entitled "Constitution of the Female education society of Amherst," declared the membership of such a society was open to any female wishing "to aid indigent young men of piety and talents, in obtaining an education, with a view of the gospel ministry." A life membership of five dollars or an annual fee of fifty cents for those over fourteen years of age, twenty five cents if under, would promote the cause. Courtesy of MAJ.

35. 26 June 1846, in *Letters*, 1:34.

36. Green, *Mary Lyon*, p. 337. I am especially indebted to Green's objective and comprehensive account of Mary Lyon and Mount Holyoke.

37. Lavinia Dickinson was to attend Ipswich Female Seminary in 1850.

38. Hannah White taught at Amherst Academy in 1833 (Green, *Mary Lyon*, p. 98). A "Hannah White" was principal of the Amherst Female Seminary in 1835.

39. Mary Lyon to Zilpah Polly Grant, 4 February 1833, in Edward Hitchcock, *The Power of Christian Benevolence Illustrated in the Life and Labors of Mary Lyon*, comp. with the assistance of others, 3d ed. (Northampton, Mass.: Hopkins, Bridgman, and Company, 1852), p. 172.

40. Green, *Mary Lyon*, p. 341.

41. An article in the *Boston Recorder*, May 1836, quoted in Green, *Mary Lyon*. p. 117.

42. Richard Chase, *Emily Dickinson* (New York: William Sloane Associates, 1951), p. 186: "Emily Dickinson's eschatological cast of mind, on the whole a departure from New England Puritanism, was entirely a personal vision of life and has no direct historical or social implications." I find a statement Chase makes shortly afterward much more convincing: "The strongest influence on her thought was undoubtedly Calvinism and to her historical relation to this religion we must attribute much of what is pre-eminent in her work" (p. 187). No Puritan doctrine is more pervasive throughout Dickinson's intellectual milieu than the belief that this life is preparatory to another.

43. Carpenter and Morehouse, *History of Amherst*, p. 253; William Seymour Tyler, "Relation of the Church to the Educational Institutions of Amherst," in *An Historical Review: One Hundred and Fiftieth Anniversary of the First Church of*

Christ in Amherst, Massachusetts, November 7, 1889 (Amherst, Mass.: Press of the Amherst Record, 1890), p. 47.

A tiny rhymed alphabet book in the Dickinson library makes reference to the Sunday School, "where you / Can sing and join in prayer." *The Poetic Gift: or Alphabet in Rhyme* (New Haven, Conn.: S. Babcock, 1842).

44. At least two copies of the *Primer* were in the Dickinson library. One, published in Worcester, Mass., by S. A. Howland, bears no publication date. It includes, however, an historical introduction by Heman Humphrey, president of Amherst College 1823–45. A second copy, published in Hartford, Conn., by Ira Webster in 1843, is a later copy, since it contains a partial text of Humphrey's introduction taken from the "Worcester" edition. It bears Edward Dickinson's inscription on the front cover, and may have been the edition presented to Edward Dickinson at a Yale College function in 1850 (Leyda, *Dickinson*, 1:178). The text is presented as "an exact reprint" from one of the earliest copies of the primer, published by Edward Draper in 1777. Though variances are slight, I have used the "Worcester" edition as the one published before 1843 and presumably available in the Dickinson home before 1850.

45. Heman Humphrey, "Introduction" to *The New England Primer: Containing the Assembly's Catechism; The Account of the Burning of John Rogers; A Dialogue between Christ, a Youth, and the Devil . . . with an Historical Introduction by Rev. H. Humphrey, President of Amherst College* (Worcester, Mass.: S. A. Howland, n.d.), pp. 4–7.

46. "Records of Town Meetings," in Carpenter and Morehouse, *History of Amherst*, p. 222.

47. Everett E. Thompson, "Noah Webster and Amherst College," *Amherst Graduates' Quarterly*, 12 (August 1933): 290, 293.

48. Tyler, *History of Amherst College*, p. 109.

49. Noah Webster, *The American Spelling Book, containing the Rudiments of the English Language. For the Use of Schools in the United States*, rev. ed. (Middletown, Conn.: William H. Niles, 1828 [c1804]).

50. Noah Webster, *The Pictorial Elementary Spelling Book: Being an Improvement on the American Spelling Book* (New York: George F. Cooledge & Brother, 1845 [c1829]).

51. Benjamin Dudley Emerson, *The National Spelling-Book with Progressive Reading Lessons*, "58th edition" (Boston: Carter, Hendee, 1835 [c1828]), "70th edition," 1837. These two books are listed in an "inhouse" catalogue of books from the Dickinson library purchased by Gilbert H. Montague from Alfred Leete Hampson and presented to Harvard University, Montague's alma mater, in 1949–50. They were not among those accepted.

52. George Frisbee Whicher, "In Emily Dickinson's Garden," *Atlantic Monthly*, 177 (February 1946): 65.

53. Whicher, *This Was a Poet*, p. 41.

54. Thomas LeDuc, *Piety and Intellect at Amherst College* (New York: Columbia University Press, 1946), p. 2. It is noteworthy that Amherst College, unlike other older New England colleges, took its name not from a particular founder or benefactor, but from the community of Amherst.

55. LeDuc, *Amherst*, p. 3.

56. Edward Strong Dwight, *A Teaching Ministry the conservators of Social*

Welfare: A Sermon Delivered at Searsport, June 23, 1853, before the Maine Missionary Society, at its Forty-Fifth Anniversary (Augusta, Me.: W. T. Johnson, 1852).

57. Tyler, "Relation of the Church to the Educational Institutions of Amherst," p. 43.

58. Tyler, "Relation," p. 44.

59. Tyler, "Relation," p. 48.

60. Tyler, "Relation," p. 44.

61. Tyler, *History of Amherst College*, p. 120.

62. Hitchcock, *Reminiscences of Amherst College*, p. 5.

63. Tyler, *History of Amherst College*, p. 107. "Dr." is generally used to distinguish this minister from the elder David Parsons, who was his father and who preceded him in the pulpit of First Church.

64. Webster, in *A Plea for a Miserable World*, p. 8.

65. Webster, in *A Plea for a Miserable World*, p. 11.

66. Clark, in *A Plea for a Miserable World*, pp. 28–29.

67. "Bill for establishing Amherst Academy," in Carpenter and Morehouse, *History of Amherst*, p. 145.

68. Claude Moore Fuess, *Amherst: The Story of a New England College* (Boston: Little, Brown, 1935), p. 31.

69. Whicher, *This Was a Poet*, p. 42: "Two of them [principals at the academy while Dickinson attended] subsequently entered the ministry, two became missionaries, and one died before completing his theological training." Tuckerman names seven principals for this period: Nahum Gale, Joel S. Everett, William Ward Whipple, Daniel Taggart Fiske, Jeremiah Taylor, Lyman Coleman, and Leonard Humphrey. Perhaps Whicher was omitting Gale and Coleman, who were ministers already.

70. Heman Humphrey, *Valedictory Address, Delivered at Amherst College* (Amherst, Mass.: J. S. & C. Adams, 1845), p. 15.

71. Fuess, *Amherst*, p. 180.

72. LeDuc, *Amherst*, p. 7.

73. Fuess, *Amherst*, p. 170; Humphrey in 1845 claimed that "of the 765 graduates of this College, at least 400 are already in the ministry, or in a course of preparation for it" (*Valedictory Address*, p. 17).

74. 21 November 1853, in *Letters*, 1:272.

75. Richard Salter Storrs, "Tribute," in Edwards Amasa Park, *Memorial Collection of Sermons*, comp. by his daughter (Boston and Chicago: Pilgrim Press, n.d.), p. 12.

76. 13 February 1859, in *Letters*, 2:346. This often quoted remark by Dickinson scarcely obviates the tremendous impact the doctrinal content of New England Puritanism, or orthodox Congregationalism of the nineteenth century, made upon her mind and art.

77. Edwards Amasa Park, "The Theology of the Intellect and That of the Feelings," in his *Memorial Collection of Sermons*, p. 91.

78. Henry Boynton Smith, "The Relations of Faith and Philosophy: An Address before the Porter Rhetorical Society of Andover Theological Seminary," 4 September 1849, *Bibliotheca Sacra*, 6 (November 1849): 697. Dickinson heard Smith preach not at the First Church in Amherst, but at the Congregational church in South Hadley during her year at Mount Holyoke; see her letter to Austin on 17 February 1848, in *Letters*, 1:64.

79. Humphrey, *Valedictory Address*, p. 16.
80. Humphrey, *Valedictory Address*, pp. 18–20.
81. Edward Hitchcock, *The Highest Use of Learning: An Address Delivered at His Inauguration to the Presidency of Amherst College* (Amherst, Mass.: J. S. & C. Adams, 1845), p. 6.
82. William Augustus Stearns, "Inaugural Address," in *Discourses and Addresses at the Installation of the Rev. William A. Stearns, D.D. as President of Amherst College, and Pastor of the College Church, Amherst* (Amherst, Mass.: J. S. & C. Adams, 1855), pp. 100–101.
83. Stearns, "Inaugural Address," p. 103.
84. Bylaws of Amherst Academy, in Tuckerman, *Amherst Academy*, p. 97.
85. This requirement appears in the Amherst Academy catalogues for these years, as do the rules regarding daily prayers and regular Sabbath worship.
86. 12 May 1842, in *Letters*, 1:6–7; 7 May 1845, in *Letters*, 1:13; 12 January 1846, in *Letters*, 1:24; and 14 March 1847, in *Letters* 1:45.
87. Joseph Emerson, "Editor's Introduction," *The Improvement of the Mind* by Issac Watts, with corrections, questions and supplement, rev. stereotype ed. (Boston: James Loring, 1832), p. iii. No claim can be made that the editions of textbooks I will cite are those actually used by Dickinson. Working within the framework of holdings in the Jones Library at Amherst, Frost Library at Amherst College, and Williston Library at Mount Holyoke, I have attempted to locate ones whose dates came closest to the year or years she would have used the texts at the academy or seminary. Jack L. Capps, in *Emily Dickinson's Reading* (Cambridge: Harvard University Press, 1966), pp. 103–111, provides additional comment on Dickinson's academy and seminary books. Appendix B to his work lists texts in use at Mount Holyoke during the appropriate period.
88. Watts, *The Improvement of the Mind*, p. 18.
89. Watts, *The Improvement of the Mind*, p. 32.
90. Watts, *The Improvement of the Mind*, p. 220
91. Watts, *The Improvement of the Mind*, p. 67.
92. Watts, *The Improvement of the Mind*, p. 151.
93. Watts, *The Improvement of the Mind*, p. 133.
94. Watts, *The Improvement of the Mind*, p. 192.
95. Watts, *The Improvement of the Mind*, p. 197.
96. Watts, *The Improvement of the Mind*, p. 199.
97. Watts, *The Improvement of the Mind*, p. 81.
98. Watts, *The Improvement of the Mind*, p. 76.
99. Watts, *The Improvement of the Mind*, p. 148.
100. Watts, *The Improvement of the Mind*, p. 232.
101. Emerson, "Hints for Teaching Watts on the Mind," *The Improvement of the Mind*, p. ii.
102. Watts, *The Improvement of the Mind*, pp. 31–32, 35, 60–61, 69–71, 75, 114–115, 219.
103. 7 May 1845, in *Letters*, 1:13.
104. Thomas Cogswell Upham, *Elements of Mental Philosophy, Abridged and Designed as a Text-Book for Academies and High Schools* (New York: Harper & Brothers, 1840). Upham's text appears first in the 1846–47 catalogue, but may have been introduced during the three years for which no catalogue exists. In 1841–43, mental philosophy was studied at the academy from John Abercrombie,

Inquiries concerning the Intellectual Powers, and the Investigation of Truth (Boston: John Allen; Philadelphia: Alexander Tower, 1835). The scope of the two books is similar; Abercrombie's religious orientation is marked. "The highest state of man," he concludes, "consists in his purity as a moral being," whose capacities cannot be satisfied until "they rest in the contemplation of God" (p. 281).

105. "The 'Mental Philosophy' recited by a girl of fifteen from Upham's manual cannot be taken seriously, nor can her acquaintance with Ecclesiastical History be supposed to have been more than perfunctory" (Whicher, *This Was a Poet*, p. 47).

106. Charles A. Goodrich, *The Ecclesiastical Class Book or History of the Church from the Birth of Christ to the Present Time: Adapted to the Use of Academies and Schools* (Hartford, Conn.: F. J. Huntington, 1835).

107. Susan L. Tolman, Rebecca Fiske, and Mary Whitman, "Mount Holyoke Seminary Journal Letter, September, 1847, to August 3, 1848" (typescript 1930), entry for 5 October (MAJ).

108. *Letters*, 1:54.

109. *Eleventh Annual Catalogue of the Mount Holyoke Female Seminary in South Hadley, Mass., 1847–8.*

110. 2 November 1847, in *Letters*, 1:50; 6 November 1847, in *Letters*, 1:54; 11 December 1847, in *Letters*, 1:57; 17 January 1848, in *Letters*, 1:59; 16 May 1848, in *Letters*, 1:67.

111. Green, *Mary Lyon*, pp. 65, 221, 373n4.

112. Green, *Mary Lyon*, p. 67.

113. Joseph Emerson Worcester, *Elements of History*, 3d ed. (Boston: William J. Reynolds, 1849), p. 2. One of several impressions from stereotype plates made in 1830 for the third edition, this reprinting very well may have been the same as those used at the academy and seminary while Dickinson was a student.

114. Mary Lyon's enthusiasm for Edwards' work, which attempts to demonstrate the operation of divine sovereignty from creation to judgment, was so keen that she solicited subscriptions to have it reprinted at the same time that she was seeking financial support to launch a female seminary.

115. John Marsh, *An Epitome of General Ecclesiastical History from the Earliest Period of Antiquity to the Present Time*, 5th ed. (New York: J. Tilden, 1838).

116. Archibald Alexander, *The Evidences of the Christian Religion*, 6th ed. enl. (New York: Jonathan Leavitt; Boston: Crocker and Brewster, 1832).

117. Green, *Mary Lyon*, p. 37.

118. Whicher, *This Was a Poet*, p. 48.

119. LeDuc, *Amherst*, p. 9.

120. Sewall, *Dickinson*, 1:344–48.

121. Green, *Mary Lyon*, p. 239.

122. Edward Hitchcock, "Prefatory," *Religious Lectures on Peculiar Phenomena in the Four Seasons* (Amherst, Mass.: J. S. & C. Adams, 1850), p. v.

123. 1 Corinthians 15:35; Hitchcock, *Religious Lectures*, p. 13.

124. Hitchcock, *Religious Lectures*, p. 17.

125. Hitchcock, *Religious Lectures*, p. 23.

126. Hitchcock, *Religious Lectures*, p. 37.

127. Hitchcock, *Religious Lectures*, pp. 61, 63.

128. Hitchcock, *Religious Lectures*, pp. 68–69.

129. Hitchcock, *Religious Lectures*, pp. 75–77.

130. Hitchcock, *Religious Lectures*, p. 94.

131. Hitchcock, *Religious Lectures*, p. 95.

132. Hitchcock, *Religious Lectures*, p. 110.

133. Alphonse Wood, *A Class-Book of Botany Designed for Colleges, Academies, and Other Seminaries*, 17th ed. rev. and enl. (Claremont, N.H.: Manufacturing Company, 1851), I: "Preface" written in 1847 by the author; Almira H. Lincoln, *Familiar Lectures on Botany . . . for the Use of Higher Schools and Academies* (Hartford, Conn.: H. and F. J. Huntington, 1829), p. vii; Denison Olmstead, *Rudiments of Natural Philosophy and Astronomy: Designed for the Younger Classes in Academies, and for Common Schools*, stereotype ed. (New York: Collins & Brothers; New Haven, Conn.: S. Babcock, 1847), p. 288; Elijah H. Burritt, *The Geography of the Heavens, and Class Book of Astronomy*, 5th ed. (New York: F. J. Huntington, 1839), "Preface" by the author. Dickinson specifically refers to studying botany, though not astronomy, while at the academy. Her references, of course, do not constitute a complete list of the courses she took. Both subjects were in the English curriculum she followed for at least two years. At the academy, Mrs. Lincoln's text was in use in 1842, when Dickinson refers to having studied botany. Olmstead and Burritt appear in each of the extant academy catalogues for 1841–47.

134. William Paley, *Natural Theology, or, Evidences of the Existence and Attributes of the Deity, Collected from the Appearances of Nature*, stereotype ed. (Boston: Gould, Kendall, and Lincoln, 1835); Joseph Butler, *The Analogy of Religion Natural and Revealed, to the Constitution and Course of Nature*, 15th ed. (New York: Mark H. Newmann, 1843). Both were required textbooks at Amherst Academy also.

135. Edward Hitchcock, *The Power of Christian Benevolence*, p. 293.

136. Sarah D. Stow, *History of Mount Holyoke Seminary, South Hadley, Mass., During Its First Half Century, 1837–1887* (South Hadley, Mass.: Mount Holyoke Seminary, 1887), p. 360.

137. Mary Lyon, "Tendencies of the Principles Embraced, and the System Adopted in the Mount Holyoke Female Seminary," 1839, in Hitchcock, *The Power of Christian Benevolence*, p. 299. The religious and moral aims of Mount Holyoke are represented well in a textbook required of those in the Senior Class in 1847–48, and also listed for the English course at the academy when Dickinson attended: Francis Wayland, *Elements of Moral Science* (Boston: Gould, Kendall & Lincoln, 1835). The "constant object" of the instructor of this subject, wrote Wayland in his preface, should be to "convict" the student of her "obligation to obey God." The source of moral "truth," of course, was the "Sacred Scriptures."

138. *Letters*, 1:54–55.

139. The original account of this meeting appeared in Sydney McLean, "Emily Dickinson at Mount Holyoke," *New England Quarterly*, 7 (March 1934): 25–42. The author draws in part upon the entry for 17 January in the "Mount Holyoke Seminary Journal Letter."

140. 17 January 1848, in *Letters*, 1:60, and 17 May 1848, in *Letters*, 1:67–68. Two other relevant letters are Emily L. Norcross to Mrs. Porter, 11 January 1848, and Mary C. Whitman to Mrs. Porter, 17 January 1848, in Leyda, *Dickinson*, 1:135–36. Miss Whitman, who was in charge of the group "without hope," was also the person who refused Dickinson's request to go home one Sabbath. It is possible that their relations entered into the poet's non-cooperation; see 17 February 1848, 29 May 1848, in *Letters*, 1:62–64, 68.

Similar struggles are recorded in the letters Dickinson sent Abiah Root two years earlier, showing that the "pressure" at Mount Holyoke was already familiar to this daughter of Amherst (see 31 January 1846, 28 March 1846, and 8 September 1846, in *Letters*, 1:27–29, 30–31, 38).

141. Hitchcock, *Reminiscences of Amherst College*, p. 162.

142. In Hitchcock, *The Power of Christian Benevolence*, p. 299.

A CALENDAR OF THE CORRESPONDENCE OF HENRY D. THOREAU

Carolyn Kappes, Walter Harding, Randy F. Nelson, and Elizabeth Witherell

THIS CALENDAR OF LETTERS is a preliminary report on the new edition of the correspondence of Henry D. Thoreau being prepared as part of the Princeton Edition of *The Writings of Henry D. Thoreau*. It is hoped that not only will it prove useful to scholars working in the field, calling their attention to new letters that have surfaced since the publication more than twenty years ago of the most recent edition of Thoreau's correspondence (*The Correspondence of Henry David Thoreau*, ed. Walter Harding and Carl Bode [New York: New York University Press, 1958]), but also that anyone noting any errors or omissions in the calendar will call them to our attention so that the new edition may be that much more comprehensive.

It is our intention to list herein every letter written either by or to Henry David Thoreau that is known to have existed. The letters are listed in chronological order. When we have been able to determine only a terminal date, we have entered the letter at the latest possible date and labeled it "before" that date. When we were able to determine only the earliest possible date, we have entered the letter at the earliest possible date and labeled it "after" that date. When we have been able to determine only an approximate date, the letter has been entered at the appropriate place and labeled "*circa*." Where letters can be dated only by month or by year or other extended period of time, they are entered chronologically at the end of that period. The few letters for which we have been unable to determine any date at all are listed at the end of the chronology. When more than one letter bears the same date, those written by Thoreau precede those he received; otherwise, they are alphabetized by the name of his correspondent. Letters with italic numbers are known to have existed, but no part of them is either extant or available to us. Some of these are mentioned or implied in biographies or extant letters, others are only listed in dealers' catalogues. Any new information about these letters, particularly locations of the manuscript, would be a great help to the editors.

Each entry gives as much of the following information as possible or necessary: date; name of correspondent; geographic origin of letter; present or most recently known location of the manuscript; location of the earliest known published text of the letter; editorial comments. Names of correspondents, dates, and geographic origins of the letters have been silently regularized. Square brackets surround information supplied by the editors.

Each letter not included in the 1958 edition of the *Correspondence* is marked with a single asterisk (*); where a manuscript source is newly available, the letter is marked with a double asterisk (**).

The location of manuscripts in libararies or other public institutions is indicated by the standard National Union Catalog abbreviation; the call number is given when the library has assigned one. Manuscripts in private hands are identified as "privately owned." It should be noted that those manuscripts outside public institutions often change hands and their present location may be other than that indicated. This is particularly true of manuscripts listed as in the possession of dealers.

The only previous checklist of Thoreau's correspondence was "Henry David Thoreau: A Check List of His Correspondence," by Walter Harding and Carl Bode, in the *Bulletin of the New York Public Library*, 59 (May 1955): 227–52. One hundred and eighteen new letters or drafts of letters are included in this list. Three letters conjectured in the earlier list have surfaced and fifty-seven letters then listed with only a printed source for their text now can be based on manuscripts. A few additional conjectured letters have resulted from a study of the new texts.

We are greatly indebted to the literally hundreds of Thoreau scholars and enthusiasts, the book and manuscript dealers, and staffs of the many libraries and other public institutions consulted. Unfortunately there is not space to identify them here, but we will make full acknowledgment in the edition when that appears. Special thanks are due to Lorna Carey Mack of the Textual Center Staff who assisted in the preparation of this checklist.

SHORT TITLES

Atlantic Monthly (May 1892)	F. B. Sanborn, "The Emerson-Thoreau Correspondence," *Atlantic Monthly*, 69 (May 1892): 577–96.
Atlantic Monthly (June 1892)	F. B. Sanborn, "The Emerson-Thoreau Correspondence," *Atlantic Monthly*, 69 (June 1882): 736–53.
Atlantic Monthly (December 1893)	F. B. Sanborn, "Thoreau and His English Friend Thomas Cholmondeley," *Atlantic Monthly*, 72 (December 1893): 742–56.
Atlantic Monthly (September 1902)	E. Harlow Russell, "A Bit of Unpublished Correspondence between Henry Thoreau and Isaac Hecker," *Atlantic Monthly*, 90 (September 1902): 370–76.
Bode	Carl Bode, "Thoreau and His Last Publishers," *New England Quarterly*, 26 (September 1953): 383–87.
Cameron, *Companion*	Kenneth Walter Cameron, *Companion to Thoreau's Correspondence*. Hartford, Conn.: Transcendental Books, 1964.
Cameron, *Minerva*	Kenneth Walter Cameron, *The Transcendentalists and Minerva*. Hartford, Conn.: Transcendental Books, 1958.
Cook	Reginald Cook, *The Concord Saunterer*. Middlebury, Vt.: Middlebury College Press, 1940.
Davenport	Elizabeth B. Davenport, "Thoreau in Vermont in 1856," *Vermont Botanical Club Bulletin*, no. 3 (April 1908): 36–38.
Emerson (1865)	Henry D. Thoreau, *Letters to Various Persons*, ed. R. W. Emerson. Boston: Ticknor & Fields, 1865.
Familiar Letters (1894)	Henry D. Thoreau, *Familiar Letters of Henry David Thoreau*, ed. F. B. Sanborn. Boston & New York: Houghton, Mifflin, 1894.
Familiar Letters (1906)	Henry David Thoreau, *Familiar Letters*, enl. ed., ed. F. B. Sanborn, vol. 6 in *The Writings of Henry David Thoreau*. Boston & New York: Houghton Mifflin, 1906.
Harding	Henry David Thoreau, *The Correspondence of Henry David Thoreau*, ed. Walter Harding and Carl Bode. New York: New York University Press, 1958.

Jones	Samuel Arthur Jones, *Some Unpublished Letters of Henry D. and Sophia E. Thoreau*. Jamaica, N.Y.: Marion Press, 1899.
Journal	Henry David Thoreau, *Journal*, ed. Bradford Torrey and Francis H. Allen, 14 vols., *The Writings of Henry David Thoreau*. Boston & New York: Houghton Mifflin, 1906.
Ricketson	Anna and Walton Ricketson, *Daniel Ricketson and His Friends*. Boston & New York: Houghton, Mifflin, 1902.
Rusk	Ralph Waldo Emerson, *The Letters of Ralph Waldo Emerson*, ed. Ralph L. Rusk, 6 vols. New York: Columbia University Press, 1939.
Sanborn, *Alcott*	F. B. Sanborn and William T. Harris, *A. Bronson Alcott: His Life and Philosophy*, 2 vols. Boston: Roberts Brothers, 1893.
Sanborn, *Critic*	F. B. Sanborn, "A Concord Note-Book," *Critic*, 48 (April 1906): 338–50.
Sanborn, *Thoreau* (1882)	F. B. Sanborn, *Henry D. Thoreau*. Boston & New York: Houghton, Mifflin, 1882.

1834

1. before 11 July 1834   [Concord]
    To "Faculty of Harvard College." Mentioned in
    Records of the Harvard College Faculty Meeting
    of 30 June 1834, MH.

1836

2. 30 May 1836   Cambridge
    From A. G. Peabody. NNPM, MA 920. Printed in
    Harding, pp. 4–6.

3. 5 July 1836   Concord
    To Henry Vose. CSmH, HM 7002. Printed in
    Fifth Year Book (Boston: The Bibliophile
    Society, 1906), p. 55.

4.*   31 July 1836   Brookfield, Mass.
    From Charles Wyatt Rice. Privately owned.

5. 5 August 1836   Concord
    To Charles Wyatt Rice. ICarbS, copy by L. P.

Gould. Printed in Edwin B. Hill, *Two Thoreau Letters* (Mesa, Ariz.: Edwin B. Hill, 1916).

1837

6.   7 September 1837   Dedham, Mass.
   From James Richardson, Jr. NN, Berg Collection.
   Printed in Harding, pp. 11–12.

7.   13 October 1837   Concord
   To Henry Vose. NN, Berg Collection. Printed in
   Raymond Adams, "Thoreau at Harvard: Some
   Unpublished Records," *New England Quarterly*,
   13 (March 1940): 28.

8.   22 October 1837   Butternuts
   From Henry Vose. NNPM, MA 920. Printed in
   Harding, pp. 14–15.

9.   27 October 1837   Concord
   To Helen Thoreau. NN, Berg Collection, copy by
   Emerson. Printed in *Familiar Letters* (1894),
   pp. 12–13.

10.   11 November 1837   Concord
    To John Thoreau, Jr. NN, Berg Collection.
    Printed in *Familiar Letters* (1894), pp. 14–18.

11.   30 December 1837   Concord
    To Orestes A. Brownson. InNd. Printed in
    Henry F. Brownson, *Orestes A. Brownson's Early
    Life* (Detroit: H. F. Brownson, 1898), p. 204.

1838

12.   5 February 1838   [Concord]
    To [Henry] Hawkins. Mentioned in
    9 February 1838 letter to Haskins.

13.   before 9 February 1838   [Boston]
    From [Charles] Hayward. Mentioned in
    9 February 1838 letter to Haskins.

14.*   9 February 1838   Concord
    To David Greene Haskins. NjP, Taylor Collection.

15.**   10 February 1838   Concord
    To John Thoreau, Jr. OMC. Printed in *Familiar
    Letters* (1894), pp. 20–21.

16.	17 March 1838 To John Thoreau, Jr. CSmH, HM 7003. Printed in *Familiar Letters* (1894), pp. 21–23.	Concord
17.	12 April 1838 From Josiah Quincy. Privately owned. Printed in Sanborn, *Thoreau* (1882), p. 61.	Cambridge
18.*	28 May 1838 To Henry Vose. ViU, Barrett Collection, 6345–e.	Concord
19.	8 July 1838 To John Thoreau, Jr. RPB, A55872[3]. Printed in *Familiar Letters* (1894), pp. 25–26.	Concord
20.	Summer 1838 From David Greene Haskins. Mentioned in David Greene Haskins, *Ralph Waldo Emerson: His Maternal Ancestors* (Boston: Cupples, Upham, 1887), p. 48.	[Roxbury, Mass.]
21.	6 October 1838 To A. Bigelow. Privately owned. Printed in Harding, p. 656.	Concord
22.	6 October 1838 To Helen Thoreau. NN, Berg Collection. Printed in *Familiar Letters* (1894), pp. 27–30.	Concord
23.	[12 November 1838] From Ralph Waldo Emerson. NN, Berg Collection. Printed in Sanborn, *Thoreau* (1882), p. 155.	Concord
24.*	28 November 1838 To Charles Stearns Wheeler. Facsimile printed in Goodspeed's catalogue, "The Flying Quill" (August 1967).	Concord

1839

25.	15 February [1839] From Ralph Waldo Emerson. MCo, Hosmer Collection. Printed in Harding, p. 32.	Concord

1840

26.*	3 January 1840 To Charles Stearns Wheeler. NjP, Taylor Collection.	Concord

Calendar of Correspondence of Henry D. Thoreau 331

27.*   6 January 1840   Cambridge
From Charles Stearns Wheeler. Privately owned.

28.   [21 or 23 January] 1840   Concord
To Helen Thoreau. NNPM, MS torn; approximately nine lines missing. Printed in *Familiar Letters* (1894), pp. 30–33. Thoreau's date, written in Latin, means "ten days from the first of February"; there are two ways of counting to determine the intended date.

29.*   2 March 1840   Concord
To Charles Stearns Wheeler. Privately owned.

30.*   4 March 1840   [Cambridge]
From Charles Stearns Wheeler. Privately owned.

31.*   6 April 1840   Concord
To David Green Haskins. Paul C. Richards Autographs. Description and excerpt printed in Richards catalog 141, item 79.

32.** 13 June 1840   Concord
To Helen Thoreau. ViU, Barrett Collection. Printed in Emerson (1865), pp. 1–3.

33.   20 June 1840   Concord
To [?]. MHi, Norcross Collection. Printed in Harding, pp. 40–41.

34.   before 10 November 1840   [Concord]
To Ellen Sewall. Mentioned in T. M. Raysor, "The Love Story of Thoreau," *Studies in Philology*, 23 (October 1926): 459.

35.   10 November 1840   [Watertown, N.Y.]
From Ellen Sewall. Mentioned in T. M. Raysor, "The Love Story of Thoreau," *Studies in Philology*, 23 (October 1926): 459, as 9 November 1840; Henry Seidel Canby, *Thoreau* (Boston: Houghton Mifflin, 1939), p. 120, establishes 10 November 1840 as correct date.

36.   1 December [1840]   Jamaica Plains, N.Y.
From Margaret Fuller. NNPM. Printed in Harding, pp. 41–42.

1841

37.*   6 January 1841   Concord
To "Concord Town Clerk." MCo. Printed in
"A New Thoreau Document," *Thoreau Society Bulletin*, no. 120 (Summer 1972): 7.

38.*   9 March 1841   Concord
To Samuel G. Howe. MWatP. Printed in Raymond Adams, "Thoreau Applies for a Position," *Lantern*, 29 (1960): 2.

39.   June 1841   Concord
From Ralph Waldo Emerson. NN, Berg Collection. Printed in *Atlantic Monthly* (May 1892): 577.

40.   21 July 1841   Concord
To Lucy Brown. Printed in Emerson (1865), pp. 3–5.

41.   before 8 September 1841   [————?]
From Lucy Brown. Mentioned in 8 September [1841] letter to Brown.

42.**   8 September [1841]   Concord
To Lucy Brown. ViU, Barrett Collection, 6345-e. Printed in Emerson (1865), pp. 5–8.

43.**   24 September 1841   Buffalo
From Isaiah Williams. NN, Berg Collection. Printed in Harding, p. 47.

44.   5 October 1841   Concord
To Lucy Brown. Printed in Emerson (1865), pp. 8–9.

45.**   8 [October] 1841   Concord
To Isaiah Williams. NNPM. Printed in Harding, pp. 51–53. Although manuscript is dated "Sept.," it is a response to Williams' 24 September letter; envelope is postmarked October.

46.   9 October 1841   Concord
To Rufus Griswold. NN, Berg Collection. Printed in Harding, p. 54.

47.   18 October 1841   Concord
From Margaret Fuller. TxU, Thoreau Letters. Printed in Sanborn, *Thoreau* (1882), pp. 169–72.

Calendar of Correspondence of Henry D. Thoreau 333

48.**	27 November 1841 From Isaiah Williams. NN, Berg Collection. Printed in Harding, pp. 58–60.	Buffalo

1842

49.	2 March 1842 To Lucy Brown. MH, bMS Am 1280.226. Printed in Emerson (1865), pp. 9–11.	Concord
50.	11 March 1842 To Ralph Waldo Emerson. NN, Berg Collection. Printed in F. B. Sanborn, "Thoreau's Poems of Nature," *Scribner's Magazine*, 17 (March 1895): 352–53.	Concord
51.**	14 March 1842 To Isaiah Williams. NN, Berg Collection, copy by Elizabeth Hoar. Printed in Harding, pp. 66–68.	Concord
52.*	15 June 1842 To Charles Stearns Wheeler. Privately owned.	Concord
53.	23 June 1842 From Isaiah Williams. NN, Berg Collection. Printed in Harding, pp. 69–71.	Buffalo
54.*	10 October 1842 To Isaiah Williams. CSmH, HM 926, incomplete draft.	Concord
55.*	29 November 1842 From Orestes A. Brownson. NNPM, Cooley Collection, MA 2101.	Boston
56.	9 December [1842] From James Richardson, Jr. NNPM, MA 920. Printed in Harding, p. 71.	Cambridge

1843

57.	16 January 1843 To Richard Fuller. NNPM, MA 2107. Printed in Emerson (1865), pp. 11–12.	Concord
58.	24 January 1843 To Lucy Brown. DFo, Corr. Box 101. Printed in Emerson (1865), pp. 13–15.	Concord

59.**	24 January 1843 To Ralph Waldo Emerson. InU. Printed in *Atlantic Monthly* (May 1892): 578–79.	Concord
60.	25 January 1843 To Lucy Brown. Printed in Emerson (1865), pp. 15–18.	Concord
61.	[7–11] February 1843 From Ralph Waldo Emerson. NN, Berg Collection. Printed in *Atlantic Monthly* (May 1892): 581–82.	New York
62.	10 February 1843 To Ralph Waldo Emerson. Printed in *Atlantic Monthly* (May 1892): 579–80.	Concord
63.	12 February 1843 To Ralph Waldo Emerson. Printed in *Atlantic Monthly* (May 1892): 580–81.	Concord
64.	12 February [1843] From Ralph Waldo Emerson. MCo, Hosmer Collection. Printed in *Atlantic Monthly* (May 1892): 582.	New York
65.**	15 February 1843 To Ralph Waldo Emerson. NNC. Printed in *Atlantic Monthly* (May 1892): 583.	Concord
66.	20 February 1843 To Ralph Waldo Emerson. Printed in *Atlantic Monthly* (May 1892): 584.	Concord
67.**	26 February 1843 From Elizabeth Palmer Peabody. ViU, Barrett Collection, 6952–a. Printed in Sanborn, *Critic*, 346.	Boston
68.	[1 March 1843] To Ralph Waldo Emerson. NN, Berg Collection. Printed in *Atlantic Monthly* (May 1892): 583–84, where it is dated 16 February.	[Concord]
69.	before 2 April 1843 From Richard Fuller. Mentioned in 2 April 1843 letter to Fuller.	[Cambridge]
70.**	2 April 1843 To Richard Fuller. Privately owned. Printed in Emerson (1865), pp. 18–20.	Concord

71.	11 April 1843 To Henry Vose. RPB, A 55872[4]. Printed in Harding, p. 95.	Concord
72.	[before 1 May 1843] From [William Ellery Channing]. VtMiM, incomplete; signature missing. Printed in Harding, p. 96.	[Cambridge]
73.	1 May 1843 From William Ellery Channing. Description and excerpts printed in *The Stephen H. Wakeman Collection of Books of Nineteenth Century American Writers* (New York: American Art Association, 1924), item 997.	Cambridge
74.	2 May 1843 From Elizabeth Hoar. Printed in *Atlantic Monthly* (May 1892): 595n.	Boston
75.**	11 May 1843 To Cynthia Thoreau. ViU, Barrett Collection, 6345–e. Printed in *Familiar Letters* (1894), pp. 80–83.	Staten Island
76.	12 May 1843 From Henry James, Sr. NNPM, MA 920. Printed in Harding, p. 101.	New York
77.	21 May 1843 From Ralph Waldo Emerson. NNPM, MA 920. Printed in *Atlantic Monthly* (May 1892): 585–86.	Concord
78.**	22 May 1843 To Lidian Emerson. MBU. Printed in Emerson (1865), pp. 20–23.	Staten Island
79.	22 May 1843 To Sophia Thoreau. NN, Berg Collection. Printed in *Familiar Letters* (1894), pp. 84–87.	Staten Island
80.	23 May [1843] To Ralph Waldo Emerson. CSmH, HM 22230. Printed in *Familiar Letters* (1894), pp. 92–94.	Staten Island
81.	23 May 1843 To Helen Thoreau. VtMiM; incomplete, signature missing. Printed in *Familiar Letters* (1894), p. 87.	Staten Island
82.*	2 June 1843 From Giles Waldo. Privately owned.	[New York]

83.	8 June 1843 To Ralph Waldo Emerson. Printed in *Atlantic Monthly* (May 1892): 587–88.	Staten Island
84.	8 June 1843 To Mr. and Mrs. John Thoreau, Sr. NHi. Printed in *Familiar Letters* (1894), pp. 100–102.	Staten Island
85.	[7–9] June 1843 From Charles Lane. Printed in Sanborn, *Thoreau* (1882), pp. 137–40, where it is dated 9 June 1843. Excerpts printed in Sanborn, *Alcott*, 2:377–78, are dated 7 June 1843.	Cambridge
86.	10–15 June 1843 From Ralph Waldo Emerson. NN, Berg Collection. Printed in *Atlantic Monthly* (May 1892): 589–90.	Concord
87.	before 19 June 1843 From Lidian Emerson. Mentioned in 20 June 1843 letter to Lidian Emerson.	[Concord]
88.	20 June 1843 To Lidian Emerson. CtGreB, No. g 255. Printed in Emerson (1865), pp. 23–26.	Staten Island
89.	before 7 July 1843 From Cynthia Thoreau. Mentioned in 7 July 1843 letter to Cynthia Thoreau.	[Concord]
90.	7 July [1843] To Cynthia Thoreau. CSmH, HM 7004. Printed in Emerson (1865), pp. 31–33.	Staten Island
91.	8 July 1843 To Mr. and Mrs. R. W. Emerson. NN, Berg Collection. Printed in *Familiar Letters* (1894), pp. 109–13.	Staten Island
92.	[14 July 1843?] To "Publishers of The Dial." Described as "relating to a 'paper which was sent for the Dial . . . ,'" in *The Stephen H. Wakeman Collection of Books of Nineteenth Century American Writers*, item 984. Either the date or the address is incorrect. Thoreau was in Staten Island in July 1843.	[Concord?]
93.	20 July 1843 From Ralph Waldo Emerson. NNC. Printed in *Atlantic Monthly* (May 1892): 591–92.	Concord

Calendar of Correspondence of Henry D. Thoreau 337

94.	21 July 1843 To Helen Thoreau. CSmH, HM 7005. Printed in *Familiar Letters* (1894), pp. 113–17.	Staten Island
95.	28 July 1843 From J. L. O'Sullivan. NN, Berg Collection. Printed in Harding, p. 130.	New York
96.*	1 August 1843 [To J. L. O'Sullivan]. CSmH, HM 13193 (draft).	Staten Island
97.	before 6 August 1843 From Helen Thoreau. Mentioned in 6 August 1843 letter to Cynthia Thoreau.	[Roxbury, Mass.]
98.**	6 August 1843 To Cynthia Thoreau. ViU, Barrett Collection, 6345–e. Printed in *Familiar Letters* (1894), pp. 117–20.	Staten Island
99.	7 August 1843 To Ralph Waldo Emerson. NN, Berg Collection. Printed in Emerson (1864), pp. 26–28.	Staten Island
100.	29 August 1843 To Cynthia Thoreau. NNPM, MA 920. Printed in *Familiar Letters* (1894), pp. 124–27.	Staten Island
101.	8 September 1843 From Ralph Waldo Emerson. Printed in *Atlantic Monthly* (May 1892): 592–93.	Concord
102.**	14 September [1843] To Ralph Waldo Emerson. MBU. Printed in *Atlantic Monthly* (May 1892): 593–94.	Staten Island
103.*	25 September 1843 From Margaret Fuller. ICarbS, Feinberg Collection. Printed in Cameron, *Companion*, p. 182.	Concord
104.	1 October 1843 To Cynthia Thoreau. CSmH, HM 7006. Printed in *Familiar Letters* (1894), pp. 129–33.	Staten Island
105.	16 October 1843 To Lidian Emerson. NN, Berg Collection. Printed in Harding, pp. 143–44.	Staten Island
106.	17 October [1843] To Ralph Waldo Emerson. NN, Berg Collection. Printed in *Familiar Letters* (1894), pp. 135–39.	Staten Island

107.	18 October 1843 To Helen Thoreau. CSmH, HM 7007, incomplete; approximately four-fifths of pp. 3 and 4 have been cut off. Printed in Harding, pp. 147–48.	Staten Island
108.	25 October 1843 From Ralph Waldo Emerson. NN, Berg Collection. Printed in *Atlantic Monthly* (May 1892): 595–96.	Concord
109.	[1 November 1843] To H. S. McKean. VtMiM, Thoreau Letters (draft fragment). Printed in Harding, p. 150.	[Staten Island]
110.	[23 November 1843] From Ralph Waldo Emerson. CSmH, HM 7321. Printed in *Atlantic Monthly* (June 1892): 736	Concord
111.	3 December 1843 From Sophia Hawthorne. NNPM, MA 920. Printed in Harding, p. 151.	Concord
112.	3 December 1843 From Charles Lane. MHarF. Printed in *Familiar Letters* (1894), pp. 146–47.	Boston
113.	before 17 December 1843. From William Emerson. Mentioned in Rusk, 3:228.	[Staten Island]

1844

114.	31 July 1844 From Isaac Hecker. CSmH, HM 20110. Printed in *Atlantic Monthly* (September 1902): 371.	New York
115.	14 August 1844 To Isaac Hecker. CSmH, HM 20109. Printed in *Familiar Letters* (1906), pp. 405–407.	Concord
116.	15 August 1844 From Isaac Hecker. CSmH, HM 20108. Printed in *Atlantic Monthly* (September 1902): 373.	New York
117.	after 15 August 1844 To Isaac Hecker. CSmH, HM 20107. Printed in *Atlantic Monthly* (September 1902): 374.	Concord
118.	14 October [1844] To James Munroe & Co. MB, Ch B 6.16. Printed in Harding, p. 159.	Concord

Calendar of Correspondence of Henry D. Thoreau 339

1845

119.	before 5 March 1845 To William Ellery Channing. Mentioned in 5 March 1845 letter from Channing.	[Concord]
120.	5 March 1845 From William Ellery Channing. VtMiM, M-Z 249. Printed in Harding, pp. 161–63.	New York
121.*	5 March 1845 From Horace Greeley. Privately owned.	[New York]
122.*	24 May 1845 From D. W. Stevens. Privately owned.	Charlestown, Mass.
123.*	17 September 1845 To James Munroe & Co. PHC.	Concord
124.*	[8 October 1845] From Ralph Waldo Emerson. MH, bMS Am 1189. Printed in Kenneth Walter Cameron, "A Bundle of Emerson Letters," *Emerson Society Quarterly*, no. 22 (1st Quarter 1961): 96.	Concord
125.	[late Fall 1845] From Ralph Waldo Emerson. NN, Berg Collection. Printed in Harding, p. 33.	[Concord]

1846

126.	17 February 1846 From Charles Lane. Privately owned. Printed in *Familiar Letters* (1894), p. 147.	New York
127.	26 February 1846 To Charles Lane, or Wiley & Putnam. Mentioned in 30 March 1846 letter from Charles Lane.	[Concord]
128.**	30 March 1846 From Charles Lane. ViU, Barrett Collection, 6345-H. Printed in *Familiar Letters* (1894), pp. 147–48.	Boonton, N.J.
129.	16 August 1846 From Horace Greeley. RPB, HA 55872[1]. Printed in Sanborn, *Thoreau* (1882). p. 219.	New York
130.	Summer 1846 To Horace Greeley. Implied in Sanborn, *Thoreau* (1882), p. 218.	[Concord]

131.	30 September 1846 From Horace Greeley. Printed in Sanborn, *Thoreau* (1882), pp. 219–20.	New York
132.	[late September 1846] From Ralph Waldo Emerson. NN, Berg Collection. Printed in *Atlantic Monthly* (June 1892): 742, as part of 2 December 1847 letter from Emerson.	[Concord]
133.	26 October 1846 From Horace Greeley. Printed in Sanborn, *Thoreau* (1882), pp. 221–22.	New York

1847

134.*	17 January 1847 From Horatio R. Storer. Privately owned.	Boston
135.	before 5 February 1847 To Horace Greeley. Mentioned in 5 February 1847 letter from Greeley.	[Concord]
136.	5 February 1847 From Horace Greeley. VtMiM, M–2 251. Printed in Sanborn, *Thoreau* (1882), pp. 222–24.	New York
137.	15 February 1847 To Horatio R. Storer. VtMiM, Thoreau Letters. Printed in Cook, p. 62.	Concord
138.	1 March 1847 From Henry Williams, Jr. MH, Class of 1837 Records. Form letter and questionnaire sent to all members of the Harvard Class of 1837; manuscript at MH is not Thoreau's copy. Printed in Harding, p. 176.	Boston
139.	3 May 1847 From James Elliot Cabot. Printed in Harding, pp. 177–78.	[Boston]
140.	before 8 May 1847 From James Elliot Cabot. Implied in 8 May 1847 letter to Cabot.	[Boston]
141.**	8 May 1847 To James Elliot Cabot. MCR–S, Cabot Papers, A 99, Folder 96. Printed in *Familiar Letters* (1894), pp. 150–53.	Concord

142.*	15 May 1847 From Isaac Hecker. NNPa.	Wittem, Holland
143.	27 May 1847 From James Elliot Cabot. Printed in Harding, p. 181.	[Boston]
144.	28 May 1847 To Evert Duyckinck. NN, Manuscript Room. Printed in Harding, pp. 181–82.	Concord
145.**	1 June 1847 To James Elliot Cabot. MCR-S, Cabot Papers, A 99, Folder 96. Printed in *Familiar Letters* (1894), pp. 153–54.	Concord
146.	1 June 1847 From James Elliot Cabot. Printed in *Familiar Letters* (1894), p. 157.	[Boston]
147.	14 [June] 1847 To [Evert Duyckinck]. Printed in Adrian Joline, *Rambles in Autograph Land* (New York: Putnams, 1913), p. 293, dated 14 January 1847.	Concord
148.	3 July 1847 To Evert Duyckinck. NN, Manuscript Room. Printed in Harding, p. 184.	Concord
149.	27 July 1847 To Evert Duyckinck. MHarF. Printed in Harding, p. 184.	Concord
150.	28 August 1847 To James Munroe & Co. PHi, Dreer Collection. Printed in Roger J. Harmon, "Thoreau to His Publishers," *American Literature*, 25 (January 1954): 497.	Concord
151.	30 September 1847 To Henry Williams, Jr. MH, Class of 1837 Records. Printed in Henry Williams, *Memorials of the Class of 1837 of Harvard University* (Boston: George H. Ellis, 1887), p. 38.	Concord
152.	September 1847 To William Emerson. Mentioned in Rusk, 3:413.	[Concord]

153.**	24 October 1847 To Sophia Thoreau. NjP, Taylor Collection. Printed in *Atlantic Monthly* (June 1892): 736–37.	Concord
154.	29 October 1847 To Ralph Waldo Emerson. Mentioned in Rusk, 3:439.	[Concord]
155.	before 14 November 1847 From Sophia Ford. Mentioned in 14 November 1847 letter to Emerson.	[———?]
156.	before 14 November 1847 To Sophia Ford. Mentioned in 14 November 1847 letter to Emerson.	[Concord]
157.**	14 November 1847 To Ralph Waldo Emerson. NjP, Taylor Collection. Printed in *Atlantic Monthly* (June 1892): 737–40.	Concord
158.	15 November 1847 To [Abel Adams]. MHi, Washburn Collection. Printed in Harding, p. 193.	Concord
159.	2 December 1847 From Ralph Waldo Emerson. NN, Berg Collection. Printed in *Atlantic Monthly* (June 1892): 741–42.	Manchester, England
160.	15 December 1847 To Ralph Waldo Emerson. ViU, Barrett Collection, 6345–e. Printed in *Familiar Letters* (1894), pp. 170–73.	Concord
161.	27 December 1847 To [James Munroe & Co.]. MB, Ch B 6.15. Printed in Harding, p. 198.	Concord
162.	29 December 1847 To Ralph Waldo Emerson. NN, Berg Collection. Printed in *Familiar Letters* (1894), pp. 173–77.	Concord

1848

163.**	12 January 1848 To Ralph Waldo Emerson. ViU, Barrett Collection, 6345–e. Printed in *Familiar Letters* (1894), pp. 177–81.	Concord
164.	28 January 1848 From Ralph Waldo Emerson. NN, Berg Collection. Printed in *Atlantic Monthly* (June 1892): 745–46.	Manchester, England

Calendar of Correspondence of Henry D. Thoreau 343

165.**	23 February 1848 To Ralph Waldo Emerson. NN, Berg Collection. Printed in *Atlantic Monthly* (June 1892): 746–48.	Concord
166.**	8 March 1848 To James Elliot Cabot. MCR–S, Cabot Papers, A 99, Folder 96. Printed in *Familiar Letters* (1894), pp. 186–88.	Concord
167.	[23 March 1848] To Ralph Waldo Emerson. ViU, Barrett Collection, 6345–e. Printed in *Familiar Letters* (1894), p. 189.	Concord
168.	25 March 1848 From Ralph Waldo Emerson. NN, Berg Collection. Printed in *Atlantic Monthly* (June 1892): 749.	London
169.	before 27 March 1848 From H. G. O. Blake. Printed in *Familiar Letters* (1894), pp. 190–91.	Worcester
170.	27 March 1848 To H. G. O. Blake. NN, Berg Collection (two leaves). Printed in Emerson (1865), pp. 41–46.	Concord
171.	31 March 1848 To Horace Greeley. Mentioned in 3 April 1848 letter from Greeley.	[Concord]
172.	3 April 1848 From Horace Greeley. NNPM, MA 920. Printed in Harding, p. 217.	New York
173.	17 April 1848 From Horace Greeley. CtY, ZA Letter File. Printed in Harding, pp. 218–19.	New York
174.	before 2 May 1848 From H. G. O. Blake. Implied in 2 May 1848 letter to Blake.	[Worcester]
175.	2 May 1848 To H. G. O. Blake. Printed in Emerson (1865), pp. 47–52.	Concord
176.**	17 May 1848 From Horace Greeley. ViU, Barrett Collection, 7669. Printed in Harding, pp. 222–23.	New York

177.	19 May 1848 To Horace Greeley. MB, Griswold MSS. No. 1080. Printed in Harding, pp. 223–25.	Concord
178.	before 21 May 1848 From H. G. O. Blake. Mentioned in 21 May 1848 letter to Emerson.	[Worcester]
179.	21 May 1848 To Ralph Waldo Emerson. MH, bMS Am 1280.3212. Printed in Harding, pp. 225–27.	Concord
180.**	25 May 1848 From Horace Greeley. ViU, Barrett Collection, 7669. Printed in Harding, pp. 228–29.	New York
181.	before 27 June 1848 To Horace Greeley. Mentioned in Henry Luther Stoddard, *Horace Greeley* (New York: Putnams, 1946), p. 117.	[Concord]
182.	before 24 August 1848 From George Thatcher. Mentioned in 24 August 1848 letter to Thatcher.	[Bangor]
183.	24 August 1848 To George Thatcher. VtMiM, Thoreau Letters. Printed in Cook, p. 64.	Concord
184.	21 October 1848 From Nathaniel Hawthorne. NN, Berg Collection. Printed in Sanborn, *Thoreau* (1882), pp. 275–76.	Salem
185.	28 October 1848 From Horace Greeley. Described in C. F. Libbie & Co., Hathaway-Richardson Sale Catalog, 9–10 May 1911. Printed in Sanborn, *Thoreau* (1882), p. 227.	New York
186.	17 November 1848 To Horace Greeley. Mentioned in 19 November 1848 letter from Greeley.	[Concord]
187.	19 November 1848 From Horace Greeley. VtMiM, M–2 251. Printed in Sanborn, *Thoreau* (1882), pp. 229–30.	New York
188.	20 November 1848 From Nathaniel Hawthorne. NNPM, V–2 71B (1835–60), MA 920. Printed in Sanborn, *Thoreau* (1882), p. 276.	Boston

Calendar of Correspondence of Henry D. Thoreau 345

189.	[November] 1848 To Horace Greeley. Printed in Bayard Taylor, "Reminiscence of Thoreau," *New York Daily Tribune*, 28 August 1875, p. 10.	[Concord]
190.	26 December 1848 To George Thatcher. Excerpt and description printed in Anderson Auction Co., Joline Sale Catalog, 28–29 April 1915, item 536.	Concord

1849

191.	before 8 February 1849 To Ticknor & Co. Implied in 8 February 1849 letter from Ticknor & Co.	[Concord]
192.	8 February 1849 From Ticknor & Co. MH, bMS Am 1185, 1:332. Printed in Harding, p. 236.	Boston
193.	before 9 February 1849 From George Thatcher. Mentioned in 9 February 1849 letter to George Thatcher.	[Bangor]
194.*	9 February 1849 To George Thatcher. Privately owned.	Concord
195.	10 February 1849 To Ticknor & Co. Mentioned in 16 February 1849 letter from Ticknor & Co.	[Concord]
196.	16 February 1849 To George Thatcher. TxU, Thoreau Letters. Printed in Harding, pp. 236–37.	Concord
197.	16 February 1849 From Ticknor & Co. MH, fms Am 1185, 1:333. Printed in Harding, p. 237.	Boston
198.	19 February 1849 From Nathaniel Hawthorne. NNPM, V-2 71B (1835–60), MA 920. Printed in Sanborn, *Thoreau* (1882), p. 277.	Salem, Mass.
199.*	20 February 1849 To Nathaniel Hawthorne, MSaE, E H399 1821 C1. Printed in Cameron, *Companion*, p. 184.	Concord
200.	20 February 1849 From Bronson Alcott. Printed in Sanborn, *Alcott*, 2:461.	Boston

201.	16 March 1849 To George Thatcher. Privately owned. Printed in Harding, pp. 240–41.	Concord
202.**	22 March 1849 To George Thatcher. MBU. Printed in Anderson Galleries, Haber Sale Catalog, 7–8 December 1909, item 1636.	Portland, Maine
203.	5 April 1849 To Elizabeth Palmer Peabody. PHi, Gratz Collection, Case b, Box 36. Printed in Harding, p. 242.	Concord
204.	17 April 1849 To H. G. O. Blake. NN, Berg Collection, copy by Blake; original envelope. Printed in Harding, p. 242.	Concord
205.	30 June 1849 To Louis Agassiz. MH, bMS Am 1419(634). Printed in Harding, p. 243.	Concord
206.	[5 July 1849] From Louis Agassiz. NNPM, V–2 71B (1835–60), MA 920. Printed in *Familiar Letters* (1894), p. 154, with a date of October 1849.	Cambridge
207.	31 July 1849 To Ellen Emerson. Privately owned. Printed in Edward Waldo Emerson, *Henry D. Thoreau as Remembered by a Young Friend* (Boston and New York: Houghton Mifflin, 1917), p. 131.	Concord
208.	before 10 August 1849 From H. G. O. Blake. Implied in 10 August 1849 letter to Blake.	[Worcester]
209.**	10 August 1849 To H. G. O. Blake. ViU, Barrett Collection, 6345–e. Printed in Emerson (1865), pp. 52–53.	Concord
210.	3 September 1849 From James Anthony Froude. MCo, Hosmer Collection, copy in an unknown hand, tipped in grangerized Salt biography. Printed in Jones, p. 11.	Manchester, England
211.	17 September 1849 To Jared Sparks, MH, Harvard College Records, 1837. Printed in Perry Miller, *Consciousness in Concord* (Boston: Houghton Mifflin, 1958), p. 37.	Concord

Calendar of Correspondence of Henry D. Thoreau 347

212.*	[Summer 1849] From Isaac Hecker. NNPa.	London
213.	20 November 1849 To H. G. O. Blake. MCo, Hosmer Collection, tipped in grangerized Salt biography. Printed in Emerson (1865), pp. 54–56.	Concord
214.*	3 December 1849 From M. M. Colburn. Privately owned.	Andover, Mass.
215.	18 December 1849 From [Samuel] Cabot. Printed in *Familiar Letters* (1894), p. 227.	Boston

1850

216.	6 February [1850] From Ralph Waldo Emerson. NN, Berg Collection. Printed in Harding, p. 255.	Saco, Maine
217.	11 March 1850 From Ralph Waldo Emerson. NNPM, V–2 71B (1835–60), MA 920. Printed in *Atlantic Monthly* (June 1892): 750.	Concord
218.	before 3 April 1850 From H. G. O. Blake. Mentioned in 3 April 1850 letter to Blake.	[Milton, Mass.]
219.	3 April 1850 To H. G. O. Blake. Printed in Emerson (1865), pp. 57–60.	Concord
220.	1 May 1850 From [Charles] H. Dunbar. MH, 278.5(17D). Printed in Harding, pp. 258–59.	Haverhill, Mass.
221.	before 28 May 1850 From H. G. O. Blake. Implied in 28 May 1850 letter to Blake.	[Milton, Mass.]
222.	28 May 1850 To H. G. O. Blake. ViU, Barrett Collection, 6345–e. Printed in Emerson (1865), pp. 60–62.	Concord
223.	before 24 July 1850 From H. G. O. Blake. In 9 August 1850 letter to Blake, Thoreau mentions receiving letter before leaving for Fire Island. He went to Fire Island on 24 July 1850.	[Milton, Mass.]

224.	[24 July 1850] To Horace Greeley. NN, Berg Collection. Printed in Harding, p. 261.	Concord
225.	25 July 1850 To Ralph Waldo Emerson. MH, ALS file. Printed in *Atlantic Monthly* (June 1892): 750–51.	Fire Island, N.Y.
226.	29 July 1850 To Charles Sumner. MH, bMS Am 1.14–89. Printed in Harding, p. 263.	Springfield Depot, Mass.
227.	31 July 1850 From Charles Sumner. VtMiM, M–2–189. Printed in Harding, p. 264.	Boston
228.**	9 August 1850 To H. G. O. Blake, TxU, Thoreau Letters. Printed in Emerson (1865), pp. 63–66.	Concord
229.*	7 October 1850 From George Bailey. Privately owned.	Portland, Maine
230.	18 October 1850 From Josiah Pierce. NN, Berg Collection. Printed in Harding, p. 267.	Portland, Maine
231.	14 November 1850 From Franklin Forbes. NN, Berg Collection. Printed in Harding, pp. 267–68.	Clinton, Mass.
232.	15 November 1850 To Franklin Forbes. CCamarSJ A–1065. Printed in Harding, p. 268.	Concord
233.	before 20 November 1850 From Josiah Pierce. Implied in 20 November 1850 letter from Pierce.	[Portland, Maine]
234.	before 20 November 1850 To Josiah Pierce. Implied in 20 November 1850 letter from Pierce.	[Concord]
235.	20 November 1850 From Josiah Pierce. NN, Berg Collection. Printed in Harding, p. 269.	Portland, Maine
236.	3 December 1850 From Thomas Wentworth Higginson. NN, Berg Collection. Printed in Harding, p. 269.	Newburyport, Mass.

Calendar of Correspondence of Henry D. Thoreau 349

237.*	9 December 1850 To H. G. O. Blake. NN, Berg Collection.	[Concord]
238.	27 December 1850 From Samuel Cabot. Printed in *Familiar Letters* (1894), pp. 226–27.	Boston
239.*	late 1850 To H. G. O. Blake. MH, 278.5(1), draft. Printed in Cameron, *Companion,* pp. 187–88.	[Concord]

1851

240.	10 February 1851 To Thaddeus W. Harris. MH, ALS file. Printed in Harding, p. 272.	Concord
241.	7 March 1851 From William W. Greenough, William J. Dale, David Greene Haskins, and J. H. Adams, Jr. MH, ALS file. Form letter sent to all members of Harvard Class of 1837; not Thoreau's copy. Printed in Kenneth Walter Cameron, "The Solitary Thoreau of the Alumni Notes," *Emerson Society Quarterly,* no. 7 (2d Quarter 1957): 32.	Boston
242.	[April 1851] From William Cushing. ICarbS, incomplete. Printed in Harding, p. 653.	[Bedford, Mass.]
243.	[26 July 1851] From Isaac Hecker. NNPa.	New York

1852

244.*	15 February [1852] From Marston Watson. MPlPS.	Plymouth
245.	17 February 1852 To Marston Watson. Printed in Sanborn, *Alcott,* 2:483.	[Concord]
246.	before 24 February 1852 To Horace Greeley. Mentioned in 24 February 1852 letter from Greeley.	[Concord]
247.	24 February 1852 From Horace Greeley. Described in American Art Association, Gable Sale Catalog, 10–11 March 1924. Printed in Sanborn, *Thoreau* (1882), p. 231.	New York

248.	5 March 1852 To Horace Greeley. Mentioned in 18 March 1852 letter from Greeley.	[Concord]
249.	18 March 1852 From Horace Greeley. NNPM, V-271B (1835-60). Printed in Harding, p. 277.	New York
250.	[25] March 1852 From Horace Greeley. Printed in Sanborn, *Thoreau* (1882), p. 232.	New York
251.	before 2 April 1852 From Thomas Wentworth Higginson. Implied in 2 April 1852 letter to Higginson.	[Boston]
252.	2 April 1852 To Thomas Wentworth Higginson. ViU, Barrett Collection, 6345-e (envelope only). Facsimile of holograph letter in Thomas Wentworth Higginson, *Part of A Man's Life* (Boston and New York: Houghton Mifflin, 1905), p. 16. Printed in Harding, pp. 278-79.	Concord
253.	before 3 April 1852 From Thomas Wentworth Higginson. While Thoreau's letter of 2 April 1853 asks Higginson to make arrangements for a lecture, his letter of 3 April states that the arrangements have been made, thus implying that in the meantime Thoreau had received a letter from Higginson.	[Boston]
254.	3 April 1852 To Thomas Wentworth Higginson. TxU, Thoreau Letters. Printed in Harding, p. 280.	Concord
255.**	3 April 1852 From Horace Greeley. ViU, Barrett Collection, 7669. Printed in Sanborn, *Thoreau* (1882), pp. 233-34.	New York
256.	before 17 April 1852 To Horace Greeley. Mentioned in 20 April 1852 letter from Greeley.	[Concord]
257.	20 April 1852 From Horace Greeley. Privately owned. Printed in Harding, p. 281.	New York

258. before 26 May 1852   [Concord]
      To Horace Greeley. Mentioned in 26 May 1852
      letter from Greeley.

259. 26 May 1852   New York
      From Horace Greeley. NN, Berg Collection. Printed
      in Harding, pp. 281–82.

260. 25 June 1852   New York
      From Horace Greeley. MCo, Hosmer Collection,
      tipped in grangerized Salt biography at p. 60.
      Printed in Sanborn, *Thoreau* (1882), pp. 234–35.

261. before 8 July 1852   [Concord]
      To Horace Greeley. Mentioned in 8 July 1852
      letter from Greeley.

262.** 8 July 1852   New York
      From Horace Greeley. Joseph Rubinfine Books.
      Printed in Sanborn, *Thoreau* (1882), p. 235.

263. 13 July 1852   Concord
      To Sophia Thoreau. CSmH, HM 7008. Printed in
      Harding, pp. 283–84.

264. before 21 July 1852   [Worcester]
      From H. G. O. Blake. Implied in 21 July 1852
      letter to Blake.

265. 21 July 1852   Concord
      To H. G. O. Blake. ViU, Barrett Collection, 6345–e.
      Printed in Emerson (1865), pp. 68–71.

266. 21 July 1852   Charlestown, Mass.
      From William Sweetser. NN, Berg Collection.
      Printed in Harding, p. 287.

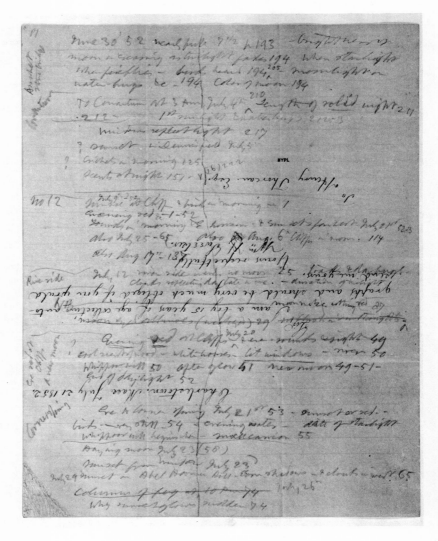

PLATE NINE
William Sweetser's letter of 21 July 1852 to Thoreau.
Courtesy NN

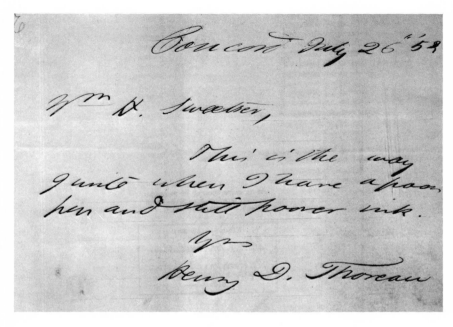

PLATE TEN
Thoreau's letter of 26 July 1852 to William Sweetser.
Courtesy NN

267.	26 July 1852 To William Sweetser. NN, Berg Collection. Printed in *Thoreau Society Bulletin,* no. 2 (January 1942): 2.	Concord
268.	[September 1852] To H. G. O. Blake. IaU. Printed in Emerson (1865), pp. 71–84.	[Concord]
269.	16 November 1852 To George William Curtis. MH, bMS Am 1124.4. Printed in Harding, pp. 288–89.	Concord
270.	before 23 November 1852 To Horace Greeley. Implied in 23 November 1852 letter from Greeley.	[Concord]
271.	23 November 1852 From Horace Greeley. CSmH, HM 1203. Printed in Harding, pp. 289–90.	New York

272.	29 December 1852 To Horace Greeley. Mentioned in 2 January 1853 letter from Greeley.	[Concord]
273.	before 31 December 1852 From Marston Watson. Implied in 31 December 1852 letter to Watson.	[Plymouth]
274.**	31 December 1852 To Marston Watson. VtMiM, Thoreau Letters. Printed in *Familiar Letters* (1894), p. 230.	Concord

1853

275.	2 January 1853 From Horace Greeley. Described in Paul C. Richards Autographs, catalogue 143, item 93. Printed in Sanborn, *Thoreau* (1882), p. 237.	New York
276.	9 February 1853 To Horace Greeley. NNPM, V-2 71B (1835-60), MA 920. Printed in Harding, p. 294.	Concord
277.	26 February [1853] To Elijah Wood. CSmH, HM 924. Printed in Harding, p. 294.	Concord
278.	before 27 February 1853 From H. G. O. Blake. Mentioned in 27 February 1853 letter to Blake.	[Worcester]
279.	27 February 1853 To H. G. O. Blake. NN, Berg Collection. Printed in Emerson (1865), pp. 85-93.	Concord
280.	before 5 March 1853 From "Secretary of the Association for the Advancement of Science." Mentioned in 5 March 1853 *Journal*, 5:4.	[Washington]
281.	9 March 1853 To Horace Greeley. Mentioned in 16 March 1853 letter from Greeley.	[Concord]
282.	11 March 1853 To George William Curtis. ViU, Barrett Collection, 6345-e. Printed in Edwin B. Hill, *Henry D. Thoreau to George William Curtis* (Ysleta, Texas: Edwin B. Hill, 1942).	Concord

Calendar of Correspondence of Henry D. Thoreau 355

283.	11 March 1853 From Horace Greeley. Described in American Auction Company Catalog, 11 March 1924.	[———?]
284.	after 11 March 1853 From Horace Greeley. Described in American Auction Company Catalog, 11 March 1924.	[———?]
285.	16 March 1853 From Horace Greeley. Printed in Sanborn, *Thoreau* (1882), pp. 237–38.	New York
286.	before 10 April 1853 From H. G. O. Blake. Mentioned in 10 April 1853 letter to Blake.	[Worcester]
287.**	10 April 1853 To H. G. O. Blake. NNPM, R–V Auto Misc. Amer. MA 2025. Printed in Emerson (1865), pp. 94–98.	Concord
288.	13 April 1853 To "Mr. Editor." Described in Clara Louise Dentler, *A Privately-owned Collection of Letters, Autographs and Manuscripts* (Florence, Italy: privately printed, 1947), p. 44.	[———?]
289.*	April [1853] From Loring H. Austin. ViU, Barrett Collection, 6345–e, incomplete.	Lincoln, Mass.
290.*	18 June 1853 To Eben Loomis. CtY, Box 8, Folder 90 (typescript).	Concord
291.*	29 July 1853 To James Spooner. MPlPS.	Concord
292.*	12 October 1853 To Michael Flannery. ViU, Barrett Collection, 6345–e.	Concord
293.	before 25 October 1853 From James Munroe & Co. Implied in 28 October 1853 *Journal*, 5:459.	[Boston]
294.	25 October 1853 From James Munroe & Co. CSmH, FI 4243. Sophia Thoreau's holograph of 24 February 1862 contains quotation from 25 October 1853 letter. Printed in Harding, p. 305.	Boston

295.*	[October 1853] From William Ellery Channing. MCo, Surveying Papers.	[Concord]
296.	22 November 1853 To [Francis Underwood]. NN, Berg Collection. Printed in Bliss Perry, *Park-Street Papers* (Boston and New York: Houghton Mifflin, 1908), p. 216.	Concord
297.	before 2 December 1853 From Francis Underwood. Mentioned in *Atlantic Monthly* (November 1907): 661.	[Boston]
298.	2 December 1853 To Francis Underwood. Printed in Perry, *Park-Street Papers*, p. 217.	Concord
299.	5 December 1853 From Francis Underwood. NN, Berg Collection. Printed in Harding, pp. 308–309.	Boston
300.	before 19 December 1853 From H. G. O. Blake. Mentioned in 19 December 1853 letter to Blake.	[Worcester]
301.	19 December 1853 To Spencer Baird. NNPM, MA 2108(1) and (2). Printed in Walter Harding, *Mr. Thoreau Declines an Invitation* (Richmond, Virginia: Attic Press, 1956), unpaged.	Concord
302.**	19 December 1853 To H. G. O. Blake. NjP, Taylor Collection. Printed in Emerson (1865), pp. 98–103.	Concord
303.*	[1853] From Louis Agassiz. MH (printed form letter addressed to Thoreau). Printed in Cameron, *Companion*, pp. 194–97.	Cambridge

1854

304.	1 January 1854 From Ralph Waldo Emerson. NNPM, MA 920. Printed in Harding, p. 317.	Concord
305.	18 January 1854 From L. Marett. CSmH, HM 13198. Printed in Harding, p. 318.	Concord

306.	21 January 1854 To H. G. O. Blake. Privately owned. Printed in Emerson (1865), p. 104.	Concord
307.	before 15 February 1854 From Ralph Waldo Emerson. Mentioned in *Atlantic Monthly* (June 1892): 751.	[Concord]
308.	23 February 1854 From Thomas Smith. NN, Berg Collection. Printed in Harding, p. 321.	New York
309.	before 25 February 1854 From George Thatcher. Mentioned in 25 February 1854 letter to Thatcher.	[Bangor]
310.	25 February 1854 To George Thatcher. ViU, Barrett Collection, 6345–e. Printed in Harding, pp. 321–22.	Concord
311.	1 March 1854 To Thaddeus W. Harris. MH, VA 111 50.6(1854). Printed in Cameron, *Minerva*, p. 481.	Concord
312.	before 3 March 1854 To Horace Greeley. Mentioned in 6 March 1854 letter from Greeley.	[Concord]
313.	3 March 1854 To Horace Greeley. Mentioned in 6 March 1854 letter from Greeley.	[Concord]
314.*	6 March 1854 From Horace Greeley. NNPM, R–V, 12C, MA 610.	New York
315.**	6 March 1854 From Horace Greeley. ViU, Barrett Collection, 7669. Printed in Sanborn, *Thoreau* (1882), pp. 238–39.	New York
316.	before 23 March 1854 To Horace Greeley. Implied in 23 March 1854 letter from Greeley.	[Concord]
317.	23 March 1854 From Horace Greeley. NjP, Taylor Collection. Printed in Harding, pp. 324–25.	New York
318.*	30 March 1854 To Ralph Waldo Emerson. MH, C 7495L.1854.3.30.	[Concord]

319.	2 April 1854 From Horace Greeley. Printed in Sanborn, *Thoreau* (1882), p. 240.	New York
320.	18 April 1854 To Thaddeus W. Harris. MH, ALS file. Printed in Harding, p. 326.	Concord
321.*	3 May 1854 To [Edmund] Hosmer. NNPM, MA 1302:23 (draft); laid in.	Concord
322.	May 1854 From Charles Scribner. CSmH, HM 954 (printed form letter requesting information for the *Cyclopædia of American Literature*). Printed in Harding, pp. 326–27.	New York
323.	after May 1854 To Charles Scribner. Since the *Cyclopædia of American Literature* contains a biographical notice of Thoreau, it can be assumed that Thoreau replied to the May 1854 letter from Scribner.	[Concord]
324.	10 June 1854 From Ticknor & Fields. MH, bMs Am 1185. Printed in Harding, p. 328.	Boston
325.	25 June 1854 To Thaddeus W. Harris. Mentioned in 27 June 1854 letter from Harris.	[Concord]
326.	27 June 1854 From Thaddeus W. Harris. NNPM, V–27 1B (1835–60), MA 920. Printed in Harding, p. 329.	Cambridge
327.**	8 August 1854 To H. G. O. Blake. ViU, Barrett Collection, 6345-e. Printed in Emerson (1865), pp. 107–10.	Concord
328.*	11 August 1854 To James T. Fields. Described in Paul C. Richards Autographs, catalog 141, item 16.	[Concord]
329.	12 August 1854 From Daniel Ricketson. CSmH, HM 6895. Printed in Ricketson, pp. 25–31.	New Bedford, Mass.
330.	13 August 1854 From Thomas Wentworth Higginson. Described in	Newburyport, Mass.

Calendar of Correspondence of Henry D. Thoreau 359

	C. F. Libbie & Co., Garfield Sale Catalog, 27–28 January 1914, item 1565. Printed in Harding, p. 336.	
331.*	31 August 1854 From Richard Fuller. Privately owned.	Boston
332.*	11 September 1854 From Catherine V. [Devero]. Privately owned.	Millbury, Mass.
333.	before 15 September 1854 From Sarah E. Webb. Mentioned in 15 September 1854 letter to Webb.	Brooklyn
334.	15 September 1854 To Sarah E. Webb. NN, Berg Collection. Printed in Harding, p. 337.	Concord
335.	17 September [1854] From Marston Watson. MPlPS, K.xx.5 (typescript). Printed in Harding, pp. 337–38.	Plymouth, Mass.
336.	19 September 1854 To Marston Watson. CSmH, HM 13205. Printed in *Familiar Letters* (1894), p. 280.	Concord
337.	before 21 September 1854 From H. G. O. Blake. Mentioned in 21 September 1854 letter to Blake.	[Worcester]
338.**	21 September 1854 To H. G. O. Blake. VtMiM and MPlPS. Printed in *Familiar Letters* (1894), p. 281.	Concord
339.	27 September [1854] From Marston Watson. MPlPS, K.xx.4 (typescript). Printed in Harding, pp. 339–40.	Plymouth
340.	30 [September] 1854 From Marston Watson. MPlPS, K.xx.6 (typescript). Printed in Harding, p. 340.	Plymouth
341.	1 October 1854 To Daniel Ricketson. CSmH, HM 7010. Printed in Emerson (1865), pp. 111–12.	Concord
342.*	4 October 1854 To Marston Watson. MPlPS.	Concord

343.	5 October 1854 To H. G. O. Blake. NN, Berg Collection, copy by Blake. Printed in *Familiar Letters* (1894), p. 282.	Concord
344.	before 6 October 1854 From William Thomas. Implied in 6 October 1854 letter from Thomas.	Philadelphia
345.	before 6 October 1854 To William Thomas. Mentioned in 6 October 1854 letter from Thomas.	[Concord]
346.*	6 October 1854 From William Thomas. Privately owned.	Philadelphia
347.	12 October 1854 From Daniel Ricketson. Printed in Ricketson, pp. 32–34.	New Bedford, Mass.
348.	14 October 1854 To H. G. O. Blake. Privately owned. Printed in *Familiar Letters* (1894), pp. 282–83.	Concord
349.	14 October 1854 From A. Fairbanks. CSmH, HM 954. Printed in Harding, pp. 345–46.	Providence
350.	23 October 1854 To Thaddeus W. Harris. NN, Berg Collection. Printed in Harding, p. 346.	Concord
351.	26 October 1854 From C. B. Bernard. NN, Berg Collection. Printed in Harding, p. 347.	Akron
352.**	30 October 1854 To Charles Sumner. InU. Printed in Harding, p. 347.	Concord
353.	31 October 1854 From Charles Sumner. TxU, Thoreau Letters. Printed in Harding, p. 348.	Boston
354.*	[October 1854] From Mary Moody Emerson. ViU, Barrett Collection, 6248-a.	[Concord]

Calendar of Correspondence of Henry D. Thoreau 361

355.*   1 November 1854   New Orleans
From A. Rouquette. Privately owned.

356.   4 November 1854   [Concord]
To A. Fairbanks. Mentioned in 6 November 1854 letter from Fairbanks.

357.   6 November 1854   Providence
From A. Fairbanks. CSmH, HM 954. Printed in Harding, pp. 348–49.

358.*   6 November 1854   East Princeton, Mass.
From Daniel Foster. Privately owned.

359.   13 November 1854   Concord
To A. Rouquette. MH, 278.5 (draft). Printed in Harding, p. 349.

360.   15 November 1854   Concord
To Bronson Alcott. MH; incomplete, signature missing. Printed in Harding, p. 350.

361.   15 November 1854   Concord
To Thaddeus W. Harris. MH, ALS file. Printed in Harding, pp. 350–51.

362.   17 November 1854   Concord
To William Sheldon. MH, 278.5(17) (draft). Printed in Harding, p. 351.

363.   20 November 1854   Concord
To C. B. Bernard. MH, 278.5(17F) (draft fragment). Printed in Harding, p. 352.

364.   23 November 1854   New York
From Horace Greeley. Described in Anderson Art Galleries Catalog, 28 February 1917.

365.   before 25 November 1854   [Nantucket]
From Andrew Whitney. Implied in 27 November 1854 letter from Whitney.

366.   25 November 1854   [Concord]
To Andrew Whitney. Mentioned in 27 November 1854 letter from Whitney.

367.   27 November 1854   Nantucket
From Andrew Whitney. CSmH, HM 954. Printed in Harding, pp. 352–53.

368.	5 December 1854 To Charles Sumner. MH, bMS Am 1–25–134. Printed in Harding, p. 353.	Concord
369.	14 December 1854 From Daniel Ricketson. Mentioned in Ricketson, p. 280.	[New Bedford, Mass.]
370.	before 19 December 1854 To Walter Mitchell. Mentioned in 19 December 1854 letter to Ricketson.	[Concord]
371.**	19 December 1854 To H. G. O. Blake. ViU, Barrett Collection, two leaves; one leaf privately owned; approximately two leaves missing. Complete printing in Emerson (1865), pp. 112–16.	Concord
372.	19 December 1854 To Daniel Ricketson. CSmH, HM 7011. Printed in Ricketson, pp. 34–35.	Concord
373.	20 December 1854 From Daniel Ricketson. Printed in Ricketson, p. 35.	New Bedford, Mass.
374.	22 December 1854 To H. G. O. Blake. Privately owned. Part of one line and signature have been removed and rewritten by Blake. Printed in *Familiar Letters* (1894), p. 289.	Concord
375.	22 December 1854 To Jocelyn & Co. Henry Seidel Canby, *Thoreau* (Boston: Houghton Mifflin, 1939), p. 476, states that there is manuscript of a letter of this date to Jocelyn & Co. at VtMiM in which Thoreau states he is prepared to supply graphite for stereotype use. However, the library has no such manuscript; it is possible that the location of the manuscript is in error and the manuscript is owned by a private collector.	[Concord]
376.	after 22 December 1854 From H. G. O. Blake. Implied in 22 December 1854 letter to Blake.	[Worcester]
377.	[1854–1856] From William Tuttle. CSmH, HM 954. Printed in Harding, p. 462.	[———?]

1855

378. 4 January 1855 — New Bedford, Mass.
      From Daniel Ricketson. Printed in
      Ricketson, p. 36.

379. 6 January 1855 — Concord
      To Daniel Ricketson. CSmM, HM 7012.
      Printed in Ricketson, pp. 36–37.

380. 9 January 1855 — New Bedford, Mass.
      From Daniel Ricketson. Printed in
      Ricketson, pp. 37–39.

381.* 25 January 1855 — Brattleboro, Vt.
      From Ann E. Brown. Privately owned.

382. 26 January 1855 — New Bedford, Mass.
      From Daniel Ricketson. Printed in
      Ricketson, pp. 39–40.

383. [30 January] 1855 — Salop, Shropshire, England

      From Thomas Cholmondeley. MCo, Hosmer Collection, tipped in grangerized Salt biography at p. 114. Printed in *Atlantic Monthly* (December 1893): 742–43, where it is dated 20 January 1855.

384. 30 January 1855 — Hampton Falls, N. H.

      From F. B. Sanborn. Described in Walter R. Benjamin Autographs, "The Collector" (November 1977), item K–856. Printed in Sanborn, *Thoreau* (1882), pp. 196–97.

385.* 1 February 1855 — Concord
      To [Ann E.] Brown. VtU, Pringle
      Herbarium, 855–151–1.

386.** 1 February 1855 — Concord
      To Daniel Ricketson. ICarbS. Printed
      in Ricketson, p. 40.

387. 2 February 1855 — Concord
      To F. B. Sanborn. ViU, Barrett Collection,
      3127. Printed in *Familiar Letters* (1894), p. 300.

388. 7 February 1855 — Concord
      To Thomas Cholmondeley. Privately owned.
      Printed in *Familiar Letters* (1894), pp. 295–98.

389.*	14 February 1855 From Elizabeth Oakes Smith. Privately owned.	Brooklyn
390.	19 February 1855 To Elizabeth Oakes Smith. MCo, Bernstein Collection. Printed in Harding, pp. 372–73.	Concord
391.	27 February 1855 To Thaddeus W. Harris. ViU, Barrett Collection. Printed in Harding, p. 373.	Concord
392.*	29 February 1855 To Mrs. Brown. ViBlbV.	Concord
393.	12 March 1855 To Charles Sumner. MH, bMS AM 1–27–64. Printed in Harding, p. 374.	Concord
394.**	13 April 1855 To George W. Curtis. ICarbS. Printed in Cameron, *Companion,* p. 207.	Concord
395.*	20 April 1855 To George William Curtis. ViU, Barrett Collection.	Concord
396.	30 April 1855 [To Ticknor & Fields]. NN, Berg Collection. Printed in Harding, p. 375.	Concord
397.	before 27 June 1855 From H. G. O. Blake. Implied in 27 June 1855 letter to Blake.	[Worcester]
398.	27 June 1855 To H. G. O. Blake. Privately owned (last of five leaves a copy by B. B. Thatcher). Printed in *Familiar Letters* (1894), pp. 301–303.	Concord
399.	8 July 1855 To H. G. O. Blake. Printed in *Familiar Letters* (1894), pp. 303–304.	N. Truro, Mass.
400.	before 14 July 1855 From H. G. O. Blake. Implied in 14 July 1855 letter to Blake.	[Worcester]
401.	14 July 1855 To H. G. O. Blake. Printed in *Familiar Letters* (1894), pp. 304–305.	N. Truro, Mass.

Calendar of Correspondence of Henry D. Thoreau 365

402.**   3 August 1855   Concord
         To Dix & Edwards. ViU, Barrett Collection,
         6345-e. Printed in Harding, p. 379.

403.**   8 August 1855   Concord
         To George William Curtis. ICarbS. Printed
         in Harding, p. 379.

404.   17 August 1855   New York
         From Horace Greeley. Privately owned.
         Printed in Harding, p. 380.

405.*   August–September 1855   [Concord]
         To [George William Curtis]. TxU, Thoreau
         Letters (draft).

406.   7 September 1855   Concord
         To Horace Greeley. NNPM, V–2 71B (1835–60),
         MA 920. Printed in Harding, p. 381.

407.   23 September 1855   New Bedford, Mass.
         From Daniel Ricketson. Printed in
         Ricketson, pp. 40–42.

408.**   26 September 1855   Concord
         To H. G. O. Blake. ViU, Barrett Collection,
         6345-e. Printed in Emerson (1865), pp. 116–19.

409.   27 September 1855   Concord
         To Daniel Ricketson. CSmH, HM 7013.
         Printed in Emerson (1865), pp. 120–21.

410.   29 September 1855   Boston
         From Ticknor & Fields. MH, fms Am 1185, 4:758.
         Printed in Harding, p. 387.

411.*   3 October 1855   East Bridgewater, Mass.
         From William Allen. CtW and privately owned.

412.   3 October [1855]   [England]
         From Thomas Cholmondeley. NN, Berg
         Collection. Printed in Harding, pp. 387–88.

413.   12 October 1855   Concord
         To Daniel Ricketson. CSmH, HM 7009.
         Printed in Emerson (1865), pp. 122–24.

414.   13 October 1855   New Bedford, Mass.
         From Daniel Ricketson. Printed in
         Ricketson, pp. 47–48.

415.	13 October 1855 From Daniel Ricketson. Printed in Ricketson, pp. 48–49.	New Bedford, Mass.
416.	16 October 1855 To Daniel Ricketson, VtMiM, Thoreau Letters. Printed in Emerson (1865), pp. 125–26.	Concord
417.*	17 October 1855 To Charles Sumner. MHi, Whitwell Collection.	Concord
418.	18 October 1855 From Daniel Ricketson. Printed in Ricketson, p. 51.	New Bedford, Mass.
419.	26 October 1855 From John Chapman. NN, Berg Collection, and VtMiM, M–2–253. Printed in Harding, pp. 395–96.	London
420.*	30 October 1855 From Kennedy Furlong. Privately owned.	New York
421.	2 November 1855 To E. W. Gardiner. Mentioned in 10 November 1855 letter from Gardiner.	[Concord]
422.	2 November 1855 From John Chapman. NN, Berg Collection. Printed in Harding, p. 396.	London
423.	8 November 1855 To Thomas Cholmondeley. NN, Berg Collection, copy in an unknown hand. Printed in Harding, pp. 397–99.	Concord
424.	*circa* 9 November 1855 From Crosby & Nichols. MH, 278.5(13); incomplete. Printed in Harding, p. 400.	[———?]
425.*	10 November 1855 From E. W. Gardiner. Privately owned.	Nantucket
426.*	[25 November 1855] From Frank Bellew. MCo, Surveying Papers.	Concord
427.*	4 December 1855 From Daniel Ricketson. Privately owned.	New Bedford, Mass.

428. 9 December 1855   Concord
      To H. G. O. Blake. Printed in Emerson
      (1865), pp. 126–29.

429.* 22 December 1855   New Bedford, Mass.
      From Daniel Ricketson. Privately owned.

430. 25 December 1855   Concord
      To Daniel Ricketson. CSmH, HM 7014.
      Printed in Emerson (1865), pp. 130–31.

431.** 26 December 1855   Boston
      From Ralph Waldo Emerson. Paul C. Richards
      Autographs, catalogue 144, item 174.
      Printed in *Atlantic Monthly* (June 1892): 751.

432. 1855   [Concord]
      To Ticknor & Fields. Described in Anderson Galleries
      Catalogue, 16 February 1906, as concerning changes
      in proof, perhaps for *Walden*. Since *Walden* was pub-
      lished a year earlier, the proof may be for his *Cape Cod*
      articles published in *Putnam's Monthly Magazine* in
      1855.

                                1856

433. before 18 January 1856   [Rochester, Mich.]
      From Calvin Greene. Mentioned in 18 January
      1856 letter to Greene.

434. 18 January 1856   Concord
      To Calvin Greene. NjP, Taylor Collection.
      Printed in Jones, p. 27.

435. before 31 January 1856   [Rochester, Mich.]
      From Calvin Greene. Implied in 10 February
      1856 letter to Greene.

436. 10 February 1856   Concord
      To Calvin Greene. NjP, Taylor Collection.
      Printed in Jones, p. 31.

437.** 26 February 1856   New Bedford, Mass.
      From Daniel Ricketson. Printed in
      Ricketson, pp. 53–57.

438. 27 February 1856   New York
      From Gerret Smith et al. MH, 278.5(13D),
      printed form letter (petition).

439.	29 February 1856 From Daniel Ricketson. Printed in Ricketson, p. 57.	[New Bedford, Mass.]
440.	2 March 1856 From Horace Greeley. Privately owned. Photostat of manuscript has been misplaced by owner.	[Washington]
441.*	3 March 1856 From Daniel Ricketson. Privately owned.	New Bedford, Mass.
442.	4 [March] 1856 From Horace Greeley. Excerpt and description in Charles F. Libbie & Co., Garfield Sale Catalogue, 27–28 January 1914, item 1566.	Washington
443.	5 March 1856 To Daniel Ricketson. CSmH, HM 7015. Printed in Emerson (1865), pp. 131–33.	Concord
444.	7 March 1856 From Daniel Ricketson. MCo, Hosmer Collection, tipped in grangerized Salt biography at p. 116. Printed in Ricketson, pp. 61–64.	New Bedford, Mass.
445.	after 7 March 1856 From Daniel Ricketson. MCo, Hosmer Collection, tipped in grangerized Salt biography at p. 116. Printed in Ricketson, p. 64.	New Bedford, Mass.
446.	10 March 1856 To Horace Greeley. Mentioned in 12 March 1856 letter from Greeley.	[Concord]
447.	12 March 1856 From Horace Greeley. Privately owned. Printed in Harding, p. 419.	Washington
448.	before 13 March 1856 From H. G. O. Blake. Implied in 13 March 1856 letter to Blake.	[Worcester]
449.	13 March 1856 To H. G. O. Blake. ViU, Barrett Collection, 6345-e. Printed in Emerson (1865), pp. 134–37.	Concord

Calendar of Correspondence of Henry D. Thoreau 369

450.*	17 April 1856 To Eben Loomis. CtY, Box 8, Folder 90 (typescript).	Concord
451.	before 30 April 1856 To Horace Greeley. Mentioned in 30 April 1856 letter from Greeley.	[Concord]
452.	30 April 1856 From Horace Greeley. VtMiM, M–2, 251. Printed in Harding, pp. 422–23.	New York
453.	5 May 1856 To Horace Greeley. Mentioned in 7 May 1856 letter from Greeley.	[Concord]
454.*	7 May 1856 From Horace Greeley. Description in Paul C. Richards Autographs, catalogue 142, item 189.	New York
455.*	10 May 1856 From Daniel Ricketson. Privately owned.	New Bedford, Mass.
456.	before 21 May 1856 From H. G. O. Blake. Implied in 21 May 1856 letter to Blake.	[Worcester]
457.	21 May 1856 To H. G. O. Blake. MHi. Printed in Emerson (1865), pp. 137–39.	Concord
458.	*circa* 21 May 1856 From Calvin Greene. Mentioned in 31 May 1856 letter to Greene.	[Rochester, Mich.]
459.	27 May 1856 To Thaddeus W. Harris. MH, ALS file. Printed in Harding, p. 425.	Concord
460.	31 May 1856 To Calvin Greene. NjP, Taylor Collection. Printed in Jones, p. 34.	Concord
461.*	31 May 1856 To John Russell. Described in Paul C. Richards Autographs, Catalogue 142, item 143. Printed in Richard Lebeaux, "An Unpublished Letter to Russell," *Thoreau Society Bulletin*, no. 151 (Spring 1980): 3–4.	Concord

462. before 12 June 1856 [Rochester, Mich.]
From Calvin Greene. Implied in 21 June
1856 letter to Greene.

463.* 12 June 1856 Worcester
From Sophia Thoreau. Reference in 12 June
1856 *Journal*, 8:377.

464. 21 June 1856 Concord
To Calvin Greene. NjP, Taylor Collection.
Printed in *Familiar Letters* (1906), pp. 411–12.

465.** [12 July 1856] Concord
From Mary Moody Emerson. ViU, Barrett Collection,
6248-a. Printed in Sanborn, *Critic*, 344.

466.** 17 July [1856] Concord
From Mary Moody Emerson. ViU, Barrett Collection,
6248-a. Printed in Sanborn, *Critic*, 345.

467.* before 21 July 1856 [———?]
From John Russell. Reference in 21 July
1856 *Journal*, 8:421.

468. 1 September 1856 Concord
To Bronson Alcott. MH, Pratt Papers, 59M–312(156),
copy by Alcott. Printed in Emerson (1865), p. 140.

469. 2 September 1856 Concord
To Daniel Ricketson. CSmH, HM 7016.
Printed in Ricketson, pp. 66–67.

470.* 4 September 1856 [Walpole, N.H.]
From Bronson Alcott. MH, copy in Alcott's Journal,
pp. 817–18. Printed in Frederick Wagner, "Eighty-six
Letters (1814–1882) of A. Bronson Alcott (Part Two),"
STUDIES IN THE AMERICAN RENAISSANCE 1980, p. 205.

471. 4 September 1856 Providence
From B. B. Wiley. NN, Berg Collection.
Printed in Harding, pp. 431–32.

472. before 5 September 1856 [Concord]
To Addison Brown. Mentioned in Davenport, 37.

473. before 5 September 1856 [———?]
From Addison Brown. Mentioned in Davenport, 37.

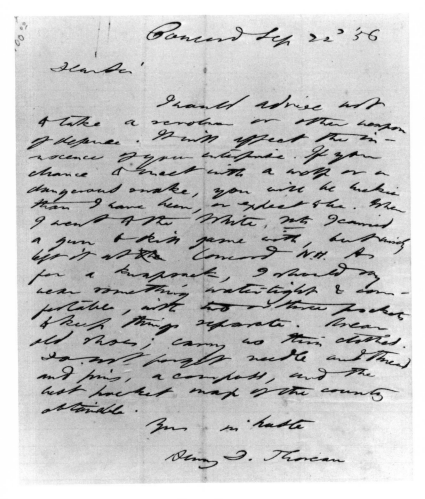

PLATE ELEVEN
Thoreau's letter of 22 September 1856 to B. B. Wiley.
Courtesy InU

474.*   22 September 1856   Concord
To B. B. Wiley. InU. Printed in Goodspeed's
catalogue 189 (1929), item 247.

475.   23 September 1856   Concord
To Daniel Ricketson. MCo, Hosmer Collection,
tipped in grangerized Salt biography at p. 116.
Printed in Ricketson, pp. 67–68.

476.   24 September 1856   New Bedford, Mass.
From Daniel Ricketson. Printed in Ricketson,
pp. 68–69.

477.   [September 1856]   [———?]
From Sarah Ripley. NN, Berg Collection.
Printed in Harding, p. 434.

478.   20 October 1856   Concord
To Thomas Cholmondeley. NN, Berg Collection,
copy by Sophia Thoreau. Printed in Harding,
pp. 435–37.

479.   31 October 1856   Providence
From B. B. Wiley. NN, Berg Collection.
Printed in Harding, pp. 437–38.

480.*   October 1856   [Concord]
To Marcus Spring. MCo (draft fragment).

481.   October 1856   [Perth Amboy, N.J.]
From Marcus Spring. Mentioned in F. B.
Sanborn, *The Life of Henry David Thoreau* (Boston
and New York: Houghton Mifflin, 1917), p. 380.

482.   1 November 1856   Perth Amboy, N.J.
To Sophia Thoreau. CSmH, HM 7017. Printed
in *Familiar Letters* (1894), pp. 335–39.

483.   before 19 November 1856   [Worcester]
From H. G. O. Blake. Implied in 19 November
1856 letter to Blake.

484.   19 November 1856   Perth Amboy, N.J.
To H. G. O. Blake. VtMiM and MCo (draft).
Printed in Emerson (1865), p. 141.

485.   6–7 December 1856   Concord
To H. G. O. Blake. NN, Berg Collection.
Printed in Emerson (1865), pp. 143–48.

Calendar of Correspondence of Henry D. Thoreau 373

486.	12 December 1856 To B. B. Wiley. NN, Berg Collection. Printed in Emerson (1865), pp. 148–50.	Concord
487.	16 December 1856 From Thomas Cholmondeley. Printed in *Atlantic Monthly* (December 1893): 746–47.	Rome
488.	21 December 1856 From B. B. Wiley. NN, Berg Collection. Printed in Harding, pp. 456–60.	Chicago
489.	31 December 1856 To H. G. O. Blake. VtMiM, Thoreau Letters. Printed in Emerson (1865), pp. 151–52.	Concord

1857

490.	6 February 1857 To H. G. O. Blake. NN, Berg Collection, copy by Blake. Printed in Harding, p. 465.	Concord
491.	16 February 1857 From Ticknor & Fields. MH, bMS Am 1185, 5:637. Printed in Harding, pp. 466–67.	Boston
492.*	17 February 1857 From [Isaiah Williams]. MH, 278.5(13) (fragment).	Buffalo
493.	22 February 1857 From Thomas Cholmondeley. NN, Berg Collection. Printed in *Atlantic Monthly* (December 1893): 751–52.	London
494.	23 February 1857 From John Burt. MH, 278.5(13). Printed in Harding, p. 468.	Bellvale, N.Y.
495.	26 February 1857 To John Burt. MWiW-C. Printed in Harding, p. 469.	Concord
496.	27 February 1857 From Ticknor & Fields. MH, bMS Am 1185, 5:660. Printed in Harding, p. 469.	Boston
497.**	8 March 1857 To Mary H. Brown. Excerpt and description in Sotheby-	Concord

Parke Bernet catalogue, 26 May 1980, item 1025. Partial printing in Davenport, 37.

498.* circa 16 March 1857 [Concord]
To Thomas Cholmondeley. NNPM, MA 595 (draft).

499.** 28 March 1857 Concord
To Daniel Ricketson. ViU, Barrett Collection, 6345-e.
Printed in Ricketson, pp. 70–71.

500.   29 March 1857 New Bedford, Mass.
From Daniel Ricketson. Printed in Ricketson,
pp. 71–72.

501.* [March–July 1857] Concord
To [?] Adams. NNPM, 1302:30 (draft); laid in.
Printed in Cameron, *Companion*, p. 216.

502.   1 April 1857 Concord
To Daniel Ricketson. MCoMx, on loan to the Thoreau
Lyceum. Printed in *Familiar Letters* (1906),
pp. 305–306.

503.   7 April 1857 Chicago
From B. B. Wiley. NN, Berg Collection.
Printed in Harding, pp. 473–75.

504.   before 16 April 1857 [————?]
From Caroline C. Andrews. Mentioned in
16 April 1857 letter to Andrews.

505.   16 April 1857 Concord
To Caroline C. Andrews. ICarbS. Printed
in Harding, p. 475.

506.   17 April 1857 Concord
To H. G. O. Blake. VtMiM. Printed in
Familiar Letters (1894), pp. 357–59.

507.* 20 April 1857 [Concord]
To Eben Loomis. Reference in Loomis Diary,
CtY, Loomis-Wilder Papers, Box 16, Folder 313.

508.* 21 April 1857 [Cambridge]
From Eben Loomis. NNPM. Reference in 21
April 1857 *Journal*, 9:332.

509.   26 April 1857 Concord
To B. B. Wiley. NN, Berg Collection.
Printed in Emerson (1865), pp. 153–54.

510.	13 May 1857 To Daniel Ricketson. CSmH, HM 7018. Printed in Carl Bode, "Thoreau Finds a House," *Saturday Review of Literature*, 29 (20 July 1946): 15.	Concord
511.*	15 May 1857 From Daniel Ricketson. Privately owned.	New Bedford, Mass.
512.*	16 May 1857 To Daniel Ricketson. Printed in Americana Mail Auction catalogue, 20 October 1980, item 211.	Concord
513.	26 May 1857 From Thomas Cholmondeley. NN, Berg Collection. Printed in Harding, p. 480.	London
514.	before June 1857 To [John Langdon Sibley]. NNPM, MA 1302:30 (envelope only); laid in.	[Concord]
515.*	1 June 1857 To [John Langdon Sibley]. ViU, Barrett Collection, 6345-e.	Concord
516.	before 6 June 1857 From H. G. O. Blake. Mentioned in 6 June 1857 letter to Blake.	[Worcester]
517.	6 June 1857 To William Ellery Channing. Mentioned in 6 June 1857 letter to Blake.	[Concord]
518.	6 June 1857 To H. G. O. Blake. Printed in *Familiar Letters* (1894), pp. 359–60.	Concord
519.*	circa 21 June 1857 To [?]. NNPM, draft attached to p. 170 of MA 1302:29. Printed in Cameron, *Companion*, p. 217.	[Concord]
520.	23 June 1857 To H. G. O. Blake. CtWaG. Printed in *Familiar Letters* (1894), pp. 359–60.	Concord
521.	before 8 July 1857 From Calvin Greene. Mentioned in 8 July 1857 letter to Greene.	[Rochester, Mich.]

522.	8 July 1857 To Calvin Greene. NjP, Taylor Collection. Printed in Jones, p. 42.	Concord
523.*	11 July 1857 To Eben Loomis. CtY, Box 8, Folder 90 (typescript).	Concord
524.	11 July 1857 To George Thatcher. NN, Berg Collection. Printed in Hill, *Two Thoreau Letters*.	Concord
525.	14 July 1857 From [Edwin Brown]. NN, Berg Collection (fragment). Printed in Harding, p. 487.	Boston
526.*	20 July 1857 From Marston Watson. NNPM. Excerpts in 8 August 1857 *Journal*, 10:3.	Plymouth
527.	17 August 1857 To Marston Watson. Printed in *Familiar Letters* (1894), pp. 360–62.	Concord
528.**	18 August 1857 To H. G. O. Blake. TxU, Thoreau Letters. Printed in Emerson (1865), pp. 155–57.	Concord
529.	18 August 1857 To Daniel Ricketson. NNPM, MA 920. Printed in Emerson (1865), pp. 157–59.	Concord
530.*	19 August 1857 From Daniel Ricketson. Privately owned.	New Bedford, Mass.
531.	7 September 1857 From Daniel Ricketson. Printed in Ricketson, p. 76.	New Bedford, Mass.
532.	9 September 1857 To Daniel Ricketson. CSmH, HM 7019. Printed in Emerson (1865), p. 160.	Concord
533.	10 September 1857 From Daniel Ricketson. VtMiM, M–2 248. Printed in Harding, p. 494.	New Bedford, Mass.
534.	12 November 1857 To George Thatcher. VtMiM, Thoreau Letters. Printed in Harding, p. 495.	Concord

Calendar of Correspondence of Henry D. Thoreau 377

535.	before 16 November 1857 From H. G. O. Blake. Implied in 16 November 1857 letter to Blake.	[Worcester]
536.**	16 November 1857 To H. G. O. Blake. MH, bMS AM 1280.214(4) and MiKC. Printed in Emerson (1865), p. 161.	Concord
537.	11 December 1857 From Daniel Ricketson. Printed in Ricketson, pp. 77–79.	New Bedford, Mass.
538.	1857 To Ticknor & Fields. Mentioned in 7 December 1858 letter from Ticknor & Fields.	[Concord]
539.	1857 From Ticknor & Fields. Mentioned in 7 December 1858 letter from Ticknor & Fields.	Boston

1858

540.	1 January 1858 To George Thatcher. NN, Berg Collection. Printed in Harding, pp. 502–503.	Concord
541.	before 16 January 1858 From Jones Very. Mentioned in 16 January 1858 letter to Very.	[———?]
542.	16 January 1858 To Jones Very. MSaE. Printed in Harding, pp. 503–504.	Concord
543.	23 January 1858 To James Russell Lowell. MH, bMS Am 765. Printed in Harding, p. 504.	Concord
544.	25 January 1858 From [?]. RPB, A 55872[7] (fragment). Printed in Harding, p. 505.	[Athol, Mass.]
545.	27 January 1858 From Thomas Wentworth Higginson. MH, 278.5(17). Printed in Harding, p. 506.	Worcester
546.	28 January 1858 To Thomas Wentworth Higginson. NN, Berg Collection. Printed in *Familiar Letters* (1894), pp. 379–83.	Concord

547.	before 22 February 1858 To James Russell Lowell. Implied in 22 February 1858 letter to Lowell.	Concord
548.	before 22 February 1858 From James Russell Lowell. Implied in 22 February 1858 letter to Lowell.	[Boston?]
549.	22 February 1858 To James Russell Lowell. MH, bMS Am 765(751); incomplete, signature missing. Printed in Harding, p. 509.	Concord
550.	5 March 1858 To James Russell Lowell. MH, bMS Am 1483(443). Printed in Harding, p. 509.	Concord
551.	after March 1858 From James Russell Lowell. Lowell has written "answered" on back of 5 March 1858 letter from Thoreau.	[Boston?]
552.	10 April 1858 From R. Warner. NN, Berg Collection. Printed in Harding, p. 510.	Boston
553.	before 23 April 1858 From Mary H. Brown. Mentioned in before 19 May 1859 letter to Brown.	[——?]
554.*	[23 April 1858] To F. B. Sanborn. ViU, Barrett Collection, 6345-e.	Concord
555.	after 23 April 1858 To Mary H. Brown. Excerpts printed in Davenport, 37–38.	[Concord]
556.*	24 April 1858 To John Langdon Sibley. Excerpt and description printed in Paul C. Richards Autographs, catalogue 15, item 299.	Concord
557.	25 April 1858 To Marston Watson. MPlPS, cxxxiv.6 Printed in *Familiar Letters* (1894), pp. 362–64.	Concord
558.	26 April 1858 From B. B. Wiley. NN, Berg Collection. Printed in Harding, pp. 512–14.	Chicago

559.	18 May 1858 To James Russell Lowell. MH, bMS Am 1484.1 (492). Printed in Harding, p. 514.	Concord
560.*	18 May 1858 From [W. R. Palmer]. MH, 278.5(13A) (fragment).	Washington
561.*	18 May 1858 From R. Warner. ICarbS, VFM 1098. Printed in *Henry David Thoreau, 1817–1862* (Detroit: Wayne State University Library, 1962), pp. 9–10.	Boston
562.	24 May 1858 From James Russell Lowell. Notation "answered 24th May" appears on back of 18 May 1858 letter to Lowell.	[Boston]
563.	1 June 1858 To H. G. O. Blake. MCo, Hosmer Collection, tipped in grangerized Salt biography at p. 130. Printed in Harding, pp. 514–15.	Concord
564.*	18 June 1858 From Daniel Ricketson. Privately owned.	New Bedford, Mass.
565.	22 June 1858 To James Russell Lowell. MH, bMS Am 765 (751). Printed in Canby, *Thoreau*, pp. 375–76.	Concord
566.	29 June 1858 To H. G. O. Blake. Printed in *Familiar Letters* (1894), pp. 385–86.	Concord
567.	before 30 June 1858 From Daniel Ricketson. Three notes received from Ricketson; mentioned in 30 June 1858 letter to Ricketson.	[New Bedford, Mass.]
568.	30 June 1858 To Daniel Ricketson. Printed in Emerson (1865), pp. 168–69.	Concord
569.	1 July 1858 To H. G. O. Blake. Printed in *Familiar Letters* (1894), pp. 385–86.	Concord
570.	before 18 August 1858 From George William Curtis. Implied in 18 August 1858 letter to Curtis.	[New York]

571.	18 August 1858 To George William Curtis. VtMiM, Thoreau Letters. Printed in Cook, p. 67.	Concord
572.	[1 September 1858] To James Russell Lowell. Excerpt and description printed in Merwin-Clayton Co., Moulton Sale Catalogue, 9 November 1905.	Concord
573.*	27 September 1858 To Eben Loomis. CtY, Loomis-Wilder Collection, Box 8, Folder 10 (photostat).	Concord
574.	4 October 1858 To James Russell Lowell. MH, bMS Am 765(751). Printed in Harding, pp. 520–21.	Concord
575.	31 October 1858 To Daniel Ricketson. CSmH, HM 7021. Printed in Ricketson, pp. 69–70.	Concord
576.	3 November 1858 From Daniel Ricketson. Printed in Ricketson, pp. 81–83.	New Bedford, Mass.
577.*	5 November 1858 From John O. Wattles. Privately owned.	Moneka, Kansas
578.	6 November 1858 To Daniel Ricketson. CSmH, HM 7022. Printed in Emerson (1865), pp. 170–72.	Concord
579.	10 November 1858 From Daniel Ricketson. Printed in Ricketson, pp. 86–88.	New Bedford, Mass.
580.	22 November 1858 To Daniel Ricketson. CSmH, HM 7020. Printed in Ricketson, pp. 88–89.	Concord
581.	26 [November 1858] From Thomas Cholmondeley. NN, Berg Collection. Printed in *Atlantic Monthly* (December 1893): 755.	Montreal
582.	1 December 1858 From Thomas G. Cary, George Livermore, and Henry G. Denny. MH, printed form letter, not Thoreau's copy. Printed in Cameron, *Minerva*, p. 486.	Boston

583.	6 December 1858 To Daniel Ricketson. VtMiM, Thoreau Letters. Printed in Ricketson, p. 89.	Concord
584.	before 7 December 1858 To Ticknor & Fields. Mentioned in 7 December 1858 letter from Ticknor & Fields.	[Concord]
585.	before 7 December 1858 From Ticknor & Fields. Mentioned in 7 December 1858 letter from Ticknor & Fields.	Boston
586.	7 December 1858 From Ticknor & Fields. MH, bMS Am 1185, 6:688. Printed in Harding, p. 532.	Boston
587.	15 December 1858 From Ticknor & Fields. MH, bMS Am 1185, 6:697. Printed in Harding, pp. 532–33.	Boston
588.	19 December 1858 To John Langdon Sibley. CtY, 2 A 8–10. Printed in Harding, p. 533.	Concord

1859

589.	before 1 January 1859 To William Ellery Channing. Mentioned in 1 January 1859 letter to Blake.	[Concord]
590.	before 1 January 1859 From H. G. O. Blake. Implied in 1 January 1859 letter to Blake.	[Worcester]
591.	before 1 January 1859 From William Ellery Channing. Mentioned in 1 January 1859 letter to Blake.	[———?]
592.	1 January 1859 To H. G. O. Blake. Described in C. F. Libbie & Co., Hathaway-Richardson Sale Catalogue, 9–10 May 1911. Printed in Emerson (1865), pp. 173–78.	Concord
593.	7 January 1859 From Henry Walker Frost. NNPM, MA 605 (fragment). Printed in Harding, p. 539.	Boston
594.	before 19 January 1859 From H. G. O. Blake. Mentioned in 19 January 1859 letter to Blake.	[Worcester]

595.	19 January 1859 To H. G. O. Blake. Printed in *Familiar Letters* (1894), pp. 405–406.	Concord
596.	21 January 1859 From Thomas G. Cary and Henry G. Denny. MH, printed form letter, not Thoreau's copy. Printed in Cameron, *Minerva*, p. 487.	Boston
597.	7 February 1859 To H. G. O. Blake. NN, Berg Collection, copy by Blake. Printed in Harding, p. 542.	Concord
598.	9 February 1859 From Daniel Ricketson. Printed in Ricketson, p. 89.	New Bedford, Mass.
599.**	before 11 February 1859 To Henry G. Denny. Privately owned. Printed in Cameron, *Minerva*, p. 489.	Concord
600.	11 February 1859 From Henry G. Denny. Privately owned. Printed in Harding, p. 545.	Boston
601.	12 February 1859 To Daniel Ricketson. CSmH, HM 7023. Printed in Ricketson, pp. 92–94.	Concord
602.*	16 February 1859 From Sophia Ripley. TxU, 818 T 39A2, vol. 1. Printed in Joseph J. Moldenhauer, "A Recently-Discovered Addition to the Thoreau Correspondence," *Thoreau Society Bulletin*, no. 84 (Summer 1963): 4.	Concord
603.	6 March 1859 From Daniel Ricketson. Printed in Ricketson, pp. 94–98.	New Bedford, Mass.
604.	6 April 1859 From Charles C. Shackford. Mentioned in 13 April 1859 letter to Shackford.	[Lynn, Mass.]
605.	7 April 1859 To Charles C. Shackford. Mentioned in 13 April 1859 letter to Shackford.	[Concord]
606.*	12 April 1859 From J. M. Macrum. Privately owned.	Pittsburgh
607.*	13 April 1859 To Charles C. Shackford. MH, 278.5(13D), draft.	Concord

Calendar of Correspondence of Henry D. Thoreau 383

608.*	16 April 1859 To Jonathan Buffum. NNPM, laid in front of MA 606, draft.	Concord
609.*	after 16 April 1859 From Charles C. Shackford. MCo, Surveying Papers.	Lynn, Mass.
610.*	22 April 1859 From Hobart & Robbins. NNPM, MA 1302:38; laid in. Printed in Cameron, *Companion*, p. 222.	Boston
611.	before 19 May 1859 From Mary H. Brown. CSmH, HM 13206, fragment. Printed in Harding, pp. 550–51.	[Brattleboro, Vt.]
612.	19 May 1859 To Mary H. Brown. VtMiM, Thoreau Letters. Printed in Cook, p. 68.	Concord
613.*	4 June 1859 From Simon Brown, David Heard, John W. Simonds, and Samuel H. Rhoades. MCo.	[Concord]
614.	30 June 1859 To David Heard. Mentioned in 1 July 1859 letter from Heard.	[Concord]
615.*	1 July 1859 From David Heard. MCo, Surveying Papers.	Wayland, Mass.
616.	8 July 1859 To David Heard. VtMiM, Thoreau Letters. Printed in Harding, p. 552.	Concord
617.*	25 July 1859 From Jonathan Hill. MCo, Surveying Papers.	Billerica, Mass.
618.	26 July 1859 From Lucas Brothers. MH, 278.5(13F). Printed in Harding, p. 553.	Baltimore
619.	30 July 1859 To William A. Wilson. Described in George MacManus Co., catalogue 257. Printed in Harding, p. 553.	Concord
620.*	8 August 1859 From [?]. NN, Berg Collection, fragment.	Philadelphia

621.	12 August 1859 From Thomas H. Mumford. NN, Berg Collection. Printed in Harding, p. 554.	Philadelphia
622.	18 August [1859] From Welch, Bigelow & Co. NN, Berg Collection. Printed in Harding, p. 554.	Cambridge
623.	22 August 1859 From Hobart & Robbins. NN, Berg Collection. Printed in Harding, p. 555.	Boston
624.	25 August 1859 To George Thatcher. PHi, Gratz Collection, Case b, Box 36. Printed in Harding, pp. 555–56.	Concord
625.	before 5 September 1859 From E. G. Dudley. Implied in 5 September 1859 letter to Dudley.	[Boston]
626.	5 September 1859 To E. G. Dudley. RPB A 55872(5). Printed in Harding, p. 557.	Concord
627.**	26 September 1859 To H. G. O. Blake. TxU, Thoreau Letters. Printed in Emerson (1865), pp. 179–82.	Concord
628.	5 October 1859 From Edward Bangs. VtMiM, M–2 250. Printed in Harding, p. 559.	Boston
629.	14 October 1859 From Daniel Ricketson. Printed in Ricketson, pp. 99–101.	New Bedford, Mass.
630.	10 October [1859] From Theophilus Brown. NN, Berg Collection. Printed in Harding, p. 562.	Worcester
631.**	31 October [1859] To H. G. O. Blake. TxU, Thoreau Letters. Printed in *Familiar Letters* (1894), p. 413.	Concord
632.	31 October 1859 From Charles W. Slack. NN, Berg Collection (telegram). Printed in Harding, p. 564.	Boston

Calendar of Correspondence of Henry D. Thoreau 385

633.	*circa* 31 October 1859 From Charles W. Slack. Mentioned in 31 October 1859 telegram from Slack.	[Boston]
634.*	7 November 1859 From Mary J. Tappan. Privately owned.	Bradford, N.H.
635.	19 November 1859 From Moncure D. Conway. NRU, MS Collection, 1859 N 19. Printed in Harding, pp. 564–65.	Cincinnati
636.	23 November 1859 To Moncure D. Conway. NRU, MS Collection, 1859 N 23 (draft). Printed in Harding, p. 565.	Concord
637.	before 24 November 1859 From Calvin Greene. Implied in 24 November 1859 letter to Greene.	[Rochester, Mich.]
638.	24 November 1859 To Calvin Greene, NjP, Taylor Collection. Printed in Jones, p. 46.	Concord

1860

639.	9 January 1860 From R. Allison. NN, Berg Collection. Printed in Harding, p. 569.	Cincinnati
640.	[9 January 1860] From Edward Bangs. NN, Berg Collection. Printed in Harding, p. 569.	Boston
641.	9 January 1860 From Hobart & Robbins. NN, Berg Collection. Printed in Harding, p. 570.	Boston
642.	15 January 1860 From Daniel Ricketson. Printed in Ricketson, pp. 101–103.	New Bedford, Mass.
643.*	17 January [1860] From Samuel Ripley Bartlett. CSmH, HM 13206.	Boston
644.	19 January 1860 To Samuel Ripley Bartlett. DLC, Bancroft-Bliss Container 14 (draft). Printed in Harding, p. 572.	Concord

645.*	19 January 1860 To Ticknor & Fields. CSmH, HM 13206 (draft).	Concord
646.	23 January 1860 From Chauncey Smith. CSmH, HM 13192. Printed in Harding, p. 573.	Boston
647.*	1 February 1860 From R. Redington. NN, Berg Collection (Nature Notes).	[———?]
648.	6 February 1860 From James Redpath. VtMiM, M-2 254. Printed in Harding, pp. 574–75.	[New York]
649.	7 February 1860 From Welch, Bigelow & Co. NN, Berg Collection. Printed in Harding, p. 576.	Cambridge
650.	9 February 1860 From Henry Williams, Jr. MH, printed form letter to members of Harvard Class of 1837; not Thoreau's copy. Printed in Harding, p. 576.	Boston
651.*	24 February 1860 From W. R. Palmer. NN, Berg Collection.	Washington
652.*	17 March [1860] From Edwin Morton. Privately owned.	Peterboro, N.Y.
653.	22 March 1860 From Jane Andrews. MH, 278.5(9). Printed in Harding, p. 577.	Newburyport, Mass.
654.	20 April 1860 From L. Johnson & Co. NNPM, R–V 12 C (Nature Notes). Printed in Harding, p. 577.	Philadelphia
655.	2 May 1860 From L. Johnson & Co. NNPM, MA 610. Printed in Harding, p. 578.	Philadelphia
656.*	9 May 1860 From L. L. & C. H. Smith. MCoA.	New York
657.	before 10 May 1860 From H. G. O. Blake. Implied in 20 May 1860 letter to Blake.	[Worcester]

Calendar of Correspondence of Henry D. Thoreau 387

658.	20 May 1860 To H. G. O. Blake. CCS. Printed in Emerson (1865), pp. 182–85.	Concord
659.	[23 May 1860] From Abby Alcott. NN, Berg Collection. Printed in Harding, p. 580.	Concord
660.	1 June 1860 From Chauncey Smith. CSmH, HM 13206. Printed in Harding, p. 581.	Boston
661.**	23 June 1860 To E. H. Russell. NjP, Taylor Collection. Printed in Harding, p. 603.	Concord
662.	8 July 1860 To Sophia Thoreau. NNPM, V–2 71B (1835–60), MA 920. Printed in *Familiar Letters* (1894), pp. 419–21.	Concord
663.	before 12 July 1860 From C. Morse. CSmH, HM 20592. Printed in Harding, p. 583.	Rochester, N.Y.
664.	12 July 1860 To C. Morse. CSmH, HM 20592, draft. Printed in Harding, p. 583.	Concord
665.	before 16 July 1860 From Benjamin H. Austin. Implied in 16 July 1860 letter to Austin.	[Buffalo]
666.	16 July 1860 To Benjamin H. Austin. NBu. Printed in Harding, p. 584.	Concord
667.	16 July 1860 To Charles Sumner. MH, bMS Am 1 (45–33). Printed in Harding, p. 585.	Concord
668.	27 July 1860 To Welch, Bigelow & Co. NN, Berg Collection, copy in Thoreau's hand. Printed in Harding, p. 586.	Concord
669.	3 August 1860 To H. G. O. Blake. Printed in *Familiar Letters* (1894), pp. 421–22.	Concord

670.	before 31 August 1860 To Charles Ricker. Implied in 31 August 1860 letter from Ricker.	[Concord]
671.	31 August 1860 From Charles Ricker. NN, Berg Collection. Printed in Harding, pp. 588–89.	Lowell, Mass.
672.	31 August 1860 To Charles Ricker. Mentioned in 6 September 1860 letter from Ricker.	[Concord]
673.	[6] September 1860 From Charles Ricker. NN, Berg Collection. Printed in Harding, p. 589	Lowell, Mass.
674.	17 September 1860 To "Publishers of The World." NN, Berg Collection, draft. Holograph described in American Art Association, John Heise Sale Catalogue, 6 May 1915.	Concord
675.	22 September 1860 To A. S. Chase. Mentioned in 5 October 1860 letter from Chase.	[Concord]
676.*	24 September 1860 To R. M. S. Jackson. PSt. Printed in Cameron, *Companion*, p. 223.	Concord
677.	29 September 1860 To Horace Greeley. NN, Manuscript Room. Printed in Harding, p. 590.	Concord
678.	5 October 1860 From A. S. Chase. NN, Berg Collection. Printed in Harding, p. 591.	Waterbury, Conn.
679.	13 October 1860 To Samuel Kneeland. MBN. Printed in Harding, pp. 591–92.	Concord
680.	14 October 1860 From Daniel Ricketson. Privately owned. Printed in Ricketson, pp. 104–106.	New Bedford, Mass.
681.	30 October 1860 From Welch, Bigelow & Co. NN, Berg Collection. Printed in Harding, p. 595.	Cambridge

Calendar of Correspondence of Henry D. Thoreau 389

682. before 4 November 1860   [Worcester, Mass.]
      From H. G. O. Blake. Implied in 4
      November 1860 letter to Blake.

683. before 4 November 1860   [Worcester]
      From Theophilus Brown. Mentioned in 4 November
      1860 letter to Blake.

684. 4 November 1860   Concord
      To H. G. O. Blake. RPB, A 55872(6) (2).
      Printed in Emerson (1865), pp. 188–94.

685. 4 November 1860   Concord
      To Daniel Ricketson. CSmH, HM 7024. Printed in
      Emerson (1865), pp. 186–88.

686.* 17 November 1860   Elmira, N.Y.
      From Isaac Wellington. Privately owned.

687. 26 November [1860]   Cincinnati
      From Moncure D. Conway. NN, Berg Collection.
      Printed in Harding, p. 601.

688. 2 December 1860   Concord
      To H. G. O. Blake. NN, Berg Collection, copy
      by Blake. Printed in Harding, p. 601.

689. 3 December 1860   Boston
      From Hobart & Robbins. NN, Berg Collection.
      Printed in Harding, p. 602.

690. 17 December 1860   Concord
      To Louis A. Surette. CSmH, HM 26183. Printed
      in Harding, p. 602.

1861

691.* 7 January 1861   New York
      From L. L. & C. H. Smith. MH, 278.5(9). Printed
      in Cameron, *Companion,* p. 224.

692. 31 January 1861   Baltimore
      From Joseph Stubbs. NN, Berg Collection, printed
      form letter. Printed in Harding, p. 605.

693. 11 February 1861   [Concord]
      To Frederic Tudor. Mentioned in 12 February
      1861 letter from Tudor.

694.	12 February 1861 From Frederic Tudor (written by Benjamin F. Field). NN, Berg Collection. Printed in Harding, pp. 605–606.	Boston
695.	27 February 1861 From Daniel Ricketson. Printed in Ricketson, pp. 108–11.	[New Bedford, Mass.]
696.	22 March 1861 To Daniel Ricketson. CSmH, HM 7025. Printed in Ricketson, pp. 111–13.	Concord
697.	22 March 1861 From L. Johnson & Co. NN, Berg Collection. Printed in Harding, p. 608.	Philadelphia
698.*	31 March 1861 To George Thatcher. MeHi.	Concord
699.	9 April 1861 From Parker Pillsbury. Excerpt and description printed in C. F. Libbie & Co., Abbott-Sprague Sale Catalogue, 25–26 February 1909, p. 101.	Concord, N.H.
700.	10 April 1861 To Parker Pillsbury. MB, Mss. Acc. 2653. Printed in Emerson (1865), pp. 195–96.	Concord
701.	13 April 1861 From Parker Pillsbury. Listed in C. F. Libbie & Co., Abbott-Sprague Sale Catalogue, 25–26 February 1909, p. 101.	[Concord, N.H.]
702.	23 April 1861 From Thomas Cholmondeley. NN, Berg Collection. Printed in *Familiar Letters* (1894), pp. 439–43.	Shrewsbury, England
703.	[April 1861] From Mary Mann. CSmH, HM 13192. Printed in Harding, p. 614.	Concord
704.	3 May 1861 To H. G. O. Blake. NHi, Thoreau MS. Printed in Emerson (1865), pp. 196–98.	Concord
705.	11 May 1861 From Ralph Waldo Emerson. MCo, D–2030 K. Printed in Harding, p. 616.	Concord

706.**	15–19 May 1861 To [Cynthia and Sophia Thoreau]. CSmH, HM 13192, draft. Printed in Harding, p. 618.	[Niagara Falls, N.Y.]
707.	22 May [1861] From Robert Collyer. MCoA, D–2030 K. Printed in Harding, p. 617.	Chicago
708.**	27 May 1861 To Sophia Thoreau. CSmH, HM 13192, draft. Printed in *The First and Last Journeys of Thoreau*, ed. F. B. Sanborn (Boston: Bibliophile Society, 1905), 1:44.	St. Paul
709.	before 14 June 1861 To Cynthia Thoreau. Mentioned in Robert L. Straker, "Thoreau's Journey to Minnesota," *New England Quarterly*, 14 (September 1941): 553.	[———?]
710.	before 23 June 1861 From F. B. Sanborn. Mentioned in 25 June 1861 letter to Sanborn.	[Concord]
711.	before 23 June 1861 From Sophia Thoreau. Mentioned in 25 June 1861 letter to Sanborn.	[Concord]
712.	25 June 1861 To F. B. Sanborn. VtMiM. Printed in Emerson (1865), pp. 198–206.	Redwing, Minn.
713.	before 27 June 1861 From Daniel Ricketson. Mentioned in 15 August 1861 letter to Ricketson.	[New Bedford, Mass.]
714.*	28 June 1861 To Dr. Anderson. MnM, Emerson Room.	Milwaukee
715.*	30 June 1861 From Daniel Ricketson. Privately owned.	New Bedford, Mass.
716.	before 15 July 1861 From "Worcester Minister." Mentioned in "A Reminiscence," *National Baptist*, 20 July 1876.	[Worcester]
717.	15 July 1861 To "Worcester Minister." Mentioned in "A Reminiscence," *National Baptist*, 20 July 1876.	Concord

718.	[15] August 1961 To Daniel Ricketson. CSmH, HM 7026. Printed in Ricketson, pp. 113–15.	Concord
719.*	16 August 1861 From Daniel Ricketson. Privately owned.	New Bedford, Mass.
720.	1 September 1861 From Daniel Ricketson. Printed in Ricketson, p. 319.	New Bedford, Mass.
721.	17 September 1861 From Daniel Ricketson. Printed in Ricketson, pp. 115–16.	New Bedford, Mass.
722.	before 11 October 1861 From [M.] Stearns. Mentioned in 11 October 1861 letter to Stone.	[———?]
723.*	11 October 1861 To J. M. Stone. OKentU.	Concord
724.	14 October 1861 To Daniel Ricketson. CSmH, HM 7027. Printed in Ricketson, pp. 116–17.	Concord
725.	13 November 1861 To L. L. & C. H. Smith. VtMiM, draft. Printed in Harding, p. 629.	Concord
726.	15 November 1861 To George Thatcher. NjP, Mather Collection. Printed in Harding, p. 630.	Concord
727.	6 December 1861 From L. Johnson. CSmH, HM 536. Printed in Harding, p. 630.	Philadelphia

1862

728.**	6 January 1862 From Myron Benton. Privately owned. Printed in *Familiar Letters* (1894), pp. 461–62.	Leedsville, N.Y.
729.	1 January 1862 From Daniel Ricketson. Printed in Ricketson, pp. 117–18.	New Bedford, Mass.

730.	10 January 1862 From Theophilus Brown. NN, Berg Collection. Printed in Harding, p. 634.	Worcester
731.	12 January [1862] From F. B. Sanborn. CSmH, HM 954. Printed in Harding, p. 635.	[Concord]
732.	before 11 February 1862 From [James T. Fields]. Mentioned in 11 February 1862 letter to Fields.	[Boston]
733.	11 February 1862 To [James T. Fields]. CSmH, FI 4241, in Sophia Thoreau's hand. Draft by Thoreau in HM 209. Printed in Bode, 384.	Concord
734.	before 18 February 1862 From Ticknor & Fields. Implied in 18 February 1862 letter to Ticknor & Fields.	Boston
735.*	18 February 1862 To Ticknor & Fields. Privately owned.	Concord
736.	20 February 1862 To Ticknor & Fields. CSmH, FI 4244, in Sophia Thoreau's hand. Printed in Bode, 384.	Concord
737.*	23 February 1862 From M. Stearns. Privately owned.	Medford, Mass.
738.	24 February 1862 To Ticknor & Fields. CSmH, FI 4243 in Sophia Thoreau's hand. Printed in Bode, 385.	Concord
739.	28 February 1862 To Ticknor & Fields, CSmH, FI 4242, in Sophia Thoreau's hand. Printed in Bode, 385.	Concord
740.	1 March 1862 To Ticknor & Fields. CSmH, FI 4247, in Sophia Thoreau's hand. Printed in Bode, 386.	Concord
741.	before 4 March 1862 From Ticknor & Fields. Implied in 4 March 1862 letter to Ticknor & Fields.	Boston
742.	4 March 1862 To Ticknor & Fields. CSmH, FI 4246, in Sophia Thoreau's hand. Printed in Bode, 386.	Concord

743.*	10 March 1862 From Sias & Hill. MConA.	Milwaukee
744.	before 11 March 1862 From Ticknor & Fields. Mentioned in 11 March 1862 letter to Ticknor & Fields.	Boston
745.	11 March 1862 To Ticknor & Fields. CSmH, FI 4245, in Sophia Thoreau's hand. Printed in Bode, 386.	Concord
746.	21 March 1862 To Myron Benton. Printed in Emerson (1865), pp. 206–207.	Concord
747.**	23 March 1862 From Daniel Ricketson. Privately owned. Printed in Ricketson, pp. 119–21.	New Bedford, Mass.
748.	30 March 1862 From Daniel Ricketson. Printed in Ricketson, pp. 121–23.	New Bedford, Mass.
749.	2 April 1862 To Ticknor & Fields. CSmH, FI 4248, in Sophia Thoreau's hand. Printed in Carl Bode, "Thoreau's Last Letter," *New England Quarterly*, 19 (June 1946): 244.	Concord
750.*	2 April 1862 From Marston Watson. MPlPS, Box K, Folder XX.	Plymouth
751.	6 April 1862 From Daniel Ricketson. Printed in Ricketson, pp. 123–25.	New Bedford, Mass.
752.	6 April 1862 From Ticknor & Fields. CSmH, HM 945. Printed in Bode, 387.	Boston
753.	13 April 1862 From Daniel Ricketson. Printed in Ricketson, pp. 125–28.	New Bedford, Mass.
754.**	4 May 1862 From Daniel Ricketson. Privately owned. Printed in Ricketson, pp. 128–31.	New Bedford, Mass.

UNDATED

755.   3 May [n.y.]   [———?]
       From Mary Moody Emerson. Excerpt and description in
       C. F. Libbie & Co., Willard Sale Catalogue, 15–16
       February 1910. Printed in Harding, p. 654.

756.   n.d.   [Concord]
       To William Ellery Channing. Printed in
       Sanborn, *Thoreau* (1882), pp. 178–79.

757.   n.d.   [Concord?]
       To Henry Williams, Jr. Printed in Williams,
       Memorials of the Class of 1837 of Harvard
       University, p. 38.

758.* n.d.   [———?]
       From R. Carter. MCoMx, on loan to the
       Thoreau Lyceum.

759.   n.d.   [———?]
       From William Ellery Channing. MH, 278.5(1B).
       Printed in Harding. p. 653.

760.* n.d.   [Concord?]
       To [?]. CSmH, Minnesota Notes, draft fragment.

761.* n.d.   [———?]
       From [?]. ViU, Barrett Collection,
       Miscellaneous Journal MS, fragment.

762.* n.d.   [———?]
       From [?]. VtMiM, fragment laid into
       Thoreau's copy of Gray's *Botany*.

763.* n.d.   [———?]
       To "a publisher." Excerpt in F. M. Holland, "Emerson
       and the Concord School of Philosophy," *Index*, 5
       (7 August 1884): 64.

INDEX TO CORRESPONDENTS

Adams, [?], 501
Adams, Abel, 158
Adams, J. H., Jr., *from*, 241
Agassiz, Louis, 205; *from*, 206, 303
Alcott, Abby, *from*, 659
Alcott, Bronson, 360, 468; *from*, 200, 470
Allen, William, *from*, 411
Allison, R., *from*, 639
Anderson, Dr., 714
Andrews, Caroline C., 505; *from, 504*
Andrews, Jane, *from*, 653
Austin, Benjamin H., 666; *from, 665*

Austin, Loring H., *from,* 289
Bailey, George, *from,* 229
Baird, Spenser, 301
Bangs, Edward, *from,* 628, 640
Bartlett, Samuel Ripley, 644; *from,* 643
Bigelow, A., 21
Bellew, Frank, *from,* 426
Benton, Myron, 746; *from,* 728
Bernard, C. B., 363; *from,* 351
Blake, H. G. O., 170, 175, 204, 209, 213, 219, 222, 228, 237, 239, 265, 268, 279, 287, 302, 306, 327, 338, 343, 348, 371, 374, 398, 399, 401, 408, 428, 449, 457, 484, 485, 489, 490, 506, 518, 520, 528, 536, 563, 566, 569, 592, 595, 597, 627, 631, 658, 669, 684, 688, 704; *from,* 169, *174, 178, 208, 218, 221, 223, 264, 278, 286, 300, 337, 376, 397, 400, 448, 456, 483, 516, 535, 590, 594, 657, 682*
Brown, Addison, 472; *from,* 473
Brown, Ann E., 385; *from,* 381
Brown, Edwin, *from,* 525
Brown, Lucy, 40, 42, 44, 49, 58, 60; *from, 41.*
Brown, Mary H., 497, 555, 612; *from,* 553, 611
Brown, Mrs., 392
Brown, Simon, *from,* 613
Brown, Theophilus, *from,* 630, *683,* 730
Brownson, Orestes A., 11; *from,* 55
Buffum, Jonathan, 608
Burt, John, 495; *from,* 494
Cabot, James Elliot, 141, 145, 166; *from,* 139, *140,* 143, 146
Cabot, Samuel, *from,* 215, 238
Carter, R., *from,* 758
Cary, Thomas G., *from,* 582, 596
Channing, William Ellery, 119, *517, 589,* 756; *from,* 72, 73, 120, 295, *591,* 759
Chapman, John, *from,* 419, 422
Chase, A. S., *675; from,* 678
Cholmondeley, Thomas, 388, 423, 478, 498; *from,* 383, 412, 487, 493, 513, 581, 702
Colburn, M. M., *from,* 214
Collyer, Robert, *from,* 707
"Concord Town Clerk," 37
Conway, Moncure D., 636; *from,* 635, 687
Crosby & Nichols, *from,* 424
Curtis, George William, 269, 282, 394, 395, 403, 405, 571; *from,* 570
Cushing, William, *from,* 242
Dale, William J., *from,* 241

Denny, Henry G., 599; *from,* 582, 596, 600
Devero, Catherine V., *from,* 332
Dix & Edwards, 402
Dudley, E. G., 626; *from, 625*
Dunbar, Charles H., *from,* 220
Duyckinck, Evert, 144, 147, 148, 149
Emerson, Ellen, 207
Emerson, Lidian, 78, 88, 91, 105; *from,* 87
Emerson, Mary Moody, *from,* 354, 465, 466, 755
Emerson, Ralph Waldo, 50, 59, 62, 63, 65, 66, 68, 80, 83, 91, 99, 102, 106, *154,* 157, 160, 162, 163, 165, 167, 179, 225, 318; *from,* 23, 25, 39, 61, 64, 77, 86, 93, 101, 108, 110, 124, 125, 132, 159, 164, 168, 216, 217, 304, *307,* 431, 705
Emerson, William, *152; from, 113*
"Faculty of Harvard College," 1
Fairbanks, A., 356; *from,* 349, 357
Fields, James T., 328, 733; *from, 732*
Flannery, Michael, 292
Forbes, Franklin, 232; *from,* 231
Ford, Sophia, *156; from,* 155
Foster, Daniel, *from* 358
Frost, Henry Walker, *from,* 593
Froude, James Anthony, *from,* 210
Fuller, Margaret, *from,* 36, 47, 103
Fuller, Richard, 57, 70; *from, 69,* 331
Furlong, Kennedy, *from,* 420
Gardiner, E. W., *421; from,* 425
Greeley, Horace, 129, *130, 135, 171,* 177, *181, 186,* 189, 224, *246, 248, 256, 258, 261, 270, 272, 276, 281, 312, 313, 316,* 406, *446, 451, 453,* 677; *from,* 121, 131 133, 136, 172, 173, 176, 180, 185, 187, 247, 249, 250, 255, 257, 259, 260, 262, 271, 275, 283, *284,* 285, 314, 315, 317, 319, *364,* 404, *440,* 442, 447, 452, 454
Greene, Calvin, 434, 436, 460, 464, 522, 683; *from, 433, 435, 458, 462, 521,* 637
Greenough, William W., *from,* 241
Griswold, Rufus, 46
Harris, Thaddeus W., 240, 311, 320, *325,* 350, 361, 391, 459; *from,* 326
Haskins, David Greene, 14, 31; *from,* 20, 241
Hawkins, Henry, *12*
Hawthorne, Nathaniel, 199; *from,* 184, 188, 198
Hawthorne, Sophia, *from,* 111
Hayward, Charles, *from, 13*
Heard, David, *614,* 616; *from,* 613, 615

Calendar of Correspondence of Henry D. Thoreau 397

Hecker, Isaac, 115, 117; *from,* 114, 116, 142, 212, 243
Higginson, Thomas Wentworth, 252, 254, 546; *from,* 236, *251, 253,* 330, 545
Hill, Jonathan, *from,* 617
Hoar, Elizabeth, *from,* 74
Hobart & Robbins, *from,* 610, 623, 641, 689
Hosmer, Edmund, 321
Howe, Samuel G., 38
Jackson, R. M. S., 676
James, Henry, Sr., *from,* 76
Jocelyn & Co., 375
Johnson, L., & Co., *from,* 654, 655, 697, 727
Kneeland, Samuel, 679
Lane, Charles, *127; from,* 85, 112, 126, 128
Livermore, George, *from,* 582
Loomis, Eben, 290, 450, 507, 523, 573; *from,* 508
Lowell, James Russell, 543, *547,* 549, 550, 559, 565, 572, 574; *from, 548, 551, 562*
Lucas Brothers, *from* 618
Macrum, J. M., *from,* 606
Mann, Mary, *from,* 703
Marett, L., *from,* 305
McKean, H. S., 109
Mitchell, Walter, 370
Morse, C., 664; *from,* 663
Morton, Edwin, *from,* 652
"Mr. Editor," 288
Mumford, Thomas H., *from,* 621
Munroe, James, & Co., 118, 123, 150, 161; *from, 293,* 294
O'Sullivan, J. L., 96; *from,* 95
Palmer, W. R., *from,* 560, 651
Peabody, A. G., *from,* 2
Peabody, Elizabeth Palmer, 203; *from,* 67
Pierce, Josiah, *234; from,* 230, *233,* 235
Pillsbury, Parker, 700; *from,* 699, *701*
"Publishers of The Dial," 92
"Publishers of The World," 674
Quincy, Josiah, *from,* 17
Redington, R., *from,* 647
Redpath, James, *from,* 648
Rhoades, Samuel H., *from,* 613
Rice, Charles Wyatt, 5; *from,* 4
Richardson, James, Jr., *from,* 6, 56
Ricker, Charles, *670, 672; from,* 671, 673
Ricketson, Daniel, 341, 372, 379, 386, 409, 413, 416, 430, 443, 469, 475, 499, 502, 510, 529, 532, 568, 575, 578, 580, 583, 601, 685, 696, 718, 724; *from,* 329, 347, 369, 373, 378, 380, 382, 407, 414, 415, 418, 427, 429, 437, 439, 441, 444, 445, 455, 476, 500, 511, 512, 530, 531, 533, 537, 564, 567, 576, 579, 598, 603, 629, 642, 680, 695, *713,* 715, 719, 720, 721, 729, 747, 748, 751, 753, 754
Ripley, Sarah, *from,* 477
Ripley, Sophia, *from,* 602
Rouquette, A., 359; *from,* 355
Russell, E. H., 661
Russell, John, 461; *from,* 467
Sanborn, F. B., 387, 554, 712; *from,* 384, *710,* 731
Scribner, Charles, *323; from,* 322
"Secretary of the Association for the Advancement of Science," *from,* 280
Sewall, Ellen, *34; from,* 35
Shackford, Charles C., 605, 607; *from, 604,* 609
Sheldon, William, 362
Sias & Hill, *from,* 743
Sibley, John Langdon, 514, 515, 556, 588
Simonds, John W., *from,* 613
Slack, Charles W., *from,* 632, 633
Smith, Chauncey, *from,* 646, 660
Smith, Elizabeth Oakes, 390; *from,* 389
Smith, Gerret, *from,* 438
Smith, L. L. & C. H., 725; *from,* 656, 691
Smith, Thomas, *from,* 308
Sparks, Jared, 211
Spooner, James, 291
Spring, Marcus, 480; *from, 481*
Stearns, M., *from,* 722, 737
Stevens, D. W., *from,* 122
Stone, J. M., 723
Storer, Horatio R., 137; *from,* 134
Stubbs, Joseph, *from,* 692
Sumner, Charles, 226, 352, 368, 393, **417,** 667; *from,* 227, 353
Surette, Louis A., 690
Sweetser, William, 267; *from,* 266
Tappan, Mary J., *from,* 634
Thatcher, George, 183, 190, 194, 196, 201, 202, 310, 524, 534, 540, 624, 698, 726; *from, 182, 193,* 309
Thomas, William, *345; from, 344, 346*
Thoreau, Cynthia, 75, 84, 90, 98, **100,** 104, 706, *709; from,* 89
Thoreau, Helen, 9, 22, 28, 32, 81, **94,** 107; *from,* 97
Thoreau, John, Jr., 10, 15, 16, 19
Thoreau, John, Sr., 84
Thoreau, Sophia, 79, 153, 263, 482, 662, 706, 708; *from,* 463, *711*
Ticknor & Co., *191, 195; from, 192,* 197

Ticknor & Fields, 396, 432, 538, 584, 645, 735, 736, 738, 739, 740, 742, 745, 749; *from*, 324, 410, 491, 496, 539, 585, 586, 587, 734, 741, 744, 752
Tudor, Frederic, 693; *from*, 694
Tuttle, William, *from*, 377
Underwood, Francis, 296, 298; *from*, 297, 299
Very, Jones, 542; *from*, 541
Vose, Henry, 3, 7, 18, 71; *from*, 8
Waldo, Giles, *from*, 82
Warner, R., *from*, 552, 561
Watson, Marston, 245, 274, 336, 342, 527, 557; *from*, 244, 273, 335, 339, 340, 526, 750
Wattles, John O., *from*, 577
Webb, Sarah E., 334; *from*, 333

Welch, Bigelow & Co., 668; *from*, 622, 649, 681
Wellington, Isaac, *from*, 686
Wheeler, Charles Stearns, 24, 26, 29, 52; *from*, 27, 30
Whitney, Andrew, 366; *from*, 365, 367
Wiley & Putnam, 127
Wiley, B. B., 474, 486, 509; *from*, 471, 479, 488, 503, 558
Williams, Henry, Jr., 151, 757; *from*, 138, 650
Williams, Isaiah, 45, 51, 54; *from*, 43, 48, 53, 492
Wilson, William A., 619
Wood, Elijah, 277
"Worcester Minister," 717; *from*, 716
Unidentified, 33, 288, 519, 760, 763*; *from*, 544, 620, 761, 762

INDEX TO LIBRARIES

Boston Museum of Science (MBN), 679
Boston Public Library (MB), 118, 161, 177, 700
Boston University (MBU), 78, 102, 202
Brown University (RPB), 19, 71, 129, 544, 626, 684
Bruce Museum (CtGreB), 88
Buffalo and Erie County Public Library (NBu), 666
Chapin Library, Williams College (MWiW-C), 495
Columbia University (NNC), 65, 93
Concord Antiquarian Society (MCoA), 656, 707, 743
Concord Free Public Library (MCo), 25, 37, 64, 210, 213, 260, 295, 383, 390, 426, 444, 445, 475, 480, 484, 563, 609, 613, 615, 617, 705
Essex Institute (MSaE), 199, 542
Folger Shakespeare Library (DFo), 58
Fruitlands Museums (MHarF), 112, 149
Gunn Memorial Library (CtWaG), 520
Harvard University (MH), 49, 124, 138, 151, 179, 192, 197, 205, 211, 220, 225, 226, 239, 240, 241, 269, 303, 311, 318, 320, 324, 359, 360, 361, 362, 363, 368, 393, 410, 424, 438, 459, 468, 470, 491, 492, 494, 496, 536, 543, 545, 549, 550, 559, 560, 565, 574, 582, 586, 587, 596, 607, 618, 650, 653, 667, 691, 759
Haverford College (PHC), 123

Henry E. Huntington Library (CSmH), 3, 16, 54, 80, 90, 94, 96, 104, 107, 110, 114, 115, 116, 117, 263, 271, 277, 294, 305, 322, 329, 336, 341, 349, 357, 367, 372, 377, 379, 409, 413, 430, 443, 469, 482, 510, 532, 575, 578, 580, 601, 611, 643, 645, 646, 660, 663, 664, 685, 690, 696, 703, 706, 708, 718, 724, 727, 731, 733, 736, 738, 739, 740, 742, 745, 749, 752, 760
Indiana University (InU), 59, 352, 474
Iowa, University of (IaU), 268
Kalamazoo College (KiMC), 536
Kent State University (OKentU), 723
Library of Congress (DLC), 644
Maine Historical Society (MeHi), 698
Marietta College (OMC), 15
Massachusetts Historical Society (MHi), 33, 158, 417, 457
Middlebury College (VtMiM), 72, 81, 109, 120, 136, 137, 183, 187, 227, 274, 338, 416, 419, 452, 484, 489, 506, 533, 534, 571, 583, 612, 616, 628, 648, 712, 725, 762
Middlesex School (MCoMx), 502, 758
Minneapolis Public Library (MnM), 714
New-York Historical Society (NHi), 84, 704
New York Public Library (NN), 6, 7, 9, 10, 22, 23, 39, 43, 46, 48, 50, 51, 53, 61, 68, 79, 86, 91, 95, 99, 105, 106,

108, 125, 132, 144, 148, 159, 162, 164, 165, 168, 170, 184, 204, 216, 224, 230, 231, 235, 236, 237, 259, 266, 267, 279, 296, 299, 308, 334, 343, 350, 351, 396, 412, 419, 422, 423, 471, 477, 478, 479, 485, 486, 488, 490, 493, 503, 509, 513, 524, 525, 540, 546, 552, 558, 581, 597, 620, 621, 622, 623, 630, 632, 639, 640, 641, 647, 649, 651, 659, 668, 671, 673, 674, 677, 678, 681, 687, 688, 689, 692, 694, 697, 702, 730
Notre Dame, University of (InNd), 11
Paulist Fathers Archives (NNPa) 142, 212, 243
Pennsylvania Historical Society (PHi), 150, 203
Pennsylvania State University (PSt), 676
Perkins School for the Blind (MWatP), 38
Pierpont Morgan Library (NNPM), 2, 8, 28, 36, 45, 55, 56, 57, 76, 77, 100, 111, 172, 188, 198, 206, 217, 249, 276, 287, 301, 304, 314, 321, 326, 406, 498, 501, 508, 514, 519, 526, 529, 593, 608, 610, 654, 655, 662
Pilgrim Society (MPlPS), 244, 291, 335, 338, 339, 340, 342, 557, 750
Princeton University (NjP), 14, 26, 153, 157, 302, 317, 434, 436, 460, 464, 522, 638, 661, 726
Radcliffe College (MCR-S), 141, 145, 166
Rochester, University of (NRU), 635, 636
St. John's Seminary (CCamarSJ), 232
Scripps College (CCS), 658
Southern Illinois University (ICarbS), 5, 103, 242, 386, 394, 403, 505, 561
Texas, University of (TxU), 47, 196, 228, 254, 353, 405, 528, 602, 627, 631
Vermont, University of (VtU), 385
Virginia, University of (ViU), 18, 32, 42, 67, 75, 98, 128, 160, 163, 167, 176, 180, 209, 222, 252, 255, 265, 282, 289, 292, 310, 315, 327, 354, 371, 387, 391, 395, 402, 408, 449, 465, 466, 499, 515, 554, 761
Virginia Polytechnic Institute and State University (ViBlbV), 392
Wesleyan University (CtW), 411
Yale University (CtY), 173, 290, 450, 507, 523, 573, 588

WITHDRAWAL AND RESUMPTION: WHITMAN AND SOCIETY IN THE LAST TWO PARTS OF *SPECIMEN DAYS*

William Aarnes

IN *DRUM TAPS*, Whitman included a two-part poem, "Give Me the Splendid Silent Sun," that addresses a tension embodied in *Specimen Days*—Whitman's desire to retreat to Nature and his equally strong, although contradictory desire for intense involvement in the life of his country. The poem opens with the chant of a poet "tired with senseless excitement, and rack'd by war-strife," and asking for the joys of a more simple life:

> Give me the splendid silent sun with all his beams full-dazzling. . . .
> Give me for marriage a sweet-breath'd woman of whom I should not tire,
> Give me a perfect child, give me away aside from the noise of the world a rural domestic life,
> Give me to warble spontaneous songs recluse by myself, for my own ears only,
> Give me solitude, give me Nature, give me again O Nature your primal sanities!

Although the picture of "domestic life" Whitman draws here may seem uncharacteristic of him, this chant does express that part of him that wishes for a secluded life close to Nature. Yet, while "incessantly" asking for the "primal sanities" of such a life, the poet is at the same time "enchained" by an opposite desire that refuses to give him up and causes him to "adhere to my city." In the second part of the poem, the poet's soul tramples "down what it ask'd for" and demands continued involvement in the city:

> Keep your splendid silent sun,
> Keep your woods O Nature, and the quiet places by the woods, . . .
> Give me faces and streets—give me these phantoms incessant and endless along the trottoirs!
> . . . .
> O such for me! O an intense life, full to repletion and varied!
> The life of the theatre, bar-room, huge hotel, for me!
> The saloon of the steamer! the crowded excursion for me! the torchlight procession![1]

A similar tension between the pull toward solitude in nature and the opposite pull toward involvement in society informs *Specimen Days*. Ostensibly *Specimen Days* divides into four parts: an account of Whitman's formative years, the war memoranda, the nature notes, and the closing travel and literary observations. If we discount the first section—which resembles the fourth in being written later than the other two parts and in being based, to an extent, on Whitman's travels—we can see that *Specimen Days* records three distinct stages in Whitman's involvement in American society. First, the war memoranda record a period of intense social interaction on Whitman's part. Second, the nature notes record Whitman's withdrawal from society to the seclusion of Timber Creek in New Jersey. Third, the remaining notes record Whitman's reinvolvement in society by offering his observations on Eastern cities, the West, and Canada. By presenting Whitman's life as one that includes a period of intense involvement, a period of withdrawal, and a period of reinvolvement, *Specimen Days* reveals Whitman's ambiguous relationship with American society. Indeed, although a dominant thrust of the book is to record a specimen American life that will help reunify the United States, *Specimen Days* is not simply, as Linck C. Johnson calls it, a "story of personal and national success."[2] The book also reflects what Newton Arvin has called Whitman's "genial acceptance and troubled repudiation" of the Gilded Age.[3] It is the work of a writer at times troubled with and unable to identify completely with the society in which he lives.

In this article I will focus on this uneasy relationships as it is revealed in the nature notes that record Whitman's withdrawal from society and in the following notes that chronicle his resumption of social activity. On the whole, these two sections reflect a simple rejection of society in favor of Nature and then a reacceptance of society. But each section (the withdrawal section to a lesser extent than the resumption section) reflects the ambiguity of Whitman's attitude towards society. Whitman's account of his withdrawal is a literary excursion that, in the manner of Thoreau, expresses both Whitman's desire, on the one hand, to effect, as much as is possible with a literary work, a revitalization of society by incorporating the energies of Nature, and, on the other hand, his willingness to reject society for lacking those strengths. In part, Whitman's account of his resumption of social activity paradoxically records a withdrawal from society—an escape from present society into recollecting the past and anticipating death. To the extent Whitman focuses on contemporary American society, however, he shows himself involved in it and trying to celebrate it. In fact, by revising the thinking behind a passage in *Democratic Vistas* that praises American society only to point out its failure, he repeats the praise and responds to the criticism. Yet, despite the overall positive thrust of this last section, Whitman reveals himself, particularly in one confusing note, to be ill at ease with American society.

I. WHITMAN'S WITHDRAWAL

In contrast to the thrust of "Give Me the Splendid Silent Sun" the notes introducing the pages following the war memoranda in *Specimen Days* reveal Whitman, not as willing to "adhere to my city," but as so "tired of ceaseless excitement, and rack'd by war-strife" as to wish, if not to warble, simply to jot "spontaneous" notes "recluse by myself." In these five notes, instead of a "crowded excursion," he both calls for and begins to record an excursion into the solitude of Nature.

In the first of these notes, "An Interregnum Paragraph," Whitman summarizes the years following the Civil War in a way that suggests, as far as significant occurrences are concerned, his life, as his account of it does, shifted almost immediately from involvement in the war to seclusion in Nature. He collapses his account of his life from the end of the war until 1876 into brief mentions of his work "in the Attorney-General's department," his paralytic stroke in 1873, and his move from Washington to Camden, where he was "quite unwell" in " '74 and '75."[4] As recorded in this note, these years simply "elapse"; Whitman treats them as an unimportant interlude between the war and his excursion into Nature. And, having dismissed these years and their events, he begins to focus, at more length, on the subject of the following notes, his retreat at Timber Creek: "—but after that began to grow better; commenc'd going for weeks at a time, even for months, down in the country, to a charmingly recluse and rural spot along Timber Creek, twelve or thirteen miles from where it enters the Delaware river. Domicil'd at the farm-house of my friends, the Staffords, near by, I lived half the time along this creek and its adjacent fields and lanes" (p. 118).

The following introductory notes insist on this focus on the "recluse and rural"—the natural. In "New Themes Entered Upon," Whitman writes that, besides recuperating from his paralysis and the war, he has learned that only Nature permanently wears (pp. 119–20). In "Entering a Long Farm-Lane" and "To the Spring and the Brook," he takes a verbal saunter through his spot at Timber Creek, celebrating his "hobby-liking" for the "farm lane" and "irregular paths" that lead "to the pond, the expansion of the creek" and "to the spring under the willows" (pp. 120–21). In the final introductory note, "An Early Summer Reveille," he sounds a call, not to martial or social duties, but to the neglected virtues of Nature:

> Away then to loosen, to unstring the divine bow, so tense, so long. Away from curtain, carpet, sofa, book—from "society"—from city house, street, and modern improvements and luxuries—away to the primitive winding, aforementioned wooded creek, with its untrimm'd bushes and turfy banks—away from . . . entourage of artificial store, machine, studio, office, parlor—from tailordom and fashion's clothes. . . . Away . . . to the breast of the great silent savage all-acceptive Mother. (pp. 121–22)

To be sure, Whitman intends these five introductory notes to preface *all* the notes coming after the war memoranda. He certainly wants to create a natural atmosphere that will dominate the rest of the book. These five notes serve more particularly, however, to introduce a sequence of notes consisting mostly of nature notes and recording the years 1876, 1877, and 1878, the years Whitman had easy access to Timber Creek because of his friendship with the Staffords.[5] There are two indications that Whitman saw this sequence as discrete. One is the distribution of nature notes. Of the 137 titled notes that follow "An Early Summer Reveille," only forty-seven are nature notes—notes based on Whitman's activities and observations at Timber Creek and other outdoor spots. The other notes are travel observations, pieces on literary figures, and comments on Whitman's intentions in *Specimen Days*. Significantly, forty of the nature notes, along with ten other notes, appear within the 1876–78 period. The second indication is what seems to be a conclusion to the three-year sequence. Because Whitman overlaps travel notes with nature notes in his treatment of 1878, this conclusion may seem oddly placed, coming, as it does, after a record trip to New York. But the last note for 1878, "A Civility Too Long Neglected," seems to

Withdrawal and Resumption: Specimen Days 405

bring the sequence, if not to an end, to a pause that suggests a moving away from a consideration of Nature. In this note Whitman dedicates "the last half of these Specimen Days" to an assortment of insects, weeds, trees, and, in a gesture of leave-taking, "to the spots and memories of those days, and of the creek" (p. 181). Before this note Whitman focuses mostly on Nature; after it, he focuses more on the social than the natural.

In the prefatory notes and the nature notes following them occur some passages that seemingly paraphrase passages from Thoreau's *A Week on the Concord and Merrimack Rivers* and *Walden*. For example, Thoreau writes in *A Week*: "It is not easy to write in a journal what interests us at any time, because to write it is not what interests us."[6] And Whitman writes parenthetically in his nature notes: "(Though perhaps my best moments I never jot down; when they come I cannot afford to break the charm by inditing memoranda. I just abandon myself to the mood, and let it float on, carrying me in its placid extacy)" (p. 134). Thoreau writes in *Walden* that his "greatest skill has been to want but little."[7] Whitman writes that "The trick is, I find, to tone your wants and tastes low down enough, and make much of negatives, and of mere daylight and the skies." (p. 119). Thoreau writes in *Walden*: "I love to be alone. I never found the companion that was so companionable as solitude."[8] And Whitman seems to echo these words: "Here [at Timber Creek] I realize the meaning of that old fellow [Thoreau?] who said he was seldom less alone than when alone" (p. 151).

These parallels merely reinforce what is obvious to anyone reading the nature notes in *Specimen Days*: Whitman's nature observations are comparable to Thoreau's. Although Whitman may get the worse of the comparison[9] and although Whitman's friendship with John Burroughs ("a second Thoreau," Whitman once wrote him in a letter[10]) may have prompted him to note down his nature observations,[11] the comparison of Whitman's nature notes to Thoreau's works needs to be pressed. For within *Specimen Days* Whitman has shaped the nature notes, in ways similar to Thoreau's handling of *A Week* and *Walden*, into a literary excursion. Moreover, if we stress the social concerns of the nature notes,[12] we can see that Whitman like Thoreau has created a record of an excursion embodying the dual intention of criticizing, rejecting, society for lacking the virtues of Nature and of restoring society to those very virtues.

Whitman has selected and ordered his material for the years 1876–78 into a record presenting this period of his life, not as he actually lived it, but as a withdrawal from society, as an extended excursion into Nature. In *Walden* Thoreau presents himself not as someone who "bivouacked' at the pond and at times went home to his family—as, in fact, he did—but as a recluse who isolated himself "within the great ocean of solitude."[13] In the nature notes Whitman's treatment of his actual experience is similar. Particularly in the 1876 and 1877 notes, he deemphasizes his activities with people. Although he includes some notes showing him engaged in family activities—eating "a good breakfast (cook'd by the hands I love, my dear sister[-in-law] Lou's)" (p. 137) —in social occasions (speaking at the anniversary of Thomas Paine's birthday) and in journeys to Atlantic City and New York, he describes little of his actual activity among people. To be sure, Whitman is candid about what he is doing; he suggests that the nature notes are not a complete record of the period they represent: in the footnote to "A Happy Hour's Command" he writes that he lived only "portions of several seasons, especially summers" at Timber Creek (pp. 2–3). Nevertheless, he has collected his notes in such a way that, if *Specimen Days* were the only source available on Whitman's life at this period, we might conclude that, instead of spending only three or four months a year for three years at Timber Creek, Whitman spent most of his time there—and most of that in solitude.

Indeed, the nature notes give only a few hints of the true extent of Whitman's involvement with people and society. Although he mentions Mrs. Anne Gilchrist in a note toward the end of *Specimen Days* as among the "friends of my soul—staunchest friends of my other soul, my poems" (p. 283), his nature notes neither indicate that this passionate woman came from England to Philadelphia in September 1876 to court Whitman nor that he spent some time at her home, living in a room she had set aside for him. In one nature note, "A Night Rememberance," Whitman writes of being down at the pond at Timber Creek "with a friend till after midnight" (p. 179). If this friend is Harry Stafford— there is no way of knowing this for sure—then this note is the only indication in *Specimen Days* of his friendship with this young comrade, an attachment E. H. Miller calls "the emotional experience" of this period of Whitman's life. And despite the few notes reflecting occasional returns to cities and society, the nature notes gives little sense of Whitman's continued, even positive interest in cities. For instance, besides discounting the amount of time he actually spent in Camden and Philadelphia, Whitman includes no record of a trip he took to New York and John Burroughs' home on the Hudson in March 1877. In addition the notes do not indicate that in 1876 Whitman had helped create a transAtlantic controversy over the inadequacy of his reception in America. Nor do we learn that Whitman earned money jobbing *Leaves of Grass*

Withdrawal and Resumption: Specimen Days 407

and *Two Rivulets.*[14] Clearly, Whitman has been selective about what he treats in this three-year sequence.

In "An Early Summer Reveille," he claims that "There is little consecutiveness in dates" (p. 122) in the nature notes. This claim is part of an attempt to suggest that Whitman has treated his nature notes with a fitting naturalness and spontaneity, but it belies his actual practice. Just as Thoreau's record of his excursion in *A Week* embodies the shift from summer to fall, and the latter part of his record of his sojourn at Walden expresses the natural progress from winter to the rebirth of spring, Whitman's notes for the years 1876–78 are arranged to emphasize the rhythm of the seasons. After the five introductory nature notes, Whitman places fourteen notes that he intends as a record of 1876. And, the dates of these pieces, with one exception—a paragraph dated 4 August (p. 131) appears among material from September—follow chronological order. The pieces themselves reflect Whitman's interest in the way "Nature marches in procession" (p. 124), and they record the passage of the seasons from spring ("Birds Migrating at Midnight") through summer ("A July Afternoon by the Pond") and into fall ("Autumn Side-Bits"). The two remaining notes, "A Winter Day on the Sea-Beach" and "Sea-Shore Fancies," while not nature notes, continue to reflect, as the title of the first suggests, the seasonal emphasis Whitman gives his notes for the year. These two notes suggest that winter is a time when Whitman's attention tends to turn away from Nature to more seemingly social activities that cause him to recall the past. Interestingly, in *Walden*, winter is a time for Thoreau to dwell on the past, "to conjure up the former inhabitants of these woods."[15] For Whitman, too, in this sequence of nature notes, winter is a time in which he conjures up the past. A day on the Atlantic City beach reminds him "of 'the mash' and south bay of my native island" (p. 137) and seems to cause him to recall the part the sea-shore plays in his art.

The notes collected in the 1877 sequence repeat the same seasonal pattern found in the 1876 notes. The opening note, "In Memory of Thomas Paine," and the closing note, "Three Young Men's Deaths," are both winter notes in which Whitman dwells on the past. Besides two notes about riding the ferry between Camden and Philadelphia in the winter and again in May and August, the rest of this year's notes are nature notes. Beginning with the "Spring Overtures" Whitman notices in February, they conclude with "The First Frost." In the 1878 sequence, Whitman begins with "February Days" and moves through spring up to the "Clover and Hay Perfume" of early July. After this note, however, in part because Whitman interpolates notes on a June and July trip to New York and John Burroughs' home on the Hudson, the chronological arrangement breaks down,[16] to be restored only briefly before the dedication that concludes the sequence. But, despite this break in the order of the 1878 notes, he has not arranged his notes with "little consecutiveness in dates." Instead, his notes for the years 1876–78 are arranged to suggest the extent to which, for nearly three years, his observations are dependent upon and express the seasonal rhythm of Nature.

In a copy of *A Week* that Thoreau had given him in 1856, Whitman bracketed the following passage, underlining the first three sentences:

> There are other, savager, and more primeval aspects of nature than our poets have sung. It is only white men's poetry. Homer and Ossian even can never revive in London or Boston. And yet behold how these cities are refreshed by the mere tradition, or the imperfectly transmitted fragrance and flavor of these wild fruits. If we could listen but for an instant to the chant of the Indian muse, we should understand why he will not exchange his savageness for civilization. Nations are not whimsical. Steel and baskets are strong temptations: but the Indian does well to continue Indian.[17]

Whitman must have agreed with Thoreau's assessment of "white men's poetry." In another passage Thoreau wrote that, while nature itself did not realize his "youthful conceptions of the woodland depths," "Still less have I seen such strong and wilderness tints on any poet's string." Whitman underlined this complaint.[18] But he also must have been interested that the poetry might be natural enough to "revive in London and Boston" and that cities should be "refreshed" by such writing. And Whitman also must have seen that both *A Week* and *Walden* were records of excursions into Nature that attempt to give "the relief of ... a background, where the pine flourishes and the jay still screams,"[19] to "restore mankind by truly Indian, botanic, magnetic, or natural means."[20] At any rate, his nature notes in *Specimen Days*, which exclude the social and emphasize the natural, are surely an attempt at such writing.

Indeed, it is clear that the nature notes are restorative for Whitman and intended to be so for his readers, for his book, and for American society. Whitman sees the hours he spent at Timber Creek as "soothing, healthy, restoration-hours" (p. 120) that helped him to a "partial recovery" (p. 118) from his paralytic stroke in 1873 and from the effects of "the long strain of the war, and its wounds and death" (p. 120). He also hopes his pages will "serve as cooling breeze ... to some fever'd mouth or latent pulse" (p. 120). Besides celebrating his own partial recovery and hoping that the notes will help the reader, Whitman suggests that the nature notes will have a restorative effect on *Specimen Days*, which in the pages before the nature notes dwells on scenes of wounds and death. In a footnote to "New Themes Entered Upon," he writes, "Without apology for the abrupt change of field and atmosphere—after what I have put in the preceding fifty or sixty pages—temporary episodes, thank heavens!—I restore my book to the bracing and buoyant equilibrium of concrete outdoor Nature, the only permanent reliance for sanity of book or human life" (p. 120).

Whitman has yet another reason for including the nature notes in *Specimen Days*. They restore nature not only to his own book but also to literature, an act he sees as important to American society. In the final note in *Specimen Days*, "Nature and Democracy—Morality," Whitman suggests that Democracy, as well as Art, needs something to restrain it "from excess, morbidity." He points out that "only with Nature" is society "hardy and sane." Whitman stresses this "very old lesson and requisite": "American Democracy, in its myriad personalities, in factories, work-shops, stores, offices—through the dense streets and houses of the cities, and all their manifold sophisticated life—must either be fibred, vitalized, by regular contact with out-door light and air and growths, farm-scenes, animals, fields, trees, birds, sun-warmth and free skies, or it will certainly dwindle and pale" (p. 294). He believes that the "Nature-element" must form the main part of society, that it must "really underlie the whole politics, sanity, religion, and art of the New World" (p. 295). His inclusion of the nature notes in *Specimen Days* is an attempt to bring society back into contact with this essential "Nature-element." But, of course, such an attempt means that Whitman sees society as lacking this "Nature-element." And, indeed, the nature notes are in part a criticism of society for this deficiency.

For Thoreau an excursion into nature, a withdrawal from society, is an opportunity to take a critical stance toward society. To climb a mountain, to journey up a river, to sojourn at Walden is to put oneself, as he puns, in "critical circumstances"[21]—new perspectives from which to evaluate society. Accordingly, when Thoreau records his "uncivil" excursion on the Concord and Merrimack River, he breaks away from the text to interpolate critical commentaries on such "civil" concerns as gardening, religion, the political state, and poetry.[22] His sojourn at Walden also puts him in a place where he can "speak critically."[23] In his nature notes, Whitman, who after all, is adopting a characteristic mode[24] of a man he once described as having "a morbid dislike of humanity,"[25] also writes from similarly "critical circumstances."

Whitman's critical stance in the nature notes is based, like Thoreau's, on the belief that to be close to Nature and away from society is to be closer to what *is* than to what *appears to be*. Whitman establishes this critical perspective most explicitly in "The Lesson of a Tree." The lesson Whitman writes of learning from trees is the difference between natural "*being*, as against the human trait of mere *seeming*" (p. 130). He contrasts "a fine yellow poplar," which "rebukes by its tough and equable serenity all weathers," to "this gusty-temper'd little whiffet, man, that runs indoors at a mite of rain or snow." For Whitman a tree, or any natural object, simply is, and this ability to simply be is what it has to teach man:

> One lesson from affiliating a tree—perhaps the greatest moral lesson anyhow from earth, rocks, animals, is that same lesson of inherency, of *what is,* without the least regard to what the looker-on (the critic) supposes or says, or whether he likes or dislikes. What worse—what more general malady pervades each and all of us, our literature, education, attitude toward each other, (even toward ourselves,) than a morbid trouble about *seems,* (generally temporarily seems too,) and no trouble at all, or hardly any, about the sane, slow-growing, perennial real parts of character, books, friendship, marriage—humanity's invisible foundations and hold-together. (pp. 130–31)

The other nature notes reflect this contrast between the natural as real and the social as seeming. They celebrate the contrast between "the great patches of dingy-blossom'd horse-mint wafting a spicy odor through the air" and "New York's or Philadelphia's streets" (p. 164). They celebrate the real in Nature while rejecting—or ignoring—the unreal manifestations of society.

Perhaps Whitman's strongest criticism of the seeming in society occurs in those notes in which he emphasizes his "satisfaction" (p. 151) with having "Every day, seclusion—every day at least two or three hours of freedom, bathing, no talk, no bonds, no dress, no books, no *manners*" (p. 150). For example, he writes in "A Sun-Bath—Nakedness":

> An hour or so after breakfast I wended my way down to the recesses of the aforesaid dell.... It was just the place and time for my Adamic air-bath and flesh-brushing from head to foot. So hanging clothes on a rail near by, keeping old broadbrim straw on head and easy shoes on feet, haven't I had a good time the last two hours! First with the stiff-elastic bristles rasping arms, breast, sides, till they turn'd scarlet—then partially bathing in the clear waters of the running brook—taking everything very leisurely, with many rests and pauses—stepping about barefooted every few minutes now and then in some neighboring black ooze, for unctuous mud-bath to my feet—a brief second and third rinsing in the crystal running waters—rubbing with the fragrant towel—slow negligent promenades on the turf up and down in the

sun, varied with occasional rests, and further frictions of the bristle-brush . . . feeling quite secure from intrusions, (and that indeed I am not at all nervous about, if it accidentally happens). (pp. 151-52)

Such a passage speaks for itself, but in this case Whitman makes the critical aspect of his activity clear:

> Sweet, same still Nakedness in Nature!—ah if poor, sick, prurient humanity in cities might readily know you once more! Is not nakedness then indecent? No, not inherently. It is your thought, your sophistication, your fear, your respectability, that is indecent. There come moods where these clothes of ours are not only too irksome to wear, but are themselves indecent. Perhaps indeed he or she to whom the free exhilirating extasy of nakedness in Nature has never been eligible (and how many thousands there are!) has not really known what purity is—nor what faith or art or health really is. (p. 152)

As can be seen from "The Lesson of a Tree" and "A Sun-Bath—Nakedness," Whitman's criticism of society in the nature notes rests more on generalized and unfocused contrast than on specific and direct comment. Accordingly, in suggesting that Whitman speaks critically in the nature notes, I am not claiming that, even when he calls humanity "poor, sick prurient," this section contains the explicit, discerning, cutting criticism the 1870s deserve, that Whitman himself calls for, and that he could himself write. Indeed, the criticism he did write in other places is a sharp, yet illuminating contrast to the more implicit comment that is usually suggested by the nature notes.

The years the nature notes deal with, 1876–78, cried for specific critical comment. During these years the United States was suffering through an economic depression that had begun with the financial collapse of 1873. Wages reportedly fell from 37.5% to 60% between 1873 and 1877.[26] There were more workers unemployed than "ever before in [American] history"[27]—3,000,000.[28] One condition of the depression was what was termed the "tramp evil," a problem so bad that "in Massachusetts alone there were said to be a thousand vagabonds roaming the rural communities," forcing people on the outskirts of towns to leave their homes.[29] Another condition was the increasing tension between laborers and their employers. In the summer of 1877, incensed at a 10% pay cut, railroad workers carried out a strike that "half-paralyzed" the railroads in the North and led to riots in which strikers and their supporters fought with police, state militia, and even federal troops. People were killed in Balitmore, Pittsburgh, Reading, Chicago, and other cities before the strike collapsed.[30] Accompanying the depression was a high tariff. In 1875, with the Democrats about to become a majority in the House as a result of the 1874 elections, the Republicans argued that the depression had reduced the government's income and gave the manufacturers an increase in protective tariff rates while also increasing the tax burden on the average American by increasing rates on such items as tobacco and sugar. By the early 1880s the government had "acquired unwieldy surpluses of funds" and "protected industries such as Carnegie's steel companies were reporting profits of more than 200 percent per annum upon their invested capital."[31]

Political events demanded as much critical comment as economic events. The exposures of 1876 revealed the corruption not only of the Grant administration but also of state and local governments.[32] The settlement of the disputed Tilden-Hayes election, although it ended Reconstruction and was accepted by the public, was still a political deal intended to keep the Republicans in power rather than to honor the choice of the voters.[33]

Whitman's response to such economic conditions is most clearly rendered not in *Specimen Days* but in some of the pieces he has assembled in *Collect*. Although he at times suggests that such "morbid facts of American politics and society everywhere are but passing incidents and flanges of our unbounded impetus of growth,"[34] Whitman calls for writing that is critical of what happens in the United States. In "Democracy in the New World," first published in *Two Rivulets* in 1876, he writes, "I can conceive of no better service in the United States, henceforth, by democrats of thorough and heart-felt faith, than boldly exposing the weaknesses, liabilities, and infinite corruption of democracy."[35] He reiterates this call in "Poetry To-day in America—Shakespeare—The Future," first published in 1881. Here he states that there is an "imperative need of a race of giant bards in the future, to hold up high to the eyes of land and race the eternal antiseptic models, and to dauntlessly confront greed, injustice, and all forms of that wiliness and tyranny whose roots never die." We will want to return to the phrase "antiseptic model," but in "Poetry To-day" Whitman stresses "dauntlessly confronting" the evils he lists. He adds parenthetically that this kind of confrontation with social wrongs "is what first class poets are for," and mentions the satirist Juvenal as one of the examples of the kind of poet he means. Moreover, he hopes for not "only poets" but also "newer, larger prophets—larger than Judea's and more passionate —to meet and penetrate those woes, as shafts of light the darkness."[36]

Besides calling for such criticism, Whitman includes *Democratic Vistas* and other pieces critical of economic and political occurrences

Withdrawal and Resumption: Specimen Days 413

in the United States in *Collect*. Two of these pieces in particular seem to address specific issues of the years of Whitman's nature notes. Focusing on economic matters in "The Tramp and Strike Questions," he asserts that wealth stands for evil, for in both Europe and, though to a lesser extent, America wealth "mainly results from, and represents, the rapine, murder, outrages, treachery, hoggishness, of hundreds of years ago, and onward." Strikes are beneficial actions similar to the American and French Revolutions, the latter being itself "a strike ... against ages of bad pay." And the existence of tramps in America is a symptom of a perhaps fatal economic disease, a suggestion that "our republican experiment ... is at heart an unhealthy failure."[37] In "Who Gets the Plunder?" he considers the protective tariffs and the wealthy class they help to create. He writes that there would be "some excuse" for the tariffs if some of the "immense revenue of annual cash" that they help to create "went to the masses of laboring-men." "But," he adds, "the fact itself is nothing of the kind. The profits of 'protection' go altogether to a few score select persons—who, by favors of Congress, State legislatures, the banks, and other special advantages, are forming a vulgar aristocracy, full as bad as anything in the British or European castes, of blood, or the dynastics there of the past."[38] What Whitman writes in these two notes is something to keep in mind when we consider the notes recording his resumption of social activity. For in that section he is not so frank about his concern that the United States, with its very poor and aristocratic rich, might be becoming a failure. But for now I offer these pieces as indications of the kind of criticism of which Whitman was capable, and as contrasts to the way Whitman deals with a specific issue in the nature notes.

In the nature notes Whitman has included only one note that seems to apply specifically to the ills of the 1870s, "November 8, '76." In this note Whitman seems to speak to a particular event—the 1876 Presidential election. But he does not "dauntlessly confront" the issue that election raises. He could have suggested that this election is another instance that proves a point he makes in what was once a general note to *Democratic Vistas*, "General Suffrage, Elections, &c.": that such offices as the Presidency are "arranged, won, by caucusing, money, the favoritism or pecuniary interest of rings, the superior manipulations of the ins over the outs, or the outs over the ins."[39] But, instead of attacking the apparent dishonesty with which the disputed election was settled, he chooses to imply his criticism by writing an "antiseptic model": "The forenoon leaden and cloudy, not cold or wet, but indicating both. As I hobble down and sit by the silent pond, how different from the excitement amid which, in the cities, millions of people are now waiting news of yesterday's Presidential election, or receiving and discussing the result—in this secluded place uncared-for, unknown" (p. 135).

Allan Nevins has described the "excitement amid which" people received the 1876 election results: "In New York crowds assembled before the bulletin boards in such numbers that traffic at certain points was virtually stopped: the second afternoon following the election the multitude in front of the *Herald* office extended across the whole area below City Hall Park and blocked the vehicles on Broadway as far south as Bowling Green. Similar scenes were enacted in other large cities."[40] At the opening of the war memoranda Whitman writes of a similar scene in New York that occurred in response to the news of the bombardment of Fort Sumter (p. 24). On that occasion Whitman was part of the crowd, but in 1876 he shows himself only involved enough to indicate his non-involvement. Rather than discussing the result or buying an extra edition of a newspaper or hearing one read to a crowd, he asserts that he is at a place where the result is not only "unknown" but also "uncared-for." A sentence Whitman had written as the end of this note but omitted when publishing *Specimen Days* makes the "critical circumstances" he is in more explicit: "Important as are the issues of that election I yield myself to try it all by this place and hour under the clear sky, in the final balance and test of Nature in the open air."[41] "To try" the election by the "balance and test of Nature" means to reject the importance of the election. In *A Week* Thoreau wrote, "While I sit here listening to the waves which ripple and break on this shore, I am absolved from all obligations to the past, and the council of nations may reconsider its notes. The grating of a pebble annuls them."[42] Thoreau also wrote in the same work that "To one who habitually endeavors to contemplate the true state of things, the political state can be hardly said to have any existence whatever."[43] Like Thoreau, Whitman has assumed a critical posture in Nature and found that Nature "annuls" the importance of elections, makes them "uncared-for."

And what "November 8, '76" implies about the 1876 election, the nature notes suggest about society. In them Whitman resorts less to explicitly criticizing society than to suggesting that, until society is restored to the "Nature-element," one does best to care only for Nature. These notes suggest, then, that the best criticism of the issues of the day is to ignore them, to withdraw to a place such as Timber Creek so that one can appreciate the *"what is"* in Nature.

II. Resumption

In "November 8, '76" and the other nature notes Whitman seems to make a choice Thoreau delighted in—"not to live in the restless, nervous, bustling, trivial Nineteenth Century, but stand or sit thoughtfully while it goes by."[44] Whitman's nature notes, however, are only one section of an autobiography meant, not to reject the nineteenth century as trivial, but to represent it as "a strange, unloosen'd, wondrous time" (p. 3). Accordingly, in contrast to Thoreau, who has shaped both *A Week* and *Walden* to emphasize his withdrawal from society, but not to recount what occurs when he becomes "a sojourner in civilized life again,"[45] Whitman has so placed his nature notes that, while recording a withdrawal from society, they also seem to record, because they record his recovery of health, his preparation for resuming involvement in society. In the notes following the nature notes Whitman records not a life of seclusion but one of social activity. His notes reflect that he "now and then take[s] long trips, by railroad or boat, hundreds of miles," and keeps his "activity and interest in life, people, progress, and the questions of the day" (p. 291). In fact, even before the end of the nature note section, Whitman records a return to New York in "Death of William Cullen Bryant," "Manhattan from the Bay," and "Human and Heroic New York."

"Death of William Cullen Bryant" is an obituary notice. As such it does not exactly focus on "the questions of the day"; thus, pausing over it will enable us to make some qualifications about the extent to which Whitman addresses such questions in the final section of *Specimen Days*. Although it is the first note to indicate Whitman's return to social concerns, it is an anticipation of notes in the final section that are not considerations of society so much as elegiac pieces that recall the past or prepare for death. For one thing, as in those winter notes in the nature note section, in this note Whitman's return to society is also a return to the past. He recalls that he "had known Mr. Bryant over thirty years ago," and that he and Bryant had taken "rambles miles long, till dark, out towards Bedford or Flatbush, in company" (p. 166). This recollection is what we might expect in a note on a distant friend's death, but in the final section of *Specimen Days* Whitman's movements often lead him to recall the past. For example, in "Some Old Acquaintances—Memories" he writes of breakfasting "at Pfaff's restaurant, 24th street," and of remembering with Pfaff the "ante-bellum times, '59 and '60, and the jovial suppers at his then Broadway place, near Bleecker street" (p. 277). In "Boston Common—More of Emerson," spending "a good deal of time on the Common" reminds him "of a bright sharp February mid-day twenty-one years ago" when Emerson tried to talk him out of including the "Children of Adam" poems in *Leaves of Grass* (pp. 281–82). Moreover, when we remember that much of the first section of *Specimen Days* is based on Whitman's return to New York and Long Island in 1881, we have an idea of the extent to which Whitman's return to social activity can be an occasion for remembering the past.

Of course, the occasion that causes Whitman to remember his "rambles" with Bryant is the older poet's death. Half of the note, in fact, is an account of Bryant's funeral. Whitman writes that the funeral ended with the singing of the "appropriate well-known lines" in which Bryant anticipates death "in flowery June, / When brooks send up a joyous tune, / And groves send up a cheerful sound" (p. 166).[46] In some of the notes in the final section of *Specimen Days*, Whitman again dwells on the deaths of others and also, as Bryant did in "June," writes in expectation of his own.

"Death of William Cullen Bryant" is the first of seven comments on literary figures Whitman includes in the final section. Like the Bryant note, "Death of Carlyle," "Death of Longfellow," and "By Emerson's Grave" were prompted by the deaths of Whitman's near contemporaries. Although in these notes he addresses the writers' relations to society, all of the notes—the other writers he considers are Poe and Whittier—show him focusing on his own dying generation of writers and not on the younger generation of Twain, Howells, and James. They show him, in other words, as more interested in commenting on the literature of the recent past than in coming to an understanding of more current literature. More than this, while focusing on these passing writers, he is conciliatory, praising even Poe, Longfellow, and—though he hedges here—Whittier.[47] These pieces of literary tribute seem to be not simply encomiums to dead and dying writers, but also a generous settling of accounts made in preparation for Whitman's own death. They seem to be written in the spirit of another note concerned with death, "An Ossianic Night—Dearest Friends." In this note Whitman writes of a night on which "absent or dead friends, the old, the past," are "somehow tenderly suggested" (p. 282). It is a night on which the "changes of moon and sheets of hurrying vapor and black clouds, with the sense of rapid action in weird silence, recall the far-back Erse belief that such above were the preparations for receiving the wraiths of just-slain warriors" (pp. 282–83). On such a night Ossian would sing a petition to the ghosts of his

Withdrawal and Resumption: Specimen Days

fathers to "Receive the falling chief" (p. 283). And on this night Whitman writes, "How or why I know not, just at the moment, but I too muse and think of my best friends in their distant homes—of William O'Connor, of Maurice Bucke, of John Burroughs, and of Mrs. Gilchrist—friends of my soul—stanchest friends of my other soul, my poems" (p. 283). This statement at once expresses concern for friends toward whom Whitman feels thankful and looks ahead to his own death. It is the statement, as are his literary comments, of a man who, as he writes in "At Present Writing—Personal," seems to have accomplished "the principal object of my life" (p. 291) and writes in anticipation of death.

While "Death of William Cullen Bryant" suggests that Whitman, in returning to society, has concerns that perhaps pull him away from complete involvement in contemporary society, the other two notes that interrupt the nature notes sequence to report Whitman's return to New York suggest an intense involvement in the present-day world around him. Moreover, they give his record of his resumption of social activity an undeniably positive thrust. Although, as I shall show, Whitman remains somewhat critical of society, on the whole the notes following the nature notes express delight with American society. "Manhattan from the Bay" and "Human and Heroic New York" announce this delight. In "Manhattan from the Bay" Whitman describes a "show" (p. 170) that he is sure exceeds everything else on earth. In "Human and Heroic New York," in a passage reminiscent of the second part of "Give Me the Splendid Silent Sun," he writes,

> After an absence of many years...again I resume with curiosity the crowds, the streets I know so well, Broadway, the ferries, the west side of the city, democratic Bowery—human appearances and manners as seen in all these, and along the wharves, and in the perpetual travel of the horse-cars, or the crowded excursion steamers, or in Wall and Nassau streets by day—in the places of amusement at night—bubbling and whirling and moving like its own environment of waters—endless humanity in all phases.... No need to specify minutely—enough to say that (making all allowances for the shadows and sidestreaks of a million-headed-city) the brief total of the impressions, the human qualities, of these vast cities, is to me comforting, even heroic, beyond statement. (pp. 171-72)

What is interesting about this resumption "with curiosity" of the crowds of New York and the other notes in the final section of *Specimen Days* is that they show Whitman not only resuming an activity but also resuming concerns he had addressed before in describing society. In particular, Whitman's report of his excursion back into society shows him resuming, recalling although adapting to new purposes, a formula—

a double perspective—for accepting yet rejecting society. He had used this formula earlier in writing an introductory passage in *Democratic Vistas*. This passage tells of a return Whitman made to New York in 1870 as a vacation from his job in Washington. Whitman uses this account to illustrate his contention that the United States, "however great a success in uplifting the masses out of their sloughs, in materialistic development, products, and in a certain highly deceptive superficial popular intellectuality, is, so far, an almost complete failure in its social aspects, and in any grand religious, moral, literary and esthetic results."[48] In this passage Whitman makes three assertions. The first two are positive: that the commercial prosperity and the resulting social activity of New York are satisfying; that the commercial and social activity is equivalent to that of Nature. The third assertion, however, unsays the first two: this activity is only the superficial manifestation of a society that is actually failing morally. In the final section of *Specimen Days*, to the extent he wishes to show himself delighted with society, Whitman addresses these three issues, reiterating the first two and responding to, and partly refuting, the third. To the extent he remains consciously critical of society—there is also at least one time when he is critical despite himself—he retains the double perspective, shifting its critical thrust in order to emphasize only the deficiency of the rich.

Whitman opens the passage in *Democratic Vistas* by celebrating the manifestations of commercial prosperity and social activity he finds upon returning to New York:

> After an absence, I am now again (September, 1870) in New York city and Brooklyn, on a few weeks' vacation. The splendor, picturesqueness, and oceanic amplitude and rush of these great cities, ... the endless ships, the tumultuous streets, Broadway, the heavy, low, musical roar, hardly ever intermitted, even at night; the jobbers' houses, the rich shops, the wharves, the great Central Park, and the Brooklyn Park of Hills, ... —the assemblages of the citizens in their groups, conversations, trades, evening amusements, or along the by-quarters—these, I say, and the like of these, completely satisfy my senses of power, fullness, motion, &c., and give me, through such senses and appetites, and through my esthetic conscience, a continued exaltation and absolute fulfilment.[49]

Except that this passage is dated eight or nine years too early and that its inclusion in *Specimen Days* would have been redundant both in idea and wording (note, for example, the similarities between this passage and the passage from "Human and Heroic New York" quoted earlier), this passage could easily have appeared in the final section of

Withdrawal and Resumption: Specimen Days 419

Specimen Days. For in that section Whitman repeats and expands upon the thrust of this passage. In "Manhattan from the Bay," Whitman notes the "great ocean Dons, iron-black, modern, magnificent in size and power, fill'd with their incalculable value of human life and precious merchandize" (p. 170), and thus begins an enjoyment of America's commercial success that shows him finding satisfaction and delight not only by returning to New York but also by traveling to the West and to other cities.

Most particularly in recording his trip West does Whitman allow himself an expansiveness about the prosperity of his country. He writes as if he were composing a pamphlet to attract immigrants. He finds that the "plain and prairie," "America's Characteristic Landscape," though "at present wild and unproductive," is an "inexhaustible land of wheat, maize, wool, flax, coal, iron, beef and pork, butter and cheeses, apples and grapes," and that, "when irrigated," it will produce "enough wheat to feed the world" (p. 220). He finds that Missouri has already developed to such an extent that he can say that the state, "in climate, soil, relative situation, wheat, grass, mines, railroads, and every important materialistic respect, stands in front rank of the Union" (p. 206). Not only does the land but also the western cities strike him as prosperous: "Lawrence and Topeka are large, bustling, half-rural, handsome cities" (p. 207). Whitman falls in love with Denver, "the Queen city of the plains and peaks," which has "plenty of people, 'business,' modernness," where he drools over the "long rows of vats, pans, cover'd by bubbling-boiling water, and filled with pure silver, four or five inches thick, many thousand dollars' worth in a pan" (pp. 215–16). He adds parenthetically "that the silver product of Colorado and Utah, with the gold product of California, New Mexico, Nevada, and Dakota, foots up an addition to the world's coin of considerably over a hundred millions every year" (p. 215). (As Newton Arvin suggests, there are times when Whitman sounds as if he were writing Andrew Carnegie's *Triumphant Democracy*.[50]) In St. Louis he finds "store-streets" that are already "showy, modern, metropolitan, with hurrying crowds, vehicles, horse-cars, hubbub, plenty of people, rich goods, plate-glass windows, iron fronts often five or six stories high" (p. 228). Actually Whitman knew that there were reasons not to be too enthusiastic about the West. In a letter he wrote to Peter Doyle from St. Louis, he says, perhaps to discourage Doyle from going west to make a living, "there are plenty of hard-up fellows in this city, & out in the mines, & all over here—you have no idea how many run ashore, get sick from exposure, poor grub &c— many young men, some old chaps, some boys of 15 or 16—I met them every where, especially at the RR stoppings, out of money & trying to get home—"[51] There is this negative side to Whitman's opinion of the West; nevertheless, in *Specimen Days* he clearly wants to present the West as prosperous.

In a note written a year-and-a-half after his return from the West, Whitman delightedly pretends to be surprised that Boston is as prosperous as the West seems to be becoming: "Boston's immense material growth—commerce, finance, commission stores, the plethora of goods, the crowded streets and sidewalks—made of course the first surprising show. In my trip out West, last year, I thought the wand of future prosperity, future empire, must soon surely be wielded by St. Louis, Chicago, beautiful Denver, perhaps San Francisco; but I see the said wand stretch'd out just as decidedly in Boston" (pp. 264–65). Prosperity, we might infer, is everywhere in the country. And wherever he goes, Whitman finds it, as he did in 1870, "a continued exaltation and absolute fulfilment."

In the passage in *Democratic Vistas* Whitman's seemingly enthusiastic response to the commercial prosperity he finds in New York spills over into his second assertion:

> Always and more and more ... I realize ... that not Nature alone is great in her fields of freedom and open air, in her storms, the snows of night and day, the mountains, forests, seas—but in the artificial, the work of man too is equally great—in this profusion of teeming humanity—in these ingenuities, streets, goods, houses, ships—these hurrying, feverish, electric crowds of men, their complicated business genius, (not least among geniuses,) and all this mighty, many-threaded wealth and industry concentrated here.[52]

Like the segment that precedes it, this one could have appeared in the final section of *Specimen Days*. It expresses a notion—that the artificial is somehow equivalent to Nature—that Whitman explores in the final section and uses to express his enthusiastic response to America's commercial prosperity. Indeed, in *Specimen Days* it is almost as if the restorative impulses behind his nature notes carry over into the following section and allow him to expand his vision into an acceptance of the artificiality of society as, in its own way, not a falling away from Nature, but a fitting accompaniment or even expression of Nature.

In "Death of William Cullen Bryant," Whitman seems to remain true to his preference for Nature established in the nature notes. Although he is in Manhattan, not only does he devote the note to "the bard who loved Nature," but he also says that he feels "at home, at peace," in Manhattan, not because he is spending his time riding buses and ob-

Withdrawal and Resumption: Specimen Days

serving crowds, but because he stays with some friends "away up on Fifth avenue, near Eighty-sixth street, quiet, breezy, overlooking the dense woody fringe of the park—plenty of space and sky, birds chirping, and air comparatively fresh and odorless" (p. 166). But perhaps he finds that this natural environment in the city has an effect on him, for when he returns to New York from a visit with John Burroughs, he writes of the city in "Manhattan from the Bay" as if it blended well with its natural surroundings: "And rising out of the midst, tall-topt, ship-hemm'd, modern, American, yet strangely oriental, V-shaped Manhattan, with its compact mass, its spires, its cloud-touching edifices, group'd at the centre—the green of the trees, and all the white, brown and gray of the architecture well blended, as I see it under a miracle of limpid sky, delicious light of heaven above, and June haze on the surface below" (pp. 170–71). In "Human and Heroic New York," he continues to suggest the apparent naturalness of New York by stressing its citizens' comparability to its watery surroundings. Its "populations" are "oceanic," its "endless humanity" is "bubbling and whirling and moving like its own environment of waters" (p. 171), and "its myriad people" are "on scale of the oceans and tides" (p. 172). New York, it seems, is a place not to be judged against Nature, but to be compared to it.

This treatment of the social as comparable to Nature continues in Whitman's notes for the spring of 1879. As I have suggested, in the nature notes section Whitman stresses the seasonal flow of the year. Although that section concludes with the end of the 1878 notes, the seasonal emphasis continues into the 1879 notes—but with a difference. The first 1879 note, "Delaware River Days and Nights," is dated "April 15" (p. 181). Whitman opens it in the manner of a nature note by pointing out that seagulls return to the Delaware when spring returns. He writes further that "The crows, plenty enough all through winter, have vanish'd with the ice." But he then shifts from natural life to artificial creations as if he intended to point out that one can recognize spring's approach by paying attention to more than birds or other natural sights: "The steamboats have again come forth—bustling up, handsome, freshly painted, for summer work" (p. 182). He follows this shift with a lengthy "bunch and catalogue" of the activity on the Delaware that is a celebration of both commerce and spring.

In "Delaware River—Days and Nights," Whitman anticipates an 1882 note, "Only a New Ferry Boat." In that note Whitman suggests that a boat might be "in its fitness comparable with the prettiest product of Nature's cunning, and rivaling it," that a boat, a "creation of artificial beauty and motion and power" is "in its way no less perfect" than the "gracefully balanced" hawks that might be circling above it (p. 284). And in "Delaware River" he also prepares the way for two 1879 notes that treat the whirl of commercial prosperity as an expression of, or at least a fitting response to, the pleasant days of spring. In "The First Spring Day on Chestnut Street'" he writes: "Winter relaxing its hold, has already allow'd us a foretaste of spring. As I write, yesterday afternoon's softness and brightness, (after the morning fog, which gave it a better setting by contrast), show'd Chestnut street—say between Broad and Fourth—to more advantage in its various asides, and all its stores, and gay-dress'd crowds generally, than for three months past" (p. 188). And in "Two City Areas, Certain Hours," he writes of the "brilliant, animated, crowded, spectacular human presentations" that occur on "these fine May afternoons" and show what New York "can do in its humanity, its choicest physique and physiognomy, and its countless prodigality of locomotion, dry goods, glitter, magnetism and happiness" (pp. 196–97). Both of these passages seem to show Whitman expressing his delight in prosperity by suggesting that "the artificial" is "equally great with Nature," is somehow an expression of the season.

In the illustrative passage in *Democratic Vistas*, having expressed pleasure with New York's prosperity and having suggested that the prosperity is somehow equivalent with Nature, Whitman changes his perspective, becomes severe and makes the points he has been moving toward—American society is "an almost complete failure":

> But sternly discarding, shutting our eyes to the glow and grandeurs of the general superficial effect, coming down to what is of the only real importance, Personalities, and examining minutely, we question, we ask, Are there indeed, *men* here worthy the name? ... Is there a great moral and religious civilization —the only justification of a great material one? Confess that to severe eyes, using the moral microscope upon humanity, a sort of dry and flat Sahara appears, these cities, crowded with petty grotesques, malformations, phantoms playing meaningless antics. Confess that everywhere, in shop, street, church, theatre, barroom, official chair, are pervading flippancy and vulgarity, low cunning, infidelity—everywhere the youth puny, impudent, foppish, prematurely ripe—everywhere an abnormal libidinousness, unhealthy forms, male, female, painted, padded, dyed, chignon'd, muddy complexions, bad blood, the capacity for good motherhood deceasing or deceas'd, shallow notions of beauty, with a range of manners, or rather lack of manners, (considering the advantages enjoy'd,) probably the meanest to be seen in the world.[53]

Thus far I have noted that the final section of *Specimen Days* parallels the illustration passage in *Democratic Vistas*. Here, however, the parallel stops because, for the most part, *Specimen Days* does not repeat the thrust of this castigation. Indeed, instead of leveling a charge of moral deficiency against American society, it answers such a charge. In *Specimen Days* Whitman raises the same question he does in *Democratic Vistas*: " 'Are there going to be *any men* there?' was the dry and pregnant reply of Emerson to one who had been crowding him with the rich material statistics and possibilities of some western or Pacific region" (p. 202). But he raises it in most cases, not to establish a critical perspective, but to praise.

During the Civil War Whitman discovered that the greatness of the United States "was in the rank and file" (p. 225). And, like the war memoranda, the final section of *Specimen Days* celebrates the average man. In "Human and Heroic New York," he writes that among "the rule and average" of the "mighty channels of men" he sees in the city he finds "Alertness, generally fine physique, clear eyes that look straight at you, a singular combination of reticence and self-possession, with good nature and friendliness." These qualities are for Whitman "a palpable outcropping of that personal comradeship I look forward to as the subtlest, strongest future hold of the many item'd Union." He writes further that "an appreciative and perceptive study of the current humanity of New York gives the directest proof yet of successful Democracy, and of the solution of the paradox, the eligibility of the free and fully developed individual with the paramount aggregate" (p. 172).

Seeing the average man as so important to his country, Whitman naturally looks for evidence of him wherever he goes. And he finds him in the person of Walter Dumont, a "quiet hero" who handles his plough oxen in an "easy and wordless, yet firm and sufficient" manner, and who risked his life to save numerous people from a steamer wrecked in the Hudson (p. 194). After talking to "a New York Park policeman" in Central Park he notes, "the Ulyssean capacity, derring-do, quick readiness in emergencies, practically, unwitting devotion and heroism, among our American young men and working-people—the firemen, the railroad employés, the steamer and ferry men, the police, the conductors, and drivers—the whole splendid average of the native stock, city and country" (p. 198). He finds the "several hundred youths" on "the United States school-ship Minnesota" to be "splendid proof of our country, our composite race, and the sample-promises of its good average capacities, its future" (pp. 201–202). On the prairies he sees the land not only as prosperous but also as having "given us our leading modern Americans, Lincoln and Grant... vast-spread, average men" (p. 208). In Denver, where Whitman becomes excited about the silver, he nonetheless writes that "The best was the men, three-fourths of them large, able, calm, alert, American," and, he might have added, average (p. 215). In Boston he finds in the "best average of houses, streets, people, that subtle something ... which effuses behind the whirl of animation, study, business, a happy and joyous public spirit" (p. 266). Nearly everywhere, even in Canada, Whitman finds examples of the "average range of the best specimens among us," who promise "to be the leaven which must eventually leaven the whole lump" (p. 240).

Whitman finds the average American nearly everywhere, but not everyone he sees is a specimen of the average. Some of the people would like to make themselves better than average and Whitman is suspicious of them, does not see the strength of America in them. He quotes himself in "An Interviewer's Item" as saying that "Our American superiority and vitality are in the bulk of our people, not in a gentry like the old world" (p. 225). In accordance with this belief, his response to his earlier criticism of America's moral deficiency is a defense of the average American—but not of the rich. Whitman remains willing to level the criticism he expressed in the illustrative passage of *Democratic Vistas* against those who would be America's "gentry."

In "A Fine Afternoon, 4 to 6," one of the notes dealing with his visit to New York in 1879, Whitman focuses on America's "gentry." Repeating the double vision he used in *Democratic Vistas*, he first writes of the "Ten thousand vehicles careening through the Park," a sight that represents to him the prosperity, "the full oceanic tides of New York's wealth and 'gentility'" (pp. 198–99). He then suggests that the show is a fitting accompaniment to the day: "It was an impressive, rich, interminable circus on a grand scale, full of action and color in the beauty of the day, under the clear sun and moderate breeze" (p. 199). That Whitman puts "gentility" in quotes—to suggest that it is not gentility at all—and calls the show of carriages a "circus" is probably meant to prepare us for what occurs next. For, as in *Democratic Vistas*, Whitman becomes severe:

> Through the windows of two or three of the richest carriages I saw faces almost corpse-like, so ashy and listless. Indeed the whole affair exhibited less of sterling America, either in spirit or countenance, than I had counted on from such a select mass-spectacle. I suppose, as a proof of limitless wealth, leisure, and the aforesaid "gentility," it was tremendous. Yet what I saw those hours ... confirms a thought that haunts me every additional glimpse I get of our top-loftical general or rather exceptional phase of wealth and fashion in this country—namely, that they are ill at ease, much too conscious, cased in too many cerements, and far from happy—that there is nothing in them which we who are poor and plain need at all envy, and that instead of the perennial smell of the grass and woods and shores, their typical redolence is of soaps and

Withdrawal and Resumption: Specimen Days 425

essences, very rare may be, but suggesting the barber shop—something that turns stale and musty in a few hours anyhow. (p. 199)

Although he no longer finds all of American society "an almost complete failure," Whitman is willing in this passage to specify the "gentility" as failing to represent "sterling America." More than this, he seems to see that their failure is bringing them to the end of their existence. He uses language that implies that these people who are different from "we who are poor and plain"—average—have become so "top-loftical" and "exceptional" as to be unnatural, decaying, and, indeed, so "corpse-like" that they need "cerements."

Curiously, the next paragraph in "A Fine Afternoon" seems to be written as if this critical passage, despite its clarity, did not come before it. Whitman writes: "Perhaps the show on the horseback road was prettiest.... As the afternoon waned, the wheel'd carriages grew less, but the saddle-riders seemed to increase. They linger'd long—and I saw some charming forms and faces" (p. 199). Perhaps all this second paragraph means is that Whitman preferred watching riders to watching carriages. Perhaps he is recalling that "His great grandmother on the paternal side... rode on horseback like a man" (p. 9) and that his "mother, as a young woman, was a daily and daring rider" (p. 8). But juxtaposed to the first paragraph, it seems strikingly inconsistent. Having made his criticism of the "gentry," he immediately seems to take it back. Having witnessed their demise, he immediately resurrects them. What caused this lapse? Is there some uneasiness behind it? Has Whitman touched upon an issue that is too serious—too full of negative possibilities—for him to consider thoroughly? I will soon look at another example of Whitman's inconsistency that may help to answer these questions.

Such is the force of Whitman's appreciation of both America's prosperity and the average American—both of which will help to bring about a stronger Union—that it is possible to conclude, as Linck C. Johnson has, that "in the last section of *Specimen Days* [Whitman] presents a country that is both healthy and united."[54] But Whitman's record of his resumption of interest in society is not a completely uncritical assessment of the United States. As we have seen, he is critical of the "gentility." In addition, some criticism occurs in his comments on the deaths of contemporary writers. In "Carlyle from American Points of View" and "Death of Longfellow," he sees the works of both writers as expressing symptoms of their societies' maladies and, at the same time, as being useful antidotes to the problems of American society. His comments make it clear that he finds fault with society. He asks, Carlyle's "rude, rasping, taunting, contradictory tones—what ones are more wanted amid the supple, polish'd, money-worshipping, Jesus-and-Judas-equalizing, suffrage-sovereignty echoes of current America?" (p. 261). And he asserts that Longfellow "is certainly the sort of bard and counteractant most needed for our materialistic, self-assertive, money-worshipping, Anglo-Saxon races, and especially for the present age in America—an age tyranically regulated with reference to the manufacturer, the merchant, the financier, the politician and the day workman" (p. 285). That Whitman allows such criticism to appear in the final section of *Specimen Days* reflects an equivocalness that underlies the record of his attempt to "resume" society. Moreover, in one of the very notes in which he wants to celebrate American prosperity, Whitman writes so confusedly that it is difficult to tell whether he is praising or means to criticize.

In "The First Spring Day on Chestnut Street," Whitman seems to want to celebrate the prosperity of Philadelphia by pointing out that its main "street any fine day, shows vividness, motion, variety, not easily to be surpass'd" (p. 189). Newton Arvin finds this note to be an example of how Whitman "wished to say Yes as sweepingly as possible," and how that "wish inevitably led him astray."[55] I believe, however, that it would be truer to say that this note is an example of the difficulty Whitman could have in saying Yes when he also needed to say No. For Whitman's praise of what he finds on Chestnut Street is definitely, although confusedly, mixed.

Whitman writes: "Doubtless, there were plenty of hard-up folks along the pavements, but nine-tenths of the myriad-moving human panorama to all appearances seem'd flush, well-fed, and fully-provided" (pp. 188–89). The "Doubtless" suggests that Whitman writes of the "hard-up folks" only to dismiss them and that he will concentrate on those who seem well-to-do. But the first items he catalogues as evidence that "At all events it was good to be on Chestnut street yesterday" belie the prosperity he suggests he finds there: "The peddlers on the sidewalk—('sleeve-buttons, three for five cents')—the handsome little fellow with canary-bird whistles—the cane men, toy men, toothpick men—the old woman squatted in a heap on the cold stone flags, with her basket of matches, pins and tape—the young negro mother, sitting, begging, with her two little coffee-color'd twins on her lap." Whitman goes on to catalogue signs of prosperity—flowers in a mansion, the meat in the restaurants, and the "costly books, pictures, curiosities in the windows" of the stores. He also includes in his catalogue, as we might

Withdrawal and Resumption: Specimen Days

expect him to, reassuring signs of the existence of average Americans. He notes, his writing becoming overly enthusiastic, the "letter carriers, so healthy and handsome and manly-looking in their gray uniforms" and "the gigantic policemen at most of the corners" (p. 189). But his initial list of poor people clashes with these indications of prosperity and national health. Indeed, given the catalogue of sights he chooses to remark on Chestnut Street, it is difficult to determine what Whitman's actual attitude is. Clearly he seems to want to emphasize the attractive, but he allows his eye to fall on the unattractive.

This lack of clarity continues. After comparing Chestnut Street favorably to the great thoroughfares of the world, Whitman adds a parenthetical question to the first paragraph of this note: "(Sparkling eyes, human faces, magnetism, well-dress'd women, ambulating to and fro—with lots of fine things in the windows—are they not about the same, the civilized world over?)" (p. 189–90). Having asked this question, he quotes a stanza from Bryant's "The Crowded Street," a poem that, although it ends with a mention of God's love, persists in asking such questions as "Who [in this crowd] writhes in throes of pain?" If the lines Whitman quotes are intended as a response to his parenthetical question, it is a response that is startlingly negative:

> How fast the flitting figures come!
> The mild, the fierce, the stony face;
> Some bright with thoughtless smiles—and some
> Where secret tears have left their trace. (p. 190)[56]

To read Whitman's question in conjunction with this quotation is to wonder if Whitman sees on Chestnut Street "Sparkling eyes" and "magnetism" or "thoughtless smiles" and traces of invisible tears. Perhaps he means to imply that he sees both.

There is yet more of this kind of inconsistency. I have suggested that "The First Spring Day on Chestnut Street" is a note in which Whitman seems to associate the "stores, and gay-dress'd crowds" with Nature. In this connection it is interesting to look at the paragraph that ends the note:

> A few days ago one of the six-story clothing stores along here had the space inside its plate-glass show-window partition'd into a little corral, and litter'd deeply with rich clover and hay (I could smell the odor outside,) on which reposed two magnificent fat sheep, full-sized but young—the handsomest creatures of the kind I ever saw. I stopp'd long and long, with the crowd, to view them—one lying down chewing the cud, and one standing up, looking

out, with dense-fringed patient eyes. Their wool, of a clear tawny color, with streaks of glistening black—altogether a queer sight amidst that crowded promenade of dandies, dollars and dry goods. (p. 190)

Something "queer" is happening here. To a note in which Whitman sees spring evidenced in social activity, he adds a paragraph that seems to undercut such a notion. He writes of two caged "magnificent sheep" that seem to be meant as a belittling contrast to the "dandies, dollars, and drygoods" around them.[57] Prosperity and its accompanying social activity are not, it seems, equivalent to Nature after all.

We cannot be sure of what is going on in this note—evidently Whitman himself is not sure. But perhaps the note is a confused registering of a perception similar to the one that led John Dos Passos, responding to the deaths of Sacco and Vanzetti, to write of America, "all right we are two nations." Although Whitman has not involved himself in events that clearly show him the distinction between what Dos Passos calls "strangers" who are "rich" and "our people," in writing about Chestnut Street he is confronting a similar double world.[58] And he is confronting, without wanting to—he is an ensemblist who sees things as uniting and not as dividing and he wants to celebrate prosperity—what is for him a serious problem. In *Democratic Vistas* he writes that there is no greater danger in the United States "than having certain portions of the people set off from the rest by a line drawn—they not privileged as others, but degraded, humiliated, and made of no account."[59] In *Collect*, in "Lacks and Wants Yet," he writes of being alarmed by "the total want of any... fusion and mutuality of love, belief, and rapport of interest, between the comparatively few successful rich, and the great masses of the unsuccessful, the poor." He asks, "As a mixed political and social question, is not this full of dark significance?"[60] What worries Whitman is that division between rich and poor might be a return to feudal conditions. In France such conditions led, as Whitman writes after looking at J. F. Millet's paintings, to generations of the "crushing of the masses of heroic people into the earth, in abject poverty, hunger—every right denied" (p. 268). In England such conditions led to "the increasing poverty and degradation of the homeless, landless twenty millions, while a few thousands, or rather a few hundreds, possess the entire soil, the money, and the fat berths" (p. 251).

In an unpublished note Whitman wrote, "The relations between the mass of employed persons on one side and the employers... on the other side is one of the vast, complicated, unsettled problems of America to-day—one of the problems to which, although I think it will be solved, I confess I do not yet see any solution or indications of solution."[61] In the final section of *Specimen Days*, perhaps out of his belief that the problem would be solved, Whitman seems to be trying to circumvent it. Attempting not to confront the disparity directly—except to criticize "gentility"—he insists on the appearance of prosperity and his hopes in the average American as proof of America's healthy success. But he is, nonetheless, worried that, as he put it in "The Tramp and Strike Questions," the United States might become "at heart an unhealthy failure." "The First Spring Day on Chestnut Street," though probably meant to conform to Whitman's celebrations of America, is both evidence that his nation has "unsettled problems" and an expression of Whitman's anxiety.

NOTES

1. *Leaves of Grass*, ed. Sculley Bradley and Harold W. Blodgett (New York: W. W. Norton, 1973), pp. 312–13.
2. Linck C. Johnson, "The Design of Walt Whitman's *Specimen Days*," *Walt Whitman Review*, 21 (March 1975): 10.
3. Newton Arvin, *Whitman* (New York: Macmillan, 1938), p. 69.
4. *Prose Works 1892*, ed. Floyd Stovall (New York: New York University Press, 1963–64), vol. 1, *Specimen Days* (1963), p. 118. Further references to *Specimen Days* will be cited in the text.
5. Whitman started visiting the Staffords sometime in the spring of 1876 (*Walt Whitman: The Correspondence*, ed. Edwin Haviland Miller [New York: New York University Press, 1961–69], 3:41). In March 1879, the Staffords moved from the farm at Timber Creek to Glendale, where they ran a store (*Correspondence*, 3:147). Whitman stopped going to Timber Creek on a regular basis after December 1878 (*Correspondence*, 3:151), but he would go from time to time, when visiting the Staffords "down in the woods"—as opposed to "down at the creek"—return to the creek (*Correspondence*, 3:193, 194, 272).
6. *The Writings of Henry D. Thoreau*, ed. Walter Harding et al., 5 volumes to date (Princeton: Princeton University Press, 1971–   ), *A Week on the Concord and Merrimack Rivers* (1980), ed. Carl F. Hovde et al., p. 332. When Thoreau visited Whitman in Brooklyn in 1856, he gave the poet a copy of *A Week*.
7. *Writings, Walden* (1971), ed. J. Lyndon Shanley, p. 69. In a letter to Myron Benton, John Burroughs described Whitman's reaction to *Walden*: "When I called on Walt this morning I found him *en dishabille*, reading 'Walden.' 'My impression of the book last night,' he said, 'was rather poor: I thought it puerile. But this morning, after I had sipped my coffee, I found it more satisfying. I opened near the end and found it so good that I turned back and commenced again'" (Clara Barrus, *Whitman and Burroughs: Comrades* [Boston: Houghton Mifflin, 1931], p. 17).
8. *Walden*, p. 135.
9. In his introduction to the Signet edition of *Specimen Days* (New York: New American Library, 1961), Richard Chase wrote that "As a nature writer Whitman

can scarcely be said to rank with the best; he is no Thoreau" (p. xiv). Other writers, however, have seen strengths in Whitman's nature notes. Gay Wilson Allen says in the *Walt Whitman Handbook* (Chicago: Packard, 1946) that, although Whitman is "more amateurish than Thoreau in his botanical and ornithilogical observations," his "enjoyment of nature is as intimate and personal as one can find in romantic prose" (p. 221). Also, Leo Marx writes that "Nowhere in all the abundant literature of natural observation is there a more convincing expression of the primary environment than in the nature notes of *Specimen Days*" (*New York Times Book Review*, 21 November 1971, p. 82).

10. *Correspondence*, 2:33.

11. Barrus writes that it is probable "that in many of his detailed observations of Nature in 'Specimen Days,' Whitman was largely indebted to Burroughs" and that "Whitman was quite as susceptible of catching from Burroughs as Burroughs had been formerly of catching from Whitman" (*Whitman and Burroughs*, pp. xxiv–xxv, 184–85). Gay Wilson Allen writes of the notes Whitman took while visiting Burroughs at Riverby: "Under the tutelage of his ornithologist friend he was especially observant of birds, though some of his notes show that he depended more on Burroughs' descriptions than on his own observations" (*The Solitary Singer: A Critical Biography of Walt Whitman* [New York: Macmillan, 1955], p. 484).

12. Of course, neither Thoreau nor Whitman is interested only in social concerns. In *A Week*, Thoreau writes that "we live on the verge of another and purer realm" (p. 381). In both *A Week* and *Walden*, Thoreau is interested in things that "betray" that "realm's vicinity" (*A Week*, p. 381). In the nature notes, as well as the rest of *Specimen Days*, Whitman also has this concern with establishing tentative contact with a realm beyond.

13. Lawrence Buell, *Literary Transcendentalism: Style and Vision in the American Renaissance* (Ithaca: Cornell University Press, 1973), p. 302. Buell quotes "bivouacked" from Ellery Channing, *Thoreau the Poet-Naturalist*, ed. F. B. Sanborn (Boston: Charles E. Goodspeed, 1902), p. 24.

14. Miller examines Whitman's relationship with Harry Stafford in the "Introduction" to the third volume of the *Correspondence*, particularly pp. 3–9. For the story of Whitman's other activities, see Allen, *The Solitary Singer*, pp. 462–90, *Correspondence*, and *Daybooks and Notebooks*, ed. William White (New York: New York University Press, 1977), vol. 1, *Daybooks: 1876-November 1881*.

15. *Walden*, p. 256.

16. The dates for 1878 run as follows: 7, 9, 19 February, 19 March, 6 May, 2, 3, 4, 5 July, 15 June, 22 August, 13, 20, 21, 22, 25 June, 22, 23 July, 17 September, 10 February, 1880, 4, 20 August, Another Later Day, 25 August.

17. This copy is in the Charles E. Feinberg Whitman Collection, DLC, no. 386 (Thoreau, *A Week on the Concord and Merrimack Rivers* [Boston: James Munroe, 1849], pp. 60–61).

18. Feinberg Collection, DLC.

19. *A Week*, p. 171.

20. *Walden*, p. 78.

21. *A Week*, p. 185.

22. *A Week*, particulary "Sunday."

23. *Walden*, p. 94.

24. Buell, *Literary Transcendentalism*, pp. 188–207.

25. *Anne Gilchrist: Her Life and Writings*, 2d ed., ed. Herbert Gilchrist (New

Withdrawal and Resumption: Specimen Days

York: AMS Press, 1973 [1887]), p. 237; see also Horace Traubel, *With Walt Whitman in Camden*, vol. 1, *March 28–July 14, 1888* (Boston: Small, Maynard, 1906), pp. 212–13.

26. Matthew Josephson, *The Politicos: 1865–1896* (New York: Harcourt, Brace & World, 1966), p. 252.
27. Allan Nevins, *The Emergence of Modern America: 1865–1878* (New York: Macmillan, 1927), p. 392.
28. Josephson, *Politicos*, p. 252.
29. Nevins, *Modern America*, pp. 301–302.
30. Nevins, *Modern America*, pp. 385–92.
31. Josephson, *Politicos*, pp. 195–96, 325–26.
32. Nevins, *Modern America*, pp. 311–12.
33. Nevins, *Modern America*, pp. 314–17, and Josephson, *Politicos*, pp. 226–36.
34. *Prose Works*, vol. 2, *Collect and Other Prose* (1964), pp. 466–67; see also p. 530.
35. *Prose Works*, 2:529.
36. *Prose Works*, 2:485–86.
37. *Prose Works*, 2:528.
38. *Prose Works*, 2:531–32.
39. *Prose Works*, 2:531.
40. Nevins, *Modern America*, pp. 316–17.
41. Feinberg Collection, Ms. 76, sheet 102, DLC; a similar statement appears in The Whitman (Livezey) Collection, folder no. 30, CU-B.
42. *A Week*, p. 359.
43. *A Week*, p. 129.
44. *Walden*, pp. 329–30.
45. *Walden*, p. 3.
46. Whitman writes "Joyous tune" for Bryant's "cheerful tune," and "cheerful sound" for "joyous sound" (*Prose Works*, 1:166n).
47. Johnson finds Whitman "profoundly conciliatory" in "My Tribute to Four Poets" ("The Design of Walt Whitman's *Specimen Days*," 15). James Bristol contends, however, that Whitman is both "praising and, through irony, quietly attacking his contemporaries," particularly Whittier ("Literary Criticism in *Specimen Days*," *Walt Whitman Review*, 12 [March 1966]: 16–19). Kenneth M. Price writes that Whitman realized "that a generous acceptance of other poets would enhance his image of national bard," but points out that Whitman's "reservations about Whittier go beyond mere circumspection to the verge of verbal attack" ("Whitman on Other Writers: Controlled 'Graciousness' in *Specimen Days*," *ESQ: A Journal of the American Renaissance*, 26 [2d Quarter 1980]: 80, 82).
48. *Prose Works*, 2:370.
49. *Prose Works*, 2:371.
50. Arvin, *Whitman*, pp. 98–99.
51. *Correspondence*, 3:168; see also 3:166.
52. *Prose Works*, 2:371.
53. *Prose Works*, 2:371–72.
54. Johnson, "The Design of Walt Whitman's *Specimen Days*," 11.
55. Arvin, *Whitman*, pp. 90, 97–98.
56. *The Complete Poems of William Cullen Bryant*, ed. H. C. Edwards (New York: Frederic A. Stokes, 1894), pp. 206–208.

57. Edward E. Chielens finds that Whitman employs "the careful use of 'oppositional' or contrasting ideas and images" in *Specimen Days*, and notes this contrast of the sheep to Chestnut Street as an example of this technique of juxtaposition ("Whitman's *Specimen Days* and the Familiar Essay Genre," *Genre*, 8 [December 1975]: 373–74).

58. John Dos Passos, *U.S.A.*, vol. 3, *The Big Money* (New York: Modern Library, 1939), pp. 461–63.

59. *Prose Works*, 2:382.

60. *Prose Works*, 2:533–34.

61. Whitman, *Notes and Fragments*, ed. Richard Maurice Bucke (London, Ontario: privately printed, 1899), p. 142.

BIOGRAPHICAL TECHNIQUE IN HORACE TRAUBEL'S *WITH WALT WHITMAN IN CAMDEN*

Tibbie E. Lynch

INTEREST IN WALT WHITMAN, both as man and artist, ran high during the early part of the twentieth century, and not too surprisingly, the appearance in 1906 of the first volume of Horace Traubel's *With Walt Whitman in Camden* caused a significant critical stir. Some contemporary reviewers gave little attention to Traubel's role in the work, choosing to view him as a simple stenographer and compiler, and focusing primarily upon the great poet himself.[1] A number of reviewers, however, acknowledged the Traubel volume as a unique literary achievement, a biography which unlike many other biographies presented an unretouched portrait of its subject.

Prepublication promotional folders had called the volume "one of the most important events in the literary history of America,"[2] and "a permanent addition to the literature of biography and character study,"[3] and after its publication, not a few critics felt that the volume had lived up to its claims. "Biography...is usually about the driest of literary work," the *Los Angeles Herald* asserted, "yet Traubel's volume is a violator of old tradition; it not only leaves all the angles and roughness, but by this very same token it gives us a most true, interesting, fascinating portrait."[4] The *Philadelphia Inquirer* termed the work "a remarkable contribution to biographical literature,"[5] and similarly, the *Philadelphia Public Ledger* asserted that it was "the most truthful biography of the language."[6] In the *London Mail*, Edmund Gosse called Traubel's chronicle "without doubt one of the most faithful pictures of a man of letters...which has ever been made public."[7] A similar accolade came from the *Kansas City Journal*, which contended that Traubel had "come as close to putting a man between covers as can be done."[8]

In addition, high regard for Traubel was shown in frequent comparisons of his work to that of the first great English biographer, James Boswell. The *Saturday Evening Post* expressed the view that Traubel's volume would "take its place with Boswell and the great biographies,"[9] and George H. Fitch, in a review in the *San Francisco Chronicle*, pointed out that Traubel had "much of Boswell's faculty of seizing characteristic things and reproducing them."[10] Some critics felt that Traubel was an even better biographer than Boswell. In a review in the *Cleveland Plain Dealer*, for example, William E. Sage asserted that Traubel had "bettered Boswell by keeping his own respect and ours. Boswell was a toady... Traubel worships Whitman but he doesn't prostrate himself."[11] The often quoted words of William Rossetti to Richard Carle also drew a Boswell-Traubel parallel, one in which Traubel emerged as the superior artist. "Traubel," Rossetti wrote, "out Boswellizes Boswell."[12]

Although, as noted earlier, several critics found the volume unwieldy and dull, suffering from the lack of a sense of "proportion" on Traubel's part and too filled with trivial and mundane information, the prevailing view of *With Walt Whitman in Camden* was that it was not only legitimate biography, but also the first biography of its kind—a singular artistic achievement. Given this view, one would expect that, for good or ill, Traubel would have earned his niche in the history of biographical narrative. Indeed, Van Wyck Brooks' statement (though perhaps a bit of dust-jacket puffery), that *With Walt Whitman in Camden* is "the greatest biographical work in American literature," suggests, at least, that the uniqueness of Traubel's accomplishment has been recognized.[13]

And yet, of the three major histories of biography written in this century, only one, Richard Altick's *Lives and Letters*, even mentions Traubel, and Altick gives the subject short shrift, calling *With Walt Whitman in Camden* a "bulky manuscript."[14] Altick later laments the fact that "no American Boswell" has appeared to "supply inspiration and challenge for the ensuing generation of biographies."[15] In none among the recent flurry of articles on the art of biography do we find any reference to or analysis of Traubel's biographical technique or achievement. Even Traubel's own biographers have devoted little attention to his reputation as a biographer, preferring instead to concentrate upon and sentimentalize his personal relationship with Whitman.[16]

Considering the silence of biographical historians on the subject of Traubel, and in the contrasting light of observations concerning his achievement, it would seem that a more detailed analysis of Traubel's biographical "formula," to use a term applied to Boswell, is in order.[17]

Such an analysis will be useful, I think, not only in helping to finally establish Traubel as a legitimate practitioner of biographical art, but also in determining the extent to which our view of Whitman in *With Walt Whitman in Camden* is being carefully shaped by the hand of his friend and admirer. This last consideration is of the utmost importance, given that many Whitman scholars use the Traubel material as a source work, rather than as an artistic creation with a rhetoric of its own. To formulate some conclusions concerning Traubel's biographical method, and to explore his manipulation of subject matter, then, is the purpose of this study.[18]

Before *With Walt Whitman in Camden* can be approached critically, an initial question must be answered: since this biography is such a radical departure from "standard" biographical practice, by what criteria should it be judged? Certainly a number of critics have wondered if this rambling sequence should be termed "biography" at all. The day-by-day chronological form, the seeming lack of selectivity, and the profession of Traubel himself that he had chosen not to "fool with its text," but rather to "leave it in its unpremeditated arrangement of light and shade,"[19] all seem to suggest that these volumes should be regarded not as biography, but as a kind of annotated diary. The legitimate biographer, or even the memoir writer should have the capability to selectively order his materials; Traubel, say many of his critics, was merely a tape recorder.

At first glance, the criticism seems valid enough; yet there also seems to be much validity in those favorable early reviews, and specifically in the Traubel-Boswell comparison. No one will dispute Boswell's key role in the development of biographical narrative. No history of biography would be complete without a full treatment of *The Life of Johnson*. Yet the biographical "deficiencies" often pointed up in Boswell's work are quite similar to those for which Traubel has been criticized. For example, in contemporary commentary, both Boswell and Traubel were faulted for recording too many trivial, insignificant details of daily life. Frequently, Boswell and Traubel have been characterized as "mindless" recorders of the words of their literary idols.[20] As with Traubel, some critics have questioned whether Boswell's work can be "termed biography at all."[21]

Clearly, the existence of similar criticisms does not make Traubel a Boswell. Recognition of these parallels, however (and consideration of the similarities in the circumstances of composition),[22] does suggest that the two biographies are at least generically related, and that *With Walt Whitman in Camden* might be more fairly tried by a

Boswellian standard than by comparison to other biographical works very different in scope and purpose. My intent here is not to assert Traubel is another Boswell, but rather to suggest that in his use of certain methods of dramatization and portraiture, Traubel deserves credit for having reasserted some of the more important biographical tenets set forth by Boswell.

It is generally agreed that one of Boswell's most important contributions to biographical art was his capacity to dramatize actual situations, revealing simultaneously the personality of his subject, and the atmosphere in which he existed. As Harold Nicholson has pointed out, biography before Boswell resembled a series of "lantern slides," in which the subject was seen in a variety of formal "attitudes."[23] Boswell was the first biographer to capture the nuances of expression and the eccentricities which characterize a flesh-and-blood human being. Allowing for the execution of a more interesting and fully realized portrait, such a technique also has an interpretive function. In dramatizing from factual material, the biographer is confronted with the same choices as an artist in the fictional mode. He underscores here; he de-emphasizes there; he allows for a constant interplay of light and shadow, while subtly manipulating the reader's response to his subject. As William Siebenschuh has noted, "we should be aware of the extent to which purely artistic choices (to dramatize or not to dramatize) shape our responses to 'facts' as well as to 'fiction,' the extent to which the making of such choices by a biographer *means*, in effect, interpretation."[24] In Boswell's case his subject was, despite his age, an active, robust, and highly social personality. Boswell used the social situation in which he frequently found his subject as a dramatic context, employing the many personalities who populated Johnson's world as foils for the great man's wit, humor, and benign wisdom.[25] Because Boswell's re-creations have such verisimilitude, the reader is largely unaware that the scene is being manipulated to show Johnson to his greatest advantage. The reader absorbs the total scene as a wholly "factual" narrative, accepting the view of Johnson depicted there. Boswell, in effect, is able to interpret without seeming to do so. (On the other hand, the biographer who does not use the dramatic mode, but who juxtaposes factual narrative with periodic editorial digression, always calls attention to his own interpretive ventures.)

Did Traubel employ a dramatic mode in *With Walt Whitman in Camden*? His introduction to the first volume is a disclaimer to that effect. Here is the record of events as they actually happened, he tells us: "I have made no attempt to improve it. I have taken nothing off and put nothing on.... I have preferred to respect its integrity.... I have done nothing negatively to disguise any poverty in the portrait and nothing affirmatively to falsely enrich it. I have had only one anxiety. To set down the record. Then to get out of the way myself."[26] The stylistic quality of the daily entries of the first volume seem an attempt to live up to this introductory statement. Traubel's prose is direct, unembellished, and often fragmentary. Certainly, he does not employ the elaborate transitional elements. He eschews extensive description. He avoids references to his own feelings and reactions. It might be said that whereas Boswell's entries are technicolor and panoramic, Traubel has chosen the stark black and white of a documentary.

In what way can such a seemingly "objective" presentation be said to be interpretive or dramatic? Let us first examine Traubel's handling of the recorded conversations in which a number of people are present. Because of Whitman's deteriorating physical condition, Traubel had to make the most of his few opportunities to observe his subject in a social milieu. Whitman's last ventures into society before he was finally confined to his bed were his Sunday trips to the home of his friend, Thomas Harned. A number of literary men of the Whitman-Traubel circle were always present at these gatherings, and lively discussion often ensued. In Boswell's recording of similar scenes, an attempt is made to capture the atmosphere of the social event by emphasizing the free exchange of ideas and recording much of the conversation of others present. He would, as one critic has noted, "gather his intelligence from various points."[27] Traubel, however, opted for a somewhat different, though no less dramatic technique. He was (like Boswell) interested in letting the reader feel the "mood" of the Sundays at Harned's, but his ultimate concern was in highlighting the fact that the aging poet, even in his infirmity, was still the dominant figure, the psychological center of the group. Thus, while he wished to portray realistically something of the give and take of normal conversational flow in which a number of people were participants, he also wanted to keep the reader's focus upon Whitman. To accomplish this, he chose to summarize briefly the subject of an argument or discussion, quoting the words of others only as "lead-ins" to especially illuminating remarks by Whitman. The effect of this method is to relegate others present to a background position and bring Whitman forward as a figure somewhat larger than life.

This kind of manipulation, I hasten to add, cannot be called dishonest distortion; Traubel undoubtedly saw Whitman in this way and wished his readers also to see him thus. The point is, to convey the desired impression of Whitman, Traubel has exercised artistic selectivity. For example, although the scene on Sunday, 1 April 1888, takes place at "a crowded table" (p. 6) where a number of those present are conversing with Whitman, Traubel chooses to isolate a free-trade argument between Whitman and Tom Dudley, retired former consul at Liverpool. Whitman, Traubel tells us, is the free-trade advocate. But the exchange of remarks, as Traubel records them, does not so much illuminate the free-trade issue as it sets up a contrast between Dudley's essentially earthbound pragmatism, and Whitman's own cosmic world view. When Dudley, described as speaking "sarcastically," accuses Whitman of wanting to " 'get down ... even the walls between the planets, if you could,' " Whitman retorts, "with spirit," " 'If I could, yes' " (p. 6). When Dudley asks whether we should not " 'take care of home [America] first,' " Whitman responds, " 'but what is home—to the humanitarian what is home?' " (p. 6). Later, when Dudley interrupts Whitman's discussion of Millet with the query " 'But what about the Constitution of the United States while all the rest is going on?' " (p. 7), Whitman laughingly replies, " 'What about the Constitution? What about last year's almanac, the weeds back there on the lot, the ash heap down the street? I guess these things crowd into the scheme after all; and after all Millet and Whitman need not feel so lonely' " (p. 7). Here, as elsewhere in his record, Traubel gives us a Walt Whitman who transcends the concerns of a particular time and place. Traubel is not so much interested in presenting Whitman's views on subjects of topical importance, as he is in isolating those statements in which Whitman appears as poet/philosopher.

Presentation of the Whitman-Dudley argument also has a second function, that of revealing Whitman's general good humor. We have seen Dudley speaking to Whitman with sarcasm, and abruptly interrupting his discourse on Millet. Whitman's responses, in contrast, are benign and wise, often accompanied by smiles and laughter. Traubel's method here is similar to one used by Boswell; he presents the evidence in dramatic form, then follows up with an editorial comment which expresses his point explicitly:[28] "Whitman is often described as lacking in humor," Traubel asserts at the end of the entry, "but this quiet play of pros and cons enters more or less into all of his conversation" (p. 7).

Some of the other Sunday entries have less continuity than this first, but Traubel's subtle manipulation is always in evidence. In his opening summation for the entry of 29 April 1888, Traubel once again establishes Whitman as the central figure, with the others present "gathered about" (p. 80) the old man. Once again, Traubel isolates the remarks of others only when they set off a Whitman response expressive of the cosmic philosophy. When someone cries out "'you're damned tolerant, Walt,'" following a Whitman discourse on "good emperors," Whitman responds: "Call it toleration, if you will. I only call it common sense philosophy. I am extreme? Perhaps. But then it is with America as it is with nature: I believe our institution can digest, absorb, all elements, good or bad, godlike or devilish, that come along'" (p. 81). When Tom Harned "annoys" Whitman by putting the cork back in the wine bottle, Whitman responds: "'Well, I forgive you. I forgive everybody ... do you know, my philosophy sees a place and a time for everybody—even Judas Iscariot—yes, for all: all of us are parties to the same bargain'" (p. 82).

By using the remarks of others as a dramatic framework, Traubel is able to create the desired impression that Whitman's cosmic and democratic utterances are spontaneous rather than part of a "formal" philosophical construct. Traubel must have perceived, wisely, that simply to catalogue Whitman's remarks, without dramatizing the circumstances in which they occurred, would be to render them less vital and immediate. One recent writer has inadvertently demonstrated the danger of such a method in his attempt to organize some of the Traubel materials by lifting Whitman remarks from context, and categorizing them according to subject matter. Although the chosen statements lose little in content, they are missing the force of personality of the speaker.[29] (Occasionally, as in the opening of the entry for 6 May 1888, Traubel will isolate "a few detached sayings," without specifying context. In these instances, however, the periodic catalogues set up a counterpoint which gives the dramatized material even greater verisimilitude.)

Another of Traubel's more effective devices is his use of Whitman's letters. The graceful incorporation of letters into factual narrative has always presented something of a problem to the biographer. Often, a proper context within the narrative itself cannot be found, and the letters, however revelatory in content, become formal digressions which only interrupt the continuity of the biographer's presentation.[30] In this regard, however, Traubel enjoyed a unique advantage that even Boswell had been denied. Not only was he allowed access to Whitman's correspondence, but, in addition, he was able to record the poet's reaction to the contents of each letter and attitude towards the sender. On almost every occasion during Traubel's daily visits to Whitman's home, the old man produced, from the chaos of paper strewn about his room, one or two "curios," as he called them, for Traubel's collection. Traubel would read the letter (aloud or silently, according to whether or not Whitman had just reread it), then record Whitman's reactions.

Traubel could easily have chosen to publish the letters separately, or simply to summarize the pertinent information within the context of each entry. But in compiling his materials, he must have realized that the letters, reproduced in entirety, could function as an effective dramatic device, a way of bringing together past and present. Each letter is a flashback, giving the reader information about past events, then providing a retrospective analysis by Whitman himself. Unlike the cold, still documents which appear in many other biographies, the letters in *With Walt Whitman in Camden* have intensity and immediacy. If the letter is a negative one, the reader feels something of Whitman's initial resentment, although that resentment may have been softened by the passage of time. If the letter is positive and supportive, the reader is allowed a view of Whitman's affection for the sender. With each successive letter, Traubel is able to define further his subject's temperament and capacity for affection.

It might be argued that Traubel's use of the letters is hardly evidence of authorial manipulation, since the reading of the letters was a normal occurrence in the course of daily conversations. Traubel, it might be asserted, was simply recording events as they happened. It is Traubel's *placement* of the letters within the narrative, however, which shows his attention to and concern for dramatic effect. Traubel seems to have realized that the areas of greatest emphasis in each entry would be the opening and closing statements. Thus, in most cases, he inserts the letter in question near the end of the entry, allowing Whitman's response, summed up in a concise paragraph, to conclude the entry. This technique has two interpretive possibilities. If the letter is effusively complimentary, the concluding paragraph is generally one in which Whitman deflects praise to the sender, thereby giving the reader a final impression of Whitman's humility. If the letter is uncomplimentary, Whitman is able to list his objection to the criticism and to gain the argumentative advantage.

By using the dramatic "framing" devices mentioned, Traubel was able to order and sharpen the focus of each entry. Nevertheless, he was faced with an additional aesthetic problem, that of giving each series of entries readable continuity. The problem was compounded by Traubel's constant desire to maintain the rough, free-form impression of the entries. For this dual purpose, several connective devices are effectively employed. The first is the linking together of three or four entries by focusing attention upon a subject of particular interest to Whitman, recording the full details of a discussion of that subject, and subordinating, in summary form, other topics discussed. For example, near the end of the entry of 3 April 1888, Whitman tells Traubel of a visit made by a tramp, an "'itinerant poet'" who had read Whitman some of his poems. Traubel concludes the entry by recording Whitman's wistful reflection that "'when I said goodbye to the tramp I was envious: I could not see what right he had to his monopoly of fresh air'" (p. 12). Then, on Wednesday, 4 April, after a summation of other subjects, Traubel presents Whitman's further thoughts upon the tramp: "'I am not so down in the mouth about it,' he explained, 'but I am still jealous of that tramp'" (p. 12). Finally, on Thursday, 5 April, the entry consists of a single quotation without commentary:

> "I feel so good again today," W. assures me, "that I no longer envy the tramp. I think that dusty cuss did me lots of good: he left me temporarily in a quarrelsome mood: I hated the room here, and my lame leg, and my dizzy head: I got hungry for the sun again, for the hills: and though Mary brought me up a good supper, she didn't bring the sort of food required to satisfy a fellow with my appetite. She didn't bring the sun and the stars and offer them to me on a plate: she brought muffins, a little jelly, a cup of tea: and I could have cried for disappointment. But later, next day, yesterday, the tramp's gift got into my veins—it was a slow process, but got there: and that has made me happy. I thought he had taken everything he had brought away with him again: that dust has taken effect." (p. 13)

Not only does the tramp motif establish continuity, but it also demonstrates Traubel's faculty of "seizing characteristic things" about Whitman.[31] Undoubtedly more conversation took place on 5 April than is recorded, but Traubel, apparently aware that Whitman's reflections on the tramp were revelatory of his way of perceiving life, chose to isolate and give emphasis to the remarks. In addition, by making the tramp the focal point of several entries, Traubel was able to present the reader with an exemplification of Whitman's tendency to reflect upon a single event over a period of time.

A final way in which Traubel sustains continuity is by concentrating upon Whitman's physical and mental condition. Here, again, the author's manipulation of the materials is evident. Whitman's first series of debilitating strokes occurred in early June 1888. Since the aging poet was subject to periods of mental confusion and disorientation during this period, and to some degree thereafter, Traubel could have chosen to downplay the illness, recording only those remarks in which Whitman demonstrated his former consistent lucidity. Instead, Traubel chose to open each entry with a "progress report" on Whitman's physical condition and general mental attitude. By so doing, Traubel not only maintains the integrity of his record, but also has the opportunity to demonstrate the affection and concern with which Whitman was regarded by numerous friends and acquaintances, as well as relative strangers. The opening of each entry with an honest admission of Whitman's periodic mental confusion, however, did create the potential hazard of discrediting his remarks as senile outpourings. Traubel handles the problem in two ways. First, he continues to reproduce Whitman's letters, many of which were entrusted to him on visits pre-dating the poet's serious illness. The letters direct the reader's attention to Whitman the artist and literary man, rather than to Whitman the invalid. Secondly, even during the critical phases of Whitman's illness, when his mind was wandering considerably, Traubel concludes each entry with a Whitman remark which reflects his still active imaginative perception. Hence, the reader is left with the continuing impression that even in his physical infirmity, Whitman retained the spirit and strength of character which is an essential part of Traubel's portrait.

In isolating some of Traubel's biographical techniques, I have undeniably only scratched the surface. An analysis of the rhetorical devices used in the other volumes needs to be undertaken. A further exploration of Traubel's interview technique, especially his use of "leading questions" would be useful. A comparison of the first three volumes with those edited by Sculley Bradley and Gertrude Traubel might yield some telling contrasts in technique. Furthermore, when the remaining two or possibly three additional volumes are edited by others, Traubel's own manipulation may become more evident. Subsequent analyses should demonstrate that Traubel's imaginative reconstructions of the conversations in Camden deserve the attention of biographical historians, as well as the informed consideration of Whitman scholars.

NOTES

1. See Donald R. Stoddard's summary of the critical reception of the volume in "Horace Traubel: A Critical Biography" (Ph.D. diss., University of Pennsylvania, 1970), pp. 239–80. Jeanette Gilder's "Whitman and His Boswell," *Critic*, 49 (1906): 185, views Traubel as an accurate but unselective reporter; similarly, George Arthur Rickett's review, "Walt Whitman," *London Tribune*, 7 November 1906, p. 8, declares that Traubel merely "gives us a phonograph record of Whitman's opinions."

2. *With Walt Whitman in Camden* [advertising folder] (Boston: Small, Maynard, 1906), p. 2.
3. *St. Louis Globe Democrat,* quoted in *With Walt Whitman in Camden* [advertising folder] (Boston: Small, Maynard, 1906), p. 2.
4. [Untitled review], *Los Angeles Herald,* 4 March 1906, p. 4.
5. "Horace Traubel's Work," *Philadelphia Inquirer,* 5 March 1906, p. 11.
6. "New Light on Walt Whitman," *Philadelphia Public Ledger,* 21 January 1906, p. 4.
7. Edmund Gosse, "The Good Grey Bard," *London Mail,* 17 November 1906, p. 9.
8. [Untitled review], *Kansas City Journal,* 19 March 1906; quoted in Stoddard, "Horace Traubel," p. 256.
9. "Walt Whitman's Self," *Saturday Evening Post,* 178 (3 June 1906): 16.
10. George Hamlin Fitch, [Untitled review], *San Francisco Chronicle,* 4 March 1906, p. 8.
11. William E. Sage, [Untitled review], *Cleveland Plain Dealer,* 16 June 1906; quoted in Stoddard, "Horace Traubel," p. 250.
12. William Rossetti to Richard Curle, 19 December 1906, InU; quoted in Stoddard, "Horace Traubel," p. 250.
13. *With Walt Whitman in Camden* [advertising folder], reproduced in the Rowman and Littlefield reprint of the first volume of Traubel's work (New York, 1961).
14. Richard Altick, *Lives and Letters* (New York: Alfred A. Knopf, 1965), p. 268. American biography has been subject to some neglect by biographical historians. Traubel is not dealt with in the major histories of biography: John A. Garraty's *The Nature of Biography* (New York: Alfred A. Knopf, 1957) and W. R. Thayer's *The Art of Biography* (New York: Scribners, 1920). Neither is Traubel dealt with in either of the two histories of American biography: Edward H. O'Neill's *A History of American Biography: 1800–1935* (Philadelphia: University of Pennsylvania Press, 1935) and Dana K. Merrill's *The Development of American Biography* (Portland, Maine: Southworth Press, 1932).
15. Altick, *Lives and Letters,* p. 270.
16. Apart from Donald Stoddard's dissertation, the three main Traubel studies are Mildred Bain's *Horace Traubel* (New York: Albert and Charles Boni, 1913), William English Walling's *Whitman and Traubel* (New York: Albert and Charles Boni, 1916), and David Karsner's *Horace Traubel: His Life and Work* (New York: Egmont Arens, 1919).
17. Stoddard calls for a reappraisal of Traubel as a biographer, pointing out that recent "encyclopedic" biographies illustrate the degree to which the modern biographer is "rediscovering the importance of extensive detail" (p. 275).
18. The extraordinary length of the complete *With Walt Whitman in Camden* (five volumes published to date) makes it impossible to explore the total compilation in a brief study. Therefore, only volume one will be drawn upon here. I believe, however, that the techniques used in volume one are generally representative of those used in volumes two and three.
19. Horace Traubel, *With Walt Whitman in Camden, March 28–July 14, 1888* (Boston: Small, Maynard, 1906), p. viii.
20. Harold Nicolson, *The Development of English Biography* (London: Hogarth Press, 1933), p. 100.

21. Donald Greene, "Reflections on a Literary Anniversary," in *Twentieth Century Interpretations of Boswell's Life of Johnson*, ed. James L. Clifford (Englewood Cliffs, N.J.: Prentice-Hall, 1970), p. 97.

22. For example, Boswell and Traubel both had direct, frequent contact with their subjects only during old age, and only for a limited number of years. Both biographers used the same method of note-taking; like Boswell, Traubel often jotted down an abbreviated version of a conversation, then wrote up the rest from memory later on. Both chose to set down the record in a day-by-day chronological form, although unlike Boswell, Traubel did not preface his record with a summary of "early years."

23. Nicolson, *English Biography*, p. 87.

24. William Siebenschuh, *Form and Purpose in Boswell's Biographical Works* (Berkeley: University of California Press, 1972), p. 54.

25. Nicolson, *English Biography*, p. 106.

26. Traubel, *With Walt Whitman*, p. viii.

27. Altick, *Lives and Letters*, p. 61.

28. Nicolson, *English Biography*, p. 103.

29. The work referred to here is Walter Teller's *Walt Whitman's Camden Conversations* (New Brunswick, N.J.: Rutgers University Press, 1973).

30. For a discussion of specific problems regarding letters see Altick, *Lives and Letters*, pp. 199, 317–20.

31. See note 10.

BOOKS RECEIVED

Caroline Bokinsky

ADAMS, ARTHUR G., editor. *The Hudson River in Literature: An Anthology.* Albany: State University of New York Press, [1980]. x, 337 pp.; 23 cm. LC 79–14862. ISBN 0-87395-407-6. Cloth, $14.95; paper, $7.95.

This volume contains excerpts from nineteenth-century writings that describe the Hudson River Valley, including works by Bryant, Cooper, Duyckinck, Poe, Whitman, and Willis.

ADLER, JOYCE SPARER. *War in Melviille's Imagination.* New York and London: New York University Press, [1981]. xi, 189 pp.; 23 cm. (Gotham Library.) Index. LC 80-20656. ISBN 0-8147-0574-X: cloth, $17.50; ISBN 0-8147-0575-8: paper, $8.00.

Traces the war-peace theme in Melville's works and points out that "Melville's passion against war was a great dynamic in his imagination and a main shaping force in his art." Although Melville felt human nature has a proclivity to war and tragedy, *Billy Budd* is his symbolic statement of man's potential to transform the world into a place of peace.

ANDREWS, WILLIAM L., editor. *Literary Romanticism in America.* Baton Rouge and London: Louisiana State University Press, [1981]. xiv, 136 pp.; 22 cm. "Notes on Contributors": pp. 135–136. LC 80–24365. ISBN 0-8071-0760-3. $14.95.

The American tradition in literature developed from the sense of wonder and reflection in romanticism. In the evolution of American literature, writers responded to their romantic birthright with social and political statements. Essays by Clarence Gohdes link Emerson's romantic idealism to the American faith in democracy and Arlin Turner point out how Hawthorne is a skeptical social commentator reflecting the conflicts of America's past.

ASPIZ, HAROLD. *Walt Whitman and the Body Beautiful.* Urbana, Chicago, London: University of Illinois Press, [1980]. xiii, 290 pp.; 23 cm. Index. LC 79–28280. ISBN 0-252-00799-9. $19.95.

Aspiz contends that Whitman's celebration of the physical body and its physiological functions in *Leaves of Grass* is the central theme and unifying metaphor of the work. While Whitman sees unity of the body and soul into one whole, the physical body is the important link to an enlightened spirituality. By focusing on the body, Whitman creates "a sensuous, emotion-charged poetic language."

ASSELINEAU, ROGER. *The Transcendentalist Constant in American Literature.* New York and London: New York University Press, [1980]. xii, 189 pp.; 23 cm. (Gotham Library.) Index LC 80–17918. ISBN 0–8147–0572–3: cloth. $17.50; ISBN 0–8147–0573–1: paper, $7.00.

Reprints essays on American writers, including one on Whitman published between 1961 and 1978.

ATTEBERY, BRIAN. *The Fantasy Tradition in American Literature: From Irving to Le Guin.* Bloomington: Indiana University Press, [1980]. viii, 212 pp.; 24 cm. "Bibliography": pp. 200–209; index. LC 80–7670. ISBN 0–253–35665–2. $17.50.

The writers of the fantasy tradition reorder reality, create a fairy land of America, and deal with the realm of the marvelous. Even though Irving's "Rip Van Winkle" is drawn from American legend, it transcends the real world and enters the marvelous enough to be a part of the fantasy tradition. The romances, however, of Hawthorne, Melville, and Poe remain grounded enough in reality, while often incorporating the fantastic, to be excluded from the tradition.

BEDELL, MADELON. *The Alcotts: Biography of a Family.* [New York]: Clarkson N. Potter, Inc./Publishers, [1980]. xv, 400 pp.: facsims., illus., ports.; 24 cm. "Bibliographical Note": pp. 335–338; index. LC 79–26741. ISBN 0–517–540312. $15.95.

Bedell's biography is the result of her "search for the Alcotts, for the real family behind the March family of *Little Women.*" Basing her sources on the Alcott manuscripts at the Houghton Library, she reveals Alcott's private life and gives a detailed impression of his wife, Abby.

BELL, MICHAEL DAVITT. *The Development of American Romance: The Sacrifice of Relation.* Chicago: The University of Chicago Press, [1980]. xiv, 291 pp.; 23 cm. "Bibliographical Appendix": pp. 277–279; index. LC 80–12241. ISBN 0–226–04211–1. $22.50.

Bell wants to reveal the essence of American Romance through Brown, Irving, Poe, Hawthorne, and Melville, and show how the European concept of romance must be reassessed by American standards where the national literature, based on native materials, was imbued with romance.

BENEDICT, STEWART, consultant editor. *The Literary Guide to the United States.* New York: Facts on File, [1981]. [x], 246 pp.: illus.; 23 cm. Bibliography: pp. 234–239; index. LC 80–26823. ISBN 0–87196–304–3. $15.95.

Benedict's *Guide* explores the American literary heritage by following a regional format. He finds that because America's diverse heritage produced an arbitrary cultural heritage, American writers have been forced to redefine their identity with respect to their sense of place in the country.

BETTS, GLYNNE ROBINSON. *Writers in Residence: American Authors at Home.* Introduction by Christopher Lehmann-Haupt. New York: Viking, [1981]. 159 pp. LC 80–20887. ISBN 0–670–79108–3. $16.95.

The photographs of writers' residences convey Betts's idea of the importance of "a sense of place" to a writer. Included are photographs of the houses of Longfellow, Stowe, Melville, Irving Poe, and the Alcotts.

BOSWELL, JEANETTA. *Herman Melville and the Critics: A Checklist of Criticism, 1900–1978.* Metuchen, N.J.: The Scarecrow Press, 1981. [xii], 247 pp.: front.; 22 cm. (The Scarecrow Author Bibliographies, Number 53.) Index. LC 80–25959. ISBN 0–8108–1385–8. $13.50.

This unannotated collection lists in alphabetical order by author 3,215 books, articles and essays on Melville.

BOSWELL, JEANETTA. *Walt Whitman and the Critics: A Checklist of Criticism, 1900–1978.* Metuchen, N.J.: The Scarecrow Press, 1980. xiii, 257 pp.; 22 cm. (The Scarecrow Author Bibliographies, No. 51.) Index. LC 80–20528. ISBN 0–8108–1355–6. $14.50.

This unannotated collection lists in alphabetical order by author 2,752 books, articles, and essays on Whitman.

BOSWELL, JEANETTA, and SARAH CROUCH. *Henry David Thoreau and the Critics: A Checklist of Criticism, 1900–1978.* Metuchen, N.J.: The Scarecrow Press, 1981. [x], 204 pp.; 22 cm. (The Scarecrow Author Bibliographies, Number 56.) Index. LC 81–929. ISBN 0–8108–1416–1. $11.00.

This unannotated collection lists in alphabetical order by author 2,150 books, articles, and essays on Thoreau.

BOWDEN, MARY WEATHERSPOON. *Washington Irving.* Boston: Twayne, [1981]. 201 pp.: front.; 20 cm. (Twayne's United States Authors Series: TUSAS 379.) "Selected Bibliography": pp. 190–194; index. LC 80–21364. ISBN 0–8057–7314–2. $9.95.

A biographical and critical study pointing out Irving's influence during his lifetime and discussing his works from an historical and political perspective.

BRUCE, DICKSON D., JR. *Violence and Culture in the Antebellum South.* Austin: University of Texas Press, [1979]. x, 322 pp.; 23 cm. "Bibliography": pp. 284–310; index. LC 79–4571. ISBN 0–292–77018–9. $16.95.

Bruce's study explores the proclivity toward violence in Southern culture. He concludes that, because Southerners were insecure about their moral condition, misunderstood human passion, and were pessimistic about the world, they assumed violence was an inevitable and unavoidable consequence. Bruce refers to Francis James Child, Cooper, Douglass, and Garrison, and shows how Poe expressed this Southern view in his tales by exploring "the irresistible power of passion and perversity."

BULLOCK, CHRIS, and DAVID PECK, compilers. *Guide to Marxist Literary Criticism.* Bloomington: Indiana University Press, [1980]. xi, 176 pp.; 21 cm. "Appendix: A Reading List on Mass Culture": pp. 148–168; index. LC 79–3627. ISBN 0–253–13144–8. $12.95.

A partially annotated bibliography of Marxist criticism, in English or translated into English, on British, American, and Canadian writers. Among the authors included are Emerson, Hawthorne, Howells, Melville, and Poe.

BUSHMAN, CLAUDIA L. *"A Good Poor Man's Wife": Being a Chronicle of Harriet Hanson Robinson and Her Family in Nineteenth-Century New England.* Hanover, N.H.: The University Press of New England, 1981. xvi, 276 pp.: front., illus., ports.; 22 cm. Bibliography: pp. 253–265; index. LC 80–54470. ISBN 0–87451–193–8. $18.00.

The biography of a neglected New England writer whose books, family records, and commentary on her affiliation with social movements disclose facts about the nineteenth-century woman, family history, and urban living.

CAVELL, STANLEY. *The Senses of Walden: An Expanded Edition.* San Francisco: North Point Press, 1981. xvii, 160 pp.; 18 cm. LC 80–28315. ISBN 0–86547–031–6: cloth, $15.00; ISBN 0–86547–032–4: paper, $7.50.

Reprints *The Senses of Walden* (1972) and prints an address at Kalamazoo College recalling Emerson's "The American Scholar," and "Thinking of Emerson," comparing Emerson to European philosophers.

CHERRY, CONRAD. *Nature and Religious Imagination: From Edwards to Bushnell.* Philadelphia: Fortress Press [1980]. x, 242 pp.; 22 cm. Index. LC 79–7374. ISBN 0–8006–0550–0. $12.95.

In the American quest for self-identity, man's response to external nature was shaped by his religious views. Channing used metaphors from nature in his sermons to evoke an awareness of man's moral duty and potential for religious perfection. Bushnell interpreted nature as a symbol of God's creative activity and a metaphor for man's spiritual life.

CHEYFITZ, ERIC. *The Trans-Parent: Sexual Politics in the Language of Emerson.* Baltimore: The Johns Hopkins University Press, [1981]. xv, 188 pp.; 23 cm. Index. LC 80–25750. ISBN 0–8018–2450–8. $13.50.

A psychoanalytic reading seeing a conflict between masculine and feminine figures surfacing from Emerson's works in which he experiments with language, particularly in *Nature* and some of the essays. There is a "strain of irony" arising from the works because of Emerson's ambivalence toward sexuality, his struggle for identity, and his attempt to find the meaning of democratic America.

COOPER, JAMES FENIMORE. *Gleanings in Europe: Italy.* Historical Introduction and Explanatory Notes by John Conron and Constance Ayers Denne; Text Established by Constance Ayers Denne. Albany: State University of New York Press, [1981]. xlvi, 377 pp.; illus.; 23 cm. (The Writings of James Fenimore

Cooper.) Appendixes ("Explanatory Notes," "Appendix A: Bentley's analytical Table of Contents," "Appendix B: Guide to parallel passages in 1828 Journal and expanded 1837 Text," "Textual Commentary," "Textual Notes," "Emendations," "Rejected Readings," "Word-Division"): pp. 305–361; index. LC 79-15177. ISBN 0-87395-365-7: cloth, $27.50; ISBN 0-87395-460-2: paper, $8.95.

A CSE-approved edition based on the last of Cooper's five travel sketches. The editors explain that this sketch is less political than the one on *Switzerland* and that Cooper intended to make the picturesque mode "a little unique" by maintaining a true fidelity to the facts of natural scenes and typography while incorporating a more poetical style of prose.

COOPER, JAMES FENIMORE. *Gleanings in Europe: Switzerland.* Historical Introduction and Explanatory Notes by Robert E. Spiller and James F. Beard; Text Established by Kenneth W. Staggs and James P. Elliott. Albany: State University of New York Press, [1980]. xliii, 361 pp.; illus.; 23 cm. (The Writings of James Fenimore Cooper.) Appendixes ("Explanatory Notes," "Appendix A: Bentley's analytical Table of Contents," "Appendix B: Guide to parallel passages in 1828 Swiss Journal and expanded 1836 Text," "Textual Commentary," "Textual Notes," "Emendations," "Word-Division"): pp. 301–347; index. LC 79-13133. ISBN 0-87395-364-9. $24.95.

A CEAA-approved edition based on the first of the five travel sketches written between 1826 and 1833. The editorial introduction notes that Cooper draws on the popular conventional form of the "pittoresque" to convey his impressions of the scenes, but his version of the picturesque mode is framed with a personal narrative and political commentary.

COOPER, JAMES FENIMORE. *The Pathfinder, or The Inland Sea.* Edited with an Historical Introduction by Richard Dilworth Rust. Albany: State University of New York Press, [1981]. xxvi, 569 pp.: illus, facsims.; 23 cm. (The Writings of James Fenimore Cooper.) Appendixes ("Textual Commentary," "Note on the Manuscript," "Textual Notes," "Emendations," "Rejected Readings," "Word-Division"): pp. 471–569. LC 79-15598. ISBN 0-87395-360-6. $24.95.

A CSE-approved edition, based on Cooper's manuscript.

COOPER, JAMES FENIMORE. *The Pioneers, or the Sources of the Susquehanna; A Descriptive Tale.* Historical Introduction and Explanatory Notes by James Franklin Beard. Text Established by Lance Schachterle and Kenneth M. Andersen, Jr. Albany: State University of New York Press, [1980]. lvii, 565 pp.: illus.; 23 cm. (The Writings of James Fenimore Cooper.) Appendixes ("Explanatory Notes," "Textual Commentary," "Textual Notes," "Emendations," "Rejected Readings," "Word-Division"): pp. 457–565. LC 77-21795. ISBN 0-87395-359-2. $24.95.

This CEAA-approved edition uses the third variant of the Wiley-Clayton first edition of Cooper's text. Beard's commentary explains the circumstances around the publication of the book in 1823, the various editions, and Cooper's problems with piracies of his most popular novel.

DEDMOND, FRANCIS B. *Sylvester Judd.* Boston: Twayne, [1980]. 161 pp.: front.; 20 cm. (Twayne's United States Authors Series: TUSAS 365.) "Selected Bibliography": pp. 154–158; index. LC 79-27605. ISBN 0-8057-7305-3. $11.95.

This biographical, analytical, and critical overview of the writer and his works puts Judd in a significant place in the history of American literature. Dedmond devotes a chapter to each of Judd's works, including contemporary reviews and criticism. Dedmond disclaims any attempts by recent critics to label Judd a Transcendentalist and notes that "with *Margaret* he awakened anew the possibility of a fiction distinctively American."

DELBANCO, ANDREW. *William Ellery Channing: An Essay on the Liberal Spirit in America.* [Cambridge: Harvard University Press, 1981]. xviii, 203 pp.; 21 cm. Index. LC 80-19304. ISBN 0-674-95335-5. $15.00.

Channing's liberalism, which seems conservative to modern interpreters, must be judged within the context of early nineteenth-century ideas, and from the standpoint of his basic beliefs as a Unitarian minister. Before his liberalism became manifest, though, he agonized over choosing an uncertain radical stand, but he was too ambitious to settle for a neutral position.

DUBLIN, THOMAS, editor. *Farm to Factory: Women's Letters, 1830–1860.* New York: Columbia University Press, 1981. x, 191 pp.: front., illus., ports., facsims.; 23 cm. LC 80-28084 ISBN 0-231-05118-2 $17.50.

The collection of four groups of letters by women mill workers reveals their personal experiences, working conditions, and a common theme in women's history during the middle of the nineteenth century.

EITNER, WALTER H. *Walt Whitman's Western Jaunt.* Lawrence: The Regents Press of Kansas, [1981]. xvi, 123 pp.: front., illus.; 23 cm. "Bibliography Essay": pp. 117–118; index. LC 80-29336. ISBN 0-7006-0212-7. $18.00.

A comparison of Whitman's published record of his western experience, *Specimen Days,* with his diary and records kept during the four-month travel, suggests that he took pretenses to reconstruct a version of the facts into fiction "to have them support a bardic pose he wished to maintain."

EMERSON, ELLEN TUCKER. *The Life of Lidian Jackson Emerson.* Edited by Delores Bird Carpenter. Boston: Twayne, 1980. xlix, 269 pp.: front., facsims., illus.; 23 cm. (Twayne's American Literary Manuscripts Series.) Index. LC 80-14908. ISBN 0-8057-9651-7. $25.00.

This is the first publication of Ellen Tucker Emerson's manuscript. Carpenter notes that the *Life*: reveals the strength, wit, and vitality of Mrs. Emerson; shows the ability of Ellen Emerson to overcome the restraints of subjectivity in writing a truthful biography of her mother; and portrays the domestic environment of Ralph Waldo Emerson.

FOYE, RAYMOND, editor. *The Unknown Poe: An Anthology of Fugitive Writings by Edgar Allan Poe, with Appreciations by Charles Baudelaire, Stephane Mallarmé,*

Paul Valéry, J. K. Huysmans and André Breton. San Francisco: City Lights, [1980]. x, 117 pp.: front., illus.; 20 cm. LC 80-24321. ISBN 0-87286-119-8: cloth, $10.95; ISBN 0-87286-110-4: paper, $5.95.

This edition collects in one volume translations of essays by the French writers who have extoled Poe and those works of his that they admired: "the arcana of Edgar Allan Poe: writings on wit, humor, dreams, drunkenness, genius, madness, and apocalypse."

GARMON, GERALD M. *John Reuben Thompson.* Boston: Twayne, [1979]. 174 pp.: front.; 20 cm. (Twayne's United States Authors Series: TUSAS 346.) "Selected Bibliography": pp. 165-168; index. LC 79-15602. ISBN 0-8057-7284-7. $13.50.

Garmon's critical and biographical study of Thompson, ignored and discredited because of his injustice to Poe, is to renew interest in the editor of the *Southern Literary Messenger,* "perhaps the most polished prose stylist of his age."

GILHOOLEY, LEONARD, editor. *No Divided Allegiance: Essays in Brownson's Thought.* With a Foreword by Arthur M. Schlesinger, Jr. Bronx, New York: Fordham University Press, 1980. xiii, 193 pp.: front.; 23 cm. LC 79-56139. ISBN 0-8232-1056-1: cloth, $20.00; ISBN 0-8232-1057-X: paper, $8.00.

In the volume are the following essays: John A. Coleman, "Vision and Praxis in American Theology: Orestes Brownson, John A. Ryan, and John Courtney Murray": points out how Brownson was in search of a unity between God and the world and a correlation between science and religion; C. Carroll Hollis, "Orestes Brownson: Jacksonian Literary Critic": Brownson's support of Jacksonian democracy is reflected in his criticism of works that reveal his concern for social theories of the time; Armand A. Maurer, "Orestes Brownson: Philosopher of Freedom": suggests that even though Brownson was called a "'weathercock'" because of his changes of opinions, he continued to be guided toward truth and a "love and defense of freedom" in religion, politics, and philosophy; A. Robert Caponigri, "European Influences on the Thought of Orestes Brownson: Pierre Leroux and Vincenzo Gioberti": because Brownson felt the "need for religious certainty and the need for social order," Caponigri feels that Brownson found these needs fulfilled by two European figures: Leroux for the derivation of Leibniz's law of continuity in the perfectibility of man and the importance of religion binding mankind throughout history; Gioberti for the belief in intuition, inner illumination, and the transcendent ability of mind to reveal reality as the basis of faith; Leonard Gilhooley, "Brownson, the American Idea, and the Early Civil War": argues that the editor's attacks in *Brownson's Quarterly Review* reflected the basic philosophy of the "American Idea," respecting the Constitution, for a free united republic and individual liberties, and that, to Brownson, the South was inhibiting both union and individual freedom; Peter J. Stanlis, "Orestes Brownson's *The American Republic* Today": the hope for new freedom in America "lies in Brownson's concept of the providential constitution of the American republic"; Russell Kirk, "Orestes Brownson and T. S. Eliot": shows similarities, not influences as Allen Guttman argues, between the two writers: Eliot did not read Brownson until 1953, according to Kirk's report from Eliot; Alvan S. Ryan, "Brownson's Significance for American Democracy Today": suggests that Brownson's "profoundly historical sense" makes his insights and thoughts in his own time as important for us today.

GREENE, DANA, editor. *Lucretia Mott: Her Complete Speeches and Sermons.* New York: Edwin Mellen Press, [1980]. ix, 401 pp.; 23 cm. (Studies in Women and Religion, vol. 4.) "Annotated Index of Proper Names": pp. 395–401. LC 80–81885. ISBN 0-88946-968-7. Paper, $24.95.

Greene's introduction states that Mott's reform philosophy is well defined in her speeches and sermons and that many of her ideas were affirmed by Unitarian and Transcendental beliefs.

GURA, PHILIP F. *The Wisdom of Words: Language, Theology, and Literature in the New England Renaissance.* Middletown, Conn.: Wesleyan University Press, [1981]. x, 201 pp.; 23 cm. "Selected Bibliography of Primary Sources": pp. 191–194. Index. LC 80–25041. ISBN 0-8195-5053-1. $17.50.

A study of the way the nineteenth century interpreted language, beginning early in the century with Unitarians, whose empirical interpretation of the biblical word spurred the mid-century shift to a more figurative acceptance of the transcendent power of language between the natural world and the spiritual. Emerson saw in this transcendent correspondence of language a symbol of universal analogy and spiritual truth; for Thoreau, philology unveiled the secrets of nature, the basis of the symbolic meaning of words; Hawthorne used "rhetorical ambiguity"; and Melville's linguistic vision could find no sure symbol of words or things—the only truth, to him, was ambiguity.

HABERSTROH, CHARLES J., JR. *Melville and Male Identity.* Rutherford, [N.J.]: Fairleigh Dickinson University Press, [1980]. 147 pp.; 21 cm. "Bibliography": pp. 137–144; index. LC 78–75178. ISBN 0-8386-2321-2. $14.50.

Melville, suffering from an identity crisis after the death of his father, created strong assertive males in the earlier novels, but ambiguous, disoriented ones in the later novels before arriving at a resolution in *Billy Budd* through Captain Vere, the example of "dutiful masculine conduct."

HARRISON, CYNTHIA E., editor. *Women in American History: A Bibliography.* Introduction by Anne Firor Scott. Santa Barbara, Calif.: [Clio Press, 1979]. xi, 374 pp.; 28 cm. (Clio Bibliography Series No. 5.) Author and Subject Indexes. LC 78–26194. ISBN 0-87436-260-1. $58.00.

Contains 3,395 abstracts of articles selected from *America: History and Life* (1964–77) that deal specifically with women.

HAWTHORNE, NATHANIEL. *The French and Italian Notebooks.* Edited by Thomas Woodson. [Columbus]: Ohio State University Press, [1980]. [xi], 1045 pp.; 23 cm. (The Centenary Edition of the Works of Nathaniel Hawthorne, Volume XIV.) Appendixes ("Explanatory Notes," "Historical Commentary," "Textual Commentary," "Editorial Emendations in the Copy-Text," "Word-Division," "Alterations in the Manuscripts," "Cross-references with *The Marble Faun*"): pp. 713–1008; index. LC 63–750. ISBN 0-8142-0256-X. $36.00.

This CSE-approved edition is the first complete publication of the notebooks which Hawthorne kept between January 1858 and June 1859 while in Europe.

HEFFERNAN, THOMAS FAREL. *Stove by a Whale: Owen Chase and the* Essex. Middletown, Conn.: Wesleyan University Press, [1981]. xiii, 273 pp.: front., facsims., illus.; 23 cm. Appendixes ("Herman Melville's Annotations and Markings in His Copy of Owen Chase's *Narrative*," "The Story of the Essex Shipwreck Presented in Captain Pollard's Interview with George Bennet," "Thomas Chapple's Account of the Loss of the *Essex*," "March 7, 1821, Letter of Commodore Ridgely to the Secretary of the Navy," "The 'Paddack Letter' on the Rescue of Captain Pollard and Charles Ramsdell," "Report of the *Essex* Shipwreck and Rescue in the *Sydney Gazette*, June 9, 1821," "Table of Islands from Bowditch's *Navigator*," "Chase Genealogy"): pp. 184–251; index: LC 80–21603. ISBN 0–8195–5052–3. $19.95.

Heffernan reprints Owen Chase's *Narrative of the Most Extraordinary and Distressing Shipwreck of the Whaleship* Essex, *of Nantucket*, gives an extensive historical overview of the factual accounts of the *Essex* disaster compared to Chase's work, and analyzes Melville's adaptation of Chase's story in *Moby Dick*.

HELLERSTEIN, ERNA OLAFSON, LESLIE PARKER HUME, and KAREN M. OFFEN, editors. *Victorian Women: A Documentary Account of Women's Lives in Nineteenth-Century England, France, and the United States.* Stanford: Stanford University Press, 1981. xvi, 534 pp.: illus.; 23 cm. "Works Cited in the Introductions": pp. 511–522; index. LC 79–67770. ISBN 0–8047–1088–0: cloth, $27.50; ISBN 0–8047–1096–1: paper, $11.95.

The editors use autobiographical and historical sources from diaries, letters, medical and legal case studies, and various publications to depict the experience of the nineteenth-century woman. Writings of and references to Alcott, Beecher, Child, Fuller, and Stowe are included.

HERBERT, T. WALTER, JR. *Marquesan Encounters: Melville and the Meaning of Civilization.* Cambridge: Harvard University Press, 1980. viii, 237 pp.: illus.; 24 cm. "Bibliography": pp. 227–230; index. LC 80–15979. ISBN 0–674–55066–8. $15.00.

In examining the responses by three Americans, representative of rival schools of nineteenth-century thought—Captain David Porter, spokesman for the Enlightenment, Rev. Charles Stewart, Calvinist, and Melville, Romantic—Herbert analyzes their versions of the meaning of civilization when they encountered the savage inhabitants of the Marquesas Islands. Melville's impression in *Typee*, unlike the factual accounts of Porter and Stewart, was criticized for inaccuracies and unconventional views, especially his ambiguous romantic stance—"between horror and profound admiration for the islanders,... between hatred for civilization and a frantic desire to return to it."

HOLMES, OLIVER WENDELL. *Ralph Waldo Emerson.* Introduction by Joel Porte. New York: Chelsea House, 1980. xxvii, 339 pp.: front.; 21 cm. (American Men and Women of Letters Series.) Index. LC 80–23687. ISBN 0–87754–157–4. $5.95.

Facsimile reprinting of the 1884 edition published by Houghton Mifflin. As Porte points out, this is a more critical and realistic treatment of Emerson than most portraits by his admiring disciples of the time. While it tends to dispel the aura of Transcendentalism, Holmes' *Emerson* endures because of the vivid recreation of the man and perceptive criticism of the poetry.

HOMANS, MARGARET. *Women Writers and Poetic Identity: Dorothy Wordsworth, Emily Bronte, and Emily Dickinson.* Princeton: Princeton University Press, [1980]. 260 pp.; 22 cm. Index. LC 80–7527. ISBN 0–691–06440–7. $14.75.

Because nineteenth-century literature inherited from the Romantic tradition a focus on masculine identity, women poets, unlike women novelists, had to struggle to transcend the impediments of the masculine bias. Dickinson's success rests with her dual self-concept in her poetry which "allows her to avoid direct competition with the masculine unitary self, while at the same time also allowing her a power of her own."

HOWELLS, W. D. *Selected Letters.* Volume 3: 1882–1891. Edited and Annotated by Robert C. Leitz III with Richard H. Ballinger and Christoph K. Lohmann; Textual Editor, Christoph K. Lohmann. Boston: Twayne, 1980. xiv, 405 pp.: front.; 24 cm. (Selected Letters of W. D. Howells.) "Textual Apparatus": pp. 331–375; "List of Howells' Correspondents": pp. 377–379; index. LC 78–27247. ISBN 0–8057–8529–9. $27.50.

A CEAA-approved text of a selection of letters in the period from when Howells resigned from his position with the *Atlantic* to work on his novels up to the end of 1891, when he took over editorship of *Cosmopolitan*. During this period Howells spent a year in Europe, suffered the declining health and eventual death of his daughter, and, in assuming a position with *Harper's* in 1885, became a strong advocate of social reform and literary realism.

HOYLE, PAMELA. *The Boston Ambience, an Exhibition of Nineteenth Century Photographs.* Boston: The Boston Athenæum, [1981]. 44 pp.: photo.; 22 cm. "Catalogue of the Exhibition": pp. 37–43; "A Short Bibliography of Nineteenth-Century Photography in Boston": p. 44. LC 81–65004. ISBN 0–934552–36–3. Paper, $5.00.

The catalogue, mentioning Edward Everett Hale's interest in photography, gives a history of the six major photographers and reproduces their photographs and daguerreotypes. The exhibit included photographs of Louis Agassiz, Emerson, and Whittier.

HULL, RAYMONA E. *Nathaniel Hawthorne: The English Experience, 1853–1864.* Pittsburgh: University of Pittsburgh Press, [1980]. xvi. 307 pp.: front., illus.; 23 cm. Appendix ("Biographical Sketches"): pp. 269–297; index. LC 79–26616. ISBN 0–8229–3418–3. $21.95.

Analyzes Hawthorne's years abroad by drawing on letters, diaries, unpublished family accounts, and the *English* and *Italian Notebooks*.

IREY, EUGENE F., editor. *A Concordance to Five Essays of Ralph Waldo Emerson.* New York: Garland, 1981. xvi, 468 pp.; 28 cm. (Garland Reference Library of the Humanities, vol. 250.) LC 80-8520. ISBN 0-8240-9464-6. $100.00.

A computerized concordance to *Nature,* "The American Scholar," "The Divinity School Address," "Self-Reliance," and "Fate," keyed to the 1903 Centenary Edition, and giving the words in context.

IRVING, WASHINGTON. *Journals and Notebooks.* Volume II: 1807-1822. Edited by Walter A. Reichart and Lillian Schlissel. Boston: Twayne, 1981. xxiii, 407 pp.: front., illus.; 24 cm. (The Complete Works of Washington Irving, vol. 2.) Index. LC 80-18822. ISBN 0-8057-8501-9. $32.00.

A CEAA-approved text of Irving's journals, during the period in which he was establishing his writing talent. Portions of the manuscripts between 1810 and 1822 are published for the first time.

IRVING, WASHINGTON. *The Life and Voyages of Christopher Columbus.* Edited by John Harmon McElroy. Boston: Twayne, 1981. xcvii, 1110 pp.: front., illus.; 24 cm. (The Complete Works of Washington Irving, vol. 11.) Appendixes ("List of Abbreviations," "Textual Commentary," "Discussions of Adopted Readings," "List of Emendations," "List of Rejected Substantives," "List of Compound Words Hyphenated at End of Line"): pp. 573-1110. LC 78-32075. ISBN 0-8057-8516-7. $60.00.

A CEAA-approved edition of Irving's work, printed from a copy-text based on four manuscript variants.

IRVING, WASHINGTON. *Miscellaneous Writings.* Volumes I and II: 1803-1859. Edited by Wayne R. Kime. Boston: Twayne, 1981. xcvi, 464 pp.; 697 pp.: front., illus.; 24 cm. (The Complete Works of Washington Irving, vols. 28-29.) Appendixes ("List of Abbreviations," "Explanatory Notes," "Textual Commentary," "Discussions of Adopted Readings," "List of Emendations," "List of Rejected Variants," "List of Rejected Precopy-Text Variants," "List of Compound Words Hyphenated at end of Line"): pp. 229-454; pp. 348-688; indexes. LC 80-19108. ISBN 0-8057-8520-5 (set). $75.00.

The CEAA-approved text includes Irving's prose works, plays, "Narratives of Spanish History Left Unpublished at Irving's Death," and "Other Prose Writings Left Unpublished at Irving's Death."

IRWIN, JOHN T. *American Hieroglyphics: The Symbol of the Egyptian Hieroglyphics in the American Renaissance.* New Haven: Yale University Press, [1980]. xii, 371 pp.; 23 cm. Index. LC 80-130. ISBN 0-300-02471-1. $19.50.

The six major writers of the American Renaissance significantly reflect the impact Champollion had on nineteenth-century America when he deciphered the Egyptian hieroglyphic with the Rosetta Stone. For each writer the hieroglyphics represented something different: Emerson, "a basic understanding of the universe"; Thoreau, nature is an emblem "whose meanings are hidden" from men; Whitman, *Leaves of Grass* is "the hieroglyphical book of nature; Poe, the decipherer/scientist/analyst of the mystery; Hawthorne and Melville, the ambiguous meaning associated with symbols.

JOHNSON, BARBARA. *The Critical Difference: Essays in the Contemporary Rhetoric of Reading.* Baltimore: Johns Hopkins University Press, [1980]. xii, 156 pp.; 23 cm. Index. LC 80–21533. ISBN 0–8018–2458–3. $12.00.

Using the process of deconstructive criticism in several literary works, Johnson explains that Melville intended both naive and ironic readings of *Billy Budd* and that understanding and misinterpreting unexplained actions help shape the plot. She uses Poe's "The Purloined Letter," Jacques Lacan's criticism of the story, and Jacques Derrida's response to Lacan as examples of how the analyses transform the story, in effect, into three texts.

JOHNSON, CLAUDIA D. *The Productive Tension of Hawthorne's Art.* University, Ala.: University of Alabama Press, [1981]. 158 pp.; 22 cm. "Bibliography": pp. 140–151; index. LC 80–15634. ISBN 0–8173–0050–3: cloth, $14.00; ISBN 0–8173–0051–1: paper, $5.95.

This view of Hawthorne proposes that his aesthetic evolved from the psychological conflict of his dual legacy between the artistic tension of the romantic temperament and his moral stance of Puritanism. In *The Marble Faun* he reconciles this tension by creating an organic regenerative work in the romantic tradition which actively engages the reader in the creative process.

KLINKOWITZ, JEROME. *The Practice of Fiction in America: Writers from Hawthorne to the Present.* Ames: The Iowa State University Press, [1980]. vii, 140 pp.; 23 cm. Index. LC 80–13608. ISBN 0–8138–1420–0. $10.25.

Klinkowitz feels that Hawthorne's *The House of Seven Gables* is the starting point of America's experimental fiction in which the writer's "self-conscious critical attention to matters of theme and form will be the yardstick by which our fiction grows." Although *The House of Seven Gables* is his one conscious attempt to work out the conflict between the reality of history and the ideality of romance, Hawthorne fails because he tries to resolve what is historically irresolvable.

KRAMER, JOHN E. JR. *The American College Novel: An Annotated Bibliography.* New York: Garland, 1981. xv, 286 pp.; 22 cm. (Garland Reference Library of the Humanities, vol. 253.) Appendix ("Major American College Novels"): pp. 273–274. Indexes. LC 80–8971. ISBN 0–8240–9365–8. $40.00.

Chronologically lists 425 "college novels"—set on an American college or university campus and having protagonists who are affiliated with the institutions—published between 1828 and 1979.

KRIBBS, JAYNE K., editor. *Critical Essays on John Greenleaf Whittier.* Boston: G. K. Hall, [1980]. xl, 228 pp.; 23 cm. (Critical Essays on American Literature.) Index. LC 80–14207. ISBN 0–8161–8308–2. $22.50.

A collection of essays reflecting an overview of Whittier scholarship which Kribbs sees falling into four periods of criticism: (1) from the first review of Whittier by William Lloyd Garrison in 1826 to 1865; (2) 1866, with the publication of *Snow-Bound*, to 1919; (3) 1920 to 1950; (4) 1950 to the present. In her introduction, Kribbs discusses the critics' assessment of Whittier and concludes that "he will survive for perceptive readers as a spokesman for significant historical events and literary trends."

KUNTZ, JOSEPH M., and NANCY C. MARTINEZ. *Poetry Explication: A Checklist of Interpretation Since 1925 of British and American Poems Past and Present.* Boston. G. K. Hall, [1980]. xi, 570 pp.; 25 cm. "Main Sources Consulted": pp. 553–570. LC 80–10291. ISBN 0–8161–8313–9. $35.00.

Indexes poetry explications printed during 1925–77 for a selection of major British and American Poets, including Emerson, Melville, Poe, Thoreau, and Whitman.

LOCKWOOD, ALLISON. *Passionate Pilgrims: The American Traveler in Great Britain, 1800–1914.* [Rutherford, N.J.]: Fairleigh Dickinson University Press, [1981]. 551 pp.: illus.; 24 cm. Bibliography: pp. 521–538; index. LC 78–68808. ISBN 0–8386–2272–0. $30.00.

Basing her study on records, commentaries, books, and essays, Lockwood classifies and analyzes the American pilgrims in search of Britain and her people, seeing this as a quest for themselves as well. Among the authors surveyed are Irving, Cooper, Emerson, Hawthorne, Fuller, and Stowe.

LOWANCE, MASON I., JR. *The Language of Canaan: Metaphor and Symbol in New England from the Puritans to the Transcendentalists.* Cambridge: Harvard University Press, 1980. x, 335 pp.; 23 cm. Index. LC 79–21179. ISBN 0–674–50949–8. $20.00.

American literature is utopian, with a basis in "a biblical impulse" or "a prophetic strain" found in the language of Canaan originating with Puritan biblical symbolism and extending into the nineteenth century with Emerson and Thoreau. While Emerson replaces the symbolism with Platonic and mystical allusions, Thoreau continues the symbolism of prophecy in his major works.

MCNALL, SALLY ALLEN. *Who Is In the House?: A Psychological Study of Two Centuries of Women's Fiction in America, 1795 to the Present.* New York: Elsevier, [1981]. xii, 153 pp.; 23 cm. Index. LC 80–26601. ISBN 0–444–99081–X. $17.95. This book may be ordered from Greenwood Press, Westport, Conn.

The images of women, portrayed by women writers, in popular fiction (i.e., read for pleasure) reflect the social and psychological realities of each period. Discusses the works of Caroline Lee Hentz and Catharine Maria Sedgwich.

MCNEIL, BARBARA, and MIRANDA C. HERBERT, editors. *Author Biographies Master Index: Supplement.* Detroit: Gale Research, 1980. xi, 587 pp.; 28 cm. (Gale Biographical Index Series, Number 3.) ISBN 0–8103–1088–9. Paper, $65.00.

Updates *Author Biographies Master Index* (1978) with additional biographical and critical sources of information.

MALE, ROY R., editor. *Money Talks: Language and Lucre in American Fiction.* Foreword by Ronald Schleifer. Norman: University of Oklahoma Press, [1980]. xiii, 149 pp.; 23 cm. Index. LC 80–5945. ISBN 0–8061–1754–0. $14.95.

A collection of essays based on the American myth of "money" and the theme of the value of money, language, and fiction, all illusory, deceptive, untrustworthy, yet invaluable as a means of exchange. Leslie A. Fiedler's "Literature and Lucre: A Meditation" discusses the lucrative writer versus the poor writer; Poe and Melville, writers who dreamed of success, were destroyed by a "money-grubbing society" because they failed "to provide what the market place demanded," while writers like Harriet Beecher Stowe died "honored and rich." Marc Shell's "The Gold Bug" deciphers the tale as an economic and linguistic cryptogram—the value of paper money or the meaning of language depend on how the imagination relates the symbol to the thing.

MELVILLE, ANNETTE, compiler. *Special Collections in the Library of Congress: A Selective Guide*. Washington: [U.S. Government Printing Office], 1980. xv, 464 pp.: front., facsims., illus.; 23 cm. Index. LC 79–607780. ISBN 0–8444–0297–4. $12.00.

Describes 269 of the special collections in the Library of Congress and gives a brief essay describing each.

MILLER, TICE L. *Bohemians and Critics: American Theatre Criticism in the Nineteenth Century*. Metuchen, N.J., and London: The Scarecrow Press, 1981. x, 190 pp.; 22 cm. "Selected Bibliography": pp. 177–180; index. LC 80–24430. ISBN 0–8108–1377–7. $12.00.

Miller focuses on five mid-19th-century drama critics (Henry Clapp, Jr., Edward G. P. Wilkins, William Winter, Stephen Ryder Fiske, and Andrew C. Wheeler) who significantly helped shape American theatre criticism into the established school it evolved into by the end of the century. Prior to 1850 Whitman and Poe were among the early critics who advocated reforms in theatre criticism, because they "wanted a quality American stage as well as objective and knowledgeable criticism."

MITCHELL, LEE CLARK. *Witnesses to a Vanishing America: The Nineteenth-Century Response*. [Princeton]: Princeton University Press, [1981]. xvii, 320 pp.: front., illus.; 24 cm. "Selected Bibliography": pp. 281–312; index. LC 80–8567. ISBN 0–691–06461–X. $18.50.

The uniquely American movement in conservation originated in the nineteenth century when Americans first became apprehensive about the rapid westward expansion and sensed the possible extinction of the wilderness. In order to capture the vanishing legacy of America, Americans "attempted to preserve its landscape in words, oils, and photographs."

MYERSON, JOEL. *The New England Transcendentalists and the* Dial: *A History of the Magazine and Contributors*. Rutherford, [N.J.]: Fairleigh Dickinson University Press, [1980]. 345 pp.: facsims., illus.; 24 cm. "Appendix": pp. 289–315; "Bibliography": pp. 316–333; index. LC 78–66814. ISBN 0–8386–2294–1. $25.00.

A history of the *Dial*, beginning with the founding of the Transcendental Club, and including a brief biographical sketch of each of the contributors. Rather than focusing on aesthetics or philosophy, Myerson concentrates on the publication procedures and problems, the contemporary reception, the editorial judgments and policies, and the selection of the contents of each issue.

NAGEL, JAMES, and RICHARD ASTRO, editors. *American Literature: The New England Heritage.* New York: Garland, 1981. viii, 204 pp.; 22 cm. (Papers presented at a conference held at Northeastern University, May 9-10, 1980.) Index. LC 80-8517. ISBN 0-8240-9467-0. $25.00.

A collection of essays on different aspects of New England literary culture, from the beginning to the present. Included are Joel Myerson, "Historic Notes on Life and Letters in Transcendental New England": Emerson's various essays, lectures, and journals imply an optimistic vision of New England—a combination of the best traits transposed from Old England and inherited from the Puritans—and her inhabitant— an eclectic, but ideal individual; and Hershel Parker, "Melville and the Berkshires: Emotion-Laden Terrain, 'Reckless Sky-Assaulting Mood,' and Encroaching Wordsworthianism": Melville's trauma in 1852, after the appearance of *Pierre,* was the culmination of two years of trauma: an idyllic summer retreat in the Berkshires in 1850 that made him more aware of Wordsworth's nature, recalling sadness and vanishing youth, coupled with Harpers meager terms for *Pierre* in 1851, incited him to revise the novel into a disunified product that even he felt was a "botch."

NELSON, RANDY F. *The Almanac of American Letters.* Los Altos, Calif.: William Kaufmann, [1981]. xii, 325 pp.; 23 cm. Bibliography: pp. 293-300; index. LC 80-27571. ISBN 0-86576-008-X. $16.95.

A collection of anecdotes, facts, important information, and minutiae about American authors from the seventeenth century to the present.

NISSENBAUM, STEPHEN. *Sex, Diet, and Debility in Jacksonian America: Sylvester Graham and Health Reform.* Westport, Conn.: Greenwood Press, [1980]. [xix], 198 pp.; 21 cm. (Contributions in Medical History, Number 4.) "Bibliography": pp. 175-189; index. LC 79-8280. ISBN 0-313-21415-8. $22.95.

Graham, his followers, and those who influenced him formulated their ideas for "a physiology of subsistence" to counteract the degradation of man by capitalism, industrialism, and urbanization. Thoreau's practices at Walden may have been an adaptation of the Grahamite system.

OSBORNE, WILLIAM S. *Lydia Maria Child.* Boston: Twayne, [1980]. 196 pp.: front.; 20 cm. (Twayne's United States Authors Series: TUSAS 380.) "Appendix": pp. 164-172; "Selected Bibliography": pp 191-193; index. LC 80-432. ISBN 0-8057-7315-0. $12.95.

This biographical and literary analysis focuses on Child's strength as a writer—her social criticism and her contribution to the development of American literature— rather than her weakness—her lack of innovation in her fiction.

POE, EDGAR ALLAN. *The Imaginary Voyages: The Narrative of Arthur Gordon Pym, The Unparalled Adventure of one Hans Pfaal, The Journal of Julius Rodman.* Edited by Burton R. Pollin. Boston: Twayne, 1981. xix, 667 pp.: illus., facsims.; 24 cm. (Collected Writings of Edgar Allan Poe, vol. 1.) Appendixes

("Variant Readings in the *Southern Literary Messenger*," "Notes and Comments," pp. 211–363; "Variants for 'Hans Pfaall,'" "The 'Manuscript Notes' of Poe," "Notes and Comments," pp. 436–506; "Notes and Comments," pp. 582–653). Index. LC 81–2915. ISBN 0–8057–8534–5. $40.00.

A critical edition of Poe's works based on available manuscripts and with full annotation.

PORTER, DAVID. *Dickinson: The Modern Idiom*. Cambridge: Harvard University Press, 1981. ix, 316 pp.; 24 cm. Indexes. LC 80–24322. ISBN 0–674–20444–1. $20.00.

Sees Emily Dickinson at the beginning of a new strain in American poetry, diverging from her forerunners and deviating from Emerson and Whitman. She is a modern idiom in the nineteenth century, anticipating the dilemma of the modern poets concerned with the limitation and function of language, how the chaos of external reality is reflected in the fragmented structure of a poem, the problem and freedom of spontaneity, and the disconnection between reality and imagination.

PRED, ALLAN. *Urban Growth and City-Systems in the United States, 1840–1860*. Cambridge: Harvard University Press, 1980. xv, 282 pp.: tables; 24 cm. (Harvard Studies in Urban History.) Appendix: pp. 175–232; index. LC 80–12098. ISBN 0–674–93091–6. $28.00.

The transformation and growth of urban centers during the pivotal period between 1840 and 1860 hinged on prior economic prosperity within a city-system before cities like Boston, New York, Philadelphia, Richmond, and Charleston gradually made the transition into industrialized complexes.

RAO, ADAPA RAMAKRISHNA. *Emerson and Social Reform*. [Atlantic Highlands, N.J.]: Humanities Press, [1981]. 133 pp.; 21 cm. "Selective Bibliography": pp. 123–130; index. ISBN 0–391–02199–0. $10.25.

Since Emerson took no active part in social reform movements, yet supported the reformers and their ideals, his ambivalent attitude was conditioned by the serenity of Transcendental optimism and his strong belief in individual self-reliance.

REYNOLDS, DAVID S. *Faith in Fiction: The Emergence of Religious Literature in America*. Cambridge: Harvard University Press, 1981. 269 pp.: illus.; 24 cm. Appendixes ("Selected Bibliography," "Chronology of Fiction"): pp. 219–257; index. LC 80–20885. ISBN 0–674–29172–7. $22.50.

The religious fiction written between 1785 and 1850 was initiated as a reaction against the conventional religious literature of the Puritans, but its role became significant in the literary history of a skeptical nineteenth-century culture by providing solace from the crisis of reality and maintaining optimism when other novelists were expressing pessimism.

ROBERTSON, JAMES OLIVER. *American Myth, American Reality*. New York: Hill and Wang, [1980]. xvii, 398 pp.; 23 cm. "Bibliography": pp. 355–381; index. LC 80–18557. ISBN 0–8090–2504–3. $16.95.

This exploration into the reasoning behind American myths mentions Whitman's vision of the individual and Cooper's Leatherstocking in the frontier. Thoreau was influential in establishing the wilderness myth by "consciously creating myth in *Walden.*"

ROLLINS, RICHARD M. *The Long Journey of Noah Webster.* [Philadelphia]: University of Pennsylvania Press, 1980. xi, 195 pp.; 23 cm. "Bibliography": pp. 173–190; index. LC 79–5257. ISBN 0–8122–7778–3. $16.00.

This biography places Webster within American literary history and attempts "to understand the ways in which an individual internalized the events, ideas, values, and beliefs of his age, and to show how these affected his work."

ROSENTHAL, BERNARD. *City of Nature: Journeys to Nature in the Age of American Romanticism.* Newark: University of Delaware Press, [1980]. 273 pp.: front.; 21 cm. "Selected Bibliography": pp. 248–261; index. LC 78–68879. ISBN 0–87413–147–2. $16.50.

The American Romantics had their own private myths about nature which differed from the preconceived concept of nature. The American wilderness of the land and sea, envisioned both as real and mythic realms of nature, was a place to be transformed into "its purest form, civilization."

RUETHER, ROSEMARY RADFORD, and ROSEMARY SKINNER KELLER, general editors. *Women and Religion in America: Volume I: The Nineteenth Century.* San Francisco: Harper and Row, [1981]. xiv, 353 pp.: illus.; 24 cm. Index. LC 80–8346. ISBN 0–06–066829–6. $15.00.

A collection of original essays and reprinted primary documents on women and religion in the nineteenth century, a significant period for redefining religion in America, when women became involved in church leadership and in religious and reform movements. Among the essays are several dealing with Brook Farm.

RUGOFF, MILTON. *The Beechers: An American Family in the Nineteenth Century.* New York: Harper and Row, [1981]. xvii, 653 pp.: front., illus., facsims.; 24 cm. Appendix ("A Note on Letter Writing in the Nineteenth Century"): p. 603; "Selected Bibliography": pp. 627–633; index. LC 80–8696. ISBN 0–06–014859–4. $19.95.

Chronicle of a family dynasty that played a significant part in the transformation of America in the nineteenth century. The focus is on the father, Lyman, a Calvinist minister, who dictated to his eleven children, as if to servants of God, a strong belief in themselves because their ideas for social and religious reform were for the betterment of all mankind.

SALIBA, DAVID R. *A Psychology of Fear: The Nightmare Formula of Edgar Allan Poe.* [Lanham, Md.]: University Press of America, [1980]. ix, 267 pp.; 21 cm. "Selected Bibliography": pp. 243–254; index. LC 80–8267. ISBN 0–8191–1269–0: cloth, $18.50; ISBN 0–8191–1270–4: paper, $10.25.

Poe, in experimenting with psychological techniques in his fiction, perfected "the nightmare as literary form" by 1838 with "Ligeia." Poe's formula elicits a fear response by recreating a nightmare experience whereby the reader, losing conscious control and rational understanding of the events, is forced to submit to Poe's art.

SANBORN, FRANK B. *Henry David Thoreau*. Introduction by Leo Marx. New York: Chelsea House, 1980. xxiv, 324 pp.: front.; 21 cm. (American Men and Women of Letters Series.) Index. LC 80–23945. ISBN 0–87754–155–8. Paper, $5.95.

Facsimile reprinting of the 1882 edition, published by Houghton, Mifflin. Marx notes, "Sanborn's *Thoreau* is a casual piece of writing," in the "19th-century genre of the informal biographical memoir."

SEDLAK, MICHAEL W., and TIMOTHY WALCH. *American Educational History: A Guide to Information Sources*. Detroit: Gale Research, [1981]. xi, 265 pp.; 22 cm. (American Government and History Information Guide Series, vol. 10.) Indexes. LC 80–19646. ISBN 0–8103–1478–9. $32.00.

An annotated bibliography of material relating to American education and its history from 1632 to 1975.

SHERMAN, CLAIRE RICHTER, and ADELE M. HOLCOMB, editors. *Women as Interpreters of the Visual Arts, 1820–1979*. Westport, Conn.: Greenwood Press, [1981]. xxiv, 487 pp.: illus.; 24 cm. (Contributions in Women's Studies, No. 18.) "Selected Bibliography": pp. 441–457; index. LC 80–785. ISBN 0–313–22056–5. $35.00.

The volume contains biographical and critical essays on important women who have contributed criticism interpreting the visual arts. An essay on Margaret Fuller brings in the art criticism appearing in the *Dial*, by her and other contributors, to analyze the Transcendentalist theory of art.

SIEGEL, ADRIENNE. *The Image of the American City in Popular Literature: 1820–1870*. Port Washington, N.Y.: Kennikat Press, 1981. [viii], 211 pp.; 21 cm. (National University Publications: Interdisciplinary Urban Series.) Bibliography: pp. 186–205; index. LC 80–19277. ISBN 0–8046–9271–8. $15.00.

Although Siegel's focus is more on the image of urban life, particularly in New York City, portrayed in "pulp prose," she does make reference to comments by Hawthorne, Melville, Poe, Whitman, and Cooper, and to Boston's "reputation in the popular book as an American Athens, the intellectual center of the nation."

SINCLAIR, ANDREW. *The Facts in the Case of E. A. Poe*. New York: Holt, Rinehart and Winston, [1980]. 181 pp.; 21 cm. LC 80–14147. ISBN 0–03–022091–2. $10.95.

Sinclair's novel, a reconstruction of the life of Poe in his character, Ernest Albert Pons, incorporates biographical facts of Poe's life and fictional accounts from his art within a framework based on *The Narrative of Arthur Gordon Pym*.

SMITH, ALLAN GARDNER. *The Analysis of Motives: Early American Psychology and Fiction*. [Amsterdam: Rodopi, 1980]. v, 195 pp.; 22 cm. "Appendix: The

Psychological Context": pp. 125–164; Bibliography: pp. 189–195. ISBN 90–6203–861–1. Paper, $23.00. This book may be ordered from Humanities Press, Atlantic Highlands, N.J.

The psychological and philosophical theories of Europe that were becoming commonly known in America in the 19th century provided Charles Brockden Brown, Poe, and Hawthorne bases for their characters. Poe, who drew from all sources, even contradicting the accepted theories of sanity/insanity, focused on "the passions of the mind." Hawthorne's psychological truth of the human heart, more consistent with theories at the time than was Poe, explored realms of the subconscious which were not realized until later in the century by psychologists.

SPILLER, ROBERT E. *Late Harvest: Essays and Addresses in American Literature and Culture.* Westport, Conn.: Greenwood Press, [1981]. xi, 280 pp.; 21 cm. (Contributions in American Studies, No. 49.) "Bibliography of the Writings of Robert E. Spiller": pp. 251–262; index. LC 80–543. ISBN 0–313–22023–9. $25.00.

This is a collection of Spiller's essays and addresses, some published for the first time, from 1920 to 1979 that deal with the cultural awakening of America, the part nineteenth-century writers, especially Emerson, played in establishing an American identity, and the role textual editors play in editing literary texts.

STAFFORD, WILLIAM T. *Books Speaking to Books: A Contextual Approach to American Fiction.* Chapel Hill: University of North Carolina Press, [1981]. ix, 165 pp.; 21 cm. Index. LC 80–25892. ISBN 0–8078–1469–5. $16.50.

A collection of essays previously published or presented as lectures, including: "A Whale, an Heiress, and a Southern Demigod: Three Symbolic Americas," "Truth's Ragged Edges: Melville's Loyalties in *Billy Budd*—The Commitment of Form in the Digressions," and "Afterword: 'Knower, Doer, and Sayer'—The James Family View of Emerson."

STROUT, CUSHING. *The Veracious Imagination: Essays on American History, Literature, and Biography.* Middletown, Conn.: Wesleyan University Press, [1981]. xiv, 301 pp.; 21 cm. Index. LC 80–17436. ISBN 0–8195–5048–5. $17.50.

There is a close analogy between history and fiction because, where novels have tried "to make prose represent history's complexity" and where there are "fictive structures in historical writing," both attempt to explain the truth of reality. Stowe's *Uncle Tom's Cabin* and the political novel tradition, in which Hawthorne, Cooper, and Melville are representative writers, are examples of this thesis.

TEST, GEORGE A. *James Fenimore Cooper His Country and His Art: Papers from the 1980 Conference at State University College of New York, Oneonta and Cooperstown.* 93 pp.; 28 cm. (Cooper Seminar, no. 3.) Paper, $5.00.

Contains the following papers read at the Cooper Seminar: Thomas Philbrick, "Cooper in Europe: The Travel Books": emphasizes the autobiographical importance of the travel books and the functional part the writing of them played in enhancing his artistic technique; Constance Ayers Denne, "Cooper in Italy": gives a biographical overview of Cooper's experience in Italy and the circumstances involved in writing and publishing the last of the travel books; Warren S. Walker, "Cooper's Fictional Use of the Oral Tradition": how Cooper applied the oral tradition to his works to provide comic relief and a dimension of realism, including a bibliography on the subject; Leonard R. N. Ashley, "The Onomastics of Cooper's Verbal Art in *The Deerslayer* and Elsewhere": examines the importance of Cooper's choice of names in his works; Constance Ayers Denne, "Cooper's Use of Setting in the European Trilogy": says Cooper's artistic merit rests with his settings which give the meaning and intrinsic value of the novels in the trilogy; Warren S. Walker, "Cooper's Yorkers and Yankees in the Jeffersonian Garden": Cooper's settings for eight of his novels in New York State reflect the pastoral mood of Jeffersonian virtues and agrarianism; Lakshmi Mani, "James Fenimore Cooper and the Apocalypse": Cooper's earlier fiction depicts his dream of an ideal world, but his last work, *The Crater*, envisions an apocalyptic nightmare.

THOMPSON, G. R. and VIRGIL L. LOKKE, editors. *Ruined Eden of the Present: Hawthorne, Melville, and Poe: Critical Essays in Honor of Darrel Abel.* West Lafayette, Ind.: Purdue University Press, 1981. xix, 383 pp.: front.; 23 cm. "Contributors": pp. 375–377; "Selected Bibliography of the Writings of Darrel Abel": pp. 379–383. LC 80–80816. ISBN 0–911198–60–1. $15.75.

The festschrift contains seventeen essays by scholars in the period of American Romanticism. The variety in the selection of critical approaches following Abel's manner of criticism represents: a comparison of authors, biographical and bibliographical studies, thematic and textual analyses, and essays on the history of ideas approach.

TINGLEY, ELIZABETH, and DONALD F. TINGLEY. *Women and Feminism in American History: A Guide to Information Sources.* Detroit: Gale Research, [1981]. xi, 289 pp.; 22 cm. (American Government and History Information Guide Series, vol. 12.) Indexes. LC 80–19793. ISBN 0–8103–1477–0. $36.00.

An annotated bibliography of selected material pertaining to women, from the Colonial era to the present, with emphasis on all aspects of feminist writing that proposes improving the condition of women. The book is divided into chapters on biographies, historical periods, periodicals, professions, psychology, sexuality, medical issues, motherhood, and anti-feminism.

VINSON, JAMES, editor. *American Literature to 1900.* Introduction by Lewis Leary. New York: St. Martin's Press, [1980]. vii, 340 pp.; 24 cm. (Great Writers Student Library.) "Notes on Contributors": pp. 333–340. LC 79–5251. ISBN 0–312–34711–1. Paper, $8.95.

Gives biographical and bibliographical information and a brief critical essay on each of the major American authors included.

WAGENKNECHT, EDWARD. *Henry David Thoreau: What Manner of Man?* Amherst: University of Massachusetts Press, 1981. 211 pp.; 23 cm. "Selected Bibliography": pp. 201–206; index. LC 80–23542. ISBN 0–87023–136–7: cloth, $12.50; ISBN 0–87023–137–5: paper, $5.95.

Taking a biographical approach, Wagenknecht wants to find out what kind of individual Thoreau was and to be able to assess "what manner man he was at every period."

WARE, W. PORTER, and THADDEUS C. LOCKARD, JR. *P. T. Barnum Presents Jenny Lind: The American Tour of the Swedish Nightingale*. Baton Rouge: Louisiana State University Press, [1980]. xiv, 204 pp.: front, illus., facsims.; 23 cm. Appendixes ("Jenny Lind's Letters to Charlotte Birch-Pfeiffer," "Jenny Lind's Letters to Otto Goldschmidt," "Contract Between Jenny Lind and P. T. Barnum," "Financial Account of the Jenny Lind Tour") pp. 141–185; Bibliography: pp. 197–200; index. LC 80–1150. ISBN 0–8071–0687–9. $20.00.

Follows the Swedish opera singer through her two-year American tour accompanied by the showman Barnum.

WELCH, JEFFREY EGAN. *Literature and Film: An Annotated Bibliography, 1909–1977*. New York: Garland, 1981. xi, 315 pp.; 22 cm. (Garland Reference Library of the Humanities, vol. 241.) "Appendix": pp. 199–285. Index. LC 80–8509. ISBN 0–8240–9478–6. $40.00.

Chronologically lists British and American books "having to do with the special relationship between films and works of literature."

WESTBROOK, WAYNE W. *Wall Street in the American Novel*. New York: New York University Press, [1980]. vii, 213 pp.; 23 cm. Index. LC 79–47997. ISBN 0–8147–9194–8: cloth, $20.00; ISBN 0–8147–9195–6: paper, $8.00.

Based on the premise that Wall Street inspired many American novelists, Westbrook notes that even though Emerson "never got too excited about Wall Street," Hawthorne and Melville were the first to link money to evil in the American financial marketplace.

WHITMAN, SARAH HELEN. *Edgar Poe and His Critics*. Introduction and Notes by Oral Sumner Coad. New York: Gordian Press, 1981. 105 pp.: front.; 22 cm. LC 80–26202. ISBN 0–87752–214–6. $9.00.

Facsimile reprinting of the 1949 edition, reprinted by the Rutgers University from the original book by Whitman, published in 1860. Coad's introduction gives an overview of Poe's contemporary critical reception that led up to Mrs. Whitman's defense, and surveys the critical response to her work.

WOODRESS, JAMES, editor. *American Literary Scholarship: An Annual / 1979*. Durham: Duke University Press, 1981. xvii, 574 pp.; 22 cm. Indexes. LC 65–19450. ISBN 0–8223–04554. $27.75.

Includes reviews of research for 1979 in the following areas: "Emerson, Thoreau, and Transcendentalism," by Wendell Glick; "Hawthorne," by David B. Kesterson; "Poe," by J. Albert Robbins; "Melville," by Hershel Parker; "Whitman and Dickinson," by Willis J. Buckingham; and "19th-century Literature," by Kermit Vanderbilt.

ZIFF, LARZER. *Literary Democracy: The Declaration of Cultural Independence in America.* New York: Viking Press, [1981]. xxv, 333 pp.; 23 cm. Index. LC 80-54085. ISBN 0-670-43026-9. $20.00.

Focuses on the major authors who contributed toward the concept of an independent and democratic national literature by emphasizing "how a major literature arose in the United States between the great panic of 1837 and the outbreak of the Civil War."

CONTRIBUTORS

WILLIAM AARNES is Assistant Professor of English at Furman University.

CAROLINE BOKINSKY, a graduate student in English at the University of South Carolina, is the STUDIES IN THE AMERICAN RENAISSANCE Editorial Assistant.

LARRY A. CARLSON, Assistant Professor of English at the College of Charleston, is currently editing Bronson Alcott's "Journal for 1838."

PHYLLIS COLE is Assistant Professor of English at Wellesley College. She has held fellowships from the National Endowment for the Humanities and the Charles Warren Center for Studies in American History, and is presently working on a generational study of the Emerson family.

WALTER HARDING, Secretary of the Thoreau Society, is Distinguished Professor of English, State University of New York, College at Geneseo.

ROWENA REVIS JONES is Professor of English at Northern Michigan University. Her article is part of a larger study in progress focusing on Dickinson's poems in the context of her religious heritage.

CAROLYN KAPPES is Editorial Assistant for *The Writings of Henry D. Thoreau*.

RICHARD KOPLEY recently completed his dissertation on *The Narrative of Arthur Gordon Pym* at the State University of New York at Buffalo. He is writing a book on *Pym*.

TIBBIE E. LYNCH recently completed her dissertation on Evelyn Waugh and the American black humorists at Texas A&M University.

RANDY F. NELSON, Assistant Professor of Engilsh at Davidson College, has published *An Almanac of American Letters.*

LEONARD NEUFELDT is Professor of English and American Studies at Purdue University. The author of numerous articles on the Transcendentalists, he is also an editor of Thoreau's *Journal* in *The Writings of Henry D. Thoreau*, a published poet, and author of *The House of Emerson.*

GLEN A. OMANS is Associate Professor of English at Temple University. His article on Poe and Immanuel Kant appeared in STUDIES IN THE AMERICAN RENAISSANCE 1980.

ELIZABETH WITHERELL is Editor-in-Chief of *The Writings of Henry D. Thoreau.* She is co-editor of *A Week on the Concord and Merrimack Rivers* and *Journal 1: 1837–1844*, and is editing Thoreau's poems.

GUY R. WOODALL, Professor of English at Tennessee Technological University, is the author of numerous articles on the figures and journals of the American Renaissance. He is currently editing Convers Francis' sermons and preparing a biography of him.

DAVID A. ZONDERMAN is a graduate student in the Department of American Studies at Yale University.

Also available:

STUDIES IN THE AMERICAN RENAISSANCE 1977

Edited by Joel Myerson

Contents:

Among the fifteen articles are **The Ideology of Brook Farm** *by Richard Francis* • **A Calendar of the Letters of Margaret Fuller** *by Robert N. Hudspeth* • **Poe's "The Spectacles": A New Text from Manuscript** *by Joseph J. Moldenhauer* • **A Guide to Primary Source Materials for the Study of Hawthorne's Old Manse Period** *by John J. McDonald* • With twenty-eight illustrations.

ISBN 0-8057-9007-1   424 pp. $25.00

STUDIES IN THE AMERICAN RENAISSANCE 1978

Edited by Joel Myerson

Contents:

Among the fourteen articles are **Bronson Alcott's "Journal for 1836"** *by Joel Myerson* • **Emerson's Prose: An Annotated Checklist of Literary Criticism Through 1976** *by Annette Woodlief* • **Apparatus for a Definitive Edition of Poe's** *Eureka* *by Roland W. Nelson* • **Melville's Marginalia: Hawthorne** *by Walker Cowan* • **An Annotated Edition of Nathaniel Hawthorne's Official Dispatches to the State Department, 1853-1857 (Part One)** *by Mark F. Sweeney* • **Louisa Alcott's Feminist Letters** *by Madeleine B. Stern* • With nineteen illustrations.

ISBN 0-8057-9009-8   480 pp. $25.00

Also available:

STUDIES IN THE AMERICAN RENAISSANCE 1979

Edited by Joel Myerson

Contents:

The Transcendentalists and Language: The Unitarian Exegetical Background *by Philip F. Gura*

Emerson's "Thoreau": A New Edition from Manuscript *by Joel Myerson*

The Pinto Letters of Charles Frederick Briggs *by Bette S. Weidman*

A Calendar of the Letters of Theodore Parker (Part One) *by Gary L. Collison*

Completing the Sphere: Emerson's Revisions of the Mottoes of *Nature* *by Richard Lee Francis*

Eighty-Six Letters (1814-1882) of A. Bronson Alcott (Part One) *by Frederick Wagner*

The Bible and the Composition of *Walden* *by Larry R. Long*

An Annotated Edition of Nathaniel Hawthorne's Official Dispatches to the State Deparment, 1853-1857 (Part Two) *by Mark F. Sweeney*

Cyrus Bartol's Transcendental Capitalism *by William G. Heath, Jr.*

Ellery Channing's "Major Leviticus: His Three Days in Town": An Unpublished Satire *by Francis B. Dedmond*

Walt Whitman's Plans for the Perfect Dictionary *by Michael Rowan Dressman*

What's in a Title? Whitman's "Calamus" and Bucke's *Calamus* *by Artem Lozynsky*

Books Received *by Robert E. Burkholder*

Includes twelve illustrations.

ISBN 0-8057-9011-X   508 pp. $25.00

Also available:

STUDIES IN THE AMERICAN RENAISSANCE 1980

Edited by Joel Myerson

Contents:

A Thoreau Iconography *by Thomas Blanding and Walter Harding*
Emerson: "A Friendly Thinker" *by James Gould Cozzens*
The Underlying Structure of the Divinity School Address: Emerson as Jeremiah *by Carol Johnston*
Emerson's Craft of Revision: The Composition of *Essays* (1841) *by Glen M. Johnson*
Necessitated Freedom: Emerson's *The Conduct of Life* *by Richard Lee Francis*
Lidian Emerson's "Transcendental Bible" *by Delores Bird Carpenter*
Hawthorne and the Mannings *by Gloria C. Erlich*
Fenimore Cooper to Rufus Griswold: A Puff *by R. D. Madison*
"Intellect, Taste, and the Moral Sense": Poe's Debt to Immanuel Kant *by Glen A. Omans*
Poe and the Dance *by Burton R. Pollin*
Eighty-Six Letters (1814–1882) of A. Bronson Alcott (Part Two) *by Frederick Wagner*
Margaret Fuller and the Phrenologist-Publishers *by Madeleine B. Stern*
Thoreau's Projected Work on the English Poets *by Robert Sattelmeyer*
An Index to Quotations in Thoreau's *A Week on the Concord and Merrimack Rivers* *by William Brennen*
The Sources for Thoreau's Greek Translations *by Kevin P. Van Anglen*
Thoreau's Rescue of John Brown from History *by Michael Meyer*
A Calendar of the Letters of Theodore Parker (Part Two) *by Gary L. Collison*
The Southron as American: William Gilmore Simms *by Miriam J. Shillingsburg*
The Marietta Lecture Series of 1866–1867: Emerson, Douglass, and Others *by Owen Hawley*
Books Received *by Robert E. Burkholder*

Includes twenty-four illustrations

ISBN 0–8057–9013–6   479 pp. $30.00

Also available:

STUDIES IN THE AMERICAN RENAISSANCE 1981

Edited by Joel Myerson

Contents:

Life as Art in America: The Case of Margaret Fuller *by Albert J. von Frank*

Bronson Alcott's "Journal for 1837" *by Larry A. Carlson*

George Partridge Bradford: Friend of Transcendentalists *by James W. Mathews*

Lydia Maria Child as a Nineteenth-Century Professional Author *by Patricia G. Holland*

Revised Check List of the Correspondence of Edgar Allan Poe *by John Ward Ostrom*

Emerson and the New Bedford Affair *by Len Gougeon*

The Journals of Convers Francis (Part One) *by Guy R. Woodall*

"A pencil in the grasp of your graphic wit": An Illustrated Letter from C. P. Cranch to Theodore Parker *by Francis B. Dedmond*

"Sugar Maple Man": Middle-aged Thoreau's Generativity Crisis *by Richard Lebeaux*

The Matthew Brady Photographs of Nathaniel Hawthorne *by Rita K. Gollin*

The Hawthornes' "Golden Dora" *by Rita K. Gollin*

Bronson Alcott and Free Religion *by Fordyce Richard Bennett*

Books Received *by Stephen Garrison*

Includes seventeen illustrations

ISBN 0-8057-9014-4   450 pp. $30.00